HISTORICAL PERSPECTIVES
OF THE
OPERATIONAL ART

Center of Military History
United States Army
Washington, D.C., 2005

Library of Congress Cataloging-in-Publication Data

Historical perspectives of the operational art / Michael D. Krause and R. Cody Phillips, general editors.
   p. cm.
   Includes bibliographical references.
   1. Operational art (Military science)—History. I. Krause, Michael D. (Michael Detlef), 1942– II. Phillips, R. Cody.

U163.H57 2005
355.4'09—dc22

2004057948

CMH Pub 70–89–1

Foreword

As we begin a new millennium and witness the rapid and complex changes happening around the world, the study of the operational art of war becomes even more critical. Today our Army is facing a multitude of challenges ranging from disaster relief and peacekeeping operations to open hostilities and war. To keep pace with both those demands and the growth of new technologies, we are currently transforming our service from a primarily heavy, forward-deployed force to a lighter, more agile, but also more deadly CONUS-based one. At the same time, the scope of our operations and our strategy is becoming increasingly influenced by our participation in international coalitions and alliances. The time-honored focus of operational art on the planning and execution of military campaigns has thus become even more diverse and complex, placing great demands on the military professional. Although operational art must be adjusted to accommodate these changing circumstances, it should not be done without some understanding—a frame of reference—of the history of the operational level of war so as to clarify the nature of the problems we can expect in the future.

Historical Perspectives of the Operational Art is an anthology of essays by historians and scholars who trace the origin and development of the operational level of warfare, the critical link between strategy and tactics. Col. Michael D. Krause, former deputy commander of the U.S. Army Center of Military History, made the initial selections for this anthology. As a student of the subject and instructor at the National War College, Colonel Krause was well qualified for the task. This volume may be regarded as a continuation of an earlier publication that he coedited on a similar subject, *On Operational Art*, which is a collection of pieces by senior military commanders and theorists dealing with the contemporary application of the operational art of war. For the soldier and student alike, *Historical Perspectives of the Operational Art* should stimulate thought and provide a deeper understanding of military history and its ability to shed light on the problems and challenges of the present.

Washington, D.C.
17 May 2005

JOHN S. BROWN
Brigadier General, USA (Ret.)
Chief of Military History

Preface

Historical Perspectives of the Operational Art is a unique study in the field of military history. Relying on the expertise of scholars and military historians from the United States, Great Britain, and Germany, it highlights some of the significant developments in the modern evolution of the operational level of war. Our intention was not to include every major military power in recent history—and certainly not every conflict. Yet students of the operational art may want to look at past wars to see how this added dimension of armed conflict might have surfaced or been applied. This study deals only with land warfare and is designed to show the doctrinal development and application of operational art in modern history. Thus, while the British, Chinese, and Japanese clearly demonstrated techniques associated with the operational art of war, their experiences tended to parallel practices already developed and implemented elsewhere.

Operational art has its origins in Western Europe. Beginning with the skillful adaptations of Napoleon Bonaparte, military commanders began to recognize the middle ground that linked national strategic goals with tactical objectives on the battlefield. The Germans, following the example of Field Marshal Helmuth von Moltke, devised the initial concepts about the operational art of war, while French contemporaries wrestled with devising a satisfactory doctrine of their own. The Russians and Soviets learned from their military brethren in Western Europe and also developed a vibrant doctrine that was masterfully implemented during the latter half of World War II. The United States, in contrast, entered the field of study belatedly. Although there clearly were moments when the operational art could be observed in selected campaigns, it is apparent that the U.S. Army's doctrinal development of this connection between strategy and tactics progressed in an irregular manner and reached fruition only recently—most notably in Operations DESERT SHIELD and DESERT STORM.

Strategy, operations, and tactics routinely affect the dimensions of military conflict, each in a different manner. For instance, the strategist aims at the enemy center of gravity, which often is the nation's will to fight, or perhaps the key resources or the delicate bond that holds an alliance together. The operational artist's center of gravity is the mass of the enemy's military force and its ability to command and control its forces. At the tactical level, the battlefield commander has a more limited and proximate perspective and focuses on his immediate foe. Strategy may dictate whether or not to fight, but operations will determine where and when to fight and tactics how to conduct the fight. In turn, tacticians employ fire and maneuver to achieve a limited objective, while operational commanders use fire and maneuver on a larger scale to create an imbalance against the enemy and set the tempo of a campaign. For a tactician, intelligence is concerned with capabilities; but at the operational level, intelligence is focused on enemy intentions. A tactical commander will use deception to hide his forces; an operational commander will use deception to mask his intentions.

The use of reserves is critical to the operational artist. Yet these are not reserves that might represent an inactive force waiting to be put into action, which is customarily how reserves are seen at the tactical level. Rather, reserves at the operational level are thought of as the future employment of forces that may or may not already be engaged in the battle or campaign. Logistics too is a factor in this discussion. At the strategic level, force generation capability and logistics are applied in broad terms and viewed as long-term reserves. At the operational level, the logistics capability is another form of reserve and an asset that affects the outcome of an armed conflict. At the tactical level, however, logistics affects only the battle in progress.

From the strategic level, a commander looks toward the outcome of campaigns and battles as a means of achieving national policy objectives. This process requires a focus on a distant goal. The operational commander often looks to a closer goal, which would be achieved following a campaign or series of battles. Obviously, the tactical commander is focused on the outcome of specific engagements or battles.

Simply stated, the strategist identifies broad goals and generates the capabilities to achieve those goals, while the operational commander seeks a unity of effort over a specific period of time, and the tactician initiates immediate action on the field of battle. The operational art of war is thus different in sum and part. It is more than large-scale tactics, but it is not small-scale strategy either. It has both a tactical and a strategic dimension, because it must create a vision of unity of action on the battlefield that ultimately achieves a strategic objective.

For both the soldier and the student of military history, this anthology will provide an orientation to significant battles and campaigns from the past. Rather than view the sound generalship of Napoleon and the tactical displacement of his divisions at Jena, the reader might also consider how this battle and the entire campaign affected both the French and Prussian strategies. Even the dramatic clash at Gettysburg becomes more than simply Little Round Top, Cemetery Ridge, Culp's Hill, and Pickett's Charge, especially when given an operational perspective. *Historical Perspectives of the Operational Art* encourages students and soldiers alike to think beyond the battle that is before them. Isolated and taken out of context, tactical maneuvers can provide a surreal comprehension of their importance and encourage a detachment from the larger strategy. The Allies were so focused on successful landings at Normandy, for example, that they had invested little planning to breaking out from the beachheads. And when that time came, despite the clear opportunity to inflict a crushing blow to the German Army, the Allies elected to squander their resources on more limited tactical objectives. Finally, particularly for soldiers, the enclosed essays might assist in understanding what operational art is and how it is applied in contemporary doctrine.

A number of people contributed to the final compilation and publication of this anthology—not the least were the individual contributors whose works are in this text. We owe a debt of appreciation to the Center of Military History and its chief, Brig. Gen. John S. Brown, as well as its chief historian, Dr. Jeffrey J. Clarke, who helped revive this project at a moment when it seemed certain to die stillborn. Four individuals in particular merit special recognition for lending their technical expertise to this anthology and its subsequent publication: Ms. Beth MacKenzie, chief of the Center's Graphics Branch, diligently guided the final manuscript through the publication process; Ms. Diane Donovan, a senior editor in the Editorial Branch, demonstrated patience and literary skills that far exceeded our abilities to articulate; Ms. Susan Carroll compiled the index; and Ms. Linda Moten assisted in the final review and editing of individual essays. We edited individual contributions to ensure a standardized format, while being careful not to mask or alter individual writing styles, not to mention the views and conclusions presented in each essay. Reprinted essays were rarely altered from their original versions, except for either space considerations or clarification of technical matters. The views expressed in these selections are those of the individual authors and do not reflect the official policy or positions of the Departments of the Army and Defense or the U.S. government.

Washington, D.C. MICHAEL D. KRAUSE
22 July 2004 R. CODY PHILLIPS

Contents

	Page
Operational Art's Origins	3
Bruce W. Menning, Ph.D.	

Part One: France

Introduction	25
Napoleon, Operational Art, and the Jena Campaign	27
David G. Chandler, Ph.D.	
French Operational Art: 1888–1940	69
Col. Robert A. Doughty	

Part Two: Germany

Introduction	111
Moltke and the Origins of the Operational Level of War	113
Col. Michael D. Krause, U.S. Army, Retired	
Operational Thought from Schlieffen to Manstein	149
Brig. Gen. Günter R. Roth	
Panzer Group Kleist and the Breakthrough in France, 1940	169
Karl-Heinz Frieser, Ph.D.	

Part Three: Russia and the Soviet Union

Introduction	185
The Imperial Russian Legacy of Operational Art, 1878–1914	189
Bruce W. Menning, Ph.D.	
The Origins of Soviet Operational Art, 1917–1936	213
Jacob W. Kipp, Ph.D.	
Soviet Operational Art Since 1936: The Triumph of Maneuver War	247
Col. David M. Glantz, U.S. Army, Retired	
Soviet Operational Logistics, 1939–1990	293
Graham H. Turbiville, Jr., Ph.D.	

Part Four: The United States

	Page
Introduction	329
The Origins of Operational Art *Brig. Gen. Harold W. Nelson, U.S. Army, Retired*	333
Operational Art and the Gettysburg Campaign *Col. Arthur V. Grant, U.S. Army, Retired*	349
Normandy to Falaise: A Critique of Allied Operational Planning in 1944 *Russell F. Weigley, Ph.D.*	393
After Inch'on: MacArthur's 1950 Campaign in North Korea *Col. Stanlis David Milkowski, U.S. Army, Retired*	415
The Maturation of Operational Art: Operations DESERT SHIELD and DESERT STORM *Brig. Gen. John S. Brown*	439
Afterword	483
List of Contributors	485
Index	489

Tables

1. The French *Grand Armée*'s Reinforcement Schedule, 13–14 October 1806 ... 50
2. Soviet Tank Army Composition, June 1942 ... 252
3. Soviet Mechanized Corps Types, September 1942 ... 252

Maps

1. Jena and Vicinity, 1806: Battles of Jena and Auerstädt ... 54
2. The Campaign in Bohemia, 1866: Army Concentration Areas and Moltke's Plan of Advance ... 122
3. Franco-Prussian War, 1870–1871: Concentration and Initial Operations ... 128
4. Franco-Prussian War, 1870–1871: Siege of Paris ... 132
5. The Schlieffen Plan, 1905 ... 152

		Page
6.	The Marne Campaign, August/September 1914	153
7.	1st Deployment Plan "Yellow"	159
8.	The Advance to Avesnes and Le Cateau, 17 May 1940	177
9.	The Planned Pincer Movement by the Allies on the "Corridor of Arras," 21 May 1940	179
10.	Gettysburg Campaign: Situation as of 28 June 1863	362
11.	Gettysburg Campaign: Situation as of 1430 Hours, 1 July 1863	368
12.	Gettysburg Campaign: Situation as of Evening, 2 July 1863	375
13.	Gettysburg Campaign: Situation as of 1430 Hours, 3 July 1863	377
14.	OVERLORD Area: 1944	394
15.	Closing the Falaise-Argentan Pocket and the Mortain Counterattack, 6–17 August 1944	404
16.	Korea	417
17.	Race to the Yalu	425
18.	Operation DESERT STORM: 24–28 February 1991	450

HISTORICAL PERSPECTIVES OF THE OPERATIONAL ART

Operational Art's Origins[1]

Bruce W. Menning

Over the last decade, and especially since coalition victory in the Gulf War, the term operational art has achieved buzzword status within the Army and joint communities. However, despite growing acceptance, a good deal of confusion surrounds the meaning and significance of operational art. For some, the term merely signifies tactical arrows drawn larger. For others, it is a cumbersome transplant from foreign military usage. For still others, it remains a key to recent and future victories, but one whose origins are murky and whose nature and content are difficult to define.

The term operational art long antedates U.S. Army usage. Six decades before operational art gained currency in the West, it was used by the Soviets. A rough equivalent also had appeared among the Germans before World War I, but the term did not enter the U.S. military vernacular for two possible reasons. Before World War II and the Cold War, there was no persistent requirement in peacetime to prepare for the conduct of extended military operations on a vast scale; and during a less complex era it was possible—even comfortable—to remain firmly wedded to a nineteenth-century inheritance that taught that military art consisted of strategy and tactics.

For the Soviet military culture of the 1920s and 1930s, this was not the case. Fresh from the seemingly contradictory experiences of World War I (1914–1918) and the Russian Civil War (1918–1920), Soviet Army theorists and practitioners sought systematic explanations for the complexities underlying victory and defeat in modern war. Armed with an ideology that emphasized theory and scientific method in military affairs, they brought new perspective to the study of military history and refreshing rigor to views on the nature of possible future war, including the conduct of operations.[2] By the late 1920s they had emerged with an altered view of the constituent components of military art, and it is to this period—a golden age of military thought—that we owe the origins of our basic understanding of operational art. To understand why the Soviets developed this concept when they did, the reader must understand their perspectives and preoccupations.

Military Art's Changing Nature

A chief problem bedeviling all military theorists of the period was the changing nature of modern operations. Historically, the term operation had been in use at least since the end of the seventeenth century to describe what European armies did in the field. Initially, during the age of preindustrial warfare, generals and kings raised professional armies to fight limited wars for the dynastic state's limited objectives. Within limited war's framework, the conduct of operations formed an integral part of strategy, and strategy was conceived as simply "the tactics of theater-level operations."[3] By the eighteenth century's end, Napoleon imparted new meaning to the traditional calculus when he raised larger armies to fight decisively for objectives that called for the annihilation of enemy forces and gave rise to empires.

Still, the basic technologies remained the same, and with room for alteration and even poetic license, the next generation of military thinkers, led by Henri Jomini and his disciples, redefined the traditional preindustrial paradigm to describe Napoleonic military art. Their view was that military strategy remained the domain of large-unit operations and that the essence of Napoleonic genius could be understood in his pursuit of "the strategy of the single point." Napoleon's columns march-maneuvered within theater to force convergence with the enemy at a single point—finite in time and space—for climactic battle to determine the outcome of a season's campaign, perhaps even the outcome of an entire war. Strategy described a limited complex of actions, including approaches, marches, countermarches, and maneuvers, which took place within theater to leverage mass for decisive battle. Tactics described what happened within the limited confines of the battlefield.[4]

During the nineteenth century's latter half, about the time when most military thinkers had grown comfortable with this understanding of strategy and tactics, the industrial revolution went to war, thereby altering the basic paradigm in ways not fully understood until after World War I:

- The evolution of the modern industrial state during the nineteenth century enabled governments to tap vast manpower resources to produce true mass armies based on the cadre and reserve principle of recruitment and organization.
- The application of steam and electricity to military ends enabled governments to mobilize these armies and project them into potential theaters with unprecedented rapidity and predictability.
- The size of these armies and their preparation for deployment in future conflict mandated the application of industrial-style planning and directing methods.
- The new firepower based first on rifled, breech-loading weaponry, then on its magazine-fed, smokeless powder variant, increased lethality and ranges and with them, the scale of modern combat.

These changes revolutionized the conduct of war and set the stage for an altered understanding of military art and its component parts. Except for the Prussians, few practitioners understood that strategy now had to account for movement of forces in theater and for their mobilization and movement to theater. In addition, something else was occurring that only a few obscure East European thinkers perceived: As modern conflict drew increasingly on the will and resources of entire populations, notions of strategy also had to take into account linkages between fighting front and deep supporting rear.

Even more perplexing for the practitioner, the novel combination of mass and firepower meant that the strategy of the "single point" within theater had lost relevance. To avoid lethal frontal confrontation and to avail themselves of mass and speed of deployment, commanders now sought to stretch Napoleon's "single point" of troop confrontation laterally in pursuit of an extended line. The idea was to pin frontally, then extend to the soft flank, with an eye toward either the envelopment or the turning movement. Thus, the Napoleonic strategy of the single point gave way within theater to the strategy of the "extended line." This development, which was already evident in the American Civil War's later stages, found its tragic culmination with the extended trench lines of World War I on the Western Front.[5]

If these changes were not challenging enough, traditional notions of tactical-level battle also underwent fundamental alteration. As ranges extended, battlefield limits increased geometrically and the commander's ability to control his troops diminished dramatically. Although more troops than ever before inhabited the battlefield, they now became invisible as they went to ground to avoid lethal firepower. Battles began to lose whatever internal logic and coherence they once had: From a mixture of controlled mayhem and chaos within a limited area mercifully lasting only hours or perhaps several days, they had now evolved to rattle across time and space to produce an outcome from which even the triumphant might emerge without final victory. As the slaughter of World War I–style positional warfare indicated, the sum of tactical successes was no sure predictor of larger strategic success.[6]

Though not fully apparent until after 1918, a key to understanding what had occurred was a perception of how the nature of military operations had changed over the course of the late nineteenth and early twentieth centuries. In traditional Napoleonic-style strategic perspective, operations described what occurred within theater as armies, already assembled and deployed, were concentrated and maneuvered against each other to force a single, climactic battle. Logistics had always been a significant, but subsidiary part of the calculus: Troops got by on what had been stockpiled before the onset of a season's campaign or on what they could scrounge from a grudging population within theater.

However, the overall picture had changed by the beginning of the twentieth century. Campaigns were no longer governed by the seasons. The nature of operations was increasingly dictated by the thrust of higher-level preparation and planning, and operations themselves were no longer finite affairs leading to a single decisive battle. Operations, a complex of military actions and battles linked by time, place, and intent, might extend for several weeks or longer. An operation's course might witness a major regroupment of forces and require changed command, control, and logistic arrangements, all within the altered limits of greatly expanded space and time. The growing realization was that the preparation for and conduct of operations had expanded beyond the limits of traditional military strategy to incorporate new content, methods, and concerns. The most important issue was one of linkages, and within a conceptual framework for the conduct of operations, how to fashion linkages to contend with changes in time, timing, duration, support, scale, range, and distance.

World War I simply reinforced and added more wrinkles to these and related considerations. Combat experience demonstrated conclusively that single operations no longer dictated the outcome of a campaign or war. Decision came only as a result of successive operations linked by intent, location, allocation of resources, and concerted action. Combat experience also demonstrated the bankruptcy of the extended-line strategy—once flanks were denied, adversaries were left with two unpalatable options: Effect a penetration or attack in another theater. Penetrations presented formidable challenges because the hard school of experience taught that defending forces could fall back on a combination of deep reserves, a relatively undamaged rail net and a coherent rear area to reconstitute a viable defense in what later was called operational depths. Consequently, after only limited tactical gains at great cost, the attackers would have to pause and prepare for follow-on offensive operations.

World War I also suggested solutions for the bloody impasse from outside the theater. One was to have a potential ally available with vast manpower reserves to tip the scales at the eleventh hour. Another was to attack the enemy's deep supporting rear, either indirectly through surface blockade or a submarine *guerre de course*. Still another came from technological innovation: Aircraft could fly over trench lines, while armored vehicles could crush and shoot their way through. But before any of these innovations could be applied with any degree of consistent success in future war, practitioners had to understand what had happened and why and what the implications were for the future. In the course of pondering these variables, theorists and practitioners would begin to fashion not only a common vocabulary, including a rudimentary understanding of operational art, but also a common conceptual framework for the conduct of operations.

New Vocabulary and Solutions

I have described a world of complex military realities that Soviet thinkers confronted during the 1920s and 1930s. To be sure, other military cultures and thinkers, including Giulio Douhet, William "Billy" Mitchell, J. F. C. Fuller, and Basil H. Liddell Hart, also contributed to intellectual ferment and "new thinking" during the same era. The Soviets were distinctive for the following reasons:

- They maintained a consistent focus on the conduct of large-scale, ground-oriented operations.
- They worried obsessively about linking separate aspects of their thought about the changing nature of operations to larger and smaller military realities.
- They produced an entire school of thinkers, not just individuals laboring in isolation from one another and their military cultures.
- They undertook a systematic historical study of operations since Napoleon's time to understand what had changed and why.

Soviet Army theorists emerged from this quest with what they felt were fundamental keys to understanding change: the shifting content of military strategy, the evolving nature of operations themselves, and the disaggregation of military structures. An important underlying assumption was that these developments owed much of their significance to the impact of changing technology over time.

The Soviets perceived that evolving military theory and practice had led to a situation in which the strategy of an entire nation at war had become a kind of intellectual and organizational continuum, linking broad fighting front with large supporting rear. That is, strategy was what guided a nation in preparing for and waging contemporary and future war, while the conduct of operations was rapidly assuming sufficient identity to warrant attention in itself, albeit not in isolation from strategy and tactics. The conscious understanding was that strategy—more precisely, military strategy—had ballooned to encompass a host of activities, including higher-level planning and preparation, resource orchestration and priority, and objective identification, all of which culminated in the direct application of military power for the state's goals.[7] In short, strategy had come to mean something akin to what Col. Arthur F. Lykke, Jr., would later define as orchestrating and linking "ends, ways and means" to attain national security objectives.[8]

This development, when coupled with the increasing complexity of operations, caused a gap to open between the traditional understanding of strategy and tactics. Some commentators filled this gap with the term "grand tactics," while others searched for analogous terms, including "applied strategy" and *operarika* (Russia, circa 1907), to define what the more traditional understanding of strategy had once described as happening within theater.[9] For a time, under military theorist Sigismund W. von Schlichting's influence, the Germans toyed with *operativ*, but they do not appear to have elaborated it with any degree of persistence and consistency.[10] Under the influence of varied perspectives and preoccupations, other commentators saw no gap and therefore found little reason to worry about it, continuing to regard tactics and strategy as directly linked.

In contrast, by 1922 the Soviets were beginning to fill the "terminological gap" with something they called operational art, and they would spend much of the 1920s and 1930s developing a more complete understanding of this concept and its implications.[11] At first, Soviet Army thinkers used the term to bridge the gap between strategy and tactics and to describe more precisely the discipline that governed the preparation for and conduct of operations. In 1926 a Soviet theorist and former Imperial Russian General Staff officer, Aleksandr A. Svechin, captured the essence of linkages among the new three-part understanding of military art when he wrote, "Tactics makes up the steps from which operational leaps are assembled. Strategy points out the path."[12] Not surprisingly, a new department, Conduct of Operations, appeared alongside the conventional Departments of Strategy and Tactics at the Soviet Staff Academy.

The new understanding of the relationship among the three components of military art provided the impetus for a second factor—steady focus on the evolving nature of operations, with implications for future war. In accordance with the foregoing discussion, the Soviets understood that the industrial revolution had changed the face of modern operations. They knew that operations now had to be consciously differentiated from battles, which were shorter in duration, more limited in scope and outcome, and more episodic in nature. Moreover, World War I had driven home the realization that single operations in themselves rarely produced strategic decision. Decision now came as the result of a whole complex of successive, simultaneous, and related operations. The Soviets also perceived that operations as diverse as those of World War I and their own civil war had much in common. This realization came primarily from an understanding that logistics and rail and road nets played a key role in determining the scale, scope, and depth of modern military operations.[13] During the mid-1920s Soviet Army Staff Chief Mikhail N. Tukhachevskiy ordered the faculty that taught the conduct of operations at the staff academy to incorporate logistics into their operational-level exercises. Some Russian commentators later asserted that consideration of support in tandem with operations actually gave birth to the concept of Soviet operational art.[14]

Soviet theorist Georgiy S. Isserson provided the necessary insight: that armies since the onset of World War I had witnessed a "disaggregation of forces." Between 1914 and the early 1930s, the steady march of technology had resulted in the structural evolution of armed forces whose organizations now reflected greater diversity and whose weaponry had become increasingly differentiated by range and combat effect. For continental-style armies, these forces bore only superficial resemblance to their past counterparts. In 1914, for example, despite differences in movement and combat technique, infantry and cavalry represented two aspects of a fairly homogeneous force moved by muscle on the battlefield and supported by similar kinds of artillery. The operational radius and combat effects of these forces were still relatively limited in depth and scope. However, by the 1930s new structures and weapons had evolved to accompany the introduction of aircraft, armor, and long-range artillery into battles and operations. What resulted was a more heterogeneous force, but, more important, a force whose qualities and attributes required a new order of thought and preparation before they could be systematically applied to military ends.

Isserson saw that a primary purpose of operational art was to reaggregate the diverse effects and operational characteristics of these forces either simultaneously or sequentially across a much larger theater of combat operations.[15]

These and related impulses came together during the 1930s to produce the Soviet concept of deep operations. With the massive application of new technologies, the Soviets swept away the older geometry of point and line to settle on the advantages of extending a force vector in depth. The requirement was to mobilize a diverse combat array, including infantry, armor, airborne, long-range artillery, and air power, then orchestrate this array's multiple effects through an operation both sequentially and simultaneously in three dimensions. The object in the offensive was to attack an enemy's defenses as near simultaneously as possible throughout their depth to effect a catastrophic disintegration of their entire defense system. The concept was to accomplish a penetration by blasting and crushing a path through the tactical zone then inserting a powerful mobile group for exploitation into the operational depths. For maximum decisive effect, the Soviets envisioned these operations as driven from the top down, starting at *front* (army group) and proceeding down through army and corps levels.[16]

Although the Soviets did not ignore other operational issues, the theory and practice of deep operations occupied center stage for Soviet operational art during the 1930s. Operational art required the practitioner to:

- Identify strategic objectives within theater.
- Visualize a theater in three dimensions.
- Determine what sequence of military actions—preparation, organization, support, battles, and command arrangements—would bring the attainment of those objectives.

After analyzing previous operations, and assuming massive injections of armor and air power, the Soviets calculated that future operations might occupy up to 300 kilometers of frontage, extend to a depth of about 250 kilometers, and have a duration of thirty to forty-five days. Consequently, these operations would be closely tied to the attainment of objectives determined by larger strategic requirements, while overall success would rest on the ability to integrate logistics and tactics into the larger design.

Linkages between fighting front and large supporting rear were also clear. For various reasons, including a close reading of Carl von Clausewitz's work, the digestion of lessons from the home front in World War I and a growing sense that victory in future war would depend on the state's total resources, the Soviets gravitated to a view that future conflict would be systemic and protracted. During the 1930s, Joseph Stalin's policies of agricultural collectivization and massive industrialization amounted to a peacetime mobilization of Soviet society. A succession of five-year plans built infrastructure for future war and produced much of the military hardware required for deep operations. The transformation—even militarization—of Soviet society stood as grim testimony to linkages between strategic vision and operational-level capability.[17]

Stalin's potential German adversaries inherited a different military legacy and worked from a different philosophical base. After lightning victories over the French in 1870 and 1871, much of the rationale behind German military planning had been to devise initial operations of sufficient scope and speed that they would bring about the enemy's capitulation during a single brief campaign of annihilation. The Germans assumed that modern society had become too fragile to withstand the dislocations of extended military conflict. The World War I experience seemed to confirm earlier apprehensions: Protractedness had brought the "Hydra-headed" dangers of attrition, domestic exhaustion, and political instability—even revolution.

As the German *Reichswehr* emerged from the Versailles-imposed 1920s cocoon to become Hitler's *Wehrmacht* in the late 1930s, emphasis once again fell upon avoidance. From a near-intuitive grasp of the military potential resident in the same technologies the Soviets were developing, the Germans fashioned *Blitzkrieg*, a stunning response to the challenges, including protractedness, inherent in positional warfare. The marriage of air power and armor with combat technique gave birth to a combined arms concept with immediate tactical application and important operational implications. Once again the siren-like calls of annihilation and rapid decision summoned the Germans to rocky military shores.[18]

In retrospect, the new German vision for "lightning war" had at least two major shortcomings, one of which was accepted as self-imposed.

The first was that operators and planners failed to embed *Blitzkrieg* in a coherent vision for the conduct of operations, something that might have come about if the Germans had bothered with developing their own legacy of *operativ*.[19] Experience could overcome this problem. The second and more important shortcoming was that the Germans failed beyond the obvious and superficial to consider important systemic linkages between fighting front and supporting domestic rear. Nevertheless, Hitler found the new vision congenial with his own grasp of strategy, while the successes of 1939 to 1942 obscured the more profound difficulties of mobilizing the home front.[20]

In contrast, the Soviet vision possessed impressive coherence, but it is important to note that Moscow did not initially have all the answers. The very nature of Soviet military culture, coupled with the requirements of continental-style warfare, meant that the Soviets retained a very limited view of operational art's air and naval components. The chief purpose of air power was to serve the ground operation, while the primary role of naval forces was to defend the coastline and to extend the geographical limits of conventional land-oriented theaters of military action. In addition, other circumstances peculiar to the Soviet situation prevented the Soviet Army from drawing timely benefit from an understanding of operational art. Thanks to a series of circumstances, including Stalin's purge of the officer corps in 1937 and 1938, misinterpretation of lessons learned from the Spanish Civil War (1936–1939), the necessity to assimilate huge quantities of troops and new technology and Hitler's ability to effect surprise in 1941, the Soviets did poorly in World War II's opening stages on the Eastern Front.[21] Not until 1943 did they emerge from the hard school of experience to return to a more perfect version of operational art—with devastating consequences for the *Wehrmacht*.

From Stalingrad to Berlin during 1943 to 1945, the Soviets perfected *front* and *multifront* sequential and simultaneous operations. Stalin's marshals learned to command and control these operations in depth and breadth while coordinating air support with armored thrusts. From 1944 on, mobility and maneuver assumed increasing significance, in part because the Germans could no longer replace losses and because lend-lease trucks enabled the Soviets to stretch the limits of logistic support. Doctrine and practice gradually evolved to emphasize the most complex of modern ground operations, the encirclement, which the Soviets successfully executed about fifty times on the Eastern Front. The Soviets decisively turned the tables on the Germans and in so doing demonstrated a mastery of the military art that compared favorably with earlier German successes.[22]

The World War II and Cold War Legacies

World War II also left the U.S. armed forces with considerable experience in conducting modern operations. However, operational mastery had come neither easily nor quickly, in part because the period between the world wars offered scant intellectual, doctrinal, and organizational precedent. At the U.S. Army Command and General Staff School (USACGSC) during the 1930s, theater operations were taught according to nineteenth-century precedent as "military strategy." The Army's capstone field manual, FM 100–5, *Operations*, appeared in draft form in 1939, but its focus, as befitting a small, peacetime ground force, was primarily tactical. The Louisiana Maneuvers of 1940 and 1941 offered only belated and limited practical experience with large-unit operations.[23] For its part, the Army Air Corps had to support ground operations, but much of its attention was riveted on acquiring the expertise and hardware to conduct strategic bombing campaigns.[24]

To its credit, the U.S. Navy, drawing from its experience in World War I and anticipating the possibility of a protracted two-ocean war, seriously considered the planning challenges inherent in conducting multidimensional operations over time and across large expanses.[25] Yet, the overall U.S. picture was one of Isserson's disaggregated forces translated into American terms. Unfortunately, the services and their offspring remained largely preoccupied with their own perspectives, problems, and self-interests. For these and other reasons, the background for preparing and conducting operations constituted at best a mixed bag. The result was that U.S. military forces during World War II had to learn on the job from the hard school of experience. To their credit, commanders and their staffs gradually perfected the art of conducting massive combined and joint operations across vast distances to reach strategic objectives. It would be difficult, in retrospect, to argue that major operations by Admiral Chester W. Nimitz in the Central Pacific, General Douglas MacArthur in the Southwest Pacific, General Dwight D. Eisenhower in Europe, and General George S. Patton, Jr., across northern France did not match the majesty and significance of Soviet World War II operations.

Despite the richness of experience in conducting World War II operations, the United States and the Soviet Union followed different paths of postwar doctrinal and organizational evolution. For a time, neither former ally focused consistently on large-scale operations. The Cold War precluded doctrinal interchange, while demobilization and the advent of nuclear weaponry produced varying responses that affected the way the two armed powers viewed their roles and the nature of possible military operations.

In the U.S. Army, theater armies and support commands atrophied or disappeared in the rush to demobilize, leaving the Army to seek parochial comfort in tactical-level concerns. During the Cold War's first decade, the United States increasingly sought military capital in reliance on strategic and battlefield-level nuclear devices, which further dampened doctrinal interest in large-unit operations.[26]

When the Korean War intervened, a mixture of improvisation and difficulties associated with theater geography at first precluded serious thought about sweeping operations on a vast scale. The one subsequent bright spot, MacArthur's landing at Inch'on and advance to the Yalu River, was soon forgotten as tactical stalemate set in along the 38th Parallel. Meanwhile, the Soviets began to reconsider their own hasty post–World War II demobilization. Because Stalin initially did not have the atom bomb, the best he could do was to modernize Soviet forces to field a better variant of what had brought them victory on the Eastern Front. Until 1953, Stalin's presence clouded analysis of lessons learned from World War II. Subsequently, Nikita S. Khrushchev's rush to downsize the Soviet military through reliance on nuclear weapons also deemphasized operational art's importance.[27]

For the U.S. Army, three important circumstances prompted a doctrinal evolution that culminated in the adoption of operational art as a doctrinal concept. The first was the Vietnam War, in which field forces scored a series of tactical triumphs but were unable to transform them into strategic outcomes. Debate over the reasons for this failure, along with the necessity to rebuild the U.S. Army, eventually prompted a far-reaching series of doctrinal and organizational changes that cut to the core of how the Army expected to do business in future war. As the Army resurrected itself and peered into the future, some officers looked to the military classics, especially those by Clausewitz, both to afford insight into recent failure and to provide inspiration and vocabulary for what needed to be done. Meanwhile, threat analysis identified the task's magnitude—major confrontation with Soviet and Warsaw Pact forces in Europe assumed overriding significance as the most challenging version of possible future war. The very nature and scale of this threat led naturally to a rebirth of interest in the conduct of large-unit operations.[28]

A second important factor in the Army's doctrinal evolution was the technological content of possible future war. The Vietnam War had witnessed the limited introduction of sophisticated precision-guided weaponry, but there was little coherent sense of the overall implications the new gadgetry and related technologies might hold for conventional war. Much of that sense came from the 1973 Middle East War, during which the massive application of new munitions appeared to revise conventional wisdom about the calculus for air superiority, the role of armor in ground combat, and the relationships among various components within the conduct of operations. Meanwhile, a new organization, the U.S. Army Training and Doctrine Command, attempted to digest the lessons of the

Middle East War and respond to the challenge of possible conflict with Warsaw Pact hordes on the northern European plain. The result was the 1976 version of FM 100–5, which emphasized "active defense."[29]

Dissatisfaction with this concept and the search for alternatives was a third major factor in the Army's post-Vietnam doctrinal evolution. On one hand, the geopolitical realities of NATO dictated both a forward defense and national contributions of corps-size formations, both of which lobbied strongly for a continuing tactical-level focus. The 1976 FM 100–5 accurately reflected this focus. On the other hand, increasingly obvious considerations, including the necessity for defense in depth and the requirement to apply and integrate sophisticated technologies at higher levels, argued for new departures in thought and organization. As critics and writers of doctrine turned to the promise inherent in conducting a future war of maneuver with large-scale units, they sought historical and doctrinal precedent. Earlier, advocates of active defense had seized upon the dogged German defense against the Soviet onslaught from 1943 to 1945 as key to the doctrinal secret of "fighting outnumbered and winning." The belated realization was that the Germans had fought outnumbered and lost.

Now, the advocates of maneuver war seized upon *Blitzkrieg* and initial German successes in World War II to advance doctrinal departures that would emphasize the marriage of technology and technique while conducting modern mobile operations. Almost as an afterthought, other thinkers began seriously to examine the doctrine and military art of the Soviet adversary that had inflicted defeat on "the devil's disciples." From Soviet military history there gradually emerged a mature understanding of the three-part nature of Soviet military art, along with notions about why the Soviets chose to place separate emphasis on operational art as the theory and practice of conducting operations. The term found immediate resonance among U.S. Army doctrine writers, who were now more attuned to the nuances and complexities of modern operations.[30]

Meanwhile, the Soviets themselves emerged from the doctrinal torpor induced by Stalinist and early nuclear-era rigidities. From the mid-1960s on into the 1970s, as the Soviets slowly clawed their way to nuclear parity with the United States, military art theorists filled the pages of the serious Soviet military press with works that amounted to a renaissance of operational art and its contemporary legacy. Under conditions of nuclear parity, a major assumption was that in a future European war, the nature of operations might remain conventional, either initially or for an extended period. Consequently, it was necessary once again to focus singlemindedly on the preparation and conduct of large-scale conventional operations—albeit under conditions that might witness a rapid escalation to nuclear war.[31] During the late 1970s and early 1980s, this train of thought lay at the heart of the conceptual evolution of the theater strategic offensive operation. This series of integrated operations envisioned a massive offensive built around the echeloned introduction of forces that would develop attacks to facilitate the insertion of operational maneuver groups for exploitation within the shallow NATO rear area.

U.S. Operational Art

When open-source materials on Soviet operational art and scattered intelligence about the theater strategic operation reached U.S. and NATO audiences, they added fuel to the fire of doctrinal and technologically inspired innovation. Already in the early 1980s, NATO leaders had begun to adopt the follow-on forces attack (FOFA) concept as a way of striking at highly echeloned Warsaw Pact formations in depth by employing new and more powerful long-range precision weaponry.

The promise of new technology, along with a NATO-oriented military buildup and the emerging emphasis on maneuver war, prompted doctrine writers to alter their focus, examine linkages, and contend with the thorny issues of scale, content, scope, and duration.[32] As a result, the U.S. Army doctrinal community conceded operational art was necessary within theater to link new concepts and technologies with higher (strategic) and lower (tactical) level concerns.

Not surprisingly, when the 1982 FM 100–5 appeared, it recognized three levels of war and asserted "the operational level of war uses available military resources to attain strategic goals within a theater of war." The new field manual emphasized agility, initiative, depth, and synchronization. It also addressed the problem of reaggregation by acknowledging the necessity for close cooperation with the U.S. Air Force in waging AirLand Battle. Despite the tactical overtones implicit in the word "battle," the 1982 FM 100–5 clearly encouraged a focus on the operational level of war, which involved planning and conducting campaigns. For their part, campaigns were conceived as "sustained operations designed to defeat an enemy force in a specified space and time with simultaneous and sequential battles."[33]

Four years later the 1986 FM 100–5 deepened and extended the Army's understanding of contemporary operations; and for the first time in U.S. military usage, the Army capstone manual actually defined operational art. Under the U.S. rubric, operational art was "the employment of military forces to attain strategic goals in a theater of war or theater of operations through the design, organization, and conduct of campaigns and major operations." This definition was no mere copying of Soviet precedent but rather an attempt to apply the concept to future U.S. operations from the perspective of an informed and updated understanding.

The elaboration of operational art in the United States' view reflected many of the preoccupations and intellectual growing pains with which Army doctrine writers had contended since the Vietnam War. From a curious mixture of modified Clausewitz and Jomini doctrines came the concepts of operational design, including *center of gravity*, *lines of operation*, *decisive points*, and *culmination*, which underlay operational art and its application to campaign planning.[34] From a sense that technology and circumstance were changing the nature and content of operations flowed a generic understanding of operational-level functions—intelligence, fires, maneuver, logistics, protection, and command and control—which entered either sequentially or simultaneously into planning for major operations and campaigns. From a realization that operational art would remain an enemy concept unless closely tied to education and application came a gradual introduction of campaign planning into the curricula of the U.S. Army War College and the USACGSC.[35]

Joint Impact

Although the Army had dealt convincingly with issues of concept, vocabulary, and application, there was no immediate guarantee that the joint community would pick up on one service's fixation with operational art. Of the other services, only the U.S. Air Force had increasingly become a party to the Army's doctrinal evolution, thanks to the explicit and implicit implications of FOFA and AirLand Battle. Indeed, doctrinal evolution might have stopped in the mid-1980s had it not been for several subsequent, near-simultaneous developments.

The 1986 Goldwater-Nichols Department of Defense Reorganization Act had several important and at first almost unnoticeable consequences for the U.S. defense establishment. The new congressional legislation enhanced the stature and functions of the warfighting commanders in chief (CINCs), who now exercised increased responsibility in planning for and conducting future joint and combined military operations.

A mandated emphasis on jointness forced the services to write doctrine with an eye toward a common understanding of the conduct of operations, both jointly and separately. With the creation of J–7, a new Joint Staff directorate, joint-level doctrinal stress fell increasingly on the development of common joint-level vocabulary and concepts. Under these circumstances, it was no accident that the U.S. Navy began to talk about operational art in maritime theaters. It was also no accident that Joint Publication 3–0, *Doctrine for Joint Operations*, and Joint Publication 5–0, *Doctrine for Planning Joint Operations*, focused more clearly and consistently on operational art.[36]

Another factor in contemporary doctrinal development was the end of the Cold War. One major result of vanishing bipolarity was a renewed effort to integrate regional perspectives and priorities into the crafting of U.S. national security and military strategies. These concepts provided guidance and a sense of larger context. The same concepts reinforced the impact of Goldwater-Nichols, causing CINCs to focus more distinctly on the development of theater-level strategies with an attendant but sometimes unspoken emphasis on operational art concerns. Campaign planning also had a role to play. It incorporated elements of operational art and theater-level strategy but also gradually evolved to contend with regional threats. Thus, another Cold War consequence had figured into the development of doctrine and concept: the emergence, or perhaps rediscovery, of major regional threats outside the context of traditional ideological conflict. Still another consequence was a deemphasis on the likelihood of nuclear war, a realization that forced all the U.S. services to ponder the challenges inherent in conducting extended conventional operations within the context of regional military conflict.

The post–Cold War era brought force reductions, force projection, and a scarcity of resources, all of which argued that future conflict would leave little room for service parochialism and little time for World War II–style on-the-job training. Key components of modern operations, especially logistics and sustainment, suddenly assumed greater significance. If during the 1970s and 1980s the Army worried about "first battles" in future war, now the joint community had to worry about "first operations" in future campaigns and wars.[37]

To prove this point, the 1990–1991 Gulf War erupted to provide an important impulse for a doctrinal reincarnation of operational art in joint guise. Operations in DESERT SHIELD/STORM reinforced the evolutionary flow in several ways. First, they unconsciously revisited Isserson's legacy by drawing attention to the complexities of planning and action required to bring about a reaggregation of combat effects within theater over time by disparate armed forces with disparate capabilities.[38] This realization lay at the heart of modern joint warfare and continues to provide fertile ground for continued doctrinal growth. Second, the conceptual tools inherent in the U.S. understanding of operational art, including center of gravity, played an important part in the calculus that brought allied victory. And third, with all the attention devoted to "high-tech" weaponry, the Gulf War reminded both the military and the public at large that a revolution in military affairs (RMA) was continuing apace, with important implications for the future.[39] One way of placing the RMA within context for theater application would be to view it within the intellectual and doctrinal perspective of operational art. After all, operational art was born in an era when the advent of air power and ground mechanization contributed to a specific theater-level focus, and there is no reason to believe that operational art as it has entered U.S. usage cannot again serve as a doctrinal catalyst for new ways to envision the conduct of future operations.

This operational art evolution overview demonstrates some of the verities and ironies inherent in the history of a concept. Concepts are based on ideas, and ideas over time can be picked up, dropped, and either reborn or refashioned to suit fresh circumstances and changed situations. In general, operational art first appeared during the 1920s in response to the shifting content of strategy, the changing nature of operations, and the evolving nature of military structures. The larger context included the appearance of major new elements within the international order and the constant intrusion of new technology into military conflict. During the late 1980s and early 1990s, all these conditions were once again present; and in one of the ironies of intellectual and military history, they elicited a rebirth of interest in operational art under different circumstances. The productive elaboration of this concept in contemporary context supports the contention that military thinkers and doctrine writers should always draw inspiration from the past but should not be bound by it. Indeed, the term's potential for retaining future significance argues that theorists should seek to expand and refine the limits of operational art. It and related concepts remain dynamic, and dynamism, while sometimes a source of confusion, is also an important sign of vitality and growth.

Notes

1. This article originally appeared in *Military Review* 77, no. 5 (September–October 1997): 32–47. It is reprinted here by permission of the author and the editors of *Military Review*.
2. The developments of the 1920s are summarized in James J. Schneider, *The Structure of Strategic Revolution: Total War and the Roots of the Soviet Warfare State* (Novato, Calif.: Presidio Press, 1994), chs. 5 and 6.
3. R. A. Savushkin, "K voprosu o zarozhdenii teoni posledovatel'nykh operatsiy" [Toward the Question of the Origin of the Theory of Successive Operations], *Voyenno-istoricheskiy zhurnal* [Military-Historical Journal] (hereafter cited as *VIZh*) (May 1983): 79–81.
4. A superb analysis of the changing nature of strategy within a theater is Georgiy S. Isserson, *Evolyutsiya operativnogo iskusstva* [The Evolution of Operational Art], 2d ed. (Moscow: Gosvoyenizdat, 1937), pp. 18–28.
5. Ibid., pp. 34–37.
6. The acute perceptions of a contemporary appear in Freiherr Hugo F. P. von Freytag-Loringhoven, *Deductions from the World War* (New York: G. P. Putnam's Sons, 1918), pp. 101–06.
7. The classic example of this trend was Aleksandr A. Svechin's textbook, *Strategiya* [Strategy], 2d ed. (Moscow: Voyennyî Vestnik, 1927), which has been edited by Kent D. Lee and translated into English as Aleksandr A. Svechin, *Strategy* (Minneapolis, Minn.: East View Publications, 1992); the first chapter describes "strategy in a number of military disciplines."
8. Arthur F. Lykke, Jr., "Toward an Understanding of Military Strategy" in *Military Strategy: Theory and Application*, ed. Arthur F. Lykke, Jr. (Carlisle Barracks, Pa.: U.S. Army War College, 1989), pp. 3–7.
9. Anton A. Kersnovskiy, *Filosofiya voyny* [The Philosophy of War] (Belgrade: Izd. Tsarskogo Vestnilka, 1939), p. 31.
10. See the commentary in Freiherr Hugo F. P. von Freytag-Loringhoven, *Heerführung im Weltkriege*, 2 vols. (Berlin: E. S. Mittler, 1920–1921), I: iii, 41, 45–46; cf. John English, "The Operational Art: Developments in the Theories of War," in *The Operational Art: Developments in the Theories of War*, ed. B. J. C. McKercher and Michael Hennessy (Westport, Conn.: Praeger, 1996), p. 13.
11. The origin of the term is categorically ascribed to Svechin by N. Varfolomeev, an early student of operational art, in "Stategiya v akademicheskoy postanovke" [Strategy in an Academic Setting], *Voyna i revolyutsiya* [War and Revolution] (November 1928): 84.
12. Svechin, *Strategy*, p. 269; see also Jacob W. Kipp, "Two Views of Warsaw: The Russian Civil War and Soviet Operational Art," in McKercher and Hennessy, *Operational Art*, pp. 61–65.
13. The officer most frequently associated with the comparative analysis of operations was V. K. Triandafillov, whose ground-breaking *Kharakter operatsiy sovremennykh armiy* [The Nature of the Operations at Modern Armies], 3d ed. (Moscow: Voyenizdat, 1936) has been edited by Jacob W. Kipp and translated into English as *The Nature of the Operations*

of Modern Armies (Essex, U.K.: Frank Cass and Co., Ltd., 1994); see especially part two.

14. Varfolomeev, "Strategiya v akademicheskoy postanovke," pp. 84–85.

15. This argument is clearly enunciated in Georgiy S. Isserson, "Osnovy glubokoy operatsii" [Fundamentals of the Deep Operation], as cited by Cynthia A. Roberts, "Planning for War: The Red Army and the Catastrophe of 1941," *Europe-Asia Studies* (December 1995): 1323.

16. R. A. Savushkin, *Razvitiye sovetskikh vooruzhyennykh sil voyennogo iskusstva v mezhvoyennyy period (1921–1941 gg.)* [The Development of the Soviet Armed Forces and Military Art during the Inter-War Period (1921–1941)] (Moscow: VPA, 1989), pp. 90–100.

17. Schneider, *Structure of Strategic Revolution*, pp. 231–65.

18. A comprehensive and provocative account of these and other continuities in modern German military development is Jehuda L. Wallach's *The Dogma of the Battle of Annihilation: The Theories of Clausewitz and Schlieffen and Their Impact on the German Conduct of Two World Wars* (Westport, Conn.: Greenwood Press, 1986), especially pp. 229–81.

19. See the discussion, for example, in John Keegan, *Six Armies in Normandy* (New York: Viking Press, 1982), p. 243.

20. The most recent critique of *Blitzkrieg* in operational-strategic perspective is Karl-Heinz Frieser, *Blitzkrieg-Legende*, 2d ed. (Munich: R. Oldenbourg Verlag, 1996), chs. 1 and 2; for the Soviet-German comparative perspective, see Shimon Naveh, *In Pursuit of Military Excellence: The Evolution of Operational Theory* (London: Frank Cass, 1997), pp. 221–38.

21. The attainments and difficulties of the prewar era are summarized in Georgiy S. Isserson, "Razvitiye teorii sovetskogo operativnogo iskusstva v 30-ye gody" [The Development at the Theory of Soviet Operational Art during the 1930s], *VIZh* (March 1965), especially pp. 54–59.

22. The most recent treatment of the Eastern Front in World War II is David M. Glantz and Jonathan M. House, *When Titans Clashed* (Lawrence: University Press of Kansas, 1995); the classic account of 1943 to 1945 in English remains John Erickson's *The Road to Berlin* (Boulder, Colo.: Westview Press, 1983).

23. Christopher R. Gabel, *The U.S. Army GHQ Maneuvers of 1941* (Washington, D.C.: U.S. Army Center of Military History 1992), pp. 185–94.

24. An eloquent summary with an emphasis on military geography is John Keegan, *Fields of Battle: The Wars for North America* (New York: Alfred A. Knopf, 1996), pp. 325–33.

25. See the overview in James J. Schneider, "War Plan RAINBOW 5," *Defense Analysis* (December 1994): 289–92.

26. L. D. Holder, "Educating and Training for Theater Warfare," in *On Operational Art*, ed. Clayton R. Newell and Michael D. Krause (Washington, D.C.: U.S. Army Center of Military History, 1994), pp.171–72.

27. Thomas W. Wolfe, *Soviet Power and Europe* (Baltimore: Johns Hopkins Press, 1970), pp. 32–49, 128–56.

28. The most recent account is Roger J. Spiller, "In the Shadow of the Dragon: Doctrine and the U.S. Army After Vietnam," *RUSI Journal* 142, no. 6 (December 1997): 41–54.

29. Paul H. Herbert, *Deciding What Has To Be Done: General William E. DePuy and the 1976 Edition of FM 100–5* (Fort Leavenworth, Kans.: Combat Studies Institute, 1988), pp. 25–36.

30. An engaging survey of doctrinal development between 1976 and 1982 is Richard Swain's "Filling the Void: The Operational Art and the U.S. Army," in McKercher and Hennessy, *Operational Art*, pp. 154–65.

31. For an indication of the renewed emphasis on operational art, see then Chief of the Soviet General Staff M. V. Zakharov's "O teorii giubokoy operatsii" [On the Theory of the Deep Operation] *VIZh* (October 1970): 10, 20. Overall context is provided by David M. Glantz, "The Intellectual Dimension of Soviet (Russian) Operational Art," in McKercher and Hennessy, *Operational Art*, pp. 135–39.

32. John English, "The Operational Art: Developments in the Theories of War," in McKercher and Hennessy, *Operational Art*, pp. 17–18.

33. For an overview, see John L. Romjue, *From Active Defense to AirLand Battle: The Development of Army Doctrine, 1973–1982* (Fort Monroe, Va.: U.S. Army Training and Doctrine Command, 1984), pp. 66–73.

34. William R. Richardson, "FM 100-5: The AirLand Battle in 1986," *Military Review* 66, no. 3 (March 1986): 4–11.

35. See, for example, William W. Mendel and Floyd T. Banks, Jr., *Campaign Planning* (Carlisle Barracks, Pa.: U.S. Army War College, 1988), pp. 5–15.

36. David A. Sawyer, "The Joint Doctrine Development System," *Joint Force Quarterly* (Winter 1996–1997): 36–39.

37. See chapter 5, "Doctrine for a New Time," in John L. Romjue, *American Army Doctrine for the Post–Cold War* (Fort Monroe, Va.: U.S. Army Training and Doctrine Command, 1996).

38. On the legacy of Isserson, see Frederick Kagan, "Army Doctrine and Modern War: Notes Toward a New Edition of FM 100–5," *Parameters* (Spring 1997): 139–40.

39. See, for example, James K. Morningstar, "Technologies, Doctrine, and Organization for RMA," *Joint Force Quarterly* (Spring 1997): 37–43.

PART ONE: FRANCE

Introduction

Clearly, one of the most influential personalities from military history is Napoleon Bonaparte. His ability to deploy and maneuver large independent forces simultaneously to concentrate them at the critical moment of battle set an operational tone that successive commanders around the world have labored to replicate. Napoleon's campaigns were the antecedent to later developments that became known as the operational art of war.

David Chandler, the world-renowned British historian, develops this idea, particularly regarding Napoleon's contribution to the evolution of operational art through his organizational innovations. The emperor's corps-size organizations could operate independently against larger enemy forces, while additional personnel and materiel resources were introduced to the battle. Aiding these efforts were his aggressive tactics, focused objectives, active intelligence, and firm command of all aspects of a campaign. The Jena-Auerstadt campaign of 1806 is the example that Dr. Chandler cites as the beginnings of the successful application of the operational art.

Robert Doughty continues the analysis of French operational art as the country began to alter its military doctrine in light of its losses suffered from the Franco-Prussian War. As the country's military leaders grappled with improving its military educational system, organization, and doctrine, they set out to redefine both the methods and the means by which the next European war would be fought on the frontiers of France. The start of the Great War witnessed massive military maneuvers reminiscent of Napoleon's Grand Armée, but with the exception of "The Miracle of the Marne," these campaigns were fruitless. By the latter half of the war, preponderant firepower and limited objectives had replaced large-scale maneuvers and more aggressive goals. Sadly, they assumed that what seemed to work at the close of World War I would set the pace for the next European conflict. Perhaps, if the *Wehrmacht* had been more conventional and less aggressive, French military doctrine in 1940 might have been vindicated. Unfortunately, the French never seemed to fully grasp the difference between tactics and the operational level of war, which ultimately contributed to the horrific casualties of World War I and the tragic defeat of World War II.

Napoleon, Operational Art, and the Jena Campaign

David G. Chandler

Napoleon would have had no difficulty in understanding and applying the modern concept of operational art. Napoleon's philosophy of war was simple and to the point. It ensured the predominance of the political aim to achieve the "continuation of policy by other means." He ensured an objective setting from the political perspective and then set the military aim. As early as 1787 we find the young General Bonaparte professing this conviction: "There are in Europe today many good generals, but they see too many things at once. I see only one thing, namely the enemy's main body. I strive to crush it, confident that secondary matters will then settle themselves."[1] Here lies the heart, the central theme, of Napoleon's concept of warfare: the *Blitzkrieg* attack aimed at the main repository of the enemy, the center of gravity, his army. Such is the kernel of Napoleon's understanding of what we today term operational art.

To the end of his days Napoleon denied he had operated according to any hard and fast set of precepts or principles. Between 1796 and 1809, he practiced warfare's apparently limitless variation and flexibility. Two phrases require elucidation. First, "a careful balancing of means and ends, efforts and obstacles"[2] brings out the true economy of force, the careful allocation of available military and political power to the achievement of the politico-military aim. It further connotes the need to avoid keeping large reserves in pointless inactivity to the rear and, equally important, employing large forces to achieve minor, secondary objectives. It calls for the correct timing of the employment of sufficient force and above all requires the achievement of a carefully calculated balance at all stages of military operations between ends and means, between inevitably conflicting priorities for the employment of strictly finite resources. The object of everything at the levels of both strategy and operational art is the destruction of the enemy's state of equilibrium, ideally by means of psychological domination before the decisive battle physically opens.

Second, the need "to make war a real science." By real, Napoleon meant living and effective. Warfare must be conducted in a realistic, practical, and decisive fashion. There is no place for posturing or "phoneywar" attitudes—chessboard maneuvers designed to avoid a major battle at all costs. The attritional stage, battle, is only intended as preparation for the third, or mobile stage, which leads to the coup de grâce. But of course it must be appreciated that Napoleon was head of state as well as supreme military commander in the field. Thus, he decided policy at the strategic level as well as implemented its military objectives at the operational level. His key subordinates, the commanders of *corps d'armée*, the vital building blocks of Napoleonic warfare, were rarely if ever permitted to indulge in free interpretation of their orders. In this fact lay both the strength and weakness of Napoleon's conduct of war. Highly motivated and closely controlled marshals of the empire were redoubtable instruments in achieving victory at the operational and tactical levels. Left on their own or divided by many hundreds of miles from their master, the emperor, the results could be (and frequently were) rampant indecision, rivalry, indiscipline—and failure. Any study of the campaigns in Spain and Portugal, particularly from 1812 when Napoleon was 2,000 miles away in Russia or in 1813 deep in central Germany, will bear this out. Thus, the supreme centralization of Napoleonic warfare had serious potential weakness as well as important strengths. But when Napoleon was present and controlling a manageable force by the lights of the time—say, some 250,000 men (as in 1805, 1806, or 1809)—there were few things he was incapable of achieving. The military concepts flowed smoothly into the political goals that the emperor could rapidly adjust.

Napoleon had a masterly grasp of military geography. He would tax his librarian for books on historical, descriptive, geographical, and topical aspects of Europe. He appreciated the political and geographical realities of each of the regions in Europe. He does not, however, appear to have appreciated the overall immensity of the physical problems presented by the campaigns in the Iberian Peninsula, "where small armies are swallowed up and large armies starve,"[3] or by the expanse of Russia.

For Napoleon, the concept of a successful campaign connoted one that achieved its real object for the most economical expenditure in terms of time and resources. The conquest and occupation of terrain was secondary in importance. Considerations of time spent or wasted were far more significant. "The loss of time is irreparable in war." "Strategy is the art of making use of time and space. I am less chary of the latter than the former; space we can recover, time never." "I may lose a battle, but I shall never lose a minute." "Time is the great element between weight and force."[4]

The proper use of available time usually called for speed and accuracy of movement by large bodies of troops, all of them integrated and synchronized according to the requirement of a campaign plan.

Napoleon commanded by means of the Imperial Headquarters (*le grand quartier-général*, or *GQG*). This organization was not only the headquarters for the army in the field, but it also comprised virtually the entire government of France. It was divided into the military component, headed by a chief of staff (under Berthier) who headed a general staff, an administrative headquarters (headed by the *intendant*, Count Daru), and a personal staff, including troubleshooting general officers. The tasks of the staff on campaign were fourfold. First, it supervised and controlled the movements of large bodies of men, equipment, and convoys, moving in two directions: toward the front and toward the rear. Second, it acquired and evaluated intelligence from the entire theater of war. Third, it controlled all military activity on up to a seventy-mile front. And fourth, it transmitted and received reports and orders over a large area, thus maintaining the critically important flow of information, which alone made possible "the ever shifting kaleidoscope of moves and intentions."[5]

Napoleon on campaign often operated with the aid of his *petit quartier-général* (or battle headquarters), which accompanied him on his incessant daily tours of inspection, for the emperor was a staunch believer in "seeing and being seen." This group usually comprised Berthier, Caulaincourt, the marshal-of-the-day on headquarters duty, a pair of aides-de-camp selected by roster, four orderly officers, one page of the household entrusted with Napoleon's telescope, the bodyguard Roustam, an imperial groom, an officer-interpreter and a soldier of the escort carrying the portfolio of maps. Four squadrons of Guard Cavalry formed the escort commanded by a general, to which was added on days of battle a section of *artillerie volante* (portable artillery, which customarily consisted of four guns) that deployed themselves whenever the entourage halted to command all four approaches to the main group. Normally Napoleon rode carefully trained, quiet Arab horses, but for longer distances he would transfer to his calèche or his large post-chaise (organized as a mobile office).

His campaign routine was designed to suit the workings of the staff system, and to pack as much as was possible into a 24-hour period. Each evening Napoleon would retire to sleep at 2000 and rise at midnight. In his office tent, he would find abstracts prepared by Berthier of the latest reports from the corps commanders sent the previous evening. After dictating any necessary orders, the emperor would retire for another hour or two of sleep. By 0600 he would have dressed and breakfasted. A first conference with Bacler d'Albe in the map office would be followed by important interviews. Returning to his desk, he would find the reports *abrégé* from outlying formations and the expanded and finally prepared orders of earlier that morning awaiting his signature. Any he disapproved he flung on the floor or, if of particularly grave importance, put carefully to one side with the remark: "Until tomorrow; of night brings counsel."[6] More dictation and interviews followed, and by 1000 the latest batch of fair-written orders would be ready for final approval and dispatch.

Napoleon would next call for his horse and set off with the *petit quartier-général* to inspect troops, award the occasional unexpected medal to a delighted veteran at the roadside, visit subordinates and (less popularly) their headquarters' staffs, and, when necessary, conduct reconnaissance often at considerable personal risk, to the anxiety of his officers and escort. By 1500 or 1600 he would be back at main *GQG* (which would probably have moved forward to a new location during his absence—he detested disorder and always tried to avoid the bustle of packing and unpacking) to hold a second map-tent conference with d'Albe, consider any recent messages, and then dictate more orders and grant further interviews. Meals were haphazardly taken and rarely lasted more than twenty minutes. An hour's relaxation might follow at 1900, involving reminiscing over old battles with intimates or the occasional card game that the emperor invariably won by fair means or foul—such was the understanding. A final conference with the indispensable d'Albe and possibly Berthier, and the emperor's eighteen-hour day was over. He would enter his sleeping tent, Roustam would place himself across the doorway, while the aides-de-camp and secretary on duty settled down in the anteroom-tent for, they hoped, a few hours of relative rest; and a silence zone of 100 meters would come into effect around the sleeping genius.

Serving Napoleon was no sinecure. His work capacity appeared limitless and he expected the same dedication from all around him. Once around 1812 Berthier was found in tears: "I am being killed by hard work; a mere private soldier is happier than I."[7] The emperor could fly into sudden rage and strike out with his riding crop at any within range; but his ability to snatch at will occasional short sleep at quiet moments of the day (even amidst the din of battle, as at Wagram in 1809) helped him recharge his mental and physical energies.

Napoleon also operated a completely separate information gleaning and overseeing system. Attached to his person rather than to the staff were up to a dozen *adjutants-général*—hand-picked young colonels who were given temporary rank of *général de brigade* or (more rarely) *général de division*, none aged over forty, who were used as his "eyes and ears" and as "trouble shooters." They would be expected to undertake everything from boiling an egg to commanding a critical attack and required tact as well as stamina. Each of these trusted aides had a couple of personal assistants. They could also call upon the dozen *officers d'ordonnance*—subalterns and captains under twenty-four years of age, noted for their intelligence, courage, and absolute devotion to the emperor, many being engineers and gunners (selected in later years from the annual classes emerging from *L'École Polytechnique de Paris*)—who were often entrusted with carrying Napoleon's own messages.

The staff's ability to effect the conduct of warfare at operational level was in large measure determined by Berthier's ceaseless supervision and urging, and by the extension of the staff system to the levels of *corps d'armée* and to the divisions of infantry and cavalry they contained. Each corps had a miniaturized form of the *GQG*. Its commander would have an *adjutant-général* (or senior adviser)—a chief of staff—up to eight aides-de-camp for intelligence gathering, five officers of the general staff (one for each section under a coordinator), and perhaps half-a-dozen spare officers—perhaps two dozen officers in all, supplemented by up to twelve more specialists—logisticians, convoy directors, a senior surgeon, and two representatives from Daru's administrative staff. Lower down the chain of command came the divisional staffs, once again reflecting the main branches of the *GQG*, and once again standardized, containing eleven officers. All in all, this was a logical if in some ways over-exclusive and top-heavy system, but it is surprising to note that there was no formal training for staff officers, nothing resembling a staff college. Staff officers were carefully selected by commanding generals from experienced subordinates whom they could trust, and below *GQG* level (where most appointments except the most junior were permanent) officers rotated between line and staff.

Napoleon was extremely thorough in his planning, leaving as little as possible to chance. He researched possible future campaigns by voracious reading to build up a clear picture and estimation of his opponent. "I am accustomed to thinking out what I shall do three or four months in advance, and I base my calculations on the worst conceivable situations."[8] This statement reveals the emperor's thoroughness—but he was not tied to a master plan. He was convinced that any plan needed many branches or alternative courses of action built into it, so as to be adaptable to actual circumstances. To that extent there is validity in his other claim: "one engages, then one sees." But his normal rule is far more methodical in tone: "Nothing is attained in war except by calculation. During a campaign whatever is not profoundly considered in all its detail is without result. Every enterprise should be conducted according to a system; chance alone can never bring success."[9]

At the same time Napoleon never underestimated the part sheer chance played in the prosecution of war. It was an important "unknown factor" that had to be placed almost algebraically within his calculations. Careful foresight could reduce the detrimental effects of chance, and every plan included a margin of time available for making good any damage so caused or for exploiting any unforeseen windfall. On campaign or in battle, Napoleon's operational mind was continually assessing and reassessing the odds:

> Military science ... consists in calculating all the chances accurately in the first place and then giving accident exactly, almost mathematically, its place in one's calculations. It is upon this point that one must not deceive oneself, and yet a decimal point more or less may change all. Now this apportioning of accident and science cannot get into any head except that of a genius.... Accident, hazard, chance, call it what you may—a mystery to ordinary minds—becomes a reality to superior men.[10]

A major purpose of seeking accurate intelligence in war is to reduce the unknown to manageable proportions. Napoleon used embassies at the strategic level. He used cavalry and spies at the operational level. He sought to use cavalry not only to gather intelligence but also to deceive an opponent as to his own strength and intentions. Napoleon served as his own intelligence evaluator, cutting out intermediate intelligence tiers—and this could lead to rapid decision-making and orders issued.[11]

The reverse side of achieving surprise and good intelligence is the ensuring of security for one's own operations, including the deception of the foe. Napoleon was a past master at concealing his own strength and intention from the enemy. Long before a campaign opened a security curtain would be lowered. The press was ruthlessly controlled and "tuned" to produce only the information—more often disinformation—that the Emperor wished the foe to comprehend. Weeks before a major military movement the frontiers would be closed to foreigners and the surveillance by Fouché's secret police redoubled. At the same time elaborate deception schemes would be implemented to create apparent military threats in areas where none in fact existed.

Once a military movement had begun, a dense mobile screen of light cavalry and dragoons would deny the enemy's probing patrols any inkling of what lay behind. Cavalry screens would equally be employed in wholly irrelevant areas to increase the bewilderment of the enemy. They also would protect the French line of communication snaking back to the *place de campagne* (operational base) or the intermediate *centres des opérations*, because Napoleon believed in keeping his links to his supply and munitions dumps, hospitals, and the like as short as possible. Napoleon frequently changed the composition of major formations in mid-campaign for operational or administrative reasons, inevitably increasing the confusion of the enemy's intelligence services as they strove to keep abreast of developments.

One of the most successful ways of achieving surprise in war is using speed to confound enemy intelligence and to present his command, control, communications, and intelligence (C3I) functions with either fait accompli or with the discouraging need to be forever adjusting to hostile initiatives. This would induce paralysis in decision-making and lead to psychological collapse. Napoleon was highly adept at inducing this state of affairs.

Napoleon's armies most certainly could move fast. In the First Italian Campaign of 1796, General Fiorella marched Augereau's division from the siege lines before Mantua to Castiglione—a matter of fifty miles—in thirty-six hours. Early the next year, Masséna force-marched his division from Verona (where it had been in action) on 13 January to join General Bonaparte at Rivoli. He fought a day-long battle there (the fourteenth), was put back on the road to Mantua that evening, and reached La Favorita on its outskirts on the sixteenth—thus ending up with having fought three actions and covered fifty-four miles of ground in just 120 hours. This was no mean feat. In 1805 Napoleon moved 210,000 men from the Rhine to the Danube around Donauwörth in between eleven and twenty-five days, the more outlying formations in the great wheel across central Germany having to cover all of 250 miles. Soult's IV Corps, for example, marched 275 miles between September 24 and October 16 in that operation. Between November 30 and the early hours of December 2, 1805, Davout drove Friant's division of III Corps over 140 kilometers in little over forty-eight hours, thirty-five of them spent on the road. Similar examples of sustained marching are to be found as late as 1814. Well indeed might Napoleon declare that "Marches are war," and his men wryly comment that "the Emperor has discovered a new way of making war; he makes use of our legs instead of our arms!"[12] Well might the emperor claim that he was more chary of losing time than space. But in fact he wrung the utmost out of both.

The basic building block for operational utilization was the *corps d'armée*. It was a self-contained fighting formation of infantry, cavalry, and artillery, together with supply and medical services, the whole controlled by a carefully designed staff of from 25,000 to 30,000 men. The basic calculation was that a *corps d'armée* could fight alone for up to twenty-four hours before having to be reinforced by neighboring formations moving up to its aid. Writing to his stepson, Eugène Beauharnais, Viceroy of Italy, on 7 June 1809, the emperor discussed this feature:

> Here is a general principle of war: ... a corps ... can be left on its own. Well handled, it can fight or alternatively avoid action, and maneuver according to circumstances without any harm coming to it, because an opponent cannot force it to accept an engagement—but if it chooses to do so it can fight alone for a long time.[13]

This requirement formed one basis for the operational "square battalion" formation made up of a number of army corps acting like the tentacles of an octopus. The composition of an individual corps was rarely a fixed matter but fluctuated considerably during a campaign or even on the eve of battle, because Napoleon frequently made alterations to confuse the enemy or to meet some special requirements. This type of flexibility obviously conferred important operational advantage.

There was another important implication in this relative invulnerability of a major French formation for up to a day's duration. This was that the corps could be routed through enemy countryside along its own axis of advance. This capacity could often increase both the overall speed of advance and general flexibility of operational employment. In short, it gave simultaneity to the operational advance of the corps. The ultimate aim of all this carefully coordinated activity was to produce the greatest number of troops on the battlefield, which could decide the outcome of the campaign. It was axiomatic for Napoleon to mass as many bayonets and sabers on the battlefield as possible. But dispersal before battle was as important as concentration in battle. On the eve of a major engagement it was more important that troops should be assembled than concentrated. By assembly, Napoleon understood the placing of his formations within close-support marching distance, not shoulder to shoulder on the battle line. It was vital to have sufficient troops disengaged to provide an enveloping or outflanking force. Equally, it was necessary to have sufficiently elastic disposition to be able to meet any unforeseen threat or development (the question of reserves figured large in this consideration). And third, the interests of field security and concealment of French intentions for as long as possible had to be taken into account. From these principles derives the true meaning of the dictum: "The army must be kept assembled and the greatest possible force concentrated on the field of battle."[14]

Much of the success of Napoleon's operational concepts lay in his creation of a web of carefully positioned formations. At the outset of a campaign, the net was widely spread; it almost resembled a cordon. Thus, for example, in the Jena campaign in October 1806, Napoleon's frontage was reduced from the initial 200 to just 45 kilometers for the passage of the problematical Thüringer Wald. Once that obstacle had been successfully negotiated, the front expanded again to 60 kilometers for the northward advance toward Leipzig. Then the crash concentration of all the forces west in the direction of Weimar was ordered when "the veil [of uncertainty] was torn" and the elusive Prussian Army was discovered beyond the River Saale. This broad base of Napoleonic operational deployment was not allowed to contradict the principle of "concentration." The enemy was steadily enveloped in the weaving tentacles, and then finally enmeshed by the last-minute "pounce" achieved by the ordering of a forced march (up to twenty-two miles), largely under cover of darkness. In this way Napoleon fused maneuver with battle, and thereafter, with pursuit, thereby making probably his greatest original contribution to the art and science of war, at least at the operational level. Napoleon succeeded more than any other soldier did before his time in fusing marching, fighting, and pursuit into one continuous and remorseless process. The development of the campaign of 1806 against Prussia is the model example.

To facilitate this process the emperor laid down a series of different operational alignments for his *corps d'armée*. These included the deployment of his major formations in a wedge-shaped disposition, or in echelon (with one flank refused), or with one flank *en potence*—loosely akin to Frederick the Great's "oblique order"—according to circumstances and the requirements of the overall general plan. But his most favored formation was *le bataillon carré* (the battalion of square). By this the army corps were disposed in a diamond-shaped rectangular formation, with an advance guard preceded by the cavalry screen in the presumed direction of the main enemy army, a right and a left wing, in the center the *GQG*, and in rear a reserve. Each component might be made up of one or more corps. It was critically important that no single corps should be more than one day's marching distance from at least one (better two) neighboring formations; and ideally the entire army should be so placed as to be able to achieve a crash concentration at the threatened or decisive point within the space of forty-eight to seventy-two hours. The great advantage conferred by *le bataillon carré* was that it permitted the emperor to take greater risks than a more formal deployment would permit, thus retaining the vital initiative by the sheer boldness of his offensive. For, given the high mobility rate, the logistical self-sufficiency, and the ability to fight alone for up to twenty-four hours (if necessary) of each individual corps, Napoleon was provided with the highest possible level of operational flexibility. He could advance—as in October 1806—without any clear knowledge as to where the enemy main body was situated and adjust his line of attack according to circumstances. Self-sufficiency and mutual support were the keys to success.

No better example of Napoleon's applying his principles of operational art can be found than the campaign he waged in central Europe against Prussia in late 1806. The military events that took place during the thirty-three days of active campaigning between 8 October 1806 (when French troops first entered Saxony) and 10 November (which saw Mortier's occupation of Hamburg) constitute a military masterpiece of the first order, and merit the most careful study. At the outset, however, two general observations must be made. However brilliant Napoleon's military achievement in 1806, it must be stressed that in one important political respect, the French campaign failed to achieve its purpose. For although Napoleon accomplished the strategic design by the defeat of Prussia, Jena-Auerstädt and the brilliant followup failed to achieve a favorable political pacification. Second, even the military achievements of 1806 contain no less than six major Napoleonic errors and miscalculations of command, control, communications, and intelligence, which will be described and analyzed below. Thus, it was the inherent adaptability of Napoleon's grasp of operational art that was arguably the most important (even, dare we suggest, the saving?) aspect of his performance. His mastery of the "alternative plan"[15] was to prove essential to success. This may be termed the inherent flexibility in the Napoleonic application of operational art.

Without detailing the entire diplomatic and political background that led Prussia to war, the Napoleonic efforts to achieve the consolidation of his political position in Europe with the announcement of the creation of the French-oriented Confederation of the Rhine on 12 July, and on 6 August 1806 the final and irrevocable dissolution of the anachronistic Holy Roman Empire, there seemed to be no bounds to Napoleon's ambition. The argument still rages whether Napoleon set out deliberately to provoke a war with Prussia. Not that weak-willed Frederick-William III and his Francophile minister Haugwitz together with "the Peace Party" at Potsdam might have found it impossible to accept the new condition; but it was wholly unacceptable to the king's beautiful and strong-minded spouse, Queen Louise, who headed the war party at court that included the Gallophobic Hardenburg and two senior generals, the Duke of Brunswick and Prince Hohenlohe. The argument raged behind closed doors, and in the end the war party triumphed, but only, it is often claimed, after the strong-willed queen had persistently denied conjugal rights to her uxorious husband until he fell into line. In August 1807 the decision for war was at last taken in secret—and for once French diplomatic intelligence did not fully discover the secret for a full month.

Prussian Armies and War Plans

The Prussian Army of 1806 could place 171,000 troops into first-line formations (including 35,000 cavalry and 550 guns), supported by a further 83,000 men in garrison. Its reputation as the creation of the august Frederick still hung like an aura around its name. In fact, however, as Clausewitz remarked, "behind the fine facade all was mildewed."[16] As General Fuller has pronounced, "the Prussian Army was a museum piece."[17] Clinging to outdated concepts, ferocious discipline was imposed to achieve uniformity, which was deemed more important than inspiration. Rigid linear drills were regarded as de rigueur, and the precision was considered more important than speed or flexibility. The supply trains were enormous in extent, the army depended upon magazines and depots for food and munitions, and as a consequence a day's march of twelve miles was considered the outside limit.

The cult of the past was carried to unreasonable lengths. The infantry were brave and well disciplined after the fashion of "walking muskets," but their muskets were the worst in Europe, most of them being of the 1754 pattern. Formal tactics discouraged all thought of initiative. The Prussian cavalry was bold and dashing, as became the heirs of von Seydlitz, and exceptionally well mounted (the horse studs of Prussia were a major resource that France would not be slow to exploit after October), but they were highly conservative as to role and employment on campaign. The artillery was imposing in size but often badly handled. Morale—despite the setbacks sustained from Valmy onward in the War of the First Coalition—was exceedingly (but unrealistically) high. Yet the Prussian soldier would fight bravely and tenaciously—their Saxon comrades a little less so.

The worst attribute lay at staff level. Leadership was not on a par with that of the 1760s, and by 1806 had become entrusted to a junta of septuagenarians. Under the king, whom nobody, least of all himself, regarded as a soldier, the chief command devolved on the Duke of Brunswick, 71 years of age. The senior royal adviser was Field Marshal von Mollendorf, aged 82 years. Blücher—regarded as unreliably youthful for senior command—was already 64, while Prince Hohenlohe and General Schmettau were striplings of 60. Had there been even a weak predecessor of the "Great General Staff" of von Moltke the Elder and the mid nineteenth century, all might have been compensated for, but in 1806 there was not even an embryonic staff corps. Worse, there were no less than three chiefs of staff, General Phull and Colonels Scharnhorst and Massenbach. The Prussian Army of 1806 presents the nigh-perfect example of an army (and behind it a government and nation) putting all its faith in dimming memories of past achievements. In doing so, it was committing the cardinal errors of falling into complacency and purblind conservatism, whilst falling victim to persistent demands for retrenchment and economy.

In August 1806 the French had approximately 160,000 men and 300 guns in southern Germany, with half as many on the River Main and the Middle Rhine. These troops were probably the best in terms of experience that Napoleon ever commanded. Fresh from their two successes at Ulm and Austerlitz, the survivors were aware of their mettle—and that of their leaders. The infantry and artillery were particularly strong, although the cavalry was still capable of improvement. At the peak of their reputation, the French were led by the eighteen marshals created in May 1804—Berthier, Soult, Davout, Lannes, Bernadotte, Augereau, Mortier, and the rest—whose average age was 36 years,[18] the same as that of their incomparable leader. That of the Prussian high command, by contrast, was all of 60 years. If it came to war with Prussia it would be a case of youth and energy against supposedly superior experience. All in all, Napoleon's army of 1806 was a finely geared and ruthlessly efficient war machine. It was, however, deployed over a wide area carrying out occupation duties. Placed in cantonments stretching from the River Main to Vienna, and south from the Danube to the approaches to the Alps, it might appear at first glance to be overextended, tempting a foe to attempt a surprise attack to defeat it in detail before concentration could be completed. The decisive battle might be expected, therefore, the Prussian generals considered, behind the Saale or Main.

On no other point than French overextension was the hydra-headed Prussian high command found to be in general agreement. Their uncertainties and rivalries provide an excellent example of the depths to which the planning side of operational art can be allowed to sink. Clearly, no concept of contingency planning existed. For a full month the complexities of military protocol were allowed to hold sway, and only in early September did anything like a Prussian order of battle begin to emerge.

Eventually, three field armies were organized. The first, under Brunswick, numbered 70,000 men drawn from the Berlin and Magdeburg districts to form between Leipzig and Naumburg. The second, commanded by Hohenlohe, initially 50,000 strong but ultimately 70,000 men following the forcible assimilation of the Saxon Army, drew up around Dresden. The third, under Generals Rüchel and Blücher, took post near Mühlhausen and Göttingen, respectively. Of their total pieces of artillery, served by 15,000 men, 300 were heavy and medium guns, the balance being regimental pieces. Such were the Prussian dispositions on 25 September.

As to how this force, imposing on paper, was best to be used became the subject of prolonged and often acrimonious debate. No less than five main plans emerged. Scharnhorst (Blücher's chief of staff) put forward the most sensible scheme—to await the arrival of the tsar's army already assembling under General Bennigsen on the River Bug. If necessary (especially if Napoleon struck first), space could be traded for time in a series of holding actions in the Thüringer Wald, along the Elbe, or even in extremity on the Oder. Nobody else came out in support of this suggestion, which several claimed would compromise the army's honor, and it was therefore dropped. Second, the idea of awaiting Napoleon around Erfurt and Hof, taking up positions to outflank the *Grand Armée*, was mooted. This also was dropped as too defensive. Third, Brunswick pressed for the superficially attractive concept of moving a single, strong army through Erfurt toward Würzburg and thence on to threaten Stuttgart in the hope of catching the French in their cantonment areas, or if not to at least compromise their communications with France. The jealous Hohenlohe spoke strongly against this plan, advocating instead a more easterly move through Hof on Bamberg. The high command also ruled out this plan when it was realized that it would involve stringing out the three armies along a ninety-mile front, with only the smallest of reserves near Naumburg. The sinister (or incompetent) Massenbach put forward the wildest idea of all—an apparently pointless military parade by the Silesian Army (his own, naturally) through Hof to the Danube and thence back into Saxony. At last the king intervened in the wrangling, and imposed a fifth plan, involving the implementation of the main features of both Brunswick's and Hohenlohe's operational schemes—a compromise that pleased nobody.

This notwithstanding, the reams of preliminary orders had already been issued to implement the king's compromise plan, when on 27 September the council of war suddenly reverted to the adoption of Brunswick's original plan in total. The rusty cogs of the Prussian military machine agonizingly went into reverse as further quires of contradictory orders were rushed to the regiments, and a state of chaos ensued as attempts were made to reorganize. Hardly had this process started when Captain Muffling returned from a reconnaissance on 5 October with the alarming news that Napoleon himself had some days before already left the Würzburg/Bamberg area and was advancing with a large force toward Bayreuth and Coburg as if intending to invade Saxony. At once the whole issue returned into the melting pot and more time was wasted as the news and its implications were hotly debated. Should the Prussians draw up behind the Saale, or should the three armies join near Leipzig? Nobody, however, reverted to Scharnhorst's plan. He lamented: "What we ought to do I know right well; what we shall do, only the gods know."[19]

At last Brunswick made up his mind—or rather had his decision forced upon him by developing circumstances, for Napoleon had already taken the initiative. In order "to defeat them by an oblique and rapid movement against the direction they will be following,"[20] he ordered the army to mass west of the Saale to threaten the French western flank. Strong cavalry forces, supported by the Duke of Weimar's infantry detachment, were to probe the French communications toward Neustadt and Hildburghausen. The remainder of Brunswick's army was to reach Weimar by 9 October and then move on toward Blankenheim, while Hohenlohe was to reach Hochdorf on the same day, before concentrating at Rudolstadt to the west of the Saale. A small part of Tauenzien's reconnaissance force was left to watch Hof, while Rüchel was to send detachments toward the already famous Fulda Gap to increase the perils to Napoleon's rear, his main force marching from Eisenach to make contact with Brunswick between Gotha and Fulda. The 13,000-strong general reserve was to move from Magdeburg to Halle, ready to join Brunswick at Leipzig or Naumburg as events dictated.

Granted that this was a wholly defensive operational scheme, all in all it represented a sound plan, but the detail was excessive. This permitted Hohenlohe, jubilant that his senior's plan for driving on Würzburg had been abandoned, to presume that his concept for a massing of troops east of the Saale was thereby agreed, at least by implication. Accordingly, without reference to his commander-in-chief, he promptly ordered the Saxon corps to Auma and Schleiz, while a further division under Prince Louis Ferdinand was moved to Saalfeld. The result was to place these troops directly in the path of Napoleon's advance.

Napoleon's Operational Plan

While the Prussians wavered from one course of action to another, Napoleon was completing his own mobilization plans, calling to the tricolors 30,000 reservists and calling up 50,000 conscripts of the class of 1806 on 5 September. The tsar's refusal to ratify the pact convinced the emperor that there was trouble afoot; and even if the Prussians were a month ahead of him in terms of preparations for war, he intended to preempt their offensive. Accordingly, the same day found Berthier ordered "to send engineer officers to make full reconnaissance of the roads from

Bamberg to Berlin, taking all necessary risks."[21] He was further ordered to make ready to assemble Soult's IV, Ney's VI, and Augereau's VII Corps at Bamberg within a week of receiving the executive order. Four days later the chief of staff was informed that in the event of war the line of communications would most likely run from Strasburg to Mannheim, Mainz, and Würzburg, utilizing the Rhine and Main Rivers for barge traffic.[22]

Paradoxically, the very indecision and continuous redeployments of the Prussian forces caused Napoleon considerable difficulty. As intelligence reports began to arrive at *GQG*, he found their reported movements impossible to understand—as well he might. Why were they not preparing to hold the mighty Elbe River line, "the Rhine of Prussia"? Why were they placing themselves so far forward and to the west of the Elbe barrier when any rudimentary knowledge of the basic principles of operational art should have convinced Frederick-William III of the advantages he could acquire by trading time for space (particularly as Napoleon now had good reason to believe that Russia was on the point of allying herself to Prussia and doubtless "infamous Albion" to form a fourth coalition)? "Prussian movements continue to be most extraordinary," he informed Berthier on 10 September. "They need to be taught a lesson. My horses leave [Paris] tomorrow and the Guard will follow in a few days time.... If the news continues to indicate that the Prussians have lost their heads, I shall travel directly to Würzburg or Bamberg."[23] Clearly, Napoleon was still leaving his options open. If the enemy marched for the Upper Main, then Würzburg would constitute the better center of operations. If they continued to hesitate, then Bamberg would be his choice.

Napoleon is known to have considered three possible operational plans for the campaign of 1806. His problem was to devise a means of ensuring the decisive defeat of Prussia without exposing French territory—or that of its allies—to Prussian (or conceivably British) invasion and ideally before Russia could intervene in the struggle.

The three courses of action open to him were as follows. First, the most direct route to Berlin lay from Wesel through Münster and Hanover. Much of this area was already in French hands, and its proximity to the Channel and North Sea would facilitate warding off any British landing in the area. On the other hand, there were several major disadvantages in this option. The redeployment of the *Grand Armée* from its present location in cantonments around the Main and Danube Rivers would take no little time to achieve. It might not be complete before the onset of winter, and this could earn the Prussian foe time to appreciate Napoleon's purposes, to bring Bennigsen's Russian army from the east, and even make it possible for Austria, anxious to avenge the humiliations of 1805, to throw over the Peace of Pressburg and enter the struggle, which would thus become one of continental extent. Two final disadvantages clinched the issue. A series of major river lines bisected this route of advance upon

Berlin, offering Prussia a series of natural defensive positions. Furthermore, the greater distance the Prussians retreated the closer they would come to their Russian friends.

Second, there was the possibility of an offensive directed from a center of operations at Mainz through the Fulda Gap toward Eisenach, where after a line of operations through either Magdeburg or Leipzig and Dessau—or both—would force through a road to Berlin and Potsdam. Such an operational scheme held the advantages of being closer to the present French cantonments, and of using the tried invasion route of the Fulda Gap. But after Fulda the terrain became far less favorable; the Unstrut, Saale, and Elbe Rivers would have to be crossed in turn; once again, any Prussian retreat eastward would bring them closer to the Russians; and it would be difficult to keep a close eye on Austria.

Third, there was an operational plan based upon Würzburg and Bamberg, leading to a major drive northeastward, toward Gera, Leipzig, and, once again, Berlin. The advantages of such an operational plan were substantial. First, at strategic level, Napoleon would be able to represent his offensive as an attempt to assist Saxony against the Prussian invaders who had already crossed its frontiers unbidden. It was also evident from the map that the forming-up areas were closest to the present dispersal zones of the *corps d'armée*—and close enough to the Danube to continue to overawe Austria—provided the generally north-flowing Saale and Pleisse as useful flank guards once the main movement was established. It also offered the possibility of driving a salient between the Prussians west of the Saale and any possible Russian intervention.

Of course, there were also disadvantages. The opening of the campaign would involve the passage of the difficult Thüringer Wald over only three available passes of which one or more might be blocked if the Prussians divulged the French intentions. During this early part of the incursion into Saxony, moreover, there would be no viable lateral roads to permit intercommunication between the three French columns. However, Napoleon doubted the Prussians would be able to block all three passes, and whichever routes proved open would permit the more fortunate column or columns to take the defenders of any blocking position in the flank or rear. However, this route, like both of the others, would inevitably lead to the mighty Elbe, which would have to be crossed. And third, as this operational plan was placed farthest from the English Channel, special security measures would have to be taken to provide for any British raiding activities against the northern coasts of the French empire. These measures might nevertheless be used to create the appearances of a major Franco-Dutch drive into north Germany, thus distracting Prussian attention and resources northward during the critical period just before and during the first period of the main attack. Such a diversionary effort could only be advantageous.

By 15 September Napoleon was in a position provisionally to make up his mind. News had arrived of the Prussian border incursion into Saxony. That being the case, the best routes toward Dresden or Leipzig and ultimately Berlin and Potsdam evidently lay through Bamberg. Its proximity to the three roads traversing the Thüringer Wald, the chain of forested mountains, presented problems associated with their crossing that also provided a convenient "curtain of maneuver" to conceal the French operational concentration from prying Prussian patrols. Furthermore, the *Grand Armée*'s advance from Bamberg to Leipzig and Berlin would sooner or later compel the Prussian generals to offer battle to save their capital from occupation by the French.

Three days later, on 18 September, more details reached Napoleon of the Prussian actions proceeding in Saxony, including their forcible incorporation of that state's small army into Frederick-William III's armament, and Napoleon no longer hesitated. The time for determined action had come. Over a period of forty-eight hours in a prodigious demonstration of his working capacity Napoleon dictated no less than 120 separate orders. The whole army was forthwith placed on a fully mobilized status. The Imperial Guard at once left Paris in convoys of special wagons to cover the 550 kilometers to beyond Mainz, reaching that city on the twenty-seventh. Most important of all was the lengthy "General Disposition for the Assembly of the Grand Army," a document that formed the basis for the whole campaign about to unfold. It emphasized three crucial dates. By 2 October Augereau's VII, Ney's VI, and Bernadotte's I Corps were to have concentrated at Frankfurt, Nürnburg, and Ansbach, respectively, ready in all respects to march. By the end of 3 October Davout's III Corps was to have moved from Nördlingen to Bamberg, there to join *GQG*, while Lefebvre's V Corps was to have reached Königshofen, and the artillery and baggage trains were to be massed at Würzburg. By 4 October Soult's IV Corps was to be at Amberg, following a lengthy march from its cantonments on the River Inn. Sent out by galloping staff couriers early on the twentieth, this missive was in Berthier's hands at Munich four days later.

Another vital document had already been sent posthaste two weeks earlier to Louis Bonaparte, ruler of Holland. This memorandum spelled out the role Louis was to assume during the prelude to and the early days of the campaign. "Hasten to mobilize your troops," Napoleon enjoined his younger *fratello*: "Reunite all available forces so as to deceive them [the Prussians] and protect your frontiers while I leap into the center of Prussia with my army, marching directly on Berlin. Keep all this secret."[24] On 19 September the emperor continued with his instructions. "As my intention is not to attack from your side, I desire you to open your campaign on 1st October by threatening the enemy. The ramparts of the Wesel and Rhine will serve you as refuge in any unforeseen eventuality."[25] To strengthen the right flank of the Dutch forces and to protect his magazines and depots along the lower Rhine, Napoleon ordered Marshal Mortier to form the VIII Corps at Mainz. In the event of a rapid French victory in central Germany, Louis and Mortier were to advance and occupy Kassel. These forces would also serve conveniently as the "anvil" for Napoleon's "hammer," should the Prussians after all march to occupy the weakly defended area between Bamberg and Mainz.

Thus, the operational requirements of security, deception, and exploitation were all carefully balanced. "I only count on your forces to serve as a means of diversion to amuse the enemy up to October 12," the emperor continued in a missive dated the thirtieth,

> The date [12 October] upon which my plans will be revealed.... The least check to you will cause me anxiety; my measures could thereby be disconcerted, and such an event might leave the whole north of my kingdom without a head. On the other hand, no matter what happens to me, as long as I know you are behind the Rhine, I will be able to act with greater freedom.[26]

To complete his precautionary measures the emperor mobilized Eugène Beauharnais and a reinforced army of Italy to keep a watch on Austrian reactions. As for the possibility of an inconvenient British descent on France or toward Hanover, Napoleon relied on Marshal Brune's 16,000 men split up in town garrisons, supported by the *gendarmerie* and local National Guard units, being able to hold up any exploitation of such a landing until Louis could put in train measures from Holland while Marshal Kellerman marched up the 8,000-strong strategic reserve from Paris and a force of 2,000 cavalry drawn from the departments. These operational plans reveal Napoleon at his best as a master of operational art.

The time for action had come. Napoleon's entourage set out at 0430 on Thursday, 25 September. He was soon burning the roads toward Mainz, traveling almost nonstop by way of Verdun, Saarbrücken, and Kaiserslautern. From Mainz, after a welcome two-day pause, his coaches and escort headed for Frankfurt. On 2 October Napoleon reached Würzburg and took over formal command from a very relieved Berthier. On the sixth he moved on Bamberg amidst welcome signs of converging French forces.[27]

Still there was no formal declaration of war—but it was not now to be long delayed. On 24 September, just before Napoleon left Paris, the Prussian government issued its long-anticipated ultimatum. Unless the French withdrew all their troops west of the Rhine, accepted the formation of a north German confederation of states under the aegis of Prussia, immediately returned the territory of Wesel, agreed to an international summit to discuss the remaining outstanding issues, and notified acceptance of these conditions to arrive in Berlin by 8 October at the latest, then a state of open war would exist between Prussia and the French empire. The forwarded ultimatum only reached Napoleon at Bamberg on

7 October. At dawn the next day the *Grand Armée* marched into Prussian-occupied Saxon territory. Such was Napoleon's immediate reply. And by ironic chance, France's written reply, forwarded from Berlin, only reached Frederick-William's hands on the fourteenth, in the middle of the Jena-Auerstädt campaign.

A major clash of arms was now obviously imminent. From Würzburg, Napoleon had issued to Marshal Soult a full operational order:

> I have caused Würzburg, Forcheim and Kronach to be occupied, armed and provisioned, and I propose to debouch into Saxony with my whole army in three columns. You are at the head of the right-hand column with Marshal Ney's Corps half a day's march behind you and 10,000 Bavarians a day's march behind him, making altogether more than 50,000 men. Marshal Bernadotte leads the center, followed by Marshal Davout's Corps, the greater part of the reserve Cavalry, and the Guard, making more than 70,000 men. He will march by way of Kronach, Lebenstein and Schleiz. The V Corps [under command of Lannes, Lefebvre reverting to his Guard command] is at the head of the way to Coburg, Grafenthal and Saalfeld, and musters over 40,000 men. The day you reach Hof the remainder of the army will have reached positions on the same alignment. I shall march with the center.
>
> With this immense superiority of force united in so small a place you will realize that I am determined to leave nothing to chance, and can attack the foe wherever he chooses to stand with nearly double his strength....
>
> If the enemy opposes you with a force not exceeding 30,000 men, you should concert with Marshal Ney and attack him.... On reaching Hof, your first care should be to open communications between Lebenstein, Ebersdorf and Schleiz.... From news that has come in today [5 October] it appears that if the foe makes any move it will be towards my left; the bulk of his forces seem to be near Erfurt.... I cannot press you too earnestly to write to me frequently and keep me fully informed of all you learn from the direction of Dresden. You may well think that it will be a fine thing to move around this area in a "battalion square" of 200,000 men. Still, this will require a little [operational] art and certain events.[28]

And so, indeed, it was to prove. Early on 8 October the move into the defiles of the Thüringer Wald began, crossing the Saxon frontier without encountering opposition in the process. A force of light cavalry, who, following their orders, began to empty every letterbox and to interrogate every peasant they met amid the passes, headed each of the three columns. Napoleon was aware that he was taking considerable risks and that his knowledge of Prussian military movements was incomplete.

Le bataillon carré in Action

Napoleon's plan for crossing the difficult Thüringer Wald region illustrates his mastery of the principles of flexibility, mutual support, and the achievement of local superiority at one or more of the three exits from the Franconian forest. Napoleon tentatively believed on incomplete evidence that the enemy's main body was either near Leipzig to the north or Erfurt to the west, and that some problems (possibly Russian intervention) might take place from around Dresden to the northeast. He tended to think that the first hypothesis, supplemented by the second, was the most likely combination. In this analysis of Prussian likely force movements, he was both right and wrong. In fact Prince Hohenlohe (with 35,000 men) was near Erfurt but already far nearer to the River Saale and Jena to his east than Napoleon believed to be the case. As for Brunswick's main army (60,000 strong) and Rüchel's third force (a weak 15,000, barely worth the designation army), both were also in fact well to the west of the Saale but within supporting distance of Hohenlohe. That officer had approved the placing of two forward detachments without Brunswick's full knowledge, namely 8,300 men under Prince Louis Ferdinand of Prussia (at thirty-three years, acknowledged as a gifted young commander of great promise, "the white-hot hope of Prussia" and a prominent member of the Prussian court War Party) at Saalfeld, and General Bolesas Friedrich Tauenzien (commander of Hohenlohe's advance guard) with 9,000 men (including 3,000 pressed Saxons) near Schleiz. Both of them were east of the River Saale and right in the path of Napoleon's proposed line of operations. There were no large concentrations of Prussian troops near Leipzig (as Napoleon believed there must be, to guard the approaches to the River Elbe, which he still expected to become the scene of the main Prussian stand) except the Prussian Reserve. Thirteen thousand men at Halle under command of Eugen of Württemberg had a triple role: being prepared to reinforce Brunswick at Naumburg or at Leipzig as might be deemed necessary by the unfolding of events and also charged with the security of the great fortress-city of Magdeburg on the Elbe far to his rear. Thus, Napoleon was indeed largely operating in the dark when his movement began on 8 October.

This notwithstanding, within seventy-two hours *le bataillon carré* had successfully crossed the Thüringer Wald and established itself beyond. Marshal Murat's advance guard of cavalry engaged in a few skirmishes with Prussian pickets. By dusk on the eighth the heads of the three main columns had reached their designated halting places at Coburg, Lobenstein, and Münchberg, respectively. The first two were just short of the Franconian forest, and the third (Soult's IV Corps) almost through it. The first real opposition was encountered on the morning of the ninth, when Murat's cavalry, joined in due course by Bernadotte's hard-marching I Corps after passing the Thüringer Wald and crossing the upper reaches of the Saale, ran into Tauenzien's force near Schleiz. A mainly cavalry and dragoon action ensued, which forced the Prussians and Saxons to retreat and thus opened the road for the French center column toward Auma and distant Gera. By dusk the remaining two columns had safely reached Saalfeld (Lannes' V Corps) and Hof (Soult's IV Corps) and taken or established bridges over the Upper Saale.

Confusion and misunderstandings of intent continued to dog the Prussian high command. Hohenlohe, on news of the action at Schleiz, had ordered his army to cross the Middle Saale and advance to Auma, there to support and rally Tauenzien, covered by a delaying action to be fought by Prince Louis Ferdinand. But Hohenlohe's superior, Brunswick, countermanded the move, substituting an advance toward Rudolstadt, and for once the prince acceded. Prince Louis Ferdinand was now instructed to fall back to Rudolstadt and avoid battle if possible. But this new order reached its addressee too late. From early on the tenth Lannes and the Prussian prince had been locked in combat near Saalfeld. The 14,000 French troops available (Augereau's VII Corps had fallen behind) routed their 7,000 opponents when Quartermaster Guindet of the 10th Hussars killed Prince Louis Ferdinand in a man-to-man mounted combat. This triggered a disaster that caused his men to flee, which resulted in 2,700 casualties (including 1,800 prisoners) and the loss of 33 guns, compared to the French with 172 killed and wounded.

It now appeared to the Prussian generals that Napoleon was indeed breaking through toward Leipzig—thus placing their communications in peril—so Hohenlohe pulled back toward Kahla en route for Jena, while the other two armies set out to re-concentrate at Weimar. The emperor, informed by Soult that the garrison of Plauen had fled northward, now believed that battle would be given by the Prussians at Gera in order to protect Leipzig ("I doubt, however, whether he can unite [his forces] before I can"[29]) and ordered all formations to press ahead northward to forestall the Prussians there. If there were no major battle there, it would doubtlessly occur at Leipzig or on the Elbe. Once again, therefore, Napoleon had reached an erroneous conclusion, although had Hohenlohe's plan of the ninth been implemented, he might have been correct in large measure. Thus, the Prussians in confusion were even now puzzling their great opponent.

Everywhere the French light cavalry and dragoons were seeking information. During the eleventh it became clear that there were no Prussians near Gera nor, even more surprisingly, in the region of Leipzig. Late that night Lannes reported that large Prussian forces were still west of the Middle Saale. Napoleon at once recast his operational plan. Expecting that the battle he was seeking would now take place near Erfurt, probably on 16 October, his orders for implementation of the twelfth inaugurated the famous wheel of *le bataillon carré* through 90 degrees to move westward, toward the Middle Saale instead of toward Leipzig as hitherto planned. Lannes and Augereau became the new advance guard, Davout and Bernadotte the new right wing, the Guard and Reserve Cavalry the new left, and Soult and Ney the reserve positioned to the east. Auma was designated the new "center of operations," which the trains and hospitals were to reach as soon as possible. Davout was to press ahead for Naumburg, and Lannes and Augereau were to approach Jena and keep in contact with the enemy. At this stage Napoleon envisaged his army's crossing the Middle Saale on the fourteenth. Meanwhile, Murat and the light cavalry were to continue to scour the land toward Leipzig in search of corroborative intelligence information, and Soult was to stay around Gera, watching for any sign of enemy activity to the north or east. These were indications that Napoleon was still not wholly convinced about the accuracy of his recast intention analysis and his operational assumptions. As always, he allowed for as many alternative situations as possible. "I am completely enveloping the enemy," wrote Napoleon to Soult, "but I have to take measures against what he might attempt to do."[30]

This lack of hard information was not, however, of critical importance. The beautiful flexibility of the *corps d'armée* system would permit him to meet almost any situation. If, as Napoleon now expected, the Prussians chose to accept battle near Erfurt (their presently presumed location) on 16 October (the assumed date), then Lannes, Augereau, and Ney would be in a position to attack the enemy frontally. Soult could move up to assume the role of the *masse de décision*. Bernadotte and Davout could sweep down from Naumburg in the north against the Prussian left flank and rear, severing their communications running back to Halle. If, on the other hand, the Prussians tried to avoid battle and set out for Halle (there to assimilate their army reserves) in an attempt to regain Leipzig or the Elbe, the French roles would be reversed. The I and III Corps would block the enemy's line of retreat and hold until the *masse débordante*—now comprising V, VII, and VI Corps, with IV and the Guard in reserve—could sweep up against the Prussian rear. And, theoretically, if a hypothetical Russo-Prussian force should appear most inopportunely from Dresden to the east, Soult should still be strong enough with the Bavarians and possibly Ney (if still within marching distance) to hold up the unwelcome newcomers while the main army completed its business with the main Prussian Army before countermarching to relieve the embattled Soult. This flexible range of options open to the French illustrates the value of Napoleon's operational formation: it could adjust itself to almost any eventuality. And the whole concept rested upon the fighting power of Napoleon's key "operational fire," the balanced, all-arm, individual *corps d'armée*.

"On the other side of the hill" the Prussian generals met in anxious conclave early on the thirteenth. Hohenlohe had to report that his withdrawal through Kahla and then from Jena the previous day had been complicated by a panic among his remaining Saxon troops as Lannes' cavalry patrols came into sight from the south. News had also arrived on the twelfth that the French were in Naumburg, threatening to close the line of the River Unstrutt—and this developing crisis caused Frederick-William III to convene a new council of war. A few argued for a major confrontation at Jena, but most advised an immediate retreat on Leipzig by way of Auerstädt, the Kosen Pass, Freiburg, and Merseberg, collecting the reserve from Halle en route to safeguard the armies' links with the Elbe. After long and often fiery debate, Brunswick announced his decision. Hohenlohe's force was to take post at Kapellendorf between Weimar and Jena, with Rüchel's force in support at Weimar itself, to cover the main army's march on Auerstädt. Once the king and Brunswick and their troops were clear of that town, Hohenlohe would assume duties of rearguard commander and follow his seniors northward. These orders were to become operative with effect from 1000 hours that same morning.

The Operational Climax Approaches

Napoleon reached Gera about 2000 on the twelfth and there impatiently bided his time waiting for definite news from Lannes. In the early hours he had issued preliminary orders for the thirteenth, which reflects the degree to which the *Grand Armée* was "marking time." Apart from two formations—Ney's VI Corps and Bernadotte's I Corps—which were ordered to close up on Roda and Naumburg, respectively, all the rest were told to stay where they were, collect stragglers, reprovision, and rest. The emperor even found time to write a line to Josephine:

> I am today at Gera, my dearest love, and everything is going very well, quite as I hoped would.... My health remains excellent, and I have put on weight since my departure [from Paris]. Yet I travel from 20 to 25 leagues each day, on horseback, in my carriage, etc. I retire to rest at eight o'clock and rise at midnight. I sometimes imagine that you will not yet have retired to bed. Ever thine.[31]

This doubtlessly welcome pause in operations was rudely shattered at 0900, when three pieces of critical intelligence information reached *GQG*. The first was a secret agent's report, relayed by Murat, that the king and queen of Prussia had been seen at Erfurt on the eleventh, that a Prussian pontoon train had moved northwest from Weissenfels on the twelfth, and that there were unmistakable signs of large-scale troop movements on the Fulda-Erfurt-Naumburg highroad. Next a courier from Davout at Naumburg arrived. Interrogations of prisoners of war, Prussian deserters, and civilians had revealed beyond doubt that the main Prussian army was between Weimar and Erfurt, that the king of Prussia had certainly been at Erfurt on the eleventh, and that there were no signs whatsoever of Prussian troops between Naumburg and Leipzig. Third, an aide from Augereau at Kahla reported that certain enemy formations, originally identified as being at Jena, were in fact moving on Erfurt through Weimar to join the enemy main body.

Although there was still no word from Lannes, close to the Saale near Jena with his V Corps, Napoleon believed that he had now at last penetrated the Prussian intentions. "At last the veil is torn," he wrote to Murat at about 0930:

> The enemy begins his retreat towards Magdeburg. Move as quickly as possible with Bernadotte's Corps on Dornburg [a town midway between Naumburg and Jena on the Saale]. I believe that the enemy will either attempt to attack Marshal Lannes at Jena or that he will retreat. If he attacks Lannes, your being at Dornburg will enable you to assist him. From two o'clock this afternoon I shall be at Jena.[32]

It is important to note that Napoleon was still prey to a degree of doubt and that indeed he had uncovered only about 90 percent of the enemy's plans. Napoleon was by no means infallible, as we have seen, but his operational concepts and methods were highly flexible, capable of rapid adjustment in the light of revealed developments.

Riding fast with his "little headquarters" and escort of Guard cavalry, Napoleon was intercepted at 0300 by the long-awaited courier from Lannes. The occasional thunder of guns could be heard a few miles to the west. Breaking the seal and quickly glancing at its contents, Berthier handed the dispatch to his master. Writing that morning from west of the Saale, the marshal reported that 12,000–15,000 enemy troops were presently in position immediately north of Jena and that an estimated 20,000–25,000 more were still between Jena and Weimar. Questing patrols were out seeking confirmation. "I desire to know whether it is the intention of Your Majesty that I should advance my corps towards Weimar. I dare not assume responsibility of ordering such a move in case Your Majesty may have some other destination for me."[33]

Loyal but cautious subordinate! The total dependence of senior commanders on Napoleon's support in advance for anything that might smack of independent thought is well illustrated. On the morrow the perils of presuming to do so would cause Napoleon to berate Ney. Although indubitably one of the most courageous, Ney also was one of the less intelligent of the marshalcy ("thickest of the thick," perhaps, as well as "bravest of the brave").

Now at last Napoleon realized the error of his belief that the "bloody solution to the crisis" would not take place until 16 October. The enemy was nearer than he thought. Accordingly, Napoleon dictated the day's third set of orders from the saddle. As it was now clear that the battle would take place on the fourteenth, Davout was to maneuver west from Naumburg on the evening of the thirteenth "so as to fall on the enemy's left" if he heard the sound of guns firing from the south. Bernadotte was to continue to Dornburg, ready to support Lannes should he be attacked. If these corps heard no firing, both were to await the morrow's first orders before crossing the Saale. Murat's cavalry was to hasten for Dornburg, and both Soult's IV and Ney's VI Corps were to force-march toward Jena, where Lefebvre and the infantry component of the Imperial Guard was to rejoin the emperor at the earliest possible moment.

Riding over the Saale, Napoleon joined Lannes at his forward headquarters on the steep Landgrafen-Berg feature northwest of Jena town. The marshal quickly briefed him on the current situation. The V Corps had reached Jena unopposed in a thick fog early that morning. General Suchet's division had pressed ahead to the Landgrafen-Berg, where he had run into Prussian pickets and driven them off to the nearby villages of Lützeroda and Closewitz. He respectfully but strongly asserted that at least 40,000 opponents were present and that the French should remain west of the Saale. Napoleon approved these suggestions and ordered the remainder of V Corps and the Guard Infantry (when arrived) to be ready to pass the Saale as soon as dusk would conceal their movement. He clearly also believed he was in the presence of the main Prussian Army.

The development of the French "intelligence picture" between 9 and 13 October is an excellent and revealing example of Napoleon's operational art in action. Although far from infallible, it eventually worked with the minimum of confusion, despite a number of serious miscalculations—and indeed a virtual 72-hour "blackout"—which might have thrown a lesser army into chaos.

Table 1 illustrates the *Grand Armée*'s reinforcement capacity from late on the thirteenth to the afternoon of the fourteenth:

TABLE 1—THE *GRAND ARMÉE'S* REINFORCEMENT SCHEDULE, 13–14 OCTOBER 1806

	Arriving Formations	Number of Troops Present
13 October		
1200	Lannes' Corps	21,000
2359	The above plus the Guard infantry	25,000
14 October		
1000	The above plus VII and part IV Corps	50,500
1200	The above plus remainder of IV Corps, VI Corps, and the Heavy Cavalry	90,500
1600	The above plus the Light Cavalry and III and I Corps from the north	145,500

Such a concentration of force within twenty-eight hours is a further tribute to Napoleon's concept and Berthier's staff work. Some forty miles were at this stage separating the two wings of the army. Messages may be calculated to have moved at about 5.5 miles an hour. As *GQG* was about equidistant from Davout and Ney and the usual time between receipt of an order and its actual implementation was in the region of at least two hours, the time that passed between an order issued and its execution by a wing commander can be said to have been about six hours. Napoleon grew in his conviction that he was pinning the main Prussian Army, and he grew anxious to strengthen the envelopment aspect of the forthcoming battle.

Plans of Battle

Napoleon's provisional operational plan was now clear in his mind. From 0600 on the morrow (14 October), Lannes, supported by the Guard in reserve, would enlarge the French bridgehead over the Saale, taking control of as much of the plateau beyond the Landgrafen-Berg as possible and occupying the villages of Lützeroda and Closewitz. This would make room for the arrival on the field of the next wave of converging French forces. About 1000, immediately to the north, the leading elements of Soult's powerful IV Corps (eventually 27,000 strong in all) would extend the battlefield to the right by moving to Lobstädt and thence through Zwätzen up on to the plateau to capture Rödigen and feel for the tactical left flank of the Prussians. Simultaneously, Augereau's VII Corps (16,500 strong) would advance from the direction of Kahla on the French left, crossing the Mühlbach Stream west of Jena before swinging half-left up the Schnecke Pass to mount the Flomberg and feel for the Prussian right flank. By midday the remainder of his corps should have reinforced Soult, and passing through Jena the newly arrived VI Corps of Ney would take over the central plateau area from Lannes' long-engaged divisions assisted by heavy cavalry. (*See Map 1.*)

Napoleon was confident that these formations and dispositions would suffice to hold and ultimately defeat the Prussian Army, but if success was to be transformed into triumph the arrival of sufficient force in the Prussian rear at the correct time and place had to occur. Up to the midafternoon issue of orders, Napoleon had planned for Davout to sweep down from Naumburg, while Bernadotte and Murat attacked over the Saale closer to Jena. Now, at 2200 hours, Napoleon saw that the true key to the Prussian communications (recently revealed to be running north toward the distant Elbe) lay in the town of Apolda, eight miles northwest of Jena. This could be reached either from Naumburg through Auerstädt or due west through Dornburg. A single, double-corps intervention would be more effective than two separate advances on Apolda. So Napoleon sent out yet another order to Davout, setting Apolda as his ultimate objective for the fourteenth, and including the atypically ambiguous phrase from which much trouble was to stem for Bernadotte: "If the Duke of Ponte Corvo [Bernadotte] is still with you, you can march together. The Emperor hopes, however, that he will be in the position which he has assigned for him at Dornburg."[34] In fact Bernadotte was still with Davout, who communicated the emperor's order to him personally in the early hours of the fourteenth, but Bernadotte's dislike for Davout and refusal to be seen as in any way under his orders caused him to disregard the imperial caveat, instead insisting on marching south toward Dornburg with his men. This act of disobedience was to place Davout in the greatest peril later that morning. The commander of I Corps in due course attempted to justify his actions on the grounds of the rather vague second sentence. It was almost to bring him before a court-martial and a possible firing squad for gross dereliction of duty.

Thus, Napoleon had envisaged a classical operational plan of battle based on a maneuver of envelopment. But between intention and actual execution there could only be a large gulf, as 14 October was clearly to demonstrate.

The night of 13–14 October found Napoleon laboring alongside his engineers and *fantassins*. To extemporize a road up the Landgrafen-Berg and its culminating peak, the Windknollen, suitable for artillery, every battalion in turn was required to labor for an hour, according to Marbot.[35] The torches to illuminate the work were hidden from the foe by the blaze of Jena's lights beyond. The security of these peaks was critical for the development of the operational plan at daylight. The work completed on his orders for the morrow issue, and 25,000 men and forty-two cannon safely deployed on and about the two summits, Napoleon slept soundly, bivouacked in the midst of a square formed by the Grenadiers of the Guard.

Over the valley, Prince Hohenlohe slept more fitfully amid his 38,000 men, but with no idea that he was facing the main French Army. He considered the French on the Landgrafen-Berg to be merely a flank-guard that, together with another French force reportedly at Naumburg, were between them covering the presumed major French advance continuing north, toward Leipzig. Both commanders were therefore in for some surprises on the fourteenth. The "fog of war" was supplemented by a thick mist that spread down the Saale River valley before dawn. Napoleon was confident of fighting with an overall superiority of force. And so he would, indeed—and to a far greater extent than he ever envisaged. But the same would not be the case for Davout.

Operational Considerations in the Battle 14 October 1806

At Jena Napoleon fought from 0400 for ten hours with a force that began the action at a strength of 46,000 men and 70 guns and ultimately reached 96,000 men and 120 guns from shortly after midday. Right through the day he believed he was fighting Brunswick's main army, which might have been 100,000 men and 350 guns strong had it all been present. In fact, Napoleon only faced Hohenlohe's flank guard of 38,000 men and 120 guns, reinforced very belatedly at 1500 by General Rüchel's command, 15,000 strong, from Weimar. His intervention only served to increase the scale of the Prussian disaster. By the approach of the autumnal dusk, the Prussians had suffered 25,000 casualties, including 15,000 taken prisoner (or 47 percent of their effective battle strength, Rüchel included). The French casualties stood at approximately 5,000 (or 5 percent) as Hohenlohe's and Rüchel's survivors fled for Erfurt hotly pursued by the Reserve Cavalry led in flamboyant style by Murat in person, who signified his scorn for the enemy by wielding only a riding-crop, refusing to draw his saber. By 1700 he was in the streets of Weimar. Two days later he would enter Erfurt.[36]

The battle did not go exactly according to the operational plan, and three events require mention. First, Lannes' initial attack against General Tauenzien's advance guard, after making considerable early progress and capturing the villages of Closewitz, Cospeda, and Lützeroda, ran into serious trouble when Tauenzien managed to launch a telling counterstroke with 5,000 rallied troops to split the French corps in two and regain much ground. Fortunately for the French (for Ney was not yet in the field), the progress of Soult's and Augereau's probing advances on the flanks induced the Prussian advance guard commander to halt his successful follow-through, and, fearful of tactical envelopment, to fall back to join Prince Hohenlohe's main body farther to the west. Thus, Napoleon's operational concept of supporting a beleaguered formation with neighboring outflanking forces was well demonstrated. By 1000 the French had secured most of the plateau.

Second, there is the matter of Marshal Ney's ill-judged intervention in the battle. By 1100 Hohenlohe launched General Grawert in an attempt to regain the plateau. Eleven battalions, deployed into line to face Lannes' tiring men, and Prussian cavalry was soon massing in force behind them. Suddenly an unanticipated struggle blazed into furious life south of the village of Vierzehnheiligen. This proved to be the work of some impatient French newcomers, namely the advance guard of VI Corps, with just two light cavalry regiments and five battalions, the fiery, addlepated Marshal Ney at their head. After chafing for several hours awaiting the arrival of the main part of his command, Ney's lion heart overruled his head and he plunged straight into battle, blithely accepting odds of two to one and heading for a strong Prussian battery. Against all probability his attack reached the cannon, scattered the gunners, and forced the postponement of an attack on Lannes by forty-five Prussian squadrons. There Ney's good fortune ran out; massively counterattacked, and out of supporting distance of Lannes or Augereau, his survivors were

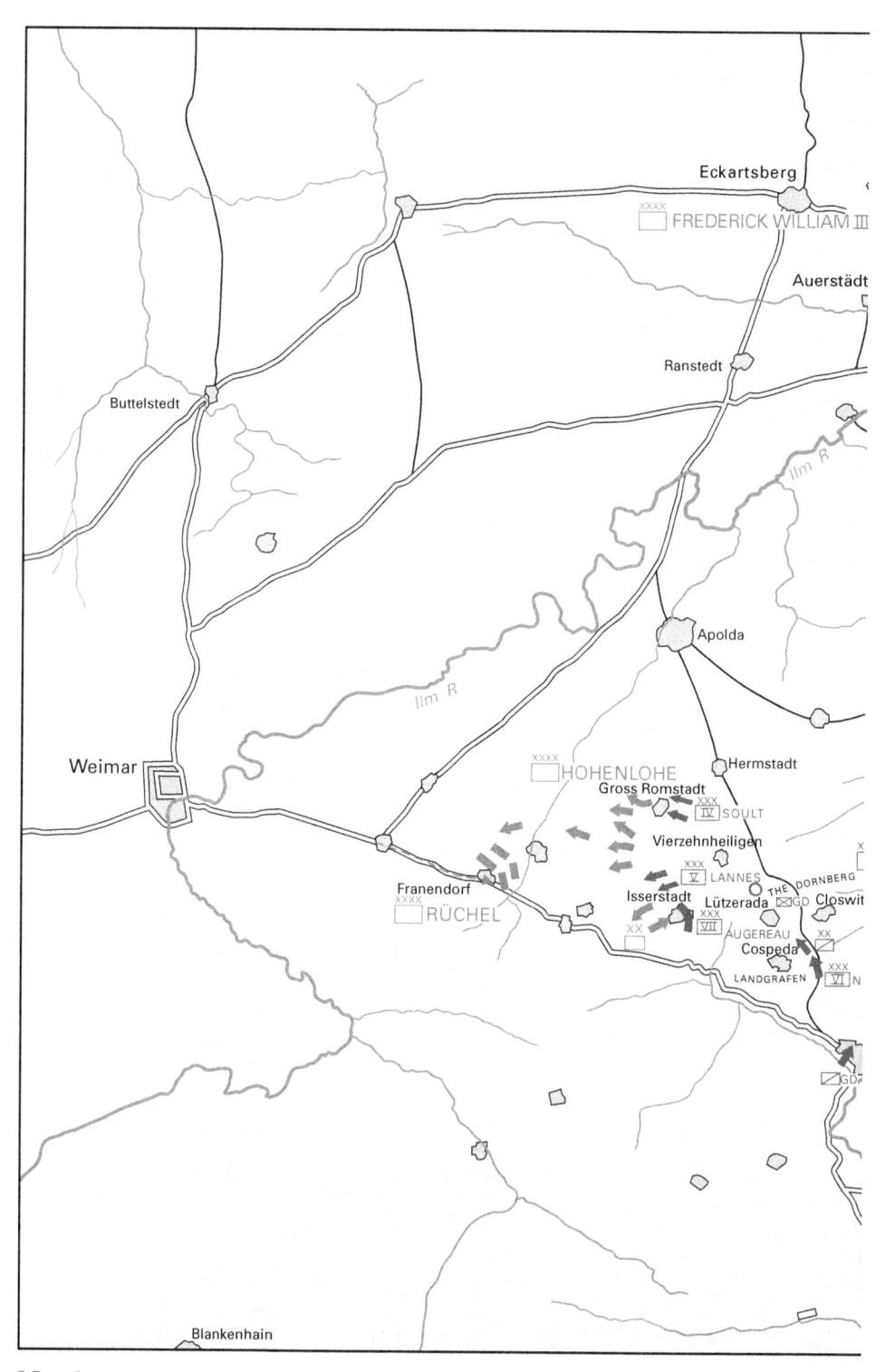

MAP 1

JENA AND VICINITY, 1806

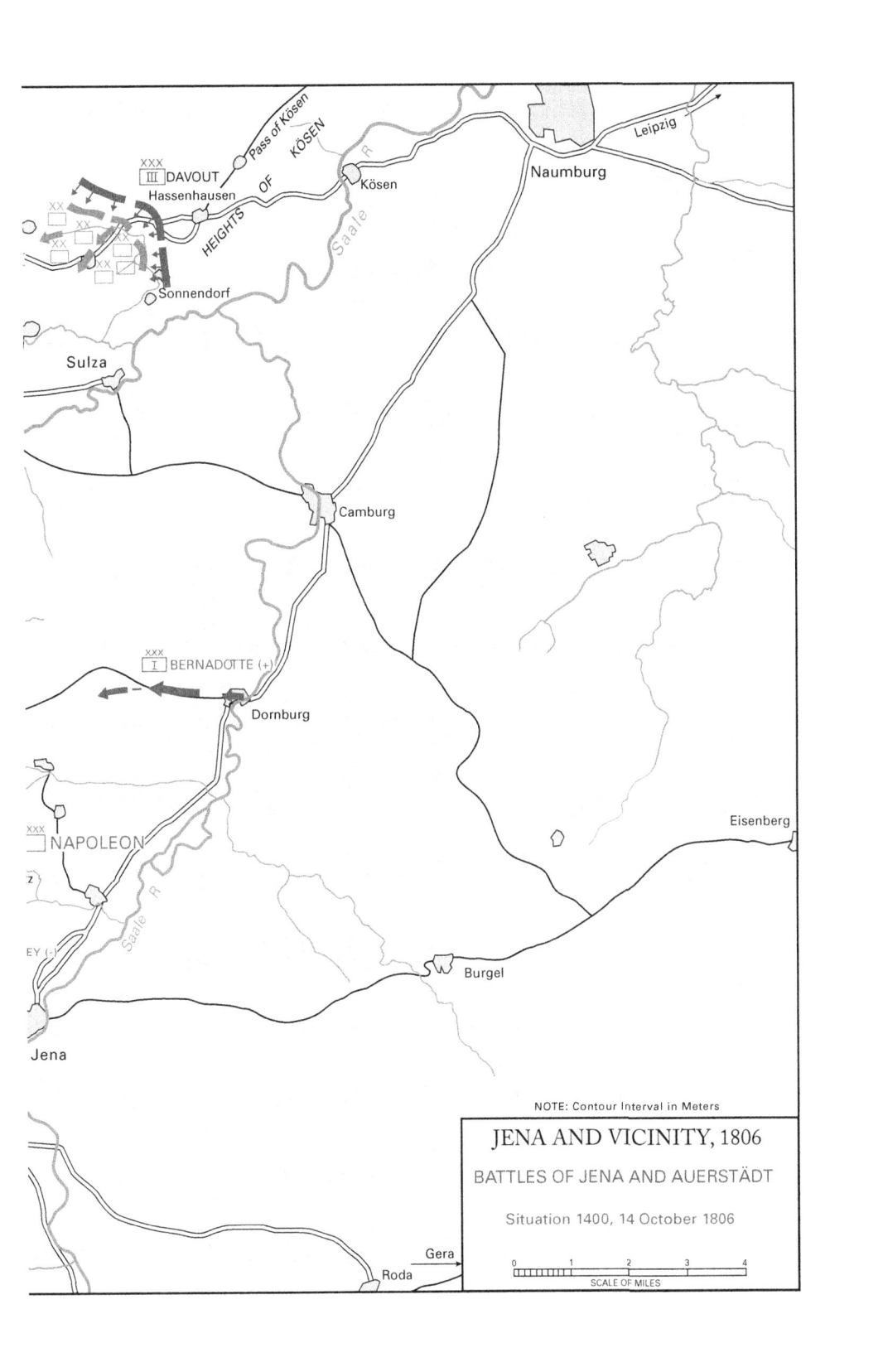

BATTLES OF JENA AND AUERSTÄDT

Situation 1400, 14 October 1806

NOTE: Contour Interval in Meters

forced to form a square. It took Napoleon's personal order to General Bertrand to lead the only two cavalry regiments in reserve (Murat had yet to reach the field) in a desperate and a costly rescue operation, supported by a determined drive by the men of the nigh-exhausted V Corps toward Vierzehnheiligen. Both attacks were ultimately driven back, but their intervention enabled Ney to return to the French lines, surrendering the village of Isserstädt on the way. Napoleon was not best pleased by this unauthorized adventure; Ney was in any case supposed to have attacked, when the time was right, on Lannes' farther (not nearer) flank. "The Emperor was very much displeased at Marshal Ney's obstinacy," recalled General Rapp. "He said a few words to him on the subject—but with delicacy."[37] According to other accounts, this was the occasion when Napoleon declared that Ney knew less about warfare "than the last-joined drummer-boy."[38] This incident illustrates how Napoleon's control of his subordinates could on occasion falter at the operational level.

The third aspect of Jena relates to the Napoleonic equivalent of operational fires. At Jena, we find the development of the use of concentrated artillery fire. Now, six years after Marengo and ten months after Austerlitz, the emperor produced his first massed battery as an extemporization to counter a moment of French weakness toward the end of the battle. It happened as follows. After Hohenlohe's defeat, Rüchel's force of 15,000 men made their appearance—belated but fresh—along the Weimar road. The sight of Lannes' and Ney's hurrying columns gave the newcomers reason for pause, but their withdrawal began as a model operation, infantry and cavalry alternately covering each other's retreats by bounds. Napoleon, eager to exploit the Prussian defeat and having no wish to be held up by this valiant enemy rearguard, called for several batteries of guns (probably three—accounts vary) and had them drawn up to pour close-range fire into Rüchel's masses. A dozen salvoes wrecked the Prussian forces' cohesion, and when the French infantry swarmed forward again their foes turned and fled. The result was another 5,000 prisoners and five colors taken. The guns were largely to thank for this sudden resolution of local difficulty.

In future years Napoleon would use artillery in large numbers on many critical occasions. One thinks of the brilliant handling of Senarmount's guns at Friedland, used as an offensive weapon, or the extemporized great battery at Wagram's second day in July 1809 that plugged a large gap in the French center and repulsed the Archduke Charles' threatening counterattack. Although the massed guns at Waterloo did not do their desired work on account of wet ground and Wellington's skillful placing of troops on the reverse slopes out of sight of the French gunners, Napoleon was right when he claimed "It is with guns that war is made." His employment of guns at Jena forms part of the evolution of his massed batteries used for operational effect.

Napoleon, weary but elated, made his way back to his headquarters in Jena at about 1700 to find the building decorated with thirty captured Prussian colors. Only two matters remained to be resolved: Where was Davout? And where was Bernadotte? So far there had been no sight or (still worse) sound of the turning movement and blocking actions by way of Apolda and Dornburg, save for the timely arrival of Murat and the light cavalry through the latter in midafternoon.

His tired musings were rudely interrupted. Awaiting his return outside his office was a wounded and travel-stained French officer, Colonel Falcon of III Corps. The news he brought stopped the emperor in his tracks. "Your master must have been seeing double," he ungraciously snapped in an unworthy reference to the bespectacled Marshal's shortsightedness. Little by little, however, he came to accept that Davout had in fact fought—and beaten—the main Prussian army at Auerstädt at unfavorable odds of at least two-to-one. Napoleon had to admit that he had made one of the grossest miscalculations in his career to date. Yet the French operational system and the fine fighting qualities of an individual *corps d'armée* under the brilliant command of "the Iron Marshal" had adjusted to wholly unforeseen circumstances and wrested decisive victory out of seemingly inevitable defeat. But why had III Corps been left to fight so valiantly alone? And, above all, where in the name of *le bon Dieu* was the Duke of Ponte Corvo and his I Corps? Had the earth swallowed them?

The Military Miracle of Auerstädt

Fifteen miles to the north of Jena, Marshal Louis-Nicolas Davout, age thirty-six, at the head of only 27,000 men and 40 guns of his III Corps, had spent an eventful day. After conveying Napoleon's late-evening order to Bernadotte at 0230 and being massively snubbed by the *Gascon*, Davout set his corps in motion westward from Naumburg, as ordered, at 0400 on the fourteenth. There were reports of military movements detectable to the west, moving from south to north, but nothing could be confirmed owing to the dense mist. Part of the Corps cavalry leading, followed by the divisions of General Gudin, Morand, and Friant in order of march, Davout's cautious progress westward along the north bank of the River Saale was both concealed and hindered by the fog. The leading troops were well through the village of Hassenhausen en route to Rehausen and distant Auerstädt, when at 0700 on that foggy morning they abruptly ran into four Prussian cavalry squadrons and one battery of artillery at the village of Poppel. This encounter battle of Auerstädt once and for all earned Davout his martial reputation and, somewhat less favorably, a measure of his master's jealousy and the greater hatred of his colleague Bernadotte.

Details of the famous battle are not part of this discussion.[39] Suffice it to say that Davout, unreinforced by Bernadotte despite what was plainly that officer's simple duty, fought a steadily escalating encounter battle until he found himself engaged with fully 63,500 Prussians supported by 230 guns, forming the Duke of Brunswick's entire army. By superlative handling of his limited resources, peering around the battle area through his special battle spectacles, ever present at the forward edge of the battle area (FEBA) despite huge risks, and doubtless aided by a number of Prussian errors (especially after Brunswick and the aged von Mollendorf had been killed or mortally wounded and King Frederick-William III had insisted on taking over command), Davout fought magnificently for nine-and-a-half hours and thoroughly defeated the Prussians. By last light the III Corps had inflicted 13,000 casualties (including 3,000 prisoners) or 20.5 percent, and captured 115 Prussian guns—for the loss of 26 percent of its effective strength on entering battle: namely, 258 officers and 6,974 rank-and-file soldiers dead or wounded. Gudin's division, the worst hit, lost all of 40 percent of its strength. It was only when he had driven the fleeing foe back through Auerstädt, southwestward to the final crest of the Eckartsberg feature (short of Apolda), that Davout at last halted his exhausted men and sent Colonel Falcon to take the news to the emperor.[40] The final compliment payable to Davout's showing on this occasion is the fact that the Prussian high command freely admitted after the battle that they had believed they had been fighting not only at least 100,000 Frenchmen all day but also Napoleon in person.

Once again the strengths of the *corps d'armée* system had been brilliantly displayed, above all its sustained fighting power and, under the right leadership, its adaptability to meet triumphantly almost any unforeseen situation. It also permitted Napoleon to survive important mistakes of calculation. He found it hard to appreciate that he had only been fighting one-third of the Prussian Army at Jena, while an isolated subordinate had dealt with the balance single-handed, as it were. But where was Bernadotte? The answer to that would have to wait until the morrow. Napoleon was so weary that he fell asleep while dictating orders for the fifteenth. At a sign from Marshal Lefebvre, the Grenadiers of the Imperial Guard silently formed their habitual square around their sleeping master—sitting on a chair alongside his customary bonfire—and guarded his slumber through the night. Ten miles away, the survivors of Davout's decimated but victorious corps also slept the sleep of exhaustion. One man, however, spent a troubled night. Near Apolda, Marshal Bernadotte had received a peremptory order from Berthier to report to *GQG* early next morning and to be ready to explain his actions, or lack of them, on 14 October.

These had indeed been incredible. Bernadotte, as we have seen, refused to obey the emperor's order dictated at 2200 on the thirteenth, preferring to hold to his previous instructions, namely to march on Dornburg. Even this simple maneuver down a reasonable road along the east bank of the Saale had been poorly conducted, and it was only at 1100 on the fourteenth that the head of I Corps had reached Dornburg, a distance of just nine miles from its starting place near Naumburg. This was not a performance that would place I Corps' march among the record-breakers of the French Army! Even worse, it transpired that the Duke of Ponte Corvo ignored three separate messages from the heavily engaged Davout, imploring his assistance during the morning. The I Corps eventually proceeded across the Saale and on its leisurely way over the eight miles to Apolda, arriving there about 1600—after both battles were over and without having fired a single shot all day.

On the fifteenth Bernadotte found himself refused access to the emperor's inner sanctum. Instead he was searchingly interrogated by an ice-cold Berthier. He blustered away as was his Gascon wont and attempted to excuse his poor marching record on roads that he described as execrable. This he repeated in his written report. The army held its breath: news of Bernadotte's misdoing was of course soon common knowledge and the subject of much speculative debate. "The army expected to see Bernadotte severely punished," recalled Marbot.[41] On St. Helena, Napoleon revealed that he had actually signed an order for the marshal's court-martial, but he then had second thoughts and destroyed it.

It was only on 23 October that the emperor, through Berthier, deigned any reply to Bernadotte's report.

> According to a very precise order you ought to have been already at Dornburg ... on the same day that Marshal Lannes was at Jena and Davout reached Naumburg. In case you had failed to execute these orders, I informed you during the night that if you were still at Naumburg when this order arrived you should march with Marshal Davout and support him. You were at Naumburg when this order arrived; it was communicated to you; this notwithstanding, you chose to execute a false march in order to head for Dornburg, and in consequence you took no part in the battle and Marshal Davout bore the principal efforts of the enemy army.[42]

Napoleon resolved not to court-martial Bernadotte but to continue to use him.

By this date, as we shall see below, a very chastened Bernadotte was performing wonders in the forefront of one of the most decisive pursuits in all military history. Perhaps Napoleon was right to have left him in command of his corps after all. But had he been either with Davout or at Apolda by early afternoon, the fate of the Prussians would have been dramatically worse, though bad enough it had turned out to be.

This incident elicits two comments. First, no matter how carefully organized, the Napoleonic operational art could be gravely compromised by the failure of one corps formation commander. The chain was only as strong as its weakest link. Second, human nature is one of the imponderables of warfare in any age. Nevertheless, Bernadotte would prove a determined survivor, and he would in the end profit by becoming the only Napoleonic marshal to found a royal dynasty (in Sweden) that has survived to the present day.

The Employment of Operational Reserves
The Pursuit after Jena-Auerstädt

The ruthless and successful pursuit after the double battle of 14 October 1806 has justly gone down into the annals of military history as a masterpiece of what we today would term operational art. The correct employment of reserves above the tactical level is one of the major sub-themes of this study, and the events of late 1806 demonstrate what could be achieved against a defeated enemy by a great captain of warfare—as well as certain limitations.

The operational pursuit was not launched immediately after the double battle. Napoleon's exhaustion and his lack of certainty concerning what had befallen I and III Corps during the fourteenth caused a short delay in mounting a major, carefully considered, operational hue and cry. Apart from Murat—already noted as leading his light cavalry with great élan toward Erfurt on the heels of Hohenlohe and Rüchel—there is little doubt that most unwounded officers and men, including their emperor, succumbed to weariness and, after a brief period of euphoria, to depression, as they sought missing friends over the battlefield and extemporized some sort of meal after so many hours of combat. Of course, it may be said that for once Napoleon showed human weakness in succumbing to slumber at such a moment. It is in the moment and the immediate aftermath of victory, as in the time of defeat, that the senior commander must show energy and determination—and drive his equally weary subordinates to still greater efforts to exploit the foe's difficulties and afford him no time to recover his equilibrium and re-form. And this was usually Napoleon's way, to be sure.

In mid-October 1806 there was no immediate cause for anxiety on the last score. The chaos and confusion among the fleeing Prussian armies must have beggared belief. This became particularly the case when men of Hohenlohe and Rüchel, attempting to flee west and northwest, collided with Brunswick's columns trying to force their way south from Auerstädt. Had Bernadotte only been at Apolda earlier than 1600—or remained with Davout, the Prussian cataclysm must have become far greater than was in fact the case.

So it was only at 0500 on the fifteenth that orders for a general pursuit were issued—and of course took several hours to put into full implementation. Napoleon's eventual plan for the pursuit closely reflects his favorite operational maneuver. Murat, Soult, and Ney were to apply the maximum frontal pressure against the retiring enemy, while *la masse débordante*, formed by Bernadotte's, Lannes', Davout's, and Augereau's corps, were to strive to outmarch and outflank the Prussians, and seize Halle and Dessau behind them and then the distant Elbe crossings. Of course, only I Corps was fresh on the fifteenth, the rest having been heavily engaged the previous day.

But Bernadotte now made up to a certain degree for his earlier negligence. While Murat rounded up between 9,000 and 14,000 prisoners (authorities differ) at Erfurt on the sixteenth, the leading division of I Corps commanded by General Dupont marched flat out for Halle, reaching it on the seventeenth to fight a brisk engagement against the Duke of Württemberg's Reserve, capturing 11 cannon and 5,000 men (practically half his force of 11,300 infantry, 1,675 cavalry and 38 guns) for a cost of some 800 casualties. Much more of the same was to follow.

Perhaps, therefore, we may suggest that Bernadotte's misbehavior on the fourteenth proved a blessing in disguise as it provided Napoleon, unintentionally to be sure, with a substantial reserve force of fresh troops capable of heading the subsequent pursuit, imbued with a genuine desire to refurbish their dulled reputation in the eyes of the *Grand Armée* and its chief. Certainly such a psychological reaction can be hazarded for Bernadotte, who over the following weeks was to produce a virtuoso performance.

On the eighteenth the French lines of communication were switched from distant Würzburg and Bamberg nearer to Mainz, the line running in ten stages over 160 miles to Erfurt—the newly designated center of operations—by way of Frankfurt, Eisenach, and Gotha.

Two days later and the French had reached the Elbe on a broad front. The same day, Frederick-William III left his army for the River Oder, heading for East Prussia and, he hoped, signs of a Russian deliverance. A bewildered Hohenlohe was ordered to extemporize a strong garrison for Magdeburg. Instead, he decided to head first for Berlin and then for Stettin at the mouth of the River Oder, fearful that Napoleon's pursuit would otherwise catch up with him. Meanwhile, farther to the west, Blücher retreated northward through Brunswick City with his cavalry and many Prussian heavier guns, which hampered his progress more than a little.

Davout was first over the Elbe in strength at Wittenberg—completing the operation by 1500 on the twentieth with the aid of the apprehensive townsfolk, who prevented the Prussian engineers from blowing the bridge. Farther west, Bernadotte—subject to repeated verbal lashings from Napoleon, dutifully (and with just a touch of malice) forwarded in writing by the tireless Berthier (who had scores of his own to settle with Ponte Corvo)—was energetically seeking boats at Bary, successfully by the next day. Thus, Napoleon had two sizeable bridgeheads over the Elbe by 22 October, while Murat, Soult, and Ney were fast closing on Magdeburg. The only disturbing event was growing indiscipline in the French ranks taking the form of uncontrolled looting.

Indiscipline at all levels notwithstanding, the *Grand Armée* drove on through Rothenau, Ziesar, and Potsdam (where Napoleon took time off to ponder alone at Frederick the Great's tomb and ordered the removal of that military monarch's sword, sash, and Ribbon of the Black Eagle for transfer to the *Hôtel des Invalides* in Paris). The evening of the twenty-fourth found the French advance cavalry in the suburbs of Berlin, and the next day Napoleon accorded to Davout's III Corps the honor of marching first into the Prussian capital—to the chagrin of Murat. Thus did Napoleon make amends for his less-than-charitable remark of the late afternoon eleven days earlier by a handsome gesture; he had already made a clear admission of the debt he owed to Davout—later awarded the title of *Duc d'Auerstädt* (1808)—in the postbattle Fifth Bulletin of the *Grand Armée* published on the fifteenth, although he did imply that it was all part of a master operational plan! "On our right, Marshal Davout's Corps performed wonders. Not only did he contain, but he pushed back, and defeated, the bulk of the enemy's troops, which were to debouch through Kosen. This marshal displayed distinguished bravery and firmness of character—the first qualities in a warrior."[43] And so they remain to the present, not least at the operational level of command.

The continuing pursuit was only briefly interrupted by this and similar ceremonies, for now Napoleon had determined to secure the line of the River Oder and to head off any Russian intervention. The new IX Corps was already near Glogau, and now Davout was moved northeast to secure Küstrin and Frankfurt on der Oder, while Lannes made for Stettin. The remainder of the army—less Ney's VI Corps carrying out the siege of Magdeburg from 20 October (which would surrender to him on 6 November)—continued northward, allowing the Prussian formations still in the field no rest. Hohenlohe was caught up with at Prenzlau on 28 October and forced to surrender with 10,000 men and 64 guns, impressed by Murat's bluster and bluff that fully 100,000 French troops were surrounding him. And so it went with a number of other Prussian garrisons.

This left only Blücher's and the Duke of Weimar's detachments unaccounted for (22,000 men in all), currently at Schwerin and the Danish port of Lübeck to the northwest. But Bernadotte was hot on their heels, with Soult (laden with loot) a few days behind him. All the Prussians were within the walls of Lübeck on 4 November, still hoping to find shipping for England. The next day, however, Chief of Staff Scharnhorst surrendered with 10,000 men, followed by his commander, Blücher, on the fifth with as many more at the neighboring township of Ratgau. An additional prize was a division of Swedish troops' belatedly landing. Bernadotte's courtesy so impressed the nobly born officers that four years later they would suggest their conqueror's name for the vacant position of Crown Prince of Sweden. (Thus in the long term the "miserable Ponte Corvo" collected the jackpot that eluded all his other comrades and rivals in the marshalcy—a royal crown.) Next day the surrender of General Kleist with 22,000 men and 600 guns to Ney at Magdeburg 100 miles away virtually ended the formal campaign of 1806, save for the occupation of Hamburg four days later.

Indeed, the whole campaign of 1806 forms a masterly example of Napoleonic operational art in action.

Operational Art and the Campaign of 1806 Some Conclusions

In summing up Napoleon's conduct of the campaign of Jena-Auerstädt in 1806 it is necessary to repeat that despite all the achievements—including the reduction of the Prussian Army from a strength of approximately 171,000 originally operating in Saxony to a mere 35,000 (all in a period of thirty-three days)—the immense military victory did not end in immediately commensurate political gains. King Frederick-William III, as we have noted, retired over the River Oder in mid-October with the remnants of his armed forces, there to await Tsar Alexander I's implementation of Russia's part of the Fourth Coalition concluded earlier the same month. It is clear that, if left a real choice, the king of Prussia and his ministry would have sought peace without further ado. But that would be to ignore the powerful influence of the "War Party"—even in this hour of cataclysmic defeat—and above all that of its leader, the beautiful Amazonian royal consort, Queen Louise of Prussia. It was not without reason that Napoleon once half-wryly, half-admiringly, referred to her as "the only real man in Prussia."[44] As a result of her influence, reinforced by that of Chief Minister Hardenburg, the patriotic party continued to dominate the Prussian court and government. The direct result of this determination to fight on, together with the tsar's honorable insistence on honoring his treaty obligations, however dire the present situation, effectively compelled Napoleon to fight three more campaigns—that of November–December 1806 (leading to the occupation of Warsaw), that of January–late February 1807 (which climaxed in the desperate battle of Eylau), and that of early May–mid-June 1807 (including the siege of Danzig, the battles of Heilsberg and, above all, Friedland). Only then was he able—at the Tilsit meetings—to impose, inter alia, a dictated peace on Prussia.

Thus, at the level of strategy and policy, the dramatic and hard-fought campaign of 1806 failed to produce the required political results, at least immediately. It would take the aforementioned additional campaigns to achieve the desired political objectives.

The feature that makes the Napoleonic system of operational art so intriguing is the way it almost automatically allowed for the emperor's human errors and still made ultimate martial success possible. From the operational art perspective, there had been a number of serious errors and confusion during the unfolding of this short campaign. Thus, I Corps and III Corps received orders at the start of the operational movements that sent them across each other's lines of march. A little later Augereau's VII Corps was left without orders from 7–10 October and failed to keep in touch with V Corps over the same period. Indeed, Napoleon had moved off into the virtually unknown on 8 October, so inadequate had been intelligence coverage, and even those reports that came in hardly clarified the situation—if anything the reverse. Only on the thirteenth did any hard information become available, and even then some of that was misinterpreted. Yet, somehow, the system pulled through.

As has been mentioned earlier in this essay, Napoleon was indubitably guilty of at least six errors of judgment and calculation, as well as "faults of command" during 13 and 14 October alone. These six errors during the critical day preceding battle and that of the battle itself, were (it is easy to discern after the fact), taken in turn, as follows:

First, Napoleon failed to realize that Hohenlohe's command constituted only a flank covering force. Here incomplete reconnaissance and habitual "fog of war" were largely to blame, but Napoleon had traveled to join Lannes at Jena on the thirteenth to see for himself. He conducted two reconnaissances, but remained convinced that he was engaging the main enemy army right to the end of the battle the next day.

His second misjudgment, which could have proved fatal for Davout, was his failure to realize that the Prussian main body was in fact moving toward Naumburg, which made Auerstädt the most important battle of the double engagement. Once again, there were intelligence indicators of this move, but because Napoleon miscalculated the likely date of battle to be 15 October at the earliest and more likely the sixteenth, and continued to do so until about 1500 on the fifteenth, when the "veil" was truly rent, he seriously miscalculated the main Prussian locations and prebattle intentions.

Third, the emperor failed to issue Bernadotte with a cut-and-dried order at 2200 on the thirteenth to accompany Davout if he was still in company with him. The slight possibility of placing different interpretations on his actual instructions (or to be able to pretend to do so) at least partially exculpates Ponte Corvo; but by no means entirely.

Fourth, Napoleon totally failed to keep in touch with either or both of I and III Corps during the hours of battle on the fourteenth. Granted, he had enough preoccupation close to hand, but it is the duty of the operational artist and commander to use all of the instrumentation at hand, not just to focus on the local picture. Once again, therefore, Napoleon stands accused of a lapse in his powers of orchestration. Berthier also bears some of this responsibility.

Fifth, through an oversight, Soult's IV Corps did not receive one vital prebattle order. Fortunately, the "standing orders" for handling a corps in the immediately preceding and actual hours of battle were well understood by as able a commander as Nicolas Jean-de-Dieu Soult, whom Napoleon had already dubbed "the foremost maneuverer in Europe" the previous year. "I and Soult understand one another," Napoleon had sagely remarked at Austerlitz. As a result, Soult understood his commander's intention and his own likely role without having specific, full instructions delivered to him, even though his final division only reached Jena at 1300 instead of at noon. It was, however, fortunate that the most severe fighting at Jena took place on the left, rather than Soult's sector on the right.

Sixth, the emperor also failed to keep adequate control over one of the formations that was immediately under his eye at Jena—or rather its commander. Ney was already well known as an impulsive *poil-de-carotte* (hot-head), yet he was allowed to start an attack at the wrong place at the wrong time with barely half his force present. Napoleon only became aware of this when VI Corps was already in peril of annihilation. The fact that he then extemporized a successful rescue operation does not disguise the fact that Napoleon might even have lost the battle of Jena at this point; but on this occasion he may be said to have "muddled through," thanks to his gift for rapid extemporization.

It can be argued—admittedly with the benefit of historical hindsight—that any or all of these errors might well have led to disaster for part, or even all, of the *Grand Armée*. Without a doubt the inadequacies of Prussian comprehension of and reaction to what was taking place were major factors in their own ultimate cataclysm. And yet the robustly adaptable operational system of *le bataillon carré* that Napoleon developed from the basic building block of the highly flexible all-purpose *corps d'armée* system enabled him to come through triumphantly (albeit with an immense debt to Davout, but also in spite of Bernadotte's flagrant indiscipline). As van Creveld says in just summary, "For all these faults in command, Napoleon won what was probably the greatest single triumph in his entire career."[45]

We have, it is hoped, shown how the campaign of 1806 demonstrated, "warts and all," the capabilities of Napoleon's operational art in its fully developed heyday. Perfect it most certainly was not, but superior to all contemporary equivalents it equally indubitably was. We have examined how Napoleon converted doctrinal conviction into achievable practice. We have seen how he built up a conception of operations, and perfected the necessary instrument for carrying it out at the operational level of warfare. In the French army corps of the period, we have seen how his methods of operational maneuver were extremely flexible and capable of conforming to changing circumstances. Other considerations included the development of operational fires through massed artillery, the use of all forces and reserves in pursuit, the attempt at intention analysis to see beyond the "veil," and how "the system of campaign" did indeed reveal "the system of battle." All went as planned—if not exactly as fought. Such, then, was the state of operational art at its highest development in the days before the development of the "continuous front," railways, and telegraphic communication. We must surely aver that it was, all in all, impressive to say the very least.[46]

Notes

1. E. F. Berthezene, *Souvenirs militaires* (Paris, 1855), p. 243.
2. Napoleon Bonaparte, *The Military Maxims of Napoleon* (Paris, 1874), no. 112; and *La correspondence de Napoléon Ier*, vol. 31 (Paris, 1856), pp. 448–50, 509, 596 (hereafter cited as *Correspondence*).
3. Attributed to Henri IV of France.
4. *Correspondence*, vol. 18, no. 14707, p. 218.
5. David G. Chandler, *The Campaigns of Napoleon* (New York: Macmillan, 1966), p. 368 (hereafter cited as *Campaigns*).
6. Details of Napoleon's schedule are to be found in E. Las Casas, *Memoirs of Napoleon* (London, 1836), p. 236ff.
7. Martin van Creveld, *Command in War* (Cambridge, Mass.: Harvard University Press, 1985), pp. 58–102.
8. *Correspondence*, vol. 13, no. 10810, p. 210.
9. Herbert Sargent, *Napoleon Bonaparte's First Campaign* (London, 1895), p. 15.
10. Claire de Rémusat, *Memoirs, 1802–1819* (London, 1895), p. 154.
11. Van Creveld, *Command in War*, p. 68.
12. *Correspondence*, vol. 11, no. 9392, p. 336.
13. Ibid., vol. 19, no. 15, p. 310.
14. Ibid., vol. 31, no. 40, p. 418.
15. Sources include van Creveld, *Command in War*, ch. 3; Chandler, *Campaigns*, pt. eight. Attention is also drawn to F. L. Petre, *Napoleon's Campaign in Prussia* (London, 1907; reissued 1977); C. von Lettow-Vorbeck, *Der Krieg von 1806–1807* (Berlin, 1892); H. Bonnal, *La manoeuvre de Jena* (Paris, 1904); and Frederic N. Maude, *The Jena Campaign, 1806* (London, 1909). Extremely good on Auerstädt is Daniel Reichel, *Davout et l'Art de la Guerre* (Paris: Delachaux et Neistlé, 1975), final section. Much of value may be culled from J. Colin's chapter in *Les Grandes Batailles de l'histoire* (Paris, 1915); J. F. C. Fuller's *The Decisive Battles of the Western World*, vol. 2 (London, 1955); and the British Military Ordnance Department (MOD), *Non-Technical Research Paper No. 12* ("Application of the Indirect Approach to Land/Air Operations in the Central Region") (London, 1984).
16. Cited by Chandler, *Campaigns*, p. 454.
17. Fuller, *Decisive Battles*, 2:418.
18. On the French marshalcy, see David G. Chandler, ed., *Napoleon's Marshals* (New York: Macmillan, 1987), especially the introduction.
19. See von Lettow-Vorbeck, *Der Krieg*, p. 163.
20. Colin, *Les Grandes Batailles*, p. 104.
21. *Correspondence*, vol. 13, no. 10744, p. 150.
22. Ibid., no. 10756, p. 160.
23. Ibid., no. 10757, p. 162.
24. Ibid., no. 10792, pp. 193–94.
25. Ibid., no. 10815, p. 213.
26. Ibid., no. 10920, p. 296.
27. David G. Chandler, *Dictionary of the Napoleonic Wars* (New York, 1979), App.: "Napoleon's Military Movements," p. 524.

28. *Correspondence*, vol. 13, no. 10941, pp. 309–10.
29. *Correspondence*, vol. 13, no. 10992, p. 344. See Carl von Clausewitz, *Nachrichten über Preussen in seiner großen Katastrophe* (Berlin, 1898); Antoine H. Baron de Jomini, *Atlas portatif... pour la vie de Napoléon* (Brussels, 1840); Chandler, *Campaigns*. Both Jean Baptiste M. E. Vachee, *Napoleon at Work* (London: A. and C. Black, 1914), and van Creveld, *Command in War*, concentrate on command, control, communications, and intelligence (C3I) aspects.
30. Colin, *Les Grandes Batailles*, p. 107.
31. *Correspondence*, vol. 13, no. 10992, p. 344.
32. Ibid., vol. 13, no. 1100, p. 348.
33. See Chandler, *Campaigns*, p. 475.
34. Bonnal, *La Manoeuvre*, p. 421.
35. Baron M. de Marbot, *Mémoirs*, vol. 1 (Paris, 1891), p. 297.
36. For details of the battle, see Chandler, *Campaigns*, pp. 479–98; MOD, *Non-Technical Research Paper* (no. 12), pp. 30–31.
37. General Rapp's account, in Louis A. F. de Bourrienne, *Memoirs of Napoleon Bonaparte*, vol. 2 (London, 1844), p. 384.
38. See Chandler, *Marshals*, p. xlvi.
39. See Chandler, *Campaigns*, pp. 489–98, and for an impressive reconstruction of Auerstädt, W. J. Wood, *Leaders and Battles—The Art of Military Leadership* (Novato, Calif.: Presidio Press, 1984), pp. 79–106; also Reichel, *l'Art de la Guerre*, final part.
40. For a further account of Davout's career, see Reichel, *l'Art de la Guerre* (to Auerstädt—a second volume was to follow, but Reichel's sad death in 1992 halted the project), and Chandler, *Marshals*, pp. 93–117.
41. Marbot, *Memoirs*, I:303.
42. *Correspondence*, vol. 13, no. 11060, pp. 393–94.
43. Chandler, *Marshals*, pp. 114–15.
44. See Chandler, *Campaigns*, p. 457.
45. Van Creveld, *Command in War*, p. 96.
46. For a fuller treatment and analysis of Napoleon's contributions to operational art, see Jay Luvaas, ed., *Napoleon on the Art of War* (New York: Free Press, 1999).

French Operational Art 1888–1940

Robert A. Doughty

Although the French acknowledged between 1888 and 1940 the existence of a level of war between the strategic and tactical levels, they did not believe it was fundamentally different from the other two levels. Essentially, they saw the operational level, or in their words grand tactics, as being a transition between the other two levels. From their perspective, the key aspect of grand tactics was the combining of units into effective combat organizations and employing them in a coordinated fashion toward a common goal. While devoting very little time and effort to studying the theoretical aspects of grand tactics, French military leaders and thinkers devoted considerable effort to developing corps, field armies, and army groups as combat organizations and to studying the practical aspects of their employment. They believed the essence of grand tactics concerned the employment of these large formations.

Despite their interest in large formations, the French failed to develop a sophisticated understanding of the operational art of war. Even worse, they deformed its very nature by having operational concepts distort their tactical methods before World War I and by having tactical concepts distort their operational methods before World War II. These distortions significantly affected the performance of the French Army in both wars.

Origins of the Operational Level of War

The evolution of the operational art is rooted in institutional and conceptual developments, for the introduction in turn of the corps, field army, and army group as military organizations led thinkers to develop new ideas about their employment. In the late eighteenth century, French military leaders conceived and nourished the concept of grand tactics when they addressed the problem of moving and concentrating forces on the battlefield. As military forces became larger on the eve of the French Revolution and as the challenge of controlling and supplying them became more difficult, Marshal Victor de Broglie in 1760 came up with the idea of breaking large armies into divisions that could move to the battlefields separately. By marching in a number of individual divisional columns, rather than in one or two huge columns, an army could approach a battlefield more quickly and enter into action much more decisively.[1] Thus, the initial idea relating to grand tactics was an organizational one that provided better command, control, and movement of large formations.

The next step, which was conceptual, occurred when General Pierre de Bourcet developed a better system for controlling divisions and, more important, addressed the issue of fighting them. In his seminal work, *Principes de la guerre de montagnes*, completed in 1764–1771, de Bourcet analyzed the operations of an army in mountainous terrain. Since such terrain would compel an armed force to operate in a number of separate, compartmented areas, de Bourcet recognized the importance of the divisions' being able to function on their own. His ideas came from his having served in the Franco-Spanish campaign against Savoy-Piedmont in 1744 and provided basic concepts for the employment in battle of an army organized on a divisional basis. In 1787–1788 the French Army adopted the main points of his proposal.[2]

Amidst the development of the new organizational structure, General Jacques Guibert recognized that warfare was changing and offered a definition of grand tactics. In his *Essai général de tactique*, which was first published in 1772, Guibert wrote:

> I have attempted, in the preceding part, to trace the principles by which the different units which comprise an army should be constituted and trained.... It is necessary to assemble these units, combine them, make them unite in the execution of the great maneuvers in a war. It is the art of conceiving the [method of] execution, planning it, directing it, that one calls grand tactics.[3]

The next step in the evolution of French ideas about grand tactics came with the development of the corps. In March 1796 General Jean Moreau formed a provisional corps in his Army of the Rhine and Moselle,[4] and then in January 1800 Napoleon grouped his infantry divisions into corps, each of which had its own staff.[5] When Napoleon formed his *Grand Armée* in 1805, it had seven corps, each of which included two to four infantry divisions, a brigade or division of light cavalry, approximately forty cannon, and appropriate detachments of engineers and supply troops. In subsequent years, Napoleon's success often came from his ability to move his corps over long distances in a coordinated manner and to flexibly employ their combination of infantry, artillery, and cavalry. With these three arms organic, a Napoleonic corps could engage an enemy force much larger than itself for a limited period. As Napoleon's subordinate commanders became more adept at their duties, his reliance upon the corps system provided him with a great deal of maneuverability and offensive capability. Moreover, his converging columns of corps often achieved victory over opponents whose organizational structure and operational methods were not as modern or flexible.[6]

Napoleon's brand of operational art strongly emphasized the offensive and always focused on actions throughout the depth of an enemy's position. His ideal battle usually included an enveloping attack by one or more of his corps that would create the opportunity for breaking through the enemy's main position and unleashing an exploitation force. He disliked unimaginative frontal assaults and used them only in those cases when he thought he had no choice. He explained, "It is by turning the enemy, by attacking his flank, that battles are won."[7] Thus, Napoleon capitalized upon his ability to conduct war at the operational level and often used his corps to fix an enemy force, move deep into its rear, or deliver the decisive blow at a weakened but critical point. He explained, "The art of war consists, with an inferior army, of always having more forces than the enemy at the point of attack, or the point being attacked; but this art is learned neither from books nor from practice; it is a knack for command that appropriately constitutes the genius of war."[8]

By the end of the Napoleonic wars, most French military thinkers thought of Napoleon's battles when they thought of grand tactics. For many of them, his ability to move large forces simply and swiftly, shift units from one mission to another, combine separate columns near or on the battlefield, and achieve decisive success demonstrated the main characteristic of the operational art.

Despite the demonstrated success of Napoleonic corps, French political leaders remained reluctant to form corps in peacetime, and for much of the nineteenth century the French Army had only twenty divisional headquarters with nothing more than a bare skeletal command structure linking them to Paris. During the same period little or no effort was expended by the French officer corps in studying the operational level of war. Far more effort was expended in regimental schools in which reading, writing, and basic tactics were taught than in professional schools in which officers studied the operational art.[9] A few officers attended staff schools, but their knowledge was not deeply appreciated and their influence limited. Despite the contributions of de Broglie, de Bourcet, Guibert, and Napoleon to the development of the operational level of war, most officers knew little or nothing about operational art on the eve of the Franco-Prussian War.

Institutional Changes After the Franco-Prussian War

The dramatic defeat of 1871 initiated a period of modernization and reform of the military, for the French could not ignore the ineffectiveness of their performance and the superiority of German methods and organizations. As part of their effort to catch up with the Germans, the army's leaders sought to establish corps and field armies in peacetime. Before 1870 France did not have corps headquarters in peacetime, much less functioning field armies, and the army's performance in combat in 1870–1871 suffered because of the newly formed units' inexperience. After 1871 French political leaders permitted the establishment of corps in peacetime, but fearing a possible threat to the republican government, many of them opposed the creation of field army headquarters.[10] They feared another Louis Napoleon could overthrow the republican government if he had the support and prestige of higher-level army commanders behind him.

In 1888 France took an important step toward creating a de facto headquarters for field armies. The Minister of War inserted a provision into the army's budget that allocated financial credits for the "inspection" of the nineteen army corps. After sharp debate in the Chamber of Deputies about the role and powers of these inspectors, the Minister of War was required to ensure that the missions for inspection were of "limited duration and constantly revocable."[11] The Chamber of Deputies and the Senate then adopted the measure. Some progress had occurred, but the establishment of field army headquarters in peacetime had not been permitted.

To an eager military, however, the door was open for change, and Charles de Freycinet, the first civilian Minister of War in the Third Republic, led the way. He declared that the changes he proposed were "inspired" by the deliberations of the request for credits for conducting inspections of corps-size units. On 26 May 1888, Freycinet submitted a proposed decree to the president of the Third Republic that would permit the establishment of field army headquarters as temporary, skeleton units during peacetime. The army commanders and their staffs would be officially designated but would be brought together only for short periods each year. The designated commanders had limited authority with "no right of interference in the command of the corps" and "no actual right of command." Despite opposition in the Chamber of Deputies, the president of the republic soon approved the decree.[12]

Two years later another improvement occurred. A decree of 10 April 1890 more clearly defined the authority of the officers who had been designated as field army commanders. They could now be charged officially with the inspection of one or more corps to determine the degree of their preparations for war and for mobilization. Although the inspections could only be conducted when ordered by the Minister of War, the power of the inspectors was great. They could "prescribe reviews and order, as an exercise, the immediate mobilization of the combat troops or [combat service] support forces of a corps, and then have them conduct the defense of a fort or defensive works."[13] If any corps commander had questions about the authority of the designated army commanders, this decree probably answered them.

The Freycinet reforms thus prepared the way for the establishment of French field armies during peacetime. As one contemporary British observer noted, commanders and staffs met as often as once a week by 1891.[14] Such meetings obviously facilitated the exchange of ideas about the employment of field armies and thereby strengthened France's abilities at the operational level of war. In 1899 another decree expanded the authority of the designated field army commanders, giving them power to inspect those army corps that would make up their wartime armies.[15]

Another improvement in France's capabilities at the operational level came with the expansion of annual fall maneuvers so high-level commanders and staffs could improve their functioning in the field. Freycinet also played a key role in this important development. In the maneuvers of September 1891, which were held in Champagne on the northeast frontier, two out of the four designated field army commanders and their staffs participated. They controlled four infantry corps, two cavalry divisions, and other supporting troops, including artillery and engineers.[16] The maneuvers were the largest heretofore conducted in France and involved more than 100,000 men.

The maneuvers were an obvious success. One British journalist noted, "Germany has this year lost that uncontested supremacy in Europe which she has enjoyed for twenty years." He added, "The results of these [maneuvers of 1891] have been able to show that which was the weakest point in France in 1870 [staff organization and efficiency] is almost her strongest now."[17] In a speech at a banquet for the generals participating in the maneuvers and for the foreign representatives observing them, Freycinet emphasized the importance of the reforms and concluded, "No one doubts today that we are strong."[18]

Operational Thinking Before World War I

As the French Army modified its organizational structure and conducted peacetime maneuvers with corps and field armies, thinkers, military schools, and publications devoted considerable effort to analyzing the techniques of employing large formations. The major concepts that came from this process and their evolution are most evident in the field manuals on large-unit operations that were published in 1895 and 1913. The 1895 edition was entitled *Regulations on the Service of Armies in the Field* and explained: "The army corps is the basic unit of all army formations. The combining of several army corps under a single leader forms a [field] army. When several [field] armies operate in the same theater of war, they are combined under a single commander and form an army group."[19] Despite the discussion of the field army and army group, the 1895 regulation devoted only a small portion of its attention to their employment in combat. In sharp contrast the 1913 edition was entitled *Regulation on the Conduct of Large Units* and included detailed information about field armies in combat. The report of the committee that wrote the later regulation explained: "Studies undertaken in France for about twenty years on the operations of [field] armies and army groups have provided evidence about a certain number of principles that dominate the employment of large units. These principles have never, until the present, been assembled in an official document."[20] Thus, the 1913 regulation included the latest information available to the French Army about the operational level of war and reflected concepts learned through more than two decades of development. In essence, the 1913 manual was the first official publication in France dealing with the operational level of war and its application through operational art.

A key difference between the 1895 and 1913 regulations pertained to the employment of the corps. While the 1895 regulation did not emphasize operations by units larger than corps and envisaged corps acting in a relatively autonomous fashion, the 1913 regulation strongly emphasized operations by field armies while acting as part of army groups. The 1913 regulation explained, "The objective of the maneuver of an army group is to impose on the enemy a ... battle under conditions which may lead to decisive results and end the war."[21] The regulation made it clear that the maneuver of an army group came from the movement and actions of field armies whose subordinate corps were always united and acted closely in concert with the other corps. Thus, the relative autonomy that was foreseen in the 1895 regulation for corps was accorded to field armies in the 1913 regulation. French operational thinking thereby reflected the important changes in organizational structure that had occurred after 1871.

Despite the greater emphasis on units larger than corps, the influence of Napoleon and the "cult" of the offensive captivated French concepts for operations. This unfortunate development occurred even though interest in the intellectual study of war increased dramatically after 1871, particularly after the 1878 founding of the *École Militaire Supérieure*, which was renamed the *École Supérieure de Guerre* in 1880. In a remarkable about-face from the pre-1870 approach, which had frowned on having educated officers, the French energetically studied the many facets of waging war successfully.[22] As officers returned eagerly to the academic study of warfare, they "rediscovered" the ideas of Clausewitz and the methods of Napoleon.[23] The study of the two important figures went hand in hand. Since Clausewitz's works dealt primarily with Napoleonic warfare, his ideas were used to awaken interest in one of France's greatest and most successful military leaders.

In the late 1880s and the 1890s, the ideas of Clausewitz and the examples of Napoleon dominated the *École Supérieure de Guerre*, which concentrated more on operations than strategy. One of the most influential of the instructors at the War College was Henri Bonnal, who frequently lectured on Napoleonic warfare. In a 1901 work on the battle of Sadowa, Bonnal argued:

> The war of 1866 was prepared, undertaken, and carried out by [German] leaders and soldiers without any war experience.... Nevertheless, despite numerous errors ... the Prussian army maneuvered, fought, and won a decisive victory by adhering to the Napoleonic principles of war, [which had] fallen into disuse or even [had been] completely forgotten in other armies of Europe.[24]

Such words linked the German victory to Napoleonic methods and obviously served to heighten interest among French officers. Nonetheless, the intense interest in Napoleonic warfare led many French military thinkers to emphasize maneuver rather than firepower, misunderstand the effect of newly introduced weapons (breech-loading rifles, machine guns, rapidly firing artillery, etc.), and blur the distinction between the tactical, operational, and strategic levels of war.

The effects of this can best be seen in France's adoption of the ill-fated *offensive à outrance*. Of those most responsible, Col. Louis de Grandmaison played a particularly important role in the development of the disastrous doctrine upon which the French offensives of 1914 were based. Grandmaison was highly interested in the employment of large formations.[25] Despite this focus on larger units, numerous officers attempted to apply his ideas at the tactical level in 1914. Many of those who died in 1914 were weaned on some of Grandmaison's phrases, such as "To fight means to advance despite enemy fire."[26] Most had paid little or no attention to the careful qualification he had made to the notion of infantrymen always advancing. In 1910, for example, he had written, "In open terrain, a frontal infantry attack is impossible. During the attack, it is the role of the artillery to establish superiority of fire needed to suppress the enemy."[27] Instead of focusing on Grandmaison's ideas about security and the operations of larger units, many officers concentrated instead on the will to attack and the need to overcome bullets and artillery fire with infantry charges. In this process they, without encountering strong disagreement from Grandmaison, thoughtlessly applied operational concepts to the tactical realm. The unfortunate result was heavy losses in 1914 among some of France's best and most dedicated officers and soldiers.

Similarly, institutional changes fostered the development of the capability to perform at the operational level of warfare, but concepts within French doctrine for employment of field armies bore a strong resemblance to the mobile manner in which Napoleonic corps had been employed. The main difference was that a field army in 1914 was much larger than Napoleon's corps in 1815. While primarily emphasizing maneuver and the offensive, and by seeking sharp, intensive battles relying on "curtains" of artillery fire and energetic infantry charges, the French army developed its abilities to fight mobile battles and campaigns with field armies in support of strategic goals. These capabilities enabled the army to survive the initial battles of World War I, but they proved woefully inadequate for the static trench warfare that replaced mobile operations a few months after the beginning of the war.

The First Battles of 1914

Offensive ideas also dominated the formulation of strategy. In the decade before 1914, France had gradually tightened its relations with Russia and slowly developed a coalition strategy with Russia that relied on simultaneous offensives on the east and west borders of Germany. By forcing Germany to fight a two-front war, French military planners anticipated an eventual victory no matter what the outcome of the initial battles between Germany and France. In March 1910 one officer asserted, "Even if beaten the French army will have opened the way for the Russian offensive and assured the final success [of the two allies]."[28]

When General Joseph Joffre became Chief of the General Staff in July 1911, he shaped French strategy and doctrine to conform to the demands of the Franco-Russian Alliance and to his own preference for the offensive. Only six weeks after becoming Chief of the General Staff, he published the first change to Plan XVI[29] and in February 1914 replaced it with Plan XVII. Though the new plan was a concentration plan and not a war plan,[30] the main body of the document stated, "The intention of the commander-in-chief is to deliver, with all forces assembled, an attack against the German armies."[31] While refusing to reveal the details of his campaign strategy or the objectives of his operations, Joffre organized and prepared French forces to attack north or south of Metz-Thionville or north into Belgium toward Arlon and Neufchâteau. Depending on German actions, the French could attack into either Alsace-Lorraine or Belgium or both.

When the Germans began their attack against France in August 1914, they adhered to the outline of Count Alfred von Schlieffen's plan and attempted to conduct a gigantic turning movement deep into the rear of the Allied forces. While maintaining minimum but sufficient forces on their left flank and center, the Germans concentrated the great mass of their forces on their right wing and planned on moving these forces through central Belgium and then north and west around Paris. Their attack began with a *coup de main* on the Belgian fortifications around Liège.[32]

During the twelve days it took the Germans to clear these fortifications, General Joffre began revealing elements of his closely held strategy, first by launching a small, ineffective offensive into Alsace on his extreme right flank on 7 August.[33] This operation not only signaled to Russia France's intentions to fulfill its obligations to the Franco-Russian Alliance for an early offensive and protected the flank of the subsequent attack by First and Second Armies, it also boosted the morale of the French people. On 8 August Joffre revealed his entire operational concept when he issued General Instructions No. 1. He intended to send First and Second Armies on his right into Lorraine, south of the Metz-Thionville fortifications, and Third, Fourth, and Fifth Armies on his left into Belgium and Luxembourg, north of the fortifications. While the supporting attack on the right fixed the German left, drew enemy forces to the south, and fulfilled alliance obligations, the subsequent main attack on the left would strike the German center and unhinge the enemy forces advancing into central Belgium.[34] Though many critics such as Basil H. Liddell Hart have mistakenly characterized French strategy as being nothing more than a "frontal and whole front offensive,"[35] Joffre retained a high level of flexibility and aimed his main attack toward what he thought would be a lightly defended armpit of an enemy arm swinging a fist no deeper than Sedan or Mézières. But the initial attacks into Alsace-Lorraine went badly.

On the morning of the fourteenth, Joffre's First and Second Armies advanced on the southern prong of what would be a two-pronged attack. In consonance with General Helmuth von Moltke's orchestration of Schlieffen's concept, the German Sixth and Seventh Armies fell back, but they made the advancing French columns pay dearly. German machine-gunners extracted a high toll from the charging French infantry, and German long-range howitzers, aided by aerial spotters, skillfully silenced the shorter-range French 75-mm. batteries early in the fighting. The two French armies crossed the frontier on 15 August, but their advance had halted by 20 August.

In one of the final attacks near Sarrebourg (fifty kilometers west of Strasbourg), the two brigades of the French 15th Infantry Division made a frontal assault at dawn on 20 August against entrenched German infantry. Since heavy artillery had not yet arrived, the French infantry gallantly moved forward in the open in their dark-blue overcoats and red trousers and kepis. With bugles blaring and banners waving, they charged forward with bayonets fixed against the German machine guns and artillery. By 0700 the attack had collapsed.[36]

During the first battles of the campaign, the misplaced ardor and tactics of the *offensive à outrance* led some commanders to charge forward and commit their troops in ill-coordinated and poorly timed piecemeal attacks. French officers advanced as quickly as they could, usually refusing to prepare trenches and strong points on which their troops could fall back if the attack failed. When the suicidal charges did collapse, the French had nothing behind them to halt a German counterattack, and some units collapsed completely, their withdrawals turning into routs.

As the French offensive on Joffre's right wing ground to a halt on the nineteenth and twentieth, the German Sixth and Seventh Armies under Crown Prince Rupprecht of Bavaria launched a counteroffensive at noon on the twentieth. Prior to the beginning of hostilities, General Moltke, chief of the German General Staff, decided the forces on his left wing should conduct an early counterattack, thereby limiting the French penetration into Germany. After the French First and Second Armies began their attacks, he strengthened Crown Prince Rupprecht on his left wing with six more divisions. The German counterattack caught the French by surprise. While the French First Army withdrew in relatively good order, Second Army had two corps that, according to Joffre, "fell back under conditions that almost resembled a rout."[37] Only the strong performance of General Foch's XXth Corps prevented disaster.[38] By 22 August First and Second Armies had withdrawn to their starting position.

During the first days of First and Second Armies' advance into Alsace, Joffre became aware of the Germans' moving farther west through Belgium than previously anticipated, and he responded by moving Fifth Army farther to his left. He expected Fifth Army, as well as the Belgians and the soon-to-arrive British Expeditionary Forces (BEF), to meet the German forces on his left flank. He also thought that such a deep movement would result in even fewer enemy forces in eastern Belgium and make the task of his Third and Fourth Armies easier. Late on 20 August, the day the Germans unleashed their counterattack against First and Second Armies in Alsace-Lorraine, Joffre ordered Third and Fourth Armies to attack.[39] He expected the two armies to advance the following day in a northeasterly direction in eastern Belgium toward Longwy, Virton, and Neufchâteau[40] and to strike marching German columns (which were supposed to be heading west) in the flank or rear and rout them. Confident of success, he told the two army commanders, "The enemy will be attacked wherever he is encountered."[41]

Meanwhile, the German Fourth and Fifth Armies had crossed the Ardennes in eastern Belgium and bided their time, waiting for the First, Second, and Third German Armies on their right to sweep through central Belgium. As they waited, the troops dug entrenchments and organized strong defensive positions. On the twenty-second, the French Third Army blindly bumped into the German Fifth Army near Longwy and the Luxembourg border. Though the terrain was hilly and heavily forested, the French had paid little attention to having advance or flank guards. Hoping to hit an advancing German army in the flank, the French instead stumbled into a killing zone and suffered thousands of casualties. Just as in the Lorraine offensive, the French infantry failed to coordinate their actions with those of the artillery and often did not bother to suppress machine-gun fire before advancing. True to their doctrine to the bloody end, they tried to dig out the Germans with bayonets, but were decimated by machine guns and artillery fire. Farther to the northwest, the French Fourth Army was no more lucky than the Third. Following several disastrous actions, the commander of Fourth Army used the word "disorderly" when he reported to the *Grand Quartier General* (GQG) that he was withdrawing.[42] After a futile attempt to renew the attack, Joffre reluctantly permitted the two armies to return to their defensive positions.

The collapse of the Lorraine and Ardennes offensives placed the French in an extremely awkward position. Without a reserve, much depended on the abilities of Fifth Army and the now arriving BEF, which was moving into position on the French left flank. Between 15 and 21 August, Joffre had moved Fifth Army north toward the angle formed by the Sambre and Meuse Rivers, but on 23 August the Germans crossed the Meuse River and forced Fifth Army to retreat. This was the final step in the collapse of Joffre's strategy. Instead of concentrating superior force against the weak point or a decisive point, Joffre had diffused his offensive power in three separate and almost unrelated attacks, none of which succeeded. French forces soon began a demoralizing withdrawal.

The first battles on the French frontier thus relied on the maneuver of field armies, almost as if they were remnants of Napoleon's *Grand Armée*. Though this resulted in huge casualties and disastrous defeats, the capability to maneuver at operational level soon enabled the French to avoid an even larger defeat.

The "Miracle of the Marne"

Despite the initial failures, the French had not yet lost the campaign and had some reason for hope. Unlike the Germans, they had an effective command and control system and a commander who did not lose his composure after the first losses. While the German communication system collapsed,[43] the French system continued to pass information smoothly and dependably. Joffre kept in close touch with the rapidly changing situation and moved forward on several occasions to meet with his major subordinate commanders. The French also had excellent and dependable railways at their disposal. After defeat in 1871, the French had made substantial improvements in their railway system and built several new lines to facilitate the movement of large bodies of troops and equipment from one portion of the frontier to another. In 1914 these improvements greatly increased Joffre's ability to respond to the threat on his left wing by moving troops and equipment from his right to his left.

Although Joffre was slow to comprehend the German strategy and the location of the main attack, he carefully recast French operational dispositions after he understood what the Germans were doing. Fortunately for France, Moltke's strategy played into Joffre's hands by permitting him to reform shaken units and then transport them west rapidly to face the German First and Second Armies. On 24 August Joffre ordered First and Second Armies on his right to hold in place, while the Third, Fourth, Fifth, and British Armies withdrew to the south. He hoped they could hold the Germans along a line extending from the Somme River to Verdun. To strengthen his left flank, he assembled two new armies. The new Sixth Army assembled under General Michel J. Maunoury around Paris; the new Ninth Army assembled under General Ferdinand Foch behind the retreating Fourth and Fifth Armies and soon entered the line when a gap appeared between the two armies.[44]

Other changes increased French effectiveness. With regard to tactics, Joffre informed his army commanders that the infantry should attack only after artillery preparation, and he forbade mass attacks.[45] This bit of tactical wisdom had been learned only after nearly 300,000 casualties. Joffre also continued to weed out the command structure, including the commanders of Third and Fifth Armies. While dozens of brigade and division commanders were also relieved,[46] sometimes unjustly, the movement of officers such as General Louis Franchet d'Espèrey into the command structure signaled the promotion of hard-nosed, self-confident fighters. It also signaled the demotion of officers who had done well in the peacetime army but who had not done well in combat.[47]

While Joffre acted to strengthen his left, the German operational plan continued to change. The key modification was the decision by the German First Army commander, General Alexander von Kluck, to move his army around the eastern edge of Paris, rather than encircling it by moving his army around the western edge. As the gigantic Schlieffen wheel continued to turn, Kluck's decision exposed the German left flank to an attack from Paris and fundamentally altered the German operational concept.[48]

On 2 September the French government placed General Joseph Gallieni in charge of defending Paris. After Maunoury's Sixth Army entered the fortified city and came under Gallieni's command, its strength slowly increased as reserve and colonial units arrived to join it. The French initially focused on defending the city, but as the strength of Sixth Army increased, and as the German right flank became more exposed toward the English Channel, the opportunity for decisive action appeared.

On 4 September Gallieni dispatched several aircraft to reconnoiter the area north and west of Paris. When the pilots returned, they informed him that four corps in Kluck's First Army had crossed the Marne River northeast of Paris and that only one corps remained to protect the entire German flank. On the same day, Franchet d'Espèrey met with the British, and after he promised that elements in Paris would protect the BEF's left flank, they agreed to participate in an offensive.[49] Later that evening Joffre received a message from Franchet d'Espèrey concerning his meeting with the British and also engaged in a heated telephone conversation with Gallieni, who demanded that a counterattack be made quickly against the vulnerable German flank. Though the extent of Gallieni's influence is not clear, Joffre decided the counterattack would take place on the morning of 6 September.[50]

At the German headquarters in Luxembourg on 4 September, Moltke learned, more than a day after Kluck made his fateful decision, that First Army's right flank—the right flank of the entire German line—stood exposed to an attack from the French Sixth Army in Paris. Moltke had no choice but to halt the advance of First and Second Armies on his right wing. Recognizing a victory on his right could not come from First and Second Armies, he ordered Third, Fourth, and Fifth Armies in his center to continue attacking, while the armies on his left continued attacking in the south. First and Second Armies were ordered to face Paris and protect the Germans' right flank. Kluck's First Army not only had to stay north of the Marne but also had to pull back from its exposed position.[51]

When the Allies launched their counteroffensive on the sixth, success or failure lay in the hands of Maunoury's Sixth Army, Sir John French's BEF, and d'Espèrey's Fifth Army. The situation favored them, for Kluck's army was split, with one portion south of the Marne and the other farther north facing west. Only the arrival of a message from Moltke finally convinced Kluck that he had no real choice but to pull his leading elements back across the Marne. As he shifted his forces north so he could concentrate his army against the French coming from Paris, he caused a gap to appear between his army and the German Second Army. Meanwhile French attacks against the right of the German Second Army resulted in an even larger gap between First and Second Armies.

As if on cue, the British Expeditionary Forces (BEF) and elements from the left wing of the French Fifth Army moved north through this gap, opposed only by reconnaissance elements. Unaware of the significance of what they were doing as they passed between the German First and Second Armies, the Allied soldiers moved slowly. On the morning of 9 September, the British crossed the Meuse River near Chateau-Thierry and insured Allied possession of a bridgehead across the Meuse and between the two German field armies.[52] This accomplishment made the position untenable for the two German armies.

As the British edged forward, Gallieni desperately reinforced Maunoury's Sixth Army, using more than 600 taxicabs to transport one division from Paris. Kluck appeared capable of repulsing Sixth Army and perhaps moving into Paris, but neither the German First nor Second had any forces available for closing the gap between their armies or responding to the Allied forces moving through this gap. Though Joffre's attempt to attack from Paris against the German left flank had failed, the advance of the British and French forces into the gap between the German First and Second Armies left the Germans little choice but to withdraw.

With the withdrawal of the Germans from the vicinity of Paris, the opening campaign of the war on the western front ended. The simultaneous withdrawal of the other field armies on the German right and the subsequent failure of the Germans and Allies to outflank the other in the "race to the sea" resulted in a long line of entrenchments running roughly from Nieuport on the English Channel, south to Noyon (100 kilometers northeast of Paris), east to Verdun, and then southeast toward Colmar. While Joffre had not saved France from a long and bloody war and had made some inexcusable mistakes in the opening phases of the campaign, he had prevented the Germans from winning a decisive victory. In essence, the ability of the French Army to perform at the operational level enabled him to achieve the "miracle of the Marne."

The Nivelle Offensive

From late 1914 through late 1917, the French continued to launch huge offensives with objectives deep in the enemy's rear. To achieve a penetration, they concentrated massive amounts of men and materiel in desperate attempts to break through the extensive German defensives. Most of the assaults, however, yielded little more than long lists of casualties, and gains were measured in meters, rather than kilometers.

From the first desperate months of war, military leaders on both sides recognized the effectiveness of artillery in suppressing enemy fires and reducing friendly casualties,[53] and with each passing month the role of artillery became more and more important. As the amount of artillery fire in support of attacks began to be measured in the millions of rounds, the battlefield came to resemble a moonscape. Craters, trenches, and barbed wire served to delay the advance of the infantry, but they also served to delay the advance of artillery, which was extremely heavy and could easily become bogged down. Since the infantry could not advance without artillery support, the pace of an advance was set less by the infantry than by the ability of the artillery to displace forward and continue to provide supporting fires. Such displacements required time, thereby adding intervals or phases to attacks and making them step-by-step, methodical operations. To make matters more difficult, an army on the attack sometimes had to build roads through an area before it could make a successful advance. In contrast, the defenders' efforts to rush reserve forces into areas threatened by a penetration were generally not impeded by such delays.

Because of constraints on mobility, fighting at the operational level during World War I was greatly influenced by the ability of a defender — usually the Germans on the western front — to reinforce a threatened sector faster than an attacker could pass through it. Using railroads and roads, a defender could move reinforcements easily and did not have to contend with the destruction an attacker faced. French commanders quickly recognized the importance of somehow tying down a defender's reserves, so reinforcements could not be shifted into the area where an attack was being launched. The primary method for contending with the Germans' reserves was through the launching of multiple attacks, usually on a successive basis, across a broad front. In 1917, for example, the Allies agreed that the British would attack at Arras before the French launched the main attack at the Chemin des Dames. By carefully locating and sequencing attacks, an attacker could compel a defender to commit his reserves piecemeal and thereby prevent him from using them more effectively. Such coordinated attacks became standard fare in most operational planning conducted by the French after 1914.

Almost all the attacks launched by the French from 1914 to 1917 were part of huge offensives seeking a breakthrough and the seizure of distant objectives. One operation, which greatly affected French military thinking and which reflected the French approach to operational art, was General Robert G. Nivelle's offensive in the spring of 1917. Nivelle was an excellent officer who quickly rose from the rank of colonel in 1914 to corps and field army command. Although the French were unable to break through German defensive positions in 1915 and 1916, Nivelle developed a reputation during this period as an innovative artillery officer. He devised the first rolling barrage of the war and coined the slogan, "The artillery conquers; the infantry occupies." By creating an intricate timetable, he enabled artillerymen to maintain a moving barrage of artillery in front of advancing infantrymen. In an era without mobile radios, the rolling barrage proved to be an excellent method for coordinating infantry and artillery and added substantially to the power of the offensive.[54]

Nivelle's initial attempt to use unusually heavy artillery barrages in support of infantry attacks failed in June 1915, but in October 1916 he launched a dramatically successful attack at Verdun. After detailed rehearsals and a four-day artillery preparation,[55] he used seven divisions along a seven-kilometer front to capture the extremely important objective of Fort Douaumont, a few kilometers northeast of Verdun. Although his forces penetrated no more than three kilometers, the advance seemed miraculously deep by the standards of the day. This successful attack was followed by a second one in early November that captured Fort Vaux.[56] In these attacks, he used more than a million rounds of artillery against German positions before beginning a rolling barrage of artillery in front of attacking infantry.[57] Ironically, Nivelle was one of the first in the French Army to notice German infiltration tactics, for in June 1916 he had warned Second Army about the Germans' closely coordinating their artillery and infantry and using "infiltration" and "encirclement" to make their way through French defenses.[58] Despite this early insight, Nivelle's method emphasized the firepower of artillery, not the mobility of infantry.

Nivelle's success at Verdun suggested that he had found the "formula" for breaking through strong German defenses, and on 12 December 1916, he was named commander of all French armies. He soon began planning to smash through the German front in the spring of 1917 along the

Aisne River between Reims and Soissons. Recognizing that the intervals required for artillery preparation between successive assaults provided the defenders time to strengthen their positions and concentrate reserves, he concluded that the French should seek a rapid penetration under circumstances that prevented the enemy from reinforcing his defenses. To obtain this rapid penetration, Nivelle planned on using vast amounts of artillery (particularly from long-range, heavy artillery recently added to France's inventory) to obliterate an enemy position throughout its depth. By concentrating simultaneous barrages on successive lines of German defenses, and by preceding the advancing infantry with a rolling barrage, he expected the infantry to rush through holes blown into enemy lines. He intended to punch through German defenses in one blow and capture the heights of the Chemin des Dames to the north of the Aisne in only twenty-four to forty-eight hours.[59] Less optimistic than the new commander of French forces, Pétain recognized the difficulties of applying a tactical technique to the operational level of war and warned, "Even the waters of the Lake of Geneva would have but little effect if dispersed over the length and breadth of the Sahara Desert."[60]

Other difficulties came from the Germans' retiring from the Noyon salient, the shoulder of which ran parallel to the Aisne, and constructing a shorter defensive line to its rear. The Germans named this new line the Siegfried Position, but the Allies called it the Hindenburg Line. Adding to Nivelle's troubles, the Germans also obtained crucial intelligence about his offensive and organized their positions into elastic defenses that placed only a minimum number of infantry in forward trenches. An important part of their method was the placing of troops on the reverse slopes of hills so they could obtain some protection from the flat-trajectory artillery fire of the Allies. They also reinforced the threatened sector with an additional field army.

Despite indications that the Germans had reorganized their defenses and expected an attack on the Chemin des Dames, Nivelle insisted on launching the offensive. On 1 April, he wrote: "It is necessary to maintain the qualities of violence, brutality, and swiftness. The success of the breakthrough lies in speed and in surprise, caused by the rapid and sudden rush of our infantry onto the third and fourth positions. No consideration should intervene which will weaken the élan of the attack."[61] Ignoring criticisms from Pétain and others,[62] Nivelle scheduled the attack for 10 April, then delayed it until the fourteenth, and finally launched it on the sixteenth. Along a front of approximately sixty kilometers, he massed two armies for the attack and kept two armies in reserve, totaling 1,400,000 men in fifty-two divisions. In support of the four armies, the French had approximately 1,650 mortars and accompanying guns; 1,800 75-mm. guns; and 1,700 heavy artillery pieces. Stocks of ammunition included 24 million rounds of 75-mm. and 9 million rounds of heavy artillery ammunition. To support the attack, the French also had to extend their railways in the region.[63]

On the left, Sixth Army had fourteen infantry divisions; on the right, Fifth Army also had fourteen infantry divisions. When the infantry broke through the German defenses, Sixth Army was supposed to turn west and Fifth Army east. This would enable the Tenth Army to pass through them and to advance north. Nivelle confidently expected the Tenth Army to advance twenty-five kilometers by the end of the second day's attack. First Army remained in reserve.[64]

Before the attack began, nine days of artillery preparation pounded the German positions. After this preparation, the leading wave of attacking infantrymen occupied the first positions fairly easily, because the enemy had abandoned many of them as they had retired to the Hindenburg Line. As the French soldiers moved over the high ground of the Chemin des Dames, however, withering German machine-gun fire halted their advance. The commander of the 2d Colonial Corps on the right of Sixth Army and in the center of the offensive described the attack in his after-action report:

> At H-hour, the troops approach in order the first enemy positions. The geographic crest is attained almost without losses; the enemy's artillery barrage is not very brisk and is sporadic. Nevertheless, our infantry advances with a slower speed than anticipated. The rolling barrage is unleashed almost immediately and steadily moves ahead of the first waves, which it quickly ceases to protect. A few machine guns that are on the plateau do not halt the ... infantrymen who are able to descend the northern side of the plateau to the edge of the steep slopes descending into the valley of the Ailette [River]. There, they are welcomed and fixed in place by the deadly fire of numerous machine guns that, located on the [reverse side of the] slopes, outside the reach of our projectiles, have remained undamaged.
>
> A few groups utilizing the approaches incompletely covered [by fire] succeed in descending the slopes. But in general, the troops suffer considerable losses in a few minutes, particularly in leaders, and [after] not succeeding in crossing this deadly zone, halt, take cover, and at some point withdraw to the first trench in their rear.
>
> They are joined by the battalions [from increment] B, which depart at the scheduled hour and dissolve on the line of combat. The battalions [from increment] C, conforming to the combat plan, advance in their turn. A few of them ... occupy the first German trenches or our jump-off trenches. In less than an hour, the fighting is stabilized. All attempts to regain forward movement fail as soon as they arrive on the line covered by enemy machine guns. The only possible movement is through trenches using grenades and [soon] this encounters growing resistance.
>
> The enemy's reserves are in effect almost intact. Well protected in holes on the northern slope or in very strong dug-outs, they have not suffered from the bombardment, and the trench running along the northern edge of the plateau constitutes for them an easy way of departure.

During the rest of the day on the 16th and the days of the 17th and 18th, combat assumes the form of a series of partial attacks, preceded as much as possible by an artillery bombardment of the enemy's positions and executed under the control of the local commander according to the availability of munitions and grenades.... Combat for the units of the corps is terminated during the night of the 18–19th.[65]

Although the fighting continued until 7 May, the Nivelle offensive had failed dismally. After only three days of fighting, Nivelle concluded that Fifth and Sixth armies could not break through the strong German defenses and modified his plan. He ordered Fourth Army, which was on the right of Fifth Army, to attack in a northwesterly direction, while Fifth Army attacked to the northeast. He hoped these attacks would encircle Reims and slice off a large part of the German positions. But this effort was also doomed to failure. The Germans had assembled additional forces in the sector, and the attacks had little chance of success.

A week after the launching of Nivelle's offensive, Paris became alarmed at Nivelle's efforts to continue the offensive despite its costs and apparent failure. The casualties during the first week were approximately 117,000, including 32,000 dead. Perhaps more important, the senseless losses had sapped the morale of the French soldiers and contributed significantly to the mutinies of 1917.[66]

Pétain's Limited Offensives

Following the disastrous operation, Nivelle was relieved and replaced by General Pétain, whose first task was to end the mutinies and then restore the French soldiers' fighting spirit. As part of his reforms, Pétain abandoned the notion of breaking through German defenses and began emphasizing limited offensives. On 19 May 1917, he published Directive No. 1, which outlined the new method of attacking. The directive stated:

> Instead of great attacks in depth with distant objectives, it is preferable to conduct attacks with limited objectives, unleashed quickly on a front as large as permitted by the number and caliber of available artillery. For this concept to be realized, the attacks must be:
>
> 1) Conducted with as few infantry as possible and with the maximum amount of artillery.
> 2) Preceded by surprise which will provide the chance of acting with strong or weak forces and obtaining important results. It should be noted that surprise can be obtained only if the attack sector ... is allowed to be quiet for several weeks or even months before the operation begins.
> 3) Applied successively on different parts of the front, chosen from those that the enemy has significant reason not to abandon readily.
> 4) Followed rapidly by other attacks which fix the enemy and deprive him of his freedom of action.[67]

Instead of a single battle leading to a decisive victory, Pétain believed a series of simultaneous or successive battles had to be fought. Even then, victory in the near future was not guaranteed, but losses could be minimized and heavy casualties inflicted on the Germans.

Using the new method of limited offensives, Pétain launched an offensive at Verdun on 20 August 1917 and achieved moderate success. As soon as the Germans concentrated their reserves and offered stiff resistance, he halted the attack. From 23 through 26 October he launched a more elaborate offensive near the Fort of La Malmaison north of Soissons on the western end of the Chemin des Dames, relying on even larger amounts of artillery than had been used in the recent offensive at Verdun. With Maj. Gen. John J. Pershing watching the first large French offensive since the mutinies, the French launched an attack with Sixth Army along a front of about twelve kilometers. The objective was the high ground supporting the German right flank along the Chemin des Dames. With about 1,850 artillery tubes firing in support, including six days of preparatory fires, and with fourteen tank companies accompanying the infantry, the French advanced about five kilometers. This advance outflanked the Germans on the Chemin des Dames and forced them to withdraw behind the Ailette River.[68]

Only 4 percent of the French soldiers who participated in the attack became casualties, and the victory served to revive the morale and confidence of the army. Pétain later observed that the units that took part in the offensive were swept with a "veritable intoxication of victory."[69] The Germans had suffered heavy losses and were forced to pull back from the blood-soaked terrain of the Chemin des Dames. Pétain must have felt extremely pleased, for a limited offensive had seized the terrain that Nivelle's all-out offensive had failed to gain. No one, however, knew how to use this operational method to end the war. To his critics who still sought a formula for a quick victory, Pétain replied, "I am waiting for the Americans and the tanks."[70]

The Model of Montdidier

Examples of limited offensives, particularly the battle of La Malmaison, were important in the development of French operational art thinking, but no battle was studied more intensively after the Great War than the battle of Montdidier. This battle occurred in August 1918 when the French First Army, commanded by General Eugène Debeney, delivered one of the final and most important blows of the war to the German Army. Occurring on what General Ludendorff termed the "black day" of the war for the German Army,[71] the August attack represented a turning point in the conduct of French operations and inaugurated the form of open warfare that characterized the last months of the war. At the same time, the

French First Army was composed primarily of French units, with only the American 1st Division making an indirect contribution to the French success with the capture of Cantigny in June 1918. As such, the battle represented an extremely important achievement of French units during the Great War.

During the battle, General Debeney commanded a force of fifteen divisions (divided into four corps), supported by more than 1,600 artillery pieces and two battalions of light tanks.[72] The initial concept was for a limited offensive by the French First Army to support an attack by the British Fourth Army under General Sir Henry Rawlinson. But General Debeney recognized that his army had an opportunity to strike a deadly blow at the Germans to his front. Rather than make a massive frontal assault, Debeney resolved to strike with a French corps on his field army's left flank (near the British Fourth Army's area of attack) and seize key terrain that would destroy the equilibrium of the enemy's defenses. He would follow this attack with a second attack in the same general area and encourage the Germans to reinforce the threatened area. As the enemy reinforced his units on First Army's left flank, the French would suddenly attack with two corps on First Army's right flank.[73] By using successive operations, the French could take advantage of the Germans' having shifted forces to the point of initial attack.

As Debeney had planned, the battle began with four French corps on line, and despite difficult resistance the two corps on the left soon pushed back the enemy defenders. When the attack on the French left was followed by an attack on the right, the sudden commitment of the two corps on the right caught the Germans off guard. Since they had already concentrated most of their reserves on the French left, the Germans could not respond to the unexpected maneuver and suffered a major defeat.

Following World War I, the battle of Montdidier became the basis for officers' studying of operational methods. The French severely criticized the disastrous methods used from 1914 to 1917 and cited the controlled and deliberate operations at Montdidier as a model of centralized control and of effective planning and execution. When General Debeney reestablished the curriculum at the War College, he included the important battle fought by the field army he commanded. Since he later became a contributing author to the 1922 *Provisional Instructions for the Tactical Employment of Large Units*[74] and served as Chief of the General Staff of the French Army from 1923 to 1930, the model of his successful operation had a remarkable influence throughout the Army.

To study this battle, students at the War College after 1918 used a book written by Maj. Marius Daille, an assistant professor of military history at the War College. They often spent four days at the end of May in their second school year walking the Montdidier battlefield and studying the details of the attack.[75] Maj. Daille's analysis of the battle warned the students that Napoleonic methods no longer applied to twentieth-century warfare. Napoleon had relied on bringing decisive firepower and forces against a single point, breaking enemy lines, and destroying the cohesiveness of the enemy force. In the Great War, the French tried similar methods but had taken enormous casualties at Artois, Champagne, and Verdun. Such methods had never achieved a breakthrough. To explain this failure, Daille argued that despite initial successes, an attack would eventually slow as the direction of attack became apparent and a defender's reserves came into action. Instead of expanding like a balloon, the breach would progressively become smaller as the attacking forces pushed forward, and the friendly line ultimately would resemble a "narrow triangle" on the terrain, pointing into the enemy's position.[76] Within this triangle, concentrated enemy fire from the flanks would preclude movement and eventually the attacker's advantage would dissolve. Repeated and powerful attempts to punch through the enemy's defenses could only lead to the creation of "pockets," or salients, which were vulnerable to concentric artillery fires and enemy counterattack. Daille concluded that breaking through an organized defensive position would remain for a long time beyond the ability of an attacking army.[77]

For Major Daille, the offensive by First Army in August 1918 at Montdidier demonstrated a new method for overwhelming an organized defensive position without attempting a breakthrough. He identified the new method as juxtaposing several powerful attacks along converging lines. The enemy could not reinforce one area without weakening another and thereby could not prevent the attacker from pressing forward. While attacking across a broad front may appear to be linear attack, according to Daille it actually consisted of concentrating powerful means along several portions of a defender's line and then attacking. These simultaneous or successive operations insured that the attacker was always stronger than the defender and that the defender could not mass sufficient forces to halt the attacks. Clearly, Debeney had used this method at Montdidier, and it had succeeded beyond his wildest hopes.

While Daille preferred separate and powerful attacks along converging lines, he did not reject completely the single-axis attack in which new action was superimposed on top of another as it faltered. A single thrust sought depth, and according to Daille it could be used in the opening days of a campaign before a strongly organized defensive front had been established. It could also be used to strike at the boundary between different armies or the armies of different nations.[78] The main theme of Daille's study, nevertheless, was that the battle of Montdidier provided the formula for future success: coordinated and carefully controlled attacks (either simultaneous or successive) across a broad front with concentrated efforts at selected points.

"Maneuvering" Masses of Fire

Between the two world wars, the French made no dramatic changes in the organization of their corps, field armies, and army groups, but they did carefully analyze possible changes in their employment. Given the obvious increase in amounts and accuracy of firepower, they expected a future war to be even more deadly and consuming than the Great War had been, and they did not wish to be unprepared. Despite an intense effort that included numerous field exercises, tests, and sometimes sharp debate, the operational methods they used in the battles of 1940 represented only modest changes from those of the past and proved inadequate for the demands of mobile warfare that was waged and thrust upon them by the Germans.

As the French developed their operational doctrine, they remained concerned primarily with the effects of firepower and placed increased emphasis on centralized control by higher-level commanders, particularly of the artillery.[79] The French had begun the Great War with a doctrine in which mobile artillery provided rapid fire during an attack; they had ended the war with a doctrine emphasizing massive fire prior to and during an attack and requiring artillery to be under the control of division and higher commanders. The concept of centralizing artillery assets corresponded with the concept of maneuvering masses of fire, which became an extremely important part of French operational-level doctrine. Such control was necessary for maneuver, according to the French, since it enabled the commander to concentrate his fires on the decisive point in battle. The decisive point, however, was defined by larger-unit commanders, and maneuver was viewed in terms of the movement of larger, rather than smaller units. In other words, concerns at the operational level overshadowed those at the tactical level.

Throughout the interwar period, the concept of maneuvering masses of fire became ever more important. General Frédéric G. Herr, Inspector General of Artillery at the end of World War I, noted that if the commander should decentralize his artillery, he would lose all control over the battle and become "disarmed." By passing control of the battle to his subordinates, the higher-level commander could not maneuver and the battle would degenerate into a series of "isolated, disjointed, sterile local actions."[80] The 1926 *Regulation on Maneuver of the Artillery* warned, "Finally, the systemic allocation of all artillery to subordinate elements must be avoided; it constitutes an abdication of command."[81]

While the French recognized the need for decentralization during an advance, military leaders preferred having larger-unit commanders control major portions of the artillery. In an October 1922 meeting of the Superior Council of War, Marshal Pétain referred to some of this artillery as a "strategic reserve, suitable for great displacement."[82] Such artillery provided a means for the higher-level commander to exercise a major influence over the battlefield and acted as a readily available reserve that could be shifted rapidly to another area. The requirement for such a reserve meant that a significant portion of the artillery was long-range, heavy artillery under the control of corps and higher commanders. This had been one of the important lessons of World War I. But the use of artillery in this manner favored a more stable battlefield, rather than a highly mobile one. The resulting distortion of tactical and operational mobility can be seen in the 1926 artillery regulation, which cited railway artillery as having "great tactical" value because of its ability to "occupy and leave" a position rapidly.[83]

One of the critics of the organization of the French artillery was Marshal Foch. In a meeting of the Superior Council of War in October 1926, he stated, "It will be necessary from the first for the divisional artillery to be the most important, then the corps artillery, then the general reserves."[84] The French emphasis remained the reverse of that suggested by Foch, and after World War II, General Maurice Gamelin noted that while the French had fifty-six regiments of artillery in general reserve in May–June 1940, the Germans had nowhere near that amount of artillery in reserve.[85] By misunderstanding the reluctance of the Germans to retain artillery as a reserve, he had misunderstood the thrust of German doctrine toward mobility, penetration, and decentralization and had missed an extremely important difference between the French and German employment of artillery.

As the French developed their doctrine, they accepted a dangerous degree of rigidity within their system for command and control. They believed the locus of decision making had to remain at higher levels, because a higher commander had to manage and coordinate the actions of numerous subordinate units. The army's doctrinal and organizational system stressed the power and authority of corps, army, and army group commanders. Each lower level had less room for improvisation and adjustments than the level immediately above it. With the strongest emphasis being placed on the operational, rather than the tactical level, the entire system was designed to be propelled forward by pressure from above, rather than by being pulled from below. In contrast to a decentralized battle in which officers were expected to show initiative and flexibility, the French preferred rigid centralization and strict obedience. Unfortunately for France, this resulted in a fatal flaw: The French military establishment could not respond flexibly to unanticipated demands and could hardly capitalize upon an important gain made by a lower-level unit.

In the final analysis, the French emphasis on centralization and their doctrine of allocation of artillery placed the greatest premium on firepower and blurred the relationship between the tactical and operational levels. The resulting distortion is apparent in the changing of the name of the French field manual on large units. While the 1913 edition was entitled *Regulation on the Conduct of Large Units*, the 1936 edition was entitled *Instructions of the Tactical Employment of Large Units*.[86] French concepts for the operational level thus rested on an extremely shaky foundation.

The Methodical Battle

By the beginning of World War II, the centerpiece in French operational thinking was what they called the *bataille conduite*, or methodical battle,[87] which bore a strong resemblance to Pétain's battle at La Malmaison and Debeney's at Montdidier. By this term the French meant a rigidly controlled operation in which units and weapons were carefully marshaled and then employed in combat. Such a battle was conducted deliberately and step-by-step, with units obediently moving between phase lines and adhering to strictly scheduled timetables as they moved toward relatively shallow objectives. With few radios available, these control measures facilitated the employment of massive amounts of artillery in support of the infantry. Such methods, the French believed, were essential for the coherent employment of the enormous amounts of men and materiel demanded by modern combat. They also kept the locus of decision making at higher command levels and provided for strongly centralized control to coordinate the actions of numerous subordinates. No audacious ideas such as those propounded by Nivelle or Joffre could ever thrive in headquarters manned by officers intensely schooled in such rigid methods.

Through the interwar period, French officers focused primarily on the methodical battle. In September 1938 a lecturer at the Center of Higher Military Studies described an operation of a field army consisting of five corps with fifteen divisions along a front of sixty kilometers. His description included a step-by-step approach to organizing the forces and synchronizing their actions in battle. His solution for how the forces should be employed included having the main attack launched by six divisions, each of which had a front of about twenty-two kilometers. The lecturer also suggested concentrating artillery assets, enabling the attacking force to have a high density of artillery tubes along each kilometer of attack frontage. As for the depth of the objective, the lecturer explained that it should not be deeper than one-half the length of the attack frontage—about seventy-two kilometers.[88]

Unfortunately for France, this attack more closely resembled the battles of 1918 than those of May–June 1940. Though French doctrine placed some value on mobility, the methodical battle represented only a slight improvement over the static method employed before 1918 and signaled a decline in the French sense of maneuver. Simultaneous or successive attacks such as those at Montdidier could be used, but no dramatic improvements in tactical or operational mobility were envisaged.

French concepts for the methodical battle had a profound effect on their views about the depth of the battlefield. Napoleonic ideas about actions throughout the depth of an enemy position disappeared from the minds of officers who focused on attacks of only seventy-two kilometers by an army of fifteen divisions. Though the French planned the employment of air attacks throughout the enemy's position, notions of linking air attacks with deep land attacks appealed to few officers. In February 1939 the French published a manual on *The Provisional Use of Armored Divisions*.[89] Despite the increased power of large tank units, the manual included the concept for successive objectives and movement by bounds and anticipated the distance between the bounds to be only three or four kilometers. These shallow depths bore little or no resemblance to the depth achieved by the Germans in May 1940.

Emphasis on the methodical battle also affected French doctrine for the defense. The essence of their doctrine was the preparation and occupation of a position in depth, but the depth of their positions was far more shallow than what was required in modern warfare. When a French unit (from battalion to corps size) occupied a defensive sector, it organized its forces into three parts: an advance post line, a principal position of resistance, and a stopping line. The principal position of resistance was the most important and heavily defended portion of the French defenses. Theoretically, it could be located along an easily protected front, preferably in an area where the enemy could be channeled into carefully selected zones or fields of fire between natural and man-made obstacles. Because of the requirement for depth, the principal position of resistance rarely resembled a line. To its rear was the stopping line, along which an attacking enemy force was supposed to be halted after it had been weakened by forward defenders.[90]

If an enemy managed to penetrate a stopping line, French doctrine called for a process known as *colmater*, or filling. A commander expected to meet a penetration by having his reserves, as well as the reserves of larger units, move in front of attacking enemy troops and gradually slow them down until they were halted. By shifting additional infantry, armor, and artillery units laterally into a threatened sector or forward from reserves in the rear, an attacker could be slowed and eventually stopped. After sealing off the enemy penetration, a counterattack would follow, but this counterattack would usually rely on the use of artillery and infantry fires rather than the charges of infantry and tanks.

Doctrine for the defense thus rested upon the belief that a defender could reinforce a threatened sector more quickly than an attacker could fight through the defenses to his front. For a variety of complex reasons, the French assumed that the rate of advance and depth of attack by an army on the offensive would not be dramatically different from that during the Great War. Subsequent events at Sedan in May 1940 soon demonstrated the fallacy of this assumption.

The Battle of Sedan

With the opening of World War II, French military leaders prepared to fight a series of methodical battles as part of their defensive strategy. While holding along the fortifications of the Maginot Line on the northeastern frontier, and while placing a minimum number of forces along the Ardennes, General Gamelin planned for French forces to rush north into central and western Belgium. The French believed the German main attack would come à la Schlieffen through the broad avenue of approach known as the Gembloux Gap that extended through central Belgium from Liège to Gembloux to Mons. To meet the anticipated German attack, Gamelin concentrated his most mobile forces along the border of central and western Belgium and prepared them to move forward rapidly.[91] After these forces entered Belgium, he wanted them to avoid an encounter battle. That is, he wanted French forces to move forward and establish a strong defensive position before the Germans arrived. After weakening the enemy and building up French and Allied forces, he intended to resume the offensive and achieve victory.

As for how far forward French forces would move into Belgium, Gamelin had several alternatives, but by May 1940 he had settled on moving them to a line that ran along the Meuse River from Sedan to Namur, across to Wavre, along the Dyle River, to Antwerp. Of the alternatives available, a defense along the Namur–Dyle River–Antwerp line would be about seventy or eighty kilometers shorter.[92] By May 1940 the French and British were poised to carry out the Allied operational concept and move forward to the Dyle line. Army Group 1 had responsibility for the area between the English Channel and the western edge of the Maginot Line. From left to right in Army Group 1, Seventh Army, British Expeditionary Forces, First Army, and Ninth Army prepared to move forward and occupy the Dyle line, while Second Army (on the right of Ninth Army) remained in position in the Sedan sector.

Second Army was the easternmost field army in Army Group 1 and had responsibility for a front that extended from west of Sedan to Longuyon, a straight-line distance of about sixty-five kilometers but actually about seventy-five kilometers because of the tying of the defense to favorable terrain. Its defensive sector included portions of the Maginot Line and the area to its left, which had relatively few fortifications. Unlike the other field armies in the west, which planned on moving into Belgium when the Germans attacked, Second Army did not have to move forward and occupy new positions. While it remained in place, its western boundary served as the "hinge" for Ninth Army on its left and the other field armies that prepared to rush forward.[93]

In May 1940 General Charles Huntziger, who commanded Second Army, had two corps headquarters and five infantry divisions under his command. To defend his sector, he identified a main position of resistance, which was south of the Meuse River in the area of Sedan, and a stopping line, which ran along the high ground of La Cassine–Mont Dieu–Stonne, sixteen kilometers south of Sedan. Second Army concentrated most of its defensive preparations along the forward edge of the main position of resistance. Huntziger placed the 41st Infantry and 3d Colonial Infantry Divisions under XVIII Corps on Second Army's right and the 3d North African and 55th Infantry Divisions under X Corps on the left. For a reserve, he initially maintained control over the 71st Infantry Division. In coordination with the field armies on his right and left, he placed a security force forward of his main position of resistance and manned it with a cavalry brigade and two light cavalry divisions. He reinforced these cavalry units with the reconnaissance squadrons from the divisions in Second Army.[94]

In his decision about the placement of his divisions, General Huntziger was primarily concerned with the possibility of a German attack pushing through his right flank and then turning southeast behind the Maginot Line. Consequently, he placed his strongest divisions on the right and his weakest on the left.[95] The 55th Division, which was a Series B division and thus manned by fewer active-duty officers and soldiers than Series A or active divisions, had the dubious distinction of being the farthest left division in Second Army. It was charged with the defense of Sedan, the sector where the three divisions from the German XIX Panzer Corps crossed on the afternoon of 13 May.

When the Germans attacked at 1500 on 13 May, the 55th Division defended the Sedan sector with two regiments on line in defensive positions along the Meuse River.[96] The 2d Panzer Division crossed at Donchery (three kilometers west of Sedan), the 1st Panzer Division crossed just west of Sedan, and the 10th Panzer Division crossed just east of Sedan at Wadelincourt. The 1st and 10th Panzer Divisions attacked directly into the 147th Regiment's sector, while the 2d Panzer Division crossed just to its west in the 331st Regiment's sector. Of the seven crossings made in the Sedan sector, only those made by the 1st Panzer Division west of Sedan managed to move quickly through the French defenders. In particular, the 1st Infantry Regiment from the 1st Division crossed west of Sedan and managed to reach Cheveuges by 2200 on the thirteenth, an advance of about six kilometers. In contrast to the success of the 1st Division, the 2d Division did not cross successfully until elements of the 1st Infantry Regiment cleared out the French defenders to its front. Similarly, the 10th Division initially managed only to get two squad-size elements across the river and advanced extremely slowly against strong opposition. Because of the difficulties encountered by the 2d and 10th Panzer Divisions, the penetration was extremely narrow and very vulnerable. That night German engineers worked feverishly to build bridges across the Meuse so additional forces could be rushed across and the bridgehead expanded.

Reinforcing the Sedan Sector

Before the Germans reached the Meuse, the French High Command took significant steps to strengthen the Sedan sector. Neither General Alphonse Georges (who commanded the French forces along the northern and northeastern frontiers) nor General Gaston Billotte (who commanded Army Group 1, which included Second Army plus other field armies west to the English Channel) believed the Germans would make their main attack through the area of Sedan. Both apparently considered the German forces in the Ardennes part of a secondary effort aiming farther north and contributing to the main German effort through the Gembloux Gap. Nevertheless, the possibility existed of a German thrust moving around the left wing of the Maginot Line and then circling behind the important fortification through the Stenay Gap. Consequently, in a classic *colmater* operation, the high-level commanders began moving units toward Sedan to reinforce the sector west of the Maginot Line not long after the Germans entered Belgium.

General Huntziger, who commanded Second Army, notified X Corps on the night of 11 May that the 71st Division would be placed at its disposition and should enter the front line. The X Corps ordered the 71st Division to move forward into the main position of resistance to the right of the 55th Division.[97] Most of the units of the 71st moved into position on the night of 12–13 May and were still settling into position on the thirteenth when the Germans crossed the Meuse. On the morning of 12 May, Second Army placed two artillery regiments, which were already in the vicinity of Sedan, under the control of X Corps.[98] Increasing the artillery support for a threatened sector accorded completely with French doctrine, for such an action added to the defensive capability of the sector while placing sufficient forces on hand to conduct a counterattack with artillery fires. Moving the 71st Division and the two artillery regiments forward, however, left Second Army with extremely weak reserves.

Second Army also began moving additional infantry and tank forces into the sector and preparing for a counterattack by these forces against a possible German penetration. On 12 May at 1105 it sent out a warning order about the 4th and 7th Tank Battalions' coming under the control of X Corps. The two tank battalions came under X Corps' control at 0030 on 13 May, about half an hour before the Germans attacked across the Meuse.[99] The X Corps also sent infantry forward. On the night of 10–11

May X Corps ordered the 213th Infantry Regiment to move forward, and late on the eleventh it ordered the 205th Regiment to move forward. By the morning of 13 May both regiments occupied positions south of Sedan near high ground between Mont Dieu and Stonne. They were in excellent positions for use against the subsequent German penetration.

The French High Command took other steps to reinforce the Sedan sector. XXI Corps, under the command of General J. A. L. R. Flavigny and was part of the General Reserve, received a warning order on the evening of 11 May that it would "probably" be committed in Second Army's sector.[100] Since XXI Corps had no combat divisions and consisted only of a corps headquarters and organic support units, Flavigny expected to assume control of two to three divisions after being committed.

At 0815 on 12 May General Georges, commander of northern group of forces, met with key members of his staff and decided to retain control over XXI Corps. Though he decided in this meeting to give one infantry division to Ninth Army and another to Second Army and to move a third division to the vicinity of the hinge between the two field armies, he was not yet willing to relinquish control of Flavigny's corps headquarters.[101] On 13 May at 1330 Second Army distributed a contingency plan for the use of XXI Corps when it came under Huntziger's control.[102] This plan mentioned the commitment of the 3d Motorized Infantry Division and "eventually" the 3d Armored Division. While serving as part of the General Reserve, the 3d Motorized Division received orders at 2000 on the twelfth to move toward Stonne. With the first group departing at midnight, the bulk of the division moved on the thirteenth and the final group closed in on the morning of the fourteenth.[103] At midnight on 12–13 May Second Army told X Corps to select the exact position of the motorized division but restricted X Corps' options by saying the motorized division had to be employed in the vicinity of Stonne and the woods to its east. This restriction reflected Second Army's concern about the Germans' turning east behind the Maginot Line.

The 3d Armored Division also began moving toward Second Army's sector. After receiving a warning order issued early in the afternoon of 12 May, the newly formed division received an order around 1500 to move northeast as quickly as possible. Although the division initially expected to move only one demibrigade, the division commander soon received orders to move his entire division. He did not learn the division's final destination until 1700, but he began moving most of his combat elements forward on the night of 12–13 May and the remaining elements on the following night.[104] Both the 3d Armored and 3d Motorized Divisions soon came under the control of General Flavigny's XXI Corps.

Thus, before the Germans crossed the Meuse, significant preparations had occurred for strengthening the Sedan sector. With two infantry regiments and two tank battalions reinforcing the 55th Division, with plans being completed for the employment of six additional divisions (including the 71st), plus two regiments of artillery and a corps headquarters, and with all units already moving and soon to be in place, the French seemed well prepared for an enemy thrust against Sedan. Significantly, however, the major focus of the preparation—except for the ill-fated counterattacks by the 55th Division—had been to prevent a counterclockwise encirclement coming from east of Sedan toward the southeast. From Huntziger's perspective, the threat seemed to be a push through Second Army and then a push or turn southeast toward the rear of the Maginot Line. He did not anticipate the Germans' pivoting west, racing to the English Channel, and severing Army Group 1 from the remaining French forces.[105]

Failing to Seal the Breach

During the night of 13–14 May, the penetration by the German 1st Infantry Regiment remained narrow and small, but General Heinz Guderian, commander of XIX Panzer Corps, rushed additional troops across the Meuse and began expanding the vulnerable bridgehead. During the same night the French took action to halt the German forces. Four hours after the Germans began crossing the Meuse, the X Corps commander, General Grandsard, called the 55th Division commander, General Lafontaine, and told him that the two infantry regiments and two tank battalions were placed under his command and were to be used to establish a defensive line between Chehéry, Bulson, and Haraucourt. Half an hour later, a messenger from X Corps delivered a message to General Lafontaine to conduct a counterattack with these units.[106]

Despite the vulnerability of the German penetration, the commander of the 55th Division, General Lafontaine, delayed launching a counterattack. Though additional forces from the reserves of Second Army had been made available to him, he preferred to have his infantry occupy defensive positions and to launch a counterattack with artillery fire. Having been schooled for years in the procedures of *colmater* for halting an enemy penetration, he had no desire to hurl his infantry forward. Because of his hesitation and his preference for a counterattack by artillery, Lafontaine did not issue an order for counterattack with infantry and tanks until about nine hours after his corps commander had instructed him to counterattack.[107]

Around 0630 on the fourteenth the 55th Division's counterattack from Chémery toward Chehéry and from Maisoncelle toward Bulson by the 213th Infantry Regiment and the 7th Tank Battalion began moving forward slowly, but the Germans soon pushed the French forces back. A short while later, the 55th Division launched another counterattack farther east with the 205th Regiment and 4th Tank Battalion, but it fared even worse than the one by the 213th Regiment.[108] General Lafontaine's unwillingness to act immediately and decisively had allowed an opportunity to slip away.

During the night of 13–14 May, General Georges ordered a massive aerial attack against the German bridges over the Meuse River at Sedan. On the morning of the fourteenth, shortly after the failure of the 55th Division's counterattacks, the Allies launched their desperate aerial attack. Though the delivery means differed, the huge concentration of air power had all the trappings of a massive artillery barrage.

The attack began with ten British bombers attempting, but failing, to destroy the German bridges near Sedan. About 0900 the French launched their first attack against the concentrated enemy forces. Around noon, the few remaining French bombers (only 13) attacked the same area, but they suffered such severe losses from ground air defense fires and German fighters that they cancelled operations for the remainder of the day. Between 1500 and 1600 the entire force of British bombers in France, supported by 27 French fighters, struck at Sedan, but of the 72 bombers participating only 40 returned. The official British history notes, "No higher rate of loss in an operation of comparable size has ever been experienced by the Royal Air Force."[109] That evening, long-range bombers from the British Bomber Command made another strike. Though they encountered fewer enemy fighters than the earlier strike, they suffered 25 percent losses. According to a high-ranking French air force officer, more than 152 bombers and 250 fighters concentrated over Sedan and completed more than 550 flying hours. To oppose them, the Germans flew more than 800 sorties.[110] Despite the number of sorties and the relatively small size of the bridgehead, the attempt to halt the German advance with air power failed.

As the three Panzer divisions continued expanding the bridgehead around Sedan, the French expected the units rushed to Sedan to halt the German advance. Instead of the entire Panzer corps continuing south or turning southeast behind the Maginot Line, however, the 1st Panzer and 2d Panzer Divisions unexpectedly turned west and crossed the Bar River and the Ardennes Canal. At the same time, the 10th Panzer Division and Gross Deutschland Infantry Regiment began pushing toward the south to protect the flank of the corps as it pivoted toward the west.

Despite the awkward position of the XIX Panzer Corps, the French XXI Corps with the 3d Armored and 3d Motorized Divisions failed to launch a strong attack into the most vulnerable point of the expanding German penetration. Most of the 3d Armored Division was in place on the morning of the fourteenth, and even though General Flavigny attempted to push it forward, the newly formed division lacked confidence, communication equipment, and logistical support and responded more slowly and tentatively than did the 3d Motorized Infantry Division. Instead of boldly charging ahead, the two divisions became involved in bitter and costly fighting in the heights of Mont Dieu. By the evening of the fifteenth, after substantial reinforcements by the Germans, it was clear that another opportunity had been lost.[111]

Though General Georges did not yet know the results of the anticipated counterattacks on the fourteenth by X Corps (with two infantry regiments and two tank battalions) and on the fifteenth by XXI Corps (with the 3d Motorized and 3d Armored Divisions), he began planning on the night of 13–14 May for the possibility of a German penetration between Second and Ninth Armies. With the right of Ninth Army touching Dom-le-Mesnil along the Meuse (nine kilometers west of Sedan) and the left of Second Army touching Omont (ten kilometers west of Chémery), an opening of about twelve kilometers soon existed between the two armies. After the collapse of the 55th Division and the insertion of the 3d Motorized Infantry and the 3d Armored Divisions by Second Army into positions along the Mont Dieu, elements of the hard-pressed and tired 5th Light Cavalry Division and 3d Brigade of *Spahis* attempted to fill the gap between the 3d Motorized Division and the 53d Infantry Division, which was on the extreme right of Ninth Army. Yet, even before General Guderian's XIX Panzer Corps pivoted west it was clear that additional forces had to be moved forward to strengthen the two sorely pressed cavalry units.

In the middle of the night, General Robert Touchon received a telephone call ordering him to report to Georges' office the following morning. During two meetings on the fourteenth, Georges informed him of his intention to place Touchon in charge of a provisional field army that would "colmater the breach [in the] vicinity of Sedan." Revealing a late-blooming concern with the possibility of the Germans' heading west, Georges wanted Touchon's forces to be employed so that the avenue of advance between Sedan and Laon could be "interdicted."[112] This discussion is the first indication of a high-level French concern with a German move or pivot to the west. It may have come from the recognition that the Germans crossing the Meuse near Dinant, Monthermé, and Sedan could combine their forces and pose a serious threat to the French center. Georges also explained that the German "pocket" had become much larger and was continuing to expand at an alarming rate. Touchon was told that he must act quickly and "assist General Huntziger in sealing the breach."[113]

At 1500 on the fourteenth, Touchon left for Senuc, where he met with Huntziger. Despite the German gains, the situation probably did not appear impossible to Touchon, for by midnight he had two corps—consisting of two corps headquarters (XXIII and XLI), four divisions (including the 2d Armored), and additional units—under his control.[114] Though the Germans had penetrated French defenses and had advanced much more rapidly than expected, the experience of World War I suggested that their rapid advance soon had to halt. Major advances in that war had rarely lasted longer than a week before physical exhaustion, dwindling supplies, and heavy logistical tails usually forced the attacker to halt. Since the German attack was already in its fifth day, Touchon expected it to stall and worked to assemble his forces and reestablish another line of defenses.

As XIX Panzer Corps turned west, the 2d Panzer Division initially moved west parallel to the Meuse River, while the 1st Panzer Division (about ten kilometers to the south) advanced to the west. The 1st Panzer Division fought against the 5th Light Cavalry Division and the 1st Cavalry Brigade. After pushing these units back, it next encountered elements of the 14th Infantry and 53d Infantry Divisions. Though the 14th Infantry Division had some success, neither the 53d Infantry Division nor the 2d Armored Division to its rear managed to delay the Germans, even though they were directly in their attack zone.[115] Farther north, the 2d Panzer Division skillfully fought through French units to its front.

When General Touchon learned of the rapid advance of the German Panzer divisions, he concluded he could not halt the enemy breakthrough. During the night of 15–16 May and the morning of the sixteenth, he pulled the scattered remnants of his army back from in front of the advancing German columns and established a new defensive line running east-west along the Aisne River. As he pulled his units back, he opened the way in front of the Germans; little or nothing stood in front of them as they began their race west toward the English Channel and into the rear of most of Army Group 1. Attempts by X Corps with its two infantry regiments and two tank battalions, by XXI Corps with an armored and a motorized division, and by Touchon's provisional army had failed to plug the hole in French defensive lines. And the concept of *colmater* proved completely inadequate.

Conclusion

Throughout the late nineteenth and early twentieth centuries, the French concentrated on the practical, rather than theoretical aspects of the operational level of warfare. Though they considered the operational level to be more a transition between strategy and tactics than something fundamentally different, they expended considerable effort in analyzing and studying the employment of corps, field armies, and army groups. They believed the employment of these larger units in operations or campaigns was the essence of operational art. For a variety of reasons, however, the French neglected to specify a function for the operational level and failed to distinguish clearly between operations and tactics. Before World War I, concepts of fighting at the operational level dominated tactical thinking, and before World War II, tactical concerns dominated operational thinking. The failure to separate operational and tactical concepts distorted the French view of the operational level of warfare and profoundly affected the performance of the army in the two world wars. In sum, the French approach to the operational level of warfare never approached the sophistication of operational art.

After the Franco-Prussian War, the French implemented important institutional changes that facilitated their adherence to an operational doctrine strongly focused on the offensive. By 1914 Joffre and other military leaders expected the battlefield to be more lethal than that of the past, but they prepared field armies to maneuver in a manner reminiscent of Napoleon's employment of corps. Despite heavy losses inflicted by the Germans, the ability of the French units to maneuver contributed to Joffre's success in the "miracle of the Marne." The establishment of a continuous line of strong and extensive defenses on the western front after September 1914 reduced the possibility of maneuver. Nevertheless, the French did not abandon their hopes of achieving a penetration and continued using huge numbers of men and materiel in vain attempts to force their way through the German defenses. After the collapse of Nivelle's offensive in April 1917, Pétain began launching limited offensives and demonstrated at La Malmaison in October 1917 how significant gains could be made with such offensives. In August 1918, Debeney launched his carefully sequenced attacks at Montdidier and drove the Germans back.

Debeney's operational methods, which relied on tightly controlled and successive attacks along a broad front, differed dramatically from those with which the French had begun the war, but they became the model for the conduct of operations in the interwar period. Although the French devoted considerable time and effort to improving their operational doctrine from 1919 to 1939, they did not develop fundamentally new methods. When the Germans attacked in May 1940, they expected to fight a series of methodical battles — reminiscent of Debeney's methods at Montdidier — in which huge masses of artillery would provide them an important advantage. They also expected the battlefield to be relatively shallow and anticipated moving reserves and placing them in front of attacking enemy units to seal penetrations. While such methods may have worked against an enemy using methodical techniques, they had little chance of success against a highly mobile enemy attacking deep into a defensive position and using supporting fires throughout the depth of that position.

As the French developed their ability from 1888 to 1940 to perform at the operational level, they moved from one extreme to another. In the opening battles of World War I, they emphasized maneuver and minimized the importance of firepower. Though some ill-conceived and poorly coordinated operations cost thousands of casualties, the ability of the French units to maneuver enabled Joffre to respond successfully to the unexpected German advance toward Paris. By May 1940, however, the French had moved to the other extreme. They displayed little concern for maneuver at the operational level, particularly in launching counterattacks, and placed much greater emphasis on firepower. Though significant French forces managed to move to the vicinity of the penetration of Sedan and attempted to halt the Germans, they could not prevent a breakthrough. The Germans could maneuver far more rapidly and effectively than the French, whose sense of maneuver had been eclipsed by too strong an emphasis on firepower.

Although French military leaders studied the operational level of warfare from 1888 to 1940, they devised doctrinal formulas that reflected an unwillingness to accept the possibility of the Germans doing something unexpected or of their encountering something dramatically different from their own methods. Their doctrine may have been perfect for the classroom, but terrible inadequacies in that doctrine became immediately apparent when it was exposed to the realities of combat and to the fog and friction that invariably appear in battle. In the final analysis, the French experience demonstrates why military professionals become students of the operational art, rather than students of the operational science.

Notes

1. Robert S. Quimby, *The Background of Napoleonic Warfare* (New York: Columbia University Press, 1957), pp. 94–97. The forerunner of the division was Marshal Maurice de Saxe's "legion," which was supported with artillery and could function separately or as part of an army.
2. Pierre de Bourcet, *Principes de la guerre de montagnes* (Paris, 1888), passim; Quimby, Napoleonic Warfare, pp. 175–84; Steven T. Ross, "The Development of the Combat Division in Eighteenth-Century French Armies," French Historical Studies 4 (1965): 84–94.
3. Francois-Apolline de Guibert, *Écrits militaires, 1772–1790* (Paris: Copernic, 1977), p. 167.
4. Gunther E. Rothenberg, *The Art of Warfare in the Age of Napoleon* (Bloomington: Indiana University Press, 1978), pp. 109, 128.
5. Ltrs to Général Berthier, 25 Jan 1800, no. 4552, pp. 136–38, and 1 Mar 1800, no. 4626, pp. 196–98, both in *Correspondence de Napoléon Ier*, vol. 6 (Paris, 1860) (hereafter cited as *Correspondence*); John R. Elting, *Swords Around the Throne: Napoleon's Grande Armée* (New York, 1988), pp. 49, 58–59.
6. David G. Chandler, *The Campaigns of Napoleon* (New York: Macmillan, 1966), pp. 184–91, 332–33. Napoleon divided his *Grande Armée* into armies, usually consisting of about three mixed corps, plus one or two cavalry corps.
7. Quoted in Chandler, *Campaigns of Napoleon*, p. 184. See also "Napoleon, Operational Art and the Jena Campaign," by David Chandler, in this volume.
8. *Correspondence*, vol. 3, no. 1976 (1859), p. 216.
9. Douglas Porch, *Army and Revolution: France 1815–1848* (London, 1974), p. 29; Michael E. Howard, *The Franco-Prussian War: The German Invasion of France, 1870–1871* (New York: Macmillan, 1962), pp. 15–17.
10. *Journal Officiel de la République Française* (1873), p. 5281; Général du Barail, *Mes souvenirs*, vol. 3 (Paris, 1896), p. 459.
11. *Journal Officiel de la République Française: Chambre Débats* (1888), pp. 791, 817.
12. Ibid., pp. 2177–78; Charles de Freycinet, *Souvenirs*, vol. 2 (Paris, 1914), p. 405.
13. *Journal Officiel* (1890), pp. 1869–70.
14. Charles W. Dilke, "The French Armies," *The Fortnightly Review* 56, no. 299 (1 November 1891): 610.
15. *Journal Officiel* (1899), p. 1487.
16. Freycinet, *Souvenirs*, 2: 445.
17. Dilke, "French Armies," pp. 597, 620.
18. Freycinet, *Souvenirs*, 2: 470.
19. France, *Ministère de la Guerre (MG), Décret du 28 mai 1895 portant règlement sur le service des armées en campagne* (Paris: Berger-Levrault, 1895), p. 30.
20. France, MG, *Décret du 28 octobre 1913 portant règlement sur la conduite des grandes unités* (Paris: Berger-Levrault, 1913), p. 47.
21. Ibid., p. 18.

22. Jay Luvaas, *The Military Legacy of the Civil War* (Chicago: University of Chicago Press, 1959), pp. 151–52.
23. Dallas D. Irvine, "The French Discovery of Clausewitz and Napoleon," *Journal of the American Military Institute* 4 (Summer 1940): 143–61.
24. Henri Bonnal, *Sadowa: Étude de stratégie et de tactique générale* (Paris: Chapelot et ce, 1901), pp. 2–3.
25. Louis de Grandmaison, *Deux conférences faites aux officiers de l'État–Major de l'Armée* (Paris, 1911), passim; Joel A. Setzen, "The Doctrine of the Offensive in the French Army on the Eve of World War I," Ph.D. Dissertation, University of Chicago, 1972, p. 99.
26. Louis de Grandmaison, *Dressage de l'infanterie en vue du combat offensif* (Paris, 1910), p. 89.
27. Ibid., p. 24.
28. Le lieutenant-colonel Pellé, Attaché militaire de France à Berlin, au général Brun, *Ministre de la Guerre*, 24 mars 1910, *D.D.F.*, 2e série, vol. XII, an. no. 467, p. 717.
29. *MG*, Modifications à apporter au plan XVI, 6 sep 1911, in France, *MG, État-Major de l'Armée (ÉMA), Les armées françaises dans la Grande Guerre* (Paris, 1935) tome 1, vol. 1, Annexes, an. no. 5, pp. 17–18.
30. France, Chambre des Députés, Procès-verbaux de la commission d'enquête sur la rôle et la situation de la métallurgie en France (Défense du Bassin du Briey, 1 re Partie), Onzième Legislature, Session de 1919, No. 6026 (Paris, 1919), Déposition de M. le Maréchal Joffre, 4 juillet 1919, pp. 142, 163.
31. ÉMA, Plan XVII, Directives pour la concentration, 7 février 1914, *Les armées françaises*, tome 1, vol. 1, Annexes, an. no. 8, pp. 21–22; Joseph Joffre, *Mémoires du Maréchal Joffre*, vol. 1 (Paris, 1932), pp. 188–89.
32. For a recent assessment of the Schlieffen Plan and Moltke's modifications, see Terence Zuber, "The Schlieffen Plan Reconsidered," *War in History* 6, no. 3 (1999): 262–305.
33. *Grand Quartier General (GQG)*, Commandant en chef à commandant armée Épinal, 6 août 1914, *Les armées françaises*, tome 1, vol. 1, Annexes, an. no. 73, p. 98.
34. *GQG*, Instruction générale N 1, 8 août 1914, *Les armées françaises*, tome 1, vol. 1, Annexes, an. no. 103, pp. 124–26; GQG, Ordre particulier pour le 4e groupe de divisions de reserve, 8 août 1914, *Les armées françaises*, tome 1, vol. 1, Annexes, an. no. 105, p. 127.
35. Basil H. Liddell Hart, *Strategy* (New York: Meridian, 1967), p. 168.
36. Ronald H. Cole, "Forward with the Bayonet!: The French Army Prepares for Offensive Warfare, 1911–1914," Ph.D. diss., University of Maryland, 1975, pp. 391–93.
37. Joffre, *Mémoires*, 1: 285.
38. Ferdinand Foch, *The Memoirs of Marshal Foch*, trans. T. Bentley Mott (New York: Doubleday, Doran and Co., 1931), pp. 23–34.
39. *GQG*, Ordre au commandant de la IVe armée, 20 août 1914, *Les armées françaises*, tome 1, vol. 1, Annexes, an. no. 593, p. 532; GQG, Le commandant en chef au commandant de la IIIe armée, 20 août 1914, *Les armées françaises*, tome 1, vol. 1, Annexes, an. no. 592, p. 531.
40. Joffre, *Mémoires*, 1: 275–76, 278, 283.
41. *GQG*, Le commandant en chef au commandant de l'armée de Stenay, 21 août 1914, *Les armées françaises*, tome 1, vol. 1, Annexes, an. no. 696, p. 599.
42. Alphonse Grasset, *Surprise d'une division: Rossignol-Saint Vincent* (Paris, 1932), passim; Alphonse Grasset, *Un combat de rencontre: Neufchâteau (22 Août 1914)* (Paris, 1924), passim.

43. Hermann J. von Kuhl, *The Marne Campaign, 1914* (Fort Leavenworth, Kans.: Command and General Staff College Press, 1936), p. 31.
44. Joffre, *Mémoires*, 1: 320, 324, 336–37; Foch, *Memoirs*, pp. 34–35, 41–58.
45. GQG, Note pour toutes les armées, 24 août 1914, *Les armées françaises*, tome 1, vol. 2, Annexes, vol. 1, an. no. 158, pp. 128–29.
46. For an analysis of the division commanders relieved, see Commandement des division du 1er août 1914 au 1er novembre 1916, 25 novembre 1919, passim, Section historique du armee de terre (SHAT) 5N269.
47. Joffre, *Mémoires*, 1: 301–02, 350.
48. Kuhl, *Marne Campaign*, p. 142.
49. Ve Armée, Propositions pour l'offensive, 4 sep 14, *Les armées françaises*, tome 1, vol. 2, Annexes, vol. 2, an. no. 2398, pp. 704–05; Ve Armée, Commandant Ve armée à grand Q.G., 4 sep 14, *Les armées françaises*, tome 1, vol. 2, Annexes, vol. 2, an. no. 2401, p. 706.
50. Joffre, *Mémoires*, 1: 379–91; Pierre Lyet, *Joffre et Gallieni a la Marne* (Paris, 1938), pp. 40–54.
51. Kuhl, *Marne Campaign*, pp. 150–51.
52. James E. Edmonds, *History of the Great War: Military Operations, France and Belgium, 1914*, vol. 1 (London: Macmillan and Co., 1933), pp. 299–300, 310, 319, 322–24, 332–334, 338–39.
53. See Grand Quartier Général des Armées de l'Est, É.-M., 3ème Bureau, Notes pour les Armées, 2 janvier 1915, pp. 3–4, SHAT 16N1676.
54. James K. Hogue, "Puissance de Feu: The Struggle for a New Artillery Doctrine in the French Army, 1914–1916," Master's Thesis, Ohio State University, 1988, pp. 51–52.
55. Ve Armée, *Les armées françaises*, vol. 4, pt. 3, p. 382.
56. Jean de Pierrefeu, *L'Offensive du 16 avril* (Paris, 1919), p. 17; IIe Armée, IIe armée à GQG, GAC, 2 nov 16, *Les armées françaises*, tome 4, vol. 3, Annexes, vol. 2, an. no. 1449, p. 545; Ve Armée, *Les armées françaises*, tome 4, vol. 3, p. 404.
57. Stephen F. Yunker, "'I Have the Formula': The Evolution of the Tactical Doctrine of General Robert Nivelle," *Military Review* 54, no. 6 (June 1974): 17.
58. IIe Armée, Note pour les groupements, 9 juin 1916, *Les armées françaises*, tome 4, vol. 2, Annexes, vol. 1, an. no. 1077, pp. 1423–25.
59. Rapport de la Commission d'Enquête instituée par lettre Ministérielle No. 18,194, du 14 juillet 1917, Le général de division Brugère, Chargé de missions spéciales, à Monsieur le President du Conseil, Ministre de la Guerre, 4 octobre 1917, p. 7, SHAT 5N255.
60. Sir Edward L. Spears, *Prelude to Victory* (London: J. Cape, 1939), pp. 345–46.
61. Quoted in Pierrefeu, *L'Offensive*, p. 41.
62. Stephen Ryan, *Pétain the Soldier* (New York, 1969), pp. 111–13.
63. Marie L. V. H. Corda, *La Guerre Mondiale (1914–1918)* (Paris, 1922), p. 210.
64. Ibid., p. 211.
65. Général Blondet, "Rapport sur les opérations du 2ème Corps Colonial du 16 au 18 avril," in Pierrefeu, *L'Offensive*, pp. 83–84.
66. Ryan, *Pétain*, pp. 114–15; Guy Pedroncini, *Pétain: Général en Chef, 1917–1918* (Paris: Presses universitaires de France, 1974), pp. 19–21, 25–34.
67. Grand quartier général des armées du nord et du nord-est, É.M., 3ème Bureau, Pour les commandants et groupes d'armées et armées seulement, Directive no. 1, no. 17356, 19 mai 1917, P.R.O. WO 158/48/9.
68. Pedroncini, *Pétain*, pp.100–08. The density of French artillery was about one gun for every 6.5 meters of front.

69. Maréchal Pétain, *La Crise morale et militaire de 1917* (Paris, 1966), p. 146.
70. Ryan, *Pétain*, p. 136.
71. Erich von Ludendorff, *Ludendorff's Own Story*, 2 vols. (New York: Books for Libraries Press, c. 1920), 1: 326.
72. Commandant Marius Daille, *The Battle of Montdidier*, trans. Walter R. Wheeler (typescript), pp. 49, 55. The British to the north had ten heavy and two light battalions of tanks.
73. General Debeney's letter explaining his concept, thought process, and actions are in Daille, *Battle of Montdidier*, pp. 22–28.
74. France, MG, ÉMA, *Instruction provisoire sur l'emploi tactique des grandes unites* (Paris, 1921).
75. See A Graduate (anonymous), "The École Supérieure de Guerre," *Infantry Journal* 21 (October 1922): 402.
76. Daille, *Battle of Montdidier*, p. 58.
77. Ibid., p. 38.
78. Ibid., pp. 39–44.
79. Robert A. Doughty, *Seeds of Disaster: The Development of French Army Doctrine, 1919–1939* (Hamden, Conn.: Archon Books, 1986), pp. 98–99.
80. Frédéric. G. Herr, *L'Artillerie: Ce qu'elle a ete; ce qu'elle est; ce qu'elle doit être* (Paris: Berger-Levrault, 1923), p. 225.
81. France, MG, ÉMA, *Règlement de manoeuvre de l'artillerie, Deuxième partie, L'Artillerie au combat* (Paris, 1926), p. 52.
82. *Procès-verbaux des reunions du conseil supérieur de la guerre* (hereafter *PV, CSG*), 4 Oct 22, carton 50.
83. ÉMA, *Règlement de manoeuvre*, p. 52.
84. *PV, CSG*, 28 Oct 26, carton 50 bis.
85. Maurice G. Gamelin, *Servir*, 3 vols., (Paris: Plon, 1946), 1: 181.
86. France, MG, ÉMA, *Instruction sur l'emploi tactique des grandes unites* (Paris, 1937).
87. Doughty, *Seeds of Disaster*, pp. 4, 89–90, 101–02.
88. France, Centre des hautes etudes militaries (CHÉM) et stage de technique d'armée, Général Audet, "La manoeuvre de l'armée" (September 1938) (n.p., n.d.), pp. 62–65.
89. France, Ministére de la defense nationale et la guerre (MDNG), Direction de l'infanterie (DI), *Notice provisoire à l'usage des unités de la division cuirassée* (n.p., n.d.).
90. Robert A. Doughty, "French Antitank Doctrine: The Antidote that Failed," *Military Review* 56, no. 5 (May 1976): 15–19.
91. Gamelin's precise motives for placing the highly mobile Seventh Army on his far left have never been clarified, but he may have planned on using them to attack into the rear of a German force advancing through the Gembloux Gap. This idea may have come from the "miracle of the Marne" or from the lectures of Général Lucien Loizeau on "maneuvers of the wing." See Lucien Loizeau, *La manoeuvre du corps d'armée* (Courbevoie, 1932), pp. 97–129; Lucien Loizeau, *Deux manoeuvres* (Paris: Berger-Levrault, 1933), pp. 3–70.
92. Gamelin, *Servir*, vol 1., pp. 84–88. For a fuller discussion of the plans, see Henry Dutailly, *Problèmes de l'armée de terre française, 1935–1939* (Paris: Imp. Nationale, 1980), pp. 91–114.
93. Robert A. Doughty, *The Breaking Point: Sedan and the Fall of France, 1940* (Hamden, Conn.: Archon Books, 1990), pp. 12–18.
94. Edmond Ruby, *Sedan: Terre d'épreuve* (Paris, 1948), pp. 11–16; Général C. Grandsard, *Le 10eme Corps d'Armée dans Bataille 1939–1940* (Paris: Flammarion, 1948), pp. 17–23, 35–43.

95. France, Assemblée Nationale, *Commission d'enquête sur les evenements survenus en France de 1933 a 1945*, Annexes, Témoignages et documents recueillis par la commission d'enquête parlementaire (hereafter Commission ... Témoignages), Testimony of General Lacaille, vol. 4 (Paris, 1952), p. 927.
96. Rapport du Général Lafontaine, 55eme D.I., 18 mai 1940, SHAT 32N251; Rapport du Lieutenant Colonel Pinaud, 147ème R.I.F., 24 mai 1940, SHAT 34N145.
97. Angora à 10ème C.A., 11 mai 1940, 22h.20, SHAT 29N49; IIème Armée, É.-M., 3ème Bureau, No. 4662/3–Op, 11 mai 1940, SHAT 29N49.
98. IIème Armée, 3éme Bureau, É.-M., No. 4665/3–Op, 12 mai 1940, 7h.30; IIème Armée, 3ème Bureau, É.-M., No. 4668/3–Op, 12 mai 19140, 9h.35; IIème Armée, 3ème Bureau, É.-M., No. 4674/3–Op, 12 mai 1940, 11h.20, all in SHAT 29N49.
99. IIème Armée, É.-M., 3ème Bureau, No. 4663/3–Op, 11 mai 1940, 23h., SHAT 29N49; IIème Armée, É.-M., 3ème Bureau, No. 4672/3–Op, 12 mai 1940, 11h.05, SHAT 29N85; IIème Armée, É.-M., 3ème Bureau, No. 4669/3–Op, 13 mai 1940, 14H.30, SHAT 29N85.
100. Journal des marches et opérations du 21ème C.A. par le Général Flavigny du 3 mai au 24 juin 1940 (hereafter Général Flavigny, 21ème C.A., J.M.O.), (n.d.), pp. 6–8, SHAT 30N225.
101. Journal du Cabinet du Général Georges, 12 mai 1940, p. 2, SHAT 27N148.
102. IIème Armée, É.-M., 3ème Bureau, No. 4697/3–Op, 13h.30, SHAT 29N49.
103. Chef de Bataillon Ragot, Compte-Rendu sur les opérations de la 3ème D.I.M., n.d., p. 8, SHAT 32N8.
104. *Commission ... Témoignages*, Testimony of General Devaux, vol. 5, p. 1334 (Devaux served as chief of staff of the 3d Armored Division); Journal du cabinet du Général Georges, 12 mai 1940, pp. 10–12.
105. IIème Armée, É.-M., 3ème Bureau, No. 4713/3–Op, 14 mai 1940, 13h., SHAT 29N49.
106. Général C. Grandsard, 10ème Corps d'armée, pp. 143–44; Ltr, Lieut. Col. Cachou, 4 mars 1942, p. 2, SHAT 30N82.
107. Général Lafontaine, Renseignements sur la 55ème Division, p. 2, SHAT 32N251.
108. Rapport du Lieut. Col. Labarthe, 213ème R.I., n.d., SHAT 34N165; Rapport du Chef de Bataillon Giordani, 7ème B.C., 23 juin 1941, SHAT 34N165; Rapport du Lieut. Col. Montvignier Monnet, 204ème R.I., 27 décembre 1940, SHAT 34N164; Rapport du Chef de Bataillon Auffret, 2/205ème R.I., 20 mai 1940, SHAT 34N164.
109. Denis Richards, *Royal Air Force*, 3 vols. (London: Her Majesty's Stationery Office, 1953), 1: 120.
110. Francois d'Astier de la Vigerie, *Le Ciel n'était pas vide* (Paris, 1952), pp. 107, 109; Jeffrey A. Gunsburg, *Divided and Conquered: The French High Command and the Defeat of the West, 1940* (Westport, Conn.: Greenwood Press, 1979), p. 201.
111. J. A. L. R. Flavigny, 21ème C.A., J.M.O., n.d., SHAT 30N225; Rapport du Général Brocard, 3ème D.C.R., n.d., SHAT 32N470.
112. Détachement d'Armée, *Journal des Marches et Opérations,* 14 mai 1940, SHAT 29N321.
113. Ibid.
114. C.C.F.N.E., É.-M., 3ème Bureau, No. 1495/3–Op, 15 mai 1940, 7h.15, SHAT 27N155.
115. Ltr, Général Etcheberrigaray, 27 juillet 1943, S.H.A.T. 32N248; 2ème Division Cuirassée, No. 45/5–CD, 5 juillet 1940, SHAT 32N461; Rapport d'opérations de la 2ème Division Cuirassée (13–21 mai 1940), 16 juin 1941, SHAT 32N462.

PART TWO: GERMANY

Introduction

The nineteenth century marked a revolution in warfare brought about by industrialization and changing technology. Until then, land warfare depended on the slow movement of soldiers by horse or foot. The development of steam power harnessed to rails—the railroads—gave strategic and operational mobility to larger forces that could cover more ground in shorter periods of time and be logistically sustained in large concentrations. Other technological developments brought about a tremendous change in the range and lethality of weapons. For hundreds of years the effective range for most muskets was less than one hundred meters; with the development of the conical bullet and rifling, range and accuracy increased tenfold. Breech-loaded artillery and firearms added to tactical flexibility and improved target acquisition and marksmanship. Smokeless powder, better ordnance, and recoil-absorbing cannon also increased artillery range, lethality, and accuracy. The battlefield that had once covered a few square miles in the early nineteenth century blanketed dozens of square miles before the century ended. Within fifty years and two world wars, battles were being fought along 200-mile fronts. Campaigns that once embraced small regional areas had by World War II swallowed entire nations. The telegraph connected faraway places—where horse-borne messengers took days and hours, the telegraph could issue news and orders almost instantly. Lastly, states could now arm themselves with mass-produced weapons, so that large forces now meant million-man armies.

The change brought about by rail, rifle, artillery, and the telegraph led to the recognition of different ways in which to conduct warfare. In this section, Michael D. Krause points to German Field Marshal Helmuth von Moltke's recognition of this changed dimension of warfare. Using railroads to deploy and concentrate his forces and the telegraph to direct their movement, Moltke developed the distinction between strategy and tactics. Moltke used the term operational conduct to describe his ability to oversee the campaign and synchronize the movement of forces to battle. Because of changes in range and lethality, tactical battle had changed the relative strength of defensive versus offensive power. Moltke argued that tactical defense was made stronger than offense. Only through operational conduct on the offensive could an opponent be outflanked. Moltke, in his writings on operational art, used modern terms and meanings that could be applied to students and practitioners today. He was arguably the first to connect tactics to strategy through the operational conduct of war.

Günter R. Roth carries Moltke's contribution through the German Chief of the General Staff, Alfred Graf von Schlieffen, one step farther into the twentieth century. Schlieffen studied and developed the means to move million-man armies in a synchronized, preplanned way to outflank an opponent. Unfortunately, he undermined Moltke's efforts to tie strategy, operational conduct, and tactics together by emphasizing that operations alone could solve strategic dilemmas. Roth traces Schlieffen's effect on German operational planning and execution. With the development of the tank, plane, and radio, *Blitzkrieg* was born. Field Marshal Erich von Manstein's employment of these means in a campaign illustrated his understanding of operational conduct and its direction.

Karl-Heinz Frieser traces Manstein's operational concept for the campaign against France in 1940. Frieser points out that the strategic aim—the defeat of Allied forces—was achieved by the operational method of making a breakthrough and deep penetration at Sedan. Frieser uses the revolving door analogy to explain the campaign, with French and British forces pushing into Belgium—precisely as the Germans wanted—and the German forces pushing this same door by cutting through the Ardennes toward the Channel. Manstein's operational concept—brilliantly focused and executed—demonstrated his understanding of operational art and its application.

Moltke and the Origins of the Operational Level of War[1]

Michael D. Krause

Is the operational level of war a discrete, integral dimension of military doctrine? Certainly Field Marshal Helmuth von Moltke, the famous Prussian officer who retired in 1888 after serving thirty years as chief of the general staff, considered it to be. Among the testimonials to his lifetime of dedicated service to his nation, many revere Moltke as the architect of German unification. He made possible the defeat of the Danes in 1864, the Austrians in 1866, and the French in 1870–1871, when Prussian-German armies achieved rapid and final victories over their enemies. Place names such as Königgrätz and Sedan have been immortalized as exemplars of set-piece battles, and German leaders of Moltke's day credited him with designing and executing the campaigns that won those battles.

To astute students of military history, Moltke's name signifies far more than a list of nineteenth-century battles. He recognized that in the years to come wars would be conducted differently from the way they were in his lifetime: as short, quick, and decisive conflicts. Instead, he predicted correctly that future wars would be lengthy and total. Still others have observed his contributions to the application of emerging technologies to the conduct of operations. He evaluated the increased lethality and range of rifle and artillery fires and realized the necessity of changing basic military doctrine accordingly. He perceived that offense would give way to the preponderance of defense on the tactical level; in his view enemy attacks of the future were destined to be shattered by a wall of German tactical firepower. Moltke also foresaw that mobility on the strategic level could be multiplied by employing railroads. He planned to utilize this mode of transport to speed German armies to the battlefield and thereby to concentrate overwhelming force at the right time and in the right place to ensure victory. Finally, by applying the telegraph to warfare, Moltke was able to direct large armies in the field from great distances, thereby enhancing strategic flexibility through what he would refer to as operational direction.

One hundred years ago, as today, there were controversies over the preponderance of attack versus defense or, in other words, over the emphasis on maneuver versus attrition. By contemporary standards Moltke was an avid supporter of maneuver, particularly as a means of unhinging one's adversaries, both psychologically and physically. At the same time he confronted the problem of defending a nation that was centrally located. Given its geo-strategic position on the European Continent, Germany could be attacked simultaneously from various approaches and by a combination of forces. Over Moltke's lifetime he evolved a series of offense-defense war plans that focused on the destruction of enemy forces. He also became a proponent of the doctrine of deterrence, maintaining the means and will to wage war as an effective way of persuading one's enemies not to attack. Like contemporary military planners, Moltke faced issues involving both the qualitative and quantitative aspects of technological change. Doctrine, in his view, had to provide the balance between the realities of the battlefield and the requirements for modernization; force structure was finite and dependent on human and materiel resources. Moreover, war—as well as campaign planning and execution—had to take into account political and economic factors. Theoretical differences over short war versus long war, defense versus offense, attrition versus maneuver, and attack versus defense were all debated in military circles in Moltke's day just as they are in our own. Most important, Moltke as a leader and a perennial student of military history reconciled these debates, an achievement that led to his success in war.

Traditionally, the Germans are credited with delineating three levels of warfare: the strategic and tactical levels (as represented by the conduct of war and battle, respectively) and the operational level that Moltke conceptualized and situated between the conduct of war and battle. One way of considering the operational level and analyzing how it came into being is to seek answers to the following series of questions. What makes the operational level unique? Did Moltke recognize it as a distinct level? Is there a difference in applying the principles of war at the strategic and tactical levels as opposed to the operational level? Is this uniqueness, and hence its discovery, due to differences in the use of terrain, the employment of reserves, and the application of technology? How do functions such as intelligence, deception, maneuver, operational fires, and logistics relate to the operational level? Does the nature of command as applied to the operational level differ significantly from its role vis-à-vis the strategic and tactical level? The answers to each of these questions can be elucidated within the context of the career and writings of Field Marshal Moltke. By examining the origins of the operational level of war it can be demonstrated that there is something inherently different about this aspect of military doctrine. Moltke was the first to recognize this difference and introduced the term "operational direction" into the vocabulary of modern warfare.

The Education of a Field Marshal

Born in 1800 in the midst of an era dominated by the Napoleonic wars, Moltke served in the Danish Army before joining the Prussian Army. In 1826 he graduated from the newly established Prussian *Allgemeine Kriegsschule* (later renamed *Kriegsakademie*) after a brilliant showing in his examinations. Although he was a student during the tenure of Carl von Clausewitz, when Moltke listed the three professors who exercised the greatest influence over him, Clausewitz was not among them. Evidence that Clausewitz observed the future field marshal, however, is recorded on his report card—the officer efficiency report of his day—where the entry "exemplary" reflected the evaluation of his performance by Kriegsakademie Director Clausewitz. Later commentators on German military history have asserted that a causal link exists between Clausewitz's writings, since he did not teach at the *Kriegsakademie*, and Moltke's praxis. Yet it is only after Moltke's victories that one finds reference to Clausewitz in his writings. While at the *Kriegsakademie*, Moltke witnessed a debate over its curriculum and purpose, a controversy that centered on whether the institution's function should be training or education. For Clausewitz training was more important than education, a point on which others disagreed. During the time that Moltke matriculated at the *Kriegsakademie*, roughly 60 percent of the three-year curriculum was devoted to education and the balance comprised training.

Moltke's formal education reinforced the value he placed on the study of military history, which he avidly pursued in order to learn the concepts that guided earlier commanders. He was also a serious campaign analyst, and his first published work was a campaign history of the Russo-Turkish war of 1828–1829.[2] After leaving the *Kriegsakademie*, Moltke was detailed to the general staff on Germany's eastern frontier, where he spent much of his time surveying and mapping. His appreciation of terrain grew enormously when he was posted as an adviser to the Turkish Army, a position that began as a sojourn and developed into a four-year adventure. Initially hired to map the defenses of Constantinople, Moltke journeyed to the far-flung borders of the Ottoman Empire, traveling through present-day Syria, Iraq, Iran, and Egypt. The descriptions of these regions, which are found in his letters and travel writings, provide a vivid picture of the total environment that he encountered: the interaction of people, topography, productivity, and resources. He also saw action while serving as adviser to the Turkish commander during his campaign against Mehemet Ali of Egypt, who had revolted against the Sultan. Moltke recommended placing Turkish forces in a strong position, but his advice was ignored; the Turkish general was more attentive to the musings of the mullahs than the advice of a Prussian captain. As a result Moltke resigned as adviser and asked to be appointed commander of the

Turkish artillery, but the request came too late in light of the Sultan's defeat at Nezib. Moltke shared in this defeat, but in the process learned the importance of terrain, training, planning, concentration of effort, and the massing of artillery firepower.

In December 1839, after four years abroad and tempered by the experience of defeat in action, Moltke returned home in broken health. When he left Berlin in 1834 he was said to already display the "courtier's, scholar's, soldier's, eye, tongue, and sword." On his return he also possessed a mind that had been expanded through a variety of new, demanding experiences in foreign climes. In recognition of his achievements in the service of the Sultan, Moltke was awarded Prussia's highest military decoration, the *Pour le Mérite*. Posted once again to general staff duty, he served in Berlin and subsequently became aide to the crown prince, an assignment that afforded him an opportunity to gain considerable influence in higher military circles. As during other periods in his career, Moltke remained an autodidact, educating himself through continuous study and application of his readings to his professional situation.

Service on the general staff required Moltke to have two horses. In order to buy these mounts he sought an outside source of income and took on the formidable task of translating Edward Gibbon's monumental twelve-volume classic, *The Decline and Fall of the Roman Empire*. He also wrote a novel and a number of travel works as well as reflections on his Turkish service and a campaign analysis of the defeat he had experienced. Both his travelogues and letters became best sellers and yielded enough money for him to obtain the proper mounts.[3] The publication of Moltke's letters and the images he captured in his writings were sufficiently romantic to win the heart of a young woman who, although unknown to this promising officer, had fallen in love with him. Eventually, however, they met, became engaged, and were married. As a couple, Maria Moltke and the future field marshal complemented each other very well, but heartbreakingly she died in 1868 before her husband's operational genius was fully recognized and rewarded.

Moltke was a talented artist who drew many of the sights he saw as he traveled and chronicled his varied experiences in word pictures. His books are rich in sketches and other illustrations, which accurately complement the corresponding passages found in his narratives. Moltke's ability as a surveyor and mapmaker also were impressive, and these were skills that he continued to rely on throughout his life. By traveling he grew to appreciate different regional cultures and national traditions, which he then studied with increasing interest. He was keenly aware of major political events and followed developments abroad such as the Polish Revolution, the Dutch and Belgian problems, and the Turkish-Russian war. Moltke also possessed an understanding of the growing role of technology in society. He studied and analyzed railroads, for instance, writing in such a way as to demonstrate a technical mastery of the details of the subject; moreover, he applied his literary gifts to descriptions of the advent of steam and rail power.[4] In our age such an accomplishment would be somewhat analogous to combining technical knowledge of rocketry and a vision of its future role in opening up the frontiers of space.

While Moltke's career presented few opportunities for command, he served at regimental level in Silesia as aide to the crown prince. In 1842 he returned to Berlin and the general staff, where his advancement was relatively slow; it was only due to his association with the prince that he eventually was marked for promotion to general officer. By remaining a student of military affairs throughout much of his life, Moltke evolved a methodology that began by understanding a given problem, examining alternative solutions, and thinking through possible courses of action. This fostered a mental discipline that served him throughout his career and particularly in the conduct of operations. It allowed him to sift and weigh each course of action to arrive at an appropriate solution. In turn, he studied the modus operandi of opposing commanders and estimated what he would do in their places. Simply stated, Moltke learned to think through a problem. This required thorough study and concentration on problem solving in order for him to arrive at a decision. Then his gift of expression would come to the fore and enable him to convey his decision to those responsible for accomplishing the objective.

Furthermore, Moltke's writings demonstrate his practical method of application. Contained in them are the analysis of the problem with assumptions, the evaluation of forces — or correlation of power — and the direct, continuous review of various courses of action. What is more, each of Moltke's campaign staff rides followed this same deliberate, methodological approach.[5] At the same time as Moltke was developing a methodology and applying it to operational directions in his native Prussia, military writers in the United States — like Arthur Wagner, Emory Upton, and Eben Swift — sought methods of campaign analysis and military problem-solving. Swift evolved the five-paragraph field order that is still used today and proposed a process of making estimates that was similar to Moltke's own.

Moltke was a man of character: humble, taciturn, literate, and unassuming. He had vision, followed practical methods, displayed professional qualities grounded in an inner strength that generates the key to success in war: constancy of character. As he studied, wrote, and applied what he learned to his professional career, Moltke balanced a thorough knowledge of the past and a mastery of his own situation to achieve the outcome he desired.

Chief of the General Staff

In 1845 Moltke was named personal adjutant to Prince Henry of Prussia. While he was traveling with the prince in Italy, he surveyed Rome, which resulted in a map that was later published. In 1846 Prince Henry died and Moltke was posted to the staff of the Eighth Army Corps at Koblenz with headquarters at Magdeburg. He remained in this assignment for seven years and received two promotions, to lieutenant colonel in 1850 and to colonel in the following year. In 1855 he was appointed as first adjutant to Prince Frederick-Wilhelm (later regent and emperor) whom he accompanied on visits to England, France, and Russia. Prince Frederick-Wilhelm commanded a regiment at Breslau, and it was there that Moltke served for a year before being promoted to major general in 1856. In October 1857 King Frederick-Wilhelm IV became gravely ill and Prince Frederick-Wilhelm became regent. Within a few days, the prince regent selected Moltke for the post of chief of the general staff of the Prussian Army, an appointment that was confirmed in the New Year.

As chief of the general staff Moltke began his greatest period of activity. At fifty-seven years of age, he adopted strategic, operational, and tactical methods for a number of areas such as changes in armament, communication, and mobility; training and education of commanders and staff officers; preparation of campaign plans; and mobilization plans. In 1859 the Austrian-French-Italian war required mobilizing the Prussian Army, which revealed serious deficiencies. The subsequent reorganization of the army by the king and War Minister von Roon enabled them to nearly double its strength. Moltke followed the events of the Italian campaign closely and later published a history of this conflict.[6] As early as December 1862 Moltke had been consulted on the political turmoil over Denmark, which was becoming acute. His approach to the situation focused on the war's objective (*Kriegsobjekt*)—the defeat of Denmark—and the operational objective, namely the destruction of the Danish Army. Moltke's written note to the War Minister and his subsequent operational campaign concept tied this political (war's) objective to the operational objective.[7] The principal difficulty that Prussia faced was defeating Denmark as quickly as possible. Moltke thought there would be difficulty in bringing war to a decisive conclusion since Danish forces could retire to offshore islands and, by controlling sea approaches, thereby avoid attack. His plan outlined a turning movement of the Danish Army before the Eider and Schleswig, which was keyed to intercept the retreating army. When the war began in February 1864 Moltke was not dispatched with the field armies but instead remained in Berlin. In his absence and as events unfolded, the plan was not properly executed and the Danes managed to escape to their fortresses of Düppel and Fredericia, each of which commanded a line of communication to an island.

Although Düppel was taken by storm and Fredericia abandoned by the Danes, the Prussian and Austrian armies were checked because the Danish Army retired farther to the islands of Alsen and Fünen just as Moltke had feared they might.

At the end of April Moltke took to the field as the chief of staff of the combined Prussian-Austrian forces commanded by Prince Frederick Karl. He planned to force a passage over the Sundewith and then attack the island of Alsen. After landing successfully, the Danes evacuated Alsen. Moltke next planned to land at Fünen, but it proved unnecessary because the Danes no longer felt secure on these islands and sued for peace. His appearance on the scene had rapidly transformed a siege war into one of maneuver, an outcome that cemented his relationship with the king: Moltke's personal influence was in ascendancy.[8] This campaign was important because Moltke foresaw the difficulty of attaining the political objective — the defeat of Denmark — without attaining the destruction of the Danish Army, which was his operational objective. Hence the concept of operations centered on the quick, flexible movement of Prussian forces to attain that end. He understood that the strategy for attaining the political objective would be controlled by the king. But as chief of the general staff, Moltke was capable of influencing the operational objective, a prerogative he exercised at his own discretion. Moreover, by introducing the terms *operational concept* and *operational goal*, Moltke started to distinguish the campaign from its purpose; he also began to delineate the strategic and operational levels.

Moltke's Strategic Vision

Moltke studied the campaigns of Frederick the Great and Napoleon intensely, both as a student at the *Kriegsakademie* and then as a devotee of military history. Their methods of conducting campaigns taught him how Frederick had capitalized on the advantage of massed flank attack; the oblique order had been one of Frederick's genuine innovations. From the French at Ulm and Bautzen, Moltke learned how Napoleon's operational conduct consisted of envelopment of the flanks. At Jena, Napoleon the defeated the Prussian Army by conducting a flanking attack while holding the center. Napoleon's concentration of mass and the ability to march his corps separately and concentrate before going into battle was a way of thinking not lost on the future field marshal of Prussia. Moltke also studied the combined campaigns of the allied forces at Leipzig and Waterloo. Moreover, drawing on his own military experience, Moltke remembered how the Turks were defeated because his advice regarding central position and the threat to the flanks had been ignored.

Strategy is studied through the experiences of the past, but while Moltke was not a disciple of Jomini, neither was he a follower of Clausewitz. However, he had read *On War* after it appeared in limited circulation in 1832. Certainly, in Moltke's view, the destruction of enemy forces meant destruction of an opponent's center of gravity; more will be said on his strategic and operational thinking in due course. Moltke inferred that strategy was the practical art of adopting means to ends; as such, he developed and applied the methods of Frederick and Napoleon to the changing conditions that he faced. As the first to realize the strength of the defensive in light of modern weaponry, he believed an enveloping attack was stronger than a frontal one. Moltke also worked out a method of marching separately and concentrating upon the battlefield. He reasoned that only one army corps could move on a single road each day; if two or three corps were on the road at the same time it would mean that the second and third corps could not be made use of if the battle was to the front. Indeed, Moltke observed that concentrating several corps to a battle was "a calamity." Multiple corps could not be fed for more than a day or two, and they would have a perilous time marching or moving. To Moltke, a large force must be broken up into manageable parts or armies; the commander should be authorized to regulate its movements and actions subject to instructions received from the commander-in-chief regarding the direction and purpose of the operations.

The campaign of 1866 illustrates Moltke's strategic vision. The political objective was to exclude Austria from Germany. Shortly after taking office as chief of the general staff, he wrote that "the war between Austria and Prussia will draw all of Europe into the battle."[9] His basic concept of operation never changed insofar as the military objective was concerned: to defeat the Austrian Army. In plan after plan from 1860 to 1866, Moltke analyzed the strategic situation, evaluated the terrain, correlated forces, and then formulated a series of deployments.[10] Central to Moltke's force evaluation was splitting the Austrian effort so as to tie down their forces in northern Italy by employing the Italian Army. Moltke conferred with Bismarck on this issue a number of times. Only when a political-military alliance was made with Italy would the Prussian Army be able to engage the Austrians. If this precondition was met, then Moltke could risk denuding western Prussian territory in order to concentrate against Austria. The question was where to concentrate: Moltke worked on a number of options, all of which assumed not only an alliance with Italy but also resolute decisions on mobilization. Yet King Wilhelm of Prussia did not want to provoke Austria and bring about a German civil war that could have an uncertain outcome. Hence, while Moltke's plans recognized the political and military objective, the real need was for rapid mobilization and the execution of a concentrated effort to ensure a short war. Moreover, Moltke had to work under constraints; for instance, relations between Prussia and its Rhine provinces had to be preserved, particularly since it was assumed that Bavaria and Saxony were allied with Austria.

While the crisis approached, during the spring of 1866, Moltke pressured for an early decision. His calculations showed the manpower stream to be advantageous between the eighteenth and forty-second day of mobilization. In a memorandum to the king, Moltke warned "that the chance of success or failure in the war rests on timely decisions being made here [Berlin] rather than Vienna. We do have the advantage of being able to use five rail lines to concentrate our Army on the Saxon-Bohemian border by the 25th day of mobilization."[11] Moreover, Moltke argued for a concentration of effort. There were two main groups of enemy forces: the Austro-Saxon armies of 270,000 men and the north and south German armies of 120,000. Although the Prussians were short 67,000 men, Moltke was determined to be superior to the Austro-Saxons when the decisive moment arrived. He allocated 278,000 men against the main threat and 48,000 to the western threat. While the king resisted such a division of Prussian forces, Moltke prevailed and under his continual prodding the small force in the west managed to knock out Hanover and Hesse in less than a fortnight.[12] The use of the railways saved time, since five routes from the provinces of Prussia led to positions on the Zeitz-Halle-Görlitz-Schweidnitz line. By making use of each of these railways at the same time Moltke had several army corps moved from their garrisons to points on this line. When the move was completed the corps were formed into three armies: the Elbe Army near Torgau, the First Army of Prince Frederick Charles at the western end of Silesia, and the Second Army of Crown Prince Frederick located between Landeshut and Waldenburg.

After it was assembled the First Army marched eastward to Görlitz. The small Saxon army at Dresden now had the Elbe Army and the First Army on its right flank. The outnumbered Saxons, placed in an untenable position, fell back into Bohemia as soon as the fighting began. In Bohemia, they were joined by an Austrian corps, which formed an advance guard far to the front of the main Austrian Army now concentrated near Olmütz. The Elbe Army then marched toward Dresden, and moved to the right of the First Army. Prince Frederick Charles now commanded both armies. (*See Map 2.*)

This gave Moltke two armies about 100 miles apart. The problem was how to bring them together so as to catch the Austrians between them. If, as seemed likely, the Austrians moved upon Breslau, the First and Elbe armies could continue their eastward march to cooperate with the Second. But on June 15 Moltke came into possession of detailed intelligence on the Austrian order of battle in positions that were spread out at Wilden-Schwerdt, Olmütz, and Brunn. He calculated that they would be unable to concentrate their forces at Josephstadt in less than thirteen days. Accordingly, he determined to bring his own two armies together by directing them toward Gitschin. Moltke calculated that the Second Army

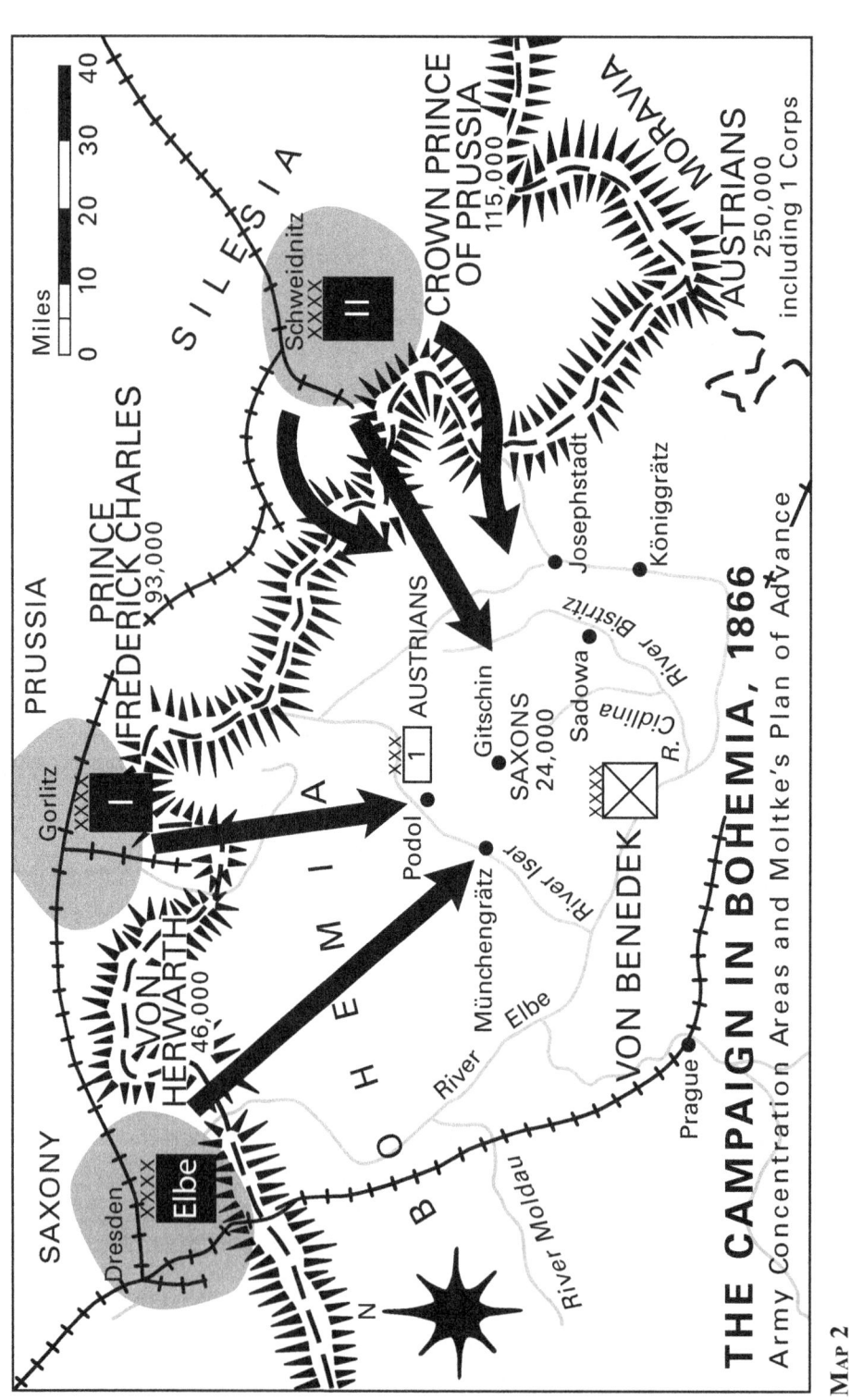

THE CAMPAIGN IN BOHEMIA, 1866
Army Concentration Areas and Moltke's Plan of Advance

MAP 2

was likely to encounter portions of the Austrian army. The crown prince had over 100,000 men, and it was unlikely that the Austrians would be able to gather a stronger force to confront him in time. The order to advance to Gitschin was issued on 22 June and resulted in the great victory at Königgrätz.

The Austrians marched faster than Moltke expected. The Austrian commander Benedek centered his attention on the First Army and allocated only four corps against the crown prince. Even these were not under common command and were beaten, as were the Saxon and Austrian advance corps opposing Frederick Charles. On 1 July Benedek collected his already-shaken forces in defensive position before Königgrätz. Moltke's two armies were now within marching distance of one another and the enemy. On 3 July they were brought into action, the First against the Austrian front and the Second against the Austrian right flank. The Austrian Army was completely defeated and the campaign decided, although an advance against Vienna was planned—but not needed—to bring about the peace terms that Prussia and Italy wanted. The night before the climactic battle, Moltke sent orders to the crown prince to attack the right Austrian flank the following morning. From a hilltop overlooking the frontal attack of the First Army, the Prussian high command anxiously awaited the crown prince's attack. The king exclaimed: "Moltke, Moltke, we will lose this battle." But Moltke calmly took a cigar from an equally nervous Bismarck and replied: "Your Majesty will not only win this battle but the entire campaign."

Not satisfied with the results of the battle, Moltke tried to have the Elbe Army brought up the river above Königgrätz in order to prevent an Austrian retreat, but its commander failed to accomplish this. He also tried to prevent the First Army from pushing its attack, hoping in that way to keep the Austrians in their positions until the crown prince's Second Army could cut off the avenues of retreat. But Moltke could not restrain the impetuosity of Prince Frederick Charles and the king. Also during the march on Vienna and Bismarck's negotiations, Moltke was confident of defeating the Austrians as well as being able to deploy against France should Napoleon III enter the conflict.

A startled Europe acclaimed Moltke's conduct of operations as brilliant. Concentration was achieved at the decisive point and the right time to annihilate the mass of enemy forces. Although Moltke termed Königgrätz his most "elegant victory," he knew the outcome had been close. In planning the operation Moltke's calculations were aided by an intimate knowledge of terrain, order of battle intelligence, and estimates of the mind of the enemy commander. He was surprised by the appointment of Benedek, since the Austrian commander was well known and respected for his abilities in northern Italy. Moltke commented on the Austrian order of battle next to Benedek's name that he was "no commander-in-chief, nor strategist; will want assistance in running an army."[13] On 30 June Benedek wrote to his wife about "this desperate situation [in which] in a few hours a great battle will be joined. I may never see you again. Better I should meet a bullet." Benedek felt that he had been beaten before the battle began, while Moltke, by contrast, made unhesitating, confident decisions with the full backing of the king.

Among the many conclusions that Moltke drew from the campaign were that the infantry, artillery, and cavalry had not worked well together on the tactical level. He thought the cavalry had not satisfactorily performed its screening, security, and reconnaissance functions. Henceforth, each division and corps was to employ its cavalry in those functions rather than holding them back to carry out saber-wielding charges. The artillery had not been concentrated enough, had changed its position too frequently, and had lacked mass; in addition, it had kept its trains to the rear of the column and therefore usually ran out of ammunition during the culmination of the battle. While Moltke thought the infantry had fought well, he believed that they should be more flexibly handled. As far as operational conduct was concerned, Moltke thought commanders at higher levels did not know how to work with the combat arms. Accordingly, he commissioned a thorough study of the 1866 campaign, the results of which were astounding for a victorious campaign.

In July 1868 Moltke gave the king a highly sensitive memorandum on the results of the 1866 campaign. Moltke explained that he did not wish to criticize the specific units, but rather in an analytical way to learn from and improve their performance. He then spoke his mind: The cavalry must perform security and reconnaissance; the artillery must be concentrated; the infantry must not rely only on superior weaponry; order of battle must be standardized; and combined actions must be improved. Also, since he believed that cavalry was crucial for operational conduct, it must develop the situation. The artillery must be massed to provide fire support. The engineers in a war of maneuver must be used early and not left in the rear of the march column. Above all, commanders must be able to integrate the combined activities of the combat arms.[14] The final part of this remarkable memorandum contains a critique of division and corps actions. The king's marginal notes indicate his support of Moltke's observations. In June 1869, under cover of a letter, the king returned the document, which led to the publication of a new regulation for the conduct of operations. Moltke was responsible for writing a large portion of this regulation, which opens with a rhetorical flourish, to wit:

> The field of reality for the army is war, but its development and its ordinary life falls in time of peace. This paradox brings out the difficulty of purposeful

training. The moral element is seldom applicable in peace, but the moral is a prerequisite for success in war. In war it is not so important what one does as how one does it. Firm determination and strong execution of a simple idea must lead surely to the objective. There must be mental preparation. Leadership of the conduct of large bodies of troops is not to be learned in peace. Previous campaigns will point the way. But progress in technology, easier means of communication, new armaments, in short, entirely changed circumstances, will prevail. Even previous victories and principles are largely inapplicable to the present.

The lessons of strategy are contained in common sense; it may hardly be termed a science.... A very large troop concentration is a calamity. A concentrated army is difficult to feed and provision; it is impossible to quarter, it can't march, it can't operate, it can't last for a long time, it can only attack.

Without the objective of seeking destruction of the enemy the decision to concentrate is a mistake. This decision is vital and requires the massing of strength down to the last battalion upon the battlefield. When approaching the enemy it will not do to be already concentrated. In the conduct of operations it is essential to remain mutually supporting and only concentrate at the right time and place: that is the task of the operational commander. Uncertainty—fog and friction—must be factored into all the calculations.

Victory through battle is the most important moment in war. Victory alone will break the will of the enemy and will subordinate his will to ours. Neither the capture of terrain, fortress, or severance of line of communication will achieve this objective. To achieve decision, breaking the will of the enemy through the destruction of his forces, that is the operational objective. This operational aim will then serve the needs of strategy.

[The] present conduct of war is to seek quick decisions.... The very strength of the army and the cost that society bears to equip and field the force makes it imperative to achieve quick decisions. The preparation for the decisive battle is the main task of military education. In peace to organize the command structure, so that in war, the commander's will can combine all the forces in the conduct of operations and apply them in battle, that is the task of understanding.[15]

Moltke argued that maneuvers of large units were valuable, but they must not be confused with the reality of war. He called for standardization of the order of battle for corps and divisions; he also stipulated what army commanders must do to make forces ready for war. He emphasized the need for cavalry at every level to perform security, screening, and reconnaissance. He included a cavalry division in the order of battle for a corps and indicated that it should be so placed in a march column as to be able to perform its functions. The same was advocated with regard to the location of artillery and engineers. Next Moltke dwelt on command relationships and the issuance of orders during the conduct of operations. "The demands on the operational commanders are such that he must conserve his energy to see the overall picture clearly and not get too immersed in detail." Moltke was aware of the need for vision and encouraged the operational commander to husband his intellectual and physical energies. He recommended that:

The commander minimize orders, he should imagine the entire operation and if too many orders are issued the subordinates begin to lose their overall concept. It is very likely that with too many orders, the most important will be lost.... The higher the commander, the shorter and simpler the orders must be.... The concept must not be lost sight of.[16]

In these orders there must not be motivation, anticipation and conjecture: it is crucial for the subordinate to understand the purpose of the operation, and then to work for its realization even if it means working against the actual orders. Within the view of the higher commander it is necessary to only tell the subordinate what is necessary to accomplish the purpose.[17]

Here Moltke's view of operational direction clearly emerged as well as his concept of the conduct of operations. Security and reconnaissance, functions of cavalry, became all important to Moltke, so as to protect the main body and to gather information on the enemy's main concentrations. Obviously, he was indicating his assessment of what had gone wrong in 1866 and also was questioning the validity of the historical function of the cavalry, the charge.[18] The regulation recognized the value of infantry firepower and the advantage of the Prussian needle gun, a subject on which he had previously written.[19] He envisioned a flexible working relationship among infantry, rangers, cavalry, and artillery.[20] On balance, this new regulation was an unequivocal statement on the need for infantry, cavalry, and artillery to collaborate on the battlefield: combined arms functioning together. In particular, Moltke believed artillery should be massed to fire in concentration.[21] According to Moltke, "the purpose of war is to accomplish the needs of policy through the use of combat." This was a fair restatement of Clausewitz's famous dictum that war was the continuation of politics by other means. Moltke continued: "Battle is the way to break the enemy's will." Although Moltke wrote about pursuit, he wanted battle to be used to achieve a distinct objective. "Only the destruction of the main forces of the enemy can lead to the realization of the main aims." Therefore it must be recognized that both the purpose and the art of command differ when applied to large and small forces; what is right for one is not right for the other. Space and time have different meanings on the level of larger units as opposed to that of smaller units. For example, mobility, the personal intervention of commanders, and the meaning of terrain are different. Moltke thought it better to continue to emphasize the maintenance of initiative and momentum. There was a reaffirmation of the principle of marching to the sound of the guns.[22]

To recapitulate, it is rare for a victorious army to conduct a review of its action and attempt to improve upon the previous campaign. With considerable risk, Moltke took on this task so that the next campaign and war might be conducted more effectively. This regulation—and what it revealed about Moltke's thoughts — was truly remarkable: He began to distinguish levels, indicated that all arms must work together, called for higher direction in the conduct of a campaign, and dared to learn from a victorious campaign. Everything considered, it was significant because it overcame the tendency to succumb to the "victor's disease."

The Defeat of France

Whereas war began suddenly in 1870, the possibility of a conflict with France had been a factor in Moltke's campaign planning almost continuously since he became chief of the general staff in 1857. A whole series of his plans are preserved and show the optimum arrangement of the Prussian-German forces for opening a campaign against the French. Preparations for the transportation of the army by railway were reviewed annually in order to adjust plans brought about by political conditions and the growth of the army as well as by improvements in the Prussian railway system. The success of 1866 strengthened Moltke's position so that when in July 1870 the orders for mobilization of the Prussian and south German forces were issued, his plans were adopted. Five days later he was named chief of the general staff of the Army at the headquarters of his majesty the king for the duration of the war. This allowed Moltke to issue orders — with the king's approval — that had the force of the king's command authority.

Moltke's plan was to assemble the entire army south of Mainz, whereby the army could best serve in defense of the whole frontier. Moltke planned for several eventualities. If the French should violate the neutrality of Belgium and Luxembourg and advance on the line from Paris to Cologne, then the German Army could strike at their flank. The Rhine itself — with the fortresses of Koblenz, Cologne (Köln), and Wesel — would be a serious obstacle in their front. If the French should attempt to invade southern Germany, a German advance up either bank of the Rhine would threaten French communications. Moltke expected that the French would be compelled by the direction of the railways to collect the greater part of their army near Metz, and a smaller portion near Strasburg. The Prussian-German forces were grouped into three armies: the First Army with 60,000 men under Steinmetz on the Moselle below Trier, the Second Army with 131,000 men under Frederick Charles centered at Homburg (with a reserve of 60,000 men behind it), and the Third Army with 100,000 men under Crown Prince Frederick centered at Landau. (*See Map 3.*) An additional three corps with approximately 100,000 men were kept separate from those three armies in order to constitute a considerable force in southeast Germany to guard against Austria's acting in concert with France.

NORTHWESTERN FRANCE

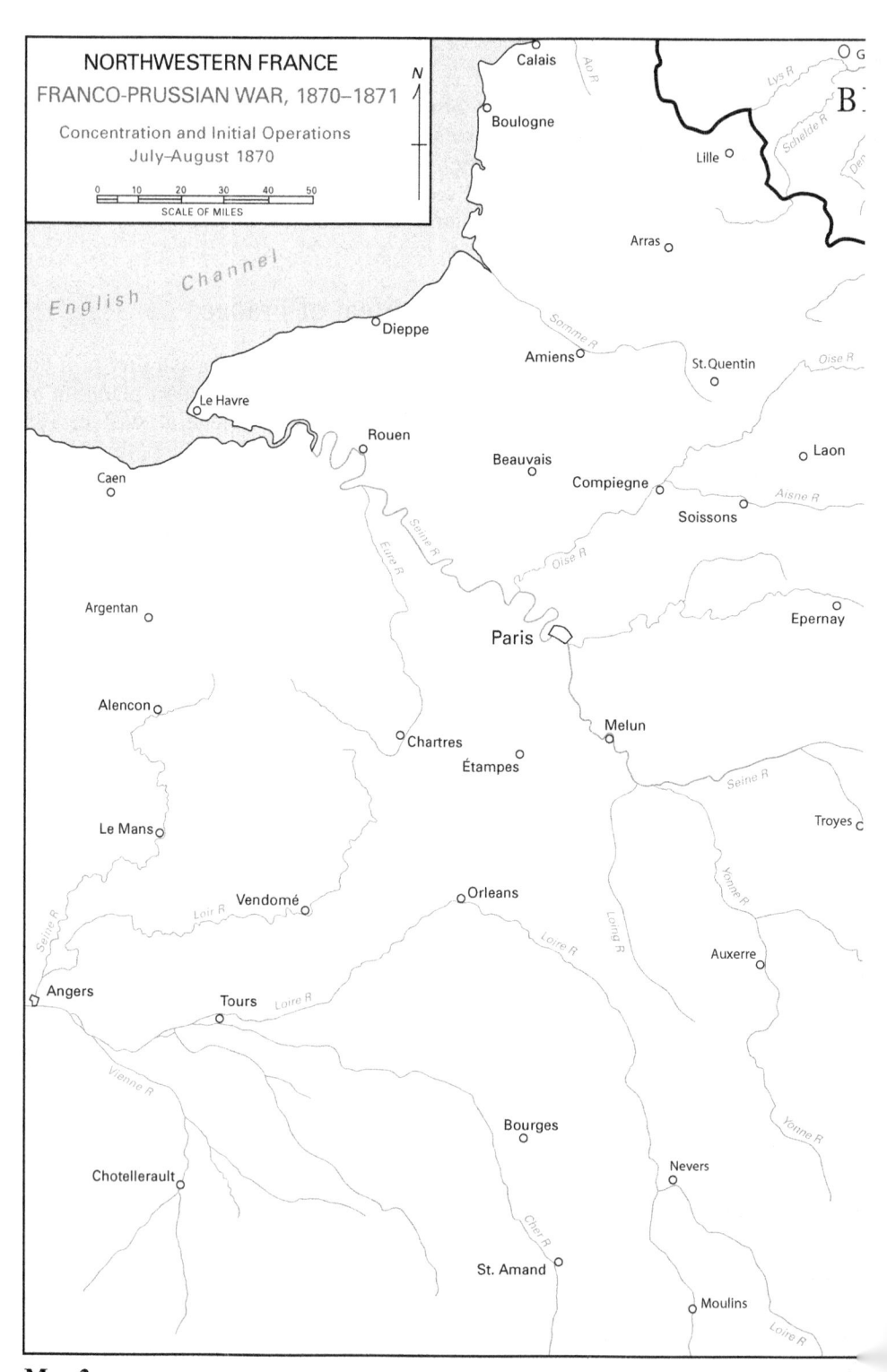

FRANCO-PRUSSIAN WAR, 1870–1871

Concentration and Initial Operations
July–August 1870

SCALE OF MILES
0 10 20 30 40 50

English Channel

Calais
Boulogne
Lille
Arras
Dieppe
Amiens
St. Quentin
Le Havre
Rouen
Beauvais
Laon
Caen
Compiegne
Soissons
Argentan
Paris
Epernay
Alencon
Melun
Chartres
Étampes
Troyes
Le Mans
Vendomé
Orleans
Auxerre
Angers
Tours
Bourges
Nevers
Chotellerault
St. Amand
Moulins

MAP 3

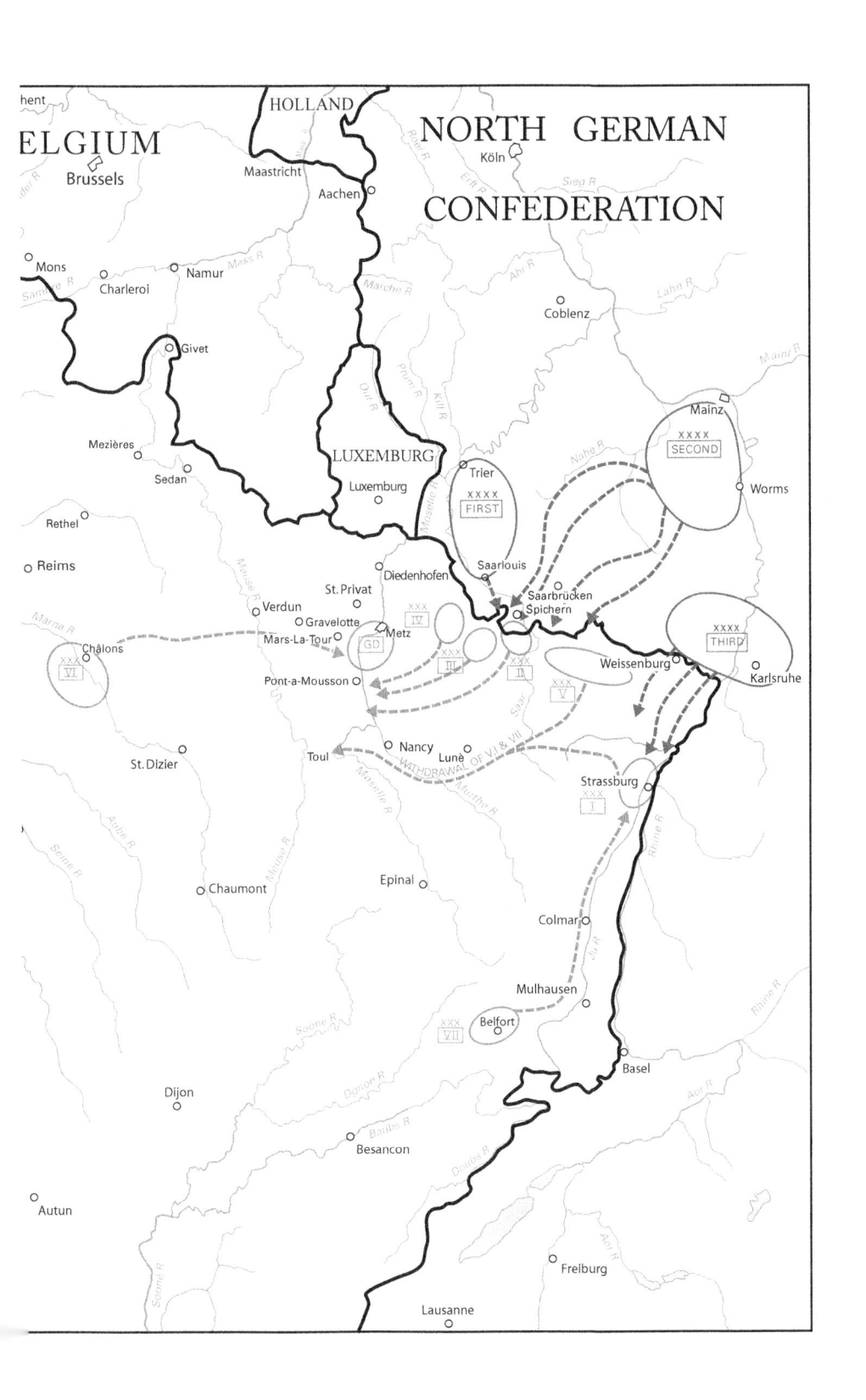

Should the French take the initiative before the German armies were prepared, as seemed likely, and advance from Metz in the direction of Mainz, Moltke would merely pull back a few miles closer to Mainz. This planned variant was actually adopted, even though the anticipated French invasion did not take place. Moltke's operational plan called for the three advancing armies to make a right wheel so the First Army on the right would reach the banks of the Moselle opposite Metz while the Second and Third Armies pushed forward. The Third Army would defeat French forces near Strasburg, and the Second Army would strike at the Moselle near Pont-à-Mousson. If the French Army should be found during this advance in front of the Second Army, it would be attacked in front by the Second Army and in the flank by the First or the Third armies or both. If it should be found on or north of the line from Saarburg to Luneville, it could still be attacked from two sides by the Second and Third Armies working in unison. Moltke used the great right wheel to attack the principal French Army from such a direction as to drive it north and cut its communications with Paris. The fortress of Metz was to be observed, and the main German forces, after defeating the main French army, were to march on Paris.

This plan was carried out in broad outline, but the battle of Wörth was brought on prematurely. It did not lead to the capture of MacMahon's army, which was the intention, but only to its defeat and hasty retreat to Chalons. Moltke also did not plan the battle of Spichern. He wanted to keep Bazaine's army on the Saar until he could attack it with the Second Army in front and the First Army on its left flank while the Third Army brought up the rear. However, these unintended victories did not disconcert Moltke. He carried out his advance on Pont-à-Mousson, where he covered the Moselle with the First and Second Armies, then faced north and wheeled round, so that the effect of the battle of Gravelotte was to drive Bazaine into the fortress of Metz and cut him off from Paris.

Nothing shows Moltke's insights and strength of purpose in a clearer light than his determination not to intervene in the attack on 18 August at a time when many strategists would have thought that an operational victory made a tactical victory unnecessary. King Wilhelm ordered this last local attack at Gravelotte, with heavy loss that Moltke blamed himself for not preventing. During the following night, Moltke decided to leave one army to guard Bazaine and Metz while setting out with the two other armies toward Paris. His southerly army led so that if MacMahon's army should be found, the main blow might be delivered from the south and MacMahon would be driven to the north.

On 25 August MacMahon's army was located while it was moving northeast to relieve Bazaine at Metz. When Moltke was satisfied with the accuracy of his intelligence, he ordered the German columns to turn to the north instead of west. MacMahon's right wing was attacked at Beaumont while he attempted to cross the Meuse, which checked his advance and forced him to gather his army at Sedan with difficulty. Here, the two German armies were brought up in order to completely surround the French. On 1 September the French Army was attacked and compelled to surrender.

After the capitulation of MacMahon's army, Moltke resumed the advance on Paris, which was surrounded and invested. (*See Map 4.*) From then on his strategy and operational conduct is remarkable for its judicious economy of force, for Moltke was wise enough not to attempt more than was practicable with the means at his disposal. The surrenders of Metz and Paris were a matter of time. The problem was to continue to invest Paris while maintaining the ability to ward off the attacks of new French armies levied for the purpose of raising the siege. Metz surrendered in October 1870, and an armistice was reached at the end of January 1871 whereby Paris and its garrison became virtual prisoners. The war was over and a treaty of peace was signed in May of that year.

The siege of Paris had lengthened the war. Chancellor Bismarck was concerned that the delay in ending the conflict would lead the other powers, especially Britain and Austria, to enter the war against Germany. Moreover, Bismarck thought that Moltke suffered from a case of the "slows" that, in a rare show of temper, provoked Moltke to accuse Bismarck of interfering in the conduct of operations where politics should have no business. Moltke raised this issue with King Wilhelm, who sided with the chancellor and argued that the conduct of strategy governed the conduct of operations.[23]

Toward a Theory of Operational Conduct

In 1871 Moltke wrote a short, theoretical "Essay on Strategy" that contains his much-quoted statement on the concept of strategy and operational conduct:

> Politics uses war for the attainment of its purpose.... There is uncertainty in war, but the aims of policy will remain. Policy must go hand in hand with strategy. The next task of strategy is to make available the military means. Next is to make possible the deployment of military force. Hereby many factors come together: political, geographic and other reasons of state. A mistake in the first deployment of the army is hardly retrievable during the entire campaign. But a great deal of prewar preparation can be accomplished. The war preparation of the force, its equipment, doctrine and training, the organization, the transport system, all should be planned before war.
> It is the task of strategy to use military means in the conduct of operations.
> Here begins the contest of wills when you encounter the independent will of the enemy. To constrain this opposing will, initiative must be maintained. This demands decision. To break the enemy's decision process can only be done through battle. The result of battle—materially and morally—are [*sic*] so far-reaching it

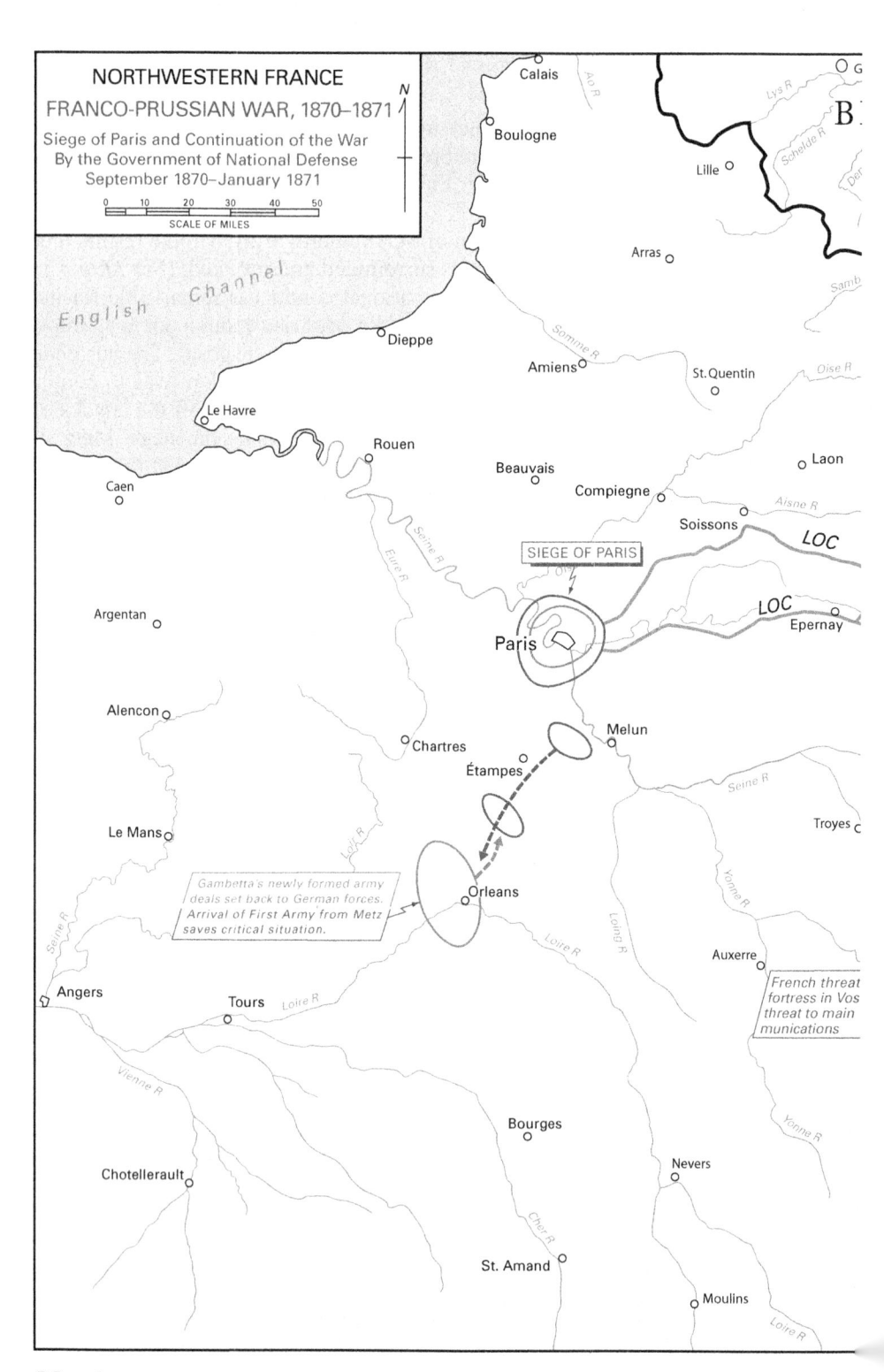

MAP 4

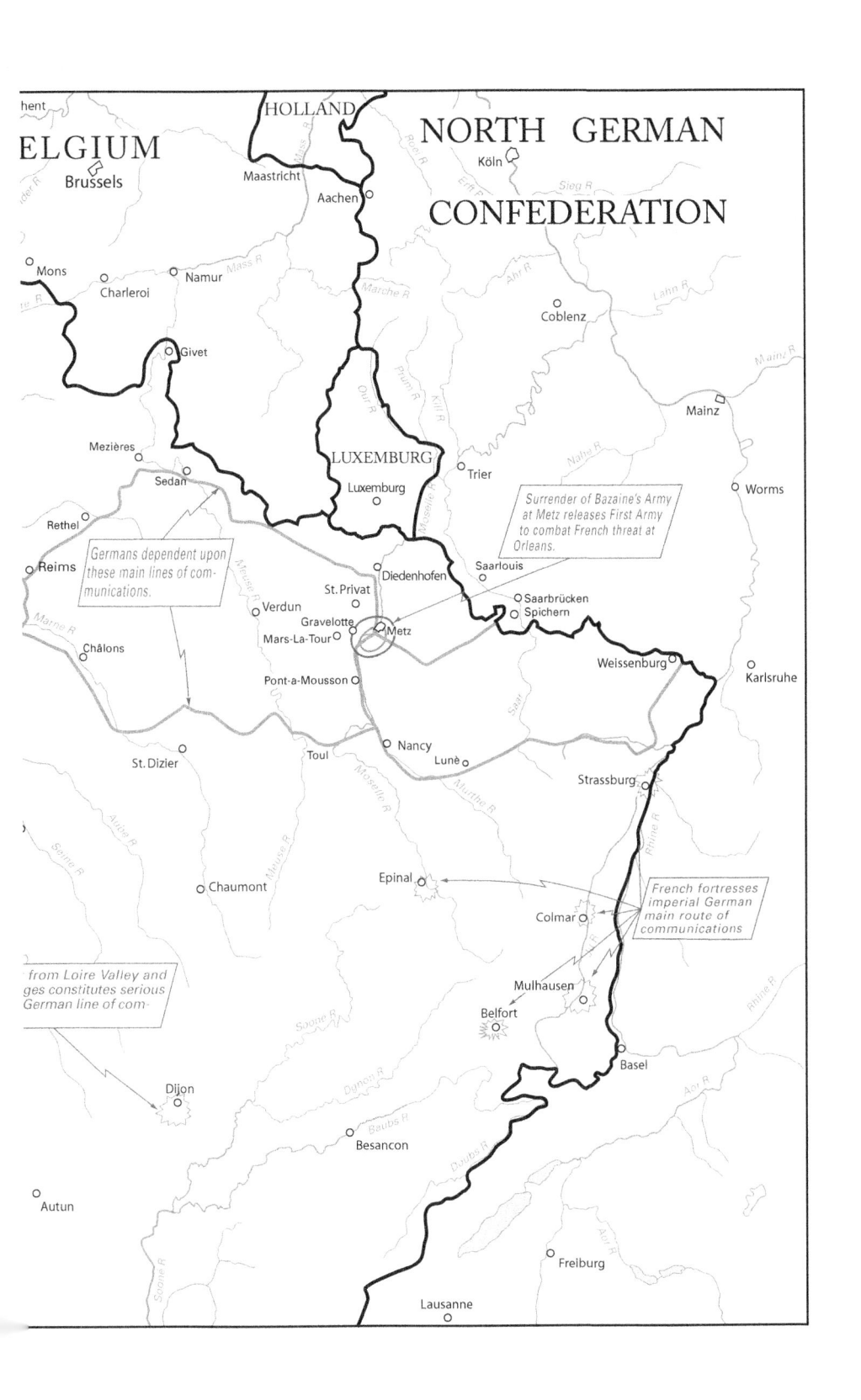

creates a new situation. A new situation calls for new measures. No operational plan can reach out with certainty beyond the encounter with the main force of the enemy. Only the layman believes that.

The commander of a campaign must keep the military objective in mind.... Throughout the entire campaign the situation will change. He must be able to react to these changes. It will require not premeditated action, but spontaneous decision, guided by military tact.... [The commander] must penetrate the fog of uncertainty, to comprehend the given, to guess the unknown, to reach quick decisions and then forcibly and unhesitatingly to execute.

In this contest of wills there enters a third factor: chance, weather, illness, railroad accidents, faulty comprehension, deception; all factors of chance enter into the balance.... [Nevertheless] will power, and rich calculation, use of chance, recalculation and constancy of the objective and reaching a timely—even if not the best decision—will be crucial.

No amount of military theoretical knowledge will prepare the commander, rather it is contained within his own character. A free, practical education, steeped in experience, schooled in military examples either from experience and military history and from practical individual experience. Upon the shoulder of the commander rests the responsibility for victory or defeat.

Responsibility may break a commander, constancy and luck have a lot to do with it.

When at the beginning of an operation, everything is uncertain other than what the commander brings in will and competence, strategy cannot bring principles and systemic rules which have any practical worth.

Archduke Charles said: "Strategy is a science, tactics is an art." He points to the science of the higher command, the art is to carry out strategic principles. Clausewitz said: "Strategy is the use of battle for the purpose of war." In the execution it is strategy that uses tactics as the means of battle. To win in leading the army to the place of battle "may be the new reality." Looked at another way "each success in battle is a building process." Before tactical success, strategy is silent, but it uses it in a new situation. Strategy is a system of expedients. It is more than a science, it is the carry-over of knowledge to practical life, the continuation of the objective with each changing circumstance, and it is the art of conducting operations under the pressure of circumstance.[24]

Herein lies Moltke's theory of operational conduct. Contained in this short essay is the concept of strategic aim, and the operational direction to accomplish it. Will, education, planning, and constancy: these were the main themes as Moltke saw it.

"Theoretical knowledge will not of itself lead to victory, but it cannot be ignored"; so Moltke quotes the German military theorist Willison. He continues: "From knowledge to doing is just one step, but from knowing to doing is a giant leap. The best lessons for the future are drawn from our own experience; but since this may be meager, we must use the study of the military historical experience of others."[25] Moltke did not write theory and his "Essay on Strategy" is an exception to the rule. The essay was revised in a number of iterations in various publications and, like Moltke's other writings on strategy and the conduct of operations, represented one of the vehicles that he used to convey his thoughts on these subjects.

These writings were closely associated with Moltke's view of himself as an educator; he saw himself as teacher, mentor, and guide to the entire Prussian-German officer corps. Among his duties was the educational development and training of officers at the *Kriegsakademie*, where a careful balance between education and training was observed. The curriculum included military history, practical application, and theory. This integrated approach centered on the applicatory technique, learning through doing, but was built on a strong theoretical foundation. Moltke expanded on this technique, not only at the *Kriegsakademie*, but also throughout the general staff. All officers were tested using the technique of the campaign staff ride. Officers attending the *Kriegsakademie* were expected to take part in various staff rides, which culminated with Moltke's personally conducting a campaign staff ride for the members of the graduating class. He would conclude each of these staff rides by offering his own observations, which subsequently were published. Officers were expected to be cross-trained in the various combat arms so that they could plan full maneuvers of corps-size units. (An equivalent approach among the United States officers would require senior service college graduates to plan maneuvers for military units from services other than their own.)

Thus, officers who had been educated and trained at the *Kriegsakademie* continued to be exposed to Moltke's educational program. As chief of the general staff, he conducted yearly staff rides for senior officers; each campaign staff ride presented an operational problem either of historical origins or as spelled out in Prussian and German defense requirements. In addition, both historical and current problems were tested in the field to emphasize an overall concept with a special situation. These staff rides did not provide military missions, but rather required working out the missions and their execution. Moltke forged a spirit of initiative, timeliness, and decision-making in the participants. Rarely—perhaps never—would Moltke give an approved solution.

Another pedagogical device that Moltke used was the tactical map problem. This could be conducted either on a tabletop or the terrain, using either historical or current practical problems. The purpose of these problems was to teach and test doctrine with battlefield experience. Moltke drew on historical studies to emphasize the experience he had gained from others. This was not a simple matter of lessons learned, but rather lessons that as yet had not been learned. Moltke believed in the value of a commonsense approach to acquiring experience; he changed the focus of military history at the *Kriegsakademie* from Frederick and Napoleon to more contemporary issues. He commissioned and personally wrote portions of the histories of the wars of 1859, 1864, 1866, and 1870–1871. In addition, Moltke required that wars other than those fought by Germany be studied in detail, including the Russo-Turkish war of 1878–1879. He brought the military history section of the general staff alive with special historical studies and other activities that chronicled and analyzed all manner of military campaigns.

Perhaps most importantly, he established campaign planning—or the imagination of future war—as a field of military specialization in its own right. These plans were based on analyses of the experience of others coupled with the requirements of the present to achieve success in future war. Moltke practiced his brand of mentorship in this area and Prusso-German campaign plans contained operational objectives. He would reevaluate each aspect of a campaign plan in order to test his concept. Moltke's theoretical construct of the why and the how of waging war came from this medium. After Moltke's death in 1891, the German General Staff codified these practical writings in three volumes entitled *War Studies: The Operational Preparations for Battle, The Tactical Preparations for Battle*, and *The Battle*. The first volume, *War Studies*, contains separate sections on war policy in peace and war, the roles of strategy and policy, the relationship between war's object and the operational objective, operational planning, high level command, operational basis, flank position, and fortresses, railroads, telegraph, and logistics, as well as examples drawn from recent European military history. The Tactical Preparations for Battle covers order of battle, transmission of orders, security and reconnaissance, marches, concentration, termination, and historical examples. In The Battle—the third and last volume—there is a reworked version of Moltke's "Essay on Strategy" and also sections devoted to battle and battle characteristics, disengagement, retreat and pursuit, lucky and unlucky commanders, and historical examples.

In all he did, Moltke differentiates between war's object and the operational objective. In most cases the operational objective is the destruction of the enemy's army, whereas war's object may be the occupation of the enemy's capital or more limited objectives. He cited the illustration of the Danish war, when the siege at Düppel was lifted by assault although Jutland was not immediately invaded and the 1866 war, when the army did not continue its advance because of a political decision. In Moltke's view, "no operational plan reaches out with certainty beyond the first engagement with the enemy."

His plans did not neglect things such as weather and included other inadvertent occurrences such as accidents, etc. Moltke described his concept of planning by turning to those campaigns in which he had a hand, most significantly, the 1870 campaign that underwent changes from its outset. The zone of concentrations for the three armies was to have been close to the border, but because the French mobilized quickly, if only partially, Moltke was compelled to move back toward the Rhine. That meant moving the First Army to Saarlouis-Merzig, the Second Army to Völkling, Saarbrücken, and Saargemund, and the Third Army to Landau and Karlsruhe—with the reserve forces moving to Homburg-Zweibrücken and Kaiserslautern as previously noted. In particular, the concentration of the Second Army had to be pushed back. While many changes had to be made, Moltke maintained the overall goal, namely, the separation of the French Army by pushing them northward and away from Paris, which was the transportation hub as well as the capital of France. The changing circumstances prompted Moltke to offer the following advice: "It is a delusion, when one believes that one can plan an entire campaign and carry out its planned end.... The first battle will determine a new situation through which much of the original plan will become inapplicable."[26]

Moltke took advantage of each new situation as he went into battle. His general ideas kept him focused, but flexible. War had a great deal of chance in it. One clear advantage upon which Moltke counted in his operational planning was a German-Prussian superiority of numbers. He calculated in his winter 1868–1869 operational plan that the German forces would face only 250,000 men while, with North German Tenth Corps, his forces would number 330,000; in addition, Moltke comments that by July 1870 another 70,000 men would be added from the South German states for a total of some 400,000.

As a planner, Moltke neither made allowances for a reserve force nor employed a reserve. But in distinguishing between the concept of directing forces from a higher level in the field, he permitted the higher level to hold forces back while also stressing that operational forces must be committed. For example, on the strategic level, Moltke initially held back forces in 1866 in the Western Prussian Rhenish Provinces to deter the French, and subsequently he held back a relatively large number of troops in 1870 in southeastern Germany to deter the Austrians. While these forces were held back, they were intended to be used in the operational conduct of the war. For once the enemy intentions and capabilities were determined and deployment occurred, there were no forces remaining to serve as a reserve. The successful integration of two or three armies was accomplished in such a way that there was never the need to hold back a reserve. Properly analyzing and calculating force requirements in order to achieve concentration in both time and space made a reserve redundant. On the strategic level, Moltke considered the ability to generate forces and to reconstitute them as tantamount to maintaining a reserve; on the operational level, he used all the forces available since he was of the opinion that once they were concentrated "great results must follow."

Moltke constantly pointed to the unexpected or unplanned, however, advising that:

> Of course the Operational Commander will need to keep his main aim constantly in mind. There will be changing circumstances so that these will not be known with certainty. He will encounter changed circumstances and he needs to think through their consequences on his main goal. All the actions of war are not concerned with premeditated execution of a plan, but rather spontaneous action, guided by military knowledge and skill.
>
> What is at issue is to be able to see through the fog-enshrouded uncertainty, to see the real situation, to guess at the unknown, to reach quick decisions and then to execute with alacrity and constancy.[27]

Accordingly, he taught repeatedly that "strategy is a system of expedients." There is a difference between war's object and the operational objective; the latter may be the destruction of the enemy force but, nonetheless, the task of strategy is to determine the operational conduct of the war. In this line of reasoning one comes to grips with the way in which Moltke differentiated the three levels of war.

Moltke's method of teaching followed from his appreciation of the operational concept. He was convinced that a mistake in the plan of concentration would not be corrected throughout the entire course of a campaign. But with proper planning—carried out through training, organization, adequate transportation, etc.—all elements of a campaign would come together and result in success.

> In wars everything is different. Our will encounters the independent will of the opponent, so that the operation hangs not only from our own intention, but also from the intention of the opponent. The first we know; the second we can only surmise. To find out the reality of the opponent's intention is the only basis upon which to act. The enemy's best course of action may be a way of finding reality.
>
> To limit the opponent's will through our own strong initiative can be done, but to break his will can only be done through tactical means in battle.
>
> But only will can steer and guide the operations. Influenced by divided council—no matter how well intentioned—the Will will lose clarity and purpose of direction.
>
> The material and moral consequences of each large battle will have consequences that will create an entirely new situation.... This changed and new situation will then call for a new direction. The aim of the destruction of the enemy can only be reached by continual adjustment of these changed directions.... Everything comes to this: to be able to recognize the changed situation, and order the foreseeable course and prepare it energetically. The tactical fall-out from battle can lead to the place of making strategically important decisions, these cannot be foreseen in the operational plan.[28]

This led Moltke to conclude by repeating Napoleon's axiom, "I never plan beyond the first battle."[29]

By calculating the will of the commander Moltke began to tie together the object, the strategy for the attainment of this object through operations, and the tactical conduct of battle. He adhered to the following concept of operational conduct: an objective on the political level with the strategy to achieve this objective. Yet the operational objective must be to destroy enemy forces and thereby break the will of the enemy through battle. One must not only prepare forces for battle, but also prepare plans of operation which explore the hypotheses of enemy action. Skill and art are requisites for the commander, force calculations must be made, hypotheses have to be reexamined, and then vision and constancy in that vision must be maintained while executing the objective.

Moltke continued to educate officers on the conduct of operations through the war college, military history, campaign staff rides, and security problems. The chief of the general staff thereby schooled the German general staff to think through the problem of attaining the end of strategy through the conduct of operations. He used this operational conduct as a level for achieving the strategic goal.

"March separately and concentrate on the battlefield" was Moltke's dictum. What did he mean? Napoleon marched separately, then concentrated before battle; Frederick marched massed. Moltke viewed concentration of force as planned to accomplish a set objective. If it held no purpose, it was "a calamity." Size, time, space, and mass entered into the equation. The size of the force increased greatly during Moltke's tenure. The time to mobilize and deploy the force decreased through preparedness, use of railways, etc. Massing had to be purposeful and to result in battle; moreover, it had to be done in such a way that the preponderance of force arrived at the right time and in the right place to produce victory in battle. Bringing the force from afar, and in a timely way, with enough mass to hold and overcome the opponent so as to defeat him in battle was therefore the essence of operational conduct. Moltke did not make too much of his dictum as a contribution to the art of operational conduct. By contrast, his contemporaries thought that it was a new secret for operational success and anointed Moltke as the most modern Napoleon. Contemporary observers argued that Moltke improved upon Napoleon's methods, but Moltke's methods simply recognized that there were different levels of war. The concentration of force must lead to battle and have the operational aim of destruction of the enemy force to support strategy.

Recognizing the defensive as the stronger form of warfare, Moltke held that firepower had made tactical attack costly; it was better to let the enemy attack first and after they are shattered to counterattack. On the strategic level, mobility was so increased that Clausewitz's evaluation of the strength of the defensive had been reconfirmed. Hence Moltke's evaluation of operational conduct as forcing the offensive, in other words, both tactical and strategic forms of warfare were stronger in the defensive. His statement on marching separately and uniting on the battlefield focused attention on the seam between the two stronger forms of war. Operational conduct would unhinge this strength and create a new situation; this was what constituted the uniqueness of the operational level.

Moltke believed in the value of flanking positions. In view of the strength of the defensive, a frontal attack was too costly. Hence he continued the practice of finding flanking positions. His campaign plans, staff rides, and historic examples attempted to create situations in which the flanks were open, particularly when the size of the force was such that a continuous line confronted an attacker. Moltke recognized that operational conduct was to attack with advantage of time through space to create open flanks. Moltke combined the capability of railways to enable his forces to concentrate faster than those of the enemy did and hence use of this form of transportation made the initial calculation of operational conduct possible.

The phrase "march separately and concentrate on the battlefield" thus signified the concept of time, mass, and space, as well as the strategic, operational, and tactical levels. Moltke also stated:

> Incomparably more favorable will things shape themselves if on the day on the field of battle itself, in other words, if the operations have been conducted in such a manner that a final short march from different points leads all the available forces simultaneously upon the front and flanks of the adversary. In that case strategy has done the best it can hope to attain, and great results must be the consequence.[30]

The Concept of Operational Direction

While the king commanded the Prussian Army, Moltke issued directives. During the 1870 war, Moltke was authorized to issue orders in the name of the king. Moltke's concept of operational direction was recognition of, and became the substance of, the operational level of war. Directive authority demanded a different approach to the conduct of operations; it was inherent in the organizational nature of the general staff. After the defeat at Jena, the general staff was formed to guard against royal and princely incompetence. The war planner advised the commander in execution of the plan of operation. Spencer Wilkinson, the British military critic, described the German general staff as the "brain of an Army."[31] The general staff at levels down through division knew the intent of the operation and, through a system of rotational assignments at unit level and with the main staff in Berlin, were guaranteed to have knowledge of the concept of operations. Thus Moltke educated and trained an entire generation of officers.

The size of Moltke's staff astonished Phil Sheridan, the American general and Civil War commander, who in 1870 met Moltke overlooking Gravelotte as he provided direction to his forces. In particular, General Sheridan was struck by Moltke's grasp of the situation and ability to brief him in fluent English as well as by the small number of officers located in his headquarters. Moltke had no more than fifteen officers with him to conduct the campaign against the French, and there were no more than eighty-five assigned to the entire general staff including those who served at army corps levels. For his part, Sheridan went on to observe Sedan and the beginning of the siege of Paris; in both instances, the size of Moltke's staff remained constant, with the chief of the general staff assisted most of the time by only two or three officers.[32] It was this limited size of the general staff that enabled its officers to effectively carry out their tasks. General staff members were able to gain insights directly from their contact with Moltke and then accurately convey his intentions to army and corps levels. Therefore, relationships developed between the general staff and individual commanders, which were neither formal nor highly structured; members of the general staff were not looked upon as authoritarian figures or demigods as they were to be depicted in later periods in German history. The combined efforts of a small, multifaceted staff whose members were capable of performing interchangeable duties and a common perception of the overarching concept of operational direction were hallmarks of Moltke's method.

Operational direction is a methodology of command used to carry out the strategic objective. It holds to the aim of breaking the will of the enemy commander through the destruction of his army. Its keynote is flexible direction. Moltke's concept of operational direction may be illustrated by an analogy of horse and rider. "Loose reins" are used when general direction is sought; when dressage or exact turns and maneuvers are demanded, then "tight reins" are used. After a period of working together, horse and rider will feel each other so that signals from rider to horse and vice versa are understood and acted upon. Again "loose reins" and "tight reins" are used, but now both horse and rider understand the intent of what is needed. Moltke used this concept in operational direction.

During the 1866 campaign neither First nor Second Army commanders understood the concept of operations. Moltke used a tight-rein concept to maneuver both armies, then had trouble restraining the First Army from attacking while prodding the Second Army to move quicker. In 1870 both commanders knew Moltke's intent and acted accordingly. In 1866 General Steinmetz received loose-rein instructions from Moltke; but in 1870 not even a tight rein kept Steinmetz from bolting. Moltke, with the king's permission, fired Steinmetz.

Communications obviously contributed to Moltke's style of executing operational direction. Moltke warned against the imposition of "a telegraph wire in the back of an operational commander." Moltke used a short, crisp, telegraphic style to issue directions. The most important of them were usually amplified through written messages delivered in the form of dispatches. In the 1870 campaign the Prussian command authorities were the king, chancellor, war minister, and Moltke himself, all located in Mainz. From there they were in a good position to observe and direct the unfolding campaign. As a rule Moltke relied on the loose-reins approach: operational direction with intent and guiding position throughout the campaign.

When great success was anticipated, Moltke used the tight-reins approach with very specific orders, even if it meant overruling the independence of the army commander. He continually emphasized in these detailed orders adherence to and an understanding of the concept of operations. Moltke orchestrated the movement of three armies in consonance with this concept. In 1870 the border crossings were left to the army commanders, but when large French forces were encountered he would unhesitatingly introduce closer and closer coordination, even down to corps level: this was a very tight rein. For instance, Moltke instituted oral explanations by general staff officers to amplify telegraphic and written orders. This tight rein did not extend to forces engaged in battle. Once the battle was joined Moltke did not give operational directions on the tactical level.

Moltke was well aware of the utility of his method and discussed the commander's relationship with command authorities at the national level in the following terms:

> The unluckiest of commanders is the one who has a control element imposed upon him. Every day, every hour, to be required to explain concepts, plans, and intentions to delegates of the highest authority or to have a telegraph wire in one's back—this is most unfortunate. Thereby the commander must lose self-confidence, initiative, decision, and daring; without these he can't wage war. A daring decision will only be made by one man.[33]

Fortunately, this is not the kind of relationship that Moltke had with King Wilhelm, Chancellor Bismarck, and War Minister Albrecht von Roon.

Moltke then turned to where the nation's command authorities should be located with respect to the operational commander: "It is always very easy to give positive orders from afar. If the highest political authority is not with the Army, then that authority must give the operational commander a free hand. War cannot be waged from the 'green table.' Decisive decisions can only be weighed."[34]

Moltke enjoyed a positive relationship with the king, chancellor, and war minister, as previously noted. In the wars of 1866 and 1870, they were together for a greater part of the campaign and Moltke's operational direction was not encumbered by their presence. One noticeable fracture in this relationship of trust between Wilhelm, Bismarck, Roon, and Moltke occurred over the bombardment in the siege of Paris. (Some modern historians have argued that it was at this point that Moltke "invented" the operational level of war to keep interfering command authorities from meddling in the conduct of operations.) Moltke believed this to be the precondition for operational direction: Trust must exist for operational direction to be effective. Moltke further commented:

> If commanders of armies in the field are surrounded by independent and negative counselors, a positive approach will encounter one hundred naysayers. They will present every difficulty, they will have foreseen all eventualities; they will always be right; they will defeat every positive idea because they have none of their own. These counselors are the spoilers; they negate the Army leader.[35]

Had a relationship of trust not existed among the so-called counselors—who were nineteenth-century equivalents of today's National Command Authorities—then the operational commander in Moltke's day could not have been effective. Moltke required the operational commander to be given both independence of action and flexibility. The selection of this commander is highly significant, Moltke noted, since "[he] not only stands in front of political authority, but before his own conscience and that of all his people.... Even so the highest commander is best the King because he places everything at risk and is in overall command." Moltke went on to observe that:

> The operational commander should only be given general instructions from the King. These instructions ought to contain primarily the political goal rather than the military goal.... It is impossible to design a plan of operations which will not change during the campaign, even change significantly in concept. Against our intentions stand those of our opponent, who has just as strong a will as ours. A thousand chance circumstances will occur; a won or lost battle can alter the entire circumstances of the war.[36]

Moltke pointed to the Danish war, when restrictions were placed on the operational commander. When these restrictions were removed, operational freedom finally yielded results. "Political authority should grant operational freedom of action and only at times point out the risks of a given operation."[37] Thus, operational direction meant separation from political authority and higher levels of military authority; it held that trust, flexibility, and freedom of action were required to achieve the military objective. As understood by Moltke, it also signified the practice of loose and tight reins and an implicit recognition of the three levels of war.

Conclusion

One hundred years ago the face of war changed. Moltke recognized this change and the effect it would have on short war as he had practiced it in his career. The last campaign in which he played a decisive role resulted in the capitulation of France. Yet, even though the French Army had been defeated at Sedan, the war continued because the French nation refused to admit defeat. New armies continued to be trained to oppose the Prussian invader; the Prussians besieging Paris were themselves attacked. The dispute between Bismarck and Moltke over the conduct of the siege gets to the heart of the matter; and Moltke understood this all too well when he quoted a letter from Clausewitz to Müffling: "It is the task of strategy to prevent policy from requiring of it those tasks which are against the nature of war, that because of not knowing about the working of the [military] instrument, will bring about failure in its utilization."[38]

Moltke regarded Bismarck's insistence on the bombardment of Paris as demanding that the military instrument be employed to do what it could not accomplish. He argued that Bismarck was meddling in operational matters, but the king was of another mind and ordered Moltke to bombard Paris.[39] Even with the bombardment, the war continued. Moltke recognized that greater and greater strength would be required and requested raising one hundred new battalions for continuation of the war. Fortunately, the raw French levies were defeated before equally untested German troops were called upon to fight, and an armistice was negotiated whereby France acknowledged defeat.

The field marshal realized that he was seeing a new form of warfare: no longer a cabinet war but the beginning of national, total war. When a young general staff officer, Colmar von der Goltz, published his history of the Franco-Prussian war under the title of *The Nation in Arms*, Moltke knew his concept of war had been validated. But Goltz was posted to a remote assignment and fate denied him the opportunity to succeed Moltke. But Moltke worked thereafter toward deterring war.[40] Strengthening the German Army could deter conflict, especially with France, and his campaign plans illustrated this point. In May 1890, near the end of his life, Moltke issued the following warning:

> The time of the cabinet wars is over, we will have only people's war. If war breaks out now, its length and outcome are not predictable. It will be the great powers of Europe, who armed as never before, will enter the list. None of the powers can be absolutely defeated in one or two campaigns.... Even if defeated and forced to make peace they will be able to renew the conflict after a year's time.... Gentlemen, it can be a war of seven or thirty years duration—and woe to him who throws the torch into the powder keg and lights Europe aflame. Great sacrifices will be called for. The lives of hundreds of thousands are at stake.... Financial considerations ought to be a secondary consideration.... Security will only be found in self reliance.[41]

He recognized the necessity to enter into the seam between strategy and tactics, knowing that strategy inherently had dual purposes: political and military. Tactics were purely military, and operations were designed to carry out purely military objectives and hence were the exclusive domain of the operational commander.

In recognizing that the seam or threshold between the strategic and the tactical levels was bound up in the conduct of operations, Moltke centered his operational theory on the simple idea of marching separately and uniting on the battlefield. This was an act that demanded orchestration and direction, planning and understanding, trust and flexibility. The more Moltke came to accept the concept of operational direction, the greater was his ability to carry out the strategic aim of campaigns such as those of 1866 and 1870. Subsequent campaign plans and staff rides demonstrated the continual growth of this concept of operational direction. Moltke separated the strategic aim from the attainment of the operational goal; his methodology for achieving the operational goal was to direct military forces toward that goal. He spent a lifetime educating and training both himself and others to realize this goal.

Instinctively, he recognized the profound significance of this third level—the operational level—situated between the strategic and tactical levels. By making this distinction, war on the strategic level was strengthened; Moltke indicated this awareness in his campaign plans. Of the two forms of war, offense and defense, defense was the stronger according to Clausewitz. Moltke accepted the validity of Clausewitz's statement on the tactical level. The question then became one of how to engage in the offensive: the answer was on the operational level.

Technological advances combined to bolster Moltke's development of war on the operational level as railroads increased strategic mobility and aided in the conduct of offensive operations. The telegraph helped to direct units coming together on the battlefield. Increased firepower contributed to tactical defense. Moltke's operational conduct utilized tactical defense in conjunction with operational offense to unhinge the opponent by flank attack. Geography, weather, and luck all became factors in operational planning and direction. Education and training were central to Moltke's promotion of the operational level. It was Schlieffen who later attempted once again to combine the strategic with the operational. His method sought to combine the strategic goal with the operational, thereby replacing Moltke's inherently flexible operational direction with precise, detailed planning and control. But that is another chapter in military history, beyond the scope of this examination of Moltke and the origins of the operational level of war.

Decisive battles, short wars, maneuver, the planning and execution of campaigns, and education of the officer corps: these are the elements of Moltke's contribution to military thought. Does the legacy of Moltke's career and writings hold within it the origins of the operational level of war, either in theory or practice? Certainly he did not formulate an elaborate theoretical hierarchy of relationships among the strategic, operational, and tactical levels of war. But Moltke implicitly recognized the fact that strategy has political content while operations have a military basis. At the risk of stating the obvious, Moltke practiced the conduct of operations and his practice resulted in the destruction of enemy forces.

Notes

1. This essay is from a manuscript prepared by the author for the National War College and published in March 1988 under the title, "Moltke and the Origins of the Operational Level of War." Extracts from this manuscript subsequently were published by the author under the title, "Moltke and the Origins of Operational Art," in *Military Review* 70, no. 9 (September 1990): 28–44. It is reproduced here with the permission of Military Review.
2. Helmuth K. B. Graf von Moltke, *The Russo-Turkish Campaign in Europe, 1828–1829*, is a classic example of campaign analysis, published in *Gesammelte Schriften und Denkwürdigkeiten*, 7 vols. (Berlin: E. S. Mittler und Sohn, 1891–1893) (hereafter cited as *GSD*).
3. Moltke's *Letters on Conditions and Events in Turkey in the Years 1835 to 1839* is an interesting account of his experiences in the service of the Sultan. His other writings during this period include a short romance novel, *Two Friends* (1827); a contemporary political analysis, *Holland and Belgium in their Natural Relations from the Separation under Philip II to their Reunion under William I*; and a volume that dealt with a burning issue of his day, i.e., the Polish Revolt and the Russian campaign to defeat it, *An Account of the Internal Circumstances and Social Conditions of Poland* (1832).
4. Moltke's interest in railways led to his appointment as a director of the Hamburg-Berlin railway. In 1843 he wrote an article entitled "What Conditions Should Determine the Choice of the Course of the Railways?" This and previously cited general works that he wrote prior to becoming chief of the General Staff were published in *Gesammelte Schriften und Denkwürdigkeiten*.
5. Helmuth K. B. Graf von Moltke, *Moltkes Militärische Werke*, 12 vols. (Berlin, 1892–1912) (hereafter cited as *MW*), contains Moltke's campaign plans through 1871; see *MW*, vol. II, no. 2, "Moltkes Taktisch-Strategische Aufsätze aus den Jahren 1857 bis 1871," and *MW*, vol. II, no. 3, "Moltkes Generalstabsreisen aus den Jahren 1858 bis 1869." His campaign plans developed after 1871 were edited by Ferdinand von Schmerfeld and are found in *Moltkes Aufmarschpläne 1871–1888* (Berlin, 1921). Another selection of Moltke's works, also edited by Ferdinand von Schmerfeld, was published under the title of *Generalfeldmarschall Graf von Moltke, Ausgewählte Werke* (Berlin: Reimar Hobbing, 1925), hereafter cited as *MAW*. The finest biography available was written by Eberhard Kessel, *Moltke* (Stuttgart: K. F. Koehler, 1957), but it has not been translated into English. E. F. Whitton's account is available in English; first published in 1921, it was reprinted in 1972. See Frederick E. Whitton, *Moltke* (New York, 1972).
6. *MW*, vol. III, no. 3, "Der Italienische Feldzug des Jahres 1859." During this campaign Moltke observed the use of railways, increased lethality of rifle and artillery fires, futility of massed bayonet charges, and changing role of cavalry.
7. *MW*, vol. I, no. 1, *Krieg 1864*, "Denkschrift vom 6. Dezember 1862 über Operationen Gegen Dänemark—An den Kriegsminister," pp. 1–6; and "Operations Entwurf vom Dezember 1863," pp. 6–16. This operational concept was criticized by Prince Friederich Karl and resulted in changes in the plans, "Bemerkungen des Prinzen Friederich Karl zu diesem Operations Entwurf," pp. 16–23.

8. *MW*, vol. I, no. 1, *Krieg 1864*, 97, "Bedingungen Einer Landung an Alsen, 8. März 1864, An den Obersten Blumenthal, Über eine Landung an Fünen, 16 März 1864, An Se, Majestät Den König," pp. 104–08. For other memoranda and orders on this subject, see particularly pp. 129ff.
9. Ibid., vol. I, no. 2, p. 4.
10. Ibid., pp. 31–43.
11. Ibid., p. 75.
12. Ibid., p. 77.
13. Whitton, *Moltke*, p. 100.
14. *MW*, vol. II, no. 2, pp. 71–148, 149–61.
15. Ibid., p. 172.
16. Ibid., p. 180.
17. Ibid., p. 183.
18. Ibid., pp. 190–94.
19. Ibid., pp. 49–65.
20. Ibid., pp. 194–200.
21. Ibid., pp. 203–06.
22. Ibid., p. 207.
23. Ibid., vol. IV, no. 1, p. 35. See Rudolf Stadelmann, *Moltke und der Staat* (Krefeld, Germany: Scherpe-Verlag, 1950), pp. 434–38, which reproduces the original memorandum in Moltke's own handwriting.
24. *MW*, vol. IV, no. 1, pp. 290–93; see also pp. 70–117.
25. Ibid., pp. 70–117.
26. Ibid.
27. *MAW*, I: 78–79.
28. Ibid., p. 76; *MW*, vol. IV, no. 1, pp. 71–73.
29. *MAW*, I: 76–77.
30. Rudolf von Caemmerer, *The Development of the Strategical Science in the 19th Century*, trans. Karl von Donat (London: Hugh Rees, Ltd., 1905), p. 218.
31. See Spencer Wilkinson, *The Brain of an Army: A Popular Account of the German General Staff* (London: Westminster, 1895).
32. Philip H. Sheridan, *Personal Memoirs of P. H. Sheridan*, 2 vols. (New York: C. L. Webster and Co., 1888), 2: 367.
33. *MAW*, I: 55.
34. Ibid.
35. Ibid., p. 54.
36. Ibid., p. 56.
37. Ibid., p. 59.
38. Ibid., IV: 135.
39. *MW*, vol. I, no. 3, pp. 413–19, 427–28, 439, 443–46, 465, 481–84; Stadelmann, *Moltke und der Staat*, pp. 212–36, 237–64, 434–38.
40. Sig Forster, "Facing People's War: Moltke the Elder and Germany's Military Options After 1871," *Journal of Strategic Studies* 10, no. 2 (June 1987): 209–30.
41. Moltke, *GSD*, 7: 139.

Operational Thought from Schlieffen to Manstein[1]

Brig. Gen. Günter R. Roth

Learning Lessons from History

Scharnhorst's conviction that history alone provides the material that sharpens man's judgment sounds quite modern, essentially meaning that we are supposed to learn not what to think, but how to think. However, this thinking process holds within itself the misunderstanding that history, including the history of war, provides rules. Thus, we were warned long ago about using the history of war to establish precepts or applying its "lessons." If it is argued that situations in history will never be repeated in exactly the same way, then by implication there is no regularity in history.[2] To forecast the problem, Clausewitz wrote this about the Battle of Jena and Auerstädt: "When in 1806 the Prussian Generals … plunged into the open jaws of disaster by using Frederick the Great's oblique order of battle, it was not just a case of a style that had outlived its usefulness but the most extreme poverty of the imagination to which routine has ever led."[3]

Dogmatist of Envelopment: Schlieffen and the Relationship between the Military and Politics

It is simply not true that General Alfred Graf von Schlieffen was keen on wrestling control from the politicians. Any tinge of "Bonapartism" appeared foreign to him. His continued influence on German policy was the fault of Bismarck's successors, who carelessly squandered his legacy. The first chancellor's alliance policy, aimed at establishing a balance of power, was not continued, and the German Reich all of a sudden found itself encircled from all sides and isolated. The politicians now looked like defaulters with a bankrupt estate on their hands.

The generals, who believed they were facing the danger of a war on two fronts, filled this vacuum. Instead of a political solution, Schlieffen could only offer the Reich a military one, which resulted in a vicious circle of political and military constraints with disastrous consequences.

In the following years, the Schlieffen Plan shackled the politicians, who were seeking diplomatic alternatives. The German Chief of the General Staff believed the assault on Belgium to be an operational condition sine qua non. However, this automatically meant the British Empire's entry into the war. The German Reich got exactly the kind of war it wanted to avoid: a war against France, Russia, and a naval power, England. For a doubtful operational success, they had thus taken the risk of a guaranteed political disaster.

In July 1914 German diplomatic circles were forced to adjust to the military deployment plans—rather than the other way around. What a perversion this was of Clausewitz's doctrine of the primacy of politics! It is inconceivable that Bismarck would have allowed a military operations plan to dictate the principles of his policies. Gerhard Ritter, the German military historian, painted an accurate picture of the situation:

> The outbreak of the war in 1914 is history's most appalling example of the political leadership's impotent dependence on the planning of the military technocrats. The historic guilt of Bismarck's successors lies in the fact that they allowed themselves to be drawn into this dependency, that without raising a voice of opposition they accepted war planning as being the privilege of the military expert.[4]

Schlieffen's Idea of Envelopment

Schlieffen's operational thinking can be condensed in the following sentence: "The flank attack is the gist of the entire history of war."[5] Schlieffen intended to lay down the art of operational command and control in a general rule; more precisely, he wanted to reduce it to a single fundamental formula, i.e., the flank attack. Spellbound he stared at the Battle of Cannae (216 B.C.), a battle of envelopment. He firmly believed that every great military leader in history, whether he realized it or not, had aspired to a repetition of this feat. But, as he said, "with the exception of Sedan, no second perfect Cannae" has ever been fought.[6] For contemporary application, he drew the following conclusion:

> A battle of annihilation, as Hannibal conceived it in the distant past, can be fought today according to the same plan. The enemy front is not the objective of the main attack, and it is not the enemy front that necessitates assembly of the masses nor the call-up of the reserves. The most important thing is to push in the flanks. This must not happen at the flank tips of the front, but rather along the entire depth and extent of the enemy's order of battle. The total defeat of the enemy will be completed by an attack into the rear.[7]

Schlieffen linked this tactical-operational maneuver encirclement with two strategic considerations. As a result of its geographical situation, the German Reich was jeopardized by a war on two fronts. There was the danger of being ground between two millstones. In the event of a long war, the second consideration, the German Reich had no chances of victory if an Anglo-French sea blockade were to sever its supply of raw materials.

Schlieffen intended to solve both problems by beating France in a fast campaign immediately after the outbreak of the war. Subsequently, it would have been possible to commit almost all forces against the cumbersome Russian colossus, whose mobilization would take more time. An instantaneous decision in the West, however, could be attained only by complete encirclement of the enemy forces, i.e., by another "Cannae."

Upon retiring from active military service in 1906, Schlieffen handed a memorandum, later to be called the Schlieffen Plan, to his successor, the younger Helmuth von Moltke. The audacity of the operational idea devised therein was breathtaking indeed: In a campaign in the West, almost the entire German Army was to march through Belgium with an excessively reinforced right wing and, bypassing Paris, advance all the way to the Swiss border in a gigantic scythe-like movement. (*See Map 5.*) The French Army would thus be encircled in a huge pocket.

The Marne Campaign of 1914

In August 1914 the German armies pushed westward at a speed and distance so far considered inconceivable. The operation was conducted with clockwork precision. Most important, however, the Germans succeeded in achieving a strategic surprise, since the enemy had not reckoned with such a gigantic outflanking move on their left flank. The French troops were swept aside by the German swivel wing, and it appeared to be only a question of days until the giant revolving door would be slammed shut behind the Allies. (*See Map 6.*)

Then there was suddenly a gap in the German right wing between the First and the Second Armies, into which the British Expeditionary Forces (BEF) thrust. The commanders in chief of these two armies made a hasty withdrawal behind the Marne River. This move brought the German attack to an abrupt halt, and the lengthy period of frustrating trench warfare now began. Was there a "miracle at the Marne," or had the German Army fallen prey to a "Schlieffen myth"?

For the French commander in chief, Joseph Joffre, this whole war had started like a nightmare. His offensive move into Lorraine, by which he intended to forestall the Germans, failed after only a few days. And it was now impossible to stop the German armies approaching his rear in an effort to envelop him. Joffre withdrew several army corps from the French Eastern Front, which was protected by strong border fortifications, and redeployed them by rail from the right to the left wing.

MAP 5

This move resembles General Erich von Manstein's famous *Rochade* (castling move) on the Dnieper River in 1943, which we shall consider in detail later, and it enabled the French commander in chief to gain a "second-strike capability." The newly formed Sixth Army thrust from the west into the flank of the First German Army attacking on the right wing. The latter found itself compelled to lunge at the threat, a move that resulted in that disastrous gap into which the BEF was able to thrust.

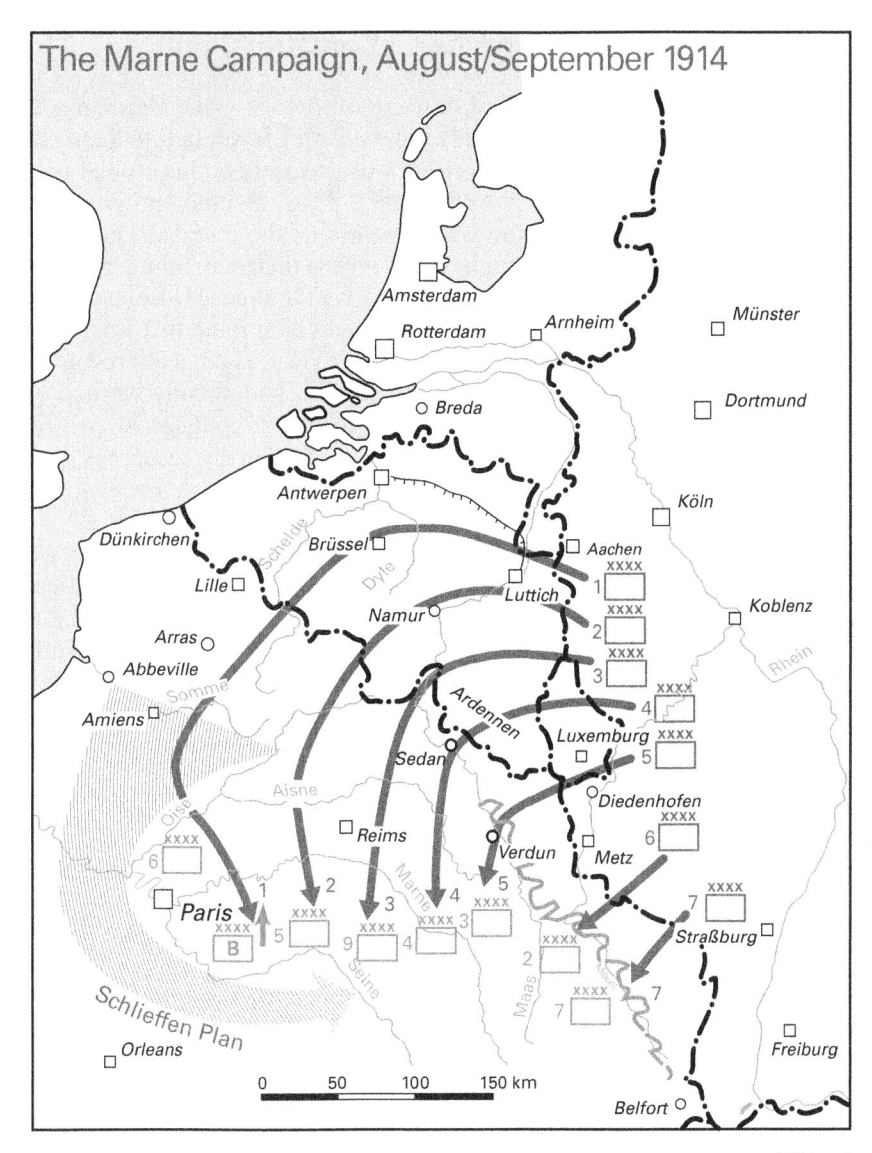

MAP 6

Now the German General Staff was beginning to get nervous. If German troops continued advancing southward, they ran the risk of being encircled by the Allies from the two cornerstones of Paris and Verdun. In other words, in attempting to encircle the enemy, the Germans were in danger of being encircled themselves. This is how the withdrawal of the two assault armies and the replacement of the younger Moltke came about.

The Principle of the Culmination Point

How was it possible that within reach of victory—the German soldiers on the right wing could already see the Eiffel Tower before them—a setback of such magnitude occurred? It was precisely at this crucial moment that there were no reserves available. Thus, a situation had come about that Clausewitz calls the transgression of the culmination point: "Most [attacks] only lead up to the point where their remaining strength is just enough to maintain a defense and wait for peace. Beyond that point the scale turns and the reaction follows with a force that is usually much stronger than that of the original attack. That is what we mean by the culminating point of the attack."[8] Schlieffen had already warned of such a development: "The experience of all former conquerors will be confirmed: offensive warfare requires and absorbs many resources, and these resources diminish as consistently as those of the defender grow, and this is particularly true in a country teeming with fortifications."[9]

Schlieffen can certainly be accused of not giving due consideration to the often-quoted gap between operational requirements and logistical reality. Moreover, he lacked Moltke's vision of future technological developments. It can be said with hindsight that the German General Staff should have attached more importance to the motorization of the supply system, especially for the armies on the right wing. However, Schlieffen's successors made crucial operational mistakes in the execution phase.

The Courage to Concentrate

The Schlieffen Plan was by no means utopian, at least not at the time of its conception in 1905, by which time an extraordinarily favorable political situation had developed: Russia had just suffered a major defeat in the war against Japan and was also weakened by internal strife. The German Reich could have pitted its entire army against France. Besides, the French Army was far from its 1914 strength, since reform of the army was not begun until much later.

When, in the First World War, the Schlieffen Plan was to be implemented, its creator had already died. In the meantime, his successor, the younger Moltke, had clearly realized that the politico-strategic conditions had drastically changed. This left him with only two options: Carry out the Schlieffen Plan no matter what, but then resolutely accept the highest risk; or devise an entirely new plan.

As it turned out later, a strategic defense with a second-strike capability would have been the right alternative. The French, for their part, were planning an offensive of their own, in order to march to "Berlin via Mainz," as General Foch demanded.[10] But the younger Moltke was so influenced by his predecessor that he did not dare to step out of his shadow. He therefore steered a middle course, which was precisely the wrong thing to do. The younger Moltke's watered-down version of the Schlieffen Plan was divested of its basic idea and thus of its operational advantages, while the political drawback, the violation of Belgium's neutrality, remained.

Certainly, the point-of-main-effort principle had never before in military history been as resolutely aspired to as in Schlieffen's plan for an offensive in the West. The force ratio of the mobile offensive wing versus the static defensive wing was seven to one. While fifty-four divisions had been massed between Metz and Aachen, Alsace-Lorraine was to be covered by only eight divisions. Upon implementation of the Schlieffen Plan in 1914, the younger Moltke had another eight additionally formed divisions at hand. He did not commit a single one of them on the right wing, however, using them instead to double the number of divisions on the left wing from eight to sixteen. In this way, he falsified—adding also qualitative factors—the force ratio sought by Schlieffen from seven to one to three to one.

When the German offensive had exceeded its culmination point on the right wing at an early stage, those divisions, which unnecessarily—and with detrimental effect, as will be explained later—were committed on the left wing, failed to provide a second echelon, a follow-on-force. Indeed, the troops needed to close the gap between the First and Second Armies threatened by the BEF were not available. But the younger Moltke committed another violation of the concentration principle. The Second Army, employed together with the First Army on the right at the point of main effort, was ordered to detach two corps to the Eastern Front after the victory on the Sambre, although no help had been requested there. Moltke himself admitted later in his memoirs that this had been his most serious mistake.[11]

The Revolving-Door Effect

The British historian Basil H. Liddell Hart has compared the functional principle of the Schlieffen Plan as well as Manstein's SICKLE CUT Plan (1940) to a revolving door.[12] In 1914 the pivot was near Diedenhofen (Thionville), to the south of Luxembourg. The more resolutely the French pushed into Lorraine, the more violently they would be hit in the back by the revolving door from the direction of Flanders. In 1940 the rotation was in exactly the opposite direction, i.e., clockwise; the farther the Allied intervention troops advanced into Belgium in accordance with the Dyle Plan, the easier it was for the German panzer units to thrust all the way to the English Channel behind their back.

In each case, the problem was to lure the enemy into a trap. Schlieffen insisted that a perfect Cannae required two people, a Hannibal and a

Terentius Varro.[13] In 1914 the French General Joffre was on the verge of playing the role of the Roman Terentius Varro. He planned an offensive toward the northeast and thus straight into the trap. In the same way, the vengeance-seeking French soldiers could not wait to advance on Alsace-Lorraine and win it back. On the battlefield of 1914, a similar configuration could have evolved as at Cannae in 216 B.C. The German troops deployed in Lorraine would have had the same role to play as Hannibal's infantry in this situation. In the final phase of the battle, the Romans had succeeded in indenting the latter in the middle, resulting in the Carthaginian infantry's closing in a semicircle around it. The deeper the Roman foot soldiers now fought their way forward, the more difficult it would be to escape backward, with the threat of encirclement by Hasdrubal's cavalry. For Schlieffen, the latter's role was to be played by the strongly reinforced right wing.

The Schlieffen Plan formed the background to the SICKLE CUT Plan developed by General Manstein. He refers to what the French Army was going to grant to the German General Staff in 1914 as the "favor of an early offensive." According to Manstein's analysis, Schlieffen had "accepted the risk of initial setbacks in the Alsace and at the same time had reason to hope that the enemy, by way of an offensive in Lorraine, would assist in making the giant German envelopment operation a full success."[14]

The younger Moltke's half-hearted planning is a classic example of a misconstrued forward defense. He was not prepared to expose the left wing and to accept the risk of temporarily leaving Alsace-Lorraine to the French. Had he done this, he would certainly have been aware of the opposition from nationalist German quarters, but especially from the Kaiser. In this respect, Schlieffen's thinking was much more consistent and not affected by ideological scruples. He went so far as to say: "If the French cross the Upper Rhine, they will meet with resistance in the Black Forest."[15] By the same token, Schlieffen also opposed the construction of a strong fortification line in the West, because he considered an advance by the French into Alsace-Lorraine even desirable.[16]

Besides, the German generals, just like the French, had opted for a wrong scenario. Both sides were caught up in a biased offensive philosophy and did not realize that the pendulum of the technique of war had in the meantime swung in favor of the defender. The troops deployed on the left wing—even had they been far fewer in number—could have bloodily repelled the French aggressors. Skillful leadership could also have lured the French into Alsace-Lorraine to be decimated by fire in the delay operation. For the French, a tactical success would have turned into an operational Pyrrhic victory. The recapture of most of Alsace-Lorraine would certainly have cost them too many lives. Now, however, the weakened aggressor would have faced a deadly danger in the rear—envelopment by the German right wing swinging in his direction.

Now Moltke had to pay for having reinforced the left wing contrary to Schlieffen's intent. The French were not only barred from falling into the trap of Lorraine; they were even expelled from the place where they would have voluntarily plunged into the abyss. Worse was to come. The now-reinforced left wing developed so much momentum of its own that it went onto the offensive. However, this thrust ground to a halt right in front of the French border fortifications.

At the operational level the tactical victory in Lorraine resulted in an about-face. The direction of the German thrust on the left wing was diametrically opposed to the planned revolving-door movement. How was the right wing supposed to prepare a Cannae in Lorraine for the French if the left wing in turn expelled them from Lorraine again? Thus, the French forces were no longer committed in the east, but were available for a counteroffensive against the German right wing, i.e., for a second strike.

The Danger of Dogmatism

Modern researchers have come to the conclusion that strictly speaking there is no Schlieffen Plan, only a memorandum. One historian states that "the memorandum may have been the basis for actual German deployment in the West; in a narrow sense, however, it did not by itself constitute a deployment or even an operations plan. This is one reason why most of Gerhard Ritter's criticism of the Schlieffen Plan is widely off the mark. On the other hand, the question arises in this connection whether Ritter is criticizing the plan itself or rather the myth surrounding it created by later epigones."[17]

This is exactly the point. Many epigones were "more Schlieffen-like than Schlieffen himself."[18] Strictly speaking, there was not just one Schlieffen Plan, but several variations. Schlieffen himself never insisted that the wide swivel movement bypassing Paris was absolutely necessary. In this connection, there is one key scene. During the last staff ride Schlieffen lead, in the summer of 1905, the "favour" version was also discussed, i.e., a French offensive into Lorraine. Schlieffen explained that in this particular situation this wide swivel movement "against Lille must not be carried out, but it would be necessary to veer sharply to the left to conduct a battle of encirclement in Lorraine."[19]

It was precisely this situation that arose in 1914. Why then did the younger Moltke not take the decision that Schlieffen would have taken? His attitude is all the more difficult to understand, as he himself had favored this solution during war games and staff rides. The Israeli military historian Jehuda Wallach practically implies that a "second Moltke" could have fought a "second Battle of Sedan."[20] The breakthrough to the south would have been achieved where his uncle had once fought this famous battle. At any rate, he missed the real chance of encircling a major section of the French Army. It would not have been a gigantic Cannae, as intended in the Schlieffen Plan of 1905, but a "Sedan in Lorraine." But in 1914, Moltke, and in fact the entire general staff, concentrated so much on the "all-embracing solution" that they could not content themselves with an early turn to the south (via Sedan).

Historians are faced with an amazing phenomenon here: an operational idea developed into a dogma to such an extent that it finally became an ideology, even an end in itself. Schlieffen's epigones paid the penalty for this envelopment mania. For Clausewitz and Moltke, the victor at Sedan, a Cannae was much more an oddity only to be achieved by a coincidence of especially favorable factors and mistakes by the enemy. Schlieffen's disciples believed that complete encirclement of the enemy should be a constant goal.

The last chance of an operational envelopment in 1914 due to the hybrid attempt to achieve a strategic envelopment can be attributed to Schlieffen's exaggerated Cannae mania. General Hans von Seeckt commented bitterly, "Cannae—no other catchword has become so disastrous for us as this one."[21]

Manstein as Creative Military Thinker and the SICKLE CUT Plan

In 1939 the German General Staff was faced with a situation similar to that in 1914. Hitler the gambler misjudged the situation when he thought he could isolate and defeat Poland in a limited war. To his surprise, France and Great Britain declared war on Germany. Thus, he had provoked the specter of World War I. Again, a shortage of raw materials meant that the German Reich was unable to endure a long war against the western naval powers. Therefore it had to attempt a *Blitzkrieg* to reach a quick military decision.

The chief of the German Army's General Staff suddenly had to submit an operations plan for the campaign against France. His deployment directive on the Case Yellow included three versions, dated 19 and 29 October 1939, as well as 30 January 1940,[22] and envisaged defeating the enemy by a more or less frontal attack in Belgium and Northern France. (*See Map 7.*) It was basically a second edition of the Schlieffen Plan. The essential difference, however, was that this time the French General Staff would be expecting it. Manstein rejected this plan, as it offered only a partial operational success, not a strategic decision. His view was based on the following estimate of the enemy situation: With skillful military leadership, the enemy could avoid a crushing defeat in Belgium. He would then succeed, as in the autumn of 1914, in establishing a strong

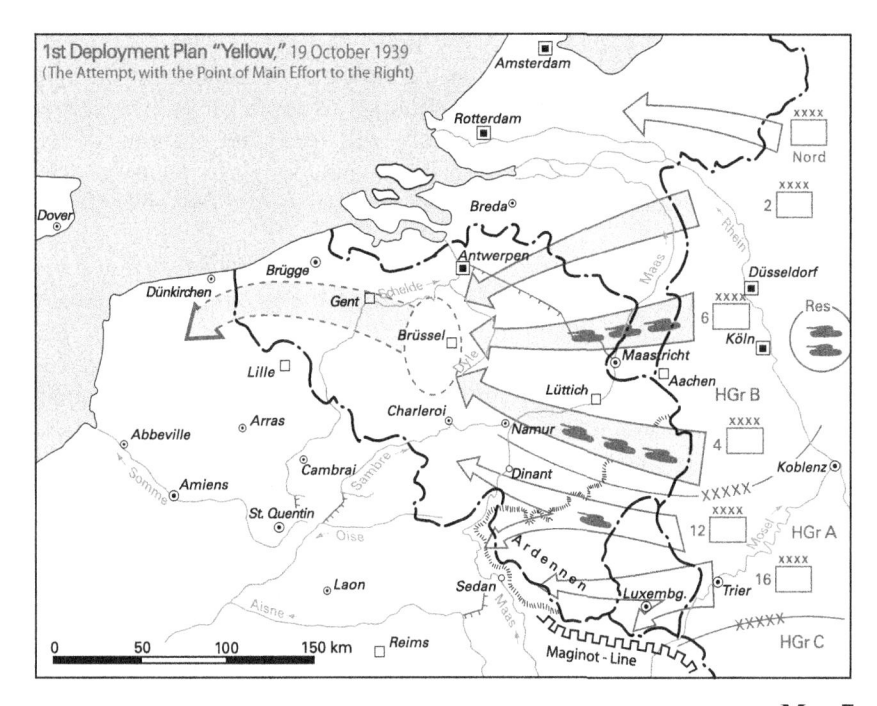

MAP 7

defensive front on the lower Somme. Besides, there was the danger of an operational counterattack into the left flank.[23]

Manstein's operational move called for the point of main effort to be shifted from Army Group B in the north to Army Group A in the south. The main thrust would have to be accelerated through the Ardennes and across the Meuse at Sedan toward the Channel coast. Thus, all the forces that the enemy might send into Belgium would not be repulsed head on but cut off behind the rear on the Somme.[24]

Furthermore, this meant that the entire operation, which was to lead to the defeat of the enemy and thus to a political decision, was to be planned in two phases and with two different points of main effort. Initially, the enemy forces deployed in Belgium and Northern France were to be cut off on the Somme and defeated there. This operation, dubbed Case Yellow, was to be followed up by a second operation, Case Red, for which it would have been necessary to veer to the south so as to crush the enemy forces still remaining behind the Somme-Sedan Line. Contrary to Schlieffen, who wanted to accomplish everything in a single operation, Clausewitz's culmination principle had thus been given due consideration.

In the meantime, the Army high command had completed an about-face and had gone over completely to Manstein's idea. The 4th Deployment Directive of the OKH (Army high command) states unequivocally: "The point of main effort of the attack to be conducted through the territory of Belgium and Luxembourg lies south of the line Liege-Charleroi. The forces committed there will force the crossing of the Meuse between Dinant and Sedan (both included) and open the way through the border defenses in Northern France toward the lower course of the Somme."[25]

Manstein simultaneously perfected and surpassed Schlieffen's operational thinking. He combined the method of envelopment proposed by Schlieffen with the method of the breakthrough rejected by the latter. Thus the sickle cut actually consisted of two partial operations: the frontal breakthrough near Sedan generated the gap for the subsequent enveloping operation toward the Channel coast. However, in this pincer movement it also became clear that there was a fundamental departure from Schlieffen's linear thinking. Schlieffen could conceive of envelopment only as the completed revolution of a wing. He wished to see entire armies swing as companies on parade. Manstein, however, had the unconventional idea of having a tank wedge penetrate deep into enemy territory without regard for exposed flanks.

This new plan constituted an operational surprise for the Allies, because the French leadership had been thinking exclusively in terms of a repetition of the Schlieffen Plan. In expecting the main German thrust through Flanders, they were being quite realistic. The Allies assumed that the Maginot Line protected their own right flank, while in the center, the Meuse and Ardennes formed a geographic double barrier. It was therefore obvious to concentrate the main force on the left. However, so as not to leave Belgium unprotected, French and British intervention troops were to advance to the so-called Dyle Line, stretching from Antwerp along the Dyle River to Namur and from there along the Belgian Meuse. When the offensive began, the main Allied forces were in the wrong place at the wrong time: To their great surprise, the Germans had concentrated seven of their ten panzer divisions where it had been least expected. They pushed through the woods of the Ardennes, a terrain allegedly unsuitable for tanks, toward the weakly defended Meuse sector near Sedan. As a result of their swivel move, the Anglo-French forces ran right into the trap of the sickle cut. The more resolutely they pushed to the north, the easier it was for the German panzer divisions to force their attack to the mouth of the Somme behind their rear. Thus we are looking at a clockwise rotation. This was, as Liddell Hart has pointed out, contrary to the rotation that had occurred in 1914 under the Schlieffen and Joffre Plans.

Liddell Hart has drawn yet another, very descriptive, comparison, and this time with a bullfight. Army Group B in the north stood for the "capa," or red cloak of the matador. It was to provoke the Allied intervention troops into racing to Belgium like an enraged bull—right into the trap. The panzer divisions concentrated in Army Group A could now thrust like the matador's sword straight into the exposed right flank.[26]

In 1940 it was a lot more difficult than in 1914 to lure the Allies into the trap. Thus, the spectacular German airborne operations in Holland and Northern Belgium (e.g., Eben-Emael) did not so much serve the tactical intention of facilitating a rapid advance by Army Group B. It was rather the operational intention to make the Allies, who were now staring northward as though hypnotized, believe that this was where the point of main effort of the attack was located. The German propaganda boasted of even the smallest success on the northern wing. The tank attack through the Ardennes Mountains and the emerging operational breakthrough near Sedan, on the other hand, were positively downplayed. On top of this, the much-feared bombers and *Stukas* were initially employed away from the actual operational point of main effort. When the Allies realized the actual scope of the German breakthrough near Sedan, it was too late. They no longer succeeded in escaping to the south, because in the meantime the German panzer divisions had forced their way to the Channel behind their rear. The trap had snapped shut.

If in 1940 the deception maneuver of the SICKLE CUT Plan worked so successfully, it was because the French were still haunted by the ghost of Schlieffen. They believed that the "dogmatic Germans"—as they saw them—would now, more than ever, attack through Flanders in accordance with the Schlieffen Plan, only this time with mechanized and motorized forces. Thus it was the irony of history that the French fell victim to the Schlieffen Plan not in 1914, but only in 1940.

Manstein's *Rochade*: The Counterstroke on the Donetz in February–March 1943

At the beginning of the Russian campaign, the German *Wehrmacht*, implementing the *Blitzkrieg* concept, succeeded in breaking through the units of the Red Army deployed far forward on the western border of the Soviet Union and crushing them in unprecedented battles of encirclement. Yet in the winter of 1941–1942 it became evident on the outskirts of Moscow that the German Eastern Army was completely exhausted, in terms of both materiel and personnel. When the first phase of the attack had reached its culmination point and when, as a result of the first counterattacks by the Red Army, there were initial signs of a setback as described by Clausewitz, there was no strategic reserve with which to overcome the crisis before Moscow.[27]

In the winter of 1942–1943, after the disaster of Stalingrad, the Red Army succeeded south of the theater of operations in going over to a

"German style" mobile war. In general, the situation had developed as follows:

- In late November 1942 the Sixth Army was encircled near Stalingrad in a pincer operation.
- In January 1943 a "Super Stalingrad" was in the offing. Two further Soviet attacks were directed at Rostov from northerly and easterly directions with the intention of cutting off all German armies positioned south of the River Don. It was just about possible to rescue the First and Fourth Panzer Armies to the north of the Don.
- Simultaneously, an unprecedented threat was developing. South of Voronezh, superior Soviet assault units had torn the front across a width of 200 miles (300 kilometers). The objective of this offensive was to thrust forward to the Dnieper bend and to seize the vital crossings near Dniepropetrovsk and Zaporozhe. This would have shut off the two most important avenues of retreat to the German armies withdrawing to the west. Now the Soviets could have attacked along the lower course of the Dnieper all the way to the Black Sea coast and the Crimea, cutting off the entire German southern wing. This could even have had a strategic impact, as the entire right flank of the German Eastern Army would have been torn open, and it could easily have led to the early collapse of the entire Eastern Front.

The Soviet plan, which was only fully revealed in the course of the operation, bears a striking resemblance to Manstein's SICKLE CUT Plan in the 1940 western campaign. Then, the German tank attack was directed at the lower course of the Somme to encircle the northern wing of the Allies on the Channel coast. In February 1943 the main Soviet thrust was directed at the lower course of the Dnieper, to sever the entire German southern wing on the Black Sea coast. Both Army Groups A and Don would have been trapped, and the possibility of a repetition of the "miracle of Dunkirk" on the Crimean peninsula was highly unlikely in view of the few German vessels on the Black Sea. Field Marshal Manstein is not only accepted as being the creator of the SICKLE CUT Plan, the most brilliant envelopment idea of the Second World War. He is also the originator of the "congenial" counterproposition: the "second strike." He implemented this operational art of countering an imminent envelopment with his counterattack from the Dnieper to the Donetz in 1943. It was Hitler himself who paradoxically turned out to be Manstein's most dangerous opponent. Hitler was still enthralled by the linear thinking of the trench warfare of the First World War and, wishing to prevent the collapse of the front, insisted on giving "hold-the-position" orders. He rejected Manstein's proposal to use the depth of the area as a "weapon" and to go over to a mobile conduct of operations. At this point, the Soviets inadvertently influenced the conflict. From 17 to 19 February Hitler had a meeting with Manstein in his headquarters near Zaporozhe. Suddenly, Soviet tanks, having broken through the German lines, drew closer to the city. Upon Hitler's departure, they were only thirty kilometers away from the airport. In view of this dramatic worsening of the situation, the supreme commander of the *Wehrmacht* agreed to make unusual concessions; he granted operational freedom to Manstein.

Unlike Hitler, the field marshal viewed the approaching Soviet tanks with the greatest of calm. He even noted their tempestuous advance with a certain satisfaction. The farther the bulk of enemy tanks advanced to the west, the deeper they would enter the trap, and the more promising the planned counterattack. In considering the situation, he was mindful of Clausewitz's principle of the culmination point. The field marshal was not going to attack until the Soviet offensive had reached its culmination. By now enemy supply lines were overstretched and their flanks exposed.

In principle, Manstein's operations plan was quite simple. It was made up of a static and a dynamic element. First he ordered the front salient to be withdrawn from the Donetz bend near Rostov to the Mius position. The Hollidt Army Task Force had to maintain that position at any cost. As a result of this shortening of the front, the First and Fourth Panzer Armies were now available for mobile operations. It was now time for the famous *Rochade*, in the process of which the Fourth Panzer Army was shifted from the right wing of the army group to its left wing. With this clever move, Manstein managed to implement an entirely new deployment of forces. He had reorganized his troops from a partly hectic retreat into a counterattack from three different directions.

Manstein's conduct of operations was facilitated by the fact that the Soviets were eccentrically fanning out their assault elements rather than concentrating their entire thrust on the main objective, the Dnieper River crossings near Dniepropetrovsk and Zaporozhe. Therefore, the field marshal decided against a classic pincer operation into the flanks. Instead, the scattering Soviet spearheads were attacked one by one and defeated with some of them wiped out after they had been enveloped. By 2 March the middle course of the Donetz River had been regained. In the immediately ensuing operation, Manstein scored a notable success by recapturing the city of Kharkov on 14 March.

Having encircled the Sixth Army on the Volga, the Soviets wanted to prepare a massive "Stalingrad" for all the German armies on the south wing. However, not only did the plan fail, the tables were turned on them. In his counterattack Manstein crushed four armies and left two more armies with heavy casualties. On this occasion, Soviet losses were considerably higher than those of the Germans at Stalingrad. The attacking Soviet soldiers believed that the German units had been beaten long ago and imagined them to be fleeing towards the Dnieper. They were all the more shocked when the latter literally turned around suddenly and confronted them with an energetic counterattack. They had run straight into the trap.

The element of surprise was decisive to this operation. As if from nowhere, out of apparent chaos, a perfectly organized battle array consisting of two panzer armies and an army detachment had suddenly formed up for a counterattack. According to Manstein the force ratio in that sector of the front was one to eight. Field Marshal Manstein thus managed to concentrate the right troops in the right place at the right time.

He explained to Hitler that he believed the strategic defensive, in conjunction with the operational counterattack, or the second strike, to be the best means of defeating the enemy who was superior in numbers. A counterstroke against a deep enemy thrust would automatically lead to a free-reeling operation. Here, the German officers could capitalize on their greatest asset, i.e. flexible command and control within the framework of *Auftragstaktik* (mission-oriented tactics).

In the summer of 1943, Hitler insisted on reverting to the strategic offensive. Unlike Manstein, he insisted on the first strike. It was the Kursk salient, which had been developed by the Soviets into an antitank fortification, that he specifically selected as the objective in Operation CITADEL.

CITADEL and SICKLE CUT Operations Compared

Operation SICKLE CUT (Case Yellow) constitutes just about the exact opposite of Operation CITADEL. Manstein's sickle cut aimed at the weakest point of the enemy front, Sedan. Operation CITADEL, however, was directed against the strongest, Kursk.

By comparison, at Sedan, the enemy antitank (AT) artillery density was 4.7; at Kursk, it was 30 guns per front kilometer.[28] The French Second Army, in whose left sector Sedan was situated, had a total of only 16,000 AT mines.[29] At the Kursk salient, however, the average for each front kilometer in the most important sectors is said to have been 1,500 AT and 1,700 antipersonnel (AP) mines.[30] The Allies never reckoned with a major German attack on Sedan. The offensive against the Kursk salient, however, hit exactly the front sector where the Soviets were expecting it. Furthermore, their intelligence had found out the precise time at which the attack was scheduled to be launched. Not only was the operational element of surprise missing, but also the tactical one. The German attack in the vicinity of Kursk resulted in a head-on collision with the numerically superior Soviet tank and antitank arm. In this offensive, as ordered by Hitler, it was decided against outmaneuvering the enemy with a far-flung operational move (like the sickle cut); attempts were to be made instead to win the battle at a tactical level. This "mobile battle of attrition" at Kursk became the "Verdun" of the German panzer arm.

It is interesting in this context that Manstein, prior to the offensive against Kursk, temporarily entertained quite an unconventional idea: He suggested cutting off the Kursk salient not in a double-pincer move from the north and the south, but instead attacking where the Soviets least expected it—head-on from the west. After the relatively easy breakthrough, deployment to the left and right would have been possible so as to push the Soviets into their own minefields. This would have resulted in an eccentric enveloping movement rather than a "classic" concentric pincer move. Hitler also pursued this idea. However, after he had postponed the start of the offensive several times, it now seemed impossible, for reasons of time, to completely regroup the units.[31]

Having chosen the line of least resistance for the breakthrough at Sedan in 1940, the Germans were now following the line of the greatest possible resistance. However, tactics was not the only deciding factor in the failure of the German offensive. The Red Army command, in anticipation of a German breakthrough, had kept available in the depth of the area mobile reserves to carry out a second-strike against the already-exhausted enemy forces.

Kursk stood for the strategic turning point in the German-Soviet war. The *Wehrmacht* lost the initiative once and for all. This also foiled the "draw" peace Manstein had sought. It transpired that the successful handling of individual military catastrophes only served to put off the final catastrophe while sustaining huge losses. Following Clausewitz, a call to end the war should have been made at that point, when there was nothing more to gain and everything to lose.

Clausewitz: The Neglected Philosopher and the Schlieffen Plan

By 1914 German foreign policy was in such a confused state that the politicians could no longer find an excuse. Schlieffen wanted to cut this Gordian knot with the sword. His military concept was meant to replace a political solution. That way, however, he had put a lot of pressure on himself in terms of the need for a move in the operational field. The Schlieffen Plan must, therefore, not be seen as an operations plan, but rather as a campaign plan. But therein lays the conceit of Schlieffen, the operational artisan. He extended Hannibal's envelopment maneuver on the battlefield of Cannae to the entire theater of war, and with a single swinging movement, he wanted to decide a war that was to become a world war. There was a very real danger of overtraining while carrying out this Herculean operation. After all, everything was to be done "in one fell swoop," in one single "battle of annihilation." The battle of Cannae should have served as a warning to him, because it also did not produce a strategic decision. In fact, the winners of Cannae were to become the losers of the Second Punic War.

Why then could such brilliant military minds as constituting the German General Staff expose themselves to such a risky, megalomaniac idea as the Schlieffen Plan? The answer lies in the military-political vicious circle that Schlieffen had conjured. The Schlieffen Plan stipulated that in the West everything had to be achieved at the same time and as soon as possible, that is, under extreme pressure. This pressure may be attributed to political constraints. These political constraints may, however, be attributed to the Schlieffen Plan. It was at this point that the vicious circle closed in around Schlieffen, who had now become entangled in his own thinking.

In 1914 an opportunity presented itself for a Cannae in the west. The German Army was considered the strongest land power in the world. The German General Staff was thoroughly drilled for envelopment maneuvers, and the French Army granted the Germans the often-quoted favor of an offensive by falling into the Lorraine trap. But Schlieffen's successors were so dazzled by a grand, absolute solution of a perfect Cannae that they completely overlooked the small solution of a Cannae in Lorraine. The First World War could have gotten off to a great start with a double "Tannenberg." In the east, a Cannae was achieved at Tannenberg because the Germans concentrated on the encirclement of a single Russian army. In the West, the entire French Army was to be enveloped all at once. At this point we can only quote Clausewitz: "the man who sacrifices the possible in search of the impossible is a fool."[32]

The Sickle Cut Plan

The fatal development that had triggered a crisis in the First World War stood in remarkable contrast to the development that was to lead to a disaster in the Second World War. This time it was exactly the other way around. In 1914 the generals had tied the hands of the politicians with a rigid operations plan. In 1940 Hitler, the politician, tied the hands of his generals in the implementation of the operations plan.

Hitler's order to halt before Dunkirk enabled the evacuation of the BEF. This way, he reduced the strategic success sought by Manstein to an operational one. He nevertheless allowed himself to be celebrated after the campaign in the West as the "greatest commander of all time." During the campaign in the East, Hitler's intervention in the course of operations was becoming an obsession, and in the end he wasted his time on the minutest tactical details. This was a violation of the Clausewitz doctrine, according to which war has no logic of its own, but it does have a grammar of its own. Hitler, the dilettante, was not familiar enough with this grammar. This was to have disastrous consequences when he shackled the art of operational command and control of his generals.

The political conceit of the German military technocrats in the First World War was followed by the military-technological conceit of Hitler the politician in World War II. Thus it was that in both world wars, the military and the political leaders of the German Reich got in the way of each other. In view of this situation, it seems like an irony of history that it was this very Germany that produced a man like Clausewitz.

Notes

1. This essay is adapted from a piece the author previously published: *Development, Planning and Realization of Operational Conceptions in World Wars I and II* (Freiburg, Germany: Military Historical Research Office, 1989), pp. 7–44. With minor revisions, it is reprinted herein by permission of the author and the Militärgeschichtliches Forschungsamt [Military Historical Research Office] of the Federal Republic of Germany. Additional contributions to this text were provided by Lt. Col. Karl-Heinz Frieser.
2. See Rudolf Stadelmann, *Scharnhorst: Schicksal und Geistige Welt* (Wiesbaden: Limes Verlag, 1952), pp. 164, 159; Berhard R. Kroener, "Vom 'extraordinari Kriegsvolk' zum 'miles perpetus': Zur Rolle der bewaffneten Macht in der europäischen Gesellschaft der Frühen Neuzeit," *Militärgeschichtlichen Mitteilungen*, 1/88, p. 141.
3. Carl von Clausewitz, *On War*, ed. and trans. Michael Howard and Peter Paret (Princeton: Princeton University Press, 1976), p. 154.
4. Gerhard Ritter, *Der Schlieffen Plan: Kritik eines Mythos* (Munich, 1956), p. 95.
5. Quote from Jeduda L. Wallach, *Das Dogma der Vernichtungsschlacht* (Frankfurt: Bernard H. Graefe, 1967), p. 64.
6. Alfred Graf von Schlieffen, *Cannae* (Berlin: E. S. Mittler und Sohn, 1925), p. 263.
7. Ibid., p. 3.
8. Clausewitz, *On War*, p. 528.
9. Ritter, *Der Schlieffen Plan*, p. 62.
10. William L. Shirer, *Der Zusammenbruch Frankreichs: Aufstieg und Fall der Dritten Republik* (Munich, 1970), p. 123.
11. Wallach, *Das Dogma*, pp. 160, 162.
12. Alistair Horne, *Über die Maas, über Schelde und Rhein: Frankreichs Niederlage 1940* (Vienna, Munich, Zurich, 1969), p. 136.
13. Schlieffen, *Cannae*, p. 262.
14. Erich von Manstein, *Verlorene Siege* (Bonn, Germany: Athenäum Verlag, 1955), p. 96ff.
15. Wallach, *Das Dogma*, p. 135.
16. Ritter, *Der Schlieffen Plan*, pp. 19, 38.
17. Heinz Ludger Borgert, "Grundzüge der Landkriegführung von Schlieffen bis Guderian," in *Handbuch zur deutschen Militärgeschichte 1848–1939*, (Munich, 1979), 5: 455.
18. Wallach, *Das Dogma*, p. 306.
19. Ritter, *Der Schlieffen Plan*, p. 56.
20. Wallach, *Das Dogma*, p. 145.
21. Hans von Seeckt, *Gedanken eines Soldaten* (Berlin: Verlag für kulturpolitik, 1928), p. 17.
22. Hans-Adolf Jacobsen, ed., *Dokumente zur Vorgeschichte des Westfeldzuges 1939–1940* (Göttingen, Germany: Musterschmidt Verlag, 1956), *Studien und Dokumente zur Geschichte des Zweiten Weltkrieges*, vol. 2a, pp. 41–46, 46–51, 59–63.
23. Hans-Adolf Jacobsen, *Der Fall Gelb: Der Kampf um den Deutschen Operationsplan zur Westoffensive 1940* (Wiesbaden: F. Steiner, 1957), p. 68.
24. Jacobsen, *Dokumente zur Vorgeschicte*, pp. 155ff.
25. Ibid., p. 64.

26. Basil H. Liddell Hart, *The Other Side of the Hill* (London: Cassell, 1948), pp. 123, 130.

27. On Manstein's *Rochade*, see Paul Carell, *Verbrannte Erde: Schlacht zwischen Wolga und Weichsel* (Frankfurt/Vienna, 1976), p. 158ff; *Geschichte des Grossen Vaterländischen Krieges, Vol. 3: Der grundlegende Umschwung im Verlauf des Grossen Vaterländischen Krieges* (East Berlin, 1964), p. 133ff; Othmar Hackl, "Operative Führungsprobleme der Heeresgruppe Don bzw ... Süd bei den Verteidigungsoperationen zwischen Donez und Dnepr im Februar und März 1942," in *Truppenpraxis* 3 (1982): 191–200, 4 (1982): 268–74; "Das Schlagen aus der Nachhand: Die Operationen der Heersgruppe Don bzw ... Süd zwischen Donez und Dnepr 1943," in *Truppendienst* 2 (1983): 132–37; Erich von Manstein, *Verlorene Siege* (Bonn: Athenäum Verlag, 1952), p. 397ff; Friedrich Wilhelm von Mellenthin, *Panzerschlachten: Eine Studie über den Einsatz von Panzerverbänden im Zweiten Weltkrieg* (Neckargemund: K. Vowinckel, 1963), p. 131ff; Walther Nehring, *Die Geschichte der deutschen Panzerwaffe 1916–1945* (Berlin: Propyläen Verlag, 1969), p. 283ff; Eberhard Schwarz, *Die Stabilisierung der Ostfront nach Stalingrad* (Göttingen: Muster-Schmidt, 1985), p. 44ff; Dieter Ose, ed., *Art of War Symposium at the Federal Armed Forces Command and General Staff College* (9 September 1986): *Ausbildung im operativen Denken unter Heranziehung von Kriegserfahrungen, dargestellt an Mansteins Gegenangriff im Frühjahr 1943* (Bonn, 1987).

28. Robert A. Doughty, "French Antitank Doctrine: The Antidote That Failed," *Military Review* 56, no. 5 (May 1976): 36–48.

29. Ibid., p. 46.

30. Ernst Klink, *Das Gesetz des Handelns: Die Operation "Zitadelle" 1943, Beiträge zur Militär-Kriegsgechichte* (Stuttgart, 1966), 7: 299.

31. Paul Carell, *Verbrannte Erde*, p. 83, writes that Manstein had this idea. According to the War Diary of Army Group South (Bundesarchiv-Militärarchiv, RH 19 VI/45), on 20 April 1943, Zeitzler reported to the Chief of the General Staff of Army Group South that Hitler was considering this "notion"; on 2 June 1943, the two men again discussed it briefly. They both "agreed to reject this operation for the reasons established previously."

32. Clausewitz, *On War*, p. 637.

Panzer Group Kleist and the Breakthrough in France, 1940[1]

Karl-Heinz Frieser

> [On 15 May 1940] I was woken up with the news that [the French Prime Minister] Reynaud was on the telephone. He spoke in English, and evidently under stress: "We have been defeated." As I did not immediately respond he said again: "We are beaten; we have lost the battle." I said: "Surely it can't have happened so soon." But he replied: "The front is broken near Sedan; they are pouring through in great numbers with tanks and armored cars."[2]
>
> —Winston Churchill

In the preceding World War, the Germans had tried in vain for four years to break through the French front. In May 1940 they succeeded after only four days. Panzer Group Kleist achieved the decisive breakthrough near Sedan. Its role in Operation S*ICHELSCHNITT* (S*ICKLE* C*UT*) can be illustrated with the famous bullfight simile coined by Liddell Hart.[3] He proposed that Army Group B in the north represented the matador's red cloak that was intended to provoke the Allied expeditionary troops to rush into Belgium like a raging bull—right into the trap. Army Group A would strike the unprotected flank like a sword, the point of which was Panzer Group Kleist.

Operational Planning

Panzer Group Kleist represented a novelty in military history. For the first time tanks were employed in an operational manner. Whereas in the Polish campaign tanks normally fought in a divisional framework—on a tactical level—here in France, five armored divisions were now combined into an operationally independent Panzer group. General Ewald von Kleist had to coordinate the attack of two panzer corps, supported by a motorized infantry corps. He commanded 1,200 battle tanks, which represented about half the German tank forces.[4]

The mission of Kleist's panzer group was to "thrust through Luxembourg and southern Belgium [and to] gain the western bank of the Meuse River in a surprise attack." During this operation, Panzer Corps Reinhardt was to operate in the area of Monthermé and Guderian's panzer corps in the Sedan region. The right, or northern, flank was to be covered by the Panzer Corps Hoth, attached to Fourth Army.[5]

Speed and surprise were of decisive importance for the success of the operation. First, from the tactical perspective the panzer divisions would have to cross the Meuse River in a coup de main before the enemy could move his reserves to the river. Second, from the operational perspective, Panzer Group Kleist had to reach the rear of the enemy's northern flank before the Allies saw through this deceptive maneuver. Otherwise, they might be able to withdraw their expeditionary force, which was now pouring to the northeast from the "Belgian trap." However, according to the German operational concept, if a fast armored thrust successfully reached the Channel coast, all enemy forces north of the Somme River would be caught in a huge encirclement. Third, the Germans needed a quick decision—in the sense of the Schlieffen concept from a political-strategic standpoint. Similar to World War I, the Germans could not cope successfully with a protracted war against the Western Allies and their sea power, which gave them virtually inexhaustible raw material resources. The *Blitzkrieg* was a race against time because time worked against the *Wehrmacht* on the tactical, operational, and strategic levels. This plan, devised by General Erich von Manstein, was initially turned down by the German General Staff as too risky.

The time factor already had been taken into consideration with respect to the organizational structure of Army Group A. It consisted of two components: The *Schnelle Truppen*, or fast troops, were key armored and motorized divisions that would cross the Meuse River in a swift coup de main; the infantry armies, the second component, would trail behind on foot.

The Conduct of Operations

Logistical Considerations

The chief of staff of Panzer Group Kleist stated prior to the start of the campaign, "If the success of an operation has ever depended on logistics, it is our operation."[6] The course of the *Blitzkrieg* was so fast-paced that mistakes made in the preparatory phase—especially in logistics—could hardly be corrected later. To ensure logistical success, the Panzer group was to carry most of its supplies. Three motor transport detachments, with a total capacity of 4,800 tons, were attached to the group to reinforce its organic logistic elements. Establishment of large fuel storage sites close to the border was also a key logistical consideration. Using an elaborate system of refueling by jerry cans, all vehicles carried their full loads of fuel when they crossed the border. As stated in the logistical after-action report, not a single crisis in logistics occurred between 10 May and the seizure of Calais that could not be handled with the resources of Kleist's group.[7]

The Advance through the Ardennes (10–12 May)

Panzer Group Kleist had more than 41,000 vehicles. If all attached and organic units were strung out in column, it would stretch for 1,000 miles, or about the distance from Washington, D.C., to New Orleans. To traverse the Ardennes Mountains, this huge armada of vehicles had been granted only four march routes. This showed that several German general officers had no understanding of the Manstein and Guderian operational concepts. Perhaps they may even have rejected these concepts outright.

General Kleist planned for the employment of two corps abreast: Panzer Corps Reinhardt on the right, toward Monthermé, and Panzer Corps Guderian on the left, toward Sedan, with the Motorized Corps Wietersheim behind both. The commander of Army Group A, however, insisted on placing the three corps in echelon behind each other, with Guderian's panzer corps' forming the first echelon. Left unanswered was how Panzer Corps Reinhardt should reach Monthermé on time if Guderian's convoys blocked the two northern march routes. This seemingly wrong decision of the army group command caused traffic chaos in the Ardennes.

To illustrate, by noon of 10 May Panzer Corps Guderian had already penetrated Belgian territory while the main body of General Reinhardt's force was still east of the Rhine River. The Wietersheim Motorized Infantry Corps had not even left its assembly area near Marburg and Giessen. This development became even more dramatic on 11 May. General Kleist ordered the northern march route to be cleared for Reinhardt's panzer corps. But the 2d Panzer Division jammed the woods of the Ardennes. In the evening Guderian's 1st Panzer Division reached Bouillon, near the French border. General Reinhardt's tanks, however, were still standing on German soil near the Luxembourg border.

On 12 May Guderian's 1st and 10th Panzer Divisions pressed into the east-bank parts of Sedan. On the northern march route, however, chaotic traffic conditions evolved. From the right, contrary to orders, elements of the III Army Corps wedged amidst the 2d Panzer Division and stalled in the Ardennes. Nevertheless, the advance detachment of Reinhardt's 6th Panzer Division successfully progressed through this mess to the French border near Monthermé. The convoys congesting the narrow Ardennes roads eventually extended all the way from the Rhine River to the Meuse River—170 miles—and would have been a sitting duck for any enemy air forces.[8]

The Breakthrough at the Meuse Line

The Sedan sector presumably formed the weakest point of the French front line.[9] But General Huntziger, commander-in-chief of the French

Second Army, thought a major German offensive on Sedan unlikely. He also believed he had enough time to deploy reserves in case of a German attack in this area. He had calculated that the Germans needed at least five days to cross the Ardennes. Undoubtedly he was still completely absorbed in the World War I operational tempo, and he reckoned with at least seven days for the preparations of the Meuse River crossing.[10] In reality, Panzer Corps Guderian reached the Meuse River after just three days and conducted an immediate surprise attack on the fourth day.

The main problem was fire support. Guderian had only about 150 artillery pieces, with several batteries arriving belatedly from the Ardennes congestion. On the other side of the Meuse River, however, the French X Corps had some 350 pieces. Thus, everything depended on the German air force, the "vertical artillery" of the *Blitzkrieg*.

On 13 May Panzer Group Kleist was supported by almost 1,500 aircraft, the bulk concentrated in the Sedan sector.[11] The employment of bombers and dive-bombers in rolling waves lasted the whole day and was intensified into a massive aerial attack shortly before the crossing. This massive aerial attack was the largest in military history at that time.[12]

The attack across the Meuse River began at 1600 hours. By 2000 hours the main line of resistance was penetrated. This breakthrough occurred at a place that had attained importance once before in Franco-German history. The Emperor Napoleon III surrendered to King William of Prussia at the Château Bellevue on 2 September 1870. Now, about 2300 hours, Hill 301 was taken. It was the very hill from which General Moltke had commanded the first battle of Sedan decades before. In the meantime the resistance of the French defenders had collapsed like a broken dam. The reason for this was not so much the violence of German arms but a dramatic development that is recorded in the history books as "the panic of Bulson." About 1900 hours a report by an artillery observer was passed on incorrectly. Suddenly, there was a rumor that German tanks had already reached Bulson. This rumor spread like a grass fire, and eventually the French 55th Infantry Division had dissolved into a wave of personnel who took flight. On the next day the division had ceased to exist. When a parliamentary commission later tried to investigate this panic, some soldiers declared they had seen the attacking German tanks with their own eyes. German war diaries, however, say that the first German tank crossed the Meuse River twelve hours later. This mass delusion was therefore called a *"phénomène d'hallucination collective."*

At Sedan, one of the strangest tank victories in history occurred. It repeatedly happened that tanks caused the enemy to take to flight without having fired a shot—simply by their physical presence. Here, however, they drove the enemy to seek refuge without even appearing. But in reality, it was not only the tanks but also the aircraft, above all the Stuka dive-bombers, which caused this mass panic. The apparently endless "rolling operation" of the air force, aimed at the nerves of the defenders, was one of the greatest tactical surprises of the war. British and French sources say that the surprise effect was even greater than that of the first employment of tanks or the first gas attacks of World War I.[13]

On the morning of 14 May the first tank crossed the pontoon bridge at Gaulier. By afternoon about 570 tanks had been moved to the other bank of the Meuse River. This did not go unnoticed by the Allies, whose air forces conducted desperate though unsuccessful attacks to destroy the pontoon bridge. During the so-called air battle of Sedan, almost 100 of about 400 Allied bombers and fighters were shot down. Before the Allied air attacks, General Guderian had ordered the deployment of 303 air defense guns around the crossing site. They wrought havoc upon the Allied air fleets. Decisive for the disaster was also the fact that the Allied aircraft were split up into twenty-seven piecemeal attacks of mostly no more than 10–20 aircraft. The Allies did not succeed in concentrating several formations for a massive strike.[14]

At 1230 hours the 1st Panzer Division crossed the Ardennes Canal at Chémery. General Guderian now faced a most difficult dilemma: Follow tactical necessity and strengthen the bridgehead to the south, or exploit the enemy's confusion and drive west toward the Channel coast with the bulk of his corps? Guderian decided in favor of the overall operational mission. Accordingly, he ordered the 1st and 2d Panzer Divisions to attack to the west with all available forces and proceed with utmost speed. Yet, until the arrival of the Motorized Corps Wietersheim, protection of the bridgehead for twenty-four hours depended solely on the 10th Panzer Division, supported by Infantry Regiment Grossdeutschland. Guderian thought he could take the risk because of the "slow and doctrinal" operational approach of the French leaders.[15]

French countermeasures were conducted without coordination and only by division-size forces. Only at Sedan was an operational counterattack attempted by the Group Flavigny. This group consisted of the 3d Armored, 3d Motorized Infantry, and 5th Light Cavalry Divisions. The counterstroke should have started in the morning of 14 May, when the 3d Armored Division reached the southern edge of the Bois du Mont Dieu. But instead of immediately attacking the weak bridgehead, the division wasted ten critical hours on servicing equipment in an assembly area. After those critical hours passed, General Flavigny reevaluated his decision to attack. He was worried by numerous alarming reports and decided on defense instead of attack. Accordingly, he distributed his tanks along a frontage of twelve miles, where he sealed all roads and bottlenecks with so-called corks. Each cork consisted of one heavy and two light tanks. When the attack was to be resumed the following morning, it became evident that it had been much easier to disperse the tanks than to concentrate them again. Besides, it was not possible to recapture the key terrain that centered on the village of Stonne. General Flavigny finally canceled his order to attack. Thus, the only operational-level counteroffensive ended before it had really started.[16]

The British General Fuller made an interesting comparison. He called Operation SICKLE CUT the Second Battle of Sedan.[17] The more famous battle of Sedan, the "Cannae of the nineteenth century," had been fought in 1870 during the Franco-Prussian War. It is indeed possible to draw a direct line of comparison from General Moltke's double envelopment of 1870 to General Manstein's single envelopment of 1940. In 1870 the linkup point of the two German armies that conducted the pincer move had been at Illy, only six miles away from Moltke's 1870 observation post. The 1940 operation was a giant outflanking movement over about 250 miles. It extended in the shape of a sickle from the Luxembourg border to the Channel coast. While in 1870 a French army of 120,000 was successfully encircled at Sedan, this time almost 1.7 million Allied soldiers were caught in the SICKLE CUT trap. The entire northern flank, where the Allies had deployed their best divisions, had been amputated. In the destruction of these Allied forces—to quote General Franz Halder—Army Group B in the north represented the anvil and Army Group A in the south was the swinging sledgehammer. French and British military historians largely agree that the defeat of France was basically inevitable after the breakthrough at Sedan. This was the time it became apparent that the Allied troops had been operationally outmaneuvered because of their ill-advised deployment.[18]

Panzer Corps Reinhardt at Monthermé (13–15 May)

On 13 May at 1600 hours—simultaneous with the operation at Sedan—the air force shifted its attacks at Monthermé into depth. What followed now was not the all-out offensive of a Panzer Corps, but the coup de main of an infantry battalion task force. The main body of Panzer Corps Reinhardt was still stalled in the Ardennes because of the miscalculated deployment planning and the chaotic traffic jam that resulted. Nevertheless, a bridgehead was established on the western bank with the first crossing attempt. On 15 May the 6th Panzer Division broke through the main resistance line and advanced within a few hours into Montcornet, about thirty-five miles away. Thus, the operational miscalculation of the army group was compensated by the tactical flexibility of the intermediate and lower echelons of command. As was to become evident later, this advance forced the French leaders to split up the counterattack of their operational reserves.[19]

The Thrust through the Depth of France to the Channel Coast (15–21 May)

The first phase of this operation had been completed in almost textbook fashion. So much so that the operations officer of the 1st Panzer Division adopted almost verbatim the exercise order he had elaborated on 21 March for a map exercise of Panzer Corps Guderian at Koblenz, which was used as a rehearsal for the operation.[20] Now, after the panzer corps crossed the Meuse River, it became evident that no clear operational concept existed for the further employment of tanks. Most of the German generals from the start had seriously doubted that the crossing of the Meuse River at Sedan by a panzer corps attacking from the move stood any chance of success at all.

What follows will necessarily be illustrated by showing two battles—the one at the front, and the rear battle within the German leadership. This conflict between the "progressives" and the "traditionalists" was argued primarily in Panzer Group Kleist.[21]

This *Blitzkrieg* showed that the German panzer divisions had become too fast not only for the French, but also for the German operational commander. On the morning of 17 May near Montcornet, General Guderian was relieved of his command. After intense lobbying, he was reinstituted a few hours later. He had been charged with continuing his westward advance beyond an expressly ordered halt line. The fact was simply that Guderian had been advancing so fast that this halt order failed to reach him in time. However, it is true that Guderian continually disregarded General Kleist's orders. Guderian was convinced he could better judge the military situation leading from the front.[22]

At the same time, another German Panzer commander, General Erwin Rommel, conducted a thrust on his own account, which earned his division the French nickname "*la division fantôme*"—the phantom division. The mission of his 7th Panzer Division, part of Hoth's panzer corps, was to cover the right flank of Panzer Group Kleist. But Rommel attacked so vigorously that he was usually far ahead of his neighbors. For example, on the evening of 16 May his first tanks stood at the French-Belgian border. On the other side lay the fortifications of the so-called "extended Maginot Line." Faced with this situation, Rommel did something typical of him. He opted not for a deliberate, but for a hasty attack. The French defenders were absolutely taken by surprise, and this hasty attack resulted in a successful breakthrough.

Another episode is a textbook example of the German system of *Auftragstaktik*, mission-oriented tactics. During the very moment of the hasty attack and breakthrough, Rommel's radio communications with higher headquarters—Hoth's panzer corps—had broken down. There simply were no orders as to how things should proceed, because none of

Rommel's superiors had foreseen such a spectacular success. Traditionally, waiting for orders would have given the enemy the opportunity to consolidate a new defensive line. However, General Rommel decided to exploit the enemy's confusion and press ahead with full momentum to ensure continued success. He was lucky, because the French 5th Infantry Division (Motorized) had set up its overnight bivouac on the road to Avesnes, leaving its vehicles neatly lined up along the roadsides. At this stage, Rommel's tanks dashed right through them, firing to both sides with all guns. Within minutes the 5th Infantry Division (Motorized) disintegrated into a wave of refugees; they had been overrun literally in their sleep. But Rommel's pace did not even slow that night. When he had reached Avesnes, he continued the assault pace by a sprint via Landrecies to Le Cateau. (*See Map 8.*) There, he stopped because of both ammunition and fuel shortages.

The success of this nighttime armored attack—contravening all doctrine and orders—was overwhelming. That night the French II Army Corps was shattered and disintegrated so that on 17 May, Rommel's soldiers could take approximately 10,000 prisoners. Their own losses, on the other hand, amounted to fewer than thirty-six men.[23]

At dawn Rommel was himself surprised when he suddenly discovered that only his vanguard had followed his tempestuous surge. This force comprised only an armored regiment, reinforced by the motorcycle battalion and a reconnaissance battalion. The division's main body, including the two rifle regiments, was still resting—literally—on Belgian soil. Radio contact had been interrupted, and nobody knew where General Rommel was located.

Thus, the 7th Panzer Division became a "phantom division," not only for the French enemy, but also for the German general staff! That night Rommel and his tanks had vanished without a trace, making the Army high command extremely nervous. Even Hitler had one of his proverbial sleepless nights. But it was impossible to court-martial such a successful general. Instead Rommel was awarded the Knight's Cross to the Iron Cross.[24]

Only a few generals, like Rommel, had quickly grasped the welcome possibilities offered by the new tank arm, provided it was employed with determination. To the contrary, many German generals regarded the tremendous successes of the panzer divisions with ever-increasing wariness; instead of being invigorated by the success, it seemed to paralyze them.[25]

During this phase, when the success of Operation SICKLE CUT was becoming increasingly evident, Hitler changed his opinion dramatically. General Halder, for example, noted this change in his diary entry of 17 May: "A rather unpleasant day. The Führer is extremely nervous. He is afraid of his own success, does not want to risk anything and therefore wants to stop us. The pretense is concern about the left flank!" On the

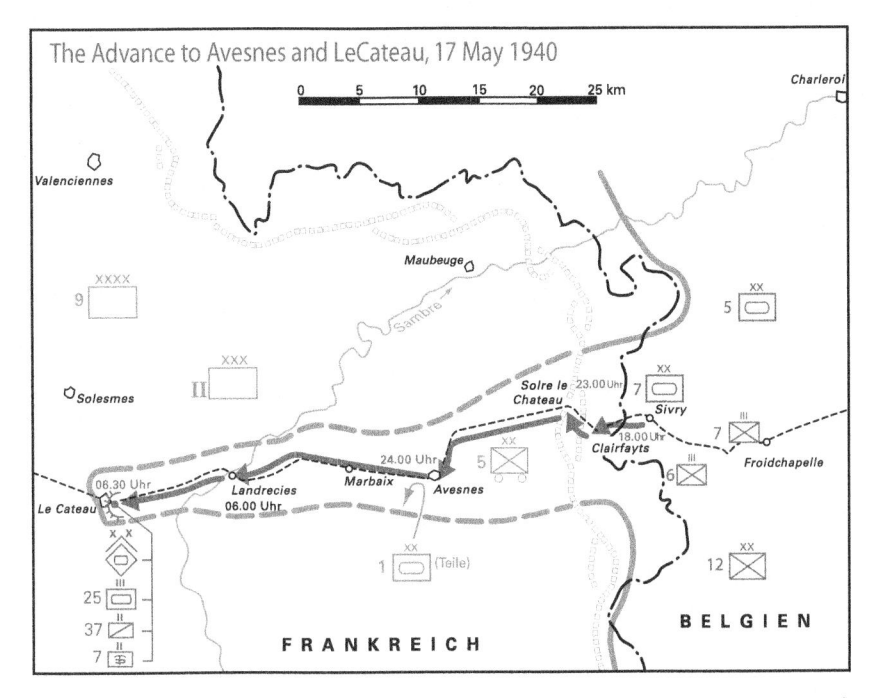

Map 8. The Advance to Avesnes and LeCateau, 17 May 1940

same subject, Halder wrote on 18 May: "The Führer has unreasonable fears for the southern flank. He rages and shouts that we are about to spoil the whole operation and to evoke the risk of defeat."[26]

But the threat to the southern flank—which mesmerized Hitler—did not exist. This is demonstrated even by Winston Churchill's memoir account. Alarmed by the German armored breakthrough at Sedan, on 16 May the Prime Minister flew to Paris, where the French commander in chief, General Gamelin, briefed him on the gloomy situation. Churchill then asked where the French operational reserves were located. In French, he asked: "*Où est la masse de manoeuvre?*" General Gamelin's answer was shattering: only one word, "*Aucune*"—there was none.[27] In fact, the core of the French operational reserves had been formed by four armored divisions whose operations developed into a sequence of escalating tragedies. The 1st Armored Division found itself caught in an encounter with Panzer Corps Hoth just when the heavy tanks had run out of fuel and were about to refill in an assembly area. The 2d Armored Division was on the way to the front, its tanks still partly loaded on trains, when Panzer Corps Reinhardt thrust right into the concentration area. The 3d Armored Division was, as discussed before, cheated out of its chance to counterattack at Sedan by the incompetence of its own commanders. And last, the 4th Armored Division was still in the process of being formed. Nevertheless its commander, Colonel de Gaulle, conducted the first and only resolute armor attack at Montcornet on 17 May. The German Air Force reacted quickly and sealed this flank attack with its dive-bombers. So much for the operational reserve.

The employment of the German *Luftwaffe* can be divided into three phases. For the first three days, the *Luftwaffe* had primarily a counterair or air superiority mission. In the second phase, on 13 and 14 May—during the breakthrough at the Meuse line—the main effort was changed to close air support of the ground forces. In the third phase—the thrust toward the Channel coast—the major task was to seal off the left flank by interdiction.

On 20 May Panzer Corps Guderian reached Abbeville at the mouth of the Somme. However, the tanks had surged so far west that a gap between them and the trailing infantry divisions had opened. The Allies then decided on a pincer attack into the only 25-mile-wide corridor of Arras, to "chop off the head of the German tortoise,"[28] quoting Winston Churchill. (*Map 9*) But the French Army was unable to mass sufficient forces quickly enough at the southern flank of the corridor to counterattack. Thus, on 21 May the British had to attack single-handed from the northern areas near Arras. This attack came to a halt after only a few miles in front of Rommel's 7th Panzer Division.[29] That same day Guderian's Panzer Corps reached the Channel coast and cut off the Allied troops in the north from their rear area. Thus ended the first phase of the SICKLE-CUT Plan.

Summary

Three conclusions may be drawn from this brief study. First, one of the fundamental causes of the Allied defeat was that their commanders could react to the operational challenge of the German tanks only on a tactical level. They were unable to concentrate their tank force, even though it was superior in quantity and quality, for an operational counterattack.

Second, this was the first instance of employment of tanks on an operational level, which was analogous to a leap in the dark. It was the first performance in military history without prior rehearsal. Exercises that could have served to test the new concept were out of the question simply for security reasons. But all deficiencies were more than compensated by the effect of surprise.

Third, the German surge of armored forces to the Channel coast led both to a climax of operational freedom of action and to its reversal when Hitler began to interfere increasingly with the control of military operations. The pace of operations in the *Blitzkrieg* was so rapid that the German panzer divisions not only outran the Allied commanders but even their own leaders. That proved the value of the principle of *Auftragstaktik*,

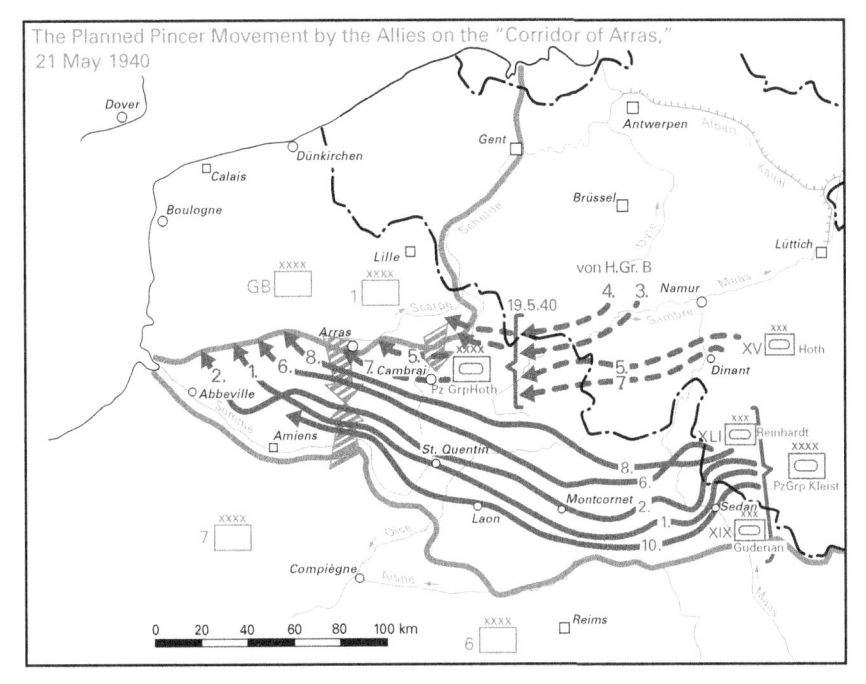

MAP 9

mission-oriented tactics. Determined leaders like Guderian or Rommel did not hesitate to take the initiative. They could, while leading from forward positions, react instantly to any enemy weakness. Then Adolf Hitler interfered. In view of the breathtaking speed of the operation, he finally lost his nerve and pulled the emergency brake. His most disastrous halt order was that of Dunkirk. With it he downgraded the strategic success that General Manstein had envisaged, to merely operational success.

Thus, going back to Schlieffen, no Cannae occurred in 1940. But even the capture of all 340,000 Allied soldiers who escaped from Dunkirk would not have meant the end of the war. Schlieffen and his successors were so thoroughly mesmerized by the envelopment at Cannae that they completely forgot that Hannibal had succeeded only on an operational level against the Roman power. The winners of Cannae were the losers of the Second Punic War. Similarly, the winners of the *Blitzkrieg* of 1940 at the operational level were to become the losers of World War II.

Notes

1. This article was published originally under the title, "The Execution of 'Case Yellow' ('Sickle Cut') Exemplified by Panzer Group Kleist (10–21 May 1940)," in *Operational Thinking in Clausewitz, Moltke, Schlieffen and Manstein*, ed. Roland G. Foerster (Freiburg, Germany: Das Amt, 1988), pp. 57–82. It is reprinted, with minor revisions, by permission of the author and the *Militärgeschichtliches Forschungsamt* [Military Historical Research Office] of the Federal Republic of Germany.
2. Quote from Alistair Horne, *To Lose a Battle: France 1940* (London, 1969), p. 333.
3. Basil H. Liddell Hart, *The Other Side of the Hill* (London: Cassell, 1948), pp. 123, 130.
4. Kurt Zeitzler, "Die Panzergruppe Kleist im Westfeldzug 1940," *Wehrkunde* 4 (1959):182–83.
5. Heeresgruppenbefehl Nr. 5, pp. 2–3, Anlagenheft zum KTB der Gruppe von Kleist, Bundesarchiv-Militärarchiv Freiburg (hereafter BA-MA, RH 21–1/19).
6. Johann Adolf Graf Kielmansegg, *Panzer zwischen Warschau und Atlantik* (Berlin, 1941), p. 161.
7. Erfahrungsbericht über die Versorgung der Gruppe von Kleist im Feldzug gegen Frankreich, BA-MA, RH 21–1/320, p. 3.
8. Gen. Kdo. XXII. A.K. (Gruppe v. Kleist), KTB (Abschrift), 10.5.–11.7.1940, BA-MA RH 21–1/22; Durchbruch der Gruppe v. Kleist über die Maas im Mai 1940 (II. Teil), BA-MA, RH 21–1/381; Gruppe v. Kleist, Mit dem "K" durch Frankreich, BA-MA, RH 21–1/382; Gen. Kdo. XIX. A.K. (Gruppe Guderian)/Ia, KTB Nr. 3 (9.5.–24.6.1940), BA-MA, RH 21–2/v. 41; XXXXI. A.K., KTB Frankreich (2.2.–8.7.1940), BA-MA, E 291, 1 and 1a.
9. Martin S. Alexander, "Prophet without Honor? The French High Command and Pierre Taittinger's Report on the Ardennes defenses, March 1940," *War and Society* (May 1986):57.
10. Claude Paillat, *La Guerre Éclair, 10 mai–24 juin 1940, Le désastre de 1940* (Paris, 1985), p. 249; H. von Dach, "Panzer durchbrechen eine Armeestellung," pt. 1, *Schweizer Soldat* 2 (1972):48.
11. Durchbruch der Gruppe v. Kleist über die Maas [see note 8], p. 23; Gen. Kdo. XXII. A.K., KTB [see note 8], p. 10; Lageberichte Luftwaffenführungsstab (9.–23.5.1940), BA-MA, RM 7/337, fol. 53 (p. 4), fol. 59–60; Study Lw 3/2: Hans Speidel, *Der Einsatz der Operativen Luftwaffe im Westfeldzug 1939/40*, pt. 3 (Bd 1), p. 166 (fol. 169), p. 230 (fol. 233).
12. Durchbruch der Gruppe v. Kleist über die Maas [see note 8], p. 17; Gen. Kdo. XIX A.K. KTB [see note 8], pp. 19, 29; Heinz Guderian, *Erinnerungen eines Soldaten* (Heidelberg: K. Vowinchel, 1951), p. 90.
13. Paillat, *La Guerre Éclair*, pp. 257–58; Horne, *To Lose a Battle*, pp. 248–49, 263–65; Len Deighton, *Blitzkrieg* (Munich, 1983), pp. 276–77; Paul Berben and Bernhard Iselin, *Die Deutschen kommen, Mai 1940, Der Überfall auf Westeuropa* (Hamburg, 1969), pp. 233.
14. Horst Adalbert Koch, *Flak: Die Geschichte der Deutschen Flakartillerie* (Bad Nauheim, Germany: Podzum, 1965), pp. 38, 164; H. von Dach, "Panzer durchbrechen" pt. 1, p. 80; Faris R. Kirkland, "The French Air Force in 1940," *Air University Review* (September/October 1985):114; Philippe de Laubier, "Le bombardement français sur la Meuse, Le 14 mai 1940," *Revue historique des armées* (Octobre 1985):96–109; Jeffery A. Gunsburg, *Divided and Conquered* (London, 1979), p. 201; Horne, *To Lose a Battle*, pp. 285–88; Paillat, *La Guerre*

Éclair, p. 260; A. Goutard, *1940: La Guerre des occasions perdues* (Paris: Hachette, 1956), p. 225; Jaques Benoist-Méchin, *Der Himmel stürzt ein* (Düsseldorf, 1958), p. 75; Berben and Iselin, *Die Deutschen Kommen,* pp. 287–88; Cajus Bekker, *Angriffshöhe 4000* (Oldenburg/Hamburg, 1964), pp. 143–44.

15. Guderian, *Erinnerungen,* p. 95; Gen. Kdo. XIX. A.K., KTB [see note 8], p. 37; 1. Pz. Div., Ia, KTB Nr. 3 (9.5.–2.6 1940), BA-MA, RH 27–1/4, fol. 33 (p. 32); Dermot Bradley, *Walter Wenck* (Osnabrück, Germany, 1981), p. 141; Berben and Iselin, *Die Deutschen Kommen,* pp. 281–82; Deighton, *Blitzkrieg,* pp. 281–82; Horne, *To Lose a Battle,* pp. 284–85.

16. Paillat, *La Guerre Éclair,* p. 268; Deighton, *Blitzkrieg,* pp. 282–83; Horne, *To Lose a Battle,* pp. 291–94, 310–15; H. von Dach, "Panzer durchbrechen eine Armeestellung," pt. 2, *Schweizer Soldat* 5 (1972):64.

17. Deighton, *Blitzkrieg,* p. 226.

18. Ibid., pp. 226–27; Horne, *To Lose a Battle,* p. 317; Michael Glover, *The Fight for the Channel Ports: Calais to Brest, 1940* (London: Leo Cooper in association with Secker & Warburg, 1985), p. 33; Gerd Brausch, "Sedan 1940. Deuxieme Bureau und strategische Überraschung," *Militärgeschichtliche Mitteilungen* 2 (1967):85–86.

19. Dach, "Panzer Durchbrechen," pt. 2, pp. 73; Hans Reinhardt, "Im Schatten Guderians," *Wehrkunde* 10 (1954):334, 337; Wolfgang Paul, *Brennpunkte: Die Geschichte der 6. Panzerdivision* (Krefeld, Germany, 1977), p. 58; XXXXI. A.K. [see note 8]; 6. Pz. Div., KTB nr. 2 (10.5.–3.7.1940), BA-MA, RH 27–6/lD.

20. Bradley, *Walter Wenck,* pp. 139–40; 1. Pz. Div., Ia, KTB [see note 15], p. 21; Durchbruch der Gruppe v. Kleist über die Maas [see note 8], p. 27; Rolf Stoves, *1. Panzerdivision* (Bad Nauheim, Germany, 1961), p. 95.

21. Stoves, *1. Panzerdivision,* p. 96; Gen. Kdo. XIX, A.K., KTB [see note 18], pp. 38–39; Durchbruch der Gruppe v. Kleist über die Maas [see note 8], p. 40.

22. Gen. Kdo. XIX. A.K., Ia, KTB [see note 8], pp. 59–60; Guderian, *Erinnerungen,* pp. 98–99; Gen. Kdo. XXII. A.K., KTB [see note 8], p. 18.

23. Armeeoberkommmando 4, KTB Nr. 4 (26.4.–31.5.1940), BA-MA, RH 20–4/54; AOK 4, Ia, Anl. 2 zum KTB Nr. 4, BA-MA, RH 20–4/69; KTB XV. A.K., Ia (10.5–4.7.1940), BA-MA, RH 21–3/36; KTB 7. Panzerdivision (6.11.1939–15.10.1940), BA-MA, RH 27–7/3; Anl. zum KTB, vol. VIII (14., 15. u. 17.5.1940), BA-MA, RH 27–7/11; Durchschriften von persönlichen Aufzeichnungen Gen. Maj. Rommels im Westfeldzug 20.5–19.6.1940, BA-MA, RH 27–7/212; Verschiedene Befehle und Berichte der 7. Pz. Div. März–Juni 1940, BA-MA, RH 27–7/213; Geschichte der 7. Pz. Div.: Kurzer Abriß über den Einsatz im Westen (Album von Generalmajor Rommel), BA-MA, RH 27–7/220.

24. Ibid.; Horne, *To Lose a Battle,* p. 354–59; David Irving, *Rommel* (Hamburg, 1978), p. 62; Erwin Rommel, *The Rommel Papers,* ed. Basil H. Liddell Hart (London, 1953), p. 20.

25. H.Gr. A, Ia, KTB West Nr. 2 (21.2.–31.5.1940), BA-MA, RH 19–1/37, p. 115.

26. Franz Halder, *Kriegstagebuch,* 3 vols. (Stuttgart: W. Kohlhammer, 1962), 1:297, 300, 302.

27. Churchill, *Their Finest Hour,* 6 vols. (Boston, Mass.: Houghton Mifflin Co., 1949), 2: 46.

28. Horne, *To Lose a Battle,* pp. 436–37, 465.

29. Rommel, *Rommel Papers,* p. 30; 7. Pz. Div., Ia, KTB (6.11.1939–15.10.1940), BA-MA, RH 27–7/3; 7. Pz. Div., Anl. zum KTB, vol. XXVI, BA-MA, RH 27–7/29; Durchschriften von Aufzeichnungen der persönlichen Erlebnisse Gen. Maj. Rommels

im Westfeldzug, BA-MA, RH 27–7/212; Geschichte der 7. Pz. Div. mit Kartenskizzen, 9.5–10.6.1940 (Album von Gen. Maj. Rommel), BA-MA, RH 27–7/220; AOK 4, KTB No. 4 (26.4.–31.5.1944), BA-MA, RH 20–4/54; Die Führung der Operation der 4. Armee durch das AOK 4 im Mai 1940, BA-MA, RH 20–4/81; XXXIX. A.K., Ia KTB 2 (17.5.–31.5.1940), BA-MA, E 63/2; Ronald Lewin, *Rommel as Military Commander* (Stuttgart, 1969), p. 30.

PART THREE:
RUSSIA AND THE SOVIET UNION

Introduction

If the seminal national events for Europe were the lightning-short wars of German unification in 1864, 1866, and 1870, the national war for Russia was in the Crimea against Turkey, England, and France. This Russian defeat led to military reforms with far-reaching consequences. The desired model for Russia became Prussia's example: an efficient military organization that could harness the powers of the state. The Prussian military model held to organization, education, and mass participation. Russian military reforms began with social reforms—the freeing of the serfs—in order to form a citizenry more capable of bearing arms. The reforms of Russian War Minister Miliutin laid the basis for the military districts' ability to mobilize human resources and to train and equip them for service. More important, educational and staff reorganizations took place, again on the German model.

Bruce W. Menning traces the results of the Miliutin reform as the intellectual setting for adaptation of operational art as practiced by German Field Marshal Helmuth von Moltke. Analyzing the western influence of theorists and practitioners, Menning highlights the teaching of Russian General Staff Academy instructor G. A. Leyer, who, as a professor of strategy, laid the foundation upon which others—notably A. A. Neznamov and M. I. Dragomirov—would erect an operational construct similar to that of Moltke. Others contributed as well, with the debate over offensive and defensive warfare (i.e., between short and long wars); over the influence of technology and doctrine; and over the legacy of Russia's premier wars before the Great War (World War I)—1877–1878 against Turkey and 1904–1905 with Japan—all feeding the development of operational thinking. If Russia did not invent operational art, it certainly embraced it, more as a result of war's experience than by conscious importation.

The failure of World War I led to a critical reappraisal. Jacob W. Kipp begins with the origins of Soviet operational art in the Civil War that followed World War I and the revolution in Russia. Kipp traces the contribution of former tsarist officers and their experience based on the failure of strategic vision in World War I. Fighting a civil war from a central position, Kipp notes, encouraged operational thinking, while strategy was almost implicit in Communist ideology. By virtue of necessity, civil wars demand that campaigns be conducted in a strategic framework that provides an operational setting. Simultaneity and sequencing of campaigns quickly becomes a critical component of such operations. Both the World

War I experience and the conduct of the Civil War thus led to the formulation of operational art within the Soviet high command. Kipp goes on to describe the rise of a department of operational art in the revamped educational system of the newly formed Red Army. The process saw the Soviet Union institutionalize operational art as a level between tactics and strategy. Thinkers and doers like Tukhachevsky and Triandafillov brought out the offensive centrality of operational conduct. Their influence upon Soviet doctrine between the Revolution and World War II created the foundations of Soviet operational doctrine and the development of tank and mechanized forces in innovative ways. These contributions to doctrine, training, and organization heralded the Red Army's full-scale adoption of operational art.

David M. Glantz takes Soviet operational art thinking a step further by delineating the organizational revolution within the Soviet Red Army. The experiment with mechanization—the right balances between tank, mechanized infantry, artillery, and cavalry formation—is discussed in light of how the Soviets anticipated fighting the next war. Glantz further shows the appreciation Soviet commanders had of operational maneuver as doctrine before the German summer offensive of 1941. He traces this concept throughout the Red Army's experience in World War II, as the Soviet command steadily developed its capabilities at the operational level. The sequencing, timing, and organization of tank corps, armies, and groups (*fronts*) and their operational conduct to achieve the military aim—the destruction of German forces—became codified by battlefield experience. At war's end, Soviet operational maneuver capabilities were such that full-scale army groups pressed continuous operations over hundreds of kilometers in sequenced, simultaneously orchestrated campaigns using continuous operational maneuver. Glantz concludes his study with an appreciation of the Soviet/Russian reaction to American AirLand Battle Doctrine and the NATO follow-on force attack concept. He notes too that Soviet doctrine went beyond synchronized operational maneuver with the use of operational maneuver groups and special force attacks.

How did logistics influence Soviet operational art? This is the basic question that Graham H. Turbiville addresses. The Soviet experiences in the Civil War and World War II gave their military leaders an acute appreciation for operational logistics. Turbiville postulates that Soviet doctrine sought to integrate logistics at the operational level so that sequenced and simultaneous offensives could be supported and sustained. It was the logistical inability to build and sustain operational forces that led to the establishment of a strategic rear force service. This organization, headed by General V. I. Vinogradov, established the organizational support structure, built the operational reserve forces, and sustained continuous offensive force application in the latter part of World War II. After the war, adaptation of logistical lessons, including the complete motorization of the logistical system at the operational level, were instituted. This recognition of operational logistics underscored the case for using operational maneuver groups.

Each of the writers on Soviet doctrine researched and wrote their essays before the breakup of the Soviet empire and the Red Army. Where appropriate or necessary, these contributions have been revised or updated. However, the fact that the authors were preparing their contributions during what was perceived by many as the height of Soviet military power lends a certain poignancy to their presentations and findings.

The Imperial Russian Legacy of Operational Art, 1878–1914

Bruce W. Menning[1]

Conventional wisdom ascribes the origins of Soviet operational art to varying experiences and perceptions of World War I on the Eastern Front and the Russian Civil War.[2] In reality, however, the roots of Soviet operational art lie embedded in the earlier imperial Russian period, when changing military circumstances and diverse intellectual influences first prompted original departures in operational theory and new approaches to application. These initiatives began with the traditional notions of G. A. Leyer and reached fruition with the novel contributions of N. P. Mikhnevich, A. A. Neznamov, and A. A. Svechin. The latter three key figures would eventually survive World War I and the revolutions of 1917 to serve as living links between the imperial Russian and Soviet military traditions.[3]

The pilgrimage from Leyer to Svechin occurred by stages within a specific intellectual context: the evolution of a theory for the conduct of operations. Between 1878 and 1914, the Russians redefined their understanding both of operations and of their preparation and conduct to produce a concept that was linked to, but theoretically and practically distinct from, either strategy or tactics. During this process, they reformulated their understanding not only of operations but also of strategy and tactics. What emerged in the aggregate were a refined interpretation of military art and military science and the glimmer of a new role for one of their most important allies, military history. It is to these developments and their consequences that the modern concept of Soviet operational art owed its origins.

Dilemmas of Application and Theory, 1878–1904
Moltke versus Napoleon

During the last quarter of the nineteenth century, the Russo-Turkish War of 1877–1878 and the Franco-Prussian War of 1870–1871 offered Russian military theorists a heady mixture of direct and vicarious combat experience. However, for reasons of misplaced emphasis, impaired institutional memory, and preoccupation with Napoleonic precedent, the Russians were unable to reap meaningful benefit from the lessons of either conflict.

In their own recent war with Turkey, the Russians had conducted a relatively successful mobilization to launch a primary effort in the Balkans and secondary operations in the Caucasus. After marching across Rumania to execute a brilliant crossing of the Danube at Sistova, the tsarist high command divided its Balkan forces into three detachments, with one each to screen right and left and a third to force the Balkan divide, thereby opening Roumelia to follow-on forces. However, the Russians failed to draw operational advantage from the tactical success of I. V. Gurko's forward detachment, which had actually seized a Balkan pass, and the tsar's offensive was soon bogged down in a time- and manpower-consuming series of battles and sieges at Plevna and its environs. Only at the end of 1877 were the Russians able to shake themselves loose, thrusting three columns through wintry Balkan passes to win a landmark battle of envelopment at Sheinovo and to seize Sofia and Philippopolis. By the spring of 1878, with the Russian Army threatening Istanbul, the Turks sued for peace at San Stefano. However, Great Power opposition forced the Russians to settle for limited gains in accordance with the Congress of Berlin.[4]

In contrast, the Franco-Prussian War of 1870–1871 had produced a clear-cut victory for Wilhelm I and Helmuth von Moltke, chief of the Prussian General Staff. Utilizing planning and railroads to the utmost, the Prussians and their German allies had concentrated well forward, driven into France across a broad front, then prevented the French armies from uniting to resist a concerted Prussian advance on Paris. After the French Marshal Bazaine had been defeated and surrounded at Metz, Marshal MacMahon marched to his rescue, only to fall victim to envelopment at Sedan. The German armies went on to lay siege to Paris, which capitulated in February 1871. The Treaty of Frankfurt ceded Alsace and parts of Lorraine to a newly proclaimed German Empire.[5]

The diverse experiences of 1877–1878 and 1870–1871 provided sufficient grounds for practitioners and commentators alike to reexamine traditional military verities. New technologies and methods had enabled commanders to assemble masses of men, equipment, and horses, then project them more quickly than ever before into potential theaters of conflict. Issues of time and space had become still more vital as theorists envisioned the outcome of future war to be determined largely by which side would win the race for deployment to and concentration within theater. The railroad and telegraph had fundamentally altered traditional conceptions of assembly, deployment, and concentration, with the result that military men were forced to accept as conditional rather than absolute long-cherished convictions about the importance of such fundamentals as interior lines and mass. Given the lethality of breech-loading weaponry and the problem of extended frontages, the solution lay, as Gunther Rothenberg has written, in "outflanking the enemy in a single, continuous strategic-operational sequence combining mobilization, concentration, movement, and fighting."[6] Moltke's oft-quoted maxim, "getrennt marschieren, zusammen schlagen" (march separately and fight together), perhaps most aptly summarized the theoretical and practical challenges confronting military thinkers of the 1880s and 1890s: The notion was at once Napoleonic and contemporary. The emphasis on mass and concentration remained traditional, but the underlying assumption was that changing technologies and methods were busily reshaping the conditions and recasting the means.[7]

In theoretical perspective, the challenge was how to understand the impact of mass armies and changing technologies and methods on the complex interplay between the offense and defense within both theater and the narrower confines of the battlefield. Again, Moltke thought he had the answer when he stressed the importance of assuming the operational offensive within the theater, then going over to the defensive, thus forcing his adversary to spend manpower and energies in a series of disastrous tactical confrontations against powerful defensive dispositions. If circumstance required offensive decision, the assailant turned to the new technologies and methods at his disposal to conduct a frontal pinning attack, then to envelop the enemy's comparatively weaker flanks to seek a classic victory of annihilation by means of encirclement. The wars of 1870–1871 and 1877–1878 offered two powerful examples: Sedan and Sheinovo.[8]

For Russian students of war, the primary task was building an effective intellectual context within which to view the complexities of Sheinovo and Sedan in all their dimensions. However, for various reasons the Russians failed to grasp the full significance of the revolution in military art embodied in Moltke's methods. Russian tactical thought, heavily mortgaged to the legacy of M. I. Dragomirov, produced only incremental adjustments to the dramatic challenges of new technology on the battlefield. Although the Imperial Russian Army devoted greater attention after 1878 to the skirmish line and open-order formations in the attack, Dragomirov and his disciples stressed the primacy of will and élan over weapon and enemy.[9]

At the same time, the Russians failed to draw maximum benefit from their own recent combat experience. The War Ministry had created a Historical Commission to produce a history of 1877–1878, but official historians soon fell victim to a combination of inertia and varying degrees of official resistance stemming from an impulse to cover up mistakes and protect careers and reputations. Although various individual studies of 1877–1878 gradually appeared, no comprehensive official account would see print until the early years of the twentieth century. The Russo-

Turkish War failed to find a place on the official historical agenda, and the curriculum of the Nicholas Academy of the General Staff suffered accordingly.[10]

The intellectual consequences were devastating. At the very time when traditional assumptions and habits required alteration or revalidation in light of combat experience, the Russians had no coherent picture of their most recent military history. With no systematic understanding of their own experience, they lacked immediate reference points to make sense of other relevant experience, including the Franco-Prussian conflict. Under these circumstances, outmoded convictions and assertions retained surprising currency, while institutional emphasis contended with broader intellectual currents to obscure change and stress continuity and system. Thus, positivist notions would mingle with prevailing wisdom to encourage the Russians to view new military realities through a conventional Napoleonic prism.

Emphasis on Napoleon corresponded with the persistent influence of his foremost interpreter, Jomini. For reasons of familiarity and simplicity, Russian thinking about war and strategy in the 1880s and 1890s gravitated heavily to Jomini, not the more complex Clausewitz.[11] Unlike Clausewitz, who asserted that strategy was complex, Jomini held that strategy was a simple discipline, limited to the art of directing masses within theater and distinct from tactics that did not admit to hard and fast rules. To retain purity of military thought, Jomini relegated political considerations to a separate discipline, military politics, thereby neatly—and dangerously—divorcing politics from strategy. Jomini also deftly sidestepped some of the more difficult questions of military art by consigning them to the imponderable realm of the great captain's genius and tact. Thus, while Clausewitz attempted to come to grips with the ambiguities of war, Jomini avoided them to retain simplicity and clarity, or as Aleksandr A. Svechin later put it, "order was attained at the expense of vitality."[12] Of more immediate importance, Clausewitz, the prophet of complexity and firm believer in the inherent strength of the defense, failed to find adherents either in St. Petersburg or within the Russian military districts. Meanwhile, the Jominian tradition reigned supreme, advocating a strategy of the shock strike (in Russian, *sokrushenie*, or "crushing") that culminated in climactic battle, in which the commander who enjoyed the fruits of victory was the commander who concentrated the greatest force at the decisive point at the decisive moment.[13]

Finally, the siren call of scientific positivism with its emphasis on method, system, and classification also figured prominently in the Russian military thinking of the time. It was no accident that strategists of the era adopted the scientific trappings of civilian academia as they sought a respectable place in the intellectual sun for their own theories of strategy and military science. It was also no accident that the neatness and clarity of Jomini at least superficially lent his thought more scientific credibility than that of Clausewitz. These and similar preoccupations lent legitimacy to a quest to demonstrate the existence of underlying laws and principles that could be studied systematically to provide the theoretical underpinnings for what some commentators exuberantly proclaimed as military science.[14]

Leyer's Strategy

The military scholar most prominently associated with this movement in Russia was Genrikh Antonovich Leyer (1829–1904). Although often identified with the emerging academic school of Russian military history, he is perhaps best remembered for his groundbreaking work on the development of strategy. Leyer taught between 1869 and 1878 as Ordinary Professor of Strategy at the Nicholas Academy of the General Staff, then served between 1889 and 1898 as commandant. His textbook, *Strategy*, went through six editions between 1867 and 1898, when disciples and detractors alike finally rose to challenge the master. Still, no other writer—save perhaps Dragomirov—exercised such a profound influence on Russian military thought between 1878 and 1904. For better or worse, Leyer's teaching formed a major part of the intellectual legacy, which a generation of Russian staff officers carried with them to Far Eastern battlefields in 1904–1905.[15]

Leyer's own intellectual baggage consisted of a devotion to Napoleon and a fixation on the seemingly diverse preoccupations of philosophical idealism and positivism. From studies of the Napoleonic campaigns he emerged with an appreciation both of military history and for individual genius as true repositories of military art. From William Lloyd and Antoine de Jomini he gained an appreciation of the rational element in Napoleonic strategy. From the positivists of his own era, Leyer drew an understanding of classification and generalization, which he would impose on his own evolving conceptions of strategy as a fledgling science. Thanks to these influences, refracted through the unique prism of Leyer's own military outlook and preoccupations, Napoleon served not as a point of departure, but as the touchstone against which all subsequent military developments were measured.[16]

Leyer's understanding of complex military phenomena began with ideas and history. For him, "always and everywhere idea came before act." When selectively and critically studied, military history enabled the discerning student to "arrive at an understanding of the idea which gave rise to the facts." In application, every military operation or sequence of operations embodied a fundamental idea from which flowed plan, lines of development, sequence of actions, establishment of priorities, and concentration of resources, all of which ultimately spelled success or failure for the commander seeking battlefield decision. From historical analysis, Leyer logically arrived at an understanding of the two forces which dominated every operation: objective (*tsel'*) as developed from idea, and direction (*napravlenie*) as represented figuratively by an operational line depicting the unfolding in reality of idea and plan.[17]

For Leyer, strategy in its most restricted sense treated operations within what he called a theater of military actions (*teatr voennykh deistvii*). His study of military history enabled him to classify strategic operations according to three types: main, preparatory, and supplemental. The first section of his text on strategy Leyer devoted to an analysis of main, or primary, operations (*glavnye operatsii*), including selection of operational line, execution of marches and maneuvers, conduct of diversions, and the concentration of forces for combat, all of which culminated in main battle as the ultimate resolution of an operation. In the second section of *Strategy*, Leyer discussed preparatory (*podgotovitel'nye*) operations, the term he used to describe the organization of armies and bases, deployment of forces in theater, and engineering preparation of the theater of military action. Finally, he outlined supplementary (*dopolnitel'nye*) operations as those involving accumulation of supplies, establishment of communication lines, and the organization of security, including planning routes of possible withdrawal and preparing fortresses and fortified lines.[18]

This intellectual framework for an understanding of operations marked one of Leyer's enduring contributions to the development of Russian military thought. Subsequent students of military art at first clung to Leyer's basic definition without a clear understanding that his conceptual umbrella emphasized Napoleonic continuities at the expense of recalculating old verities in light of recent technological and organizational innovation. Not surprisingly, in 1891 the rising young strategist N. P. Mikhnevich penned a definition of "operation" for the *Entsiklopediya voennykh i morskikh nauk* (Encyclopedia of Military and Naval Sciences), which stood virtually unchallenged until 1905. He wrote that each war consists of one or several campaigns, each campaign of one or several operations, which represent by themselves a known, finite period, from the strategic deployment of the army on the departure line of the operation to the final decision of the latter by way of victorious battle on the field of engagement."[19] The realization was that, although strategy as a whole was more complex than ever before, its main task in theater was to guide the commander to a main battle that would produce decision either by encirclement of the enemy or by the energetic pursuit of his broken forces following main battle.

Leyer was less successful in linking strategy within theater—which he called the "tactics of the theater of military actions"—with his broader conception of strategy as an all-embracing military science. He believed that strategy in its widest sense was "a synthesis of all military matters, their generalization, their philosophy."[20] Although the physical manifestations of reality might change, Leyer clung to a conviction that underlying ideas remained constant and that a selective reading of military history yielded eternal and unchanging principles that existed independently of time and place. These principles he identified as four: mutual support, concentration of superior forces at the decisive moment and place, economy of force, and surprise. He was less clear about how these "eternal and unchanging principles" might apply to specific situations.[21]

Leyer's approach thus left his students with two substantial intellectual obstacles to overcome: an obsessive and exclusionary preoccupation with Napoleonic precedent and the knotty problem of translating idea and immutable principle into action. Rather than ask how Moltke and his adherents varied from the French paradigm, he sought to demonstrate how they conformed to it. He taught that the campaigns of 1870–1871 reaffirmed the significance of Napoleonic strategy, but he completely ignored the campaign of 1866 because it did not neatly fit his preconceived pattern. In addition to charging that Leyer had his own "court complement of facts," Svechin later asserted that in Leyer's eyes, "facts were also good children or troublemakers." If the latter required a break in consciousness, Leyer's "doctrinaire thought turned away from them or ignored them."[22]

New Currents

Not everyone agreed with Leyer's impulse to delimit either by approach, definition, or geography, and one of the gravest challenges came from thinkers who actively challenged convention by crossing disciplinary lines to ponder the relationship between politics and war. In 1892, Jan S. Bloch, a Warsaw banker and amateur student of war, embarked on a pioneering study of the relationship between a nation's social and economic infrastructure and its ability to conduct war. Unlike the adherents of *sokrushenie*, who accepted 1870–1871 and, to a lesser extent, 1877–1878, as models of future lightning war, Bloch envisioned future wars as costly, drawn-out contests that would eventually lead to the exhaustion of the combatants. Thus emerged in embryonic form a complex vision of linkages between fighting front and civilian rear which, with subsequent elaboration, came to support a strategy of exhaustion (in Russian, *izmor*, in German, *Ermattungsstrategie*) as an alternative to a strategy of annihilation. Abetted by A. K. Puzyrevskii, military historian and chief of staff of the Warsaw military district, Bloch's opus by 1898 had blossomed into a five-volume compendium published in Russian in St. Petersburg.[23]

Bloch's ideas found only a few sympathetic listeners in the imperial capital. One of them, A. P. Agapeyev, openly criticized military writers who persisted in treating military matters "as something closed [and] isolated, not having a direct connection with overall state institutions and independent of the spirit of the times and the political life of society in its entirety." Lt. Col. A. A. Gulevich, another Bloch partisan and an instructor at the Academy of the General Staff, carried the argument further, asserting that:

> The final outcome of decisive war will depend not only on the perfection of the instrument of struggle and the art of its use [but also] on the vitality [*zhiznedeiatel' nost'*] of the state structure in general, on its ability to withstand protracted struggle and during its course to maintain a sufficiently strong and powerful armed force.

Gulevich maintained that the advent of mass cadre and reserve armies meant that future war would be decided not by main blows on the field of engagement, but by persistent and protracted armed struggle. Therefore, the decisive element in modern war was the strength of the state's socioeconomic infrastructure, that is, the foundation of the state's ability to wage protracted conflict.[24] In a theme to which others would return, Gulevich further maintained that Russia's apparent economic backwardness was actually a strength, since the dislocations of protracted war would have far less effect on an agrarian society than on a more industrialized society. However, Gulevich did warn that Russia's underdeveloped armaments industry and rail network would pose serious difficulties in any future European war.[25]

A. K. Puzyrevskii's direct and indirect participation as a historian in the intellectual ferment of the 1890s revealed the degree to which institutionally sponsored military history owed much of its origins and initial successes to the preoccupations of the period. Despite the absence of consistent official sanction, the assumption on the part of generalizers and fact-finders alike was that history alone in all its richness offered sufficient evidence for the discerning student to discover the underlying patterns and rhythms inherent in any body of knowledge with sufficient coherence to become the foundation for a military science. Not surprisingly, conflicting opinions over the relevance of unchanging law and changing circumstance dominated the development of Russian military historiography throughout the 1890s and early years of the twentieth century. In addition to giving rise to "academic" and "Russian" schools of Russian military thought and history, debate about the nature and meaning of military history sparked wide-ranging and original research, the results of which can be read with profit even today.[26]

Within the larger picture of growing intellectual diversity, one of the brighter spots was the emergence at the very end of the nineteenth century of N. P. Mikhnevich as a serious synthesizer of Russian military thought. By the late 1890s he had already made his mark as a military analyst and historian, having completed several article-length studies during the previous decade on cavalry and partisan operations, then having acceded in 1892 to the Chair of the History of Russian Military Art at the Staff Academy. There followed in rapid succession two groundbreaking monographs, "The Significance of the German-French War of 1870–1871" (in Russian, 1892) and "The Influence of the Most Recent Technological Inventions on Troop Tactics" (in Russian, 1893). Like Mikhnevich's encyclopedia entry for "Operations," these works revealed Leyer's persistent influence with introductory assertions that wars were eternal and that the laws and principles of the art of war were in essence "Napoleonic." However, there was also a glimmer of something new, something that was already beginning to affect many of Leyer's disciples. This was the understanding that "the phenomena to which war relates and with which it must reckon are subjected to constant change" and that "almost every epoch has its own military art, distinct from others."[27]

In an 1899 presentation to the officers of the garrison and fleet of St. Petersburg, Mikhnevich argued for the necessity of a well-founded military science. At the same time he called for a timely review of its focus, essence, and content, including especially the relationship of military science to other sciences. He placed military science with the social sciences and emphasized that its object was a study of "the laws of victory," the principles of military art, and the means of applying them to the concrete conditions of reality. In contrast with Leyer's fixation on philosophical idealism, Mikhnevich emphasized the material foundations of military science, holding that laws and principles represented "broad empirical generalizations proceeding from a multiplicity of facts" and retaining conditional significance, but he was not quite willing to divorce them completely from Leyer's emphasis on permanence. Still, in contrast with Leyer, who saw strategy as the essence of military science, Mikhnevich saw the latter as the philosophy of military affairs, linking it closely with the theory of military art. He emphasized the necessity for such a vision of military science as a science for application that would direct military thought to make correct decisions.[28]

The Russo-Japanese War of 1904–1905 and Its Aftermath

Even as Mikhnevich was groping for a new synthesis, the Russo-Japanese War provided a rude shock for Russian officers who had been brought up on a steady diet of Leyer and Dragomirov. After the initial Japanese surprise attack of 9 February 1904 on the Russian Pacific Squadron at Port Arthur, the Russians began a laborious buildup that would eventually leave several field armies under General A. N. Kuropatkin dangling at the end of a precarious 5,000-mile supply line. Meanwhile, the Russian Pacific Squadron would remain bottled up in Port Arthur. After unsuccessful Russian delaying actions, the land campaign naturally subdivided itself into two distinct parts: a siege war at Port Arthur and a maneuver war astride the railroad extending south from Mukden to Liao-yang. Both wars revealed the impact of smokeless powder technology, including the machine gun, quick-firing artillery, and the repeating rifle. However, it was the maneuver war in all its starkness that revealed the bankruptcy of Leyer's Napoleonic paradigm. Mass armies moved like lemmings to contact, pressed from contact directly into meeting engagements, then fought—sometimes sporadically and sometimes continuously—for days and even weeks. Neither side could produce a Sedan-like victory, and frontages ballooned to 100 kilometers and depths to 60.[29] In the aggregate, various disparate but related combat actions across time and space amounted to something more than large battles (*srazheniya*), and gradual recognition of this fact would argue for altered approaches to planning, organization, and implementation. Other requirements included the creation of higher commands, including army groups, and the necessity to undertake deliberate reorganization during the actual course of an operation.[30] In the parlance that the Russians would come to accept after the war, they fought three separate operations—Liao-yang, Sha-ho, and Mukden. And they lost all three because, as one young general staff officer put it, "we did not understand contemporary war."[31] Port Arthur capitulated on 20 December 1904, and the destruction of the Russian Baltic Fleet at Tsushima Straits in May 1905 wrote the last humiliating chapter to a sad war story. While the Japanese fared better, peace negotiations found the field armies of both combatants exhausted and increasingly susceptible to the vulnerabilities of the home front.

For Russian military thinkers, the post-1905 challenge lay in fashioning a new intellectual construct within which they might make sense of the Far Eastern débâcle. Leyer's understanding of strategy as a science with its own immutable laws—demonstrable through a close study of military history, and especially the campaigns of Napoleon—remained too rigid, remote, and unimaginative to convey a sense of the complexities of contemporary battles, operations, and campaigns. Modern mass armies stubbornly resisted defeat in the single climactic battle, which during the previous century had often decided the fate of an entire campaign, or even an entire war. The nature of battle itself was changing from a deadly affair mercifully lasting only several days to protracted struggle dragging on for several weeks. The railroad and the telegraph, and more recently the telephone and wireless, continued to play havoc with traditional notions of time, space, and timing. The same changes prompted a renewed call for a reevaluation of fundamental conceptions of envelopment and operation on interior and exterior lines. In a word, Jomini was out, and Clausewitz and the elder Moltke (as modified by experience and observation) were in. However, Moltke had to be understood not so much in the way he related to Napoleon as in the way that he and his disciples had revolutionized modern warfare in a new age of industrialism. This understanding accented the development of an embryonic version of the operational level of war. In the realm of tactics, General Dragomirov's principles cried out for rigorous updating in light of new weaponry and attendant requirements for more flexible application and a new emphasis on combining the effects of the combat arms, especially infantry and artillery. The lethality of smokeless powder weaponry begged for a fundamental reevaluation of the relationship between fire and shock action in both offensive and defensive battle.[32] Greater dispersion seemed inevitable, but the problem was how to achieve mass and retain control with manpower and firepower spread over larger areas. Manchurian battles delivered new experience and new data into the hands of those who would update the lessons that many tacticians had seen in the conflicts of 1870–1871 and 1877–1878.

Preliminary conclusions offered scant comfort. The Russo-Japanese War seemed to indicate that the modern tactical headache, the meeting engagement, was to remain a standard feature of military operations. To escape set-piece battles with their steep casualty rates, the sensible commander now sought both to avoid the assault of fortifications and to retain the initiative by attacking his adversary from the march while both sides were still moving to contact. It was now commonplace that commanders attempt to catch each other in the rear or on the flank to avoid costly confrontation with frontal firepower. While the defensive retained utility, only the offensive promised both decision and all-important retention of the initiative in warfare. One of the ironies of the period was that renewed emphasis on offensive battle did not occur in utter disregard of changing military technology; rather, it evolved as a way of minimizing the lethality of the new technology.

Whether or not stress on the offensive proved sound, conflict rattling across space and time had to conform to some kind of overall design. New means and methods of deploying mass armies within theater had led to engagements and battles unfolding seemingly helter-skelter across vast distances for days and even weeks until physical, moral, and materiel exhaustion called a temporary halt. But how to make sense out of chaos, how to meld apparent confusion into a coherent whole? Writing in 1907, Col. Aleksandr Gerua reflected on the teachings of Russian military thinkers and the writings of the German strategist Blume and called for a new concept to bridge the intellectual gap between Dragomirov's elementary tactics and Leyer's undying (and ethereal) principles of strategy. Gerua labeled his version of the bridge "applied strategy" (*prikladnaya strategiya*). Of emphatically modern significance, its function would be "to afford a series of firm rules for moving armies along contemporary routes of communication, securing these routes, equipping bases, maneuvering large armies toward the field of engagement, and organizing reconnaissance and so forth in the field."[33] Somewhat later, perhaps under the influence of the German *Operativ*, he would interpose between strategy and tactics something that he called *operatika*.[34] Its function was to provide an intellectual perspective from which commanders and their staffs could envision and plan for the sum of disparate activities and actions over time and space that went into the makeup of a modern military operation. Gerua's term never gained currency. In the 1920s, however, Svechin and other Soviet military writers would supplant it with the less elegant term "operational art" (*operativnoye iskusstvo*).[35]

Perhaps Gerua failed to introduce new terminology because traditional conceptions of strategy retained sufficient flexibility to be hauled back to earth from Leyer's ether. Theorists might differ with each other in their definitions of strategy, but there was common agreement that Leyer's legacy lacked practicality. A new generation of officers extended the criticisms which Leyer and his disciples had already witnessed in the 1890s, with the result that old terms and concepts were subjected to rigorous re-examination in the light of new urgencies. After 1905, Leyer's idealism was carried away in a new wave emphasizing theater and battlefield application. For the time being, few saw the inherent danger in emphasizing practice over theory that Svechin—paraphrasing a French commentator—would warn against years later in a different context: "theory strives always to go hand-in-hand with experience, and sooner or later avenges itself if it is ignored too much."[36]

Theory and practice came together at the General Staff Academy, but only imperfectly. Unfortunately, the Academy chose to meet post-1905 challenges with a combination of half-hearted reform and inertia. Consequently, the atmosphere at the Academy proved conducive only in a limited sense both to reexamining old verities and to searching for new ones. Examinations and student projects often focused on comparisons across time, and faculty members with Far Eastern experience made their presence felt in field exercises and tactical problems. In addition, many of the students themselves were veterans of the Russo-Japanese War. As Ordinary Professor of Strategy, Lt. Col. A. A. Neznamov brought a combination of background from the field and theoretical insights to his instruction. He was a brilliant tactician whose Manchurian experience and reading of German military theory prompted him to link tactical and operational conceptions with broader issues of strategy. Indeed, without using the terminology, Neznamov's course in strategy probably did a reasonable job of bridging the gap that Gerua had pointed out in 1907. B. M. Shaposhnikov, an officer-student at the time and later first chief of the Soviet General Staff, recalled that Neznamov's lectures were "something like instruction about operational art, neither grand tactics according to

Napoleon's definition nor Leyer's strategy of the theater of military action."[37] Students were at first captivated, then put off when they discovered that many of Neznamov's ideas came from a German military theorist, General Sigismund Wilhelm von Schlichting, whose works were first translated into Russian in 1909.

Reaction to Schlichting's influence indicated the degree to which segments of the military consciousness remained captive to "we-they" notions of indigenous evolution and foreign military domination. Although Neznamov went out of his way to cite Russian military authorities with great frequency in his works, he was branded a "westernizer," as were many reform-minded *genshtabisty*, or general staff officers, who soon earned for themselves and their adherents the sobriquet Young Turks. Against these westernizers were arrayed latter-day descendants of the Russian nationalist school that now championed the development of "a national military doctrine." One side preached the merits of military modernization, whatever the inspiration; the other trumpeted the necessity to search the immediate and more remote past to retain harmony with Russia's true national lines of military development. The issue, of course, was one of degree. While Neznamov considered military history an indispensable adjunct to theoretical development, the nationalist school saw historical understanding as the key to theoretical advances. In effect, the old feud between the Russian national and academic schools was now rekindled under different terms with different participants. Lines between the camps often blurred, but their discourses, definitions and debates helped establish a framework for the continued development of Russian military theory and its definition of operational art.[38]

The Mature N. P. Mikhnevich

Nikolay Petrovich Mikhnevich, the strategic thinker who inherited Leyer's mantle at the academy, stood with one foot in either camp, but his publishing record and deep regard for historical studies meant that he was usually identified with the nationalist school. A disciple of the positivist philosopher Auguste Comte, Mikhnevich firmly believed in the evolution of both human institutions and knowledge from simple to more complex forms. This conviction simultaneously put him at odds with Leyer's unchanging laws of military science and endeared him to historians wedded to an approach that stressed studying change within context over time.

For Mikhnevich and others who seriously pondered military issues a common point of departure was speculation over the nature and character of future war. Would future European conflict be a "lightning war" in the manner of 1870–1871? Or, would it follow the lines of protracted struggle in the manner of the wars of the French Revolution and Napoleon? Answers to these questions drew upon analysis and insights gleaned from a variety of sources and experiences. The same answers also determined issues and emphases across a range of war-related considerations. By now, nearly everyone acknowledged the impact of technology — although perhaps in varying degrees. Likewise, everyone acknowledged the likelihood of a coalition war waged by multimillion-man armies. However, here the similarities in outlook ended. If war were to be brief and violent, stress would fall upon immediate preparation, speedy deployment, a spirited offensive, and firm tactical and operational linkages during the initial period of conflict. If war were to be protracted, then stress would fall on strategic depth, full mobilization capacity, measured responses to operational challenges, and maintenance of internal unity and firmness of purpose.

Mikhnevich's *Strategy* (in Russian, third edition, 1911) touched on nearly all these issues with its far-reaching and integrative inquiry into the nature of military science, strategy, and tactics in an age of mass armies. In accordance with his own positivist views and in contrast with Leyer's penchant to look for many laws, Mikhnevich saw only two: the law of evolution and the law of struggle. Both military institutions and knowledge about military affairs were evolving from simpler to more complex forms. For him, such a thing as military science existed, but only in so far as it was "an objectively verifiable and systematic knowledge about real phenomena from the perspective of their regular recurrence [*zakonomernost'*] and unchanging order." Within Mikhnevich's dynamic scheme, the search for laws gave way to a search for principles with an emphasis on the need to seek unity of theory and practice. The main objective of a theory of military art, he wrote, was "to establish firmly its fundamental principles, to study the most fundamental elements of a situation, and to indicate in light of the situation how principles are to be applied in war."[39]

Mikhnevich agreed with apostles of the Russian national school that man remained the center of war, but his understanding was more complex than simple emphasis on the role of individuals. In the past, the human element had been manifested in war through strategy and tactics. Now, the evolving complexity of human society meant that emphasis fell upon the manifold aspects of humanity as a whole. Or, to put it another way, the human element remained, but it now manifested itself through more sophisticated institutions in a new, mass form. There was no romantic wistfulness for times gone by, only hardheaded acknowledgment of an emerging new order. For Mikhnevich, then, the laws of war were embodied in those social characteristics (numerical, physical, economic, intellectual, and moral superiority) that in sum determined the outcome of armed conflict. In a more limited military sense, the principles of war governed application of mass against the main objective and the attainment of moral superiority over the factors of material, accident, and surprise.[40]

In arguments reminiscent of the German theorist Colmar von der Goltz, Mikhnevich went on to assert that the competitive stakes were now so great that nations would go to war only on the basis of all their resources, physical and moral. With everything committed, modern war held the distinct possibility of transforming itself into protracted struggle that would involve the total resources of the state, a concept already advanced by Gulevich and Bloch. This vision of deliberate and calculated engagement explicitly called for a new kind of preparation and domestic and foreign policies, a position that at least implicitly criticized the tsarist government's conduct of the Russo-Japanese War.[41]

Mikhnevich also held that Russia possessed some distinct advantages in waging modern war. One was the strong monarchy, which he saw as the best form of government for waging modern war. Another was the combative spirit (*voinskyi dukh*) of the population, which promised persistent moral superiority. At the same time, Russia's comparative backwardness meant that its society was immune to the kind of wartime dislocations that would quickly imperil more complex western European societies. In different terms, his ideas were reminiscent of the nineteenth-century Slavophile conviction that Russia's backwardness was actually virtue when viewed from a different perspective. For Mikhnevich, durability and inherent spiritual strength meant that there was no need for Russia to be stampeded into a lightning war. If need be, the Russians could revert to a Scythian strategy, calling upon depth and the resources of their land to outlast the enemy in protracted conflict. "Time is the best ally of our armed forces," he wrote, "therefore, it is not dangerous for us to adopt 'a strategy of attrition and exhaustion,' at first avoiding decisive combat with the enemy on the very borders, when superiority of forces might be on his side."[42]

Yet this was no excuse for deliberately embarking on a defensive war. A theorist of strong convictions and perhaps even stronger perceptions, Mikhnevich remained enough of a historian to know that the political price could be steep when trading land and lives for time. He encouraged the monarchy to increase military expenditures and to double the size of the army "in order not to fall behind the other states." Otherwise, "in a future general European war without allies, Russia would be forced to begin on the defense as against Charles XII [of Sweden] and Napoleon, which of course is undesirable and disadvantageous."[43]

Although very much a traditionalist in cultural terms, Mikhnevich saw changing technology exerting a profound impact on war. Indeed, since the 1890s, his evolutionary model of military reality owed much of its dynamism to an acknowledgment that technology was changing the very nature of battles and operations. He saw, for example, that smokeless powder weaponry imposed new battlefield requirements for calculating distances, intervals, and depths. These requirements in turn called for new tactical and organizational structures. At the same time, other technologies, including steam propulsion and telegraphic communication, imposed still more new requirements in planning for and conducting mobilization, deployments, and operations.[44]

Mikhnevich's emphasis on planning not only called attention to the pressing need for rational economic development but also laid stress on the purely military aspects of the initial period of war. He held that strategic deployments should not occur in close proximity to the enemy so that concentrating forces would not be subject to attack before an army was fully capable of conducting operations. It seems likely that he also borrowed from the Germans and expanded upon Leyer's teaching to evolve a suitable terminology to describe what occurred in war. Just as in the 1890s, he continued to write that "every war consists of one or several campaigns, and every campaign of one or several operations."[45] However, the understanding now was that this conception underlay a more modern understanding of operations and encouraged the kind of conceptual linkages across the warfighting spectrum that Gerua had found so lacking in the pre-1905 intellectual environment.

Neznamov and the War Plan

Even more to the point were the views of Aleksandr Aleksandrovich Neznamov, who shared some of Mikhnevich's interest in history and more of his preoccupation with the war plan. Neznamov was one of the most outspoken of the Young Turks, whose views are often interpreted as diametrically opposed to the nationalists, although differences were often more of degree and approach than substance and program. Neznamov well knew the value of history but chose to use it only as a point of departure, for 1904–1905 had convinced him that the Russians simply did not understand the nature of contemporary war.[46] For Neznamov, the most pressing task confronting the Imperial Russian Army was not a generalization of past experience but an analysis of the probable means and methods of waging future war. "Even the past does not provide a full idea of the present, especially in our fast-moving century," he wrote. Therefore, "past military thought cannot be ignored, but [military thought] must constantly make corrections because of present technical advances and, where possible, also peer ahead."[47]

As if in answer to Gerua's pleading, Neznamov extended Mikhnevich's thought to evolve a modern theory of military operations that joined planning and preparation to the actual conduct of operations and battles. Central to his thought, just as to Mikhnevich's, was the war plan. Like Mikhnevich, Neznamov believed that modern war would no longer be decided by the outcome of a single climactic engagement (*srazhenie*). Rather, modern war consisted of a series of engagements and operations linked to one another by the overall concept of the war plan. The plan guided the fulfillment of discrete but related tasks; therefore, the accomplishment of general strategic objectives occurred during the actual course of operations.[48] Neznamov owed his concept not only to a close and original study of the Russian experience in the Far East, but also to a reading of contemporary European, especially German, military theory. He quoted Falkenhausen on preparedness, paraphrased Schlichting on the meeting engagement and modern battle, and believed in the relevance of Goltz's notion of the nation in arms.[49]

Neznamov's war plan was an integrated concept calling for a nation's total involvement in modern conflict. Implicit was a fundamental devotion to Clausewitz's definition of war as politics by other means, with all the attendant implications for unity of civil-military will. The necessity for a truly single-minded effort meant that before embarking on modern war, a nation had to take into account a number of considerations other than purely military factors, including economics, politics, morale, and culture. Neznamov's intent was not merely to emphasize method in war planning but also to underscore the importance of preparing the entire body politic for future conflicts, which would probably not resemble past wars. In actual war preparations, he parted ways with those who emphasized the importance of great Russian captains. Leadership was no doubt important, but the war plan itself was less the province of supreme authority than it was a function of a relatively constant set of objective factors: geography, climate, communications, strategic objectives, and centers of political and economic concentration.

The idea behind the war plan was to translate preparations into military realities, which would allow one state to impose its will on another through offensive operations. This was the essence of strategy. The army's strategic deployment remained the clearest expression of a nation's war plan and its determination to seek decision. In the past, Neznamov declared that faulty dispositions had been "a chronic Russian weakness." In contrast now with Mikhnevich, who emphasized the inherent advantages of depth and the ability to trade space for time, Neznamov asserted that dispositions must be governed by a requirement to achieve speedy and superior concentration against the main threat while lesser threats were held at arm's length. Security of concentration was an absolute necessity, but distances were to be calculated not by historical rules of thumb but in accordance with knowledge of actual rates of deployment, concentration, and advance. Above all, in determining courses of action, Neznamov repeatedly intoned that "we must know what we want."[50]

Whether the Russians wanted it or not, Neznamov read the combined lessons of the past and present theoretical projections to emphasize maneuver warfare. Along with his contemporaries, A. G. Yelchaninov and V. A. Cheremisov, Neznamov pondered the nature of contemporary and future battle to emerge with a vision that called for new attention to the application of mass through combined fire-and-maneuver tactics. The old combination of skirmish line and closed ranks in the assault had to give way to new forms of organization and attack. In addition, new ways had to be devised to concentrate all forms of firepower, for in Neznamov's view "fire was the primary factor in contemporary battle."[51] The appearance of various kinds of air assets both promised new forms of reconnaissance and attack and created the problem of air defense and active and passive security measures against air power. Despite the importance of mass, the lethality of modern weaponry opened distances and added depth at all organizational levels in the field.[52]

Battles, he believed, would be integral components of operations conducted not only by a single army, but also by groups of two or three armies, a development that would create the need for additional organizational and intellectual linkages. Under the pressure of modern combat, success beckoned to commanders at all levels, who displayed confidence and mutual trust in their own and other commanders' dispositions and decisions. Such confidence flowed from a common understanding of the nature of contemporary war and from adherence to a common plan. "Only battles are decisive in war; everything else serves only to prepare for them," Neznamov asserted. Therefore, "it is understood that each troop unit, each column must press into battle with all it has [and] under conditions in which units enter battle in the normal organizational structure."[53] Kuropatkin's Manchurian muddle had made a strong impression on Neznamov.

Manchuria also influenced the way that Neznamov viewed seemingly discrete aspects of combat within theater. He saw armed confrontation both as physical struggle and as a struggle for information and time. Speed enabled a commander to win these struggles, thus assuring retention of the initiative and constantly forcing an adversary to react. At the same time, Neznamov perceived that "just as all of a war is broken down into a whole series of operations, so is each operation broken down into a whole series of immediate tasks, in which the preceding ones condition the following ones, and all of them are combined into a single operation just as all operations are joined with one another."[54] Just as contemporary war could not be fought with older methods, neither could contemporary armies be defeated in a single engagement. Future war might well assume a protracted character. Manchuria had demonstrated that war was now a series of "separate offensive leaps forward and defensive leaps backward." Thus appeared in embryonic form a theory of successive operations.[55]

One of Neznamov's lasting contributions to military theory was to ascribe a central place to the operation as a phenomenon of contemporary war. In contrast with Leyer's more abstract categories of operations (fundamental, preparatory, and supplementary), Neznamov offered a down-to-earth classification of operations as either offensive, defensive, meeting, or delaying (*vyzhidatel'nye*), with the latter two being variants respectively of the first two. He also emphasized preparation and conduct, asserting that these aspects of operations were evolving in complexity from the concepts of individual commanders to "purely scientific" requirements that involved not only the art of army commanders but also the precise work of their staffs.[56]

From these and related ideas flowed conceptions that visualized modern war unfolding across a broad strategic front in which envelopments and breakthroughs became major operational objectives. While envelopment (shallow and deep) and encirclement operations had long held central stage in German military thought and teaching, there was increasing evidence that the breakthrough was gaining its share of adherents, both Russian and German. The objective of the breakthrough was to drive a wedge into the enemy's strategic front, then to develop success in depth and outward, thus threatening at their core an enemy's communications and organizational coherence. Individual successes during the course of the breakthrough would assure larger successes within the theater of operations. Overall success depended upon superiority in forces and means, particularly in the realm of artillery support. It was emphasized that the breakthrough would enjoy success only under conditions of the cooperative action of all arms.[57]

How to conduct Neznamov's vision of future military operations? In rejoinder to the nationalists, he asserted that the traditional Russian virtues of bravery, self-sacrifice, stolidity, and self-sufficiency—although still necessary—no longer sufficed. Now, more than ever, the army needed knowledge, training, and correct utilization of national assets, and it needed to apply them in accordance with mutually understood principles and methods. Schooling and training in advance of war were the keys to releasing the moral potential of the Russian soldier and elevating the competence of his leaders.[58]

Against the pre-1914 background of personnel turmoil and intellectual ferment, Colonel Svechin remained a voice of sober calculation. He understood the contemporary emphasis on the offensive from the beginning ("*offensive à outrance*," as the French intoned), but was careful to look ahead in case initial operations failed to produce decision. In 1913 he assessed the significance of potential coalition operations both west and east and concluded that the strategic center of gravity was slowly shifting to the east, thanks to demography, distance, and improved Russian military preparedness. In the event that French and tsarist armies failed to deliver rapid decision in any future conflict, the two nations would be well served to seek a balance between offense and defense. Svechin did his calculations and concluded that combatants might plan for an early victory but must be prepared for protracted conflict.[59] This was a theme to which he would return in the 1920s, with lamentable personal consequences. Before 1914 his voice was lost in the whirlwind accompanying overcommitment to the French and overconfidence in the decisive effect of initial operations.

Conclusion

World War I on the Eastern Front became additional grist for the combat experience mill. As early as 1918, with Russian participation scarcely terminated, military historians and commentators in the new Soviet state set to work on the history of the conflict with an eye both to distilling lessons learned and to adding more generally to the font of historical wisdom. Not surprisingly, some of the same figures involved either directly or indirectly in this effort were *voenspetsy*, or military specialists, former tsarist officers who were serving new political masters. As the Russian Civil War and allied intervention wound their course, they found their ranks swelled by younger officers who owed their fortunes more assuredly to the new revolutionary regime.

During the early and mid-1920s, the experience and outlook of these two groups of officers blended to influence the evolving military theory of the new Soviet state. What emerged from the blend was a novel understanding of military doctrine, military science, and the primary components of military science, including strategy, operational art, and tactics. While the specific definitions of these and other terms often assumed new significance and dimensions, the Soviet military theorists of the 1920s did not build on empty ground. In fact, A. A. Svechin, the *voenspets* whose name is most frequently associated with the appearance of the term operational art, was a former officer of the imperial Russian General Staff who had attained intellectual maturity during the remarkable flowering of Russian military thought in the pre-1914 period.

Notes

1. Bruce W. Menning is the author of *Bayonets Before Bullets: The Imperial Russian Army, 1861–1914* (Bloomington: Indiana University Press, 1992). The author wishes to thank Indiana University Press, which has graciously permitted him to draw substantial portions of this chapter from the book.
2. V. A. Semënov, *Kratkii ocherk razvitiya sovetskogo operativnogo iskusstva* (Moscow: n.p., 1960), p. 112.
3. Aleksandr G. Kavtaradze, *Voennye spetsialisty na sluzhbe Respubliki Sovetov 1917–1920 gg.* (Moscow: Nauka, 1988), pp. 224, 247.
4. For a survey of the Russo-Turkish War of 1877–1878, see Liubomir G. Beskrovnyi, *Russkoe voennoe iskusstvo XIX v.* (Moscow: n.p., 1974), pp. 296–359. The most recent treatments of planning may be found in these two publications: O. R. Airapetov, *Zabytaya kar'era "Russkogo Mol'tke" Nikolay Nikolaevich Obruchev (1830–1904)* (St. Petersburg: n.p., 1998), pp. 140–82; and David A. Rich, *The Tsar's Colonels: Professionalism, Strategy, and Subversion in Late Imperial Russia* (Cambridge, Mass.: Harvard University Press, 1998), pp. 115–48.
5. The classic English-language account is Michael E. Howard's *The Franco-Prussian War: The German Invasion of France, 1870–1871* (New York: Routledge, 2001).
6. Gunther E. Rothenberg, "Moltke, Schlieffen, and the Doctrine of Strategic Envelopment," in *Makers of Modern Strategy: From Machiavelli to the Nuclear Age,* ed. Peter Paret (Princeton: Princeton University Press, 1986), p. 296.
7. N. Pavlenko, "Iz istorii razvitiya teorii strategii," *Voenno-istoricheskii zhurnal* (hereafter cited as *VIZh*), no. 10 (October 1964): 111–13; see also F. F. Gaivoronskii, ed., *Evolyutsiia voennogo iskusstva: Etapy, tendentsii, printsipy* (Moscow: Voen. izd-vo, 1987), pp. 94–96.
8. On Sheinovo, see Chapter 2 of Menning, *Bayonets Before Bullets*; on Sedan, see Howard, *Franco-Prussian War*, pp. 203–23; on the legacy of Moltke, see William L. McElwee, *The Art of War: Waterloo to Mons* (Bloomington: Indiana University Press, 1974), pp. 107–09, 162, 184–87; and Michael D. Krause, "Moltke and the Origins of the Operational Level of War," in *Generalfeldmarshall von Moltke: Bedeutung und Wirkung*, ed. Roland G. Foerster (Munich: R. Oldenbourg, 1991), pp. 141–64.
9. G. P. Meshcheryakov, *Russkaya voennaya mysl' v XIX v.* (Moscow: n.p., 1973), pp. 261–72.
10. V. A. Zolotarev, *Russko-turetskaya voina 1877/78 gg. v otechestvennoi istoriografii* (Moscow: n.p., 1978), p. 40.
11. Aleksandr A. Svechin, ed., *Strategiya v trudakh voennykh klassikov*, 2 vols. (Moscow: n.p., 1924–1926), II: 102–04.
12. Ibid., p. 103.
13. Ibid., p. 101.
14. Liubomir G. Beskrovnyi, ed., *Russkaya voenno-teoreticheskaya mysl' XIX i nachala XX vekov* (Moscow: n.p., 1960), pp. 21–22.
15. Meshcheryakov, *Russkaya voennaya mysl'*, pp. 234–36; see also Peter von Wahlde, "A Pioneer of Russian Strategic Thought: G. A. Leer, 1829–1904," *Military Affairs* 35, no. 4 (December 1971): 1–2.

16. Liubomir G. Beskrovnyi, *Ocherki po istochnikovedeniiu voenno istorii Rossii* (Moscow: Izd-vo Akademii nauk SSSR, 1957), p. 379; R. Savushkin, "K voprosu vozniknoveniya i razvitiya operatsii," *VIZh* no. 5 (May 1979): 79–80, and Wahlde, "G. A. Lear," pp. 3–4.
17. Svechin, *Strategiya v trudakh voennykh*, II: 272, 276.
18. G. A. Leyer, comp., *Zapiski strategii*, 3d ed. (St. Petersburg: n.p., 1877).
19. Quoted in Savushkin, "K voprosu voziknoveniya i razvitiya operatsii," p. 80.
20. Leyer, *Zapiski strategii*, p. 1.
21. Beskrovnyi, *Ocherki*, p. 378; cf. Wahlde, "G. A. Lear," pp. 4–5.
22. Svechin, *Strategiya v trudakh voennykh*, II: 273.
23. Pavel A. Zhilin, ed., *Russkaya voennaya mysl' konets XIX—nachalo XX v.* (Moscow: Nauka, 1982), pp. 99–100.
24. Ibid., pp. 101–02; A. A. Gulevich, "Voina i narodnoye khozyaistvo," *Voyennyĭ sbornik* 241, no. 1 (January 1898): 60.
25. A. A. Gulevich, "Voina i narodnoe khozyaistvo," *Voennyi sbornik*, 241, no. 6 (June 1898): 300–01, 308–09.
26. On the origins of the two schools, see Zolotarev, *Russko-turetskaya*, p. 2129, and Liubomir G. Beskrovnyi, *Ocherki voennoi istoriografii Rossii* (Moscow: Izd-vo Akademii nauk SSSR, 1962), pp. 185–88, 203–69.
27. A. Ageyev, "Voenno-teoreticheskie vzglyady N. P. Mikhnevicha," *VIZh* no. 1 (January 1975): 91.
28. Ibid., p. 92; Zhilin, *Russkaya voennaya*, pp. 90–92.
29. For a useful survey of the Russo-Japanese War, see I. Rostunov, "Uroki russko-yaponskoi voiny 1904–1905 gg.," *VIZh* no. 2 (February 1984): 73–79.
30. Savushkin, "K voprosu voziknoveniya," pp. 81–82.
31. Aleksandr A. Neznamov, *Sovremmenaya voina* (St. Petersburg: n.p., n.d.), p. vi.
32. Dragomirov returned to Konotop to die in October 1905, but apparently not before he revised his text on tactics to account for changing battlefield conditions. See Zhilin, *Russkaya voennaya*, pp. 184–85.
33. Aleksandr V. Gerua, *Posle voiny o nashei armii* (St. Petersburg: n.p., 1907), pp. 17–18; see also Carl Van Dyke, "Culture of Soldiers: The Role of the Nicholas Academy of the General Staff in the Development of Russian Imperial Military Science, 1832–1912," Master's thesis, University of Edinburgh, 1989, pp.187–89.
34. Anton A. Kersnovskiy, *Filosofiya voiny* (Belgrade: Tsarskogo Vestnilka, 1939), p. 31; with that particularly Russian penchant for precise military definition, Kersnovskiy noted: "Strategy is the conduct of war. *Operatika* is the conduct of engagement [*srazhenie*]. Tactics—the conduct of battle [*boi*]." Cf. John Keegan, *Six Armies in Normandy* (New York: Viking Press, 1982), p. 243.
35. There is some speculation that Svechin, often credited with coining the term operational art, borrowed the concept from A. V. Gerua; see Aleksandr A. Svechin, *Strategiya*, 1st ed. (Moscow: n.p., 1926), pp. 18–19.
36. Svechin, *Strategiya v trudakh klassikov*, II: 175.
37. B. M. Shaposhnikov, *Vospominaniya. Voenno-nauchnye trudy* (Moscow: n.p., 1974), p. 143.
38. Peter von Wahlde, "Military Thought in Imperial Russia," Ph.D. diss., Indiana University, 1966, pp. 182–83.
39. N. P. Mikhnevich, comp., *Strategiya*, 3d ed. (St. Petersburg: n.p., 1911), pp. 9, 43; see also Ageyev, "N. P. Mikhnevicha," pp. 92–93.
40. Mikhnevich, *Strategiya*, p. 47.
41. Ibid., pp. 98–106.

42. Ibid., pp. 96, 144–45; see also Pavlenko, "Iz istorii razvitiya teorii strategii," pp. 114–15.
43. Quote from Beskrovnyi, *Russkaya voenno-teoreticheskaya*, p. 459.
44. Ibid., pp. 446–51.
45. Quote from Ibid., p. 497.
46. Neznamov, *Sovremmenaya voina*, p. vii; see also Walter M. Pintner, "Russian Military Thought: The Western Model and the Shadow of Suvorov," in Paret, *Makers of Modern Strategy*, p. 368.
47. Quote from Wahlde, "Military Thought in Imperial Russia," *Military Affairs* 35, no. 4 (December 1971): 223.
48. Aleksandr A. Neznamov, s.v. "Plan voiny," in *Voennaya entsiklopediya*, XVIII.
49. Neznamov, *Sovremennaya voina*, pp. 132, 145, 162; see also Beskrovnyi, *Russkaya voenno-teoreticheskaya mysl'*, pp. 640, 642, 672.
50. Wahlde, "Military Thought," pp. 225–26.
51. Aleksandr A. Neznamov, *Trebovaniya, kotorye pred'yavlyaet sovremennyi boi k podgotovke (obucheniyu) nachal'nikov i mass* (St. Petersburg: n.p., 1909), p. 4.
52. Neznamov, *Sovremennyi boi*, pp. 228–36.
53. Neznamov, s.v. "Operatsiya (voennaya)," in *Voennaya entsiklopediya*.
54. Beskrovnyi has noted that this understanding is similar to contemporary Soviet operational art: "Neznamov provided a basis for understanding operational art which is rather close to our definition." See Beskrovnyi, *Russkaya voenno-teoreticheskaya mysl'*, p. 37; and Savushkin, "K voprosu voziknoveniya," p. 80.
55. Neznamov, "Operatsiya (voennaya)," pp. 132–33, and Neznamov, *Trebovaniya*, pp.10–13; see also A. Ageyev, "Voenno-teoretichieskoe nasledie A. A. Neznamova," *VIZh* 11 (November 1983): 86.
56. Ageyev, "A. A. Neznamov," p. 86.
57. Neznamov, *Sovremennaya voina*, pp. 21–23.
58. Neznamov, *Trebovaniya*, p. 6.
59. Aleksandr A. Svechin, "Bol' shaya voennaya programma," *Russkaya mysl'* VIII (August 1913): 19–29. See also A. Y. Savinkin and A. G. Kavtaradze, et al., comps., *Postizhenie voennogo iskusstva: Ideinoe nasledie A. Svechina* (Moscow: n.p., 1999), pp. 125–43.

The Origins of Soviet Operational Art 1917–1936[1]

Jacob W. Kipp

Over the last decade Western military historians and analysts have come to appreciate the importance of operational art in modern warfare — the conduct of war at echelons above corps and on the scale of theater-strategic campaigns. Such appreciation of operational art stands in stark contrast to the situation two decades ago, when Soviet claims for the importance of operational art (*operativnoe iskusstvo*) were dismissed as mere pretension. Operational art, an artificial creation imposed between tactics and strategy — so it was thought — had no content or merit.[2]

The contributions of Soviet military theorists and practitioners to the development of operational art and the vitality of Soviet military theory in the 1920s and early 1930s are now widely acknowledged.[3] Condoleeza Rice's essay on the young Red commanders and tsarist military specialists, who laid the foundations for Soviet military art, placed their works among the ranks of the *Makers of Modern Strategy*.[4] The late Brig. Richard E. Simpkin, one of the most original and insightful students of military affairs of the last decade, in a stimulating study on the continuing relevance of the Soviet concept of deep operations, noted the special contribution of Marshal Mikhail N. Tukhachevsky to that concept.[5]

This chapter examines the development of Soviet operational art within the larger context for the formulation of Soviet military art and military science between 1918 and 1936. Operational art was more than the accomplishment of one man. This essay will trace the path to operational art from the creation of the Soviet State and the Red Army through the recruitment of tsarist military specialists (*voenspets*) to the evolution of the Red Army as a combat force fighting a revolutionary war. The issues raised by the final campaigns of the Russian Civil War are examined as they contributed to the articulation of such concepts as successive operations, deep battle, and deep operations.

For over a decade a spirited, often polemical, positive, but finally lethal debate among the leadership of the Red Army laid the foundations for the development of Soviet operational art, the theory of deep operations, and the mechanization of the Red Army. Aleksandr I. Verkhovsky (1886–1938), an officer of the tsarist general staff (*genshtabisty*), Minister of War in the Provisional Government in September–October 1917, and *voenspets* from 1919, saw those debates as a three-way contest among conservatives, realists, and futurists. In the 1920s Verkhovsky taught in and directed the Tactics Department at the Military Academy of the Red Army of Workers and Peasants (RKKA). He identified reform-minded, *voenspetsy* professors like himself as the "realist," engaged in "a war on two fronts." They had to contend with conservatives, who wanted to maintain past concepts because they were sanctioned by history and the unchanging laws of military science, and the futurists, who on the basis of the Revolution and Civil War put their faith in crude military means and political agitation and trusted in class struggle to ignite revolution behind the enemy's lines. In assessing this struggle during the Academy's first decade, 1918–1928, he concluded that it had been full of vitality and had served the Red Army quite well.[6]

One area of significant progress was the realm of "higher tactics" or "lower strategy," as studies of the operational level of war were known at the Military Academy in 1918–1923. A leading figure in the study of operations was Verkhovsky's colleague, Aleksandr A. Svechin. He too was a *genshtabist*, veteran of the Russo-Japanese War and World War I, and *voenspets* in the RKKA. Prior to World War I Svechin, as a professor at the Nikolaevskaya Academy of the General Staff, had been one of a cohort of young military thinkers and historians who had focused on the conduct of operations as the foundation of modern industrial war. Svechin in a series of lectures on strategy in 1923–1924 coined the term operational art.[7] He described operational art as the bridge between tactics and strategy, the means by which the senior commander transformed a series of tactical successes into operational "bounds" linked together by the commander's intent and plan and contributing to strategic success in a given theater of military actions.[8]

N. Varfolomeev, the deputy head of the Department of Strategy during the same period, noted that objective changes in warfare associated with the appearance of million-man armies and technological innovations had recast the face of battle, increased its spatial and temporal dimensions, broken down the conventional forms of combined arms, forced a rethinking of problems of command and control, and laid the foundation for the emergence of the operation as the bridge between strategy and tactics. Tactics became the conduct of battle/combat (*boi*), the engagement (*srazhenie*), which in the Napoleonic era had been conducted as a series of combats on a single battlefield under the observation of the commander. The engagement now took place over a much broader front and at much greater depths well beyond the ability of any commander to exercise direct control. Borodino had given way to Mukden, Tannenberg, and Warsaw. In this manner the operation emerged as the bridge to strategy. Varfolomeev described the modern operation as: "the totality of maneuvers and battles in a given sector of a theater of military actions

(TVD) which are directed toward the achievement of a common objective, which has been set as final in a given period of the campaign. The conduct of an operation is not a matter of tactics. It has become the lot of operational art."[9] Within a year operational art became a new discipline taught in the new chair on the Conduct of Operations within the Department of Strategy at the Military Academy of the RKKA, thanks to the intervention of Tukhachevsky, the newly appointed deputy chief of staff of the RKKA.

While the introduction of operational art as a separate discipline was short-lived—the chair disappeared within a year—the subject became a core topic in senior officer education and reappeared as a Department in the Frunze Military Academy in 1931. The very existence of this new category within Soviet military science had a profound impact on Soviet military art, military doctrine, and the concept of future war. This situation is quite clear from contemporary publications, articles, and regulations.[10]

Later events—the politicization of military theory and attacks upon *voenspetsy*, the blood purge of the military, the cult of Stalin, and the manufacture of an entire pseudo-history of the Civil War, conspired to rob the Red Army of its past, obscure the origins of operational art, and plant seeds of confusion and uncertainty about the contribution of individuals to the development of operational art in the interwar period. After the triumph of Stalinism, many of the most important contributors to these developments were labeled "enemies of the people," imprisoned, liquidated, and then transformed into "non-persons." This situation has greatly handicapped the study of the origins and development of operational art. The Soviet Army lost much of its own past. In spite of these problems, we can recreate that past and discuss the development of operational art from World War I and the Civil War to the articulation of the theory of deep, successive operations in *"The Temporary Field Regulations of the Workers' and Peasants' Red Army, 1936."*

World War I and Russian Operational Experience

As Professor Menning has pointed out in the previous chapter, with the industrialization of war, the problems of mass and mobility became infinitely more complex. The new weapons extended the breadth and depth of the battlefield, increased the lethality of fire, played havoc with well-established concepts of combined arms, and made possible the more rapid mobilization of manpower for the conduct of the campaign. The traditional definitions of tactics (the direction of forces on the field of battle) and strategy (the control of units as they maneuvered prior to engagement) broke down.

The experience of combat in the Far East during the Russo-Japanese War, 1904–1905, brought these problems to the attention of a group of reform-minded Russian officers associated with the general staff and the Nikolaevskaya Academy of the General Staff, who became the leaders of a postwar military reform effort. For these officers the conduct of operations, as the means of linking together tactical successes into a coherent whole and setting the stage for new methods and means of troop control, became the essence of modern warfare. The process culminated with new field regulations in 1912, an unsuccessful campaign for a "unified military doctrine," and a greater emphasis on immediate offensive operations in Russia's war plans.[11]

These interwar debates had marginal impact upon the way in which Russia went to war in 1914. The concept of a unified supreme headquarters (*Stavka*) was accepted, and the intermediary command was introduced to control the operations of a group of armies in a given sector of the theater. New Russian field regulations placed greater emphasis upon effective combined arms, the meeting engagement, and march-maneuver. In addition, thanks in part to changing diplomatic circumstances, bureaucratic politics, and the emphasis upon a short, decisive war, Russian war plans shifted from General Mikhnevich's covering-force strategy to one of initial offensive actions, even before the completion of mobilization, a position in keeping with Colonel Neznamov's views on the decisiveness of initial operations. Not all the reformers, however, agreed with this shift.[12]

War Plans A (Austro-Hungary) and G (Germany) as drafted did not provide for a decisive massing of forces and means against either opponent. When war came in the summer of 1914, after the false start of the proposed partial mobilization against Austro-Hungary, Russian forces under Plan A were committed to immediate offensive operations against the Germans in East Prussia and Austro-Hungarians in Galicia. As General Zaionchkovskiy noted later, both operational plans were remarkable for their "diffusion and distribution of means." Nowhere did Russian forces achieve an overwhelming superiority, which would have brought about a decisive victory. In their advances to contact and initial engagements the Russian armies found their logistical systems to be totally inadequate to sustain the pace of operations.[13] *Stavka* and the fronts did not effectively coordinate the armies' actions and were slow to adjust their planning to enemy actions.

While prior to the war the Academy of the General Staff had begun the study of the operational level of war, the results were not in evidence in the initial phase of the war. The Russian Army did not achieve the "steamroller" mass, which worried its adversaries and consoled its allies. Nor did it attain operational massing of forces. Zaionchkovskiy argues that failure of leadership was the responsibility of the tsarist general staff. Reformers at the Academy were cut off from the rest of the army. Its generals and colonels, who staffed the fronts and armies, were considered "professors in uniform" and thought incapable of command. The higher leadership of the state and the army did not take such ideas seriously. New concepts were proposed in *Russkiî invalid* and *Voennyi sbornik*, but they seemed to have little positive impact on either the chiefs of the general staff or the ministers of war. General Sukhomlinov's memoirs are typical of the lack of attention paid to the academy by senior officers.[14] The academy was not the "brain" of the general staff, and the general staff hardly qualified as the "brain of the army." Indeed, the process of expanding the force and simultaneously changing the nature of the war plans proved too complex for the general staff to manage in the last two years before the outbreak of hostilities.

In spite of the reformers' efforts, the Russian officer and NCO corps were hardly prepared for modern war. This was particularly true regarding the ability of Russian units and formations to maneuver with dispatch. Zaionchkovskiy argued that Russia went to war in 1914 with "good regiments, average divisions and corps and poor armies and fronts."[15] The meeting engagements fought at Gumbinnen in East Prussia and along the Gnilaia Lipa in Galicia in the first weeks of the war seem to confirm this judgment. Here, Russian regiments and divisions fought without operational direction or coordination. In both cases they won initial victories. At Gumbinnen, no follow-up advance by victorious units of the First Army ensued; the defending German forces were able to disengage and then mass against General Samsonov's ill-fated Second Army. In Galicia, the victories along the Gnilaia Lipa were the first Russian successes on a path which would culminate in the capture of Lvov.[16] Then the logistical system collapsed and the advance into the Carpathians came to a halt. In short, the army's organism had a stronger skeleton than nervous system. Its training and regimental system created good junior officers but not an effective staff system or high command structure.[17]

The experience of Russian forces on the Eastern Front during World War I proved particularly beneficial to such study. The situation at the front never degenerated into the absolute linearity of positional warfare in the trenches of the Western Front because of the correlation of area (the very length of the front, its density, and relatively lower number of forces) and means available along the front, making it difficult to create deeply echeloned defenses like those seen in the West and the underdevelopment of the transportation and communication assets of the theater, which reduced the defender's relative advantage in responding to an attack. Thus, scale, density, and economic backwardness combined to create greater opportunities for maneuver. War in the East became a *Gummikrieg* (*rezinovaya voîna*), as one captured Austrian officer described the autumn fighting in the Carpathians to his Russian interrogators at Eighth Army Headquarters.[18] Operational maneuver, such as the Lodz envelopment and counterenvelopment of the fall of 1914 during which

German and Austro-Hungarian forces sought to encircle the Second and Fifth Russian Armies and were themselves subsequently threatened with envelopment, persisted throughout three years of fighting without either side's being able to gain the upper hand. Commanders on both sides developed the techniques necessary for a breakthrough but were unable to transform a breakthrough into a sustained drive, which would destroy the opposing force, overcome the enemy's reserves as they redeployed to meet the threat, and bring about decisive victory. General Brusilov's Southwestern Front provided a model for such a breakthrough operation on the Russian side, one which Red Army staff officers would study in detail.[19] It is probably fair to describe the 1914–1917 struggle as a semi-mobile war in which neither side was able to execute decisive maneuver. Cavalry raids in the rear of the enemy army became more difficult and could not deliver any decisive results. The pauses between operations grew longer as combat losses increased and the process of regrouping forces became more complex and time-consuming.[20]

At the start of the war, on the assumption that it would be a short one, the War Ministry closed the academy and mobilized its faculty and students. As the war dragged on and the need for more staff officers became critical, the War Ministry reopened the academy in late 1916. During a turbulent year of revolution and social upheaval in which the old army disintegrated, the academy resumed its mission under these trying circumstances.[21] Following the October Revolution and the German advance toward Petrograd, the commandant of the academy ordered the faculty and students and the library moved to safety. In this case safety was Kazan, where most of those who went joined Admiral A. V. Kolchak's White Russians (counterrevolutionary forces) in Siberia. A minority of faculty and students moved to Moscow with the Soviet government. In the fall of 1918 the Soviet government set about organizing its own Academy of the General Staff.[22]

The Civil War and the Conduct of Operations

The disintegration of the old army and the mounting prospects of civil war and foreign intervention created a situation in which the newly established Bolshevik regime had to set about the creation of its own armed forces. The RKKA, or Red Army of Workers and Peasants, which emerged during the Civil War, relied heavily upon tsarist military specialists for combat leadership, staffing, and training. By the end of the Civil War about one-third of all Red Army officers were *voenspetsy*, and in the higher ranks the ratio was even greater. Thus, 82 percent of all infantry regiment commanders, 83 percent of all division and corps commanders, and 54 percent of all commanders of military districts were former tsarist officers.[23]

The forging of this union between the new Bolshevik government and the tsarist military specialists had not been easy. Lenin and his new Commissar of War, L. D. Trotsky, had faced criticism from left-wing advocates of partisan warfare and critics who doubted the loyalty of the tsarist officers. In March 1918 Trotsky wrote:

> We need a real armed force, constructed on the basis of military science. The active and systematic participation of the military specialists in all our work is therefore a matter of vital importance. The military specialists must have guaranteed to them the possibility of exerting their powers honestly and honorably in the matter of the creation of the army.[24]

As I. A. Korotkov has acknowledged, the first steps taken by Soviet military science were made by *voenspetsy* associated with the tsarist general staff and its Academy. The first Soviet professional military journal, *Voennoe delo*, carried articles on military doctrine by Neznamov, Svechin, and P. I. Izmest'ev—the last being the author of a major study on the significance of the estimate in planning military operations.[25] In this fashion the Bolshevik state, championing the proletarian world revolution, inherited the mature speculations on the conduct of operations by the best minds of the tsarist army. Izmest'ev's study on "The Significance of the Estimate in Working Out and Conducting Military Operations" had appeared in *Voennyĭ sbornik*, between March 1915 and June 1916. The author used historical analysis of military operations and the writings of Clausewitz, Schlichting, and Jomini to address the importance of staff process in planning and controlling military operations. Izmest'ev pointed out that "great captains" of the past had combined will and reason to manage risk. However, he noted that modern war had made the planning and conduct of military operations one of the most complex and demanding of human activities. Modern warfare would not tolerate an eyeball estimate (*glazomer*) of the situation. Only the intellect (*um*) could deal with the complexity of modern operations and reduce chance to a question of probability.[26] The staff in this context replaced the intuition of the "great captain" to become the instrument of rational control and planning. Kuropatkin's handling of Russian forces at the Battle of Mukden in January 1905 became a case in point of what could go wrong.[27] In a critique of Europe's war planners before 1914, Izmest'ev noted the tendency to suppose that the war plan and the plan of initial operations were the end of the estimate process. That estimate process began when the war plan moved to the campaign plan, which he defined as the preparation and execution of the plan of war in a given theater of military action. But experience had shown that the same detailed planning was necessary for subsequent operations. The staff process had to calculate march rates, transport rates, and rates of consumption of ammunition and materiel, as well as assess enemy intentions and plan those actions that would frustrate them. In short, the staff engaged in a struggle with time and space to make possible the decisive concentration of combat power on the main direction of possible attack in a timely fashion. In making such calculations, planners had to employ norms, based upon the combat experience of actual troops and not arbitrary assessments. Izmest'ev believed that the estimates upon which the war plan was based should for the most part be "mathematically absolutely exact estimate[s]." Such calculations did not end with the first operations of the initial phase of the war. After that the commander and his staff would have to engage in their own calculations based upon their assessment of the mission, theater terrain, enemy, one's own forces, and time. Failure to adjust to new circumstances would lead to defeats, like those inflicted at Tannenberg and along the Marne. He wrote:

> Only an amateur [*profan*] can think that the entire campaign will unfold according to the prearranged plan without a deviation and that the original plan could be maintained up to the end in all its features. Of course, the military commander never lets his main objective pass from view and is not distracted by accidents or changes in events but he cannot predetermine beforehand with confidence the path by which to achieve this goal.[28]

The more scientific the approach to operational planning, the greater the ability to reduce risk to manageable dimensions and the higher the probability of success in the conduct of operations.[29]

Thus, the legacy of the tsarist general staff provided the Red Army with an intellectual legacy conducive to the study and use of past operations. One of the most important vehicles for such work was the Commission for the Study and Use of the Experience of the War, 1914–1918, which the Soviet government created in 1918 and which Svechin soon headed. The focus of the commission's work was to be the operations of all belligerents.[30] However, intellectual speculation about the nature of operations took second place to the conduct of war for most officers of the newly founded Red Army. As Civil War tore apart the fabric of Russian society, the Soviet Republic created its own "new model army." By recruiting former officers, the Bolsheviks sought to exploit the professional talents of a "class enemy" to secure the survival of their new order. The recruitment of military specialists (*voenspetsy*) was to some measure the product of the Bolsheviks' and Lenin's attitude toward the professional expertise of the "*spetsy*."[31] Among the officers who joined the Red Army it was in part the product of a commitment to a transcendent Russian nationalism. Such sentiments moved General Brusilov to offer his services to the Soviet State during the Polish invasion in the spring of 1920. Finally, it was partly a matter of luck and prerevolutionary ties.

By the end of 1918 with the help of the military specialists the Soviet Republic had raised an army of 300,000 men, instituted conscription, created a main staff to direct the war, initiated the publication of *Voennoe delo*, formed a military-historical commission to study World War I and later the operations of the Civil War, and begun creation of the Academy of the General Staff.[32] Some *voenspetsy* would change sides, but the system of political commissars, making hostages of military specialists' relatives in some cases, and infusion of party cadres into the military kept such defections within bounds. S. I. Gusev, an old Bolshevik with close ties to general staff circles in the prewar period when he served as one of the editors of the *Military Encyclopedia*, noted the loyalty of the military specialists with whom he served at the front.[33]

In spite of reservations among many Bolsheviks and even among their fellow officers, the *genshtabisty* proved an increasingly vital component in the Red Army's conduct of the Civil War. Tukhachevsky, a former tsarist officer and the dashing commander of the Fifth Army, had initial reservations about the *genshtabisty*, whom he considered, with the exception of the youngest officers, to be totally unprepared for modern war or the special conditions of a civil war between social classes. Tukhachevsky called for the creation of a "Communist command cadre."[34] Tukhachevsky himself, however, as the scale of the fighting and the quality of the opposing forces improved, changed his tune. In explaining the setbacks that he suffered during the Western Front's May offensive against the "White Poles," he pointed to the lack of staff support under which he suffered at the division, army, and front levels.[35] By the end of the Civil War, S. S. Kamenev, himself a *genshtabisty* and the commander in chief of the Armed Forces of the Soviet Republic, described the secret of success as a command team, in which the Communist and *genshtabist* joined to create the perfect command team.[36] One of the best examples of such a combination was that of M. V. Frunze, who went from political commissar to Red Army commander under the guidance of such *genshtabisty* as F. F. Novitsky, A. A. Baltiîsky, and V. S. Lazarevich.[37]

On their side the Red *genshtabisty* understood the most pressing needs of the new workers' and peasants' army. A. Neznamov set the immediate goal of officer education in the Red Army at the level of Tolstoy's Captain Tushin — to give these officers the ability to lead in combat. The Red Army did not need young Fredericks or Napoleons. The basic education of junior officers was to consist of teaching them uniform tactics so that they might be "good executors" of orders.[38] Many junior officers suffered from that independence of action, associated with the *partizanshchina*, out of which many Red Army units emerged. At the operational level, Neznamov prized creativity.[39] But here the commander's plan and his concept had to limit the creativity of his subordinates to using initiative to fulfill the plan. Neznamov's approach had three specific consequences, which would shape the Red Army's officer corps. First, uniform tactics put a high premium on battle drills as a way of providing a general response to tactical developments. Second, it emphasized the dissemination of such uniform tactical views to all combat arms so that combined arms would come naturally at the tactical level. Third, it established a specific need to educate senior commanders in the conduct of operations. Creativity was to be most prized here.[40]

The marriage of the RKKA with the *voenspetsy* proved stormy but successful. However, during the war and after it a gulf opened between *voenspetsy* and the young Red commanders. Most *spetsy* dismissed the RKKA's experience, the Civil War, as a poor man's war, fought with what was at hand. Young Red commanders saw the same struggle as the embodiment of a revolutionary class warfare that would sweep the globe. The historical orientation of Marxist ideology served as a powerful stimulus for this debate, while the Academy of the General Staff provided focus, military-historical perspective, and professionally competent judgment of that distinctive experience.[41]

The ideologically correct evaluation of that experience set the context for the postwar polemics between Frunze and Trotsky within the Communist Party regarding the appropriateness of a "unified military doctrine" for the Soviet state and the Red Army. Commissar for Military Affairs Trotsky argued that the Civil War experience had not created the basis for a Marxist military science. Indeed, Marxism had no right to make any such claim regarding military art and science. Frunze, the Bolshevik commander, self-taught military intellectual, and victor over Baron Wrangel, contested that point. He argued that the revolutionary nature of the new state, the Red Army, and its combat experience had forged the conditions for the formulation of a unified military doctrine, "which determines the character of the construction of the country's armed forces, the methods of combat training for troops and command personnel." The ruling group's concept of its military system was in turn shaped by class relations, external threat, and the level of the nation's economic development.[42] Trotsky, like the prewar opponents of a unified military doctrine, worried that giving official sanction to a particular concept would invite the transformation of doctrine into an ossified dogma. He feared efforts to universalize the validity of the combat experience derived from the Civil War.[43]

This intraparty debate in the minds of many officers was an explicit echo of the prewar debate over a "unified military doctrine." Supporters of Trotsky's position within the Academy of the General Staff noted the linkage between Frunze's views and those of Svechin and Neznamov. When veterans of the Civil War returned to the Academy, they called for a revision of the curriculum to emphasize the "Higher Studies on War." This program was nothing more than the tsarist reformers' program dressed in revolutionary red. As D. Petrovsky observed, the struggle between students and faculty at the Academy reflected this earlier fight over military doctrine:

On the contrary, a close review of this very program as well as the written and oral commentaries about it leads one to the conclusion that in the struggle between two factions of the old Academy of the General Staff the students entirely have accepted the point of view of the followers of Professor Golovin and Chief of the Academy Comrade Snesarev is correct, when he stated that, in fact, the proposal of the students to replace Lukirsky by Neznamov as Director of Tactics, of course, is not just a simple change of personnel. These figures personify in themselves certain tendencies.[44]

To Petrovsky, Frunze's proposals were only an updated, Marxian expression of the same program. Reform-minded *voenspetsy* saw the Civil War as a confirmation of those trends that they had seen in the Russo-Japanese War and World War I.

The Experience of the Civil War

Clearly, the Civil War had been qualitatively different from World War I on the Western and Eastern fronts. If the Imperial Army had suffered from economic backwardness and isolation, enduring a shell crisis in 1915 that reduced its combat capabilities, the Red Army had to confront the utter disintegration of the national economy. Revolution, civil war, international boycott, and foreign intervention combined to undermine the national economy. The regime's response, War Communism, was less social utopia and more a form of barracks socialism, in which all resources were organized to field a mass army, equipped with the most basic instruments of industrial war—the rifle, machine gun, and field artillery. Even in the procurement of these vital weapons the level of production fell sharply in comparison with what had been achieved by Russian industry during World War I. Thus, in 1920 the production of rifles was only one-third of that in 1917.[45] It was the Whites who, thanks to foreign assistance, fielded in small quantities the latest weapons of war, especially the tank.[46] By the end of the Civil War the Soviet Republic put into the field a ragged force of 5.5 million men.

The Civil War was also noteworthy for a number of politico-geostrategic features, which had a profound impact on the nature of the struggle. First, it was in every sense a civil war in which neither side asked for nor gave any quarter. The Russia over which the Reds, Whites, and Greens struggled might be described as a few island-cities in a sea of peasant villages. The cities emptied as the links between town and countryside collapsed. Red Guard detachments swept through Tiutchev's "poor villages," seizing grain and recruiting soldiers. Red Terror and White Terror mounted in scale and intensity. At times it was difficult to distinguish between combatants and brigands. The Red and White armies were notoriously unstable, with a persistent problem of desertion. In 1920, as

Tukhachevsky prepared the Western Front for an offensive, he instituted a campaign to extract 40,000 deserters from Belorussia's villages for service. Within a month the Western Front found that it had extracted 100,000 deserters, whose presence taxed the supply and training capacity of the front.[47] Such reinforcements were unstable in the attack and tended to vanish at the first sign of disaster.

The second reality of the Civil War was the fact that the Bolsheviks controlled the central heartland around Moscow and managed to maintain an effective, if much reduced in scale, rail system, which permitted them to use their internal lines of communication to great effect. On the other hand, the White Armies fought on the periphery of Russia, in lands often inhabited by non-Russians who had no great interest in the revival of a centralized Russian state. The presence of the White Armies on the periphery, especially in southern Russia, the Kuban, and Siberia, meant that operations were frequently conducted in "underdeveloped [*malokul'turnye*] theaters of military action." As R. Tsiffer observed in 1928, the Civil War seemed to confirm the general rule that the more developed the theater of war, the more likely the emergence of positional forms of warfare; conversely, the less developed the theater of war, the greater the opportunities for the employment of maneuver forms of combat.[48] This situation, when linked to the low density of forces, the ineffectiveness of logistical services, and the low combat stability, created conditions for a war of maneuver. It was not uncommon, as Tukhachevsky pointed out, to have each side launch operations that would sweep 1,000 *versts* (600 miles) forward and another 1,000 *versts* back.[49] The instability of the rear in military and political terms meant that a successful offensive, if a vigorous pursuit could be maintained, would often lead to the routing of the opponent and the disintegration of his political base.

Maneuver in this case took the form of a "ram" of forces directed at the enemy in the hope of disorganizing and demoralizing him. It would be fair to characterize this operational approach as an attempt to substitute mobility for maneuver. The Red Army lacked either the staff assets or communication facilities to sustain the necessary command and control to carry out more complex maneuvers that might lead to the encirclement and destruction of enemy forces.[50] In Tukhachevsky's case this approach was linked with the concept of political subversion and class war as a combat multiplier, what he called "the revolution from without."[51]

One of the most conspicuous developments of the Civil War was the resurgence of cavalry as a combat arm. Russian cavalry had not distinguished itself particularly during World War I. Now under civil war conditions, cavalry recovered its place as the combat arm of a war of maneuver. The loyalty of the Don Cossacks and the support of many senior cavalry commanders gave the Whites substantial initial advantages in the use of this arm. Trotsky's famous call, "Proletarians to horse!" initiated the process of creating a Red Cavalry.[52] Soviet cavalry units were raised from the beginning of the war. However, greater attention was paid to creating troop cavalry detachments to provide the eyes and security screens for the newly formed infantry divisions. Army cavalry, cavalry units organized into independent brigades and divisions, were gradually formed into corps and later into armies.[53]

The raid mounted by General K. K. Mamontov's cavalry in August–September 1919 provided the stimulus for the creation of the First Red Cavalry Army, Budennyî's legendary *Konarmiya*. In order to take pressure off Denikin's forces, Mamontov's IV Don Cavalry Corps (7,500 sabers) undertook an independent raid deep into the rear of the Southern Front. The 36th and 40th Divisions that held the 100-kilometer section of the line through which Mamontov's corps passed were widely dispersed, and Mamontov used air reconnaissance to find a sector where his cavalry could slip through without serious opposition. Using his air reconnaissance to avoid contact with Bolshevik units, Mamontov struck deep into six *guberniyas*, wrecking the rail lines and destroying military stores as they advanced.[54] The *Revvoensovet* [Revolutionary Military Council] of the Republic took this threat seriously and created an internal front under the command of M. M. Lashevich to deal with Mamontov's corps. On its return to Denikin's lines the corps' pace slowed under the weight of booty, allowing Lashevich to concentrate Red Cavalry forces against its strung-out columns. Mamontov reached Denikin's lines but suffered serious losses on the retreat south from Kozlov to Voronezh.[55] The use of air assets to provide effective reconnaissance for large-scale cavalry raids was noted by the Red Army and became an important part of its own concept of the operational-strategic use of cavalry.[56]

White intelligence units and counterintelligence organs [*AZVUKI*] quickly grasped the military and political effects of such raiding maneuvers. The Eighth Red Army had been totally routed, a general panic created in the Soviets' rear area, and the most strenuous military and political measures were required to deal with the threat posed by Mamontov's Raid. These included systematic use of terror and the secret police.[57]

For their part in assessing the failure of their own offensive the Soviet leadership noted the role of Mamontov's Raid in contributing to the further disorganization of their own forces and creating a crisis in their rear. As counteraction to the threat of further raids, Trotsky proposed the creation of more partisan detachments in the rear of Denikin's Army.[58] Trotsky also began to promote the creation of larger Red Cavalry units. In November the *Revvoensovet* ordered the creation of the *Konarmiya* under the command of S. M. Budennyî, a former NCO in the tsarist army and then the commander of the I Cavalry Corps. The *Konarmiya* was initially composed of three cavalry divisions, an armor car battalion, an air group, and its own armored train. Later two other cavalry divisions were added and an independent cavalry brigade was also included.[59] The basic units of the *Konarmiya* were its cavalry divisions, armed with rifles, sabers, revolvers, and hand grenades. Each division was also to have, according to its table of organization and equipment, twenty-four machine guns mounted on *tachanki*, but in practice the number was often two or three times higher. The most effective commanders used such guns to provide concentrated fire. Each division also had its own artillery, three batteries of light field guns and one battery of 45-mm. howitzers. In offensive operations it also became common practice to assign a "mounted infantry" to each cavalry army. This force amounted to about one battalion for each cavalry division—a battalion being between 1,000 and 1,300 men—and eighteen machine guns mounted on roughly 200 *tachanki*.[60]

Budennyî's Red Cavalry quickly became the stuff of legends. Isaac Babel, who served as a political commissar with one of its units, immortalized its exploits in a series of short stories.[61] The legend later turned into official myth as Budennyî, Voroshilov, and Stalin invented history to fit their own cults of personality. In the decade after the Civil War it was still possible to give a reasonably objective evaluation to the contribution of the *Konarmiya* and strategic cavalry in general to Soviet operations on the various fronts of the Civil War.

Strategic cavalry repeatedly played the role of shock force, striking deep into the enemy rear, disrupting his command and control, and demoralizing his forces. Among the most celebrated of these operations were those in the Ukraine in June–July 1920, when the *Konarmiya* was redeployed from the Caucasian Front to the Southwestern Front to form the strike group for a drive to liberate Kiev and push the Poles out of the Ukraine. At the start of the operation, Budennyî's *Konarmiya* had 18,000 sabers, 52 guns, 350 machine guns, 5 armored trains, an armored car detachment, and 8 aircraft. The Polish Third Army was spread thin and had few effective reserves. Thus, one cavalry division was able to slip through the lines and mount a raid on Zhitomir-Berdichev in the first week of June. The Polish commander responded by shortening his lines and giving up Kiev. The blows of the *Konarmiya* were in this case combined with pressure from the Soviet Twelfth Army, and this created the impression that the Polish defenders faced the possibility of being surrounded and cut off.[62] Polish cavalry proved totally ineffective in maintaining contact with Budennyî's forces. Over the next month the *Konarmiya* took part in heavy fighting around Rovno, taking that town by a flanking maneuver on 4 July, losing it to a Polish counterattack on 9 July, and regaining it by direct assault the next day.

Budennyî's force engaged in forty-three days of intensive combat without effective logistical support. Cavalry brigades, which at the start of the campaign had numbered 1,500 sabers, were down to 500 or fewer by the end of the fighting. The fighting at Zhitomir and Rovno exemplifies the combined-arms approach that typified Soviet employment of strategic cavalry. It also showed its limited ability to engage in sustained combat.[63] At the same time, the Zhitomir and Rovno operations exemplified the psychological impact of the strategic raiding force. Marshal Pilsudski credits Budennyî's *Konarmiya* with an ability to create a powerful, irresistible fear in the deep rear. Its effect on the Polish war effort was like the opening of another and even more dangerous front within the country itself.[64]

The Red Cavalry's success at Rovno set the stage for one of the most controversial and frequently studied operations of the Civil War: Marshal Tukhachevsky's general offensive of July–August 1920, in which his Western Front struck beyond the Vistula to threaten Warsaw. Pilsudski's counterattack, coming at the very gates of Prague and resulting in the destruction of major Soviet formations pinned against the Polish–East Prussian border, became known as the Miracle of Warsaw. More realistic Soviet assessments of the campaign doubted this implied connection between the Vistula and the Marne and said that the "miracle" was that the bedraggled, unfed, poorly armed, ragtag divisions of the Western Front had gotten as far as they had. Tukhachevsky's general offensive took place without adequate reserves, effective command and control, and logistical support.[65] Believing his own theory about "revolution from without," he fell into the trap of assuming that the psychological weight of the advance would break the will of the Polish defense without his having to destroy those forces in the field. His forces did manage to push the Polish defenders back over several natural defensive positions and the line of German emplacements along the Auta.[66] However, Pilsudski's counterattack struck the overextended forces of the Western Front near Siedlce and drove a wedge between Tukhachevsky's Thirteenth Army and the Mozyr Group. The attack threw the Western Front back in disarray and trapped the RKKA's Fourth Army against the East Prussian border.[67]

The geographic peculiarities of the theater—the fact that the Pripiat Marshes dissects Belorussia and the Ukraine—created two distinct axes of advance toward the Vistula. The existing Soviet command structure called for Tukhachevsky's Western (Belorussian) Front to direct the fighting north of Polesie and Egorov's Southwestern Front (Ukrainian) to direct the fighting south of Polesie. This military case of "dual power" combined to frustrate Soviet control of the Vistula Campaign. In addition to directing the fighting in the Kiev sector, the Southwestern Front also had to combat Wrangel's army based in the Crimean and cover the potential threat of Rumanian intervention. Memoir literature by the principal commanders on both sides addressed the issue of strategic-operational direction and control. Budennyî's *Konarmiya* persisted in its attacks toward Lvov, even after Kamenev as commander in chief had ordered it and the Twelfth Army to regroup, join the Western Front, and undertake a drive toward Lublin to relieve pressure on the Western Front. Southwestern Front Commander A. I. Egorov, in the words of Triandafillov, found himself caught trying to manage operations on two axes without staff support and did not feel "the beating pulse of the operation."[68] Thus, Tukhachevsky's Western Front lacked support from the south when its Fourth, Fifteenth, and Third armies tried to turn Warsaw from the north by crossing the Vistula between Modlin and Plock. Since Joseph Stalin served as the Political Commissar of the *Konarmiya*, Budennyî's independence and insubordination became entangled in the political struggles following Lenin's death. Under Stalin's cult of personality the unpleasant truth about Lvov and Warsaw was covered up by blaming Trotsky, the Commissar of War, for ordering the regrouping of forces to support a drive on Lublin.[69]

The Development of Soviet Operational Art

Before Stalin, Budennyî, and Voroshilov were able to rewrite history to their own liking, a host of Soviet works in the 1920s addressed the Vistula Campaign in a critical and fruitful manner. Some of this was undoubtedly fueled by the usual postwar "battle of the memoirs." However, there was something more to the Soviet debates. Marshal Pilsudski caught the kernel of this difference when he observed that Tukhachevsky's published account of the campaign showed an "extraordinary penchant for the abstract." He noted that the underlying theme of the work was "an attempt at the solution of the problem of handling great masses on a large scale."[70] The Soviet military authors, including Tukhachevsky's defenders and critics, seem to have taken seriously Neznamov's assertion regarding the role of historical criticism in the development of military theory: "It would seem that nothing could be higher than experience in war itself, and yet historical experience shows us that without the criticism of science, without the book, it, too, is of no use."[71]

The emphasis was on the development of military theory, and A. Verkhovsky, a *voenspets* and professor of tactics at the Military Academy, seems close to the truth when he describes the internal struggle among military intellectuals as a contest between right and left flanks for support. The former wanted to take the realities of World War I and the Civil War and codify them into military doctrine, while the latter sought to envision a future "class war," which negated the more mundane concerns of the military art.[72] The debate and a very sharp, almost brutal criticism, which did not spare personal feelings, seem to have kept these two flanks in a dynamic balance, creating the necessary conditions for the emergence of a distinctive Soviet operational art, which addressed the conduct of initial operations in a future war.

The emergence of operational art as a specific topic of study within the Red Army coincided with the end of the Civil War, the introduction of the New Economic Policy at home, and the recognition of a temporary restabilization of the capitalist system. The party's leadership and the military had to deal with the pressing problem of postwar demobilization and the creation of a military system that would provide for standing cadre forces and mobilization potential. By the mid-1920s and simultaneous with Lenin's death and Trotsky's removal from the post of commissar of war, these reforms were enacted under the party's new collective leadership. Frunze was entrusted with the task of putting these measures into practice. For him, as for the party leadership, the nature of the threat confronting the Soviet State was quite clear. As opposed to Trotsky, who had told the Red Army's leadership that it should use the postwar period to master mundane matters of troop leadership and leave strategy to the party, Frunze had explicitly defined the threat posed by capitalist encirclement as one demanding constant vigilance and military preparations:

> Between our proletarian state and the rest of the bourgeois world there can only be one condition—that of a long, persistent, desperate war to the death: a war which demands colossal tenacity, steadfastness, inflexibility, and a unity of will.... The state of open warfare may give way to some sort of contractual relationship which permits, up to a certain level, the peaceful coexistence of the warring sides. These contractual forms do not change the fundamental character of these relations.... The common, parallel existence of our proletarian Soviet state with the states of the bourgeois world for a protracted period is impossible.[73]

This threat created a need to study future war (*budushchaya voîna*) not as an abstract proposition but as a foreseeable contingency. In the 1920s the study of past campaigns, current trends in weapons development, and force structure requirements coalesced around the concept of operational art (*operativnoe iskusstvo*). The ideological framework for such study was the application of the dialectical method to historical materialism with the goal of creating a military science directed at foresight.[74]

The linchpins in this development were Svechin, Frunze, and Tukhachevsky, who promoted the development of military scientific societies and identified a group of talented officers, some of whom were destined to become the first Red *genshtabisty*. Many of these officers entered the newly renamed Military Academy during Tukhachevsky's short tenure as its commandant in 1921–1922. Others came later, when Frunze took over as Commissar of War. Two of the Red *genshtabisty* were N. E. Varfolomeev and V. K. Triandafillov. Varfolomeev had in fact graduated from the final, wartime course of the old General Staff Academy, but his career as a staff officer coincided with his service in the RKKA.[75]

For the first few years of the Military Academy, the problem of how to conceptualize warfare on the basis of the experience of the World War and the Civil War remained unresolved. Its academic program reflected the conventional divisions of strategy and tactics, but new terms were being used to describe the more complex combat of World War I and the Civil War. "Grand tactics" and "lower strategy" were employed but without rigor or definition. Only in 1923–1924 did Svechin tackle the problem by proposing an intermediary category, which he called operational art. This he defined as the "totality of maneuvers and battles in a given part of a theater of military action directed toward the achievement of the common goal, set as final in the given period of the campaign."[76] These lectures served as the basis for Svechin's *Strategiya*, which appeared in 1926. Here Svechin for the first time wrote about the nature of "operational art" and its relationship to strategy and tactics.[77] As Svechin formulated this relation: "Then, battle is the means of the operation. Tactics are the material of operational art. The operation is the means of strategy, and operational art is the material of strategy. This is the essence of the three-part formula."[78]

Svechin's own work then turned toward the study of the problem of national preparation for war. Here he emphasized the need to address the political and economic preparation of the nation for war. His formulation of two competing strategic postures—annihilation (*sokrushenie*) and attrition (*izmor*)—raised a host of issues regarding the relationship between operational art and the paradigm of future war. Drawing on the work of Delbrueck, Svechin was critical of the German general staff's one-sided emphasis upon the conduct of decisive operations in the initial period of war.[79] Svechin saw the seeds of disaster in such short-war illusions. He stressed the need to prepare for a long war, given the geostrategic and political situation confronting the USSR. Here Svechin emphasized political and economic objectives for strategy at the expense of the enemy's armed forces as the center of gravity.

This focus led Svechin and others to consider the problem of the relationship between the civilian and military leadership in the conduct of war and in preparations for war. Svechin argued that one of the legacies of Russia's heritage of frontier warfare was the tendency of military commanders to turn their own rear areas into satrapies, where immediate supply requirements of front commands took precedence over a rational mobilization of the entire state economy. He criticized such a narrow perception of military logistics and emphasized the need for a unification of front and rear through the planned mobilization of the entire "state rear," by which he meant the national economy, to the purposes of supporting front operations.[80] With Frunze, Svechin shared a concern for the need to mobilize the entire national economy for the prosecution of what he saw as protracted warfare. Using Conrad von Hoetzendorf's memoirs as a vehicle to explore the role of the general staff in modern war and preparations for war, the *voenspets-genshtabist* Boris Mikhailovich Shaposhnikov characterized that role as "the brain of the army."[81] While Svechin emphasized the need for close cooperation between the state apparatus and the general staff, Shaposhnikov, himself also a non–party member throughout the 1920s, stressed the need for a linkage between the Communist Party and the general staff.

The problem of studying operational art was left to the newly established and only briefly sustained "chair" at the Military Academy. This chair, named Conduct of the Operation, which was founded in 1924, immediately took on the problem of studying the conduct of operations during World War I and the Civil War. Special attention was devoted to the summer campaign of 1920 against Poland. Leadership of the new chair went to N. E. Varfolomeev, who had fought with the Western Front during the Vistula operation and served as chief reporter on the large-scale maneuvers that Tukhachevsky conducted with that front in 1922.[82]

Following the Civil War, Varfolomeev had turned his attention to the difficult problem of conducting deep pursuit so as to bring about the conditions for the destruction of the enemy. The focus of his attention was the advance on Warsaw and the failure of the Western Front to turn that operation into a decisive victory. Varfolomeev emphasized the need to organize a relentless pursuit by advance guards, the use of army cavalry to turn the enemy's flanks and preclude the organization of a defense on a favorable line of terrain, the sustainment of close contact between the advance guard and main forces to allow for the timely commitment of fresh forces to the attack, and the maintenance of a viable logistical system in support of the advance. Varfolomeev still spoke in terms of pursuit to "the field of the decisive engagement," but his attention was focused on the utilization of reserves to maintain the pace of the pursuit without risking pauses in the advance that would permit the enemy to recover.[83]

Varfolomeev's arrival at the Military Academy in 1924 coincided with Tukhachevsky's return to Moscow as deputy chief of staff of the RKKA. Over the next three years, 1924–1927, the academy addressed the problem of how to conduct operations of annihilation to bring about the total destruction of enemy forces in the field. Varfolomeev summed this up in two propositions. First, there was the need to combine breakthrough and deep pursuit so as to destroy the enemy forces throughout their entire depth. Under conditions of modern warfare this could not be achieved in a single operation but required successive deep operations, "the zigzags of a whole series of operations successively developed one upon the other, logically connected and linked together by the common final objective." Second, success in such successive deep operations depended fundamentally on the "successful struggle against the consequences of the attendant operational exhaustion." Logistics, the unity of front and rear as an organizational problem, thus assumed critical importance as an aspect of operational art.[84]

In researching operational art the faculty sought means of defining the operational norms that would set the parameters of such deep operations. One of the major breakthroughs in getting students to master operational art at the Military Academy was a shift from formal lectures and special studies to actual operational-scale wargaming. Each student was expected to apply norms and do those calculations that the members of front and army staffs had to do in preparing for an operation. Young tacticians might object to calculating the veterinary support for a front offensive, but the faculty found such assignments the very best way to get across to students the relationship between staff planning and the successful conduct of operations.[85]

Varfolomeev found the roots of the theory of deep, successive operations in Tukhachevsky's attempt to use the techniques of class war and civil war in an "external war" against a much-better-prepared adversary. He saw the failure of the Vistula operation as rooted in Tukhachevsky's overoptimistic evaluation of the potential for "intensification of the revolution" within Poland by means of "a revolution from without" (*revolyutsiya izvne*) and the mounting exhaustion with the Red Army, brought on by attrition and the total disorganization of the rear services during the advance.[86] Prudent operational plans, which took into account the need to break through and penetrate the enemy's defenses throughout their depth, sobered revolutionary élan. In the 1930s he turned his attention to the employment of shock armies in the offensive and the problem of overcoming enemy operational reserves as they joined the engagement. In these studies he focused upon the German and Allied offensives of 1918, especially the Anglo-French offensive at Amien in August 1918. The Amien operation was noteworthy for both the achievement of surprise and the mass employment of armor and aviation to achieve a breakthrough.[87]

The logistical parameters of deep successive operations to a great extent depended upon the visions of the Soviet Union as a political economy and the nature of the external threat. In the hands of Svechin and those like him who emphasized the need to prepare for a long war, the maintenance of the workers' and peasants' alliance became the central reality of the Soviet Union's domestic mobilization base. Such a view assumed that Lenin's New Economic Policy, with its emphasis upon agriculture's recovery, would be the long-term policy of the USSR. At the same time, such authors cast the nature of the external threat in terms of the states immediately bordering the USSR. They could not ignore postwar developments in military technology, but they concluded that Europe was in fact divided into two parts, two military-technical systems. The west was industrial, and the potential for a mechanization of warfare was there to be seen. Eastern Europe, which included the USSR, was dominated by a peasant economy and a "peasant rear" (*krest'ianskiĭ tyl*).[88]

One of the most important advocates of an operational art adapted to the realities of a future war fought on the basis of a peasant rear was V. K. Triandafillov. Triandafillov had served in the tsarist army during

World War I, took an active part in the revolutionary politics within the army in 1917, and joined the Red Army in 1918, where he commanded a battalion, regiment, and brigade. He fought on the Ural Front against Dutov and on the South and Southwest Fronts against Denikin and Wrangel. Joining the party in 1919, he was a natural choice for education as a Red *genshtabist* posted to the Academy in the same year. During his four years with the Academy, he divided his time between theory and praxis. As a brigade commander with the 51st Rifle Division, one of the best in the Red Army, he took an active part in Frunze's successful offensive at Perekop Isthmus against Wrangel. At the same time, Triandafillov began writing military analysis of operations from the Civil War as his part in the activities of the Academy's Military Scientific Society. These included essays on the Southern Front's offensive against Denikin and the Perekop offensive against Wrangel.[89] He also took part in the suppression of the Tambov Insurrection in 1921, where he served under Tukhachevsky. Following his graduation from the Military Academy in 1923, Frunze chose his former subordinate to join the main staff of the RKKA, where he took over as chief of the Operations Section in 1924. From there he moved on to command a rifle corps and then returned to Moscow as deputy chief of staff for RKKA in 1928.

Charged with putting operational art into practice, Triandafillov authored what became the chief work on the nature of the operations of modern armies, which laid out in detail the military context of the theory of successive deep operations. Triandafillov called attention to the process of technological development, which was making possible the "machinization" of warfare, but noted its limited impact upon the economically backward regions of Eastern Europe with their peasant rear. New automatic weapons, armor, aviation, and gas would affect such a war but would not become decisive. He also treated the problem of manpower mobilization and the reality of mass war quickly becoming a war of conscripts and reservists. This brought him to the problem of addressing the means of achieving breakthrough and sustaining pursuit in successive deep operations. Here he drew upon Frunze's use of shock armies for the breakthrough and the use of echeloned forces to facilitate exploitation and pursuit. Success in such operations turned upon the organization of an effective command and control system to coordinate the operations of several fronts and the establishment of realistic logistical norms in keeping with the geographic-economic realities of the theater of military action.[90]

As deputy chief of staff to the RKKA, Triandafillov's views reflected some basic assumptions regarding the sort of war the Red Army would fight in the future. The Field Regulations of 1929 discussing the offensive touched on many of the same themes developed by Triandafillov in greater depth.[91] While the new regulations did provide for successive deep operations based upon a combined-arms offensive, the armies described by Triandafillov and the regulations were modernized versions of the Red Army from the Civil War.

This vision was in keeping with what Svechin had described as the political-military context of Soviet strategy. The threat assessment outlined in Triandafillov's book corresponded with Svechin's modest and prudent vision of the immediate threat to the USSR and the limited offensive capabilities the Soviet state could reasonably hope to field in the initial period of a future war. Recently, Russian military and civilian analysts have begun a positive reappraisal of Svechin's views in the late 1920s with their emphasis upon attrition and defense in the initial period of war.[92] For instance, in 1989 A. A. Kokoshin pointed to Svechin's early and correct assessment of German geopolitics and the threat of a rearmed Germany to Poland.[93]

The Mechanization of Deep Operations

Triandafillov died in an airplane crash in 1931, before he had a chance to complete a new and revised edition of his book. The outline for this revision, which was published in posthumous editions of his book, does contain some clues as to the major changes that he envisioned. First, in keeping with the new party line on the external threat, Triandafillov addressed both the crisis of capitalism and the increased risk of direct attack upon the USSR by one or more major capitalist powers. Second, Triandafillov began to address the problem of employing massed armor in the offensive. The first Five-Year Plan had promised to industrialize the USSR, and now it was possible to put the USSR within the ranks of the modern western European states and the United States. Third, Triandafillov specifically turned his attention to the role of mechanized combined-arms formations in the conduct of deep operations. The outline is at best a sketch without details. Russian officers have been willing to say that these few remarks anticipate the mechanization of successive deep operations as presented in the 1936 Field Regulations.[94]

There were other advocates of operational art, who argued that technological developments and the nature of the external threat made it absolutely essential to carry out a total mechanization of the Red Army and Soviet rear. One of the leading proponents of such views was Tukhachevsky, who had been Triandafillov's immediate boss as chief of the RKKA Staff from 1925 to 1928. Tukhachevsky argued that what was required to make the new operational art into a sound strategic posture was nothing less than "complete militarization" of the national economy to provide the new instruments of mechanized warfare. Committed to an operational art that would end in the total destruction of the enemy Tukhachevsky crossed pens with Svechin, whom he accused of being an advocate of attrition.[95] According to G. S. Isserson, one of his closest collaborators in the 1930s, Tukhachevsky came forward with a master plan for the mechanization of the Red Army in December 1927, only to have it turned down by the party leadership under Stalin.[96] Several years later, in 1930, Tukhachevsky's views won favor when Stalin broke with Bukharin's thesis on the stabilization of capitalism and began to associate the Depression with a rising threat of war to the Soviet Union. This threat the party leadership openly used to justify the brutal processes of industrialization and forced collectivization by now linking them with an improvement in the level of national defense.

During the intervening two years Tukhachevsky had left the RKKA Staff to take over as commander of Leningrad Military District, where he conducted a number of experiments relating to mechanization. These experiments came at a time when motorization versus mechanization emerged in Western Europe as alternative solutions to the problem of integrating the internal combustion engine into the armed forces. The former implied grafting automobile transport onto existing combat arms, while the latter called for the creation of "self-propelled combat means" with an emphasis upon armor, especially tanks, armored cars, and self-propelled artillery. Soviet officers who followed developments in France, England, and the United States noted that all armies were exploring both paths but that, owing to strategic, operational, tactical, political, and financial circumstances, the French Army was more sympathetic toward motorization and the British toward mechanization.[97] Tukhachevsky in his comments on the training exercises of the troops of the Leningrad Military District emphasized the need to increase their mobility as a combined-arms force that could engage in a multiecheloned offensive. His interest in the development of tank, aviation, and airborne forces during this period marked him as an advocate of mechanization.[98]

At the XVI Party Congress and IX Congress of the Komsomol in 1930–1931, K. E. Voroshilov, the Commissar of War and Stalin's closest collaborator, spoke out regarding the mechanization of warfare as bringing about a qualitative change in the nature of future wars. But in Voroshilov's case, mechanization would in the future bring about the possibility of a short, bloodless war, carried quickly on to the territory of the attacking enemy.[99] Such views emerged at a time when it appeared that world capitalism had gone back into a profound political-economic crisis which was creating greater instability and increased risks of war. This in turn was creating the basis for the formation of a broad anti-Soviet alliance, which threatened war on every frontier. At home the strains of the first Five-Year Plan were also underscoring the possibilities of an alliance between the external threat and the so-called internal enemy — the forces of counterrevolution.

In 1930 Tukhachevsky came forward with his own powerful arguments for a mass, mechanized army as the means to execute the new operational art. He used a number of forms to present this argument. One was the foreword to the Russian translation of Hans Delbrueck's *Geschichte der Kriegskunst im Rahmen der Politischen Geschichte*, which provided a forum in which to attack Svechin's concept of attrition as the appropriate strategy for the USSR.[100] This work was conspicuous for the tenor of the political-ideological assault mounted by Tukhachevsky against the old *genshtabist*. In a time of heightened suspicions toward all specialists as wreckers, Tukhachevsky called his colleague an idealist in Marxist dress.

Worse attacks followed within the confines of the Section for the Study of the Problems of War in the Communist Academy. This section was organized in 1929 as part of an effort to infuse Marxism-Leninism into military science. Within the section, as within the Communist Academy, the notion of a struggle between an old, bourgeois past and a young, dynamic communist future was given free rein. Tukhachevsky, armed with the appropriate citations from Stalin and Voroshilov, attacked Professors Svechin and Verkhovsky because their writings were infested with bourgeois ideology. In Svechin's case the fault was that he did not believe in the possibility of decisive operations but defended the idea of limited war. Verkhovsky was charged with favoring a professional army at the expense of a mass army. Tukhachevsky spoke positively of Triandafillov's book, but noted some shortcomings.[101] His line of criticism fit that offered in a review of Triandafillov's book, published in the spring of 1930, in which the reviewer took the author to task for talking of a peasant rear without noting the possibility of transforming that rear through industrialization. That industrialization, the reviewer pointed out, would make it possible to speed up the massing of forces and their maneuver, creating opportunities for decisive operations, if the political — revolutionary — possibilities were exploited.[102] As we have noted above, Triandafillov was himself responding to this new situation when he died in 1931.

That same year Tukhachevsky became deputy commissar of Military and Naval Affairs, a member of the *Revvoensovet*, and Director of Armaments for the RKKA. Over the next six years he directed the mechanization of the Red Army, laying the foundations for the creation of mass, mechanized forces designed to conduct successive deep operations in a war of annihilation. The Stalinist industrialization did make the USSR into a major industrial power with the capacity to mechanize its armed forces to an extent Triandafillov had never imagined. During that same period the nature of the military threat confronting the USSR became more complex and serious. To his credit Tukhachevsky never fell into the trap of assuming that mechanization would negate mass war. He was an informed critic of "*Blitzkrieg* theory," and his criticism of the works of Fuller, Liddell Hart, and others deserves serious attention. They contain a good clue about the emerging Soviet way of war. In 1931 he wrote regarding the professional mechanized army:

> Let's imagine a war between Great Britain and the USA, a war, for example, which breaks out along the Canadian border. Both armies are mechanized, but the English have, let's say, Fuller's cadres of 18 divisions, and the U.S. Army has 180 divisions. The first has 5,000 tanks and 3,000 aircraft, but the second has 50,000 tanks and 30,000 planes. The small English Army would be simply crushed. Is it not already clear that talk about small, but mobile, mechanized armies in major wars is a cock-and-bull story? Only frivolous people can take them seriously.[103]

By spring 1935 Tukhachevsky fully appreciated the fact that German rearmament and Hitler's calls for Lebensraum in the East would soon pose a serious military threat to the Soviet Union, a view he shared with Stalin and which was published in *Pravda* in March.[104]

In Tukhachevsky's Soviet military theory—building upon the work of the tsarist general staff and the combat experiences of the Russo-Japanese War, World War I, and the Civil War—focused on the mechanization of the mass army as the means to conduct decisive operations in a total war. The *Vremennyî polevoî ustav RKKA 1936*, with its emphasis upon the "decisive offensive on the main axis, completed by relentless pursuit" as the only means to bring about the total destruction of the enemy's men and equipment, underscored Tukhachevsky's twin themes of combined arms and mechanized forces. Tanks were to be used en mass, and mechanized formations, composed of tanks, motorized infantry, and self-propelled guns, were expected to strike deep into the enemy's rear, using their mobility to outflank and encircle the enemy force. Aviation formations, apart from independent air operations, were expected to act in close operational-tactical cooperation with combined-arms formations. At the same time, airborne units were to be used to disorganize enemy command and control and rear services.[105]

In one of his last publications, Tukhachevsky warned that the Red Army should not confuse mastery of theory with command of practice. Discussing the basic questions of combat covered in the new field regulations, he warned against the tendency to transform a healthy doctrine into a sterile dogma and noted that technological changes were qualitatively reshaping the combined-arms concept. The new content of mechanized combined-arms operations set the 1936 regulations apart from those of 1929. The employment of mechanized forces, constructed around "long-range tanks, mounted infantry, artillery, aviation and airborne forces," made it possible to win the "battle for the flanks" through the application of maneuver. Rapid mobility was the only means to exploit the temporary appearance of an open flank in the enemy's battle order. "Therefore the struggle for the flanks demands rapid actions, surprise, lightning blows."[106]

Tukhachevsky appreciated the threat that the *Wehrmacht* posed to the Soviet Union and warned of the dangers of *Blitzkrieg* and surprise attack by its Panzers and the Luftwaffe.[107] The purge of the military and the experience of combat in the Spanish Civil War called the theory of deep, successive operations into question on both political-ideological and military-operational grounds. The organic development of operational art stopped for almost three years. One might well wonder how much that hiatus affected the covering force engagements at the start of Operation BARBAROSSA, the German campaign against the Soviet Union, in the Belorussian and Ukrainian theater of military operations when the *Wehrmacht* won Tukhachevsky's "struggle for the flanks."[108]

During the succeeding operations attrition imposed major changes in both sides' force postures, especially their mechanized forces. The autumn fighting on the approaches to Moscow resembled more the conditions described in Triandafillov's "peasant rear" than they did Tukhachevsky's. Indeed, Soviet operational art during the winter counteroffensive before Moscow, which relied so heavily upon infantry and cavalry in the absence of tank, motorized infantry, and aviation, fit Triandafillov's early model of successive operations. Later Soviet offensives did try to put into practice the principles of operational art outlined in the 1936 Field Regulations, which bore Tukhachevsky's imprint. Gradually, through a process of trial and error, Soviet commanders achieved the skills necessary to handle the massive, mechanized forces that the marshal had championed.

None of the architects survived to witness those events. Triandafillov had died in an airplane crash in 1931. Tukhachevsky, along with much of the Soviet military elite, died at the hands of Stalin's terror, labeled a traitor and enemy of the people. Svechin, who was hounded in the early 1930s as a class enemy, outlasted his critic by less than a year, dying in 1938. Varfolomeev was arrested by the *NKVD* (*Narodnyi Kommissariat Vnutrennykh Del* [People's Commissariat of Internal Affairs, or secret police]) and imprisoned; he died in 1941. What followed was a time when the Red Army had a theory, whose authors it could not acknowledge, and a mythical past that precluded the sort of criticism necessary for the perfection of theory.

The shock of real war in Manchuria, Poland, Finland, and France cracked the myth, allowing needed reforms prior to the German invasion. These measures were too little in practical accomplishment, too late in initiation, and too radical in scale either to undo the damage of the purges or to offset German advantages in command and control and operational surprise. Painfully the young commanders of the Red Army gained the talents necessary to put into practice the deep successive operations for which their field regulations called. Gradually Soviet society forged the new weapons necessary to conduct such operations. Step by step the Red Army adjusted its force structure to provide the combined arms armies, tank armies, and tank and mechanized corps to mount such operations. In the final phase of the war Soviet operations achieved what prewar theory had promised.[109] Only after Stalin's death could historians begin to study the roots of these successes during this dynamic and tragic period in Russian and Soviet military history and thus grasp the significance of operational art.[110]

Notes

1. For the author's earlier and more complete treatment of the origins of military doctrine and operational art in the Russian and Soviet Armies, see "Soviet Military Doctrine and the Origins of Operational Art, 1917–1936," in Philip S. Gillette and Willard C. Frank, Jr., eds., *Soviet Military Doctrine from Lenin to Gorbachev: 1915–1991* (Westport, Conn.: Greenwood Press, 1992), pp. 63–84.
2. J. Walter Jacobs, "The Art of Operations," *Army* no. 11 (November 1961): 64.
3. David M. Glantz, "Soviet Operational Formation for Battle: A Perspective," *Military Review* 63, no. 2 (February 1983): 2–12; Earl F. Ziemke, "The Soviet Theory of Deep Operations," *Parameters* 13, no. 6 (June 1983): 23–33; David M. Glantz, "The Nature of Soviet Operational Art," *Parameters* 14, no. 1 (January 1984): 2–12.
4. Condoleeza Rice, "The Making of Soviet Strategy," in Peter Paret, ed., *Makers of Modern Strategy: From Machiavelli to the Nuclear Age*, 2d ed. (Princeton: Princeton University Press, 1986), pp. 648–76.
5. Richard Simpkin, *Deep Battle: The Brainchild of Marshal Tukhachevskii* (London: Brassey's Defence Publications, 1987), pp. ix, 249–70.
6. Aleksandr I. Verkhovsky, "Evolyutsiya prepodavaniya taktiki v 1918–1928 gg.," *Voîna i revolyutsia* no. 11 (November 1928): 50–52. On Verkhovsky's background and career, see *Voennyi entsiklopedicheskii slovar'* (Moscow: Voenizdat, 1983), p. 126.
7. Nikolai Varfolomeev, "Strategiya v akademicheskoi postanovke," *Voina i revolyutsya* no. 11 (November 1928): 84.
8. Aleksandr A. Svechin, *Strategiya*, 2d ed. (Moscow: Voennyî Vestnik, 1927), p. 14ff.
9. Varfolomeev, "Strategiya v akademicheskoi postanovke," pp. 83–84.
10. I. Ivanov, "Voenno-tekhnicheskaya literatura po voprosam kharaktera budushchei voiny i operatîvnogo iskusstva," *Voina i revolyutsiya* no. 2 (March–April 1934): 13–30; *Field Regulations of the Red Army* (Washington, D.C.: Foreign Broadcast Information Service, 1985); and USSR, Narodnyi Komissariat Oborony, *Vremennyî polevoî ustav RKKA 1936* (PU 36) (Moscow: Gosvoenizdat, 1937).
11. For a lengthy discussion of these issues, see Jacob W. Kipp, "Mass and Maneuver: The Origins of Soviet Operational Art, 1918–1936," in Carl Reddel, ed., *Transformation in Russian and Soviet Military History: Proceedings of the Twelfth Military History Symposium, USAF Academy, 1986* (Washington, D.C.: U.S. Air Force Academy, Office of Air Force History, 1990), pp. 87–116.
12. I. I. Rostunov, *Russkiî front Pervoî mirovoî voîny*, (Moscow: n.p., 1976), pp. 93–95; Andrei M. Zaionchkovskiy, *Mirovaa voîna 1914–1918 gg.*, 2d ed. (Moscow: n.p., 1931), pp. 50–53; and A. Zaionchkovskiy, *Podgotovka Rossii k mirovoî voîne* (Moscow: Shtab RKKA, 1926), pp. 141–54. On the attitude of Russian military reformers toward initial offensive operations, see Aleksandr Svechin, "Bol'shaya voennaya programma," *Russkaya mysl'* 8 (August 1913): 19–29. Svechin argued that the implications of the Russian rearmament program were connected with France's increasing vulnerability. Thus, while Svechin noted the need for Russia to mount and conclude decisive operations within two months of the outbreak of hostilities, he linked this to a shift by the French from an immediate offensive to strategic defense. He reasoned that "the Russian front had for Germany

become the most important theater of operations. And first-class theater of operations refers to the Russian preparations for war which are on a completely unique scale" (p. 23).

13. Zaionchkovskyi, *Mirovaya voîna*, pp. 51–52.
14. Vladamir A. Sukhomlinov, *Erinnerungen* (Berlin: Verlag von Reimar Hobbing, 1924). Sukhomlinov mentions General Leyer on five occasions, but most of these concern his own education. He never mentions Mikhnevich, Neznamov, Maslovskiî, Baîîov, or Svechin. Bonch-Bruevich, his supposed informer on Academy affairs, is mentioned once in connection with Sukhomlinov's service as chief of staff of the Kiev Military District.
15. Ibid., p. 23.
16. L. Radus-Zenkovich, "Nekotorye vyvody iz srazheniya pri Gumbinene v avguste 1914 g. (Vstrechnyi boi)," *Voenno-istoricheskii sbornik* III (1919): 74–95.
17. A. A. Bogdanov, *Vseobshchaya organizatsionnaya nauka (tektologiya)* (Moscow: n.p., 1913), I: 185–255. Bogdanov, an early Bolshevik and renaissance man — who could claim significant contributions in the fields of medicine, politics, philosophy, economics, literature, and literary criticism — quarreled with Lenin in 1909 but kept close ties to the Bolsheviks through his marriage ties with Lunacharsky. After the revolution he was one of the founders of the *Proletkul't* movement in the arts and literature and the Socialist Academy in Moscow, lecturing frequently at the Proletarian university there. One of his prerevolutionary novels, one of two science fiction works he authored, was called *Krasnaya zvezda* [Red Star]. The science of control or the scientific organization of labor as it became known in the 1920s embraced control with certain conditions: see I. I. Gludin, "NOT: Voprosy organizatsii i upravleniia," *Revolyutsiya i voina* no. 23 (1923): 20.
18. A. A. Brusilov, *Moi vospominaniya* (Moscow: Voenizdat, 1983), p. 122ff.
19. Ibid., pp. 174–217; A. Bazarskiî, *Nastupatel'naya operatsiya 9-i russkoî armii v iyune 1916 goda* (Moscow: Voenizdat, 1939), p. 9ff.
20. F. Gershel'man, "Sovremennaya voennaya obstanovka," *Voennyi sbornik* no. 6 (June 1916): 33–37.
21. B. V. Gerua, *Vospominaniya moe i zhizni* (Paris: n.p., 1969–1970), I: 273–75.
22. S. A. Fediukin, *Sovetskaya vlast' i burzhuaznye spetsialisty* (Moscow: Mysl', 1965), pp. 71–72.
23. Ibid., p. 77.
24. L. D. Trotsky, *Sochineniya* (Moscow: Gosizdat, 1925), XVII: pt. 1, p. 316.
25. I. A. Korotkov, *Istoriya sovetskoî voennoi mysli* (Moscow: Voenizdat, 1980), pp. 27, 28. Izmest'ev's study, "Znachenie raschëta pri razrabotke i vedenii voennykh operatsii," was serialized in *Voennyî sbornik* from March 1915 to June 1916.
26. P. I. Izmest'ev, "Znachenie rascheta pri razrabotke i vedenii voennykh operatsii," *Voennyi sbornik* no. 3 (March 1915): 19–28, no. 4 (April 1915): 17–30.
27. Ibid., no. 1 (January 1916): 19–28, no. 2 (February 1916): 17–32, no. 3 (March 1916): 17–29.
28. Ibid., no. 1 (January 1916): 29–30.
29. Ibid., no. 6 (June 1916): 26.
30. Aleksandr A. Svechin, "Trudy Komissii po isledovaniyu i ispol'zovaniya opyta voîny 1914–1918 gg.," *Voenno-istoricheskii sbornik* I (1919): 3–9.
31. Jacob W. Kipp, "Lenin and Clausewitz: The Militarization of Marxism," *Military Affairs* 49, no. 4 (October 1985): 184–91.
32. V. G. Kulikov, ed., *Akademiya general'nogo shtaba: Istoriya Voennoi ordenov Lenina i Suvorova. I stepeni Akademii General'nogo Shtaba Vooruzhennykh Sil SSSR imeni*

K. E. Voroshilova (Moscow: Voenizdat, 1976), pp. 6–21; Korotkov, *Istoriya sovestkoi voennoi mysli,* pp. 28–31; S. A. Tyushkevich et al., *Sovetskie Vooruzhennye Sily: Istoriya stroitel'stva* (Moscow: Voenizdat, 1978), pp. 38–39.

33. S. I. Gusev, *Grazhdanskaya voîna i krasnaya armiya* (Moscow: Voenizdat, 1952), pp. 55–56.
34. Mikhail N. Tukhachevsky, *Izbrannye proizvedeniya* (Moscow: Voenizdat, 1964), I: 27–29.
35. V. Triandafillov, "Vzaimodeîstvie mezhdu zapadnym i iugozapadnym frontami vo vremya letnego nastupleniya krasnoî armii na Vislu v 1920 g.," *Voina i revolyutsiya* no. 2 (1925): 23–24.
36. Gusev, *Grazhdanskaya voina*, p. 113.
37. M. I. Vladimirov et al., *M. V. Frunze: Voennaya i Politicheskaya deyatel'nost'* (Moscow: Voenizdat, 1984), pp. 58–60.
38. A. Neznamov, "Prepodavanie taktiki," *Voennoe znanie* no. 15 (1921): 4–5.
39. Verkhovsky, "Evolyutsiya," pp. 52–56.
40. Neznamov, "Prepodavanietaktiki," pp. 4–5.
41. D. Riazanov, "Voennoe delo i Marksizm," in B. Gorev, ed., *Voîna i voennoe iskusstvo v svete istoricheskogo materializma* (Moscow: Gosizdat, 1927), p. 5ff.
42. M. Frunze, "Edinaya voennaya doktrina i krasnaya armiya," *Voennaya nauka i revolyutsiya* no. 2 (1921): 33–39.
43. L. Trotsky, "Voennaya doktrina ili mnimo-voennoe doktrinerstvo," *Voennaya nauka i revolyutsiya* no. 2 (1921): 204–13. Later in 1921, when speaking before the Military Scientific Society of the Military Academy, Trotsky tried to occupy a middle ground between the voenspetsy and the young Red Commanders associated with Frunze, Gusev, and Tukhachevsky. He warned that a unified military doctrine carried the seeds of mysticism and metaphysics. See L. Trotsky, *Kak vooruzhalas' revolyutsiya (na voennom dele)* (Moscow: Vysshii voennyi redaktsionyi sovet, 1925), III, kn. 2, pp. 201–09.
44. D. Petrovsky, "Edinaya voennaya doktrina v A[kademii] G[eneral'nogo] Sh[taba]," *Voennoe znanie* nos. 14–15 (August 1921): 13.
45. A. S. Bubnov, *O krasnoî armii* (Moscow: Voenizdat, 1968), p. 216.
46. D. A. Kovalenko, *Oboronnaya Promyshlennost' Sovetskoî Rossii v 1918–1920 gg.* (Moscow: Nauka, 1970).
47. M. N. Tukhachevsky, "Pokhod za Vislu," *Izbrannye Proizvedeniya*, vol. I, pp. 126–27.
48. R. Tsiffer, "Zametki o voîne v malokul'turnykh teatrakh i metode eë izucheniya," *Voina i revolyutsiya* no. 11 (1928): 132–40.
49. Lev Nikulin, *Tukhachevskiî Biograficheskii ocherk* (Moscow: Voenizdat, 1963), p. 161.
50. Tukhachevsky, "Pokhod za Vislu."
51. Mikhail N. Tukhachevsky, "Revolyutsiya izvne," *Revolyutsiya i voîna* no. 3 (1920): 45–54.
52. "Konnitsa v grazhdanskoî voîne," *Revolyutsiya i voîna* nos. 6, 7 (1921): 36.
53. A. I. Soshnikov et al., *Sovetskaya kavaleriya: Voenno-istoricheskiî ocherk* (Moscow: Voenizdat, 1984), pp. 3–24.
54. M. Ryshman, *Reid Mamontova: Avgust-sentyabrya' 1919 R.* (Moscow: Gosvoenizdat, 1926), pp. 16–29.
55. Ibid., pp. 30–43.
56. K. Monigetti, *Sovmestnye deîstviya konnitsy i vozdushnogo flota* (Moscow: Gosvoenizdat, 1928), pp. 92–93.

57. Hoover Institution, Wrangel Papers, Box 33 (*delo* 146), Arkhiv Shtaba Glavkommandogo V[ooruzhennykh] S[il] na iuge Rossii, "Svodki i doneseniya razvedyvatel'nykh punktov Glavkomago V. Silami na iuge Rossii za period Yanvar'-Noyabr' 1919 goda," Nachal'nik, Khar'kov Razved. Punkt, 9 Sentyabr' 1919 g., no. 132.
58. Ibid.
59. Soshnikov et al., *Sovetskaya kavaleriya*, pp. 62–63.
60. [G. D.] Gai, "Nedostatki v organizatsii krasnoî konnitsy," *Revolyutsiya i voîna* nos. 6, 7 (1921): 49–68.
61. Isaac Babel, "Konarmiya," in *Izbrannye Proizvedeniya* (Moscow: Khudozhestvennaia Literatura, 1966), pp. 27–58.
62. [N. I.] Zotov, "Boî 1 konnoî armii v raîone Rovno v iyune 1920 g.," *Voîna i revolyutsiya* no. 2 (1929): 102–03; U.S. Army, Attaché Reports (Poland), No. 1095, "Operations of Budenny's Cavalry" 9 Dec 20, pp. 1–4.
63. Zotov, "Boi 1 konnoi armii," pp. 104–18. Other operations by strategic cavalry might also be cited regarding their role in Soviet offensive operations. In the final campaign against Baron Wrangel, Frunze used the Second Cavalry Army to blunt a raid by White cavalry across the Dnieper, then employed the newly arrived First Cavalry Army to try and encircle Wrangel's force north of the Crimea. When that failed he assigned the Second Cavalry Army to carry out the pursuit of Wrangel's forces after the breakthrough to the Crimea during the Perekop-Chongarskaia operation. In this breakthrough operation Frunze employed an echeloned attack by his Sixth Army against the Litovskiî Peninsula, ordered partisans to strike at the enemy's rear to disrupt his communications, and employed F. K. Mironov's Second Cavalry Army in a meeting engagement to counter Wrangel's last reserves, elements of General Barbovich's corps. When Barbovich's troops saw the mass of horses drawn up to their north, the White general sent his own cavalry to meet the threat. However, as the two sides closed to within 900 yards of each other, Mironov's Cavalry broke ranks to the right and left to reveal 250 *tachanki* mounting machine-guns. Before the White cavalry could break off its charge, a rain of lead cut into its ranks. The utter disorder in the enemy force allowed elements of 2d Konarmiya and the 51st Division to mount a sustained attack, which broke Barbovich's corps and sealed the fate of Wrangel's army. See Vladimirov, *M. V. Frunze*, pp. 137–47, and V. V. Dushen'kin, *Vtoraya konnaya: Voenno-istoricheskiî ocherk* (Moscow: Voenizdat, 1968), pp. 189–206.
64. Jozef Pilsudski, *Year 1920* (London: Pilsudski Institute of London, 1972), p. 83.
65. Nikulin, *Tukhachevsky*, pp. 119–22.
66. Tukhachevsky, "Pokhod za Vislu," pp. 134–52, and *Revolyutsia voîna*, pp. 85–150.
67. Pilsudski, *Year 1920*, pp. 151–208.
68. Triandafillov, "Vzaimodeistvie mezhdu zapadnym," pp. 26–27.
69. The extent of Soviet military studies on the Vistula Operation of 1920 becomes clear when we examine a bibliography on the Soviet-Polish War prepared by the Military Section of the Communist Academy in 1930 to mark the tenth anniversary of the campaign. That bibliography listed 257 titles, most of them Soviet books and articles on the Vistula Operation. See "Bibliograficheskiî ukazatel' literatury po sovetsko–pol'skoi voîne 1920 g.," in *Kommunisticheskaya akademiya: Sektsiya po izucheniyu problem voîny. Zapiski I* (1930), pp. 219–31. The Stalinist version of events is summed up in I. Apanasenko's essay on the Konarmiya, written to mark the twentieth anniversary of its founding. Here the Red Cavalry, led by Budennyî and Voroshilov, "fulfilled the strategic plan of the Great Stalin." The seizure of Lvov "would have been the single and best possible way to help the Western Front." But Trotsky, "the enemy of the people," changed the axis of advance on 1 August and betrayed the cause to Poland and the entente. See I. Apanasenko, "Pervaya konnaya," *VIZh* no. 4 (November 1939): 35–42.
70. Pilsudski, *Year 1920*, pp. 85–86.

71. Aleksandr A. Neznamov, *Trebovaniya, kotorye pred'yavlyaet sovremennyi boi k podgotovke (obucheniyu) nachal'nikov i mass* (St. Peterburg, 1909), p. 27.
72. Verkhovsky, "Evolyutisiya," pp. 56–60.
73. Frunze, "Edinaya voennaya doktrina," p. 39.
74. "Voennaya nauka i dialektika," *Morskoî sbornik* no. 1 (January 1925): 17–27.
75. A. G. Kavtaradze, *Voennye spetsialisty na sluzhbe Respubliki Sovetov, 1917–1920 gg.* (Moscow: Nauka, 1988), p. 238.
76. Varfolomeev, "Strategiya v akademicheskoi postanovke," pp. 83–84.
77. Svechin, "Trudy Komissii," p. 14ff.
78. Varfolomeev, "Strategiya v akademicheskoi postanovke," p. 84.
79. Svechin, "Trudy Komissii," pp. 6–26.
80. Aleksandr A. Svechin, "Gosudarstvennyî i frontovoî tyl," *Voîna i revolyutsiya* no. 11 (1930): 94–108.
81. Boris M. Shaposhnikov, *Mozg armii*, 3 vols. (Moscow: Voennyî Vestnik, 1927–1929), I: 112ff.
82. Nikolai Varfolomeev, "Manevry na zapfronte," *Revolyutsiya i voîna* no. 19 (1923): 5–26, no. 20 (1923): 77–104. On the influence of Frunze and Tukhachevsky upon the Academy, see A. I. Radzievsky, ed., *Akademiya imeni M. V. Frunze: Istoriya voennoi ordena Lenina Krasnoznamennoî ordena Suvorova Akademyi* (Moscow: Voenizdat, 1972), pp. 71–77.
83. Nikolai Varfolomeev, "Dvizhenie presleduyushcheî armii k polyureshitel'nogo srazheniya," *Revolyutsiya i voîna* no. 13 (1921): 69–96.
84. Varfolomeev, "Strategiya v akademicheskoî postanovke," pp. 87–88.
85. Ibid.
86. Nikolai Varfolomeev, "Strategicheskoe narastanie i istoshchenie v grazhdanskoî voîne," in A. S. Bubnov et al., eds., *Grazhdanskaya voîna 1918–1921: Voennoe iskusstvo Krasnoi armii* (Moscow: Voennyî vestnik, 1928), pp. 260–81. What Varfolomeev called strategic intensification, Tukhachevsky had termed intensification of the revolution (narostanie [sic] revolyutsii). See Tukhachevsky, "Revolyutsiya izvne," pp. 47–54.
87. Nikolai Varfolomeev, *Udarnaya armiya* (Moscow: Gosvoenizdat, 1933), pp. 169–89, and *Nastupatel'naya operatsiya (po opytu Am'enskogo srazheniya 8 avgusta 1918 g.)* (Moscow: Gosvoenizdat, 1937), pp. 169–76.
88. V. K. Triandafillov, "Vozmozhnaya chislennost' budushchikh armii," *Voîna i revolyutsiya* no. 3 (1927): 14–43. Triandafillov's assumptions about the prospect of war were those of the party's right, the advocates of the continuation of the NEP. He even cited Bukharin on the stabilization of the world capitalist economy (p. 17).
89. V. K. Triandafillov, *Kharakter operatsii sovremennykh armii*, 3d ed. (Moscow: Gosvoenizdat, 1936), pp. 7–9, 255. Triandafillov's study of the Perekop Operation was later reworked and published as part of the three-volume history of the Civil War. This essay is noteworthy for its attention to the problem of combined arms, especially the coordination of infantry and artillery in the attack, and the analysis of the role of the higher density of machine guns in this breakthrough operation. See V. K. Triandafillov, "Perekopskaya operatsiya Krasnoî armii (takticheskii etyud)," in Bubnov, *Grazhdanskaya voîna*, pp. 339–57.
90. V. K. Triandafillov, *Kharakter operatsii sovremennykh armii*, 1st ed. (Moscow: Gosizdat, Otdel Voenlit, 1929), p. 1ff.
91. *Field Regulations of the Red Army 1929* (Washington, D.C.: Foreign Broadcast Information Service, 1985), pp. 63–93. The tie between future war (*budushchaya voîna*) and operational art (*operativnoe iskusstvo*) was made by I. Ivanov in a bibliography he

published in 1934. The posthumous second (1933) edition of Triandafillov's book was listed as the basic work in four out of twelve major categories, i.e., contemporary operational means, the conduct of operations, meeting operations, and offensive operations. Under the subtopics listed for conduct of operations, *Kharakter operatsii sovremennykh armii* was listed as the basic work for studying general questions, control of operations, and transport and rear. See I. Ivanov, "Voennotekhnicheskaya literatura po voprosam kharaktera budushcheî voiny i operativnogo iskusstva," *Voîna i revolyutsiya* no. 2 (March–April 1934): 13–30.

92. V. N. Lobov, "Aktual'nye voprosy razvitiva teorii sovetskoî voennoî strategii 20-kh — serediny 30-kh godov," *VIZh* no. 2 (February 1989): 44.

93. A. A. Kokoshin, *V poiskakh vykhoda: Voenno-politicheskie aspekty mezhdunarodnoî bezopasnosti* (Moscow: Izdatel'stvo politicheskoî literatury, 1989), pp. 252–61.

94. Triandafillov, *Kharakter operatsii sovremennykh armii*, pp. 235–54.

95. M. N. Tukhachevsky, "K voprosu o sovremennoi strategiî," in *Voîna i voennoe isskustvo v svete istoricheskogo materializma* (Moscow: Gosizdat, 1927), pp. 127–33.

96. G. Isserson, "Zapiski sovremennika o M. N. Tukhachevskom," *VIZh* no. 4 (April 1964): 65–67.

97. "Motorizatsiya i mekhanizatsiya inostrannykh armii (k nachalu 1929 g.)," *Informatsionnyi sbornik* no. 12 (December 1928): 145–57.

98. Mikhail N. Tukhachevsky, "Na baze dostignutogo — k novym zadacham," in *Izbrannye Proizvedeniya*, II: 67–68; and D. N. Nikishev, "Chelovek dela," in N. I. Koritsky et al., eds., *Marshal Tukhachevskiî: Vospominaniya druzeî i soratnikov* (Moscow: Voenizdat, 1965), pp. 199–202.

99. *Sovetskaya voennaya entsiklopediya* (Moscow: Sovetskaya entsiklopediya, 1933), II: 842–43.

100. Mikhail N. Tukhachevsky, "Predislovie k knige G. Del'briuka, *Istoriia voennogo iskusstva v ramkakh politicheskoî istoriî*," in *Izbrannye proizvedeniya*, II: 116–46.

101. Mikhail N. Tukhachevsky, "O kharaktere sovremennykh reshenii VI kongressa Kominterna," in *Zapiski: Kommunisticheskaya Akademiya: Sektsiya po izucheniyu problem voîny* (Moscow: n.p., 1930), pp. 21–29.

102. *Voina i revolyutsiya* no. 3 (1930): 140–47.

103. Mikhail N. Tukhachevsky, "Predislovie k knige Dzh. Fullera," in *Izbrannye proizvedeniya*, II: 152.

104. Mikhail N. Tukhachevsky, "Rukopis' stat'i M. N. Tukhachevskogo 'Voennye plany Gitlera' s pravkoî I. V. Stalina," in "Iz Istorii Velikoî Otechestvennoi voîny," *Izvestiya TsK KPSS* no. 1 (January 1990): 161–70.

105. USSR, *Narodnyî Komissariat Oborony, Vremennyî polevoî ustav RKKA 1936 (PU 36)* (Moscow: Gosvoenizdat, 1937), pp. 9–16.

106. Tukhachevsky, "O novom polevom ustave RKKA," in *Izbrannye proizvedeniya*, II: 253–55.

107. Tukhachevsky, "Voennye plany nyneshneî Germanii," in Ibid., pp. 233–39.

108. G. S. Isserson, *Novye formy bor'by* (Moscow: Gosvoenizdat, 1940). Isserson, Tukhachevsky's colleague, warned that the war in Spain had been atypical and that the German use of mechanized mobile groups and tactical aviation against the Poles was the real threat to be met. How Isserson survived the purges, kept his position at the Military Academy, and was able to secure the publication of New Forms of Struggle remains unclear.

109. P. A. Kurochkin, *Obshchevoîskovaya armiya v nastuplenii (po opytu Velikoî Otechestvennoî voîny 1941–1945 gg.* (Moscow: Voenizdat, 1966), pp. 19–25.

110.The situation is exemplified by V. A. Semënov's study of the development of Soviet operational art, published in 1960. This work cited Triandafillov's "Nature of the Operations of Modern Armies" but provided no intellectual context and ignored the contributions of Svechin, Varfolomeev, Tukhachevsky, and others. See V. A. Semënov, *Kratkiĭ ocherk razvitiya sovetskogo operativnogo iskusstva* (Moscow: Voenizdat, 1960), pp. 103–26.

Soviet Operational Art Since 1936

The Triumph of Maneuver War

David M. Glantz

Introduction: On the Eve of War

The vital theoretical and practical work the Red Army accomplished between 1932 and 1936 in the realm of operational art created a model for offensive combat that has endured to the present. In the late 1930s, however, this model did not accord with reality. It would take years of crisis and warfare for the Red Army to realize fully the theoretical concepts it developed by 1936.

As was the case with the entire Soviet military establishment, Soviet operational maneuver concepts and forces suffered severe damage in the late 1930s, in part because Stalin purged their creators. The multiple waves of military purges, which began in 1937 and lasted into the opening months of World War II, liquidated most Red Army theoreticians and senior commanders. Inevitably, therefore, their ideas fell into disuse or outright disrepute.[1] In addition, despite the success of the Red Army's fledgling armored forces at Khalkhin-Gol in the Far East, Soviet military experiences in Spain, Poland, and Finland cast doubt on the combat utility of its large mechanized and armored formations.[2] Consequently, in November 1939 the Soviet High Command abolished its four large tank corps and replaced them with smaller motorized divisions organized on a combined-arms basis.[3]

The subsequent German victory over France in the spring of 1940 revealed the full and shocking potential of *Blitzkrieg* and alerted the Soviets to the mistake they had made when they truncated their mechanized force structure.[4] Hastily, under the direction of Defense Minister S. K. Timoshenko, the Red Army began creating new mechanized corps, twenty-nine of which were to exist, fully equipped, by mid-1942.[5] Consequently, while the Red Army's force structure, particularly that of its mechanized force, was imposing on paper by mid-1941, it was far less capable in practice.[6] In addition, the shockingly efficient performance of the German Army in Poland and France, juxtaposed against the Red Army's dismal performance during the early stages of the Finnish War, rekindled Soviet faith in the concept of deep operations and operational maneuver. Accordingly, Timoshenko reaffirmed the twin concepts (although not by name) in a speech he delivered to senior commanders in late 1940.[7] The purges, however, had eliminated the most effective large-unit commanders and those who best understood how operational maneuver fit with established offensive techniques. In addition to weak high- and mid-level leadership, the Red Army experienced a multitude of ills associated with simultaneous attempts to alter and entirely reequip its entire force structure. As a result, the Red Army was unprepared for war in 1941 in terms of leadership, command and control, logistics, and training, especially for a war begun by strategic and operational surprise.

The Test of War: Background

The surprise German invasion of June 1941 shook the Soviet nation to its very foundations, subjected the Red Army to six months of grave crisis, and subsequently led to over three years of grueling and costly war. The Red Army was utterly shattered during the first two months of war. Thereafter, it faced the arduous tasks of surviving, then reviving and maturing into an instrument that could compete with the *Wehrmacht* and achieve ultimate military victory.

Soviet military analysts and historians subdivide the war into three distinct periods, each of which reflected the basic political-military conditions that characterized its duration.[8] Although the Red Army was primarily on the strategic defensive during the first period of war (22 June 1941–19 November 1942), this period was punctuated by the Red Army's Moscow strategic counteroffensive and several operational offensives designed to wrest the initiative from German hands. The two massive German offensives during this period (October–December 1941 and June–October 1942) placed the Soviet nation in jeopardy. The second period of war (19 November 1942–31 December 1943), which commenced with the Soviet strategic counteroffensive at Stalingrad, was a transitional period marked by alternating attempts by both sides to secure strategic advantage. After the titanic Battle of Kursk, by 31 December 1943, the Soviets had firmly secured the strategic initiative and advanced beyond the Dnepr River line. The Red Army maintained the strategic initiative during the third and final period of war (1944–1945) and ultimately emerged victorious over Nazi Germany.

While each of these periods displayed unique political-military characteristics, each also reflected distinct changes in the Red Army's force structure and operational maneuver capabilities—forces and capabilities that in turn helped produce the distinct political-military nature of each period. The first period of war was a formative phase during which the *Wehrmacht* virtually dismantled the Red Army's force structure in heavy combat and forced the Soviet High Command (the *Stavka*) to reconstruct it in a painful and costly process of trial and experimentation. Soviet operational maneuver concepts and mobile forces necessary to carry them out emerged in embryonic form during the spring of 1942. Additional battlefield experimentation during 1943 led to the creation of the Red Army's "modern" operational maneuver force and refined concepts for their combat employment. The Soviets improved their mobile forces and concepts governing their use during the third period of war, providing a basis for both wartime victory and an effective military force in the postwar years.

The First Period of War

The first period of war began on 22 June 1941. During the ensuing two months, advancing German forces literally destroyed the Red Army's initial force structure in intense combat along the Soviet Union's borders. Although Soviet defensive (and counteroffensive) concepts were theoretically realistic, and the *Stavka* tried in vain to mount an effective strategic defense, the results were disastrous. German armored spearheads easily penetrated Soviet rifle armies and pushed rapidly into the depths of the Red Army's strategic defenses.[9] The new Soviet mechanized corps, hastily assembled and deployed under the ever-present threat of German air power, stumbled into combat, often in uncoordinated and piecemeal fashion, subsequently to be destroyed systematically by German forces. By early July most mechanized corps in the border military districts were fragments of their former selves. As the battle moved eastward toward Leningrad, Smolensk, and Kiev, the remaining corps suffered a similar fate, leaving the Soviets by late July with only a skeletal capability for conducting maneuver war, either tactical or operational. Throughout this entire period, the *Stavka* mounted attempt after attempt to launch counteroffensives and counterstrokes with its mobile forces, only to experience repeated failures.[10]

During the disastrous initial months of war, the Soviet High Command truncated its already-shaken force structure to match its commanders' abilities and available logistical support. The Soviets disbanded the mechanized corps not already destroyed and replaced them first with separate tank divisions and ultimately with numerous small tank brigades.[11] The tank divisions, however, also proved ineffective, and soon the *Stavka* transformed them into separate brigades or battalions. By December 1941 the Red Army's armored force consisted of 7 tank divisions, 79 separate tank brigades, and 100 separate tank battalions. In conjunction with cavalry corps, cavalry divisions, light cavalry divisions, and new ski battalions, these provided the mobile capability of the Red Army, a pale reflection of the once proud mechanized force of June 1941.[12]

Soviet offensive operations before and during the winter campaign of 1941–1942 vividly displayed the weaknesses of this force structure. Soviet rifle forces penetrated German tactical defenses and pursued into the operational depths at foot speed. They were, however, deficient in staying power; soon growing infantry casualties brought every advance to an abrupt and bloody end. Soviet cavalry corps reinforced by rifle and tank brigades also penetrated into the German operational rear. Once there and reinforced by airborne or air-landed forces, they ruled the countryside, forests, and swamps but were unable to drive the more mobile Germans from the main communications arteries and villages. At best, they could force limited German withdrawals, but only if in concert with pressure from forces along the front. At worst, these mobile forces were themselves encircled, only to be destroyed or driven from the German rear area when summer arrived.

At Rostov, in November 1941, the Soviets forced the overextended German First Panzer Army to withdraw to the Mius River line by striking German defenses with the 37th Army secretly deployed forward, supported by a cavalry corps and two separate tank brigades. However, no encirclements ensued, and German forces halted the Soviet advance at the Mius River defenses.[13] Two months later, Red Army forces were frustrated as they launched another partially successful operation south of Khar'kov (the Barvenkovo-Lozovaia offensive). During the first stage of the Red Army's Moscow counteroffensive in December 1941, the Soviets spearheaded their thrusts with rifle units on skis and tank brigades (roughly two or three per army). South of Moscow, General Belov's 1st Guards Cavalry Corps penetrated into the rear of Second Panzer Army and advanced 100 kilometers deep into the Kaluga region. During the second phase of the Moscow counteroffensive in January 1942, the 11th, 2d Guards, and 1st Guards Cavalry Corps penetrated deep into the German rear area in an attempt to encircle German Army Group Center. Despite heroic efforts and the commitment into combat of the entire 4th Airborne Corps, the cavalry corps failed to link up and became encircled in the German rear area.[14] The ambitious Soviet operation failed to achieve its ultimate strategic aim, due largely to the fragile nature of Soviet operational maneuver forces. Ultimately, in June 1942 German forces cleared "the Red louses from their hides," although the elusive Belov escaped to Red Army lines with a quarter of his original strength. The geography of the Eastern Front in the summer of 1942, with huge salients occupied by German and Soviet forces at Demyansk, at Rzhev, and south of Khar'kov, bore mute testimony to the failure of Soviet operational maneuver during its winter counteroffensive.

The *Stavka* correctly judged that these operations had failed because of the Red Army's lack of large, coherent, mechanized, and armored formations capable of performing sustained operational maneuver. To remedy the problem, in April 1942 the Soviets fielded new tank corps consisting of 3 tank brigades and 1 motorized rifle brigade and totaling

168 tanks each.[15] The *Stavka* placed these corps at the disposal of army and front commanders for use as mobile groups operating in tandem with older cavalry corps, which by now had also received a new complement of armor. The *Stavka* employed these new tank corps in an offensive role for the first time in the spring of 1942.

On 12 May 1942, the Soviet Southwestern Front attacked out of bridgeheads across the Northern Donets River north and south of Khar'kov.[16] The Soviets intended to exploit with a cavalry corps (the 3d Guards) in the north and two secretly formed and redeployed tank corps (the 21st and 23d) and a cavalry corps (the 6th) in the south. Ultimately the two mobile groups were to link up west of Khar'kov and entrap the German Sixth Army. Although the offensive surprised the Germans, the Soviets mishandled their mobile forces. Soviet infantry penetrated German defenses to the consternation of the German commanders, but the Soviets procrastinated and failed to commit the two tank corps for six days. The corps finally went into action on 17 May simultaneously with a massive surprise attack by First Panzer Army against the southern flank of the Soviet salient. Over the next two days, the two tank corps disengaged, retraced their path, and engaged the new threat. But it was too late. The German counterattack encircled and destroyed the better part of 3 Soviet armies, the 2 tank corps and 2 cavalry corps, totaling more than 250,000 men.[17]

The Khar'kov debacle and a simultaneous disaster to the south in the Crimea demonstrated to Soviet planners that they not only had to create larger armored units, but they also had to learn to employ them properly. The twin disasters, however, did not halt Soviet efforts to rejuvenate their mobile force. Throughout the summer and fall of 1942, even as the German Operation *Blau* (the Stalingrad offensive) was unfolding dramatically across southern Russia, the Soviets created even larger mobile forces. In June the *Stavka* formed four mixed-composition (rifle, cavalry, and armor) tank armies, each around the nucleus of two tank corps.[18] (*See Table 2.*) The combination of tracked, foot, and hoof forces under control of a single headquarters was dangerous, and, understandably, the new tank armies functioned poorly. The 5th Tank Army, committed to combat west of Voronezh with four separate tank corps, attracted German attention and perhaps deflected the German advance southward but failed to halt the Germans' offensive.[19] Two other Red Army tank armies (the 1st and 4th) engaged German forces on the distant approaches to Stalingrad, but suffered heavy losses and were soon renumbered as rifle armies.[20] By November 1942 the two tank armies (3d and 5th), which remained in the Soviet force structure, would soon make their presence felt with stunning effect. In September 1942, the Soviets formed eight mechanized corps, each consisting of one tank brigade (or three tank regiments) and three mechanized brigades.[21] (*See Table 3.*) The Soviets relied on these new

TABLE 2 — SOVIET TANK ARMY COMPOSITION, JUNE 1942

1st Tank Army	3d Tank Army	4th Tank Army	5th Tank Army	5th Tank Army (Second Formation)
2 tank corps	2 tank corps	2 tank corps	2 tank corps	2 tank corps
1 separate tank brigade	1 motorized rifle division	1 separate tank brigade	1 rifle division	1 cavalry corps
2 rifle divisions	2 rifle divisions	1 antitank brigade	1 separate tank brigade	1 separate tank brigade
	1 separate tank brigade	1 rifle division		6 rifle divisions

Source: I. M. Anan'yev, B.B. Vashchenko, and N.T. Konashenko, "Tankovye armii" [Tank armies], *Sovetskaya voennaya entsiklopediya* [Soviet military encyclopedia] (Moscow: Voyenizdat, 1980), 8: 665–69. For a critique of the tank armies' performance, see P. A. Rotmistrov, *Stal'naya gvardiya* [Steel guard] (Moscow: Voyenizdat, 1984), pp. 163–64.

TABLE 3 — SOVIET MECHANIZED CORPS TYPES, SEPTEMBER 1942

Type 1	Type 2	Type 3
3 mechanized brigades	3 mechanized brigades	3 mechanized brigades
1 tank brigade	2 tank brigades	2 tank regiments
Support units	Support units	Support units
Strength: 175 tanks	Strength: 224 tanks	Strength: 204 tanks

tank armies, tank corps, and mechanized corps to spearhead their offensive operations in the winter campaign of 1942–1943, which commenced in November 1942 at Stalingrad and against the Rzhev salient, west of Moscow. While these forces experimented with new force combinations and operational and tactical techniques, the *Stavka* prepared to field even more capable and powerful operational maneuver formations.

The Second Period of War

The forces of the Soviet Southwestern and Stalingrad Fronts attacked out of bridgeheads across the Don and Volga Rivers northwest and south of Stalingrad on 19 November 1942, commencing the second period of war. After penetrating Romanian defenses with infantry forces, Soviet armored and mechanized corps drove deep into the German rear, linked up, and encircled the German Sixth Army and part of the Fourth Panzer Army.[22] Although Soviet forces formed a coherent inner encirclement line around German forces, several flaws marred this first example of successful large-scale operational maneuver. Command and control was awkward because mobile corps commanders reported to both front and army commanders, and the outer encirclement line, formed by cavalry corps, was fragile and almost immediately threatened by German relief forces. Most troubling was the high attrition rate of armor in this and in subsequent stages of the winter offensive, due primarily to logistical causes.[23]

Less than a week later, the Western and Kalinin Front's forces, under the personal direction of Marshal of the Soviet Union G. I. Zhukov, struck German Ninth Army in the Rzhev salient. Delivering a massive blow along four separate axes, six Soviet armies spearheaded by two new Red Army mechanized corps, two tank corps, and a cavalry corps tried in vain to encircle German forces in the salient. Three weeks of bloody and futile fighting produced over 300,000 casualties and once again indicated that Soviet commanders had yet to learn how to coordinate complex mobile operations by so massive a force.[24]

During subsequent operations throughout the winter, the Soviets worked to correct the deficiencies apparent in November. In the Middle Don operation (17–30 December 1942), the Soviets employed two groups of mobile forces to attack across the Don and Chir Rivers and encircle the Italian Eighth Army.[25] Again mobile corps commanders were responsible to both the front and army commanders, but unlike the case at Stalingrad, one tank corps (17th) formed a more durable outer encirclement line. Despite the fact that the mobile corps advanced up to 100 kilometers and destroyed the Italian Eighth Army, the Soviets again experienced major difficulties. Armor attrition rates exceeded 60 percent in the tank corps, and the corps advanced out of mutual supporting distance and well beyond the range of supporting foot infantry and artillery. German reinforcements took advantage of the weakness and dispersion of Soviet mobile forces by counterattacking and temporarily halting the advance.

In the Donbas operation (29 January–20 February), in which the Soviets sought to encircle all of German Army Group Don, the Southwest Front commander formed four of his tank corps (3d, 10th, 18th, and 4th Guards) under a single headquarters (Group Popov) as the first Soviet front mobile group.[26] To improve the sustainability of the group, truck-mounted rifle divisions were attached to each of the tank corps. To a large degree, however, the overall weakness of the group (160 tanks) negated the group's effectiveness. The weakness of the tank corps, their propensity for being caught up in operations along their flanks, and the lack of mobility of the attached rifle divisions almost instantly fragmented the group, and Popov was unable to concentrate and achieve decisive results. Overextension and dispersion of Soviet forces provided General Erich von Manstein, commander of Army Group South, an opportunity to orchestrate a counterstroke that cut the supply lines of overextended Soviet mobile forces and destroyed them. At the same time, Manstein's forces encircled and severely damaged the 8th Cavalry and 4th Guards Mechanized Corps, which were attacking German forces in the Donbas region from the east (at Debalt'sevo and Anastasievka) and virtually cut off and annihilated the 25th Tank Corps, which had been advancing toward Zaporozh'ye.[27]

Concurrently, the *Stavka* mounted an ambitious offensive by its newly formed Central Front (the former Don Front), supported by the Western and Bryansk Fronts, against German defenses along the Orel-Bryansk-Smolensk axis. General K. K. Rokossovsky, the Central Front commander, spearheaded his offensive with the 2d Tank Army, the 2d Guards Cavalry Corps, and numerous ski brigades. In heavy fighting that endured from 25 February through mid-March, Rokossovsky's forces reached the banks of the Desna River, over one hundred kilometers into the German rear area, almost severing communications between German Army Groups Center and South. However, a combination of skillful German maneuver, poor Soviet logistical support, and clumsy operations by exhausted Red Army forces, all exacerbated by deteriorating weather and terrain conditions, spelled doom for the ambitious offensive. By mid-March the Soviet offensive fell victim to Manstein's counteroffensive. Having suffered nearly 500,000 casualties, the Red Army ceased its winter campaign and dug in around what would become the infamous Kursk bulge.[28]

An even more grisly fate befell the Voronezh Front's 3d Tank Army operating in the Khar'kov region. This tank army was encircled and annihilated by counterattacking German forces in early March 1943, and its parent front was forced to abandon Khar'kov and withdraw to positions south of Kursk and east of the Northern Donets River.[29] In the Donbas, Khar'kov, and Orel-Bryansk operations, the Soviets took a calculated risk to win a major strategic victory before spring rains interrupted operations. Soviet mobile forces shared in that risk and suffered the consequences. While the winter campaign demonstrated what operational maneuver forces could achieve, it also vividly demonstrated the problems that had to be overcome if they were to realize their full potential. Soviet armored forces would require six more months to accomplish the goals the *Stavka* assigned them in February 1943.

After the winter campaign, a three-month lull set in across the Eastern Front, during which both sides planned summer strategic operations. During this period the Soviets exploited lessons learned in the winter and reconstructed their mobile forces to make them more powerful and sustainable. Simultaneously, they refined mobile operational and tactical techniques to improve the operational maneuver capability of front and army commanders. Soviet strategic plans for the summer of 1943 increasingly relied for success on the operations of these refined mobile groups. The premier Soviet mobile forces were the five new tank armies created by a January *Stavka* order, each consisting of two tank corps, an optional mechanized corps, and a variety of mobile support units. The new armies fielded over 500 tanks each and were soon augmented by newly formed self-propelled artillery units.[30] Similarly, the Soviets refined the structure of separate tank and mechanized corps by adding more combat and combat service support units. By July 1943 the Soviets fielded twenty-four tank and thirteen mechanized corps.[31]

The new tank armies and augmented tank, mechanized, and cavalry corps provided operational maneuver capabilities to both front and army commanders. In all major operations, the *Stavka* allocated one or two tank armies to front commanders and one mechanized or tank corps to army commanders operating along main attack axes. These mobile units conducted operational maneuver under direct control of their parent headquarters. On difficult terrain or in bad weather (spring), cavalry corps served as front or army mobile groups, and by the fall of 1943 front commanders in these circumstances employed cavalry-mechanized groups (usually one mechanized or tank corps and one cavalry corps) to perform operational maneuver. In theory, rifle forces, supported by an increasing array of artillery and engineer units, penetrated enemy tactical defenses to a depth of 8–12 kilometers, and then army mobile groups began the operational exploitation. The front commander then committed his operational maneuver force to develop the offensive into the enemy's operational rear area. In practice, however, rifle forces seldom completed the tactical penetration. That task fell to the army mobile group as it advanced to begin the exploitation. As a result, the army mobile group was often significantly weakened before the exploitation phase began. Thus, the success of deep exploitation depended on the skill of commanders whose tank armies were serving as mobile groups.

The first "modern" Soviet operations in terms of operational maneuver occurred during the Kursk strategic operation (July–August 1943).[32] Soviet strategic plans called for a temporary defensive phase to weaken German forces, diversionary attacks to draw German operational reserves to other sectors of the front, and two major counteroffensives, spearheaded by mobile groups, against weakened German forces, the first at Orel and the second near Belgorod. The Orel offensive by the Western, Bryansk, and later the Central Front began on 12 July 1943, just as the Germans' Kursk assault ground to a halt. Tank corps (1st, 5th, 20th, and 1st Guards) of attacking Soviet armies joined the struggle on the second day of the operation and were later joined by two tank armies, 3d and 4th Guards, attacking under front control on the eighth and fourteenth days of the operation. Heavy German defenses and quick reaction by German reserves prevented significant Soviet advances, and the operation evolved into a slugging match between both parties.

The Belgorod-Khar'kov operation, however, better characterized deep operations and more clearly reflected what the Soviets hoped to accomplish. It began on 3 August 1943, after German operational reserves (the XXIV Panzer Corps and II SS Panzer Corps) had been drawn away to other sectors of the front by Soviet diversionary offensives.[33] The attacking armies of the Soviet Voronezh and Steppe Fronts advanced directly against the nose of the Belgorod salient to penetrate German tactical defenses. Once penetration was achieved, the army and front commanders were to commit both separate tank and mechanized corps or multiple tank armies to conduct operational maneuver and seize the Khar'kov region.

Before noon on 3 August, the Voronezh Front's 1st and 5th Guards Tank Armies advanced through the 5th Guards Army into the penetration, with a forward detachment leading each of their four subordinate tank corps. By late afternoon, the four corps had penetrated thirty kilometers to begin an operational exploitation. Separate tank corps of adjacent Soviet armies also advanced on the first day of attack but had to deal with more extensive German defenses before exploiting into the operational depths. The operational exploitation of the 1st and 5th Guards Tank Armies lasted seven days and thrust to a depth of 110–120 kilometers. On 11 August German operational reserves, returned from other sectors of the front, intervened and within days halted the precipitous Soviet advance. After heavy fighting, which severely eroded the strength of both Soviet and German mobile forces, Khar'kov fell on 23 August, signaling the end of the operation.

Despite the early deep advance and the favorable outcome of the operation, severe problems emerged for Soviet mobile forces, which they would have to remedy in the future. The tank armies and mobile corps outran supporting forces by a factor of several days, thus exposing themselves to German counterattacks. As a consequence, the Soviets recognized the need to provide them more mobile combined-arms support. Moreover, some link had to be established between armor and mechanized forces operating deep and slower follow-on forces. The Soviets remedied this problem by fielding and employing more forward detachments at army, corps, and division level.

After the Kursk strategic operation, Soviet forces launched offensives along the entire Eastern Front and forced the Germans to withdraw to its newly created Panther Defense Line, which the Germans had constructed along the Sozh, Pronya, and Dnepr Rivers. Soviet forces pursued vigorously, with operational maneuver forces leading the advance to secure crossings over these river barriers. During the pursuit the Soviets secretly shifted the 3d Guards Tank Army southward from Orel. Together with numerous separate tank, mechanized, and cavalry corps, the tank army raced forward parallel to withdrawing German units, reached the Dnepr River before the Germans, and, with forward detachments from rifle armies, seized small bridgeheads near Velikiy Bukrin, south of Kiev. Because the absence of heavy bridging equipment prevented passage of the river by the army's armored elements, for the first time the Soviets attempted a major river crossing operation employing a large-scale airborne drop.[34] The attempt failed when hastily assembled German forces thwarted both the airdrop and Soviet attempts to enlarge the bridgehead. The operation, although unsuccessful, was an attempt to fulfill Marshal of the Soviet Union M. N. Tukhachevsky's dream of combining ground and vertical aspects of operational maneuver.

To the north, after clearing German Army Group Center forces from the Smolensk and Bryansk regions, in early October the Kalinin, Western, and Central Fronts began a major operation to envelop and defeat German Army Group Center from north and south, capture Minsk, and liberate Belorussia.[35] Soviet forces hammered German defenses from Nevel' southward through Vitebsk and Orsha to Gomel' in massive offensives that pierced German defenses in the Nevel' and Gomel' region but failed to collapse German strategic defenses. The Kalinin Front succeeded in driving a wedge between Army Groups North and Center near Nevel', and the Central Front severed communications between Army Groups Center and South in a deep thrust along the Rechitsa-Bobruysk axis. However, numerous separate violent Soviet offensives against Vitebsk and Orsha failed, and by mid-December a German counterstroke restored the front in southern Belorussia. By 31 December Soviet forces threatened Vitebsk and occupied sizable bridgeheads across the Dnepr River near Rechitsa and Chernobyl'. Once again, the *Stavka* failed to achieve its strategic ends largely due to the weakness of operational maneuver forces in the three attacking fronts. Since the *Stavka* had been forced to withdraw its tank armies for refitting after the heavy losses they had incurred during the Battle of Kursk, only separate tank and cavalry corps were available to spearhead the advance into Belorussia. The *Stavka* would try again to smash German defenses in Belorussia during the following winter but would fail once again. The German bastion in Belorussia would not fall until the summer of 1944.

In the southern sector of the front, the Steppe and Southwestern Fronts advanced on the Dnepr and secured a large bridgehead south of Kremenchug and Dnepropetrovsk in October. However, despite constant heavy fighting throughout November and December, the fronts' forces failed to capture their objectives, the cities of Krivoy Rog and Nikopol', and drive the Germans from the Dnepr River's eastern bend. At the same time, the Southern Front employed a cavalry-mechanized group to conduct deep operations and drive German Army Group South back through Melitopol' toward the Dnepr River and Crimea.[36] Clumsy employment of a mechanized corps (the 4th Guards) and a tank corps (the 19th) led to the bloody failure of four separate Soviet attempts to crush German defenders of the Nikopol' bridgehead.[37]

In late fall 1943, Soviet forces wrestled with the problem of breaching the German's Dnepr River defenses near Kiev. In five separate offensives during early October, the Central Front's left wing (the 13th and 60th Armies) and the Voronezh Front's 27th, 38th, 40th, and 47th Combined-arms Armies and the 3d Guards Tank Army failed to crack German defenses near Chernobyl', Gornostaipol', Lyutezh, and Velikiy Bukrin.[38] These failures occurred despite Soviet massed employment of the 3d Guards Tank Army and three separate mobile corps in the Bukrin region. After these bloody failures, in early November the Soviets finally employed operational maneuver masked by successful deception to solve the strategic dilemma. Between 29 October and 3 November 1943, the Soviet 1st Ukrainian (formerly Voronezh) Front secretly redeployed the 3d Guards Tank Army northward into the small Lyutezh bridgehead north of Kiev, and on 3 November the front assaulted out of the bridgehead.[39]

Subsequently, the 3d Guards Tank Army advanced over one hundred kilometers southwest of Kiev before being halted by redeploying German reserves. The operation bore many similarities to the Belgorod operation, for the 3d Guards Tank Army's two forward detachments were destroyed in the German counterattacks. Subsequent German counterattacks failed to drive Soviet forces back to Kiev. During the waning stages of these counterattacks, the Soviets again secretly regrouped under the cloak of an effective deception plan and prepared a new offensive, this time spearheaded by two full tank armies (the 1st and 3d Guards).[40] While German forces attacked what they falsely assumed to be the main Soviet concentration northwest of Kiev, on 24 December the new Soviet blow struck weakened German defenses southwest of Kiev. In the ensuing Zhitomir-Berdichev operation, Soviet operational maneuver forces advanced 120–130 kilometers before being halted by redeployed German armored forces.

The Third Period of War

The Zhitomir-Berdichev operation began what the Soviets call the Right Bank of the Ukraine Strategic Offensive, which encompassed two distinct phases. The first phase, from December 1943 to the end of February 1944, consisted of five major operations conducted successively by one or two fronts.[41] During this phase, the third period of war commenced on 31 December. The second phase, which lasted from 4 March to 12 May 1944, consisted of three simultaneous and two successive operations, each by a single front.[42] Operational maneuver forces played a significant role in these operations and often resulted in the encirclement of large German forces, although at this stage most encircled forces were able to escape destruction. More disturbing for the Germans was the fact that for the first time Soviet mobile forces successfully operated during the period of the *razputitsa* [spring flooding], a time when, in earlier years, operations came to a grinding halt.

Several notable features characterized the first phase of these operations. During the Kirovograd operation, the Soviet 2d Ukrainian Front employed a portion of its operational maneuver force to deceive the Germans regarding the location of their main attack, a technique the Soviets improved upon in the future.[43] During the Korsun'-Shevchenkovskiy operation, the 2d Ukrainian Front's operational maneuver force, the 5th Guards Tank Army, continued its exploitation despite the fact that German tactical defenses temporarily solidified behind it.[44] In addition, the mobile groups of the 1st and 2d Ukrainian Fronts formed an outer encirclement line around two encircled German corps, while rifle and cavalry forces reduced the encircled German forces. This formation was designed to permit the forces manning the outer encirclement line to continue to develop the offensive while the encircled force was being destroyed. Soviet forces, however, were not able to accomplish this feat successfully until the summer operations of 1944. Elsewhere, cavalry and cavalry-mechanized forces played an important role in the offensives, particularly in swampy regions near Rovno and Lutsk and in operations during rainy periods in the southern Ukraine.[45]

During the second phase of the offensive, the *Stavka* placed three tank armies at the 1st Ukrainian Front's disposal. General Vatutin, the front commander, and Marshal Zhukov, who succeeded him when Vatutin was killed by Ukrainian partisans, regrouped these tank armies secretly from his right flank to his left. He then committed them in sequence (first two and then one) from the Lutsk area south toward the Romanian border in an attempt to encircle German Army Group South.[46] After advancing

120–180 kilometers, the three tank armies encircled German First Panzer Army, which barely escaped destruction by breaking out to the west. The offensive concluded in early May with a major offensive by the 2d Ukrainian Front toward Yassy in northern Romania. The operation, which the Germans called the Battle of Targul-Frumos, failed when German Panzer forces skillfully countered a poorly coordinated assault spearheaded by the Soviet 2d, 5th Guards, and 6th Tank Armies.

Soviet employment of multiple tank armies, mobile corps, and cavalry-mechanized corps fragmented German defenses in the Ukraine and forced German forces to withdraw from the Ukraine into Poland and Romania. Improved Soviet mobile force logistics permitted deeper operations over longer periods. Most important, the concentration of Soviet armor and mechanized units in the Ukraine convinced German planners that in the summer the Soviets would attack German forces in Poland and Romania. The Soviets reinforced this misperception by deliberately posturing offensively in the south while secretly moving large mobile formations northward into Belorussia. The *Stavka* prepared to conduct a series of devastating offensives in the summer that would rely on operational maneuver forces and deception to produce significant strategic success.

Planning for the 1944 summer-fall campaign began in May. Under the cloak of an extensive strategic deception plan, the *Stavka* planned four major successive strategic blows, each capitalizing on the results of the preceding offensive and each relying on operational maneuver forces to produce victory.[47] Each operation targeted a single German army group for destruction, and three of the four relied for success on strategic-scale maneuver by large mobile forces. For the first time, the Soviets employed large mobile formations in the terrain of Belorussia, which the Soviets previously had considered less suited to armored operations than southern Russia or the Ukraine.

During the Belorussian operation, the *Stavka* employed simultaneous and then successive encirclement operations to destroy the German Third Panzer and Ninth Armies around Vitebsk and Bobruysk and, subsequently, Fourth Army and the bulk of Army Group Center east of Minsk.[48] Separate tank corps served as army operational maneuver forces; and the 5th Guards Tank Army and two cavalry-mechanized groups formed front mobile groups for deep exploitation. In addition, tailored forward detachments created by combined-arms armies and rifle corps conducted tactical maneuver to produce shallow encirclements. These tactical and operational maneuver forces operated in concert to continue the exploitation after German forward forces had been encircled. The Belorussian offensive, code-named Operation BAGRATION, commenced on 22 June and developed rapidly and spectacularly. The armies' mobile groups exploited the success of rifle forces on the first or second day of the operation; and, in the Vitebsk region, the advancing forward detachments and rifle forces quickly encircled most of the Third Panzer Army. On the first day of operations, the cavalry-mechanized group exploited toward the Berezina River northeast of Minsk, and the 5th Guards Tank Army advanced directly toward the Berezina River and Minsk on the third day. To the south, army mobile groups committed on the first and third day of the operation reached Bobruisk and encircled major portions of the German Ninth Army, while another cavalry-mechanized group thrust northwestward on the second day to sever German communications routes running into Minsk from the south and southwest. By orienting their advance on key terrain southwest and northwest of Minsk, the fronts' operational maneuver forces had linked up west of Minsk by 3 July, secured the city without costly urban combat, and encircled large segments of Army Group Center. Unlike earlier operations, Soviet forces were able to continue the offensive westward and simultaneously destroy the bulk of three German armies, assisted by the fact that the bulk of German armor remained in the south in the expectation of a major Soviet offensive in that region.

No sooner had the *Stavka* inflicted a devastating defeat on Army Group Center than it launched a second major offensive against German Army Group North Ukraine, defending in southern Poland. The First Ukrainian Front struck German defenses northeast and east of L'vov on 13 July 1944.[49] Two tank armies (the 3d Guards and 4th) and a cavalry-mechanized group, operating as front mobile groups, assaulted L'vov from the east. Simultaneously, a secretly deployed third tank army (the 1st Guards) struck German defenses at L'vov from the northeast in cooperation with a second cavalry-mechanized group. The Germans expected the former attack but were unprepared for the latter. The armies' mobile groups (separate tank corps) advanced on the first day of operations and were followed by the tank armies and cavalry-mechanized groups.

In the south, however, the offensive did not develop as planned. Rifle forces penetrated German defenses in the 3d Guards Tank Army's commitment sector but failed to pierce German defenses in the sector where the 4th Tank Army was to join battle. Hastily, both tank armies and several tank corps regrouped and advanced through the narrow (6-kilometer) corridor in the 3d Guards Tank Army's sector. The 3d Guards Tank Army advanced on the third day, followed over the next two days by the 4th Tank Army. Once committed, the two mobile groups enveloped German defenses around L'vov.

The 1st Guards Tank Army's and the cavalry-mechanized group's operations to the north had even more devastating effect on the Germans. Prior to its commitment on the fifth day of the operation, the 1st Guards Tank Army had ordered its army's forward detachment (the 1st Guards Tank Brigade) to attack westward and deceive the Germans regarding the direction of the army's main attack.[50] Once German operational reserves (the 16th and 17th Panzer Divisions) had responded to that threat, thinking it to be the bulk of the Russian tank army, the main Russian Army advanced to the southwest, broke cleanly through German defenses, and advanced deep into their operational rear. Subsequently, Soviet operational maneuver forces drove to the Vistula River, where they secured a key bridgehead. By the end of the operation, the three Soviet tank armies had advanced up to 300 kilometers during only 15 days of continuous operations. Capitalizing on Red Army successes in Belorussia and southern Poland, on 17 July the 1st Belorussian Front's left wing advanced from the Kovel' area toward the Vistula River south of Warsaw, employing its secretly redeployed 2d Tank Army and a cavalry-mechanized group as front mobile groups.[51] The 2d Tank Army reached the banks of the Vistula River in early August and turned north toward Warsaw, only to be halted on the outskirts of Warsaw on 4 August by heavy German counterattacks.

Between 23 June and early August 1944, multiple Soviet mobile groups employed deep operational maneuver across an 800-kilometer front to thrust deep into the German rear along numerous axes. The attacking Soviet forces forced the shaken German defenders to frantically erect new defenses along the Narev and Vistula Rivers, over three hundred kilometers west of their original defense lines. Only the increased number, strength, and resilience of Soviet operational maneuver forces made this possible. To an increasing extent, the axiom held true that, where Red Army mobile forces operated successfully, Soviet offensives succeeded. Where they failed, offensives failed.

The final Soviet blow in the summer-fall campaign occurred in August 1944 where the Germans had expected the first blow to fall. On 20 August the Soviet 1st and 2d Ukrainian Fronts struck German Army Group South Ukraine in Romania.[52] The two Soviet fronts employed tank and mechanized corps, configured as army mobile groups, to conduct shallow encirclements, while the 1st Ukrainian Front's mobile group, the 6th Guards Tank Army, conducted deep operational maneuver toward Bucharest. The two Soviet fronts fully encircled and destroyed two Axis armies (the Sixth German and Third Romanian) within nine days. In the wake of this destruction, the remnants of German Army Group South Ukraine frantically erected defenses in the Carpathian Mountains to block the Soviet offensive from spreading into eastern Hungary.

Near the end of the summer-fall campaign, the *Stavka* ordered additional assaults to exploit the Germans' unprecedented defeats. The 3d Belorussian Front conducted the most important of these along the Gumbinnen-Königsberg and Goldap axes into the heartland of German East Prussia in late October. Once again, the limited availability of combat-capable operational maneuver forces at the end of a long strategic campaign (in this case, only the 2d Guards Tank Corps was available) permitted the Germans to parry the Soviet thrust. As was the case before in the Kursk and Orel regions, Belorussia, and Romania, the conquest of East Prussia would have to wait several more months.

During the winter campaign of 1944, Soviet operational maneuver forces successfully encircled German forces; but those encirclements had been either partial, or the quarry had escaped. In the summer, however, the encirclements were larger, and few of the encircled forces escaped destruction. By summer the Soviets had mastered the most difficult step of an encirclement operation, the ability to continue the exploitation while encircled forces were being destroyed. This sealed the fate of the encircled and extended the range of the operation. The increased use of forward detachments by operational maneuver forces, their refined composition, and the improved logistical structure of mobile forces overall markedly improved the Soviets' capability for sustaining operations to greater depths and for longer periods.[53]

Soviet operational maneuver forces and techniques achieved their greatest successes in 1945. This was due to more experienced Soviet commanders, improved weaponry, and the weakening of German forces, which had been dealt such devastating blows in 1944 and now had to contend with a two-front war. Mitigating these Soviet advantages was the shrunken Eastern Front, which now ran from the Baltic Sea through Hungary, and the manpower crisis facing the *Stavka*.[54] Given the catastrophic losses the Red Army had suffered in more than three years of war, success in 1945 would have to depend on sustained operational maneuver rather than wholesale expenditures of men's lives.

During the fall of 1944, the *Stavka* planned a climactic winter offensive to drive German forces to the Baltic coast and the Danzig-Poznan-Breslau-Budapest line. Since the offensive would be conducted across a more restricted front against more heavily fortified German defenses, careful planning was necessary to generate sufficient force superiority in key front sectors. The *Stavka* selected the Warsaw-Poznan-Berlin axis as the focal point for its operations after the New Year. In the meantime, Soviet forces along the strategic flanks in the Baltic region and Hungary conducted offensives to distract German attention and reserves from the critical western axis. A Red Army advance to the Danzig-Poznan-Breslau line required that it sustain offensive operations to a depth of almost three hundred kilometers, and the new area of operations was crisscrossed with well-prepared, but largely unoccupied, defense lines. An advance to this depth required rapid penetration of tactical defenses and coherent, well-coordinated conduct of deep operational maneuver into the operational depths.

The *Stavka* planned two major offensive operations along adjacent strategic axes. The most important offensive required two fronts to advance toward Poznan and Breslau from bridgeheads across the Vistula River south of Warsaw. The second required two more fronts to advance into East Prussia toward Königsberg, the lower Vistula River, and Danzig. The offensive across Poland (named the Vistula-Oder operation) was aimed at dismembering and destroying German Army Group A by deep, cutting thrusts. The offensive into East Prussia (named the East Prussian operation) was designed to pin German Army Group Center against the coast between Königsberg and the mouth of the Vistula River and destroy it. The former began on 13–14 January and the latter on 14–15 January, and Soviet mobile groups played a key role in three of the four front operations.[55]

In the Vistula-Oder operation, Marshal I. S. Konev's 1st Ukrainian Front employed separate tank corps as mobile groups for each army participating in the main attack from the Sandomierz bridgehead. He used two tank armies (the 3d Guards and 4th) to exploit the initial offensive success. The 1st Belorussian Front, now commanded personally by Marshal Zhukov, exploited his front's main attack from the smaller Magnushev bridgehead, with two tank armies (the 1st and 2d Guards), which entered the bridgehead soon after the rifle armies had commenced their assault. Zhukov supported the main effort by launching attacks from the even smaller Pulavy bridgehead with two separate tank corps functioning as army mobile groups.[56] The two fronts also committed their mobile groups to combat in different fashion. Konev orchestrated a massive blow on the first day of operations, and his three army and two front mobile groups advanced into combat on the heels of the rifle armies' assault. So close was the cooperation that tank army forward detachments deployed within the rifle army's attacking formation. On the other hand, since Zhukov initially had no room within the bridgehead to deploy his two tank armies, the armies entered combat sequentially on the second and third day of operations after rifle armies had penetrated German tactical defenses.

Both techniques were equally devastating. Deception concealed the scale of Soviet concentration and, combined with economy of force elsewhere, produced Soviet force superiority of over 10:1 in manpower and 6:1 in armor. Konev's assault swept through German defenses in a matter of hours and smashed the two reinforcing German Panzer divisions; within two days the 3d Guards and 4th Tank Armies were streaming deep into the Germans' operational rear.[57] Zhukov's forces penetrated German defenses quickly; and the 1st and 2d Guards Tank Armies began their operational exploitation on the second and third day of operations. The momentum of the four exploiting tank armies was so great that they swept around and encircled German operational reserves (Panzer Corps Grossdeutschland) deployed from East Prussia. Within a week the four Soviet tank armies and five tank corps advanced west, past Lodz and Krakow toward Poznan and Breslau, virtually obliterating organized German defenses across a 250-kilometer front.

While three tank armies raced toward the Oder River, the 3d Guards Tank Army dealt with German resistance anchored on the industrial city of Katowice in southern Poland. On the evening of 20 January, Konev ordered the tank army to turn abruptly southward 90 degrees away from its projected line of advance, west toward Breslau.[58] The army reoriented its forward detachments southward within hours, and the remainder of the army followed the next day. The attack ultimately forced the Germans to abandon their defensive bastion. By 1 February Soviet forces had reached the Oder River from Kuestrin, 60 kilometers east of Berlin, to south of Oppeln and had secured small bridgeheads across the river 100 kilometers beyond their planned objective of Poznan. The spectacular Soviet advance covered up to 650 kilometers in seventeen days and established new sustainment records for Red Army operational maneuver forces. Although part of the deep advance resulted from decreased enemy resistance after the initial battles, the distance traversed demonstrated that the Soviet capability for sustaining operational maneuver was double that of 1944 and six times that of 1943.

In East Prussia, more formidable German defenses and difficult terrain adversely affected the operation.[59] The 3d Belorussian Front's thrust toward Königsberg became a prolonged penetration operation until the commitment of a second echelon army unhinged the German defenses. The 2d Belorussian Front, however, succeeded in unleashing its operational maneuver forces. Its army mobile groups advanced on the second day and completed penetration of German tactical defenses. The front mobile group, the 5th Guards Tank Army, entered a wide-open breach in the German defenses on the fifth day. Subsequently, the tank army reached the Baltic Sea, severing communications between German Army Group Center and forces west of the Vistula. After the massive January offensive, over a period of six weeks, Soviet forces defeated troublesome German forces in Pomerania and Silesia that threatened the flanks of the Soviet salient. All the while, the Soviets prepared for the inevitable drive on the German capital.

Spurred on by their concern over the rapid Allied push toward Berlin and the upper Elbe River, the *Stavka* began their Berlin strategic offensive in mid-April. After a hasty, but major regrouping of forces, on 16 April Zhukov's 1st Belorussian and Konev's 1st Ukrainian Fronts began the Berlin operation in the form of a classic double envelopment of German forces defending the city.[60] Attacking from the Kuestrin bridgehead directly toward Berlin, Zhukov ordered his army mobile groups to penetrate German defenses and two front mobile groups (the 1st and 2d Guards Tank Armies) to encircle Berlin from the north. Konev ordered his tank armies (the 3d and 4th Guards) to advance south of Berlin as soon as the rifle armies and their mobile groups had penetrated German tactical defenses.

The two assaults, however, developed in dissimilar fashion. Zhukov committed his tank armies on the first day, before his forces penetrated the dense German tactical defenses. The resulting crush of concentrated manpower and weaponry was so great and the German defenses so effective that a prolonged, costly penetration battle ensued virtually all the way to Berlin, during which all of Zhukov's tank forces simply provided infantry support. On the other hand, Konev's infantry and armor broke cleanly through the German tactical defenses and exploited so successfully that they earned for Konev the honor of participating in the seizure of Berlin. Although the Soviets relied on time-honored and combat-proven methods for employing their mobile forces in the Berlin operation, Zhukov experienced major difficulties and failed to fulfill his mission in the requisite time or manner. Although Konev's forces operated successfully, they experienced similar difficulties to a lesser extent. The Berlin offensive made it apparent that armored and mechanized forces structured to maneuver in Eastern Europe and the Soviet Union could not do so effectively in the more heavily urban and forested terrain of Central Europe. After the Berlin operation had ended, the Soviets studied its conduct and recommended force structure changes to overcome these problems in the future.

Postscript

Although not an integral part of the third period of war, one of the most intriguing wartime operations involving operational maneuver was the Soviet's August 1945 Manchurian offensive operation, shaped by unique imperatives of time, geography, and politics.[61] Although the Japanese faced inevitable defeat, that defeat would occur far more rapidly if the Soviet Union could eradicate the large Japanese force (the Kwantung Army) in Manchuria. At the request of the Allies, the Soviets agreed to engage Japanese forces in Manchuria in August 1945. However, Japanese reinforcement of their forces in Manchuria and the U.S. employment of the atomic bomb in early August forced the *Stavka* to accelerate its offensive plans. In short, the *Stavka* considered it essential to capture Manchuria and, if possible, southern Sakhalin and the Kurile Islands, northern Korea, and a portion of Hokkaido before the Japanese surrendered, if the Soviets were to reap any political rewards from their participation in the war against the Japanese. The immense size and challenging geographical configuration of Manchuria made the task facing the *Stavka* even more daunting. Therefore, it concluded that only bold, rapid maneuver on a strategic scale could preempt Japanese defenses, paralyze Japanese command and control, overcome the imposing terrain barriers, and guarantee seizure of the region before the Japanese Empire and its military collapsed.

The Soviets conducted a Cannae-type strategic envelopment operation in Manchuria. Two fronts invaded Manchuria from east and west, while a third front exerted pressure from the north. The two enveloping fronts' operational maneuver forces penetrated deep into Manchuria and linked up in the region's central valley. The envelopment forces encircled large Japanese forces with a rapidity that paralyzed the entire Japanese force. The attacking Soviet fronts exploited their operational and tactical maneuver forces to achieve surprise and generate the maximum forward momentum necessary to preempt defenses or overcome weakened defenses before they were reinforced. Wherever possible, additional maneuver forces in the form of forward detachments exploited terrain the Japanese considered unfit for the conduct of maneuver.[62]

The rash plan succeeded beyond Soviet expectations. The operation originally planned for thirty days was over in fifteen. Soviet mobile forces reached the pinnacle of their success in the Manchurian offensive by employing operational and tactical maneuver extensively and effectively in special conditions. The Soviet offensive operation also generated a host of lessons relating to mobile operations in the future.

The First Postwar Years (1946–1954)

Even before war's end, the *Stavka* began analyzing the lessons its forces gleaned during the final year of war so as to adjust its military force structure and operational techniques to the political and physical realities of the postwar world. The most important physical reality was the geographical configuration of the central European theater of military operations, within which Soviet armies were likely to operate in future warfare. Red Army experiences in the Berlin offensive operation clearly indicated that the army needed to restructure its forces to operate effectively in the more urbanized, rougher, and more heavily forested region.

In 1946 Marshal of Tank Forces P. A. Rotmistrov, the Chief of GOFG's (the Group of Occupation Forces, Germany) armored forces, chaired a commission that analyzed the Red Army's performance in the Berlin operation and recommended appropriate force structure changes.[63] These changes included full integration of armored and mechanized forces into every level of the army's force structure, the formation of more powerful combined-arms armies, the conversion of tank and mechanized corps into tank and mechanized divisions, and the transformation of tank armies into mechanized armies.

In many ways, the new mechanized armies replicated the configuration of the 6th Guards Tank Army in the Manchurian offensive. They consisted of two mechanized and two tank divisions with improved fire and logistical support, and its component tank and mechanized divisions were more capable of conducting sustained operations in central

European terrain than the older tank-heavy tank forces.[64] The new combined-arms armies were also considerably more durable than their wartime counterparts. Each consisted of two rifle corps made up of two rifle divisions. Each rifle corps also contained a mechanized division, and each rifle division a tank and self-propelled gun battalion.[65] In addition, Soviet industry created a new generation of tanks and armored personnel carriers to improve the survivability of operational and tactical maneuver forces.

The operational and tactical techniques that this reformed force structure adopted closely resembled procedures that Red Army mobile forces employed during the final two years of war. Offensive operational maneuver by mobile groups remained the most critical ingredient for achieving offensive success. As expressed by one contemporary Soviet source, "Mechanized troops are used for the exploitation of success into the depth of the operational area."[66] A wartime front commander, with two to four combined-arms armies and one or two mechanized armies under his control, employed the combined-arms armies' rifle corps to conduct the penetration operation. The rifle corps' mechanized divisions supported the penetrating rifle divisions and, if possible, began the operational exploitation. The combined-arms army commander then committed his mobile group, which consisted of one or two tank or mechanized divisions, into combat on the first or second day of the operation, with the mission of exploiting tactical success into the shallow operational depths. Thereafter, but probably on the second or third day of the operation, the front commander was to commit his mobile group(s), the one or two mechanized armies, into combat to extend the exploitation to even greater depth. The Soviets expected these operational maneuver forces to advance to a depth of up to two hundred kilometers within five to seven days.

The Zhukov Reforms (1954–1959)

In the mid-1950s, Soviet recognition of the growing importance of atomic weaponry, reinforced by the United States' adoption of new force structures and weaponry tailored to combat in the atomic age, prompted the Soviets once again to alter their force structure and operational and tactical concepts.[67] After Stalin's death in 1953, Ministers of Defense Zhukov and R. Y. Malinovsky implemented these reforms. The central focus of the Zhukov reforms was to create a force with greater mobility and troop protection that could better perform and survive in an atomic environment. The heavy mechanized armies and corps were too large, too cumbersome, and hence too vulnerable to survive on the atomic battlefield, while the rifle corps and divisions were too light and lacked mobility and troop protection.

Therefore, Zhukov converted the mechanized armies into more streamlined tank armies and the heavy mechanized and light rifle divisions into more agile motorized rifle divisions.[68] Although this restructuring fully mechanized and motorized the Soviet Army and rendered the term mobile group superfluous, it did not alter the importance of operational maneuver. The new combined-arms armies consisted of three to four motorized rifle divisions and one tank division, while the tank army reversed the mixture of divisions. Although the Soviets recognized the significance of atomic weaponry, they considered the weapons neither unique nor dominant, but only one more combat factor (albeit a powerful one) to consider.[69] Soviet concern for retaining a strong conventional capability was reflected in the size of the Soviet force structure (175–180 divisions) and the strength of the new divisions and armies within that structure.

The operational and tactical employment of the new Soviet force remained similar to former patterns. Fronts consisting of three or four combined-arms armies conducted the penetration operation, and army-level tank divisions began the operational exploitation. The fronts' tank armies then continued the exploitation to depths of up to 270 kilometers within three to seven days and up to 500 kilometers in two weeks. Soviet theoretical works reaffirmed their faith in operational maneuver, stating: "Military operations in contemporary wars are characterized solely by maneuver. This is made possible by contemporary means of combat, especially the full mechanization and motorization of the ground forces.... The mobility and maneuverability of ground forces on the field of battle will have decisive importance in operations."[70] Although the term mobile group no longer applied to specific operational maneuver forces, Soviet definitions of the function still made it clear that specific forces would be assigned the task: "Operational maneuver is ... the organized shifting of distinct groups of forces during an operation to achieve a more favorable position with regards to an enemy in order to strike a blow against him or repel an enemy attack."[71]

The Revolution in Military Affairs (1960–1970)

In 1960 Soviet Premier N. S. Khrushchev's open declaration that a revolution had taken place in military affairs signified a major shift in Soviet military doctrine. Marshal of the Soviet Union V. D. Sokolovsky's 1962 work *Voyennaya strategiya* (military strategy) summed up the nature of the change: "The fires of nuclear weapons will play a decisive role on the battlefield; the other means of armed conflict will utilize the nuclear attack for the final defeat of the enemy."[72]

Soviet acceptance of the notion that future war would inevitably be nuclear had serious implications for traditional Soviet views concerning the nature and conduct of military operations and for the Soviet force structure. The strategic nuclear exchange became all-important, and the newly formed strategic rocket forces replaced the ground forces as the premier arm of the armed forces. Strategic considerations eclipsed the realm of operational art, and operational maneuver ceased to be an area of fundamental concern.

Reflecting this doctrinal change, the Soviet ground force structure shrank to roughly 140 divisions, each better tailored to operate in a nuclear environment. Tank and combined-arms armies decreased in manpower and weaponry, and tank armies and divisions became armor-pure entities more capable of surviving on a nuclear battlefield.[73] Ground forces would perform the simple mission of cleaning up the battlefield after the nuclear exchange.

Given the more restrictive role of the ground forces, Soviet fronts and armies would normally deploy in two-echelon configuration across larger frontages and disperse to greater depths. At every level armor forces would operate in the first echelon, because of their reduced vulnerability to the effects of nuclear weapons, and advance along numerous axes to exploit gaps created by nuclear fires. Operational maneuver was irrelevant in these chaotic scenarios, since nuclear forces would be the principal means for destroying the enemy. Consequently, Soviet commanders did not employ operational maneuver forces as specific functional entities. However, tactical maneuver became far more important on this fragmented and potentially contaminated battlefield. Numerous, tank-heavy forward detachments spearheaded ground operations, protected from the adverse effects of the nuclear environment by their small size, greater speed, and heavier armored protection. This offensive scheme also revived the utility and prestige of airborne forces, since they were particularly well suited to cooperate with tactical maneuver forces.

The Counterrevolution in Military Affairs (1971–1985)

At least in part, Khrushchev's removal from power in 1964 reflected the Soviet military establishment's growing uneasiness over existing doctrinal trends. Although displeased with the reduced size, importance, and prestige of the ground forces, Soviet military leaders and theorists had temporarily accepted the validity of the revolution in military affairs as long as the United States retained clear nuclear superiority. As that superiority waned, however, and the United States shifted from the strategy of massive retaliation to one of flexible response, the conventional option once again appeared more attractive and feasible. This transformation in Soviet military thought to renewed faith that warfare could be kept conventional took years to mature fully. First, it required that the Soviet Union checkmate U.S. nuclear capabilities at each level: strategic, theater, and tactical. Then, as the world wearied of the specter of nuclear war, Soviet leaders believed that political conditions would become conducive to reducing the quantities of these weapons and, perhaps, fully or partially abolishing them. Were this to occur, warfare would return to the conventional realm in which the Soviets were far more capable, hence more comfortable. Meanwhile, Soviet military theorists sought to develop combat techniques that could deter the use or, should they be employed, at least neutralize the effects of enemy nuclear weapons. Specifically, the Soviet military began fashioning strategic, operational, and tactical combat techniques that could in the future make any opponent's decision to use nuclear weapons militarily irrational and increasingly unlikely.

The increased attention Soviet theorists paid to the conventional option and the operational level of war in general, and to operational maneuver in particular, provided clear evidence of this change in Soviet military thought. During the 1970s and well into the 1980s, the steady trickle of articles on conventional operational and tactical maneuver ultimately turned into a flood. The threatening presence of nuclear weapons in the European theater of war prompted this intensified study. If employed by the enemy, these awesome weapons placed in jeopardy the large maneuver forces deployed deep in the Soviets' rear area, either in the second echelon or in positions from which they could support the initial penetration operation and conduct the exploitation. Therefore, Soviet theorists sought methods to neutralize or at least minimize the effects of those weapons. Based on this study, Soviet theorists formulated several concepts designed to remedy the problem. First, they transformed their traditional air offensive (developed in late 1942) into an air operation designated in part to strike and neutralize enemy nuclear weapons, particularly artillery, missiles, and aviation systems, deployed from the FLOT (forward line of troops) to the deep enemy rear. Second, they developed the concept of antinuclear maneuver (*protivoyadernyî manevr*), expressed first in defensive terms. Col. F. D. Sverdlov, a leading maneuver specialist, defined antinuclear maneuver as: "The organized shifting of subunits with the aim of withdrawing them out from under the possible blows of enemy nuclear means, to protect their survival and subsequent freedom of action to strike a blow on the enemy. Therefore, antinuclear maneuver is also one of the forms of maneuver."[74] Soon, however, offensive measures "to disperse sub-units rapidly or change the direction of their offensive and to conduct other measures related to defense against weapons of mass destruction" complemented the defensive aspect of this maneuver.[75]

The work done by Sverdlov and other military theorists in the 1970s led the Soviets to conclude that the most effective manner in which to conduct antinuclear maneuver was to rely more extensively on operational and tactical maneuver. Although Soviet theorists ceased referring directly to the term antinuclear maneuver during the late 1970s, they continued to describe the function indirectly in both defensive and offensive contexts.

As Soviet theorists developed techniques for employing contemporary operational and tactical maneuver forces, they carefully examined how these forces operated in their Great Patriotic War. In particular, because of their flexible configuration, wartime mobile groups and forward detachments seemed ideally suited to conduct antinuclear maneuver at both the operational and the tactical levels. Their organization and operating procedures during the war provided a sound basis for the emerging concepts of operational maneuver by groups—OMGs—and tactical maneuver by forward detachments.

At the same time, the Soviets deemphasized the importance of operational second echelons (at the front and army level), because of their increased vulnerability to possible nuclear strikes, and began to emphasize the concept and utility of employing multiple operational maneuver forces and reserves at front and army level. Specifically, they recommended that fronts and armies concentrate the bulk of their forces well forward prior to launching an offensive and, once the offensive began, commit numerous operational maneuver groups into combat along multiple axes early in the operation. Tactical maneuver would pave the way for advancing operational maneuver forces and main force units.[76] Employment of these antinuclear maneuver techniques provided increased opportunity to surprise the enemy with respect to the timing and form of the attack.

During the later 1970s Soviet theorists also carefully analyzed past "initial periods of war," in particular the disastrous initial months of their Great Patriotic War (June–October 1941). They did so to determine what a nation's army had to do to win quick victory or avoid precipitous defeat. Based on this study, they concluded that the most important factor contributing to offensive success was the early and surprise commitment of the bulk of one's maneuver forces deployed well forward.[77] Accordingly, the Soviets deemphasized preliminary large-scale mobilization (which had been the primary indicator of impending war) and recommended employing single strategic and operational echelons dominated by numerous tailored operational and tactical maneuver forces.

This modern variant for the employment of operational maneuver groups had fully matured by the early 1980s, and Soviet ground force strength and composition reflected these new warfighting concepts. The steady growth of the ground forces increased its total strength to well over 200 divisions by 1985. As the ground forces expanded, formations (divisions) and units (regiments) grew in size, and, although the Soviet Army still tended to be armor heavy, its force structure increasingly reflected the combined-arms balance so essential for success in conventional operations. In particular, tank armies and divisions received additional mechanized infantry, and divisions were augmented with more personnel, tanks, and artillery to improve their strength and mobility. The Soviets also streamlined their logistical support structure to better support sustained deep conventional operations.[78]

The Soviets developed, tested, and fielded a wide variety of new functional units necessary to support their expanded concepts of combat maneuver. Air-assault battalions and brigades at army and front level provided a new vertical dimension to both operational and tactical maneuver and, although fielding never occurred, thought was given to deploying smaller air-assault units at division level. Reconnaissance-diversionary (special designation [*spetsial'nye naznacheniye*, or *SPETNAZ*]) brigades at front level added a new dimension to deep operations by threatening security in a potential enemy's rear area. Assault helicopter formations employed as flying artillery or tanks assisted traditional aviation units in providing necessary air support for deep operating forces. In addition to these structural changes, the Soviets experimented with new types of maneuver forces whose organization closely resembled their former mobile groups and forward detachments.

The Soviets also modernized their specialized forces in accordance with new concepts of maneuver. They fully mechanized and restructured their airborne divisions by equipping them with the BMD combat vehicle and assault guns. They reorganized their naval infantry regiments into brigades, formed their first naval infantry divisions, and provided each with an air-assault capability. Throughout their force structure, the Soviets streamlined logistics by creating materiel support units at the tactical and operational levels. By implementing these and other changes during the 1970s and early 1980s, the Soviets sought to create more flexible forces capable of performing the critical functions of tactical and operational maneuver in theater war.

The Technological Revolution in Weaponry and its Consequences (1985–1988)

Beginning in the early 1980s, Soviet military theorists recognized that a technological revolution was taking place in conventional weaponry and that the rapid development of new, high-precision weaponry had the potential to make the conventional battlefield as deadly and complex as the nuclear battlefield described in the 1960s. Increasingly, they also realized that these developments were fundamentally altering the traditional relationship between offense and defense.[79]

Initially at least, theorists still emphasized the utility of antinuclear maneuver as the cornerstone for their operational and tactical techniques. They continued to maintain that antinuclear maneuver could preempt, preclude, or inhibit enemy resort to nuclear warfare. As articulated in 1987 by V. G. Reznichenko, "The continuous conduct of battle at a high tempo creates unfavorable conditions for enemy use of weapons of mass destruction. He cannot determine targets for nuclear strikes precisely and, besides, [he] will be forced to shift his nuclear delivery means often."[80] By the mid-1980s, however, the Soviets openly acknowledged that the Western development of a wide variety of high-precision weapons posed a major new threat. If employed skillfully, these weapons could affect attacking forces in the same fashion as tactical nuclear weapons. Worse still, they could engage attacking maneuver forces even before they made actual contact with the enemy. Initially, at least, the Soviet solution to this dilemma was to place even greater emphasis on operational and tactical maneuver to counter enemy employment of high-precision weaponry.[81] To capitalize fully on the effects of maneuver, the Soviets believed that they had to restructure their forces for maximum flexibility, reduce planning time, and execute command and control more precisely. This required the increased use of cybernetic tools, including automation of command and expanded reliance on tactical and operational calculations (nomograms, etc.).

A dialectical process of change governed this evolution of military techniques and force structure as multiple influences forced the Soviets to refine their concept of antinuclear maneuver and increasingly emphasize operational and tactical maneuver. This process continued in the 1980s as new stimuli provided impetus for Soviet definition of new forms of combat, new operational concepts, and combat structures and formations (echelonment) to carry them out. At the same time, Soviet views on the nature of contemporary combat also evolved, and the Soviets redefined the requirements for a force to achieve offensive success. One writer articulated the chief characteristics of future battle as:

- Transformation of traditional land actions into land-air actions;
- Broadening of the role of mobility in all troop actions;
- Development and dissemination of the practice of combat actions within enemy formations, especially raid actions;
- Initiation of battle at increasingly greater distances;
- Growth of the significance of the "information struggle," having as its goal the steering of the enemy in the direction of one's own plans and intentions.[82]

This offensive scheme posited certain distinct requirements, which included:

- The achievement of a degree of surprise to create necessary force superiority and to gain initial advantage, which involves deception regarding attack intentions, timing, location, and scale;
- Avoidance of major attack indicators, which requires extensive prewar theater preparations and the use of selective covert mobilization techniques

for all services of the armed forces to minimize key attack indicators prior to war;
- In the armed forces as a whole, deployment of nuclear submarines, concentration or dispersal of military transport aviation (VTA), removal of nuclear weapons warheads from permanent facilities, etc.;
- Reliance on shallow strategic, operational, and tactical echelonment to offset less-than-full mobilization, to reap maximum surprise, and to establish high initial offensive momentum;
- Preemptive destruction or neutralization of enemy nuclear delivery, command and control, and deep attack systems;
- Early commitment of tactical and operational maneuver forces to achieve rapid penetration, to enmesh forces quickly, to avoid enemy nuclear response, and to diminish the effectiveness of enemy high-precision fires;
- Development and proliferation to the lowest command level (battalion) of advanced cybernetic applications to speed planning and increase the efficiency of command and control during combat.

Increasingly, however, Soviet theorists emphasized the increased difficulty encountered in meeting these requirements.

As late as 1985, buttressed by analysis of the impact of new, high-precision weapons on combat, the Soviets still reiterated their firm belief that a combination of operational and tactical maneuver, conducted by tailored forces operating in relatively shallow echelonment and employing deception to achieve surprise, could produce success in contemporary and future war. The military solution to the problem of waging contemporary warfare seemed to rest in the creation of a force structure that encompassed in its entirety the attributes of operational and tactical maneuver forces, namely a corps, brigade, and combined-arms battalion structure. The works of Reznichenko, Dragunsky, and many other theorists conveyed this impression. At the same time, it was becoming shockingly apparent to Soviet military leaders that the Soviet Union lacked the technological know-how and economic resources to meet these challenges.

In the late 1980s, however, the dialectical process of change continued, and the Soviets were able to project possible changes in military conditions in the 1990s. The Soviets responded to these stimuli with a range of military and political options whose adoption would depend directly on future political, economic, social, and military realities:

- Political
  Arms limitations
  Force reductions
  Denuclearization of theater of operations
- Economic
  Revitalization of the "military economy" (as well as civilian) by restructuring
  Increasing research and development competitiveness

- Social
  Reducing social tensions within the military (problem of first year soldiers)
  Solving the nationalities problem
- Military
  Preemption in the initial period of war
  Surprise (deception)
  Operational and tactical maneuver (antinuclear maneuver)

The political and economic components of these realities triumphed, at least temporarily, during the late 1980s and shaped Soviet force structure and concepts for conducting operational and tactical maneuver. Impelled by economic, political, and even military considerations, in 1988 the Soviets embraced the concept of "defensiveness" in their military doctrine. They admitted that defensiveness contradicted and altered what had in reality been a long-standing offensive orientation in the component levels of Soviet military science—strategy, operational art, and tactics. They underscored their sincerity by proposing to create a new military force structure, which by its very nature had to be construed by the West as defensive.[83]

However, as the shape and form of the new Soviet force structure emerged, it became clear that there was a sharp dichotomy between the offensively oriented force so evident in Soviet writings up to and through 1985 and the new and apparently defensive force being implemented. In essence the former force, offensive in its orientation, seemed to accord with strictly military requirements, while the new defensive structure reflected the dictates of sharply adverse economic and political conditions.

Addendum: The Soviet and Russian Army After 1988

During the period 1988 through 1991, political and economic realities prompted the Soviets to enunciate a new defensive military doctrine within the context of the twin programs of *perestroika* and *glasnost'*. The central notion of defensiveness was a Soviet commitment to a strategic defensive posture based upon the principle of "defensive sufficiency" and a military strategy based upon premeditated defense. Driven by political and economic necessity, the Soviets shelved their attempts to restructure their armed forces to meet the demands of nonlinear war and temporarily abandoned public attempts to create a corps, brigade, and combined-arms force structure that could fight and survive in the fragmented modern battlefield. While doing so, however, both the economic situation within the Soviet Union and the technological dilemmas that the Soviet Army faced worsened sharply.

In accordance with defensiveness, the Soviets introduced two new divisional structures. The first, called Division 89, fielded in the forward groups of forces, was clearly defensive in nature. The new square, motorized rifle division consisted of four motorized rifle regiments and incorporated the combined-arms principle by including a tank battalion in each motorized rifle regiment. The new tank division had two tank and two motorized rifle regiments. However, both divisions were far weaker than their predecessors, and they suited political rather than military needs. The second type formation, called Division 90, and formed within the depths of the Soviet Union, was a stronger counteroffensive-type shock division. To a greater extent, these divisions were better tailored to suit their prospective combat function and the area in which they operated. At the same time, the Soviets revived the fielding of fortified regions (*ukreplenniye raiony*) as economy-of-force military formations. Although Division 90 formations realistically met military demands, they were "cumbersome and expensive," and they experienced "serious complexities in rear services and technical support." Nevertheless, they represented serious efforts by Soviet military authorities to satisfy both the requirements of defensiveness, military-technological realties, and the perceived demands of future war.

During the period from 1991 through 1993, unprecedented and revolutionary political, economic, and social changes engulfed and destroyed the Soviet Union and gave birth to the new Russian Federation. In large measure, the Soviet Union collapsed under the weight of its immense defense burden conditioned by Russian resolve that it could never permit a recurrence of the predicament in 1941. Frustrating Soviet defeat in the prolonged Afghan War, which sapped the national will, exacerbated the devastating long-term effects of the crushing weight of massive military expenditures produced by an arms race that Russians finally perceived could not be won due to the Soviet Union's weak economic and technological base. Accordingly, the Revolution of 1991 replaced the Soviet State with a Russian Federation that lacked the strength of its Communist predecessor.

Understandably, the army of the new Russian Federation brought with it many of the traditions and biases of the former Soviet Army. In addition to playing a key role in the formulation of a new military doctrine, the Russian Army and General Staff continued to perform the vital role of applying foresight and forecasting to determine the nature of future war and the defense needs of the Russian State. They did so through careful analysis of key defense issues and careful study of recent and ongoing military conflicts, in particular the Persian Gulf War.

The twin imperatives of determining State doctrinal requirements and the General Staff's appreciation of the nature of future war provided context for Russian military theory and force structuring since 1993. In accordance with the draft military doctrine, the Russian Federation announced in May 1992 and in subsequent official pronouncements that the new Russian State mandated a peacetime military establishment of about 1.5 million men. Although unattainable for a variety of reasons, this establishment was to consist of two types of forces, permanently ready forces and mobile, rapid-reaction forces, backed up by a one million-man strategic reserve. Economic and geographic constraints dictated that permanently ready forces would deploy in limited numbers along critical axes to serve as covering forces in the event of war. Mobile reserves, structured flexibly to respond to any crisis, would deploy within the depth of the state to assist ready forces in repelling aggression, while strategic reserves would mobilize and deploy in the event of major war. Given these doctrinal requirements, the most critical question facing the General Staff was determining the size, form, and shape these forces take in peacetime. The General Staff also continued to define the nature and requirements of future war.

The debate within the General Staff over the nature of future war represented a dynamic and virtually seamless continuation of the debates that dominated the 1980s. The General Staff concluded that future war would be fragmented and nonlinear and would be dominated by increasingly lethal, high-precision weapon systems. This warfare would place a premium on combat flexibility at all levels and exploitation of the time factor in decision making, planning, command and control of forces, and battlefield communications. Among the many themes Russian military theorists analyzed were:

- The future of AirLand Battle;
- The nature of the air echelon;
- Vertical maneuver and envelopment by air assault;
- The conduct of operational and tactical maneuver on the nonlinear battlefield, particularly during defensive actions, counterattacks, counterstrokes, and counteroffensives;
- The utility of raid actions;
- The modernization, reorganization, and proliferation of fire systems, organization, and tactics.

New concepts such as fire strike of the enemy and the employment of mobile fortified regions and mobile covering brigades supplemented the ongoing study of such familiar themes as reconnaissance strike, airmobile defense, raids, and antipartisan combat.

Characteristic of this analysis, one perceptive theorist concluded:

> In our view, new forms of combat operations will be established in the next 5–15 years; a massive, integrated strike by electronic, precision, laser, and super-high-frequency weapons; strikes by large groups of helicopters with simultaneous suppression of the enemy; raiding operations of air-land tactical combat groups; massive reconnaissance-fire and anti-reconnaissance strikes; and so on.[84]

So defined, this new combat environment placed immense new demands on organizations and staffs tasked with operating within it. At least, coping with the consequences of the ongoing technological revolution required Russia to fundamentally reevaluate all components of its military establishment.

The Russian Ministry of Defense attempted to structure its forces in accordance with these doctrinal constraints and theoretical discussions. The General Staff indicated that all new force structures and future strategic deployment as a whole had to satisfy four functional and interrelated components essential to conducting modern military operations. It identified these components as information, ground, air, and logistical support. The information component combined mobile command, control, and communications with reconnaissance and radio-electronic combat in a traditional headquarters structure. Beneath this headquarters were tailored building blocks of combined-arms subunits and units that could be flexibly configured to meet precise combat requirements. The air component provided vertical capability, and the logistical component was designed to sustain relatively independent combat in nonlinear circumstances.

Force tailoring for maximum flexibility predominated within this paradigm as the Russians created what may be termed a Division 2000 force structure. While the components principle was clearly applicable to all types of forces during the transition to whatever new force structure emerged, they were most applicable to a corps, brigade, and combined-arms battalion force configuration. However, continuing economic and budgetary problems and extreme turbulence in the Russian Armed Forces (particularly in recruiting) inhibited the institution of these changes. Moreover, Russian failure in the first Chechen War only compounded the problems, although it reinforced Russian resolve to solve both the Chechen and force-structure dilemmas. In the near term, it remains likely that Russia will institute military structural reforms at lower command levels (the battalion level) and in the formation of new brigades of various types and a limited number of new corps. Thus, a transitional structure consisting of mixed divisional, regimental, corps, and brigade organizations will exist. In the longer term, however, depending on political, economic, and military circumstances, these structures will evolve into a more thorough and varied corps and brigade structure. This conclusion derives from the predominate belief that as in the past flexible corps and brigade structures will better meet the demands of future war and the requirements of operational and tactical maneuver that still endure.

According to the General Staff's construct, the highest level of the force structure will likely consist of unified commands, or operational-strategic groupings organized on a geographical basis, each of which will ultimately consist of from three to five corps and associated air and supporting forces. Within these commands, permanently ready forces will consist of divisions (perhaps corps), light motorized rifle brigades, mobile fortified regions, and mobile covering brigades. Mobile forces will consist of two operational-strategic force components: immediate reaction forces and rapid deployment forces. The former will be light forces with a strong air component capable of deploying within one to three days after alert, and the latter will contain heavier combined-arms formations (probably corps) capable of reinforcing IRF forces within three to seven days.

In the near term, the nucleus of immediate reaction forces will comprise 5 airborne divisions, 8 separate airborne brigades, 6 light motorized rifle brigades; the reaction forces will be supplemented by naval infantry battalions, air assault battalions, and reconnaissance-diversionary forces. The air component will include bomber aviation, fighter ground-attack aviation, and helicopter regiments; surface-to-air missile brigades will provide air defense. Helicopter regiments and air transport divisions will provide mobility support, and a mobile signal center exploiting satellite communications will form the upper end of the information component.

The rapid deployment force will provide tailored heavier support to IRF elements. It will likely include several mobile corps of from three to five brigades (tank, mechanized, or motorized rifle, depending upon battalion mix, and at least one light motorized rifle battalion), at least one tank and one motorized rifle division during the transitional period, a large air component, and enhanced mobility and communications support.

Economic necessity dictates that the new corps and brigade structures are likely to be truncated in form and often experimental during the immediate future. In the interim, remaining motorized rifle and tank divisions and their component regiments will take on some of the characteristics of corps and brigades, particularly in terms of diverse attachments, and the Russians will field a wide variety of test brigade structures, some separate, some within corps, and some, perhaps, also within divisions.

Conclusions

Whether or not political and economic developments within Russia permit further rational and orderly development of military art and force structuring, it is clear that the Russian military will continue to be perplexed by those same issues that their Soviet forebears found daunting. Despite the past and continuing turmoil and the persistent uncertainties that now plague the Russian Federation and its military establishment, to date key and striking continuities are evident. First, examination of Russian military theoretical writings indicates a continuing keen appreciation on the part of military theorists of the altered nature and unprecedented new challenges of future war. Russian military theory remains alive and vibrant; and, in terms of operational art, tactics, and force structuring, analysis of the 1970s, 1980s, and 1990s remains accurate, seamless, and convincing.

Like the Soviets before them, Russian military theorists understand the revolutionary effect that new generations of increasingly lethal high-precision weapons have had on the face of battle. They also appreciate the unprecedented new demands these weapons have placed on modern force structures and the ability of commanders to communicate and exercise control over them in modern, nonlinear war. Since the 1980s the conclusions they have reached regarding the formation of optimum force structures for fighting, surviving, and prevailing in such a lethal environment have been remarkably consistent. Finally, they realize the importance of what they term information warfare in future war. The Russian Federation's apparent political and economic weakness, social ferment, and ignominious and embarrassing defeat in the 1995 war in Chechnya, however, has severely negated Russian progress in the realm of military theory and force structuring.

Russian political and military leaders realize that the nation faces daunting political and potential military challenges in the future that may require military response. These include challenges to the viability of the Russian state itself from within, arising from ethnic conflicts and potential new challenges from an apparently offensive-oriented NATO alliance. The Russian leadership has already begun responding to these perceived challenges, first by conducting the Second Chechen War, and second by openly renouncing its longstanding policy of no first use of nuclear weapons in the event of an attack on Russian territory.

Translating their military theories into practice will remain a formidable task. Political instability, economic deprivation, social upheaval, and technological barriers are likely to pose major obstacles to realization of these theories in terms of the reformation of the Russian military establishment and the reconfiguration of the Russian Army force structure. This applies equally to the ability of the Russian Army to perform the functions of operational and tactical maneuver, which it still deems a critical element of contemporary and future war.

Notes

1. The newly published Soviet casualty figures resulting from the purges include: 3 of 5 marshals of the Soviet Union, 14 of 16 army commanders (first and second rank), 60 of 87 corps commanders, 136 of 199 division commanders, 221 of 397 brigade commanders, all 11 vice-commissars of war, 75 of 80 members of the Supreme Military Council, and all military district commanders as of May 1937. The estimated 35,000 purged represented half the officer corps, 90 percent of all generals and 80 percent of all colonels. The purges were, in fact, still in progress when the German invasion of June 1941 began. O. F. Suvenirov, "Vsearmeiskaya tragediya" [An all-army tragedy], *Voyenno-istoricheskiy zhurnal* [Military-historical journal] (hereafter cited as *VIZh*) no. 3 (March 1989): 41. These update already published Western estimates. See Leonard Shapiro, "The Great Purge," in *The Soviet Army*, ed. Basil H. Liddell Hart (London: Weidenfeld and Nicolson, 1956), p. 69.
2. Analysis of the experiences of Soviet tank units and armored specialists who participated in the Spanish Civil War cast doubt on the feasibility of using large tank units in modern combat. The units proved difficult to command and control; enemy fire separated tanks from supporting infantry; and the light tanks were vulnerable to destruction by artillery fire and even crude infantry antitank weapons (including explosives and bottles filled with flammables). The Kulik Commission ultimately acted upon these reports. Since most high-level defenders of armored operations had been purged, the defense of armored operations before that commission was weak. The Soviet occupation of eastern Poland in September 1939 illustrated command and control difficulties experienced by the tank corps. In addition, their logistical support proved inadequate. At Khalkhin-Gol in August 1939, a large Soviet force, commanded by G. Zhukov, used mechanized and armored forces to encircle and ultimately destroy two Japanese divisions. Critiques of Zhukov's performance gave him credit for surprising and encircling the Japanese force but criticized the time it took to destroy the encircled force and the heavy casualties his force incurred.
3. The Kulik Commission recommended changes that resulted in a subsequent order to form eight motorized divisions in 1940 and seven more in the first half of 1941. Details of the commission's work are found in A. Ryzhakov, "K voprosy o stroitel'stve brone-tankovykh voîsk Krasnoy armii 30–e gody" [Concerning the question of the formation of Red Army armored forces in the thirties], *VIZh* no. 8 (August 1968): 109–11.
4. Contemporary Soviet critiques of the invasion include A. Konenenko, "Boy vo flandrii (Mai 1940 gg.)" [The battle in Flanders (May 1940)], *VIZh* no. 3 (March 1941):3–25; A. I. Starunin, "Operativnaya vnezapnost'" [Operational surprise], *Voennaya mysl'* [Military thought] no. 3 (March 1941): 27–35.
5. The new mechanized corps consisted of 2 tank divisions, 1 motorized division, a motorcycle regiment, a signal battalion, a motorized engineer battalion, and an aviation troop. Each had an armored strength of 1,031 tanks. The average materiel strength of these corps in June 1941 was 53 percent, consisting primarily of obsolete T–26 and BT–5 tanks. Just over 1,475 new T–34 and KV tanks and 10,150 older models were deployed with corps in the border military districts, but they were distributed unequally. See S. P.

Ivanov, *Nachal'nyî period voîny* [The initial period of war] (Moscow: Voyenizdat, 1974), pp. 260–62; V. P. Krikunov, "Kuda delis' tanki?" [Where were the tanks shared?], *VIZh* no. 11 (November 1988): 29.

6. For details on the state of the Red Army in June 1941, see David M. Glantz, *Stumbling Colossus: The Red Army on the Eve of World War* (Lawrence: University Press of Kansas, 1998).

7. See S. K. Timoshenko, *Zaklyuchitel'naya rech narodnogo komissara oborony soyuza SSR geroya i marshala Sovetskogo Soyuze S. K. Timoshenko no voyennom soveshchanii 31 dekabrya 1940 g.* [The concluding speech of the people's commissar of defense of the USSR, hero and marshal of the Soviet Union S. K. Timoshenko at a military conference 31 December 1941] (Moscow: Voyenizdat, 1940). Timoshenko verbally and graphically sketched out the nature and purpose of deep operations without specifically using the term.

8. For the sake of analysis, prior to 1960 Soviet theorists subdivided the war into four periods by treating 1944 and 1945 separately. See K. S. Kolganov, ed., *Razvitiye taktiki sovetskoî armii v gody Velikoy Otechestvennoy voîny (1941–1949 gg.)* [Development of Soviet Army tactics in the Great Patriotic War years, 1941–1945] (Moscow: Voyenizdat, 1958), pp. 5–6.

9. Soviet defensive plans called for covering armies to engage enemy forces as they attacked across the borders. Armies deployed corps laterally along the border, with reserve rifle corps dispersed in the depths under front control. The rifle corps deployed their divisions in depth, with divisions covering extended frontages along the border interspersed with border guards units and fortified regions. The Soviet mechanized corps were deployed in echelons, one echelon backing up forward rifle corps and a second well to the rear, with additional corps farther east in the "strategic depths." The echeloned defense conceded the German capability to penetrate border defenses but emphasized defensive fighting along successive distinct defense lines to erode German strength as *Blitzkrieg* unfolded. The mechanized corps were to launch counterattacks in support of each successive Soviet defense line to hasten the attrition of advancing German forces. Ultimately, these successive struggles and the introduction of newly mobilized Soviet armies and mechanized corps deployed from the "strategic" depths would halt and repulse the German advance (ideally along or forward of the Dnepr River line).

These plans evidenced that the Soviets clearly understood the nature of *Blitzkrieg*, but subsequent operations demonstrated that they underestimated the power of the German threat. In addition, the Soviets mistook where the main German thrust would occur: in the south rather than along the Brest-Minsk axis. The mechanized corps failed to do requisite damage to German forces, the Soviet air force was largely destroyed on the ground, and successive Soviet defense lines crumbled before they were fully prepared (Minsk, Dnepr, and Smolensk). The defensive system would have worked more effectively if forces had been fully prepared and not in the midst of both reorganization and reequipment. Ultimately, by December 1941 the Soviet defensive scheme of successive barriers worked, albeit much later than expected and at much higher cost.

10. For details, see David M. Glantz, *Forgotten Battles of the German-Soviet War (1941–1945), Vol. I: The Summer–Fall Campaign (22 June–4 December 1941)* (Carlisle, Pa.: Self-published, 1999).

11. The truncation process paralleled one in the rifle forces. The Soviets abolished the rifle corps and decreased the size of armies and rifle divisions. New armies consisted of rifle divisions and newly created rifle brigades (light divisions consisting of rifle and artil-

lery battalions). The high command stripped armor, artillery, and engineer assets from the divisions and former corps and centralized them in newly created specialized units under high command control to allocate to armies where they were most needed.

12. I. V. Pavlovsky, *Sukhoputnye voîska SSSR* [Ground forces of the USSR] (Moscow: Voyenizdat, 1985), pp. 65–69. On paper, tank brigades had forty-six tanks each.

13. I. K. Bagramyan, *Tak nachinalas' voîna* [How war begins] (Kiev: Izdatel'stvo politicheskoy literatury Ukrainy, 1984), pp. 391–435; Franz Halder, *The Halder Diaries: The Private War Journals of Colonel General Franz Halder* (Boulder, Colo.: Westview Press, 1977), pp. 1303–21.

14. For details on the use of operational maneuver forces in the Moscow counteroffensive, see I. Y. Krupchenko, ed., *Sovetskye tankovye voîska 1941–1945* [Soviet tank forces, 1941–1945] (Moscow: Voyenizdat, 1973), pp. 46–51; F. Tamanov, "Primeneniye bronetankovykh voîsk v bitve pod Moskvoî" [Use of armored forces in the battle of Moscow], *VIZh* no. 1 (January 1967): 14–23; P. A. Belov, *Za nami Moskva* [Behind us Moscow] (Moscow: Voyenizdat, 1963). Belov was 1st Guards Cavalry Corps commander. The Soviets also created and used separate ski battalions for deep maneuver in the German rear area during the Moscow operation. The weather, terrain, and unequal mobility of these diverse forces made them difficult to coordinate in combat. Their lack of firepower exacerbated the problem, as their heaviest weapon was the 50-mm. mortar. Soviet units could seize the countryside but could not expel German forces from the towns, villages, and main road network.

15. O. A. Losik, ed., *Stroitel'stvo i boevoye primenenie Sovetskykh tankovykh voîsk v gody Velikoî Otechestvennoy voiny* [The formation and combat use of Soviet tank forces in the years of the Great Patriotic War] (Moscow: Voyenizdat, 1979), pp. 50–53. Initially, the tank corps consisted of two tank brigades and one motorized rifle brigade with 100 tanks. In late April the Soviets added an additional tank brigade to the corps. The Soviets created 28 tank corps by the end of 1942. Ultimately, the tank corps' strength rose to over 200 tanks and self-propelled guns each.

16. For details on the Khar'kov operation, see David M. Glantz, *Kharkov 1942: Anatomy of a Military Disaster* (Rockville Center, N.Y.: Ian Allan and Sarpedon), 1998.

17. Krupchenko, *Sovetskye tankovye*, pp. 58–60; A. I. Radzievsky, *Proryv* [Penetration], (Moscow: Voyenizdat, 1979), pp. 25–29; I. K. Bagramyan, *Tak shli my k pobede*, [As we marched to victory] (Moscow: Voyenizdat, 1977), pp. 47–128; K. S. Moskalenko, *Na yugo-zapadnom napravlenii 1941–1943* [On the southwestern axis 1941–1943] (Moscow: Nauka, 1973), pp. 187–218. The German deception plan is discussed in E. F. Ziemke, "Operation Kreml: Deception, Strategy, and the Fortunes of War," *Parameters* 91, no. 1 (March 1979).

18. A. I. Radzievsky, *Tankovyi udar* [Tank blow] (Moscow: Voyenizdat, 1977), pp. 24–25. The actual tank army composition was as shown in *Table 2*.

19. The counterattacking forces included the 5th Tank Army (the 2d, 7th, and 11th Tank Corps); the 1st, 16th, 4th, and 24th Tank Corps; and the 8th Cavalry Corps. This force totaled about 1,500 tanks commanded by such future luminaries as Generals Katukov and Rotmistrov. Poor command and control during the month of fighting seriously reduced the forces' effectiveness. For details on these forgotten operations, see David M. Glantz, *Forgotten Battles of the German-Soviet War (1941–1945), Vol. II: The Summer Campaign (12 May–18 November 1942)* (Carlisle, Pa.: Self-published, 1999).

20. The 1st Tank Army was disbanded in August 1942, and its staff formed a nucleus for the new Southeastern Front. In October 1942 the 4th Tank Army, which its soldiers referred to derisively as "the 4-tank Army," was redesignated 65th Army. See Anan'yev, "Tankovye armii."
21. Radzievsky, *Tankovyi udar*, p. 24. Initially, the Soviets created three types of mechanized corps organized as shown on *Table 3*. The Soviets created eight mechanized corps by the end of 1942.
22. To effect this encirclement, General N. F. Vatutin, the Soviet Southwestern Front commander, employed two tank corps (the 1st and 26th) of General P. L. Romanenko's secretly regrouped 5th Tank Army, while a cavalry corps (the 8th) of 5th Tank Army formed the protective outer encirclement line. A separate mechanized corps (the 4th) and a tank corps (the 13th) of the Stalingrad Front formed the southern arm of the great pincer. By virtue of the Stalingrad experience, the Soviets identified five steps in an ideal encirclement operation, which included: (1) penetration of tactical defenses; (2) exploitation and linkup of mobile force; (3) creation of an inner encirclement; (4) formation of an outer encirclement; (5) continued exploitation by forces forming the outer encirclement.

At Stalingrad, the Soviets were able to carry out the first four steps but had difficulty with the fifth step. The 5th Tank Army's strength in the operation was about 400 tanks.
23. Armor attrition rates for the tank army and mobile corps exceeded 50 percent and at times reached 70 percent, due to purely logistical and mechanical causes. This rate would fall later in the war; but for the moment it became a major factor in the determination of future unit strength authorizations and prompted the Soviets to stress improvements in logistics. See "Nekotorye vyvody po ispol'zovaniyu tankovykh i mekhanizirovannykh korpusov dlya razvitiya proryva" [A few observations regarding the employment of tank and mechanized corps in the exploitation of the breakthrough] in *Sbornik materialov po izucheniyu opyta voîny No. 8 Avgust–oktyabr'1943 g.* [Collection of materials for the study of war experience no. 8: August–October 1943] (Moscow: Voyenizdat, 1943), pp. 48–81, classified secret. Hereafter cited as *Sbornik materialov*. For subsequent loss rates, see Radzievsky, *Tankovyi udar*, pp. 211–30.
24. For details, see David M. Glantz, *Zhukov's Greatest Defeat: The Red Army's Epic Disaster in Operation Mars, 1942* (Lawrence: University Press of Kansas, 1999); David M. Glantz, *Forgotten Battles of the German-Soviet War (1941–1945): Vol. IV: The Winter Campaign (19 November 1942–21 March 1943)* (Carlisle, Pa.: Self-Published, 1999), pp. 18–67.
25. The first group consisted of four tank corps (17th, 18th, 24th, and 25th), which attacked south and southeast from bridgeheads across the Don River along parallel axes to link up with a second mobile force (1st Guards Mechanized Corps), attacking westward across the Chir River. "Planirovaniye i podgotovka nastupatel'noy operatsii Yugo-zapadnogo fronta v dekabre 1942 g." [Planning and preparation of the offensive operations of the Southwestern Front in December 1942], in *Sbornik materialov*, vol. 8 (1943), pp. 3–24; K. K. Rokossovsky, ed., *Velikaya pobeda na Volga* [Great victory on the Volga] (Moscow: Voyenizdat, 1965), pp. 336–70. The combined strength of the four tank corps was about 660 tanks, but logistical attrition rates quickly reduced this number. By 28 December most corps counted about 25–35 tanks.
26. A. G. Yershov, *Osvobozhdeniye Donbassa* [Liberation of the Donbas] (Moscow: Voyenizdat, 1973), pp.1–68. The operations of one tank corps are detailed in A. V. Kuzmin and I. I. Krasov, *Kantemirovtsy: boyevoy put' 4–go gvardeiskogo tankovogo Kantemirovskogo ordena Lenina Krasnoznammennogo korpusa* [Kantemirovtsy: The combat path of the Kantemirovka, Order of Lenin and Red Banner 4th Guards Tank Corps] (Moscow: Voyenizdat, 1971), pp. 50–68.

27. For details on these forgotten operations, see Glantz, *Forgotten Battles*, IV: 83–183.
28. For details on the failed February–March offensive, see Ibid., pp. 213–311.
29. A. M. Zvartsev, *3-ya gvardeiskaya tankovaya* [3d Guards Tank] (Moscow: Voyenizdat, 1982), pp. 50–54. General P. S. Rybalko's 3d Tank Army, after about thirty days of continuous operations, received orders to attack directly into the path of the unfolding German counteroffensive. Already reduced in strength to as few as thirty tanks, the army was destroyed in the process. Within two months, however, Rybalko received command of the new 3d Guards Tank Army.
30. Losik, *Sovetskykh tankovykh*, pp. 70–73. A sixth tank army would be formed in January 1944. All tank army components possessed similar mobility, although Soviet efforts were still hindered by the absence of a true armored personnel carrier.
31. S. A. Tyushkevich, ed., *Sovetskiye vooruzhennye sily* [The Soviet armed forces] (Moscow: Voyenizdat, 1978), pp. 320–21. By 31 December 1943, the Soviet armored and mechanized force structure consisted of 5 tank armies, 24 tank corps, 13 mechanized corps, 80 separate tank brigades, 106 separate tank regiments, and 43 separate self-propelled artillery regiments.
32. See David M. Glantz and Jonathan M. House, *The Battle of Kursk* (Lawrence: University Press of Kansas, 1999); P. Rotmistrov, "Bronetankovye i mekhanizirovannye voîska v bitva pod Kurskom" [Armored and mechanized forces in the battle of Kursk], *VIZh* no. 1 (January 1970): 12–23; I. Krupchenko, "Osobennosti primeniya bronetankovykh i mekhanizirovannykh voîsk v Kurskoy bitve" [Characteristics of the use of armored and mechanized forces in the battle of Kursk], *VIZh* no. 7 (July 1983): 19–25. For details concerning the operations of the 1st and 5th Guards Tank Armies, see A. K. Babadzhanyan et al., *Lyuki otkryli v Berline* [They opened the hatchway to Berlin] (Moscow: Voyenizdat, 1973), pp. 62–94; P. Y. Yegorov et al., *Dorogami Pobed* [By the roads of victory] (Moscow: Voyenizdat, 1969), pp. 55–86. Initially, the 1st Tank Army contained 571 tanks and self-propelled guns and the 5th Guards Tank Army 543 tanks and self-propelled guns.
33. These diversionary offensives were conducted on 17 July by the Southwestern Front near Izyum and by the Southern Front along the Mius River. The two offensives continued until 27 July and 3 August, respectively—up to the very time the Belgorod-Khar'kov operation commenced.

During the Belgorod-Khar'kov operation, tank armies and subordinate corps led operations with forward detachments of reinforced tank-brigade size that performed tactical maneuver. The forward detachments were tasked with securing key objectives, preempting defenses, and facilitating the advance of their parent units (later with deception). The question was how large should the detachments be and how far in advance should they operate? At Belgorod-Khar'kov, they were as much as 60 tanks each, operating up to 20 kilometers in advance of the main body. The initial German counterattacks destroyed these detachments and in so doing severely reduced the strength of the parent tank army. Later, the Soviets better task-organized the detachments (principally with antitank and artillery elements) and matched their distance of advance to enemy strength and the nature of terrain to ensure support was available if needed. The Belgorod-Khar'kov experience, the first case when both front and army commanders possessed dedicated operational maneuver forces, indicated what could be achieved in the future once all problems were solved.
34. Zvartsev, *3-ya gvardeiskaya tankovaya*, pp. 86–111. The 3d Guards Tank Army began the pursuit with a strength of 686 tanks and self-propelled guns. See also David M. Glantz, *A History of Soviet Airborne Forces* (London: Frank Cass, 1994), pp. 262–89.

35. For details on the Belorussian offensive, see David M. Glantz, *Forgotten Battles of the German-Soviet War (1941–1945), Vol. V (The Summer Campaign, 22 March–31 December 1943)* (Carlisle, Pa.: Self-published, 2000), pts. 1 and 2.

36. The Soviet Southern Front employed cavalry-mechanized groups consisting of the 4th Guards Mechanized and 4th Guards Cavalry Corps in the Donbas operation (13 August–22 September 1943) and the 19th Tank and 4th Guards Cavalry Corps in the Melitopol' operation (26 September–5 November 1943).

37. For details on the lower Dnepr operations, see Glantz, *Forgotten Battles*, V: pt. 2.

38. For details on the failures near Kiev, see Ibid.

39. Zvartsev, *3-ya gvardeiskaya tankovaya*, pp. 111–13; S. Alferov, "Peregruppirovka 3–i gvardeîskoy tankovoy armii v bitve za Dnepr (oktyabr 1943g.)" [The regrouping of 3d Guards Tank Army in the battle for the Dnepr (October 1943)], *VIZh* no. 3 (March 1980): 16–17. Confirmation of the successful deception is found in the German Eighth and Fourth Panzer Armies' intelligence reports. See 8. Armee. lc/AO, Feindlage vom 2–6.11.43; Pz. A.O.K.4. Lagenkarten vom Kriegstagebuch, Feindlage am 28.10–6.11.43. The 3d Guards Tank Army regrouped and attacked with 621 tanks and self-propelled guns.

40. David M. Glantz, *Soviet Military Deception in the Second World War* (London: Frank Cass, 1989), pp. 278–85. The armored strength of the 1st Guards and 2d Guards Tank Armies was, respectively, 546 and 419 tanks and self-propelled guns.

41. Zhitomir-Berdichev, 24 December 1943–14 January 1944; Kirovograd, 5–11 January 1944; Korsun'-Shevchenkovskiy, 24 January–17 February 1944; Rovno-Lutsk, 27 January–11 February 1944; Krivoy-Rog, 30 January–29 February 1944.

42. Proskurov-Chernovtsy, 4 March–17 April 1944; Uman'-Botoshany, 4 March–17 April 1944; Bereznogevotoye-Snigirevka, 6–18 March 1944; Odessa, 26 March–14 April 1944; Crimea, 8 April–12 May 1944.

43. Glantz, *Soviet Military Deception*, pp. 130–32. Prior to the operation, the 5th Guards Army's 8th Guards Mechanized Corps conducted operations well to the north of its parent army, distracting the German attention from the point of main effort.

44. Yegorov, *Dorogami Pobed*, pp. 169–72.

45. The 1st Guards and 6th Guards Cavalry Corps acted as mobile groups for the 13th Army in the Rovno-Lutsk operation, and the 4th Guards Mechanized and 4th Guards Cavalry Corps formed a cavalry-mechanized group in the Bereznegovatoye-Snigirevka and Odessa operations.

46. A. N. Grylev, *Dnepr-Karpaty-Krym: Osvobozhdeniye pravoberezhnoy Ukraîny i Kryma v 1944 gody* [Dnepr-Carpathians-Crimea: The liberation of the right bank of the Ukraine and Crimea in 1944] (Moscow: Nauka, 1970), pp. 135–39. The 3d Guards and 4th Tank Armies conducted the initial exploitation and were joined by the 1st Guards Tank Army less than two weeks later. Armored strength of the tank armies was: 1st Guards, 239; 3d Guards, 310; and 4th, 253.

47. Glantz, *Soviet Military Deception*. In order, the planned strategic offensives and the period of their conduct were Belorussia, 22 June–29 August 1944; L'vov-Sandomierz, 13 July–31 August 1944; Baltic, 5 July–October 1944; Yassy-Kishinev, 20–29 August 1944.

48. A. M. Samsonov, ed., *Osvobozhdeniye Belorussii, 1944* [The liberation of Belorussia, 1944] (Moscow: Nauka, 1974). The 5th Guards Tank Army's strength at the beginning of the operation was 534 tanks and self-propelled guns. During the operation the army suffered heavy losses, largely due to tank ambushes, for which its commander received strong criticism. In late July Rotmistrov was replaced as army commander by General V. T. Vol'sky, probably because of these losses.

49. M. A. Polushkin, *Na sandomirskom napravlenii-L'vovsko-Sandomirskaya operatsiya (iyul'–avgust 1944g.)* [On the Sandomierz direction—The L'vov Sandomierz operation (July–August 1944)] (Moscow: Voyenizdat, 1969). The armored strength of the tank armies was 3d Guards, 555; 4th, 464; and 1st, 416.

50. S. Petrov, "Dostizheniye vnezapnost' v L'vovsko-Sandomirskoy operatsii" [The achievement of surprise in the L'vov-Sandomierz operation], *VIZh* no. 7 (July 1974): 33–36. Confirmed by German intelligence reports contained in *OKH [Oberkommando des Heeres], Kriegsgeschichtliche Abteilung*, "Der grosse Durchbruch bei HGr, Nord-Ukraine u, kampfe am grossen Weichselbruchenkopf v. 8.7–20.–.44."

51. B. Petrov, "O sozdanii udarnoy gruppirovki voîsk v lyublinsko-brestskoy nastupatel'noy operatsii" [Concerning the creation of the shock group of forces in the Lublin-Brest offensive operation], *VIZh* no. 3 (March 1978): 83; F. I. Vysotsky et al., *Gvardeyskaîa tankovaya* [Guards tank] (Moscow: Voyenizdat, 1963), pp. 109–28. This is a history of the 2d Guards Tank Army. The tank army began the operation with 732 tanks and self-propelled guns.

52. M. V. Zakharov, ed., *Osvobozhdeniye yugo-vostochnoy i tsentral'noy evropy voiskami 2-go i 3-go ukrainskikh frontov 1944–1945* [The liberation of southeastern and central Europe by forces of the 2d and 3d Ukrainian Fronts 1944–1945] (Moscow: Nauka, 1970); G. T. Zavizion and P. A. Kornyushin, *I na Tikhim Okeane* [And to the Pacific Ocean] (Moscow: Voyenizdat, 1967), pp. 60–94. This is a history of the 6th Guards Tank Army, which had 531 tanks and self-propelled guns. The Soviets treat this operation as a modern Cannae—a perfect encirclement—although the process was helped along a bit when elements of two Romanian armies quit the fight early in the operation and left their German allies to fend for themselves.

53. *Polevoy ustav Krasnoy armii 1944 (PU-44)* [Field regulation of the Red Army 1944] (Moscow: Voyenizdat, 1944]. Translated by the Office of the Assistant Chief of Staff, G–2, GSUSA, 9–16. The Soviets expressed their faith in the new operational maneuver techniques in their 1944 regulations. The 1944 *Ustav* stated: "Maneuver is one of the most important conditions for achieving success. Maneuver comprises the organized movement of troops for the purpose of creating the most favorable grouping and in placing this grouping in the most favorable position for striking the enemy a crushing blow to gain time and space. Maneuver should be simple in conception and be carried out secretly, rapidly, and in such a way as to surprise the enemy." The regulation went on to articulate the function of tank corps, mechanized corps, and cavalry. Together they formed an echelon to exploit success "for the purpose of breaking up and encircling the main groups of enemy forces and smashing them in cooperation with aviation and ground troops of the front." Cavalry, with its high degree of mobility, was capable of "executing wide operational maneuver and striking swift and sudden blows in both mounted and dismounted formation." The largest mobile force, the tank army, could perform operational maneuver with possible strategic consequences.

54. Soviet losses by late 1944 probably exceeded 9 million men. For German estimates of those losses, see Fremde Heere Ost (IIc), *Die Personelle Starke der Roten Armee. Entwicklung seit Kriegsbeginn* [The personnel strength of the Red Army, developed since the beginning of war], [1945]. Soviet sources reflect manpower deficiencies by emphasizing the low strength of rifle units and the draconian measures used to enlist soldiers in liberated regions. By 1945 Soviet rifle divisions were often below 50 percent strength, with only 3,500–5,000 men each.

55. In fact, the array of operational and tactical maneuver forces in the three fronts and the manner in which they operated resembled a graduate exercise in how such operations should be conducted and remains today as something of a Soviet model for mobile deep operations by operational maneuver forces.

56. Principal accounts of mobile operations are contained in Babadzhanyan et al., *Lyuki otkryli v Berline*, pp. 222–69; Vysotsky, *Gvardeyskaîa tankovaya*, pp. 144–69; Zvartsev, *3-ya gvardeiskaya tankovaya*, pp. 191–220; D. D. Lelyushenko, *Moskva-Stalingrad-Berlin-Praga* [Moscow-Stalingrad-Berlin-Prague] (Moscow: Nauka, 1985), pp. 276–308. The tank armies' respective armored strengths were: 1st Guards, 752; 2d, 873; 3d, 922; and 4th, 680. Separate tank and mechanized corps had between 220 and 260 tanks and self-propelled guns each.

57. The German Panzer divisions in the operation were relatively strong. For example, the 17th Panzer Division, opposite the Sandomierz bridgehead, had over two hundred tanks, half of which were heavy King Tiger models.

58. Zvartsev, *3-ya gvardeiskaya tankovaya*, pp. 212–14. This maneuver is reminiscent of the turning movement of Patton's army during the 1944 Ardennes campaign. Although Rybalko's and Patton's armored strengths were roughly equivalent, Patton's army was over twice the size of Rybalko's in manpower and supporting units. Throughout the operation the Soviets kept the entire advancing force coherent, well organized, and mutually supporting. Tank armies led advancing fronts by up to 100 kilometers and were separated from one another by as much as 80 kilometers. The tank armies marched in corps columns, usually with two tank corps leading, separated by as much as 30 kilometers. The mechanized corps either deployed forward or provided a reserve. Advancing slightly to the rear of and in between the tank armies, separate tank corps of rifle armies formed in multiple brigade columns, with one brigade in the lead as forward detachment and one brigade (usually motorized rifle) in reserve. Tank army and mobile corps forward detachments operated up to 20 kilometers in front of their parent force. Rifle armies led their advance with reinforced tank brigade–size forward detachments, which rode hard on the heels of the tank armies or separate tank corps. Rifle corps and divisions also fielded smaller forward detachments, which closely cooperated with army forward detachments and mobile groups. This well-orchestrated array of operational and tactical maneuver forces facilitated the swift and steady advance by both fronts and in large part accounted for the depth to which operational maneuver was sustained.

59. Losik, *Sovetskye tankovye*, pp. 257–65; Yegorov, *Dorogami Pobed*, pp. 289–329. The 5th Guards Tank Army's armored strength was 585 tanks and self-propelled guns.

60. In preparation for the Berlin operation, between 1–15 April, twenty-eight Soviet armies had to regroup, fifteen of them a distance of up to 385 kilometers and three between 530 and 800 kilometers. See N. M. Ramanichev, "Iz opyta peregruppirovki armii pri podgotovke Berlinskoy operatsii" [From the experience of regrouping an army during the preparation of the Berlin operation], *VIZh* no. 8 (August 1979): 9. The armored strength of the tank armies participating in the operation was 1st Guards, 709; 2d, 672; 3d, 632; and 4th, 395.

61. David M. Glantz, *August Storm: The Soviet 1945 Strategic Offensive in Manchuria*, Leavenworth Papers no. 7 (Fort Leavenworth, Kans.: Combat Studies Institute, 1983); Zavizion and Kornyushin, *I na Tikhim Okeane*, pp. 206–44. The 6th Guards Tank Army's initial strength was 1,019 tanks and self-propelled guns.

62. The average size of a forward detachment for a tank, mechanized, or rifle corps was a reinforced tank brigade. The reinforced brigade normally consisted of the tank brigade

(three tank battalions and one motorized rifle battalion), a rifle regiment or battalion (on trucks), a tank destroyer battalion, a guards mortar (*Katusha*) battalion, a light artillery battalion or regiment, a self-propelled artillery battalion, an antiaircraft regiment, a mortar battalion, and a sapper company or battalion.

63. "Iz doklada komandyushchego bronetankovymi i mekhanizirovannymi voîskami Gruppy sovetskikh voîsk v Germanii marshala bronetankovykh voîsk P. A. Rotmistrova na voenno-nauchnoy konferentsii po izucheniyu Berlinskoy operatsii" [From the report of the commander of armored and mechanized forces of the Group of Soviet Forces in Germany, Marshal of Armored Forces, P. A. Rotmistrov, at a military-scientific conference on the study of the Berlin operation], *VIZh* no. 9 (September 1985): 43–50.

64. Tyushkevich, *Sovetskiye vooruzhennye sily*, p. 393; A. Dunin, "Razvitiye sukhoputnykh voîsk v poslevoennyy period" [The development of ground forces in the postwar period], *VIZh* no. 5 (May 1978): 34–35.

65. Pavlovsky, *Sukhoputnye voîska*, pp. 208–12; Tyushkevich, *Sovetskiye vooruzhennye sily*, pp. 392–94.

66. "Osnovy obshevoyskobogo boya (Lektsiya)" [Principles of combined arms battle (a lesson)], *Vystrel'* [Advanced infantry course], trans. Directorate of Military Intelligence, Army Headquarters, Ottawa, Canada, 1954.

67. In the mid-1950s the United States reorganized its ground forces into pentomic divisions, which were designed to operate on an atomic battlefield.

68. Dunin, "Razvitiye sukhoputnykh voîsk," p. 38. At this point the Soviet description of their force structure shifts into use of generic terms and comparisons between old and new units on the basis of percentage changes in strength and firepower. More detail is available in "Recent Changes in Soviet Divisional Organization," *Intelligence Review* no. 222 (August–September 1955): 10–14; "Organizational Employment of Soviet Line Divisions," *Intelligence Review* no. 254 (July 1962): 9–12.

69. The new Soviet attitude is best articulated in V. A. Semenov, *Kratkiy ocherk razvitiya Sovetskogo operativnogo iskusstva* [A short survey of the development of Soviet military art] (Moscow: Voyenizdat, 1960), pp. 290–91.

70. Ibid., p. 296.

71. B. Arushanyan, "Manevr v nastupatel'nykh operatsiyakh Velikoy Otechestvennoy voyny" [Maneuver in offensive operations of the Great Patriotic War], *VIZh* no. 12 (December 1963): 3–12. Most Soviet works of this period replaced the term mobile group with older terms such as exploitation force or echelon to develop success.

72. V. D. Sokolovsky, *Voennaya strategiya* [Military strategy] (Moscow: Voyenizdat, 1963), p. 383.

73. Dunin, "Razvitiye sukhoputnykh voîsk," pp. 38–39; "Soviet Field Armies: Organizational and Operational Concepts," *Intelligence Research Project No. P3–10* (Washington, D.C.: Office of the Assistant Chief of Staff, Intelligence, 1962), declassified. Average-size wartime fronts would consist of a mixture of combined-arms and tank armies; the combined-arms army of three or four motorized rifle divisions, one tank division, and the tank army of two to four medium tank divisions; possibly one heavy tank division; and under special circumstances, a motorized rifle division.

74. Among the many articles, see F. Sverdlov, "K voprosy o manevre v boyu" [Concerning the question of maneuver in combat], *Voennyy vestnik* [Military herald] no. 88 (August 1972): 31; V. Savkin, "Manevr v boyu" [Maneuver in battle], *Voennyy vestnik* no. 4 (April 1972): 23.

75. Sverdlov, "K voprosy o manevre v boyu," p. 31.

76. David M. Glantz, *The Conduct of Tactical Maneuver: The Role of the Forward Detachment* (Fort Leavenworth, Kans.: Soviet Army Studies Office, 1988).
77. For further explanation of these views, see David M. Glantz, *The Soviet Conduct of War* (Fort Leavenworth, Kans.: Soviet Army Studies Office, 1987); Graham H. Turbiville, Jr. "Strategic Deployment: Mobilizing and Moving the Force," *Military Review* 68, no. 12 (December 1988): 58–70. Extensive Soviet analysis of this theme of initial war has produced many studies, including S. P. Ivanov, *Nachal'niy period voiny* [The initial period of war] (Moscow: Voyenizdat, 1974); M. Cherednichenko, "O nachal'nom periode Velikoi Otechestvennoi voîny" [Concerning the initial period of the Great Patriotic War], *VIZh* no. 4 (April 1961): 28–35; P. Korkodinov, "Fakty i mysli o nachal'nom periode Velikoy Otechestvennoy voîny" [Facts and ideas about the initial period of the Great Patriotic War], *VIZh* no. 10 (October 1965): 26–34; V. Baskakov, "Ob osobennostyakh nachal'nogo perioda voiny" [Concerning the peculiarities of the initial period of war], *VIZh* no. 2 (February 1966): 29–34; A. Grechko, "25 let tomu nazad" [125 years ago], *VIZh* no. 6 (June 1965): 3–15; I. Bagramyan, "Kharakter i osobennosti nachal'nogo perioda voîny" [The nature and peculiarities of the initial period of war], *VIZh* no. 10 (October 1981): 20–27; V. Matsulenko, "Nekotorye vyvody iz opyta nachal'nogo perioda Velikoy Otechestvennoy voîny" [Some conclusions from the experience of the initial period of the Great Patriotic War], *VIZh* no. 3 (March 1984): 35–42; A. I. Yevseev, "O nekotorykh tendentsiyakh v izmenenii soderzhaniya i kharaktera nachal'nogo perioda voîny" [Concerning some tendencies in the changing form and nature of the initial period of war], *VIZh* no. 11 (November 1985): 11–20.
78. Headquarters, Department of the Army, Field Manual 100-2-3, *Soviet Army Troops Organization and Equipment* (Washington, D.C.: Department of the Army, 1984), pp. 4–48.
79. In a review of a book by A. Babakov on the Soviet armed forces in the postwar years, A. Reznichenko challenges Babakov's description of postwar periods of military development. Babakov had postulated that the distinct periods were 1945–1953, 1954–1961, 1962–1972, and 1973–1986. Reznichenko argues that the subdivisions should be 1945–1960, 1962–1970, and 1971–1985. His argument clearly delineates the period of the revolution in military affairs (1961–1970) and the period when the Soviets adopted a dual option (1971–1985). He strongly implies that a new period began in the mid-1980s, characterized by the rapidly changing pace of conventional technology and the emergence of high-precision weaponry as the first noticeable facet of that change. The growing importance of new weaponry will probably accentuate techniques the Soviets developed in the 1970s to deal with the menacing presence of nuclear weapons. Specifically, the Soviets will further develop operational and tactical maneuver techniques aimed at preempting or neutralizing effective enemy use of any weapons of mass destruction, nuclear or conventional. See V. Reznichenko, "Sovetskiye vooruzhennye sily v poslevoyennyi period" [The Soviet armed forces in the postwar period], *Kommunist vooruzhennykh sil* [Communist of the armed forces] no. 1 (January 1988): 86–88. See also M. A. Moyseyev, "S pozitsii oboronitel'noî doktriny" [From a position of defensive doctrine], *Krasnaya zvezda* [Red Star], 10 Feb 89, pp. 1–2.
80. V. G. Reznichenko, *Taktika* [Tactics] (Moscow: Voyenizdat, 1987), p. 200.
81. For example, see I. Vorob'yev, "Novoye oruzhiye i printsipy taktiki" [New weapons and tactical principles], *Sovetskoy voyennoye obozreniye* [Soviet military review] no. 2 (February 1987): 18.

82. Stanislaw Koziej, "Anticipated Directions for Change in Tactics of Ground Forces," *Przeglad Wojsk Ladowych* [Ground Forces Review] no. 9 (September 1986): 9, trans. Harold Orenstein in *Selected Translations from the Polish Military Press* (Fort Leavenworth, Kans.: Soviet Army Studies Office, 1988), I: 7. Colonel Koziej, a graduate of the General Staff Academy of the Polish Armed Forces, has written extensively in the Polish journal of the general staff, *Mysl Woiskowa* [Military thought], on, among other topics, air-land operations and the Polish theory of operational art.

83. Jacob W. Kipp, "Gorbachev's Gambit: Soviet Military Doctrine and Conventional Arms Control in an Era of Reform," in *The Soviet Army in an Era of Reform* (Fort Leavenworth, Kans.: Soviet Army Studies Office, 1989). This article exhaustively investigates the roots of Soviet defensiveness.

84. Ibid., pp. 55–56.

Soviet Operational Logistics, 1939–1990

Graham H. Turbiville, Jr.

Introduction

The disintegration of the Soviet armed forces is continuing well after the official demise of the Soviet State at the end of 1991. Military manpower and materiel of the former Soviet Union has been divided or claimed by USSR successor states, with the largest share of these resources now incorporated into the Armed Forces of the Russian Republic. Russian military forces themselves sit in shrinking, isolated garrisons in what is now termed the "near abroad" beyond Russia's borders, on the territory of a now united Germany, or in installations spread across Russia. One consequence of this enormous and continuing military turmoil has been the shattering of a centralized logistic support system designed to sustain joint and combined operations of unprecedented size and scope, which also is integrated with the military and civilian resources of the former Soviet Union's Warsaw Pact allies. Nevertheless, Soviet concepts for the conduct of combined operations—logistics theory, organizational structure, and resources integral to their support—remain instructive for military planners and historians alike and deserve the closest study and evaluation.

The development of Soviet military art and operational logistics—that complex of rear service roles, missions, procedures, and resources intended to sustain military operations by army and front groupings—clearly occupied a prominent place within overall Soviet efforts to formulate or adapt warfighting approaches to new conditions.[1] As Soviet military theorists and planners have long emphasized, logistic theory and practice are shaped by the same historical and technological developments that influence Soviet warfighting approaches at every level. In turn, they play a major role in defining directions and parameters for Soviet warfighting approaches.

Soviet military writings point also to the need for logistic theory and practice that are wholly consistent with other components of strategy, operational art, and tactics. Despite the many changes in the political, economic, and military environment and the quickening pace of technological change, Soviet military theorists and planners continue to emphasize the importance of applying pertinent historical precedent to contemporary military problems. This process is evident now in the area of logistic support, where formulating or adapting logistic support concepts for fundamentally different circumstances is a particularly complex task.[2]

This chapter will address the development of logistic concepts and resources integral to sustaining large-scale combined-arms operations as the Soviets have conceived them over the last five decades from 1939. It will also consider what Soviet specialists see as rear service developments that will shape logistic support in the 1990s.

Prewar Preparation, Wartime Reorganization, and the Support of Strategic Operations, 1939–1945

When German forces began their rapid advance into the Soviet Union on 22 June 1941—the beginning of the Soviet-termed Great Patriotic War—the logistic support system of the Red Army and Navy was in virtually every respect unprepared for the demands that were to be placed upon it. Rear service responsibilities were largely decentralized; analogous rear service control and management entities often absent from key tactical, operational, and central command levels; existing rear service directorates understaffed; and logistic resources of all types badly deployed for dealing with the "difficult" support situations faced by Soviet military forces. Indeed, the whole concept of providing logistic support to armies and fronts—operational logistic support—proved badly flawed from both organizational and resource standpoints.

Prewar logistic planners anticipated these systemic and resource problems, though senior Soviet commanders (severely attrited by the 1930s purges) gave logistic matters only secondary attention. Thus, when a 47-year-old corps commissar named A. V. Khrulev was appointed supply chief of the Red Army in October 1939, he found himself in a job that was ill defined and possessed little real authority over those many agencies charged with logistic support.[3] Khrulev, a decorated veteran of S. M. Budennyî's First Cavalry Army in the civil war, set out with his staff to reconstruct a rear service establishment that even in peacetime seemed clearly unsuited to support large-scale combined-arms operations.

Almost from the beginning of his tenure, however, he became immersed in the numerous problems engendered by the 1939–1940 Winter War with Finland. Transportation and logistic management problems were particularly acute in the Winter War. Even from the earliest days, railway cars supplying front forces were backed up on a number of lines because of inadequate tracking and poor planning. An attempt to alleviate this problem by also supplying the Northwest Front by sea from Arkhangelsk through Murmansk instead created chaotic conditions at the Arkhangelsk port. Every Red Army branch of service (artillery, engineer, signal, etc.) operated on its own schedule with no overall coordination.

Information sent from operational levels to central logistic planning bodies was irregular and sometimes inaccurate.[4]

As a consequence of these problems, and the inability of the logistic establishment to deal with them, Khrulev pushed for the creation of a central "Quartermaster Directorate" with expanded capabilities, a request met by People's Commissar of Defense Marshal K. E. Voroshilov, in the summer of 1940. Khrulev (now a lieutenant general) was given increased authority and staff support. While this constituted a measure of progress at the central level, it was far from the sweeping restructuring envisioned as necessary at all levels by senior logisticians.

As Khrulev continued to push for greater control over rear services in the months preceding the Soviet Union's entry into World War II, there was considerable discussion and disagreement within the Soviet military establishment over the subordination of rear service bodies and responsibilities for planning logistic support at every level. These disagreements became particularly acute with the assignment of Army General G. I. Zhukov to be chief of the Soviet General Staff in January 1941.

General Zhukov "supported those on the general staff who believed that a general outline sufficed as a basis for directing the supply of the army in the field."[5] Under this approach:

> The General Staff would calculate needs and issue a directive; the quartermaster services subordinate to it would dispatch everything requested from them; and the commandant's offices of the general staff's Military Transportation Service, to which motor vehicle, rail, water, and air transport were subordinate, would deliver to the troops all types of authorized supply.[6]

In short, Zhukov wanted the general staff to retain direct control of key rear service entities.

By the start of the war, in accord with Zhukov's wishes, logistic responsibilities were divided among the several principals. As the recently retired chief of staff of the Soviet Armed Forces Rear Services, Col. Gen. I. M. Golushko, noted in a considerable understatement forty years later, "a definite separateness could be observed in the organization and, consequently, in the actions of the directorates and services related to the rear support sphere."[7] At the tactical and operational levels, the control of logistic planning within fronts, armies, and divisions rested principally with the commanders and combat staffs, not specialized rear service planning bodies. This allowed only the most superficial attention to be given to rear service support because of the other combat demands placed on the commanders and staffs.[8]

In addition to the organizational problems and resulting difficulties in the operation of the rear service system, those logistic resources intended to support Soviet operational formations in the initial period of war were badly deployed. Basically, there were depots for all classes of supply (weapons and equipment, ammunition, POL [petroleum, oil, and lubricants], repair parts, food, etc.) subordinate to the various central directorates of the Commissariat of Defense, and to military districts. These stockpiles were intended for the mobilizational deployment of operational formations. However, in addition to the lack of centralized rear service management (and likely because of it), there were dangerous anomalies in what supplies were found at which levels. For example, the General Staff's POL reserves were virtually all located at military district level or in facilities of the national economy, with almost no stocks under direct central control.[9] Thus, the general staff was limited in how quickly it could influence the POL supply of field formations.

On the other hand, ammunition stockpiles, which were the responsibility of the Main Artillery Directorate's (*GAU*) Artillery Supply Service at each level, were located in *GAU* central, military district, and field army depots. In wartime central depots were expected to supply forward army ammunition dumps directly, while army depots in turn would supply lower echelons.[10] No provision was made for a front link, though fronts would be expected to plan for the expenditure and resupply of ammunition while army entities carried out the actual resupply operations.[11] The problems and confusion resulting from this kind of arrangement were not difficult for Khrulev and his staff to imagine and indeed became quickly manifest once the war began.

It is clear that the rear service support establishment existing at the time of the German attack would have had substantial problems meeting large-scale support requirements even with adequate preparation time and favorable circumstances at the beginning of war. The German attack, however, totally disrupted prewar plans for rear service mobilization and support. Huge quantities of supplies were overrun or destroyed by German forces in the first days of the conflict. Those supplies surviving or located further in the interior were often "in the hands of various services that were not subordinated to combined-arms headquarters" and thus were not made available to combat units.[12] Rear service elements had to simultaneously provide retreating units with supplies, undertake the mobilization deployment of rear service units, and evacuate supplies.[13] In addition, because of the concurrent requirements to sustain Soviet units and operational formations in combat and evacuate over 1,300 industrial enterprises as well as agricultural and other resources, "two gigantic train flows were moving in opposite directions with incredible difficulty under constant air attack by the enemy."[14]

It is not surprising, in light of the above, that the Soviet logistic support system failed in most respects to meet the enormous demands so suddenly placed upon it. By early July 1941, by Soviet assessment, Zhukov and the General Staff were so immersed in operational matters that they had neither a conception of the logistic situation at the fronts, nor knew what the forces required in terms of logistic support. No requirements had, in fact, even been leveled on Khrulev and his staff. On 27 July a thoroughly frustrated Khrulev prepared a written proposal for a centralized rear service establishment designed to impose a measure of order on this rapidly unraveling rear support situation.[15] The proposal was passed to the Supreme Commander, I. V. Stalin, who approved Khrulev's recommendations and immediately ordered that a draft State Defense Committee (SDC) decision on the Red Army rear service organization be prepared.[16]

Working with his staff, Khrulev quickly drew up the SDC draft decree and presented it to Stalin in the predawn hours of 28 July.[17] Over Zhukov's objections, the decree was approved—a move that was to establish by 1 August the essential organizations and responsibilities of the Soviet Armed Forces Rear Services as they continued to exist through the 1980s.[18] It also institutionalized what appears to be a degree of creative tension between the national-level rear services and the General Staff.[19]

Under the rear service reorganization approved by Stalin, Khrulev was named Chief of the Red Army Rear and a Deputy Commissar (later Minister) of Defense for Rear Services. A Main Directorate for the Rear (consisting of a Main Staff, Military Railroad Directorate, Highway Directorate, and Inspectorate) was established, with Main Quartermaster, Fuel Supply, Ambulance (Medical), and Veterinary Directorates also assigned to Khrulev's direct control.[20] The Staff of the Main Directorate of the Rear had sections designated to deal with rear service planning for operational formations, planning rail and motor transport shipments, organizing logistic entities and facilities; and handling general issues.[21] Thus, Khrulev had control of vast logistic resources in the form of transport, supply stockpiles, and key services, as well as being able to speak with the authority of a Deputy Commissar of Defense. Only technical support—repair, maintenance, the supply of technical equipment including ammunition, and major end items—remained under the control of main and central technical directorates (e.g., *GAU*) and of the various branch services (artillery, armor, engineer, signal, etc.).[22] These rear service organizations and resources were in total referred to as "central" or "strategic" rear services—assets the Supreme High Command (*Verkhovnoe Glavnokomandovanie* [*VGK*]) used to influence the course of strategic operations. As the war progressed, this level of rear service support became critical to the direct logistic support of operational formations and, as a consequence, integral to Soviet operational logistics.

Within the operational logistic system itself, "chiefs of the rear," who were simultaneously deputy commanders for rear services, were set up in the fronts and armies. These officers and their staffs had duties analogous to those of Khrulev and his central apparatus. They were directly and immediately subordinate to the commander of the given operational formation, and subordinate "in a special sense" to the chief of the rear at the next higher level.[23] They were responsible for planning and controlling designated rear service activities of the fronts and armies, while the commanders and other staff officers concerned themselves with force planning and employment issues.

Stalin himself emphasized that supplying armies and fronts required an "iron discipline" and that the new deputy commanders for rear services "must be dictators in the rear zone" of their fronts.[24] The rear service chiefs at all levels exercised a coordinating role even in regard to those technical support entities that were not directly subordinate to them. They accomplished this through their control of transportation—a role that grew as the war progressed—and were thus the center for all rear service planning from strategic to tactical levels.[25] On 19 August a Chief of Rear Services of the Soviet Army Air Forces was established.[26] This officer and his staff (replicated at lower levels) handled all aviation-specific supply items for flying and ground support units in the air armies of the fronts or other air units, while coordinating with the Red Army Chief of Rear Services and staff for all other supply items.[27] Since the Main Administration of the Air Force was a component of the Red Army, the Air Force Chief of Rear Services was subordinate in a "special sense" to Khrulev.

By mid-August 1941, then, with a basic rear support structure in place, Khrulev and his subordinates undertook the staggering task of imposing order on a logistic situation that was failing at every level. He was, more specifically, charged with

> Managing the rear's organization, transporting troops and replacements, delivering all types of materiel to the fronts ..., evacuating casualties, patients and military property [and] ... maintaining information on the presence of military materiel reserves in the fronts (armies) and bases, as well as on the availability of all kinds of materiel in the field army.[28]

Each of these functions encompassed numerous and complex components that had to be thoroughly planned and coordinated in accord with developing combat operations.

In performing these myriad tasks, a workable delineation of responsibility was developed between the central rear service bodies and the general staff, and between front and army commanders and their new rear service deputies. The general staff's Main Operations Directorate (and in an analogous way the front and army operations department staffs) would communicate to the rear services general, initial data on forthcoming combat operations and possible requirements. On this basis, rear service staffs worked out detailed logistic support plans for the operation.[29]

Each of the three periods of the Great Patriotic War and the 1945 Manchurian operation against Japanese forces, as analyzed by the Soviets, featured critical developments in sustaining all levels of Soviet and coalition armed forces.[30] While it is not within the scope of this chapter to address these developments in any detail, features associated with each period are key to understanding Soviet rear service support concepts and operational logistics in particular as they developed in the post–World War II years.

In providing rear service support in the first period of the war—a period characterized by largely retreating Soviet forces conducting a strategic defense in a rapidly changing operational environment—great emphasis was placed on reducing the cumbersome organization of operational rear services and on creating strategic logistic reserves.[31] The permanent depots and repair centers that initially had been providing support to operational formations were replaced by field depots, the structure of transport support was improved, and the formation of consolidated army logistic bases stocking key supply items begun.[32] The number of units and facilities as well as the proliferation of specialized rear staff officers and sections created haphazardly in the early days of the war were reduced.[33]

Motor transport at all levels was increased to the extent possible, though this was in critically short supply. As a consequence, extensive use was made of animal-drawn transport at all levels, as well as motor transport columns under *VGK* (central rear service) control.[34] The new trend of using air transport for supplying operational formations gained momentum as the war progressed. Transport aircraft employed in such a role were also principally assets of the *VGK*.[35] Enormous experience was gained in managing military rail shipments and in building and restoring rail lines. To facilitate this, in March 1942 Khrulev became the People's Commissar of Railroads in addition to his other posts.[36]

Other significant developments during the first period of war included the extensive use of rear service operations groups. Under this practice, central rear service staffs, including sometimes Khrulev himself, were dispatched to the fronts to coordinate logistic activities and deal with special problems.[37] This approach proved useful throughout the war, especially in supporting strategic offensive operations later in the conflict, as well as in formulating approaches for theater-level or strategic rear service control and management four decades later. In March 1942 the Soviets established the Trophy Service, which had organizations subordinated to rear service chiefs at central, front, and army levels to collect, classify, and evacuate captured German war materiel.[38] The large quantities of materiel they recovered played an important role in offsetting the severe shortages of Soviet weapons and transport stocks at that time. In May 1942 the Soviets introduced rear service deputy commanders or chiefs of the rear at division and corps levels and established a Navy Chief of Rear Services.[39]

Simultaneously with supporting forces participating in the strategic defensive efforts of 1941 and 1942 the *VGK* began to build substantial strategic reserves of all types, including rear service reserves. The logistic components of these reserves comprised transport resources of all kinds, weapons systems and equipment, ammunition and POL stockpiles, and other resources. These assets, managed by central rear service organizations, could be employed only at the discretion of the *VGK*, and were intended to replace losses, create new units, and decisively influence the support of operational formations in key sectors.[40] The employment of such strategic rear service reserves was to be critical for the support of subsequent Soviet counteroffensives and strategic offensive operations throughout the war, and the experience gained in their employment has clearly been incorporated into Soviet theater logistic support planning in the 1970s and 1980s.[41]

Overall, then, by the end of the first period of the war a basic rear service support system had been established that with considerable difficulty had imposed a measure of order on what had been a chaotic rear area situation. The system was sustaining strategic defensive operations across a broad front and, in accord with strictly followed *VGK* directives, central rear service organs were building a strategic logistic base for the conduct of far more ambitious operations.[42]

The second period of the war, as the Soviets assess it, was a fundamental turning point "not only in the course of the Great Patriotic War and the strategic situation, but also in the work of all levels of the Soviet Army's rear."[43] New problems for the Soviet rear services surfaced during the November 1942 counteroffensive by the Southwestern, Don, and Stalingrad Fronts, as well as from the battles for the Caucasus in 1942–1943, the summer 1943 Battle of Kursk, and the subsequent battle for the Dnieper.[44] These centered principally on supplying huge combined-arms groupings, often poorly equipped in terms of combat and support equipment, that now were advancing over sweeping frontages and territory on which lines of communication had been largely destroyed. As in the first period of the war, the strategic rear services played a major role in this effort, amassing enormous quantities of materiel prior to the counteroffensives/offensives and directly supplying operational formations during their course. Golushko, for example, in noting that "the influence of the agencies of the strategic rear on the organization of rear support for the fronts increased with the increase in the scale of military actions" went on to indicate that "a number of central bases were prepositioned in the Transcaucasus republics when the battle for the Caucasus unfolded almost simultaneously with the enormous battle between the Volga and the Don."[45] In preparing for the Stalingrad offensive, the central rear services deployed supply bases forward to support the Stalingrad, Southern, and Briansk Fronts and managed other rear service preparation efforts.[46] In this way, the increasingly mobile central rear services acquired a role, which had not been envisioned earlier, in directly supporting operational groupings.

Great effort was given in the Stalingrad counteroffensives (in the Caucasus as well) to building and restoring roads and railways, with Khrulev requesting and receiving support from two *VGK* air transport divisions to help reduce transportation shortfalls.[47] The role of special line of communications troops—Highway and Railway Troops, as well as other special bridge-building and engineer elements—thus grew in importance as an organic component of operational rear services and one critical to the successful supply and support of advancing formations. The application of experience gained in transportation-route construction, maintenance, and management was clearly evident in the buildup for the Kursk Battle.[48]

To better manage the central rear service resources that were playing such increasingly important front support roles in the switch to offensive operations, Khrulev established in the Azerbaidzhan SSR in 1942 a "supply base for the center" to improve the control of rear service resources. This effort included the dispatch of military materiel received from the defense industry and the shipment of supplies through ports on the Caspian Sea.[49] In a subsequent effort to bring central materiel resources closer to the fronts engaging in offensive operations, central depots, for the first time in the war, were moved west of Moscow and the Volga in the spring of 1943.[50] The forward deployment of central rear services would continue throughout the war. Technical support at the central and front levels was improved as well, with central- and front-subordinated assembly and distribution points for damaged combat and support equipment established.[51]

In operational formations, the Soviets encountered considerable difficulties in keeping combat units of the fronts and armies supplied with materiel. As a consequence of State Defense Committee findings, it was directed in June 1943 that in the future, higher rear service levels would be generally responsible for supplying and otherwise supporting lower levels, rather than the motor transport of units and formations being sent back to higher echelons to pick up supplies or deliver damaged equipment.[52] This "delivery forward" principle continues as a primary tenet of the Russian logistic system today. In addition, the depths of unit and formation rear areas were greatly reduced, a trend that by the end of the war had cut rear area depths in half. This substantially reduced, of course, the distances required for supplying units and for evacuating casualties and equipment to rear bases.

Finally, the successful evacuation and restoration of Soviet defense industrial facilities began to play a major role in the supply of Soviet military forces in the second period of the war.[53] Industrial output—together with other sources of equipment, including Lend-Lease shipments—contributed also to the rapid reequipping and reorganization of the USSR's armed forces. It made possible the buildup of strategic reserves that enabled the successful switch "from strategic defense, to counteroffensive, and then to strategic offensive operations of tremendous scope."[54]

The third period of the war saw the Soviet armed forces engaged in three major campaigns that could each be fairly characterized as of "tremendous scope." Supporting the strategic offensives conducted within the course of these campaigns presented all levels of the Soviet rear services with enormous problems and necessitated the development of new support concepts. As the winter campaign developed, for example, rear services fell far behind the advancing fronts, and armies engaged in the offensive had to rely heavily on local procurement, assets provided by the Trophy Service, and repaired equipment to sustain themselves.[55] Shortages of motor transport, disrupted rail and road lines of communication, and early spring thaws compounded the problems.[56] Overcoming these difficulties involved a range of field expedients, including a renewed reliance on animal transport, the hand delivery of ammunition and other supplies by rear service personnel on foot, and the increased use of transport aviation to deliver supplies, principally ammunition, to those forces most intensively engaged.[57]

Overall, despite the numerous tactical, operational, and strategic logistic support problems encountered, the winter 1944 campaign concluded successfully and rear service preparations for the subsequent summer/fall campaign began well before its completion. These rear service support plans were predicated on the concept of successive offensives on different axes. Joint planning involving the *VGK*, the chief of the rear, *GAU*, and other central rear agencies set out supply requirements that had to be fulfilled before and during the course of the operations. Rear service support was to meet both consumption needs as the operation unfolded and, of particular importance, establish operational and strategic reserves that would enable the fronts to undertake subsequent operations without significant pauses.[58] This logistic planning approach remains key to contemporary theater rear service support concepts.

In supporting operations of the summer and fall of 1944 and the concluding 1945 campaign in eastern Europe, rear service units, reinforced with motor transport and making heavy use of rail, were brought much closer to the combat forces they would be sustaining:

> As a rule, the front rear was deployed in three echelons at the start of the Belorussian, Iassk-Kishinev, Vistula-Oder, Berlin, and other offensive operations. Usually, 70–80% of all front rear service units and facilities were in the first and second echelons, while only about 5% were deployed farther away than 220 kilometers from the front line.[59]

The extensive maneuver and regrouping of units and formations between fronts and strategic directions during the 1944–1945 operations required the simultaneous maneuver of rear service units and resources. Making more effective use of all forms of transport coordinated by those strategic and operational transportation management bodies established earlier in the war, the massive Soviet transfers of units and materiel was carried out with increasing skill. Indeed, the successful regrouping, *peregruppirovka*, of Soviet forces during this period is the focus of close Russian attention today by planners seeking applicable lessons learned.

When Soviet forces entered Eastern Europe, the Soviet rear services were given the task of managing and exploiting foreign road and rail networks. As a consequence, eleven strategic rear service transloading bases were deployed at the junction of railroads having broad Soviet and narrower east European gauge lines, as well as at some seaports.[60] These bases oversaw, prioritized, and otherwise facilitated the dispatch of military units and materiel to Soviet forces advancing into Eastern Europe. In addition, "procurement administrations" were established under the Red Army chief of the rear in Romania, Poland, Hungary, and Czechoslovakia, while fronts began to be assigned railroad operating brigades (in addition to railroad construction brigades).[61]

At the same time, "depots of central subordination—artillery, food, fuel, clothing, and others with materiel reserves, and also repair medical, transport, airfield engineering, procurement, and other rear organs—had to be moved forward with the fronts."[62] This gave the Supreme High Command the means of directly influencing the success of strategic offensives logistically, by reinforcing the rear services of designated operational formations. In an effort that Soviet planners concerned with Warsaw Pact coalition support measures have given much careful postwar analysis, the "rear services also provided support to Polish, Czechoslovak, and other foreign military organizations formed on Soviet territory, and which battled shoulder-to-shoulder with the USSR Armed Forces against a common enemy."[63]

As noted, a number of technical support services were not under the direct control of the chiefs of the rear at each level, but rather of representatives of organizations like *GAU*, the armored services, engineer services, etc. Despite this, as contemporary Soviet logisticians like I. M. Golushko emphasized, the joint planning of transportation, evacuation, rear defense, and common approaches to deployment and redeployment, all supervised and largely controlled by the chief of the rear, provided for a smooth, effective working relationship among the various components of the rear service system.[64]

A most important focus of Soviet rear service attention—particularly during the third period of the war and in Manchuria—was the logistic support of mobile groups. Mobile groups were established at army and front levels, and most often comprised reinforced tank, mechanized, or cavalry corps at army level, or tank-mechanized-cavalry groupings of up to army size at front level.[65] These mobile groupings were tasked to advance rapidly into the operational depths of the enemy, "cut up enemy groupings," and otherwise facilitate his defeat—missions that required them to operate at great distances from the main forces and their rear service bases.[66] A number of specialized supply and support procedures for the operational and exploitation groups were developed. These included the allocation of "slices" of the more mobile army, front, and central rear service assets to the mobile groups, and innovative approaches to provide for their continuing supply and technical support. As Soviet sources note, special rear service headquarters groups were sometimes organized to oversee mobile group support, which included motor transport, supply stocks, special troops (i.e., line of communications [LOC] construction and repair, combat engineer, etc.), medical support assets, and other rear service resources.[67] The direct supply of mobile groups by transport aviation resources was also provided for when practical, and by the end of the war it was considered a standard component of support for deep operations forces.[68] While transport aircraft were limited throughout the war, aviation's potential for the rear service support of mobile formations made a profound impression on Soviet planners.

Protecting, defending, and securing operational and deep rear areas was a major Soviet concern throughout the war. In the third period, this emphasis was focused on securing the rear areas of advancing front forces as well as the increasingly long lines of communication running back to the Soviet Union. This task was principally assigned to the Border Guard and Internal Troop units of the People's Commissariat of Internal Affairs, or the *NKVD*, which were most typically organized into security regiments, security battalions, and maneuver groups.

The number of security regiments or other *NKVD* units assigned to front rear areas varied widely with the perceived threat, though half a dozen or more security regiments per front was not unusual. Their actions were controlled by chief of rear security, usually a senior *NKVD* officer, by the front military council, and directly determined by the decisions of the deputy front commander for rear services in his formulation of the rear service plan.[69] In addition to the units drawn from the *NKVD*, regular line maneuver units and logistic units—all of whose actions were coordinated with *NKVD* forces—were assigned rear area security duties.[70] Overall, rear area security, carried out by both dedicated and temporarily assigned forces, was considered a rear service responsibility and remained so for the next 40 years.

The final Soviet strategic operation of World War II, the 1945 strategic offensive in Manchuria, required the redeployment of substantial

Soviet forces and supplies from Europe to the Soviet Far East. From December 1944 to August of the following year, some four armies, numerous other maneuver, aviation, and special troop units, and huge quantities of materiel were moved over distances of up to 11,000 kilometers, principally by rail. Postwar Russian planners continue to study all the dimensions of the redeployment associated with the Manchurian operation, which serves as a model considered particularly useful for the strategic movement of combined-arms forces.[71]

Planning by the Soviet Supreme High Command for the operation, which began on 9 August, called for the creation of three fronts to defeat the Japanese Kwantung Army in Manchuria: the Transbaikal, First Far Eastern, and Second Far Eastern Fronts.[72] Each of these, in accord with the organizational concepts developed during the Great Patriotic War, had rear service deputy commanders and staffs, as well as technical support and branch arms and services representatives, to direct and coordinate the overall rear service support of operational formations.

Of particular significance, however, was the establishment of a strategic rear service control body in the composition of a "High Command of Forces for the Far Eastern Theater of Military Action." The Far East High Command, which was a deployed headquarters of the Supreme High Command, was set up because of the great distance of this theater from Moscow and the enormous area and scope of operations planned.[73] The commander in chief of forces in the theater was Marshal of the Soviet Union A. M. Vasilevskiĭ, who with his staff and representatives controlled and coordinated assigned ground, air, air defense, and naval forces, including allocated reserves of the Soviet Supreme High Command (transport and strike aviation, artillery, engineer units, motor transport, etc.) and units of the Mongolian People's Republic.[74]

Within Vasilevskiĭ's High Command of Forces, a rear service operations group headed by Col. Gen. V. I. Vinogradov (a Deputy Chief of Red Army Rear Services) was established with the mission of organizing and managing overall rear service support for the 11 combined-arms, 1 tank, and 3 air defense armies, and other ground and air groupings. In addition, the rear service operations group coordinated the rear service activities of the Pacific Fleet and Amur River Flotilla.[75] Vinogradov's staff consisted of representatives from the Red Army's central rear service directorates, including the Central Directorate of Military Communications (*VOSO*) and the Main Motor Transport, the Main Road Building and Maintenance, Main Fuel Supply, Food Supply, Clothing Supply, Main Medical, and Main Trophy Directorates.[76]

As noted, counterparts to these directorate representatives were present in assigned operational formations and tactical units, where they were the support to rear service deputy commanders. At every level of command, as before, rear service deputy commanders and staffs played key roles in coordinating the activities of technical services not under their direct control.

Despite maritime materiel deliveries to Far East ports, theater-level rear services were linked principally to the "center" by the Trans-Siberian Railroad, which had extremely limited feeder lines in the Far East. Therefore, supplies for some theater forces had to be moved by motor transport to front forces and concentration areas, in some cases a distance of hundreds of kilometers. In addition, the primitive road network, insufficient motor transport, and rapid advances by many maneuver units on the fronts made it difficult to relocate operational-level logistic bases so far forward.

Front supply depots of the Transbaikal Front, for example, did not relocate during the operation because of this combination of factors, with the increasing distance between bases and supported forces causing substantial logistic problems as the operation progressed.[77] Fuel consumption in particular was extremely high. By the third day of the operation, elements of the front's fast moving Sixth Guards Tank Army had to be resupplied with fuel by air transport.[78] From 11–16 August the Sixth Guards Tank Army received as much fuel by air as it did by motor transport, with the Transbaikal Front overall receiving some 2,456 metric tons of fuel by air during the course of the operation.[79]

Certainly, the Soviets experienced problems in logistic support of Far East Theater forces in their successful twenty-four day campaign, many of which are enumerated in Soviet historical writings.[80] Notable among these, in addition to the movement and fuel problems noted above, were providing water and cooking fuel, accomplishing road maintenance, ensuring adequate levels of rear service communications, providing for the timely evacuation of casualties, dealing with motor transport shortages, and other difficulties. Regarding the overall effectiveness of rear service support, however, Soviet military historians make the following judgment:

> All the work accomplished by rear agencies in the preparatory period ensured the successful course of the operation. Despite the fact that Soviet troops advanced 300–800 kms during the first 10–15 days, they did not experience serious supply difficulties, with the exception of temporary interruptions in fuel supply for the 6th Guards Tank Army.[81]

Despite this generally positive assessment, one major rear service shortcoming highlighted in retrospective assessments of the operation has considerable implications for the contemporary support of theater operations on a strategic scale. That is, while emphasizing the importance of having the Rear Service Directorate in the headquarters of the Far Eastern High Command of Forces, the absence of logistic resources directly under its control was a major drawback to its effective operation.[82]

Since such reserves—reserves of the center—had been established and employed as a matter of course by the central rear services and *VGK* in strategic offensive and defensive operations against the Germans, their absence in the Far East was most likely a consequence of resource constraints in this remote theater of military action. In any event, the lack of such resources in the Manchurian campaign reinforced Soviet perceptions regarding the absolute necessity for such strategic logistic reserves to directly support operational formations in a theater of strategic military action.

The Soviet rear services ended World War II with a vastly different structure, governed by far more complex and sophisticated support concepts than had existed in the prewar years. It was geared to support combined-arms operations of sweeping scope, with a rear service management structure centralized at the national level and replicated at the operational and tactical levels. Thus, as a former chief of rear services of the Soviet armed forces pointed out, in July and August 1944 the rear services were "capable of simultaneously and completely supporting the participants in the strategic advance of ten of the eleven fronts which were available at that time."[83] Clear, workable delineations were made between operational and rear service planning and control, which at the same time provided for their integration at all levels. The responsibility of higher echelons to support lower echelons in accord with a center-to-front to army-to-tactical-unit scheme was confirmed, as was the requirement to establish logistic reserves at each level. These would not only support one planned operation, but they would permit formations to undertake subsequent operations without substantial pauses to resupply and regroup. To accomplish this, echeloned systems of relocatable logistic bases at the central and operational levels were created to support combat units and groupings. Echelonment of transport, repair, medical, and other assets was also specified and improved throughout the war.

The coordinated use of all forms of transport under the centralized control of rear service military transportation staffs was developed, with the use of motor transport and aviation becoming increasingly important as the war progressed. Considerable progress was made in employing both motor transport and aviation to resupply mobile groups, with innovative approaches that remain instructive for contemporary rear service planners. Special line of communications troops—railroad, highway, and engineer in particular—played a growing role in building, restoring, and maintaining routes critical to the movement and support of troops.

A development of key importance during the war was the evolution in the role of central rear services from a relatively passive storage and distribution network to that of directly sustaining operational formations engaged in strategic offensive and defensive operations. In the prewar years, planners envisioned that central rear services, fragmented and uncoordinated as they were, would serve principally as a conduit to receive materiel from the national economy and deliver it to the fronts and fleets.[84] However, the experience of the war from its earliest days caused the role of the central rear services to broaden substantially.[85]

As Russian assessments stress, the role and significance of central rear services increased, especially "during strategic offensive operations on foreign territory, when the rear service efforts of operational formations had to be augmented in the theater of strategic military action." A broad spectrum of logistic units, facilities, and materiel under central rear service subordination was moved forward with the fronts and directly supported these formations during strategic offensives, including the utilization of transport, military, and economic resources on foreign territory.[86]

At the end of the war, then, the USSR had established a large and complex logistic system from strategic to tactical levels that despite its shortcomings and limited resource base had successfully sustained the Soviet armed forces through four years of war. This logistical system was critical to sustaining operational maneuver. As with the Soviet armed forces overall, however, Soviet rear service planners and theorists were soon faced with new kinds of military problems generated by rapidly changing weapons technology and future battlefields that promised to be far more demanding for the conduct of combined-arms operations.

Operational Logistics after World War II

The wartime experience addressed above became the focus of study in the immediate postwar years, with Soviet rear service personnel who had distinguished themselves in the war selected for study or teaching at advanced military schools and academies.[87] The logistic lessons learned from the Great Patriotic War and the Manchurian Campaign began to be generalized and incorporated into rear service support concepts and planning, with relatively modest transport and equipment modernization programs simultaneously instituted. By 1950 the last animal-drawn logistic transport means were removed from rear service units and replaced by medium cargo trucks.[88] Nevertheless, motor transport was in limited supply for some years, with Lend-Lease Studebaker trucks provided by the U.S. continuing to be found in Soviet motor transport units into the 1960s.

Clearly, much of the attention of rear service personnel and organizations in the years immediately after the war was directed at the enormous problems of demobilization, force restructuring and modernization, and assistance in rebuilding the national economy that had been devastated by four years of war.[89] But at the rear service schools and academies, attention to important theoretical questions of rear service support was much in evidence, including issues that were to play such an important role in later "new" Soviet operational concepts, including such issues as the support of "operational maneuver groups" and other deep operations forces of various types.[90]

The generalization of war experience, study of theoretical questions of rear service support, and continuing transport and equipment modernization efforts were supplemented by the more direct involvement of the Soviet rear services in supporting combat operations. That is, the Soviet logistic establishment played a large role in providing weapons, equipment, and supplies to the Korean and Chinese armed forces from 1950 to 1953.[91] By 1954, however, the rear services, like the rest of the armed forces, began to address the impact of new weapons, equipment, and troop control means on military operations, including the complex issues associated with operations under nuclear conditions. These developments, which began to fundamentally shape the structure and operational concepts of the Soviet armed forces in the 1950s and beyond, collectively became known as the "revolution in military affairs."

With the overall direction of the Chief of Rear Services, Col. Gen. V. I. Vinogradov, the focus of "experimental research" on emerging rear service support problems became the newly reestablished and expanded Rear Staff of the Ministry of Defense (whose 1953 incarnation, unlike earlier versions, centralized rear control for all of the services) and the Military Academy of Rear and Supply.[92] Vinogradov had headed the Rear Service Directorate within the Far East High Command of Forces during the Manchurian campaign. He presided over a period of substantial change within the rear services and faced considerable pressure to undertake organizational changes that in the view of rear service planners would be poorly conceived. For example, it was decided about 1957 to abolish the post of deputy commander for rear services within troop units, making the position simply that of chief. That greatly undermined the authority of these officers, who no longer spoke in the name of the commander but only as staff specialists controlling only limited rear service resources. In addition, because of the reduced size of the armed forces, it was proposed that operational-level rear services be abolished.[93] Such decisions and proposals seemed to fly in the face of the rear service theory and practice ratified during four years of war.

The clear and still-vivid war experiences mustered in support of rear service arguments and positions during this period were generally successful in shaping logistic force structure and control decisions. A major rear service conference held in 1958 to resolve many of these issues resulted in the reestablishment of the rear service deputy commander position, and a reaffirmation of other structural and organizational aspects of rear service support developed or improved during the war. Following the conference, the practice of appointing line officers to rear service positions became more widespread, including appointing combined-arms commanders to the position of Deputy Minister of Defense/Armed Forces Chief of the Rear. Marshal I. Kh. Bagramian, a World War II army and front commander among other duties, was named Chief of the Rear, with all of his successors to date coming from major field/military district commands.[94] This practice was intended to further the integration of logistic support personnel, organizations, and resources within combined arms units and formations.

While the questions of rear service support under conditions of nuclear weapons employment had begun to be addressed during the 1950s, it was only at the start of the 1960s that nuclear warfighting variants became for a time the principal focus for the Soviet armed forces. Under the apocalyptic view of future war prominent in the early to mid-1960s, it seemed to some Soviet military theorists and planners that traditional methods of rear service support in part had lost their relevance. In their view, a nuclear war of short duration would reduce the requirement for the kinds of sustained logistic support associated with multifront strategic offensives of the last war. Logistic support for fast-moving maneuver forces would have to be far more mobile, and the measured buildup and movement of logistic forces and means would be both dangerous and problematic. Ammunition requirements would be reduced in any case, since nuclear strikes would create large gaps in enemy defenses formerly created by conventional artillery. The reconstitution of weakened maneuver units and formations would neither be possible nor desirable, since warfighting contingencies were based on a ten- to fourteen-day race to the Channel coast and entire divisions would replace those that had lost their combat effectiveness.[95] Such judgments sparked intense debate within the Soviet General Staff.[96]

By the mid-1960s the process of debate and discussion—centered on reconciling traditional approaches to sustaining operations with new requirements—had already modified some of the most extreme views of Soviet theorists predicated on war variants seen as nuclear from the onset of initial operations. Nevertheless, rear services during this period had been tailored to support a fast-moving war of relatively short duration, one almost certainly to be fought with the widespread employment of nuclear weapons throughout the depths of theaters and the USSR itself and with support concepts tailored in accord with such variants.

By 1965, with an emerging Soviet assessment that future general wars would have at least conventional phases, however, rear service planners began to reexamine more intensively just what would be required to support large combined-arms forces under both nuclear and nonnuclear conditions. In preparing a logistic support structure for nuclear war, they renewed their attention to the increasingly complex problems of conventional rear service support. Thus, by 1966 the current rear service chief of staff, Lt. Gen. M. Novikov, felt compelled to assert that "at present we have a logistical arm capable of ensuring mobile operations by the troops in any situation, with or without nuclear weapons involved."[97] Regardless of how Western analysts would assess the accuracy of Novikov's assertion about Soviet logistic capabilities at that time, it clearly pointed to a changing perception of future battlefield requirements by Soviet rear service planners.

Despite changing technologies and new requirements for Soviet logisticians to consider, there were five imperatives throughout the 1940s, 1950s, and 1960s that continued to shape rear service force structure and concepts. These included: (1) the need for greater rear service mobility; (2) the requirement to consolidate and centralize diverse rear service assets into more manageable, responsive units and groupings; (3) the need to establish increasingly more powerful logistic resources from lower to higher levels; (4) the requirement to create rear service control and management bodies that matched those of maneuver units in effectiveness; and (5) the need to develop measures to ensure the survivability of rear service units and resources in the face of increasing threats to rear areas from a variety of strike systems and forces.[98] Despite more than two decades of postwar rear service force modernization efforts and structural improvements introduced in response to these imperatives, the gap growing between rear service capabilities and the requirements generated by far more complex and demanding contingencies became apparent by the 1970s. As a consequence, these imperatives gained, as a Soviet planner might note, "new content" and by the end of the decade generated the largest rear service force restructuring of the postwar years.

Sustaining Theater Strategic Operations

It is clear from a variety of Soviet military writings, both open sources and openly available classified assessments, that by the early 1970s Soviet planners were postulating the conduct of multifront strategic operations without the employment of nuclear weapons. The prospect of conventional operations of increasing duration, as well as the concurrent formulation of concepts for strategic offensives designed to achieve theater goals with the use of conventional weapons only, dictated the implementation of sweeping logistic preparations and rear service force restructuring. Despite a number of at-the-time ambiguous indications throughout the 1970s, however, it was not until some ten years later that Soviet open sources began to speak more candidly about "theater strategic operations" and associated logistic support requirements.

Marshal of the Soviet Union N. V. Ogarkov announced in the summer of 1981 that the basic form of operation in a future war would be the "theater strategic operation," which highlighted for Western analysts that a fundamental change in Soviet planning for theater war had taken place.[99] The former chief of the Soviet General Staff, later commander in chief of the High Command of Forces in the Western Theater of Strategic Military Action (TSMA), went on to note that "in the implementation of complex modern operations," the nation's logistic support system "must make good in a shorter space of time the loss of a huge quantity of combat equipment and weapons, without which it is virtually impossible to maintain the armed forces' combat capability at the necessary level."[100]

In fact, the developments that Ogarkov publicly articulated in 1981 had not sprung full-blown in the 1980s. Rather, Soviet concepts for strategic combined-arms operations in continental TSMAs had been integral to Soviet planning for at least a decade and a half. Thus, by the early 1970s Soviet military educational institutions like the Voroshilov General Staff Academy were instructing Soviet officers in the conduct of all components of theater strategic operations, including rear service support.[101] As Soviet planners envisioned it, a theater strategic operation would comprise a number of major components, coordinated and integrated with each other and carried out in accord with a common plan and concept to achieve defined military-political aims of strategic significance. The Soviet goal was to achieve these aims with the use of conventional weapons only, by rapidly attriting enemy nuclear delivery means and associated control and support facilities, quickly achieving an intermingling of friendly and enemy forces, and so rapidly penetrating opposing defenses that nuclear employment was no longer a useful enemy option. Nevertheless, the constant threat of nuclear use by the enemy would shape the conduct of operations by all force groupings and require contingency nuclear fire planning and readiness for nuclear operations on the part of Soviet commanders and staffs at all levels. Control and planning for theater strategic operations would be exercised by high commands of forces in the TSMAs or, in some cases, directly by the Supreme High Command.[102]

One of the major tasks to which Soviet logistic planners addressed themselves in the early 1970s was the accelerated development of a logistic infrastructure better able to sustain such sweeping conventional operations. Many of these rear service preparations are associated with that component of strategy Soviet planners term strategic deployment and more specifically the discipline within strategic deployment, "preparing the theater of strategic military action." Theater preparation encompasses a broad spectrum of engineer, signal, line of communication, and other preparations for conducting large-scale combined-arms operations. The logistic aspects of these preparations consisted of major programs designed to establish logistic reserves of all types of supplies throughout theater areas, with particular emphasis put on pre-positioning in Eastern Europe ammunition and POL stockpiles capable of supporting many weeks of operations.[103]

The Soviets expected that establishing a theater logistic support structure is among the most complex and time-consuming elements of preparing for the conduct of theater strategic operations, a process that to the extent possible must be accomplished in peacetime. As a consequence, transportation systems and facilities with military application, both in Eastern Europe and the USSR, were improved, and stocks of construction materiel for the repair and restoration of war-damaged rail lines, roads, and bridges were established. Special troop units, notably railroad, highway, and pipeline troops intended for the construction, repair, management, and operation of transportation systems, were expanded and modernized. Among the many tasks assigned to railroad troops, for example, would be restoring the rail transloading zones along Soviet western borders, where broad and narrow gauge rail lines meet. As in the latter stages of World War II, these important facilities would fall under the control of Soviet strategic rear service bodies.[104] Russian planners expected that these other transportation facilities throughout theater areas would be subject to heavy and continuing enemy attack. The establishment and improvement of rail ferry links on the Black and Baltic Seas also constituted rear service theater preparations, which in wartime would supplement other forms of transport for military cargoes.[105]

A major feature of Russian rear service support was the requirement to mobilize large transport and other resources from the national economy to fully establish a logistic support base. Russian planners had to consider what new burdens the prolonged withdrawal of such assets would mean for the functioning of the national economies in a conventional war of extended duration.

The requirement to plan and prepare for the support of theaterwide conventional operations lasting weeks or months shaped the development of new planning norms for ammunition, POL, and other supply consumption; changed rear service deployment and relocation times; substantially increased the requirement for motor transport at all levels; placed new demands on rear service units for the sustained, incremental replacement of losses in maneuver forces and rear service units themselves; and compressed the time that rear service commanders and staffs would have to respond to more demanding support missions. It became clear to Soviet rear service planners that the gap between those support requirements generated by far more capable combat forces, and the capabilities of logistic units to meet these demands, would necessitate logistic restructuring on a large scale.[106]

In the late 1970s, driven by the above considerations, the Soviet rear services began the most sweeping logistic reorganization of the postwar years. Under this reorganization, new "materiel support units" were formed at tactical and operational levels, replacing the older unwieldy system of logistic bases, transport units, and fragmented supply and servicing units and resources. This was the component of the Soviet logistic system charged with the receipt, storage, movement, and delivery of ammunition, POL, and other consumable supply items. New, streamlined "materiel support brigades," each under a single commander, replaced the loosely coordinated and managed army mobile bases and front forward bases. At division and regimental levels, fragmented transport/supply entities were replaced by "materiel support battalions" and "materiel support companies," respectively. This reorganization increased transport lift capabilities, improved rear service responsiveness, facilitated the tailoring and allocation of logistic support packages—especially important for the support of deep operations forces—and assigned rear service units increased responsibilities for their own defense.[107] This logistic reorganization was clearly tied to force-restructuring efforts under way at the same time in other theater force components, which were intended in large measure to structure combined-armed forces for the conduct of nonnuclear theater-strategic operations.

In all these restructuring efforts, a careful examination of historical precedent, supplemented by new battlefield technologies and capabilities, characterized the Soviet approach. As noted earlier the 1981 publication of sanctioned military-historical research topics encompassing a spectrum of critical rear service issues illustrates the role of applicable military precedent in this process.[108] As the 1980s ended, however, Soviet military planners were faced with military restructuring problems the scope of which they had not imagined just a few years earlier, and whose precise direction was far from clear.

Logistics Dimensions of Military Posture in the Late Soviet Period

Even before Mikhail S. Gorbachev's 7 December 1988 unilateral troop reduction announcement, logistic restructuring programs already under way in the 1980s and the application of new technologies to logistic materiel and equipment were both streamlining and reducing the size of the Soviet logistic infrastructure.[109] As noted above, the materiel support system had already been restructured. Because the new materiel support units at all levels provided a much enhanced framework for incremental reinforcement, reductions in their active strength could be reconstituted rapidly through the addition of transport companies and battalions activated from stored equipment sets or mobilized from the national economy, as well as the addition of requisite servicing units of various types. This process would have been far more difficult under the old materiel base system used until the end of the 1970s.[110]

It was clear that both the technical and medical support components of the Soviet theater logistic system were good candidates for precisely the kind of reorganization already carried out in the area of materiel support. The creation in peacetime of multifunctional repair and medical regiments and brigades in place of apparently cumbersome and more loosely controlled technical and medical support groupings and bases would seem a likely development that responded to the same Soviet imperatives that drove the reorganization of the materiel support system.[111]

In an insightful article published early in 1988, Colonel-General Golushko stressed how substantially different the Soviet rear service establishment was going to be.[112] According to Golushko, these changes would come as a consequence of new technology, force restructuring, and "the new defensive strategy" that the Communist Party of the Soviet Union's Central Committee for the Soviet State adopted.[113] He noted in regard to technology's impact that the "qualitative 'boom' [*bum*] in the expenditure and accumulation of [resupply] reserves will diminish."[114] More specifically, these potential developments included:

> A reduction in the gross tonnage, storage, and transport requirements for conventional ammunition due to advances in caseless ammunition, the increased use of precision-guided munitions capable of destroying targets with far fewer rounds, and the employment of directed energy weapons in place of some small arms/artillery systems. Given that conventional ammunition accounts for about 40 percent of materiel consumed by weight, even modest reductions can make a substantial difference in transport and storage requirements. In this regard, Soviet sources have noted that "caseless ammunition having identical ballistic characteristics, are almost twice as light as conventional ammunition, one third smaller in volume, and four times less expensive."[115]
>
> The introduction of more fuel-efficient engines in all military vehicles will reduce fuel requirements to some extent, while the continued introduction of higher capacity cargo trucks to replace more numerous, less capable models, will both lower overall POL consumption and reduce the size of the transport fleet. Fuel-efficient wing-in-ground (WIG) vehicles used in a logistic or troop transport role may contribute to this fuel reduction as well. Like ammunition, POL accounts for approximately 40 percent of Soviet consumable supplies by weight.[116]

While the size of the deployed Russian materiel support system may well be smaller and more mobile for future Russian forces, technical support requirements will certainly increase as Soviet equipment continues to grow in sophistication and complexity. New kinds of weapon systems and equipment (e.g., directed-energy weapons, target acquisition, and communication systems) will dictate new technical support approaches and, quite likely, new kinds of repair and maintenance units.

Those more or less evolutionary changes noted above promised substantial change in the Russian logistic system. However, the sweeping Soviet/Russian military reduction and reorganization announced in December 1988, to be carried out in the context of a new defensive military doctrine, presented new considerations.[117] Additionally, the prospects for sweeping conventional arms control agreements and a rapidly changing political, economic, and international security environment pointed to a radical change in force posture. Without question, Soviet troop withdrawals from Eastern Europe, the German reunification, and the increasingly independent posture of former Warsaw Pact allies fundamentally alters Russian concepts for conducting theater strategic operations, as do nationality problems within the former Soviet bloc itself. They also changed earlier Soviet assumptions about every dimension of coalition logistic support, called into question the future of forward-based logistic stockpiles in Eastern Europe and portions of the former USSR, and raised questions about the security of transport and other support operations in some national republics. All these fears, of course, turned out to be more than justified.

Without question, all the issues noted above utterly disrupted Russian logistic force structure and support concepts in the final days of the Warsaw Pact and the Soviet State. The dismemberment of forward logistic bases in Eastern Europe, the rapid loss of those transportation systems and other military and civilian resources of Warsaw Pact states upon which theater sustainability was to be so heavily based, the declared independence of constituent republics of the USSR and the consequent disruption of cohesive transport and mobilization systems, simultaneous troop withdrawals and drawdowns, and a host of other "logistic" problems in some respects overshadowed the calamitous events of the first period of the Great Patriotic War. In any event, the elaborate, carefully conceived, and heavily resourced system of Soviet/Russian logistic support that reached its high-water mark in the late 1980s was in a few short years destroyed. Nevertheless, it should be emphasized that the concepts that underpinned this system, the historical experience and theoretical formulations upon which they were based, and emerging approaches to complex logistic support problems during the last days of the USSR armed forces all provide a rich body of material for historians and military planners alike. In this respect, Soviet approaches to logistic support in all its dimensions—especially operational logistics—remains a worthwhile focus of study and evaluation.

Notes

1. Rear service support (*tylovoî obespechenie*) comprises three principal components: materiel support, concerned with the supply of ammunition, petroleum (POL), and other consumable supply items; technical support, concerned with maintenance, repair, and the supply of major end items; and medical support in its various forms. See N. V. Ogarkov, ed., *Sovetskaya voennaya entsiklopeyia* [Soviet military encyclopedia] (hereafter cited as *SVE*) (Moscow: Voenizdat, 1980), 8: 152–58, for a discussion of key rear service terms.
2. The problems facing Soviet logisticians are particularly difficult because they must respond not only to military change in all its dimensions, but also to constraints, restructuring, and other developments in the national economy. The application of historical precedent is apparent in a number of ways. For example, an officially sanctioned list of military historical research topics published for the 1981–1990 period identified many issues of rear service experience that clearly were of concern to contemporary planners. See M. M. Kir'ian, "Perspektivnaya tematika voenno-istoricheskikh issledovanii na 1981–1990 gg." [Perspective themes for military-historical research in 1981–1990], *Voyenno-istorichesky zhurnal* [Military-historical journal] (hereafter cited as *VIZh*) (May 1981): pp. 44–47, and (June 1981): 59–61.
3. See I. Safronov, "General Armii A. V. Khrulev" [Army General A. V. Khrulev], *Tyl i snabzhenie Sovetskikh Vooruzhennykh Sil* [Rear and supply of the Soviet Armed Forces], (hereafter cited as *RS*) (September 1972): 85–87; and S. N. Skriyabin, "Iz istorii sozdaniya organov upravleniya tylom Sovetskoi Armii" [From the history of the creation of the rear control organs of the Soviet Army], *VIZh* (July 1979): 54–59, for an account of Khrulev's service, to include his early experiences. Khrulev had served as a political commissar in the First Cavalry Army during the civil war and in various quartermaster posts in the 1930s, among other assignments.
4. Skriyabin, "Iz istorii sozdaniya organov," p. 56.
5. A. V. Khrulev, "Stanovlenie strategicheskogo tyla v Velikoî Otechestvennoî Voîne" [Formation of strategic rear services in the Great Patriotic War], *VIZh* (June 1961): 65. This substantial article (pp. 64–86) is a particularly useful account of the formation of rear service control bodies in the early period of the war. Decisions made at this chaotic time largely proved themselves effective in subsequent military operations and continue to be reflected in contemporary Russian rear service control structure.
6. Ibid.
7. I. M. Golushko, "Iz opyta raboty shtaba Tyla Sovetskoi Armii v gody Velikoi Otechestvennoi voîny" [From the experience of the staff of the Rear Services of the Soviet Army in the Great Patriotic War], *VIZh* (October 1985): 37.
8. Ibid.
9. S. N. Skryiabin and N. Medvedev, "O tyle frontov v nachale Velikoî Otechestvennoî voîny" [On the rear services of the fronts at the beginning of the Great Patriotic War], *VIZh* (April 1984): 32–33.

10. I. Volkotrubenko, "Artilleriîskoe snabzhenie v pervom periode voîny" [Artillery supply in the first period of the war], *VIZh* (May 1980): 71.
11. Ibid.
12. S. K. Kurkotkin, ed., *Tyl sovetskikh vooruzhennykh sil v Velikoi Otechestvennoi voine, 1941–1945 gg.* [Rear of the Soviet Armed Forces in the Great Patriotic War, 1941–1945] (Moscow: Voenizdat, 1977), p. 75. In Khrulev, "Stanovlenie," pp. 65–66, the author blames the People's Commissar for State Control, I. Mekhlis, for the extensive concentration of stockpiles in the border areas that were subsequently lost.
13. Khrulev, "Stanovlenie," p. 65.
14. Ibid.
15. Skriyabin, "Iz istorii sozdaniya organov," p. 58.
16. Khrulev, "Stanovlenie," p. 69.
17. Skriyabin, "Iz istorii sozdaniya organov," pp. 58–59. One of Khrulev's key consultants at this time was the former chief quartermaster of the tsarist Russian Army and former assistant chief of the Red Army's Central Supply Directorate, K. E. Goretskiî. Goretskiî was one of a number of former tsarist quartermaster officers who served the new regime in the first years of Soviet power and in some cases subsequently. See A. G. Kavtaradze, *Voennye spetsialisty na sluzhbe Respubliki Sovetov. 1917–1920 gg.* [Military specialists in the service of the Soviet Republic, 1917–1920] (Moscow: Nauka, 1988), p. 180. In the process of putting together the draft (as described in Skriyabin, "Iz istorii sozdaniya organov," p. 58), Khrulev and Goretskiî disagreed again over a fundamental issue of rear service organization that had been raised first in a discussion they had in 1939. Khrulev, in delineating those rear service entities that should come under his control, "took a pencil and added one more service, artillery supply, to those under the rear service chief's jurisdiction." This would have given Khrulev direct control of all ammunition, artillery, and small-arms supply, as well as weapon repair and maintenance responsibilities. This major logistic role was then the responsibility of *GAU*. Goretskiî, however, as he had earlier, objected strongly to Khrulev's penciled annotation, and was able to dissuade him from adding the artillery supply service to the proposal on the grounds that this key function, because of its vast scope, would be incompatible with Khrulev's other proposed duties. Khrulev reluctantly agreed, thus setting in motion a division of logistic responsibility that continues to the present.
18. As mentioned, Zhukov was opposed to the centralization of rear services outside of the general staff, a view he continued to hold even in the face of the general staff's obvious inability to deal simultaneously with operational and logistic matters. Zhukov attended Khrulev's 28 July meeting with Stalin, and upon reading the draft State Defense Committee directive "declared peremptorily" that: "I do not agree. The authors of the draft want the rear services to undercut the general staff." Stalin, "casting an expressive glance at G. K. Zhukov," took back the draft and immediately signed it. Khrulev, "Stanovlenie," p. 69.
19. This is apparent in part from the continued justifications set out by senior rear service officers after the war and to the present. They reiterate the need for centralized rear service planning and execution to be undertaken by logistic commanders and staffs at the strategic and operational level and point to the consequences suffered in the initial period of the Great Patriotic War when this system was not in place.
20. Golushko, "Iz opyta raboty shtaba Tyla," p. 38.
21. Ibid.
22. Khrulev, "Stanovlenie," p. 69.

23. Skriyabin and Medvedev, "O tyle frontov v nachale," pp. 36–37, discusses the responsibilities of various rear service bodies in this period.
24. I. M. Golushko, "1. Razvitie sistemy upravleniya tylom" [Part 1. Development of the system of control of the rear], *RS* (May 1981): 1. Part 2 of this article, with the same title, was published in *RS* the following month (pp. 13–17). To illustrate how important Stalin considered the front rear service chiefs, it should be noted that the first five appointed included the Chief of the General Staff Academy (Northern Front), the Chief of the Frunze Military Academy (Southwestern Front), the Chief of the Soviet Army Directorate of Military Educational Institutions (Southern Front), the Commander of Troops, Western Military District (Western Front), and the Deputy Commander of Troops, North Caucasus Military District (Briansk Front). Kurkotkin, *Tyl sovetskikh vooruzhennykh sil*, pp.77–78.
25. Skriyabin and Medvedev, "O tyle frontov v nachale," p. 36.
26. Orgarkov, *SVE*, p. 154.
27. U.S. War Department, Technical Manual (TM) 30–430, *Handbook on U.S.S.R. Military Forces* (Washington, D.C.:, U.S. War Department, 1945), p. xi–2.
28. Kurkotkin, *Tyl sovetskikh vooruzhennykh sil*, p. 77.
29. I. M. Golushko, "2. Razvitie sistemy upravleniya tylom" [Part 2. Development of the system of control of the rear], *RS* (June 1981): 16. Typically, in the case of major operations, rear service directives were worked out by the central rear services in accord with operations plans. These directives were signed by the *VGK* commander in chief (Stalin) or the chief of the general staff, as well as by Khrulev. Rear service directives, which delineated front rear areas, transportation routes and capacities, timelines for accomplishing key tasks, and other issues, comprised "the principal operational rear service documents of the strategic rear services." Kurkotkin, *Tyl sovetskikh vooruzhennykh sil*, p. 81.
30. Soviet military historiography divides the course of the Great Patriotic War into three periods: 22 June 1941 to 18 November 1942; 19 November 1942 to 31 December 1943; and 1 January 1944 to 9 May 1945. The victory over Germany, ending the Great Patriotic War, was followed by the "defeat of militarist Japan" (9 August–2 September 1945), the last Soviet strategic operation of World War II. Ogarkov, *SVE* 2 (1976): 55–65, provides an overview of military operations within these periods.
31. Khrulev, "Stanovlenie," p. 74; N. A. Maliugin, "Sovershenstvovanie operativnogo tyla" [Improving the operational rear], *VIZh* (June 1985): 27–28; Kurkotkin, *Tyl sovetskikh vooruzhennykh sil*, pp. 81–82; I. Plotnikov and I. N. Chaban, "Rear Services of the Soviet Armed Forces During the Great Patriotic War," *Istoriya SSSR* [History of the USSR] (January 1975): 5, in the translation by Joint Publications Research Service.
32. Kurkotkin, *Tyl sovetskikh vooruzhennykh sil*, pp. 81–82.
33. Ibid.
34. Khrulev, "Stanovlenie," p. 76.
35. The use or allocation of these air resources was requested from the *VGK* by central and front rear services and often planned, organized, and monitored by rear service commanders and staffs. See Kurkotkin, *Tyl sovetskikh vooruzhennykh sil*, pp. 254–55.
36. Golushko, "Iz opyta raboty shtaba," p. 40.
37. Ibid., pp. 38–39.
38. Plotnikov and Chaban, "Rear Services," p. 7.
39. Ogarkov, *SVE*, p. 154. The navy's rear service efforts were, of course, of considerably less scope and scale than logistic support of the Red Army. In general, naval rear sup-

port during the war years was centered on permanent naval bases with modest numbers of support ships that sustained the fleets and their operations along coastal axes. As the war progressed, the navy gained increasing experience with the deployment of advanced naval bases along coastal axes for the support of amphibious operations and sustaining naval combatants. In the process, naval rear services made far greater use of land transportation and particularly of motor transport to move supplies from fleet main bases to forward facilities. V. Shlomin, "Organizatsiya i sovershenstvovanie tyla VMF" [Organization and improvement of the VMF rear], *VIZh* (November 1975): 42–47, as translated in Joint Publications Research Service, *USSR Military Affairs* no. 66518. The critical importance of rapidly and effectively establishing such advanced bases was impressed on Soviet rear service specialists and naval planners during the war and continues to be identified as a support area requiring the closest attention. Overall, cooperation between the Red Army and Navy rear services became increasingly important in the war, if not as widespread or as effective as Soviet planners judge it should have been. As one authoritative Soviet source put it:

> The experience of the past war demonstrated the importance and necessity of organizing efficient, continuous interaction of fleet rear services with those of other Services of the Armed Forces and their operational formations during joint actions in one or adjacent theaters of military action, as well as unifying designated models of armament and standardizing various Army and Navy materiel support. (Kurkotkin, *Tyl sovetskikh vooruzhennykh sil*, pp. 450–51.)

40. For a definition of strategic reserves, see Ogarkov, *SVE* 7: 553. In building strategic logistic reserves, the *GAU* retained such a tight control of artillery weapons, small arms, and ammunition in 1941 that Zhukov complained he had to beg Stalin for their release. Volkotrubenko, "Artilleriîskoe snabzhenie," p. 72.
41. See Ogarkov, *SVE*, 7: 554, for a discussion of the strategic rear services.
42. Colonel-General Golushko gave a retrospective assessment that summarized the status of Soviet rear services in this period. He noted that while many difficulties lay ahead of the Soviet rear services and changes and improvements would have to be made, "the main thing was done: the system had begun to work with confidence, and its materiel base was being used more purposefully." See Golushko, "2. Razvitie sistemy upravleniya tylom," p. 17.
43. Plotnikov and Chaban, "Rear Services," p. 8.
44. Ibid.; Golushko, "2. Razvitie sistemy upravleniya tylom," p. 17.
45. Golushko, "2. Razvitie sistemy upravleniya tylom," p. 13. See also S. N. Skriyabin, "Sozdanie baz snabzheniya Tsentra" [Creation of the supply base of the Center], *VIZh* (October 1986): 54–60, for an excellent discussion of the role of strategic rear service bases in this period.
46. Kurkotkin, *Tyl sovetskikh vooruzhennykh sil*, p. 108.
47. Ibid., p. 111.
48. As noted in Golushko, "Iz opyta raboty shtaba," p. 43:

> In the course of preparing for the Kursk Battle, the staff of the rear, on the basis of instructions from the general staff, worked out a plan for troop rear support. In behalf of the Voronezh Front, it supervised the construction of the new Starîi Oskol Rzhava railway spur and preparations for the dirt roads; the operation of motor trans-

port units; [and] the supply of personnel with new summer uniforms, good food, and medical supplies.... In the area of the Kursk salient, during the period from March through April 1943, the rear staff and VOSO [Military Transportation Service] bodies handled 141,354 cars of supply freight alone, including: 33,668 cars for Central Front, 31,948 for the Voronezh, 18,359 for the Steppe, 25,905 for the Southwestern, 21,106 for the Briansk, and 10,368 for the Western.

49. Golushko, "2. Razvitie sistemy upravleniya tylom," p. 13.
50. Kurkotkin, *Tyl sovetskikh vooruzhennykh sil*, p. 119.
51. Plotnikov and Chaban, "Rear Services," pp. 10–11. Overall, the role of the central rear services in the second period of the war was key, as Plotnikov and Chaban (p. 12) indicate:

Bases of the strategic rear organizations acquired great significance in the continuous support of forces in their preparation for, and conduct of, offensive operations. All of them made shipments, repaired combat equipment and weapons, procured rations from local resources, and supplied the fronts with ammunition, fuel, rations, and other technical materiel.

52. Kurkotkin, *Tyl sovetskikh vooruzhennykh sil*, pp. 507–08.
53. While in some cases the output of the defense industry was provided directly to operational formations, the central rear services comprised the main link between the armed forces and the national economy. The newly produced materiel was made available in substantial quantities during this period. For example, in 1942 the Soviets reported that "25,436 airplanes, 24,668 tanks, 29,561 guns, and 3,237 rocket launchers were produced." In 1943 the output of heavy industry increased by 19 percent and overall production by 17 percent. This stream of weapons, equipment, and supplies began to flow so rapidly that, for example, the Soviets assessed the ammunition production problem "solved" by the end of that year. Ibid., pp. 106, 129.
54. Plotnikov and Chaban, "Rear Services," p. 8.
55. *Ibid.*; Maliugin, "Operativnogo tyla," p. 32.
56. Plotnikov and Chaban, "Rear Services," p. 15.
57. Kurkotkin, *Tyl sovetskikh vooruzhennykh sil*, pp. 130–32.
58. Ibid., pp. 133–34.
59. Plotnikov and Chaban, "Rear Services," p. 18.
60. Ibid.
61. Ibid., pp. 18–19.
62. Kurkotkin, *Tyl sovetskikh vooruzhennykh sil*, p. 508.
63. S. K. Kurkotkin, "Tyl—pobedy" [The rear—forge of victory], *Voennye znaniya* [Military knowledge] (December 1983): 1.
64. Golushko, "2. Razvitie sistemy upravleniya tylom," p. 15.
65. K. Abramov, "Nekotorye voprosy tylovogo obespecheniya v nastupatel'nykh operatsiyakh tret'ego period voiny" [Several problems of rear support in offensive operations in the third period of the war], *VIZh* (November 1980): 32.
66. Ibid.
67. Ibid., pp. 32–33.
68. Plotnikov and Chaban, "Rear Services," pp. 16, 18.
69. B. Veselov, "Tyl armii v nastupatel'nykh operatsiyakh Velikoî Otechestvennoî voiny" [Rear of the army in offensive operations in the Great Patriotic war], *RS* (February 1979): 33–34; and Maliugin, "Operativnogo tyla," p. 31.

70. Veselov, "Tyl armii," pp. 33–34.
71. L. N. Vnotchenko, *Pobeda na dal'nem vostoke* [Victory in the Far East] (Moscow: Voenizdat, 1971), provides one the best Soviet assessments of the Manchurian campaign, particularly the preparatory activities.
72. Ibid. For a discussion of the composition and missions of the three fronts, see especially pp. 51–53 and 59–84.
73. Ibid., p. 50.
74. Ibid. The direct control of the Pacific Fleet and the Amur River Flotilla, operating in behalf of the overall plans for the strategic operation, was delegated by the Supreme High Command to Navy Commander in Chief N. G. Kuznetsov. See A. Vasilevskiî, "Pobeda na Dal'nem Vostoke" [Campaign in the Far East], *VIZh* (August 1970): 7; A. M. Vasilevskiî, *Delo vsei zhizni* [The work of an entire life] (Moscow: Politizdat, 1983), p. 505; N. G. Kuznetsov, *Kyrsom k pobede* [On a course to victory] (Moscow: Voenizdat, 1977), p. 498.
75. Kurkotkin, *Tyl sovetskikh vooruzhennykh sil*, p. 387.
76. Ibid.
77. Ibid., p. 403.
78. Ibid., pp. 408–09.
79. Ibid.
80. Ibid., pp. 342–86.
81. V. I. Achkasov, ed., "Voennoe iskusstvo osnovnykh gosudarstv, uchastvovavshikh v voine" [Military art of the principal states participating in the war], *Istoriiya vtoroî mirovoî voîny* [History of World War II] (Moscow: Voenizdat, 1980), 11: 440–41.
82. As noted in Kurkotkin, *Tyl sovetskikh vooruzhennykh sil*, p. 420:

> The absence of materiel reserves and reserves of the most important rear service units and establishments (railroad, road, motor transport, air transport, technical support, medical) at the immediate disposal of the Rear Service Directorate prevented it from reacting effectively to all crises occurring in troop rear support. It did not have the potential for extensively maneuvering rear service forces and means among the fronts or operational directions when the situation urgently required such maneuvering.

83. S. Mariakhin, "The Rear and the Front during World War II," *RS* (May 1972): 24, in the translation prepared by the Foreign Science and Technology Center, FSTC-HT23-973-73.
84. Kurkotkin, *Tyl sovetskikh vooruzhennykh sil*, p. 508.
85. As noted in Kurkotin's work cited above (p. 106), the central rear services "not only received military products from the national economy and delivered them to the fronts, fleets, and military districts, but also stockpiled designated reserves of materiel, supported operational and troop evacuation movements, and built, provided technical support to, and restored the most important lines of communication. Centrally subordinated repair facilities carried out the most complex forms of repair on weapons, combat equipment, and property, and manufactured a number of types of military items. A large network of medical institutions provided care to casualties and patients."
86. Ibid., pp. 508–09; Plotnikov and Chaban, "Rear Services," pp. 18–19.
87. For example, in 1946–1947, the faculty of the Military Academy of Rear and Supply included seventy-two generals and officers with combat experience. See I. M. Golushko,

ed., *Razvitie Tyla Sovetskikh Vooruzhennykh Sil* [Development of the rear services of the Soviet armed forces] (Moscow: Voenizdat, 1989), p. 229. Promising officers attended as students, such as Colonel-General Golushko, the chief of the Main Rear Staff in 1989 and one of the most authoritative rear service theorists and planners. Following wartime service as an engineer/technical service officer, Golushko was recognized as an officer deserving of higher military training. After being prevented temporarily from attending the Armored Troop Academy because of war wounds, he was nominated and selected for attendance at the Military Academy of Rear and Supply. Golushko's postwar service is recounted in his memoir Soldaty tyla [Soldiers of the rear services] (Moscow: Voenizdat, 1988).

88. Kurkotkin, *Tyl sovetskikh vooruzhennykh sil*, p. 525. New trucks included the GAZ–51 (2.5 metric ton capacity) and ZIL–150 (4 metric ton) models, both of which began production in 1946. Headquarters, U.S. Army Europe and Seventh Army, USAREUR PAM no. 30–60–1, *Identification Guide: Part Two, Weapons and Equipment—East European Communist Armies, Volume II, Soviet Trucks and Trailers* (Heidelberg, Germany: U.S. Army Europe and Seventh Army, 1974), pp. 14–17, 168–71.

89. Kurkotkin, *Tyl sovetskikh vooruzhennykh sil*, p. 524.

90. An experience of Golushko as a student at the Military Academy of Rear and Supply (later the Military Academy of Rear and Transport) in 1947 illustrates a dimension of the process of identifying and assessing key issues. During the course of a lecture by the distinguished faculty member, Army General F. M. Malykhin, on the topic "Rear Support of a Combined-Arms Army on the Offensive (From the Experience of the War)," Golushko asked the general about the features of logistically supporting tank forces serving as mobile groups in isolation from main supply bases. Malykhin provided only a sketchy answer and indicated that as yet the problem had not been elaborated fully. Several days later, however, Golushko was summoned to Malykhin's office and assigned the task of participating in the Academy's military-scientific research conferences and preparing a study on the topic, "Materiel Support for a Tank Mobile Group in a Combined-Arms Army, Committed to a Breakthrough." The resulting study underwent a number of revisions, was eventually presented in a 1951 military-scientific conference at the Frunze Military Academy in Moscow, and was commended by then Minister of Defense, Marshal A. M. Vasilevskiî. This process, of course, was employed in similar variants time after time to identify and study important rear service research issues. For an account of this episode, see Golushko, *Soldaty tyla*, pp. 47–54.

91. Golushko, *Razviti Tyla*, pp. 216–17.

92. Ibid., p. 220; Golushko, *Soldaty tyla*, p. 124.

93. Golusko, *Soldaty tyla*, p. 151.

94. Ibid., pp. 169–70. In addition to Khrulev, Vinogradov, and Bagramian, deputy ministers of defense/chiefs of the rear included Army General S. S. Mariakhin, a World War II tank commander, postwar Northern Group of Forces (Poland), and Military District commander; Marshal S. K. Kurkotkin, a World War II tank brigade commander and former commander of the Group of Soviet Forces, Germany; and Army General V. M. Arkhipov, who moved to the post from the position of Moscow Military District commander.

95. This 1960s Soviet view was generally accepted in the West as valid long after the Soviets had modified it substantially. See, for example, the early edition of Friedrich Wiener and William J. Lewis, *The Warsaw Pact Armies* (Vienna: Carl Ueberreuter Publishers, 1977), p. 120.

96. See Golushko, *Soldaty tyla*, p. 182. Colonel-General Golushko attended the Voroshilov General Staff Academy from 1960 to 1962, during the height of the internal debates that surfaced these views, and his somewhat understated observations from this period are worth noting:

> During those years, there was a heated debate in military circles and lecture halls over the role of the various armed services and arms of troops in modern war. Some worked for 'large' aviation and large forces of surface ships, with others, on the contrary, proposing that missiles would not only completely replace aircraft and the navy, but also even eliminate artillery. Alekseî Ivanovich Radzievskii [then 1st Deputy Chief of the Academy and later Chief of the Frunze Military Academy] participated in discussions of this question also. In relying on his rich military experience, he helped us correctly assess not only all the advantages of the new and the old so-called classic types of weapons, but also their specific role in the operations of the armed services and arms of troops. [He helped us correctly] work out a well-reasoned attitude toward new tendencies in the development of means of armament and the theory of military art.

97. M. Novikov, "Combat Logistics Today," *Soviet Military Review* (May 1966): 41.
98. These enduring areas of concern to Soviet logistic planners have been addressed in many Soviet military publications and continue to shape Soviet rear service force structure and concepts.
99. N. V. Ogarkov, "Za nashu sovetskuyu rodinu: Na strarazhe mirnogo truda" [For our soviet motherland: on guard for peaceful labor], *Kommunist* no. 10 (1981): 86.
100. Ibid. Published that same year was the two-part article by Colonel-General Golushko, chief of staff of the Rear Services of the Soviet Armed Forces, who took a clear operational-strategic focus in discussing the development of Soviet logistics in World War II and in drawing retrospective lessons from this experience. See Golushko, "Razviti sistemy." This two-part feature highlighted a number of issues key to supporting theater strategic operations that Golushko and other military authors have subsequently addressed.
101. See, for example, the Voroshilov lecture entitled "Strategic Operations in a Continental Theater of Strategic Military Action."
102. As discussed in the Voroshilov general staff lecture materials and other sources, a theater strategic operation may typically include: (1) nonnuclear air operations of combined-arms composition to destroy enemy aviation groupings, nuclear rocket and artillery strike resources, and other key targets in depth; (2) anti-air operations to protect friendly force groupings and contribute to the achievement of air superiority; (3) front operations aimed at defeating enemy ground force groupings within the theater; (4) naval operations in maritime regions of the TSMA to destroy enemy naval groupings, interdict sea lines of communication, and conduct other actions to include the conduct of amphibious landings; (5) airborne operations on an operational-strategic scale to accomplish or support missions ranging from the elimination of smaller, weaker states from an enemy coalition to opening major new areas of combat action deep in the enemy rear; and (6) in a nuclear war, the infliction of theaterwide nuclear strikes by the Strategic Rocket Forces in conjunction with other land-, air-, and sea-based nuclear strike systems. By the mid-1980s Soviet planners had established high commands of forces in four of the five TSMAs around the Soviet periphery. Within these headquarters they established deputy

commanders for rear services to control and coordinate theater rear service support, a development closely analogous to the rear service directorate established in the High Command of Forces that directed the Manchurian strategic operation. Also included in the new theater staff was a deputy commander for armament to control and coordinate theater technical support. See Graham H. Turbiville, Jr., "Sustaining Theater Strategic Operations," *The Journal of Soviet Military Studies* 1 (April 1988): 88.

103. See Ibid., pp. 82–89, for further discussion of Soviet peacetime rear service posture in continental theaters of strategic military action.

104. Kurkotkin, *Tyl sovetskikh vooruzhennykh sil*, pp. 238–40.

105. See, for example, Hans Frank, "The Significance of the Eastern Sea Routes and the Possibilities of Their Defense," *Marine-Rundschau* (September–October 1986): 265.

106. B. Bugrov and L. Morozov, "Separate Materiel Support Battalion," *RS* (October 1984): 19–22; I. M. Golushko, "Rear Services When the Enemy Is Employing Extremely Accurate Weapons," RS (July 1984): 13–17.

107. See Graham H. Turbiville, Jr., "Soviet Logistics Concepts Change," *Army Logistician* (March–April 1987): 2–7, and Turbiville, "Sustaining Theater Strategic Operations," for more complete discussions of this reorganization at the tactical and operational levels.

108. See note 2. The logistic support of mobile groups applied to the contemporary problem of supporting forward detachments, airborne and air assault forces, and "operational maneuver groups" is a particularly good example of the process, with innovations like high-capacity helicopter aviation factored into the approach. Pertinent historical articles include I. Skorodumov, "2-i gvardeîskiî tankovyî korpus v Belorusskoî operatsii" [The 2d Guards Tank Corps in the Belorussian operation], *VIZh* (June 1979): 27–33; V. Odintsov and V. Obsiannikov, "Tylovoe obespechenie podvizhnykh grup" [Rear support of mobile groups], *VIZh* (March 1983): 43–49; A. Krupchenko, "Tekhnicheskoe obespechenie tankovykh i mekhanizirovannykh korpusov, deistovavshikh v kachestve podvizhnykh grup" [Technical support of tank and mechanized corps, acting as a mobile group], *VIZh* (June 1982): 27–33. In another example, the problem of sustaining forces given encirclement missions, K. N. Abramov, "Material'noe obespechenie frontov v operatsiyakh na okruzhenie" [Materiel support of fronts in encirclement operations], *VIZh* (June 1986): 31–38, identifies a number of the special rear service support considerations associated with encirclements.

109. The unilateral Soviet force reductions that General Secretary Gorbachev announced to the United Nations on 7 December 1988 did not address rear service units or resources specifically. However, his assertions that all divisions in the forward area were being reorganized, that six divisions would be withdrawn, and that these unilateral reductions would result in the removal of 50,000 troops and 5,000 tanks from Eastern Europe, by themselves clearly point to substantial logistic restructuring and adjustments.

110. The structure of materiel support units was quite clearly designed to facilitate the rapid augmentation or detachment of unit elements to create tailored logistic support packages, a capability that has advantages for both mobilization and the rear service support of forces tasked to operate in isolation from the main body of troops, e.g., forward detachments, air assault units, and operational maneuver groups.

111. Articles in the Soviet military press continually called for the better control and coordination of all rear service components. Today, deputy commanders for rear services from tactical to operational-strategic levels are directly responsible for materiel and medical support, with a Deputy Minister of Defense for Rear Services found in the Ministry

of Defense itself. Technical support, however, is the direct responsibility of deputy commanders for armament (deputy commanders for technical matters), whose activities are coordinated with rear service deputy commanders at each level and shaped by the rear service deputy's responsibility for developing and overseeing overall rear service plans and his direct control of transportation.

112. I. M. Golushko, "The Rear Services: Yesterday, Today, Tomorrow," *Tyl vooruzhennykh sil* (February 1988): 5–10.

113. Ibid., p. 9. The use of the formulation defensive strategy [*strategiya*] instead of defensive doctrine [*doktrina*] was interesting but not expanded upon further.

114. Golushko, "Rear Services," p. 10. In addition, M. M. Kir'ian, *Voenno-tekhnicheskii progress i vooruzhennye sily SSSR* [Military-technical progress and the armed forces of the USSR] (Moscow: n.p., 1982), surveys a number of these developments in the context of overall military organizational development and technological change, with the newest developments often ascribed to U.S. or other "foreign" research and development.

115. Kir'ian, *Voenno-tekhnicheskii progress*, p. 271. Kir'ian (p. 260) also noted, in regard to foreign work on laser weapons, that such a weapon could "be used repeatedly" and would "not be constrained by the requirement to transport ammunition."

116. Ibid., p. 292, pointed out the high speed and low energy consumption associated with wing-in-ground craft, as well as their effective performance over land as well as water. The first public official U.S. acknowledgment of Soviet work on WIG craft took place in U.S. Department of Defense, *Soviet Military Power*, 5th ed. (Washington, D.C.: Department of Defense, 1986), p. 93. As *Soviet Military Power* indicated, WIG technology "takes advantage of the increased aerodynamic lift that occurs when a wing operating near the surface experiences a reduction of induced drag." Golushko, "Rear Services," p. 10, indicated that in addition to improvements in existing transportation means, "applications will also be found for entirely new transport means which, in the general opinion, will fundamentally change the structure of the rear support system." He may have had WIG developments in mind, among other innovations.

117. See *Military Review* 59, no. 11 (December 1989), for discussions by analysts of the U.S. Army's Soviet Army Studies Office of emerging Soviet military, political, strategic, operational, and tactical developments. The military situation today is in some respects analogous to the 1945–1948 period, when Soviet forces were simultaneously reorganized, reduced, and redeployed at the conclusion of World War II.

PART FOUR: THE UNITED STATES

Introduction

Responding to the American contention that "we were never defeated in battle," a North Vietnamese officer reportedly answered that the statement was "irrelevant." The American defeat was above the tactical level. Lacking was a coherent strategy and the operational objectives that might have supported it. And yet, perhaps one sanguine benefit of America's defeat in Vietnam was the initiation of a renewed interest in the operational level of war. By concentrating on the Russians and the Soviet Union and their understanding of operational art, the American Army started to reconsider its own doctrine of war. In the process, the United States slowly relearned the lessons of its own past about the operational art of war and applied these to the present.

Harold W. Nelson reminds us that the American Army has practiced operational art throughout its history. In fact, the sheer size of the nation and its major wars forced its leaders to broaden the scope of their war planning and the execution of those plans for the first one hundred years of the Republic, while the post–1898 overseas deployments have had the same result. But, as Nelson convincingly demonstrates, the intellectual and doctrinal developments, which ought to have supported such endeavors, lagged far behind and only began to catch up in the period between World Wars I and II. Even then, the postwar development of nuclear weapons appeared to have at least temporarily stalled the emergence of operational concepts in the U.S. Army until it finally chose to address the Soviet threat on its own ground.

Prior to its official inclusion in American military doctrine in the 1980s, nowhere was the practical application of the operational art of war in America more evident than during the Civil War. Arthur Grant examines the Gettysburg campaign from the perspective of the operational level of war and the battle itself. Even though the two opposing generals, Lee and Meade, did not use this specific term, it pervaded their thinking and actions throughout the contest. The author first focuses on the respective objectives that guided General Lee, commanding the Confederate Army of Northern Virginia, and General Hooker and his mid-campaign replacement, General Meade, commanding the Union Army of the Potomac. He writes that Lee's use of deception to dislodge the Union Army from Fredericksburg demonstrated an essential element of the operational art. But the Confederate general's lack of operational intelligence caused him to be surprised by the speedy movement of the Army of the Potomac, another critical component of the operational art and one that certainly affected the conduct of the campaign and the battle of Gettysburg itself. Lee simply failed to appreciate time and space in relation to the growing Union combat power. In contrast, Meade's orchestrated use of mutually supporting corps during the urgent approach marches and his subsequent deployments during the battle itself demonstrated the importance of operational maneuver while in a defensive posture.

Russell F. Weigley redefines the importance of operational-level planning and its absence in the Normandy invasion during World War II and the attempted encirclement of German forces around Argentan-Falaise in June–July 1944. Weigley credits detailed tactical planning with the success of the Normandy campaign but points out several Allied operational successes as well. These included overall intelligence and the knowledge of the main German dispositions; deception measures that tied down significant German forces in the Pas de Calais area; over-the-beach logistical support for a one-million-man force; and operational fires applied by the numbered air forces to bomb paths for a breakout from the beaches. On the other hand, Weigley postulates that lack of operational planning and vision placed the more mobile American forces on the wrong terrain. Moreover, the exploitation of the breakout at St. Lô sent American forces westward for ports in Brittany for their perceived logistical value, when the main Allied objectives were to the east. The effort diverted precious resources and prevented a full exploitation of the Allied success. Lastly, Weigley points to personalities in command and their difficult relationships. The inability to encircle German forces at Argentan-Falaise was caused by a failure to redraw army group boundaries. The blame lay on the operational commanders: Eisenhower, Montgomery, and Bradley. Weigley concludes that the Allies lacked operational objectives during the breakout and never developed an operational focus in the ensuing pursuit.

In the essay that follows, Stanlis D. Milkowski concludes that the small, ill-prepared American Army engaged in Korea achieved a brilliant operational success at Inch'on, which reversed the tide of defeat. His focus, however, is on the post-Inch'on campaign. The sense of victory gained there redefined MacArthur's campaign objectives from the defense of South Korea to the destruction of the North Korean military forces. Here Milkowski analyzes the command relationships in the theater. MacArthur's operational reserve—the U.S. X Corps, used so brilliantly at Inch'on—was subsequently kept under his control. The stroke at Wonsan on North Korea's eastern coast, conceived as a second Inch'on, fell on thin air. In turn, the Eighth Army's lack of logistical support, caused in part by the X Corps' independent movement, slowed its northward pursuit. But X Corps continued to report directly to MacArthur, while the rapid drive into North Korean forces stretched both X Corps and the Eighth Army extremely thin. When the two battlefield commands began to encounter Red Chinese forces, MacArthur chose to ignore his operational intelligence. As a result, when the Chinese intervened en mass and forced the entire Allied force into a disastrous retreat, the cumbersome and split command structure only made the withdrawal, always a most complex maneuver under fire, extremely difficult to execute effectively. Milkowski concludes his assessment by faulting MacArthur's failure to see the operational consequences of a divided command, which crippled his ability to articulate all the elements of his combat forces on or near the battlefield.

These deficiencies were not replicated forty years later, when an international coalition under U.S. leadership crushed the Iraqi Army and liberated Kuwait. By 1991 the operational art of war had become thoroughly embedded in American military doctrine, which was reflected in a variety of training modes, organizational structures, and technological advances. In the concluding essay of this section, Brig. Gen. John S. Brown, the Army's chief of military history, summarizes the most recent developments in the U.S. approach to operational art and how those initiatives were applied so effectively in the first Gulf War. As General Brown succinctly demonstrates, Operations DESERT SHIELD and DESERT STORM were virtually set-piece exercises that represented the maturation of a critical component of American military doctrine.

The Origins of Operational Art

Harold W. Nelson

The Operational Level of War uses available military resources to attain strategic goals within a theater of war. Most simply it is the theory of large unit operations. It also involves planning and conducting campaigns. Campaigns are sustained operations designed to defeat an enemy force in a specified space and time with simultaneous and sequential battles. The disposition of forces, selection of objectives, and actions taken to weaken or to outmaneuver the enemy all set the terms of the next battle and exploit tactical gains. They are all part of the operational level of war. In AirLand Battle Doctrine, this level includes the marshalling of forces and logistical support, providing direction to ground and air maneuver, applying conventional and nuclear fires in depth, and employing unconventional and psychological warfare.[1]

The U.S. fought its wars for more than 200 years without needing an "operational level." *Strategy* and *tactics* were good enough for Clausewitz and Jomini—and for our fathers and grandfathers as they fought the biggest wars known to man. They learned how to plan and conduct campaigns without any special terminology, so why do we need a new term, an intermediate level, in our hierarchy of warfighting concepts? I believe the introduction of the new term reflects a revision in our view of war rather than recent changes in the nature of war. A quick look at some of the things our predecessors wrote and studied convinces me that there was a growing awareness of what we now call the operational level of war long before we introduced the term. Its application should, therefore, help us to understand the use of military force in twentieth-century wars while helping us plan for the future.

In fact, one of the biggest problems with the new term is that it is so old. In the broad sense of the *Oxford English Dictionary*, operations has long been a useful generic term in the language of the military professional. Napoleon and his best-known publicists, Jomini and Clausewitz, all used the term. When Joachim Stocqueler published his *Military Encyclopedia* in 1853, he defined operations as "the resolute application of preconcerted measures in secrecy, despatch; regular movements, occasional encampments, and desultory combats, or pitched battles."[2] An all-encompassing definition such as this does little to clarify the role of operations within the hierarchy of military endeavors, but it does capture some of the meaning we still hope to impart—the relationship between plan and execution. It covers as well the notion of simultaneous and sequential action.

When Col. Henry L. Scott published his *Military Dictionary* during our Civil War, he provided an uninspired, circular definition: "Operations. Field operations; offensive and defensive operations; underground operations; siege operations, etc."[3] This definition reveals the truly generic meaning of the term in its old sense: "operations" didn't actually mean anything until an adjective was added, and then the noun tended to fade into the background, giving a certain ponderous elegance to the resulting phrase but adding little to its meaning. The insidious lexicological implications of this state of affairs is illustrated in Scott's definition of strategy:

> Strategy is the art of concerting a plan of campaign, combining a system of military operations determined by the end to be attained, the character of the enemy, the nature of the resources of the country, and the means of attack and defense. The *theater of operations* selected embraces the territory we seek to invade or that to be defended. It comprehends a *base of operations*; the *objective point* of the campaign; the *front of operations*, that is, the extent of the line occupied by the army in advance of its base; lines of operations, the routes followed to reach the objective point or ends proposed; the lines of communication which unite the different lines of operations together; obstacles, natural or artificial, and places of refuge.[4]

None of this gives us a clear notion of the scope of the theater or the operations to be conducted. It is vague as to space, time, and mass. While this definition reflects the Jominian influence so common in American theory of the day, clarity in the use of the term operations would not have been better served had Clausewitz held sway. When he moved up from tactics to strategy, he wrote: "At the strategic level the campaign replaces the engagement and the theater of operations takes the place of the position. At the next stage, the war as a whole replaces the campaign, and the whole country the theater of operations."[5] Clausewitz shared the common nineteenth-century tendency to define strategy in terms of operations and to think of campaigns as being strategic. Further search in *On War* only clouds the definitional issue: "No one starts a war—or rather, no one in his senses ought to do so—without being first clear in his mind what he intends to achieve by that war and how he intends to conduct it. The former is its political purpose: the latter is its operational objective."[6]

Why not use the word strategic, given Clausewitz's definitional framework? The military dictionaries and encyclopedias published near the end of the nineteenth century reflect the continued broad meaning for operations. Thomas Wilhelm's 1881 dictionary cribbed Stocqueler (quoted above) verbatim.[7] Voyle introduced in English usage the broad formulation linked to strategy and tactics that endured for generals: "Operations, Military—General movements of troops or armies in the field during mimic or real warfare. They are of two kinds, strategic or tactical. The former are undertaken before being within reach of the enemy, whilst the latter take place on the field of battle itself."[8] In fact, the last two sentences of this "definition" merely restate Jomini's definition of strategy and tactics, so we are left with the impression that military operations means little more than the field evolutions of armies.

Before the turn of the century there were two noteworthy efforts to make better use of the general term "operations" to clarify thinking on the art of war. The first of these is in Junius B. Wheeler's *A Course of Instruction in the Elements of the Art and Science of War*, designed for cadets at the U.S. Military Academy. In his preface, Wheeler states, "A correct knowledge of history is only acquired by systematic and methodical study: the study of that part relating to the operations of war should be preceded by a general knowledge of the theory of war."[9] In this formulation, operations are still undifferentiated as to levels of war, but they are separated from theory. This is the sense in which "operational history" has come down to us: We continue to use this term to describe our activity when we discuss the actions of small units or army groups.

Now that we have introduced the operational level of war into our lexicon, while retaining this older meaning, we must guard against occasional confusion. Shortly after Wheeler used operations as a term to help his students differentiate between theory and practice, an instructor at the Artillery School at Fort Monroe was using the term to bring theory up to date. William Kobbe was far more Clausewitzian than many of his contemporaries, and he was very well attuned to the situation in Europe at the turn of the century: "In modern war the opening of the campaign follows the declaration [of war] so closely that there is no time, as there was formerly, to mature plans: they must be established in peace. They will consist of 'The Plan of War' and the 'Project of Operations.'"[10]

Kobbe saw the former as largely the province of government and the latter as the responsibility of the military. He defined the art of war as that of overthrowing an enemy by an armed force:

> The means and methods of doing this are called the "operations of war" and the territory in which they are employed is called the theater of operations.
>
> The operations of war consist in overcoming the natural and artificial obstacles which may be met. Natural obstacles are the climate and topographical features of the country: artificial obstacles are temporary and permanent fortifications, the troops of the enemy, and negatively, the necessity for supplying troops and providing for their security and repose.[11]

This use of the term operations is only loosely linked to levels of war and includes both planning and the execution of plans. It also begins to reflect the idea that operations form something of a continuum, not being merely a cycle of preparation, engagement, and pursuit. This notion that war might be tending away from the climactic battle of the Napoleonic era was difficult to support at the turn of the century. Battles had expanded in space and time because of the evolution of mass armies and railroads. The evidence of the Civil War and the wars in Europe all seemed to point toward operations culminating in a single large battle. For example, Gettysburg, Sadowa, and Sedan suggested the principal feature of the military art. Siege operations (e.g., Vicksburg, Paris, and Plevna) also reflected changes flowing from the modifications of objective circumstances that had changed field operations, but these changes in scale and lethality seemed to bring nothing fundamentally new to the art of war. However, with the U.S. Army's 1905 *Field Service Regulations*, we begin to see the changes in the attitude toward the decisive battle that would ultimately result in recognition of an operational level: "Engagements are usually preceded by operations the object of which is to locate the enemy without committing the main body to action. These preliminaries begin with the action of independent cavalry and culminate in the contact of the advance guard."[12] The image here is one of building toward a crescendo—the decisive battle—but the preliminaries have begun to expand in space and time and in importance because of the nature of modern weapons.

The 1910 *Field Service Regulations* contain virtually the same characterization of preliminaries and the decisive battle,[13] but this later version discusses the implications of modern weapons in far more detail:

> Increased rapidity, accuracy, and range of small arms have increased the difficulties of a frontal attack. Without superiority of fire we may assume the frontal attack as impracticable. If we consider two lines as consisting of infantry only, this superiority cannot be secured unless the number of rifles put into action by the assailants is either greater than the number opposing them, or the assailants are decidedly better shots or more skillful in the use of cover than the defenders, or the latter are surprised or have been demoralized by previous defeats and the assailants have an unquestioned moral ascendancy over them. Frontal attacks are not impossible, but in order to be successful the assailants must gain a superiority of fire and be willing to pay the price of victory.
>
> Nearly all the factors that make frontal attack difficult inure to the advantage of the offensive in enveloping and flanking attacks. For example, the longer the range of the weapons, the greater is the capacity for converging fire on salients of the enemy's line; and the neutral color of uniform which hides the defenders, also favors the assailants by concealing their turning movements.
>
> While the improvement of small arms has benefited the defensive, improvement in field artillery has increased the advantages of the offensive, whether in frontal or flank attacks. The great range and rapidity of fire of field artillery, and its ability to fire while concealed, enable the assailants to accumulate a crushing superiority at the desired point without discovery by the defenders, to open an accurate and overwhelming fire as a surprise, and thus to acquire an ascendancy that becomes more pronounced as the power of that arm increases.
>
> It is impossible to shoot an enemy out of position. To avoid serious losses, the defender has only to lie down behind cover; but a resolute and simultaneous

advance on the front and flank of a position, made after a thorough preparation by and with the effective accompaniment of artillery and infantry fire, will generally be successful.[14]

The *Field Service Regulations* did not work out the implications of this state of affairs as completely as some independent analysts did. Rudolph von Caemmerer's insights merit attention:

> Tactical concentration of portions of the enemy's army, which is once complete, can no longer be penetrated, be the line ever so thin in the center. Tactical envelopment, owing to the armaments and the size of the armies, has gained far too great an ascendancy to make this possible. Penetration must be absolutely strategic, however near the battlefield it may have been brought about—that is to say, we must be able to beat one portion of the enemy, while the other is or will be prevented from taking part in this operation by its fire. A day's march indicates perhaps the minimum distance which will ensure protection against this contingency.[15]

While Caemmerer uses only the terms strategic and tactical to describe the levels of war, he has outlined an imperative of twentieth-century warfare—imposed by the range, rate of fire, and lethality of modern weapons—that would force professionals to think at the operational level as well. The strategic objective of destroying the enemy's army required simultaneous tactical engagements to fix his forces frontally while enveloping them, and the distances involved would be much greater than in earlier wars. The sequential linking of preliminaries and the size and complexity of the engagements that comprised the decisive battle had now resulted in a new level of planning and execution in war.

I can find no evidence that the U.S. Army had grasped this change before 1914. Under General Bell's leadership the manuals and schools were greatly improved, but the main doctrinal thrust was to standardize orders and procedures within a campaign framework that would be little changed from Civil War experience. Arthur Wagner's work is illustrative:

> The two great divisions of the Art of War are Strategy and Tactics. Tactics may be divided into maneuver tactics and fighting tactics; the first relating to the movements by which troops are brought into position on the field of battle, and the second having reference to the formations for attack and defense and the handling of troops in actual battle. Maneuver tactics furnishes the connecting link between strategy and tactics; as it consists entirely of drill movements, which, being also employed in marching, pertain as well to strategy; moreover it forms the transition from the movements in the theater of operations to those of actual conflict.[16]

Wagner knew there was a link between strategy and tactics, but his is the Napoleonic link—not fully suited to the requirements of contemporary warfare. Eben Swift suspected that demands of modern war were different from Napoleon's day: "Brilliance of the old kind has little of its old chance in these days of entrenchments and long range artillery."[17] But he devoted his efforts to teaching officers the relationship between tactics and terrain so they would be effective in the new environment. Wagner with his theory and Swift with his application were teaching officers sound, interactive, situational approaches to the use of military force. Their efforts inevitably focused on the tactical level: Their students had little professional education, the U.S. Army was small, and the sources they modified to American needs were cast in the "decisive battle" mold.

As we have been reminded so often, the material realities that made decisive battle so difficult to achieve on the major fronts in World War I surprised the military professionals of all combatant nations. Once there were no flanks to envelop the lethality of modern weapons combined with massive industrial production and manpower resources to produce formidable defenses in depth that could be penetrated but proved highly resistant to breakthroughs. After the war, American officers adjusted their thinking to reflect the larger organizations necessary to fight in this type of warfare, but they were slow to develop new concepts to deal with the larger battlefields:

> During the World War, not only was old material improved and new material of all kinds created, but the personnel engaged was so large as to involve practically a national effort. This large personnel with arms of all kinds necessitated the most careful organization, control and coordination, extending especially to the Large Units. A broad knowledge of the constitution, capabilities and functioning of these units was indispensable.[18]

Before the war ended, the U.S. Army translated the French Army's *Instruction on the Offensive Action of Large Units in Battle*.[19] This volume provided detailed discussion on force requirements and planning imperatives associated with the complex combined-arms action required to launch a penetration of sufficient size to carry through deep defensive belts with adequate residual power to roll up the flanks and exploit in the rear. The need for higher-echelon commands and staffs—armies and army groups—to deal with the masses of men, materiel, and planning details was explicit, but the battlefield function performed by these large units was perceived as tactical. Thinking in terms of decisive battle, these practitioners of the military art merely perceived higher stakes, not a new game.

After the war, the U.S. Army's doctrine and higher-level professional instruction tried to place the apparent lessons of the war on the Western Front into a larger context. The 1923 *Field Service Regulations* stressed concentrating superior force at the decisive place and time so that successful offensive operations—even when outnumbered—could destroy the enemy's armed forces. In the decisive attack, an infantry division might cover a frontage of only 2,400 to 4,000 yards, and extensive depth would be required, but penetration on a "stabilized front" was possible if the situation demanded. However, moving the army from its area of concentration through the meeting engagement to the decisive battle presented a more palatable scenario.[20]

The Army War College's early postwar effort at doctrine for large units presented the same optimistic picture of future decisive offensive battle, with one important difference. It explicitly noted:

> The modern battle is characterized by its great length and the rapid exhaustion of the troops engaged. The length of the battle is the result of various elements but most of all the power of the armament and the solidity of the organization of the ground. The wastage of troops is brought about by exhaustion of morale, losses sustained, and hardship suffered.... [T]he offensive battle takes the form of successive violent actions preceded by periods of preparation and movement, both of variable length.[21]

Unfortunately, this statement in a provisional draft was not incorporated into subsequent doctrinal manuals and was soon forgotten.

The schools at Fort Leavenworth and the Army War College continued to use map problems in their applicatory method. By concentrating on situations set, however improbably, in the United States, they managed to present problems with armies and army groups similar to those used in World War. I, but spread over longer lines with greater opportunity for maneuver, envelopment, and short, decisive battle.

By 1922 Hugh Drum had been instrumental in producing a volume of *Tactical and Strategic Studies* for use at Fort Leavenworth. It portrayed a series of problems facing an army operating along a Harrisburg-Washington, D.C., front employed as part of an army group headquartered in Pittsburgh that was attempting to defeat a Red force in Baltimore. The "plan of campaign" for this army was the basic conceptual tool underlying the studies.[22] In a related problem students were faced with a "Scarlet Coalition," Canada and Great Britian, occupying the northeastern United States and required to develop a concept of operations for a corps-level amphibious operation against Nova Scotia.[23] In both cases, the situation required bold maneuver and the relatively low density of troops in the active theater made it possible for students to think in terms of decisive battles rather than protracted conflict.

In 1923 Leavenworth raised its sights to the army group, noting that even though U.S. forces in World War I had needed no such organization, its use might be indicated in the future. Causes for such innovation were thought to include span of control imperatives when general headquarters was engaged in extremely large and disparate strategic endeavors, coordination requirements when two or more armies were operating with a common end, the need to optimally position and use mobile reserves along a single extensive front, or to provide centralized direction on a single line of operations within a large complex theater.[24] Since most of these situations could not have been derived directly from the historical record of World War I, the theoreticians were clearly using their classroom exercise with large units to derive insights into the organizational implications of the extended operations possible in industrialized warfare. By 1926 Leavenworth's treatment of the functions of larger units — army, corps, and division — had surfaced the difficulties associated with thinking at that level:

> There is, in reality, no marked dividing line between [strategy and tactics]. Commanders of small units are concerned almost entirely with tactics, whereas the commander of an army may be concerned largely with strategic questions as well as tactical ones. Where tactical and strategic considerations conflict, tactical considerations must govern. The gaining of decision in combat is of primary importance.[25]

Could that last assertion be correct? If so, what were the implications for commanders of larger units? They were encouraged to impede the tendency for the tactical tail to wag the strategic dog:

> A plan of operations always should be formulated. This includes primarily a study of the theater of operations (terrain, road/railroad, possibility of supply).... The mission and objective will determine the depth of advance. Generally speaking, a plan of operations will include five main phases, viz., mobilization, concentration, advance, occupation of positions, and combat.[26]

When we consider the phases of this plan of operations, we can clearly see that it has little to do with what we now call the operational level of war. Mobilization and concentration of forces are clearly strategic actions reflecting plans, decisions, and priorities at the highest levels — today we would associate these activities with the National Command Authority. The advance of the armies and occupation of initial positions probably match our concepts of the operational level, but combat — unless aggregated into theater-level results — is the tactical concern of divisions and corps. Confusion caused by lack of clarity in terminology is seen most clearly in the *Manual for Commanders of Large Units (Provisional)* published in 1930. This manual envisioned the commander in chief in his general headquarters commanding a theater of war with army groups and armies as his subordinate headquarters:

> [The commander in chief] draws up and issues strategic plans in accordance with the general policies prescribed by the President. He specifies the personnel and supplies of all kinds required for his field forces, requests their allocation, and establishes policies and priorities for their distribution.[27]
>
> The group of armies is a tactical unit. In accordance with missions assigned to him by GHQ, the group commander draws up tactical plans, issues orders to

armies, special troops, and reserves under his command, apportions to the armies the forces at his disposal, allots zones of action or sectors to the armies, and coordinates their movements and efforts.[28]

    The army is the fundamental unit of strategic maneuver. The army commander draws up tactical and administrative plans for the employment of the army, under instructions from higher authority.... [T]he army commander himself conducts the battle, by constantly assuring coordination of the efforts of his subordinates whom he had already informed of the general plan. He gives to the operation that unity of direction so indispensable to success, and he impresses his own determination on its execution.[29]

These quotes show that most of the elements we now associate with the operational level of war were present in these doctrinal statements, though badly obscured by the nomenclature. Given that situation, it appears that the War College faculty sidestepped the swamp of ill-defined doctrinal nomenclature when they divided their course of instruction into "Preparation for War" and "Conduct of War" phases in the early 1930s. This approach allowed them to teach much of what our generation would call national security policy, strategy, and management in the first phase and then devote the remainder of the curriculum to campaign considerations. There may have been some question as to the boundary between strategy and tactics in developing and executing war plans, but this approach cut through the confusion and gave every student a thorough grounding in what we now call the operational level.[30] Throughout the "Conduct of War" phase of the course, students were required to study at least two historical campaigns (beginning with Napoleonic warfare and ending with the Russo-Polish campaign of 1920), comment on trends, and then: "After a consideration of the present trend in development of weapons and other means of warfare, the study will culminate in a statement of the important lessons drawn from each campaign studied that may be of assistance in planning for and in the conduct of war."[31] Students were organized into subcommittees of twenty-five participants to study and present evidence on specific campaigns. A broad range of operational-level topics was covered: objectives of campaigns in furtherance of national aims, means for combat, command at the theater level, plans for war and initial operations of wars, plans, and their execution in joint operations.[32]

After honing their thinking with these analyses of historical trends, students conducted what we would call a transition-to-war command post exercise at the army level and then a map exercise based on a student version of an actual war plan—usually Plan Orange. The map exercise emphasized command decisions, and the class was reorganized as command groups to study and report on each map problem.[33]

This combination of analysis of historical trends and conduct of map exercises gave the War College graduates sound insights into the operational level of war, even though contemporary doctrine may have been confused. By looking at trends rather than merely reviewing the events on the Western Front, they continued to consider maneuver as well as administration and firepower and developed great mental flexibility. By contemplating the enormous mobilization base and force structure necessary to project power to the Philippines, they kept the mobilization and logistics requirements of global warfare firmly fixed in their minds, even though they came to the War College from a small army weakened by Depression-era budgets. We can attribute the graduates' successes in every theater of World War II at least partially to this educational experience.

Military victory in 1945 seems to have provided little impetus for revising U.S. doctrinal views to make room for an operational level of military thinking. The Army struggled for survival in a period of rapid demobilization in which many theoreticians saw the long-range bomber and the atomic bomb as instruments that would make large-scale ground operations obsolete. The situation was different in the Soviet Union, so it was natural for Soviet military thinkers to develop their thoughts on the operational art, their term for what we have now come to call the operational level of war. In their discussions, Soviet authors analyzed the military lessons of twentieth-century war and in a smug, heavy-handed, Stalinist way, congratulated themselves on having a military theory with room for the operational art. In doing so, they defined and outlined the utility of this new theoretical tool with some care. Their early postwar articles, as translated by the U.S. Army at the time, still make interesting reading. A few highlights from these articles should clarify some familiar points:

> War in the capitalistic era, with its mass armies and its great quantities of material of the most varied types, became more complicated than it had been in former years. In order to achieve the objectives of war under such conditions, as the experience of recent wars has shown, a number of relatively lengthy campaigns must be fought. Each of these in turn consists of a number of simultaneous and successive operations carried out on various sectors of the front. An operation, involving mass armies with millions of men, during the machine period of war has become a characteristic and well-defined phenomenon.[34]
>
> In the second half of the nineteenth century conditions that determine the development of the military art changed radically from what they had been in the time of Napoleon. A whole series of new factors arose, growing out of the development of industrial capitalism and the consequent rapid growth of productive capacity and equipment. The introduction of universal military service led to the establishment of mass armies. The appearance of railroads made it possible to concentrate forces far more rapidly, and they could be deployed over very broad fronts. The scale of combat became decidedly grander. In place of the single "general" battle which formerly had often decided the outcome of the war, now there usually was a number of major and smaller battles and engagements. Under these conditions, the commander had to be able skillfully to unite the efforts of his forces, deployed over

a sizable area, in order to achieve the overall aim of the war. Thus, military actions by the end of the nineteenth century had taken on new typical characteristics which in one way or another were basically similar to our present concept of operations. A number of new developments in the military art could not be considered as being in the sphere of strategy, but at the same time they did not bear directly on tactics. But the military thought of those times was incapable of dialectically taking these new experiences and setting them in the context of historical background in order to reveal the significance of the new developments.[35]

Early in World War I the conduct of an operation became the task of an army, which previously had had the task of accomplishing strategic missions. And at the same time, the number of armies grew causing the introduction of higher echelons (fronts in Russia, army groups in the West).[36]

In World War I the tempo of the offensive was still a great deal slower than the tempo of maneuver of the reserves of the defender. World War I was a step in the process of development of the operational art. But it did not solve the problem of the operational breakthrough.[37]

In the 1930s in the Soviet operational art there was formulated the theory of the deep offensive operation. The basis of this theoretical formulation was laid on the recognition that operations in future wars, in contrast to operations in World War I, could and would bear an active character, pursuing decisive ends and taking the form of crushing offensive blows through the entire depth of the operational defense. It was anticipated that in spite of the expected increase in the operational density and solidity of fronts, in the firepower and the engineer preparations of the defense, the availability of new mobile offensive weapons would make it possible, after the breakthrough of the defensive zones, to come out into broad maneuver space in the enemy's rear and carry through a decisive offensive battle for the destruction of the enemy. The depth considered possible for a blow by mobile forces was determined by the operational depth of the enemy defensive (up to 100–120 km).[38]

The Soviet doctrine writers observed our own writings on the subject:

[O]ne can detect a whole series of contradictions in the American field service regulations in definitions of strategic and tactical forces. Thus, in one part of the FSR [field service regulations] in which the actions of army groups are discussed, it is said that an army group is a tactical force. Elsewhere, army groups, armies, and corps are all defined as strategic units: while in another part of the regulations the actions are referred to as tactical. In yet another passage an army is defined as "an administrative-tactical organization with administrative, territorial and tactical functions."

In accordance with our own debate on the workings of airpower in the conduct of war and the practice of campaigns, the Soviets observed:

All this only confirms that the military art of the American Army has no strict system of scientific theory. Moreover, in the American Army, the old discredited "idealistic" military theories of the alleged obsolescence of mass armies continue to be accepted as well as theories to the effect that the Air Force alone can decide the outcome of a war (General Arnold's pet theory). Or else "atomic war" is presented as the ultimate in military affairs, with all other elements of war being crowded off the stage by atomic energy.[39]

Based on the experience of the most recent wars, Soviet military art holds that operations as a new phenomenon in the conduct of military actions has made for itself a definite and clear-cut place in the conduct of war. The modern definition of operations holds that this is the organized joint action of large military bodies (armies, army groups, and organizations of like size) carried out on a common sector or in a single direction and all arising out of a single plan of action and all aimed at the attainment of a single overall objective.[40]

The most important tasks of the operational art, in accomplishing the missions assigned to forces of operational dimensions by the overall strategy of the country's leadership, consist of: working out an operational plan; determining the forces, methods of employment and leadership of operational formations in the operation at hand; determining the means and methods by which coordination of the various arms and service will be accomplished; determining the character and order of cooperation among the various large operational formations taking part in the operation; carrying out all the preparatory measures necessary for the organization and subsequent conduct of the operation; and the carrying out of the operation and the direction of the troops during the course of the operation.[41]

The highly significant problems relating to the modern operational art [are] the organization and conduct of a defense capable of standing up to mass attacks by tanks and powerful aviation and at the same time creating favorable conditions for the launching of a decisive counteroffensive; the working out and application of new forms and methods of the conduct of the offensive designed to solve two important requirements of offensive operations, namely, the breakthrough of dense and solidly developed defenses in great depth and the exploitation of such breakthroughs in such manner as to paralyze enemy resistance in the total operational depth of his position: the organization of the direction and leadership of great masses of troops heavily equipped with various kinds of mechanized equipment and the employment of such forces for rapid maneuver and massing in the direction of the main effort; the organization of operational cooperation among the various arms and services which are brought together for participation in large-scale operations.[42]

When we recall that these Soviet thoughts have been around for nearly forty years and have been updated and perfected in a large, dedicated body of military leaders throughout that period, we have a tendency to become a bit alarmed. Before throwing up our hands in despair or surrender, two thoughts merit consideration. With the exception of the central region in Europe, the massive prolonged combat stretched over immense space and time that gave birth to the operational level cannot really flourish. As an Army with global commitments, we are wise to view operational-level thinking in a broader context than did our Soviet brethren. How much good did their forty years of thinking about the operational art really do them in five to ten years in Afghanistan? Did the absence of an operational level in our military theory really make that much difference in Vietnam? In Korea?

This situation before World War II that I have outlined above seems to indicate that our knowledge sometimes transcends our doctrinal terminology. The work done in service schools and at major command headquarters since World War II may not have been uniformly aimed at solving problems at the campaign level, but many problems have been solved and many problem-solving techniques learned. This gives us a very firm foundation for making imaginative and productive use of the operational level as we analyze the products of that work, the lessons of twentieth-century war, and our preparations to meet the challenges across the spectrum of conflict.

Notes

1. Department of the Army (DA), Field Manual (FM) 100–5, *Operations* (Washington, D.C.: Department of the Army, 1982).
2. Joachim H. Stocqueler, *The Military Encyclopedia* (London: William H. Allen, 1853), p. 203.
3. Henry L. Scott, *Military Dictionary* (New York: D. Van Nostrand, 1864), p. 433.
4. Ibid., p. 574.
5. Carl von Clausewitz, *On War*, ed. and trans. Michael Howard and Peter Paret (Princeton: Princeton University Press, 1976), p. 358.
6. Ibid., p. 579.
7. Thomas Wilhelm, *A Military Dictionary and Gazetteer* (Philadelphia, Pa.: L. R. Hamersly & Co., 1881), p. 368.
8. Maj. Gen. George E. Voyle, *A Military Dictionary* (London: William Clowes and Sons, 1876), p. 276.
9. Junius B. Wheeler, *A Course of Instruction in the Elements of the Art and Science of War* (New York: D. Van Nostrand, 1879), pp. v–vi.
10. William A. Kobbe, *Notes on Strategy and Logistics* (Fort Monroe, Va.: Artillery School Press, 1896), p. 17.
11. Ibid., p. 16.
12. U.S. Army, *Field Service Regulations* (Washington, D.C.: Government Printing Office, 1905), p. 101.
13. U.S. Army, *Field Service Regulations* (Washington, D.C.: Government Printing Office, 1910), p. 159.
14. Ibid., pp. 157–58.
15. Rudolph von Caemmerer, *The Development of Strategical Science during the 19th Century*, trans. Karl von Donat (London: Hugh Rees, Ltd., 1905), p. 263.
16. Arthur L. Wagner, *Organization and Tactics* (New York: B. Westermann and Co., 1895), pp. 1–2.
17. Eben Swift, "Remarks, Introductory to the Course in Military Art" (Fort Leavenworth, Kans.: Command and General Staff College, 1904), p. 8.
18. U.S. Army War College (AWC), *Provisional Manual of Tactics for Large Units* (Washington, D.C.: Army War College, 1923), p. 1.
19. Headquarters, American Expeditionary Forces (AEF), *Instructions on the Offensive Action of Large Units in Battle* (from the French edition of 31 October 1917) (Chaumont, France: Headquarters, Army Expeditionary Forces, 1918), pp. 69–80.
20. U.S. Army, *Field Service Regulations* (Washington, D.C.: Government Printing Office, 1923), pp. 77–100.
21. AWC, *Provisional Manual*, p. 64.
22. General Service Schools, *Tactical and Strategical Studies, Corps and Army* (Fort Leavenworth, Kans.: General Service Schools, 1922).
23. Col. Conrad H. Lanza, *"Illustrative Problem: Strategy of the North Atlantic"* (Fort Leavenworth, Kans.: General Service Schools, 1922).

24. General Service Schools, *Tactical and Strategical Studies: A Group of Armies* (Fort Leavenworth, Kans.: General Service Schools, 1923).
25. General Service Schools, *General Tactical Functions of Larger Units* (Fort Leavenworth, Kans.: General Service Schools, 1926), p. 3.
26. Ibid., pp. 1–2.
27. War Department (WD), *A Manual for Commanders of Large Units (Provisional), Vol. 1: Operations* (Washington, D.C.: Government Printing Office, 1930), p. 7.
28. Ibid., pp. 13–14.
29. Ibid., p. 21.
30. For an excellent account of the forces shaping the U.S. Army War College and its curriculum, see Harry P. Ball, *Of Responsible Command: A History of the U.S. Army War College* (Carlisle Barracks, Pa.: The Alumni Association of the U.S. Army War College, 1983).
31. AWC, *Conduct of War Course*, vol. 5, pt. 1, "Analytical Studies" (Washington, D.C.: Army War College, 1933).
32. Ibid.
33. Ibid., pt. 2.
34. L. Vetoshnikov, "The Operational Art and its Place in the Soviet Art of War," *Voennaya Mysl'* no. 4 (1949):1 (U.S. Army translation).
35. V. Zlobin and L. Vetoshnikov, "Concerning the Operational Art of the Soviet Army," *Voennaya Mysl'* no. 3, (1947): 1 (U.S. Army translation).
36. Ibid., p. 2.
37. Ibid., pp. 5–6.
38. Ibid., pp. 9–13.
39. Vetoshnikov, "Operational Art and Its Place," p. 4.
40. Ibid., p. 6.
41. Ibid., p. 7.
42. Ibid., p. 13.

Operational Art and the Gettysburg Campaign

Arthur V. Grant

It was nearly unanimous: The Army of Northern Virginia would take the war to the enemy. With the exception of the Postmaster General, the Confederate cabinet voted and approved Robert E. Lee's proposal in May 1863 to invade Pennsylvania. Confident of success, the government placed its hopes in the South's most successful commander. He would redeem the Confederacy's declining fortunes and preserve the new nation's future. The hope for a successful military strategy was now in the hands of the operational commander.[1]

As a concept, the operational level of war did not exist during the American Civil War. Strategy and tactics were frequently used terms, but even they lacked the precise meanings we assign to them today. Having rushed into a war for which neither side was prepared, both Northern and Southern leaders were more interested in finding out what worked than in academic discussions about levels of war. Nevertheless, by May 1863 both sides were aware of the intimate relationship between politics and war at the theater level. They understood that operational successes and failures determined their nation's political future.

In the previous September, the commander of the North's principal eastern army, the Army of the Potomac, was relieved from command partly for misunderstanding that relationship. Maj. Gen. George B. McClellan had been involved in political arguments with the President of the United States, but he had been unable to deliver the military victories that might have made his political opinions more important. Similarly, early the next spring, a different commander of the Army of the Potomac had also made strong political statements mentioning that the nation needed a good dictatorship to pursue its goals successfully. Abraham Lincoln told that general that if he could deliver military victories, the president was prepared to worry about the threat of dictatorship. Politics and war were on everybody's mind.[2]

Only in the western theater was the North collecting military victories that might provide political hope for the future of the United States. Maj. Gen. Ulysses S. Grant started a virtually uninterrupted series of victories at Forts Henry and Donelson in February 1862, and by May

1863 his army stood at the gates of Vicksburg, Mississippi. Everyone understood the political importance of Vicksburg. To the United States, Vicksburg represented the only remaining impediment to reopening the river-borne trade from the northwest. Its seizure would open the Mississippi River, cut the Confederacy in two, and provide important political capital for continuing the war. To the Confederate states, Vicksburg was a link to the west and the scene of four previous Northern failures. As Grant's ring of troops tightened their hold around it, Southern leaders argued over its importance and Confederate strategy. Many of the strategic discussions hinged on the issue of the political outcome that could be expected. Politics and war were closely intertwined.

Strategic Setting

The Confederacy was in a difficult strategic position. The South's resources were strained severely by the three major fronts along which the Northern armies operated. Grant was hammering at Vicksburg. In central Tennessee, Maj. Gen. William S. Rosecrans aimed the Army of the Cumberland at the heart of the Deep South. Only in northern Virginia was there hope. Robert E. Lee had checked, had outmaneuvered, and finally had driven a much larger Army of the Potomac back across the Rappahannock River near Chancellorsville in early May 1863. Lee's brilliant victory seemed to offer opportunities. But the strategic meaning of those opportunities was not clear.

In mid-May Lee discussed alternatives with President Jefferson Davis, Secretary of War James Seddon, and other members of the Confederate cabinet. As in many important strategic discussions, much of the talk focused on priorities.[3]

There was a strong move afoot to shift some troops from Lee's army to the Confederate forces in front of Vicksburg. Lee's resounding victory at Chancellorsville bolstered this argument because most of the corps under James Longstreet had been on operations in southeastern Virginia during the battle. Even without this sizable force, Lee had been able to humiliate his Federal opponent, Maj. Gen. Joseph Hooker. It appeared, therefore, that Lee could adequately defend northern Virginia without a portion of Longstreet's corps, which then could be sent to the west to help the situation there.[4]

Lee would not hear of it. To him, the choice was clear. Northern Virginia was the most important theater of operations. A Federal army that outnumbered his by three to one stood ready to seize the Confederate capital at Richmond if the situation presented itself. While Chancellorsville had been a great victory, it had not been an easy one. On several occasions an opponent more aggressive than Joe Hooker might have defeated his army in detail. Not only should he not send forces from his army to help the west, Lee argued that forces from other areas of the Confederacy should be sent to reinforce the Army of Northern Virginia. Resurrecting a concept discussed on several previous occasions and tried once before, Lee urged an invasion of the North.[5]

An operational commander must be concerned with the political objectives of his campaign. Lee's participation in the government-level discussions of his proposal should have provided him with a unique opportunity to understand the goals that his political masters wished to achieve. During the lengthy discussions, he had the chance to detect all of the nuances about the military conduct of the war that were troubling the South's leading politicians. Moreover, he was in a position to gain great insights into the thinking of his commander in chief, President Jefferson Davis, while Davis was articulating his positions on issues to both Lee and the Confederate cabinet. Later, several of the participants either wrote about or discussed the results of the meetings as they concerned Lee's campaign objectives. When analyzed carefully, it is clear that there is disagreement among their views of Lee's objectives. There are some objectives that are troubling because they display a lack of clear thinking. This tells much about why the battle of Gettysburg occurred as it did. The lengthy discussions may have contributed to the uncertainty concerning exactly what Lee was supposed to accomplish and how he was going to do it.

Lee was explicit about his desire to invade in order to draw the enemy away from its excellent defensive positions behind the Rappahannock River in northern Virginia. In its present location along the river, the Army of the Potomac was not vulnerable to a frontal assault. Additionally, an invasion around a flank would force a response from Federal forces threatening other areas of the South. Lee reasoned that reinforcements would have to be shifted north from Federal operations along the coasts of South Carolina, Georgia, and Florida to resist his invasion. Thus, an invasion would relieve Union pressure against other fronts, retain the initiative in northern Virginia, and draw Lee's enemy away from natural defensive barriers.[6]

Lee was greatly concerned about feeding his army. Northern Virginia farms had been supporting the war effort almost from the first days of combat. An invasion would allow Northern farmers to share the burden of supplying two opposing armies as they marched through the countryside. In addition, Lee would be able to gather sufficient supplies not only to subsist, but also to stockpile for future operations. It was an attractive objective for a commander constantly concerned about where sufficient supplies could be gathered.[7]

A peace movement had been gaining momentum in the North. Lee hoped that an invasion might divide the United States even further than the secession crisis of 1861. Northern farmers, seeing their crops being traded for worthless Confederate money, might demand an end to the war to eliminate the deprivations they were suffering. Northern peace parties might also be persuaded that ultimately the South only wished to be left alone in peace. A politically divided and weakened enemy was a worthy objective.[8]

Less clear was the issue of when and where to fight the Army of the Potomac. Lee had no intention of fighting it along the Rappahannock River. It was also clear to him that the Federals would pursue him if he successfully crossed the Potomac River and marched north into Pennsylvania. A battle would be virtually inevitable. But one witness to the cabinet discussions wrote that Lee's mission was to "threaten" Washington, Baltimore, and Philadelphia. Lee said after the campaign that he had hoped to occupy Philadelphia. A senior member of his staff later said that Philadelphia was not a campaign objective. Instead, he said, Lee intended to fight a major battle west of the Susquehanna River in Pennsylvania. A victory there would give him virtual control of Maryland, western Pennsylvania, and western Virginia.

Even a cursory examination shows that these objectives create decidedly different military missions. Threatening, occupying, or bringing the enemy to battle in a specified region are not objectives that necessarily support one another. Each mission could create very different requirements for the disposition of the Army of Northern Virginia. Perhaps Lee's confidence in the abilities of his army overshadowed his considerations about the precise circumstances under which he would accept battle.[9]

Lee was certain of his army's great abilities. In its two most recent major battles—Fredericksburg in December 1862 and Chancellorsville in May 1863—the Army of Northern Virginia had performed exceptionally well. Stating that "There never were such men in an army before," Lee knew they were invincible if they were properly led and organized. Believing this, then, Lee might not be too concerned about the enemy's army. Whenever and wherever the Army of the Potomac chose to fight, the men of the Army of Northern Virginia would be ready to beat them once again.[10]

Proper organization of his army had been an issue bothering Lee for some time. Each of the two Confederate corps comprising the Army of Northern Virginia had grown too large for a single commander to lead effectively. Always sensitive to his subordinate's sense of honor and dignity, Lee had been reluctant to appear dissatisfied with their performances by dividing their two corps into three. During the Battle of Chancellorsville, however, one of his corps commanders, Thomas J. "Stonewall" Jackson, was killed. A shocking loss on the one hand, it also gave Lee the opportunity to reorganize his major units on the other.[11]

Lee's reorganization did not affect only the command of his corps. As officers were moved upward into their new positions as corps commanders, they left vacancies at the division level. When officers from lower echelons filled these new vacancies, additional commanders had to be found to replace them. The net rippling effect of the reorganization was that approximately two-thirds of the major units of the Army of Northern Virginia were under new leaders when it embarked on its invasion of the North.[12]

For the Army of the Potomac in positions along the Rappahannock River, the problems were equally difficult. General Hooker's excellent plan for the spring campaign had ended in disaster at Chancellorsville. Most historians view the army's failure during the battle as having resulted principally from Hooker's lack of self-confidence. Lee had achieved a moral ascendancy over him. The Federal forces could not compensate for the vacuum in top-level leadership through any amount of hard fighting at the tactical level. Nevertheless, President Lincoln retained Hooker in command after the battle, and the army's leadership crisis at the top would create some difficult days ahead.[13]

The commander in chief, Lincoln, and his general in chief, Henry W. Halleck, visited Hooker's headquarters soon after the battle at Chancellorsville. Lincoln asked Hooker what he intended to do, mentioning that an early move against Lee could restore some of the army's morale that might have been adversely affected by the recent battle. Hooker's reply was defensive, stating that the performance of one of his corps in the battle might cause that corps to be discouraged or depressed, but that the rest of the army was ready to fight. He further indicated that he would continue to operate along the same line toward Richmond that he had chosen before the battle.[14]

Hooker then developed plans to move south of the Rappahannock River once again. On 13 May he notified Lincoln that he was going to move on the following day. Alarmed that the move might be premature, Lincoln called Hooker to Washington. Upon Hooker's arrival on the following day, the president handed him a letter giving him his objectives: "I therefore shall not complain if you do no more for a time than to keep the enemy at bay and out of other mischief by menaces and occasional cavalry raids, if practicable, and to put your own army in good condition again."[15]

Thus by the end of May, Lee was preparing the Army of Northern Virginia for an invasion of the North, while Hooker maintained the Army of the Potomac in its positions along the Rappahannock. Lee intended to gather supplies, threaten some major northern cities, promote the northern peace movement, draw the Army of the Potomac away from the Rappahannock River, and fight a battle somewhere at sometime. Hooker had his orders to keep Lee out of mischief and to rebuild his army.

Invasion!

Lt. Gen. James Longstreet's Confederate corps left its positions near Fredericksburg on 3 June. Two days later, Lt. Gen. Richard Ewell's corps also marched west for the Shenandoah Valley. Lee kept Lt. Gen. A. P. Hill's corps deployed near Fredericksburg. Keeping Hill in position as a rear guard, Lee also hoped that Hill's presence would deceive Hooker into believing that the Army of Northern Virginia's dispositions were unchanged.

Hill's position helped Lee address a bothersome course of action open to Hooker. One of Lee's intentions was to draw the Army of the Potomac northward. Hooker, however, could choose to advance south and attempt to seize Richmond. If that threat developed in his rear, Lee could not afford politically to continue an advance into Pennsylvania and leave the Confederate capital open to capture. He would have to follow Hooker south, and Hooker would then have seized the initiative. Hill's presence at Fredericksburg helped to prevent Hooker from choosing that alternative.[16]

Lee's concern for Richmond extended beyond Hooker's potential moves at Fredericksburg. Southeast of Richmond, more than two Federal corps were operating in the vicinity of the York and James Rivers. Probably too small to capture the capital, the Union force nevertheless represented a potential threat that could also upset Lee's plans. It could become a covering force for a major enemy operation along the James River. While Lee's army was in the Shenandoah Valley moving north, Hooker might shift his army rapidly by water to the James and fall in behind the two corps. McClellan had made a similar move in 1862 during the Peninsula campaign. Fortunately for Lee, this threat never materialized. The Federal troops under Maj. Gen. John A. Dix never became a more serious threat than a force to be watched carefully.[17]

Lee's moves puzzled Hooker. By 5 June Hooker had decided that the Army of Northern Virginia was up to something. Some of the Confederate camps had been abandoned, and Hooker surmised that Lee might be embarking on another invasion of the North. In order to test the strength of Lee's remaining force, he ordered the VI Corps commander to conduct a reconnaissance in force in front of some pontoon bridges south of Fredericksburg.

Maj. Gen. John Sedgwick, the VI Corps commander, already knew the answer. He quickly responded to Hooker's order and reported that the Confederates had strengthened their picket line and moved some additional artillery into forward positions. If the Federals attempted to advance more than two hundred yards, they would be decisively engaged. Apparently, Lee's directive to A. P. Hill was being carried out effectively; to the VI Corps commander, the Army of Northern Virginia's positions looked as strong as ever.[18]

Hooker was not convinced. He believed that if only a rear guard existed at Fredericksburg, he had an excellent opportunity to destroy this smaller force. Asking Lincoln's permission to cross the Rappahannock, Hooker added that there were some distinct disadvantages to his proposal. His advance might make the supply lines along the Orange and Alexandria Railroad vulnerable near Warrenton. Furthermore, Lee's army could end up between his army and a Union force at Harpers Ferry. Exposed, the force at Harpers Ferry might be defeated in detail while Hooker was south of the Rappahannock.[19]

Lincoln quickly rejected Hooker's idea. He told Hooker that by advancing south toward Richmond, the Army of the Potomac would be fighting an entrenched force—a very difficult task. While the Federal army fought the smaller force at Fredericksburg, the remainder of Lee's army would have freedom of action elsewhere. In a separate note, Halleck supported Lincoln's views and told Hooker that the enemy's march column was his proper objective. He added to Hooker's doubts about the Confederates' dispositions by suggesting that perhaps the enemy force at Fredericksburg was Lee's main army and a smaller, but still-strong force had departed for a raid into Maryland and Pennsylvania. Hooker responded appropriately by sending his main reconnaissance force, the Army of the Potomac's cavalry corps, on a raid against the Confederates.[20]

Complying with Hooker's directive, Brig. Gen. Alfred Pleasonton led his cavalry across the upper Rappahannock River on 9 June. He intended to advance on Culpeper Court House and destroy any Confederate supplies that he might find there. He never reached Culpeper; instead he struck a large force of Confederate cavalry under the famous Jeb Stuart at Brandy Station on the Orange and Alexandria Railroad. A seesaw mounted clash occurred with the Confederates eventually getting the upper hand. But the Battle of Brandy Station had many consequences for the campaign, some of which were not immediately obvious.

First, Pleasonton returned with some of the information that Hooker thought he needed. Pleasonton reported that he had caught Stuart's cavalry prepared to mount a raid. This seemed to support Halleck's suggestion to Hooker and confirm Sedgwick's report on 6 June: Lee's army was still at Fredericksburg, and only a raiding force was being assembled to threaten Maryland and Pennsylvania. Second, the Federal cavalrymen completely surprised Stuart's force and, although finally driven back across the river, gave an excellent account of themselves. To them, the famed Confederate cavalrymen were no longer invincible. Third, having his cavalry surprised by the Federal attack embarrassed Stuart. This would later be important when Stuart sought a means to redeem his reputation.[21]

After examining Pleasonton's report of the battle at Brandy Station, Hooker resurrected his previous plan to march south and seize the Confederate capital. Wiring Lincoln on 10 June, Hooker again asked permission to seize Richmond if it was determined that a sizable infantry force was accompanying Stuart on his raid. Lincoln's response was immediate and direct: "I think Lee's army, and not Richmond, is your sure objective point. If he comes toward the Upper Potomac, follow on his flank and on his inside track, shortening your lines of communications while he lengthens his. Fight him, too, when opportunity offers. If he stays where he is, fret him and fret him."[22]

While Hooker fretted over his next move, Lee's campaign continued to unfold smoothly. Ewell's corps captured almost half of the sizable Federal force located and isolated at Winchester on 14 June. Over 4,400 officers and men; 200,000 rounds of small-arms ammunition; and 23 artillery pieces fell into Confederate hands. Hooker was unaware of the magnitude of the disaster until Maj. Gen. Robert H. Milroy and 1,200 of the remainder of his force straggled into Harpers Ferry on the fifteenth and reported the extent of the debacle. To further confuse Hooker, Lee ordered Longstreet's corps to move north and remain east of the Blue Ridge Mountains. This might give the impression to the Federal commander that Lee was threatening the Orange and Alexandria Railroad in an attempt to turn Hooker out of his positions along the Rappahannock River. Three cavalry brigades covered Longstreet's front and flank. Lee attempted to deepen the deception by having Ewell advance his corps toward the Potomac. This could cause Hooker to vacate his positions along the Rappahannock to contest Ewell's crossing of the Potomac. If Hooker took the bait, A. P. Hill's corps would then be able to leave its positions at Fredericksburg unopposed and rejoin the main Confederate Army. Stuart assigned one brigade of cavalry to cover Ewell, and two brigades formed a link between Hill's corps and the main army.[23]

After arranging his corps dispositions to confuse Hooker as to his true intent, Lee then developed a plan to place his opponent on the horns of a dilemma. The Confederate commander asked President Davis on 23 June for assistance in executing the plan. Lee proposed that Davis assemble units from the Confederate forces in North and South Carolina and Georgia and reinforce General P. G. T. Beauregard's command at Richmond. Beauregard should then take this new army and march to Culpeper Court House. From that location, Beauregard's force would be in a position to threaten Washington. Davis denied Lee's request, because there was not enough time to organize the force. Moreover, Beauregard's own units could not afford to leave the vicinity of Richmond because of Dix's Federal forces' operating between the York and James Rivers near Yorktown.[24]

If implemented, Lee's proposed moves would have made a tremendous psychological impact on Hooker. Eventually, Hooker would have sifted through all of the conflicting evidence and determined the true nature of Lee's invasion. By that time, however, Beauregard would have been in Culpeper. For Hooker, it would have been a profound dilemma. Should he go after Lee's army in Pennsylvania, attack Beauregard's smaller force at Culpeper, or remain in a defensive posture to try to protect Washington, Baltimore, and Philadelphia from both Lee and Beauregard? If he kept his army massed and attacked one of his two opponents, a clear possibility would have been that the ensuing battle would have been indecisive. The unengaged Confederate force would then have a free hand to accomplish much operationally. If he piecemealed his army to try to engage both his opponents, he would have stood a strong possibility that another Chancellorsville would occur; personal ruin and disaster for the Union cause would have been very reasonable outcomes. By this stage in the campaign, the true genius of Robert E. Lee was quite clear. Hooker was clearly coming out second best in a race of two people.

Ten days after the Army of Northern Virginia had left its positions along the Rappahannock River, Hooker responded with an order to the Army of the Potomac. He shifted his line of communications to the Orange and Alexandria Railroad and directed his corps to positions making Centreville the center of mass. A relatively cautious move, it nevertheless was long overdue. Even some of Hooker's corps commanders already had surmised that Lee was off on a major invasion of the North.[25]

Hooker's frame of mind is discernible from some of his correspondence. On the day after he ordered his army to shift to Centreville, he sent a letter to Lincoln indicating the focus of his attention. Hooker asked the president if he knew whether the Confederates had seized Winchester. Obviously, this was an important question because it was at this time that Milroy's command was passing into ignominy. Hooker concluded his message with a comment that makes it clear that he was less concerned for Milroy's men than he was for himself: "I do not feel like making a move for an enemy until I am satisfied as to his whereabouts. To proceed to Winchester and have him make his appearance elsewhere, would subject me to ridicule." Clearly, Hooker was not focusing on acting aggressively or decisively. He was focused on his own appearance.[26]

From 17–24 June Hooker continued to feel his way forward in the direction of Lee's line of communications. He consolidated his army's positions east of the Blue Ridge Mountains and ordered Pleasonton's cavalry division to learn more about the Confederates. Stuart's Confederate cavalry, however, had erected an effective screen, and several large clashes occurred as Pleasonton aggressively tested the Confederate cavalry's strength.[27]

Intelligence information other than that being provided by Pleasonton reached Hooker from several sources. Probably the best information came from Maj. Gen. Darius N. Couch. Couch had been a corps commander under Hooker during the Chancellorsville campaign. Following that battle, he had left the Army of the Potomac in disgust and was appointed the head of the newly created Department of the Susquehanna. Headquartered in Harrisburg, he controlled only militia forces. Nevertheless, he became the focal point for much of the information that was being collected by agencies outside of the Army of the Potomac as Lee advanced through Maryland into Pennsylvania.

The Pennsylvania Central Railroad played an important part in this network. Probably acting as much out of self-interest as out of a sense of patriotism, the railroad organized scouting parties that worked initially out of Williamsport, Maryland, and conducted activities from Chambersburg and from the region west of the Cumberland Valley in Pennsylvania. Couch assembled information from sources such as these and forwarded them to Hooker and to the War Department.[28]

Hooker was not inspiring confidence. Beginning to shift his forces in the direction of Lee's apparent line of communications, he reported his moves to Washington on 24 June and added, "I don't know whether I am standing on my head or feet." He seemed unaware that his own fortunes were declining, because he then became involved in fatal arguments with Lincoln and Halleck.[29]

Harpers Ferry was the issue. Almost since the beginning of Lee's campaign, Hooker had been concerned over the fate of that important location. Not only was it located at the confluence of the Potomac and Shenandoah Rivers, astride the Chesapeake and Ohio Canal and along the Baltimore and Ohio Railroad, the town lay directly along the invasion route of any Confederate force marching down the Shenandoah Valley toward Maryland. Early in the campaign Hooker wanted to be in charge of the garrison there so he could withdraw the forces to his own army at the opportune time. Lincoln and Halleck retained control of the garrison and told Hooker that Harpers Ferry must be held. In a personal meeting in Washington on 23 June, Lincoln and Halleck again told the general to hold the town. Upon his return to the army, Hooker sent a corps in the direction of Harpers Ferry, but it was not the end of the issue.[30]

Hooker was also having a feud with Halleck over reinforcements. Convinced that Lee's army outnumbered his, he peppered the War Department with requests for additional troops. After his meeting with the president on the twenty-third, he sent his chief of staff, Maj. Gen. Daniel Butterfield, to Washington to seek additional reinforcements from the troops manning the capital's defenses. Over 25,000 soldiers already had been sent either to Hooker or to Dix's forces near Yorktown, so Halleck told Butterfield that no more troops were available. But Hooker still saw Harpers Ferry's 10,000 men as a ready source.[31]

Hooker did not abandon the Harpers Ferry issue. On 26 June he wired Halleck: "Is there any reason why Maryland Heights at Harpers Ferry should not be abandoned after the public stores and property are removed?... It must be borne in mind that I am here with a force inferior in numbers to that of the enemy, and must have every available man to use on the field."[32] After again being told to hold Harpers Ferry, Hooker wired Halleck on the twenty-seventh: "I have received your telegram in regard to Harper's Ferry.... [Those troops] are of no earthly account.... Now they are but bait for the rebels."[33]

Later that same day, Hooker, looking for more troops—and perhaps in his continuing mental struggle over what to do, looking for reassurances from the capital—brought matters to a head:

> My original instructions require me to cover Harper's Ferry and Washington. I have now imposed upon me, in addition, an enemy in my front of more than my number. I beg to be understood, respectfully, but firmly, that I am unable to comply with the condition with the means at my disposal, and earnestly request that I may at once be relieved from the position I occupy.[34]

Halleck quickly replied: "Your application to be relieved from your present command is received. As you were appointed to this command by the President, I have no power to relieve you. Your dispatch has been duly referred for Executive action."[35] Action was forthcoming.

Very early on the morning of 28 June the V Corps commander, Maj. Gen. George G. Meade, was awakened by an officer from Halleck's staff. Col. James A. Hardie told Meade that he brought trouble. Quickly, the V Corps commander searched his memory for any misdeed that might warrant his relief from command or his arrest. Finding none, he told Hardie that his conscience was clear. Hardie handed Meade a message. Indeed there was trouble in store for Meade; Hooker was relieved from command of the Army of the Potomac, and Meade was to replace him.[36]

Hooker's performance had been truly lackluster. When compared to Lee, he clearly was second best. By this stage of the campaign, Hooker had shown himself unable to master his own fears, to create any uncertainties in his opponent, or to cement strong ties with his own political leaders.

At first, Lincoln did not blame the defeat at Chancellorsville on Hooker. But during May he received letters and visits from generals who convinced the president that Hooker owned much of the blame for the defeat. This assessment was reinforced by Hooker's cautious response to Lee's movements in June. There is no record to show that Hooker ever had a clear campaign objective in mind for his army. Certainly he had never outlined one to his seniors or to his subordinates. He positioned his forces as though prepared to react but not to seize the initiative. His statements, which indicated that Lee possessed the psychological advantage, added to a picture of a general bewildered by his opponent and afraid to fail. The final argument over the fate of the Federal garrison at Harpers Ferry was anticlimactic. Lee had seized operational control of the theater, and Lincoln had to do something.[37]

On the other hand, Lee showed that he had mastered his opponent. Skillfully positioning his corps to provide maximum security for his army while it moved north, he continued to try to deceive Hooker. Some of his efforts were so complex that it is doubtful if Hooker ever understood the false picture, let alone the true one. Regardless of their effect, Lee used Stuart's cavalry so well that even if the Federals could see through the deceptions, they still would not know exactly what was happening. All of this occurred behind terrain that Lee used effectively to his own advantage. The comparison of the two generals is remarkable in the starkness of the contrast.

Colonel Hardie remained with the Army of the Potomac for several hours to determine the effect of the change in command. He reported that a sense of satisfaction ran through the army. The situation appeared to be under control. Halleck's orders handed to Meade by Hardie helped to achieve that control:

> Your army is free to act as you may deem proper under the circumstances as they arise. You will, however, keep in view the important fact that the Army of the Potomac is the covering army of Washington as well as the army of operation against the invading forces of the rebels. You will, therefore, maneuver and fight in such a manner as to cover the capital and also Baltimore, as far as circumstances will admit.[38]

Meade moved quickly to reassure the War Department that he had a firm grasp on the situation. Four hours after being notified that he was in command, he wired Halleck:

> Totally unexpected as it has been, and in ignorance of the exact condition of the troops and position of the enemy, I can only now say that it appears to me I must move toward the Susquehanna, keeping Washington and Baltimore well covered, and if the enemy is checked in his attempt to cross the Susquehanna, or if he turns toward Baltimore, to give him battle.[39]

To Lincoln and Halleck the contrast of this message to Hooker's previous indecision must have been remarkable. Here was a general who was talking about fighting Lee after being in command for only four hours! Indeed, Meade had formulated an operational plan that would accomplish the mission accepted as stated above.

Meade was an excellent choice to command the Army of the Potomac. A Regular Army officer, he had been a commander at every level from brigade through corps. He had led the V Corps at both Fredericksburg and Chancellorsville, and at the latter battle, had urged Hooker to remain south of the Rappahannock River and continue the fight. Quick to criticize himself if he made mistakes, he was equally hard on those who fell short of his high standards. Swiftly, this experienced combat commander set about organizing his army to find and fight the Army of Northern Virginia.[40]

He asked several officers to be his chief of staff. It was customary for a commander to appoint his own chief of staff, and Daniel Butterfield was Hooker's man. Twice turned down, Meade accepted the advice of his second choice, Brig. Gen. Gouverneur K. Warren, who said it was a bad idea to change chiefs of staff in mid-campaign. Butterfield stayed on as chief—a decision that Meade would later regret.[41]

Many historians have examined Lee's reorganization of the Army of Northern Virginia and concluded that it had an adverse effect on Confederate performance during the Gettysburg campaign. Meade, however, faced circumstances at least equally difficult. He assumed command of an army in mid-campaign, not knowing the dispositions of the enemy and unaware of his predecessor's intentions and corps-level dispositions. The II Corps received a new commander on 22 May. His own corps, the V, received a new commander when Meade assumed command of the army. The Cavalry Corps came under the direction of Alfred Pleasanton on 22 May, and the XI Corps received a new commander in April. Finally, the artillery also recently had been reorganized significantly. Each of these factors created some organizational turmoil for the new commander, but Meade proceeded with confidence.[42]

Meade attached the 1st Cavalry Division under Brig. Gen. John Buford to the trusted I Corps commander, Maj. Gen. John Reynolds. Meade told Reynolds to advance northward into Pennsylvania and seek out the enemy. If Reynolds could find suitable terrain, he was to fight Lee; Meade would reinforce Reynolds' effort with the remainder of the army. If a good battle position could not be found, Reynolds was to withdraw toward the Army of the Potomac as it was advancing northward on a wide front in the direction of York, Pennsylvania. According to this alternative plan, Meade would bring the Army of the Potomac together along Pipe Creek in Maryland. It is clear from Meade's orders that he deployed his forces for an offensive operation that embodied the important elements of what today would be called a movement to contact.[43] (*See Map 10.*)

For both Robert E. Lee and George G. Meade, 28 June was a momentous day. On that day, Lee was surprised to learn that the main Federal army was north of the Potomac River, and its exact dispositions were unknown. The source of Lee's information was a man named James Harrison, whom Longstreet had hired to spy on the Union Army. It may seem strange that Lee received his best information about the enemy from a privately hired spy instead of from his cavalry, but an unusual turn of events had occurred that had put Lee in the dark.[44]

A week previous to Harrison's report, Jeb Stuart proposed to Lee a daring plan. Hooker's forces were stationary, and Pleasanton's cavalry had been unable to penetrate the Confederate cavalry screen. The lull

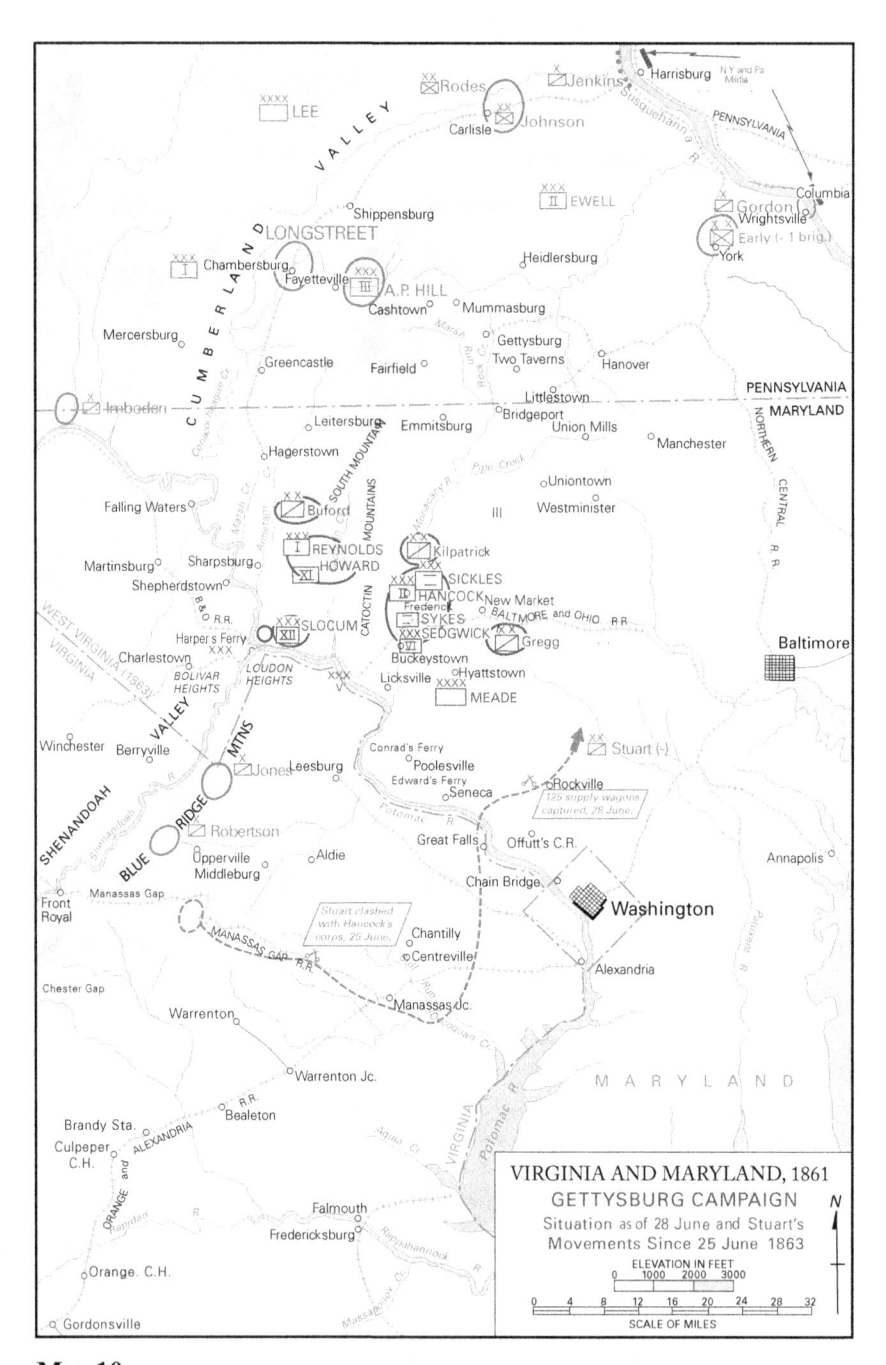

MAP 10

in action at the operational level gave Stuart the opportunity to try to convince his commander that a large Confederate cavalry force under his supervision could ride east around the Army of the Potomac and then head north, joining the remainder of the Army of Northern Virginia in Pennsylvania. It would duplicate a much-heralded feat that Stuart had performed similarly against McClellan's army a year ago during the Peninsula campaign. Not only would this dashing ride regain some of the prestige lost by his cavalry surprised at Brandy Station, it would allow Stuart's men to gather supplies separate from the main army. Lee gave his conditional consent.[45]

Lee indicated that he preferred that Stuart bring his cavalry across the Potomac River at Shepherdstown, west of Harpers Ferry. But if Stuart felt that he could pass around the Federal army "without hindrance," he could do so while "doing [the Federals] all the damage you can." After crossing the river, Stuart was to proceed north and "feel the right of Ewell's troops," which would put him in proper position to screen the most vulnerable flank of Lee's northernmost force. Stuart was authorized to take with him three of the five available cavalry brigades. The remaining two brigades were to guard the passes leading into the Shenandoah Valley. As the main army moved north, these remaining brigades were to leave pickets to guard the passes and then close up on the rear of the army as it proceeded.[46]

Stuart determined that he could pass around the Army of the Potomac "without hindrance." This decision effectively removed him from the mainstream of the campaign until 2 July. He skirmished with some Federal troops, created some consternation within the Federal ranks, and captured some supplies. But his real value to the Army of Northern Virginia was not in any of these things. Over the past year, during which he and Lee had worked together, Stuart had built up rapport and understanding that had worked extremely well. Stuart could anticipate his commander's intent. He had the capability to analyze the intelligence information his cavalrymen collected and to provide Lee with an accurate appraisal of the enemy. These characteristics were missing when the army commander needed them most. When the Federal army finally got moving and crossed the Potomac, Stuart was not around to detect the importance of the movements. Lee's surprise on 28 June was real and important.[47]

Lee apparently anticipated that he would learn of a Federal pursuit when the Union forces started to cross the Potomac River, the major obstacle between his army and the Army of the Potomac. It seems that he assumed that while the enemy's troops, artillery, and long supply trains crossed the river on pontoon bridges or at fords, he would have ample time to reassemble his army spread out over the Pennsylvania countryside. Harrison's report therefore caused consternation over the effectiveness of his cavalry reconnaissance. It also required that Lee respond quickly to avoid having his forces defeated in detail.[48]

Ewell's corps was spread between Carlisle and York, with some of his forces probing Harrisburg's defenses along the west bank of the Susquehanna. At first, Lee directed Ewell to assemble his corps and rejoin the main army at Chambersburg, but upon realizing that the congestion at Chambersburg might be overwhelming, he changed Ewell's orders and told him to march to Heidlersburg. From there, Ewell could advance on either Gettysburg or Cashtown, depending on circumstances. Lee had decided that since the Federals were approaching from the direction of Frederick, Maryland, their route of march would force them through Gettysburg or Cashtown on 30 June or 1 July. With Ewell at Heidlersburg, he would be in a position to respond accordingly. Ewell was disappointed at not being allowed to continue with his efforts to seize the capital of the North's second most politically powerful state, but he moved rapidly to comply with Lee's orders.[49]

Most of Lee's two remaining corps spent two days resting in camps along the turnpike between Chambersburg and Gettysburg. On 29 June Lee ordered Hill's corps to advance to Cashtown, and Longstreet was to follow close behind on the thirtieth. Although surprised by the Federals' appearance north of the Potomac River, Lee responded quickly. His corps were mutually supporting by the evening of 30 June. The Army of the Potomac would not find his army vulnerable to defeat in detail.[50]

Meade's actions were equally decisive. Halleck initially tended to confuse the situation by providing Meade with inaccurate and conflicting information. Early in the afternoon on which Meade assumed command, Halleck informed the new commander that the Confederates probably would mass their forces east of the Susquehanna River. Later that same afternoon Halleck added to the confusion by informing Meade that a large force of Confederates was still south of the Potomac River. Fortunately for Meade, neither of Halleck's reports proved correct. He moved his corps northward through Maryland into Pennsylvania, keeping Halleck informed of his movements.[51]

Meade's messages must have convinced Halleck of the soundness of Lincoln's decision to appoint Meade. Responding to Halleck's analysis of Confederate dispositions and intentions on 28 June, Meade told the general in chief that if Lee was en route to Baltimore, he would get his army between Lee's and the city in time to cover it. If Lee tried to cross the Susquehanna in Pennsylvania, Meade told Halleck that he was relying on Couch's forces to delay the Army of Northern Virginia until he could catch it and defeat it in detail. For the time being he was prepared to ignore Stuart's irritating but strategically and operationally harmless Confederate cavalry raid. He reassured Halleck that he would keep his corps mutually supporting and be prepared for any eventuality. It was clear that Halleck was dealing with a competent, confident commander. Meade reminded his Washington superior of his "main point being to find and fight the enemy."[52] Although to us today this may seem like a very obvious statement, it is well to remember that every commander of the Army of the Potomac who had found and fought Lee in a major battle in the past had lost.

By the evening of 30 June Meade was responding to a reasonably accurate picture of the locations of Lee's corps. Reports indicated that Ewell was in the vicinity of York and Harrisburg, Longstreet was at Chambersburg, and A. P. Hill was somewhere between Chambersburg and York. Maj. Gen. John Reynolds, now commanding a "wing" of three corps, was pushing north, toward the crossroads town of Gettysburg. His attached cavalry commander, John Buford, was already in the town. At 1030 Meade gave Reynolds a detailed account of the movements of Lee's corps and told Reynolds that Lee's army probably would assemble at Gettysburg sometime during 1 July. Reynolds informed Meade of the unfolding events and continued to push his troops hard. Although his army's grueling pace concerned Meade, he continued the effort in the hopes of catching Lee.[53]

Gettysburg

On 30 June Brig. Gen. James Pettigrew took his Confederate brigade to Gettysburg to get some shoes. Part of Maj. Gen. Henry Heth's division of A. P. Hill's corps, Pettigrew was continuing his mission of gathering supplies. On a ridge west of Gettysburg, however, he ran into some dismounted enemy cavalry. Unsure of whether this was only another brush with militia or if it was a more organized resistance by veteran soldiers, Pettigrew withdrew. He certainly had no orders to bring on a decisive engagement with the Army of the Potomac. He returned to camp at Cashtown without the shoes.

Pettigrew briefed Heth concerning his encounter at Gettysburg. During the session, the corps commander rode up and Pettigrew briefed him on the situation. Hill replied that he felt that there were no large enemy forces in the vicinity of the town and that Pettigrew probably had just run into a cavalry vedette. Heth recommended that he take his entire division to Gettysburg and get the shoes. Hill told him to go ahead.[54]

Lee was unaware that contact with major Federal forces was imminent. Stuart's absence from the main army on 30 June and 1 July was extremely important. Although Lee was in the process of gathering his corps so that they were within supporting distance of each other, he had not positioned them for an engagement. Stuart's presence and aggressive cavalry work by his troopers probably would have revealed that a major battle was in the offing. This would have caused Lee to position his corps in a manner different than they were on the morning of 1 July: Longstreet's corps in camps near Chambersburg, one of Hill's divisions out looking for shoes, and Ewell's corps approaching from Heidlersburg. Five of Lee's nine divisions were west of South Mountain and only one road through the pass at Cashtown could support a movement to Gettysburg. Although as confident as ever, Lee was poorly positioned to meet an opponent conducting a movement to contact and looking for a fight.[55]

Hill's decision to send an entire division to Gettysburg for shoes and to bag a few Federal prisoners perhaps left exposed by a careless commander was a fateful one. It essentially left Lee out of the picture at a time when his presence would have been important; Lee would arrive on the battlefield long after his corps commanders had seized what appeared to them to be an excellent opportunity and had committed his army to a major engagement. The opening phase of the battle is an example of how an operational commander can rapidly lose control of a campaign when tactical circumstances overtake his plans.

When Heth tried to force his division through the Federal cavalry screen under Buford west of Gettysburg on the morning of 1 July, he ran into a formidable opponent. Buford skillfully deployed his badly outnumbered cavalrymen and turned to Maj. Gen. John Reynolds for help. Quickly, Reynolds brought the I and XI Corps forward; in the process of leading them into battle, he was shot and killed. Federal command passed to the next senior corps commander on the battlefield, Maj. Gen. Oliver O. Howard. Repeating Reynolds' earlier call for assistance, Howard sent messages both to his nearby corps commanders and to Meade at Taneytown. Heth, his Confederates now fighting infantry as well as cavalry, deployed both to the right and to the left to try to find a weak flank in the Union positions.

Ewell's Confederate corps had left Heidlersburg en route to Cashtown when Ewell received a message from A. P. Hill indicating he was advancing to Gettysburg. Ewell redirected his corps to that same location. About four miles from the town, his men heard the sound of battle. Ewell responded swiftly and typically by marching to the sound of the guns. It was this very strength upon which the reputation of the Army of Northern Virginia was built. Commanders were expected to assist one another and to seize the initiative whenever the opportunity presented itself. Ewell's corps thus appeared north of Gettysburg and moved into battle positions opposite both the Federals deployed west of the town and those now beginning to arrive on the low ground on its northern edge. Ewell's initiative further committed Lee to battle.

When Lee heard the sounds of sustained combat coming from the direction of Gettysburg, he rode to A. P. Hill's headquarters on the Chambersburg Pike, east of South Mountain. Hill described Heth's advance on Gettysburg and explained also that he had sent Pender's division in support. Lee rode down the Pike behind Hill's two divisions. Upon his arrival on the battlefield at about 1430, he initially tried to slow down the development of the battle. Unsure of the size of the force his army was facing, he did not want to bring on a general engagement until all of his combat power was available. Unfortunately for the Confederates, Hill's third division and Longstreet's entire corps were being delayed on the solitary road that was available to support the movement of both corps. It would take a long time for all of his army to arrive at the scene of battle. In the meantime, after hearing several strong proposals from his corps commanders, Lee approved their requests to drive the Federals off the field north and west of Gettysburg. (*See Map 11.*) With the primitive communications available, it was normally wise to trust the judgments of valued subordinates and seize opportunities where they appeared.[56]

Meade, still located at Taneytown, sent two of his most able subordinates to assess the situation reported by Reynolds from Gettysburg earlier in the day. Reynolds had indicated that he might be driven from his initial positions north and west of the town, but he added that he was prepared to barricade the streets in order to hold off the inevitable Confederate onslaught. Meade sent his chief engineer, Warren, to assess the terrain and, following Reynolds' death, sent Maj. Gen. Winfield S. Hancock, the II Corps commander, to take charge of the battlefield. Upon later hearing that the Union dispositions near Gettysburg appeared favorable, Meade directed all of his corps to assemble there. His earlier assessment of the operational circumstances and the deployments he made to meet them were being vindicated. In today's terms, he quickly shifted his operations from a movement to contact to a meeting engagement. Operationally, he had disposed all his corps so they were mutually supporting each other within a hard day's march. Under these circumstances Meade would be able to rapidly concentrate his force. Although tactical circumstances were about to overwhelm the Federals at Gettysburg, Meade had the operational situation firmly in hand.[57]

The collapse of the Federal lines at Gettysburg started on the right. The battle, which had begun on the west side of the town, had been building northward and then eastward throughout the day. The Confederates, searching for an exposed flank, found the Federal left too difficult to turn. For each success in that direction, they were countered by an effective Union move as the Federal troops arrived on the battlefield from the south. Ewell's appearance north of the town near Oak Hill also tended to shift Confederate hopes for success in that direction. For the Federals, then, it became a race to extend their lines north and east as additional enemy units arrived to threaten their right. The Federals ran out of troops before the Confederates did. Outflanked, outgunned, and outnumbered by about 28,000 to 18,000 on the entire field, the Union right unraveled and fell back toward new positions already being prepared by a division of the XI Corps, south of Gettysburg on Cemetery Hill. There, Hancock carefully aligned the retreating troops from the XI and I Corps that had been ordered to withdraw following the collapse on the right.[58]

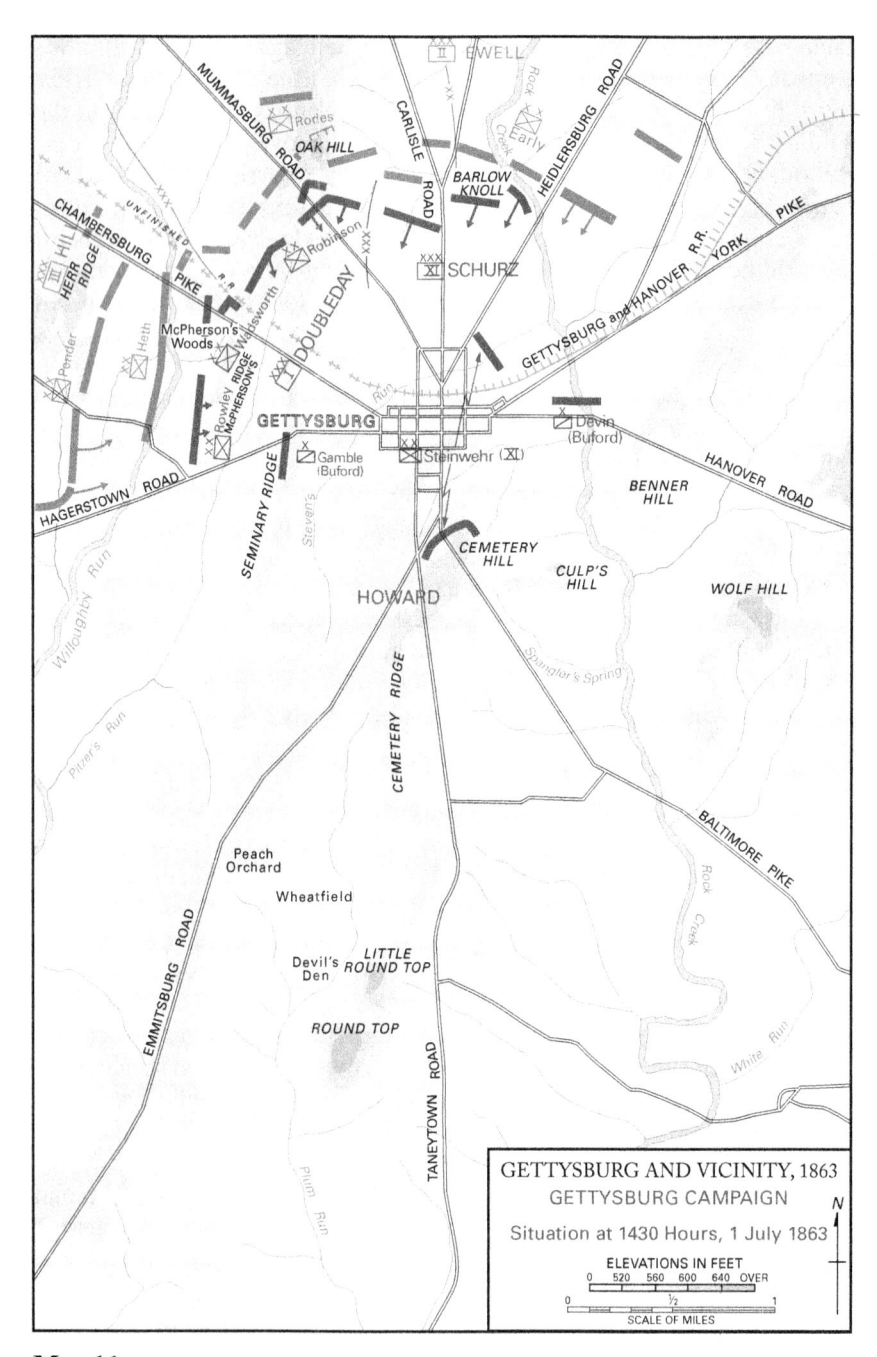

MAP 11

From his vantage point on Seminary Ridge, Lee watched the disorganized Yankees fleeing up and over Cemetery Hill at about 1630. It appeared the time was right for another blow. Lee told Ewell "to carry the hill occupied by the enemy, if he found it practicable, but to avoid a general engagement until the arrival of the other divisions of the army." Five of Lee's nine divisions were still not on the field. Piecemeal attacks carried the high risk of sustaining large casualties without achieving anything substantial because insufficient combat power was available. Pursuit of a beaten foe might have been admirable, but Federal troops on Cemetery Hill were quickly occupying and preparing new positions to meet anything that Ewell might throw against them.[59]

While Lee waited for Ewell to attack (if practicable), Longstreet rode up and joined him on Seminary Ridge. His corps had been delayed by the passage of Hill's corps at Cashtown, and elements of Ewell's corps, specifically Johnson's division, blocked the road, so Longstreet had ridden ahead to find out the situation facing the Confederates at Gettysburg. On Seminary Ridge, he learned that Lee was planning to attack the enemy. Longstreet argued against the plan. Before the start of the campaign, he had proposed that when the Confederates had brought their invasion to the point where the Yankees confronted them, the Southerners should adopt the defensive. Remembering the resounding defensive success achieved at Fredericksburg in the previous December, Longstreet believed that the tactical defensive offered the best hope for success. Lee, of course, had just completed his most brilliant tactical and operational victory at Chancellorsville in May while on the tactical offensive. The previous discussion had ended unresolved; now, on Seminary Ridge, Longstreet reopened the debate. Lee, however, was adamant. He was going to attack the enemy. Longstreet rode off to rejoin his corps as it approached Gettysburg.[60]

In one of the more important controversies surrounding the battle, Ewell decided not to attack. It took a long time for Johnson's division to get into position to launch an assault, and suitable artillery positions were difficult to find. Moreover, the Confederates captured a message indicating that the Federal V Corps was approaching Gettysburg from the direction of Ewell's left rear. If his corps was locked in a struggle on the summit of Cemetery Hill when this Federal corps appeared in their rear, disaster was sure to follow. In Ewell's view, a successful assault that avoided a general engagement was just not "practicable."[61]

Lee, however, still held the initiative. So far, the battle had been a resounding success. The Yankees had been driven from every position that they had occupied. The Army of Northern Virginia may have been caught unprepared for a battle with the entire Army of the Potomac, but in its finest tradition it had responded vigorously and effectively.

After dark Lee rode to Ewell's headquarters and explained his concept of operations for the next day. Ewell's corps was to exploit their success of the first day and attack early the next morning to drive the Federals off Cemetery Hill. One of Ewell's division commanders, Jubal Early, argued against the idea because the Yankees were continuing to improve their defensive positions. By morning they would be well prepared to receive an attack. Early added that in his view the keys to the entire battlefield were the Round Tops located to the south. From these hilltops, artillery could dominate much of the terrain to the north, to include the rear of Cemetery Hill. Based on the arguments presented by the commanders who had seen the ground, Lee changed his mind and directed Ewell to shift his corps around, toward the Confederate right. Lee was concerned over the length of his lines, and this movement would permit him to mass forces at the critical point much more quickly and shift the focus of the battle southward.

Ewell again remained silent as Early disagreed once more. If the corps shifted south, Early was concerned that morale would suffer because the severely wounded who were quartered in the town and the hotly contested ground of the fighting on 1 July would be given to the Yankees without a fight. Lee reversed himself once again. He told Ewell and his division commanders that Longstreet's corps would make the main attack against the Federal left. Ewell was to remain in position and then make a demonstration to support Longstreet. Hearing no argument against this plan, Lee rode back to his headquarters located northwest of the town along the Chambersburg Pike.[62]

When Lee reached his headquarters, he changed his mind once again. He sent a courier to Ewell ordering him to move his corps around toward the Confederate right. Longstreet's corps still was not on the field, and tightening up the lines of Hill's and Ewell's corps on the west side of town would form a solid base from which to launch an attack. Ewell responded to Lee's instructions by riding to his commander's headquarters and personally arguing in favor of his corps' making a demonstration from its present location to support Longstreet. It appeared that Culp's Hill to the east of Cemetery Hill might be vulnerable; if the Confederates captured it, they would dominate the Union positions on the lower hill to its west. Lee approved Ewell's proposal, ordering him to make a demonstration against the Federal right; the demonstration was to be turned into a full assault if an opportunity looked promising. Ewell was to open his part of the battle when he heard the sounds of Longstreet's guns commencing the attack against the other flank.[63]

Ewell's and Early's concerns about the strength of the Union positions on Cemetery and Culp's Hills were well founded. Casualties had been relatively high for both sides. The Confederates had lost about 8,000 and the Yankees about 9,000, including 4,500 captured during the hasty retreat to Cemetery Hill. But more Union troops were arriving every minute. About 1700 there were 12,000 Yankees on Cemetery Hill. An hour later, the number had grown to 20,000. By about 2100 there were 27,000 Federals in positions along Cemetery and Culp's Hills. Union strength continued to build throughout the night, and at 0300 the next day Meade arrived on the battlefield.[64]

In the early morning darkness, he met Maj. Gens. Henry W. Slocum, Daniel E. Sickles, and Oliver O. Howard at the cemetery gates on Cemetery Hill. Only Sedgwick's VI Corps was still not present, but Meade, before leaving Taneytown earlier in the evening, had ordered Sedgwick to march the thirty miles to Gettysburg as quickly as possible. The generals now facing Meade assured him their positions were strong. He informed the assembled officers that once Sedgwick's corps arrived, he intended to attack on the right. In the meantime, each corps was to continue to prepare its positions and rearrange its lines so that unit integrity, thoroughly mixed up during the momentous events of the previous afternoon and evening, would be restored.

Geary's division of the XII Corps was to move from the vicinity of Little Round Top and rejoin its parent unit now positioned on the Federal right at Culp's Hill. Sickles' III Corps was directed to extend the Federal line southward from the left flank of the II Corps and anchor its left flank on Little Round Top. Meade rode to a small house in the immediate rear of the center of his lines and set up headquarters. It was now a matter of waiting until all of his army was assembled.

As the morning of 2 July wore on and there were no discernible movements from the Confederate lines, Meade grew concerned that Lee was up to something. After Lee's resounding success on 1 July, it would be unlike him to lie dormant and only stare through the early morning hours at his Yankee foe. About 0930 Meade asked Slocum if the XII Corps could launch an attack on the right. Undoubtedly this would cause a response from Lee, and it might upset any plans that Lee had set in motion. Slocum replied that while the terrain in his corps area favored the defense, it was unsuitable for an attack. Meade abandoned the notion and soon after wired Halleck in Washington that the Army of the Potomac was in good defensive positions and if driven from them would fall back to its supply base at Westminster, Maryland.[65]

Indeed, Lee was up to something. He did not complete his final plans for the attack on 2 July until that morning. All through the previous night, Longstreet's corps had been hurrying toward Gettysburg. Since the I Corps was to make the main attack, an early morning assault was out of the question. Nonetheless, Lee continued with his plan, and in a conference that morning on Seminary Ridge he explained his concept to Longstreet and two of his division commanders, Maj. Gen. John B. Hood and Maj. Gen. Lafayette McLaws. The third division commander, Maj. Gen. George E. Pickett, and his division were still at Chambersburg.

Lee indicated that I Corps was to advance up the Emmitsburg Road and strike the Federal left flank south of Cemetery Hill. Because of the difficulty of controlling a corps-size maneuver, the road offered an excellent terrain feature along which to guide an attack. Longstreet again opened his old argument that the Confederates should be adopting a tactical defensive. Instead of attacking the Federal left directly, he argued that the Army of Northern Virginia should slip around the enemy's left and position itself so the Yankees would have to attack to dislodge them. Lee reiterated that the army would attack at Gettysburg. He turned to McLaws and showed him precisely how to position his line of battle perpendicular to the Emmitsburg Road with a direction of attack northeastward up the road. Lee added that he wanted McLaws to move by a concealed route, so the enemy would learn of the impending attack too late to respond effectively.

McLaws asked permission to conduct a personal reconnaissance. Lee mentioned that staff officers were already doing so. Longstreet interceded and denied McLaws permission, telling him to remain with his division. He then pointed to the map and indicated the position for McLaws' division to occupy. This was different from Lee's earlier location; he indicated a line parallel to the Emmitsburg Road and facing eastward in the direction that Longstreet felt the attack should proceed to bring it around the enemy's left. Lee immediately retorted, "No, General, I wish it placed just the opposite." Longstreet stood off to one side as Lee continued to explain how the attack was to unfold.[66]

During the discussion, Lee asked Captain Johnston of his staff to brief the group on the results of his reconnaissance around the Federal left. Johnston explained that he personally had climbed to the crest of Little Round Top and found the southern end of Cemetery Ridge unoccupied by the enemy. Satisfied that an attack up the Emmitsburg Road would bring the I Corps against the Yankee left flank, Lee concluded the meeting, emphasizing that the attack must start as soon as possible. Longstreet and his commanders returned to their staffs to get their units started.[67]

Johnston's report is puzzling. As soon as Meade had a clear understanding of the terrain, the Federal commander had directed units to occupy all of Cemetery Ridge, to include anchoring the left flank on the Round Tops. From a vantage point on Little Round Top, Johnston had viewed the portion of the line assigned to the Union III Corps. Since Johnston saw a vacant area, he must have made his hasty reconnaissance during the time when Geary's division of the Federal XII Corps had left its positions on Little Round Top and Cemetery Ridge. It had been ordered to return to its parent unit on Culp's Hill. For a brief period the area was unoccupied, because the III Corps had not moved from its bivouac in the rear to its assigned front on Cemetery Ridge. Johnston's report is significant because it reinforced Lee's completely inaccurate knowledge of Meade's intended dispositions.

Lee completed the issuing of his orders by riding to Ewell's headquarters to personally explain his final plan. Ewell was on a reconnaissance of his corps positions when Lee arrived. Lee, however, waited to make sure that there was not going to be any misunderstanding about the day's activities. Upon Ewell's return, Lee explained again that Ewell's corps was to conduct a demonstration in support of Longstreet's attack. If the demonstration indicated that an assault would succeed, Ewell was to proceed with a full-scale attack. Again hearing no arguments against the plan, Lee rode to a position on Seminary Ridge, where he could see most of the enemy's apparent positions.[68]

Lee was disappointed to find on his arrival that Longstreet's corps still was not in position to attack. The I Corps commander wanted to have Pickett's division available during the attack, but that was impossible because Pickett still had considerable marching to do before his troops would reach Gettysburg. Brig. Gen. Evander Law's brigade of Hood's division also had not arrived, and Longstreet asked to delay the move to his attack positions until Law arrived. Granted permission, he did not begin the approach march until a little after noon. Time was growing short.[69]

Time was playing against Meade for different reasons. About midmorning General Sickles, the III Corps commander, arrived at Meade's headquarters to request permission to move his corps to a new position. Assigned the role of tying the left flank of the II Corps to Little Round Top, Sickles believed that the area along Cemetery Ridge was "unfit for infantry, impracticable for artillery." Large boulders and trees covered the ground to the west of his area of responsibility, which sloped gradually up, toward the Confederate lines. Sickles proposed that he move his corps to the higher ground in the west at a place where a peach orchard bordered on the Emmitsburg Road. Meade explained the army's dispositions, hoping to convince Sickles of the soundness of his assigned position. Sickles left Meade's headquarters with the army's chief of artillery, Brig. Gen. Henry Hunt. The next time Meade talked with Sickles, the III Corps commander had gained sufficient time to move his corps into new positions, well in advance of his assigned area and uncoordinated with the rest of Meade's plans.[70]

Lee's attack did not start until about 1600. Longstreet's approach march was bedeviled by bad luck and poor reconnaissance. By the time he had moved by a concealed route and was ready to attack, the Federals were deployed very differently than they were at the time Lee developed his plan. As a consequence, I Corps did not strike the Federal left flank near Cemetery Hill. Instead, Longstreet's men swung around the enemy's flank that stretched northwestward on a line from near the foot of Little Round Top to the peach orchard near the Emmitsburg Road. On the opposite flank, Ewell started his demonstration with a bombardment conducted by artillery located on Benner Hill. In his typical style, Lee had decentralized the execution and remained mostly an observer throughout the remainder of the day.

Meade, on the other hand, was extremely busy. He had called a council of war for about the time that Longstreet's artillery opened up in support of the I Corps assault. He grabbed his chief engineer, Gouverneur Kemble Warren, and rode to the Union left to find out the reason for the heavy firing. He reached Sickles' assigned position and discovered that the III Corps was well out of line and had advanced into a poorly defended salient at the peach orchard. Warren rode off to find reinforcements for the defense of Little Round Top, and Meade rode forward to find Sickles.

By the time he reached Sickles' headquarters, Meade had decided that it was too late to withdraw the III Corps. If they withdrew under pressure, the entire Federal left might collapse. Meade told Sickles that he would send help from the artillery reserve and the II and V Corps; he rode back to Cemetery Ridge to coordinate this effort.[71]

Fortunately for Meade, Longstreet's and Ewell's attacks were uncoordinated. Although Ewell's artillery started firing at the right time, his infantry did not attack until almost three hours after Longstreet's infantry. But even with the poor coordination, Longstreet's infantry assaults drove the Federals back and pierced their lines in several places. Reinforced by units from the Federal II and V Corps, the III Corps fought desperately but finally retreated to Cemetery Ridge. Two Confederate brigades from Hill's corps gained a foothold in the II Corps line near a "clump of trees" in the center of Cemetery Ridge. Meade started funneling troops from the XII Corps on the right to reinforce the deteriorating situation on the left. The timely arrival of Sedgwick's VI Corps on the left also prevented a collapse. On the opposite flank, Ewell's infantry eventually attacked. They seized the trenches just vacated by the XII Corps on Culp's Hill and briefly penetrated the XI Corps front on the northeast slope of Cemetery Hill. The fighting continued until well after dark.

That evening Lee was convinced that success still could be achieved if his army's efforts were coordinated better. From his perspective, on the enemy's left the Yankees had been driven back a considerable distance from their positions in the orchard to their final lines on Cemetery Ridge. The penetration of the enemy's center near the clump of trees on Cemetery Ridge also looked promising. These results, combined with Ewell's penetration on Cemetery Hill and seizure of portions of Culp's Hill, indicated the continued dominance of the Army of Northern Virginia. (*Map 12*) Moreover, Stuart and the Confederate cavalry finally had arrived on the battlefield during the day. Although unhappy that his army had not achieved more, Lee believed that a more concerted effort on 3 July offered excellent opportunities for ultimate success.[72]

Lee did not meet simultaneously with all of his corps commanders. Instead, he dealt with them individually. He directed Ewell to continue the

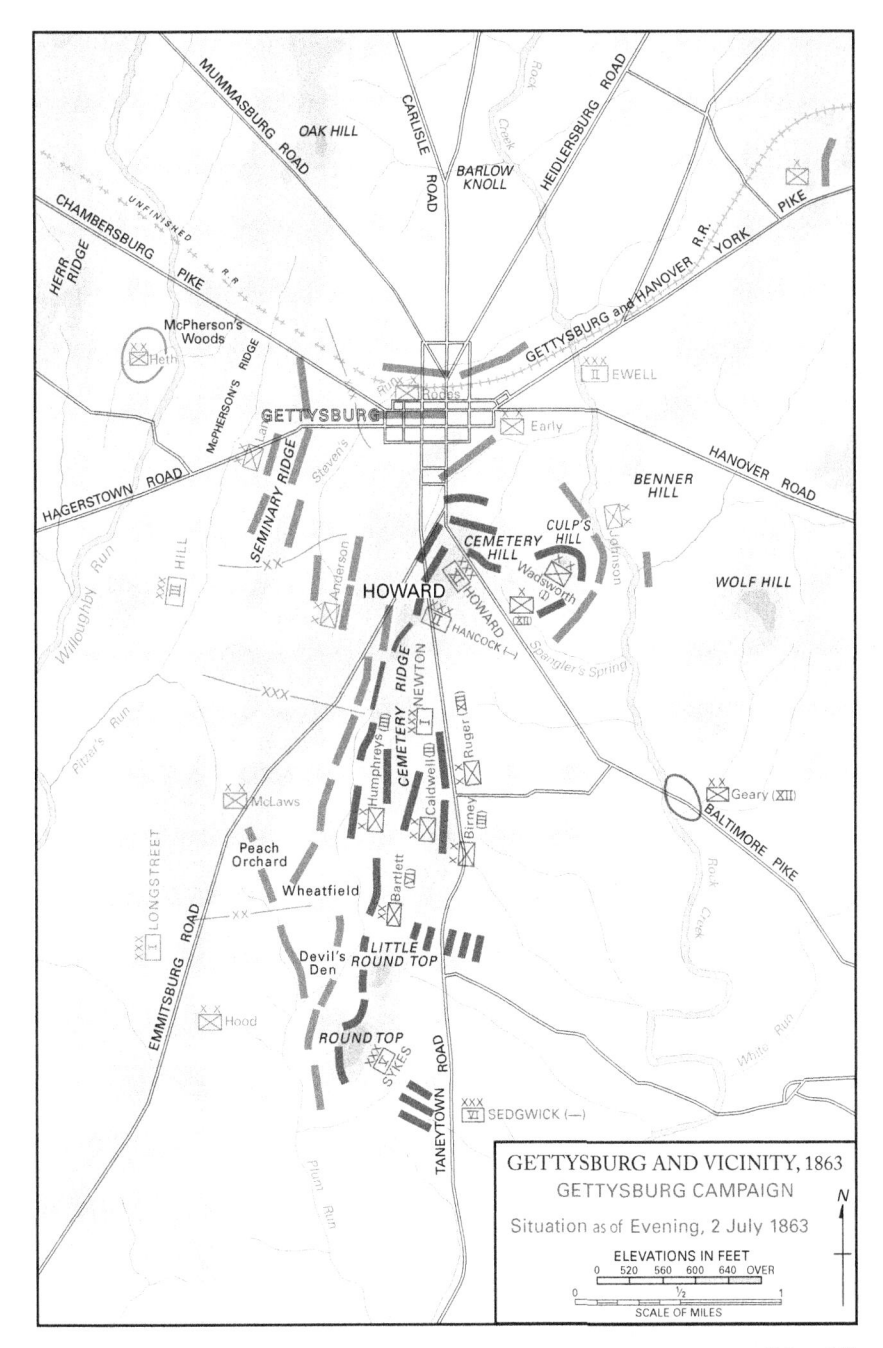

MAP 12

attack against the Yankee right on Culp's Hill. He ordered Longstreet to continue the attack started on 2 July. He assigned Hill a supporting role.

On the morning of 3 July Lee rode to Longstreet's headquarters to determine how his attack was going to be made. Almost before Lee was able to begin the conversation, Longstreet told the commanding general that I Corps scouts had conducted a reconnaissance around the Union left flank. It was still possible to slip around the enemy and position the army so the Federals would have to attack the Confederates. He was organizing his units to begin the move to the right. Amazed that Longstreet had interpreted his orders to mean that he could make a flanking march before conducting his attack, Lee rejected the idea and told Longstreet that the plan was to have the I Corps attack the enemy's center on Cemetery Ridge.

Longstreet argued that while Pickett's division was fresh, Hood's and McLaws' divisions were not. Moreover, if Hood and McLaws attacked the center, the Confederate right flank would be exposed to a counterattack. This could endanger the entire Southern position. Lee agreed with Longstreet's analysis and said that Heth's division and half of Pender's division—both from A. P. Hill's corps—would support an attack by Pickett. Hood and McLaws could remain in position to protect the right. The generals then rode to a position where they could see the enemy's center. The discussion became heated as Longstreet argued that a frontal attack could not succeed. When asked how many soldiers he intended to commit to the attack, Lee replied 15,000. Longstreet answered that there were not 15,000 men alive who could successfully attack across the open field that had been selected as the avenue of approach. Furthermore, Yankee artillery now positioned on Little Round Top could sweep the entire line of attack as it advanced across the open field. One of Lee's staff officers replied that these Federal guns could be silenced. Lee was adamant, and Longstreet acquiesced. The commanding general added that Stuart's cavalry would make a supporting attack by riding around the Federal defenses and attacking the center of the rear of the enemy's line. (*Map 13*) The instructions for "Pickett's Charge" were complete.[73]

In the meantime, Johnson's division of Ewell's corps had followed Lee's earlier instructions and at first light had opened the attack up the slopes of Culp's Hill. Instead of finding vacated trenches as they had on the previous afternoon, they now discovered that the XII Corps had returned in strength. Moreover, the Federal commanders were anxious to regain the positions that had been lost so easily the day before. Federal artillery, unanswered by Confederate guns, supported furious counterattacks. Not only did Johnson's attack falter, his soldiers were driven from the ground that they had held at first light. It was an inauspicious start for Lee's plan.[74]

Meade's commanders were confident that their positions were strong. During the previous evening, Meade had called a meeting of his principal

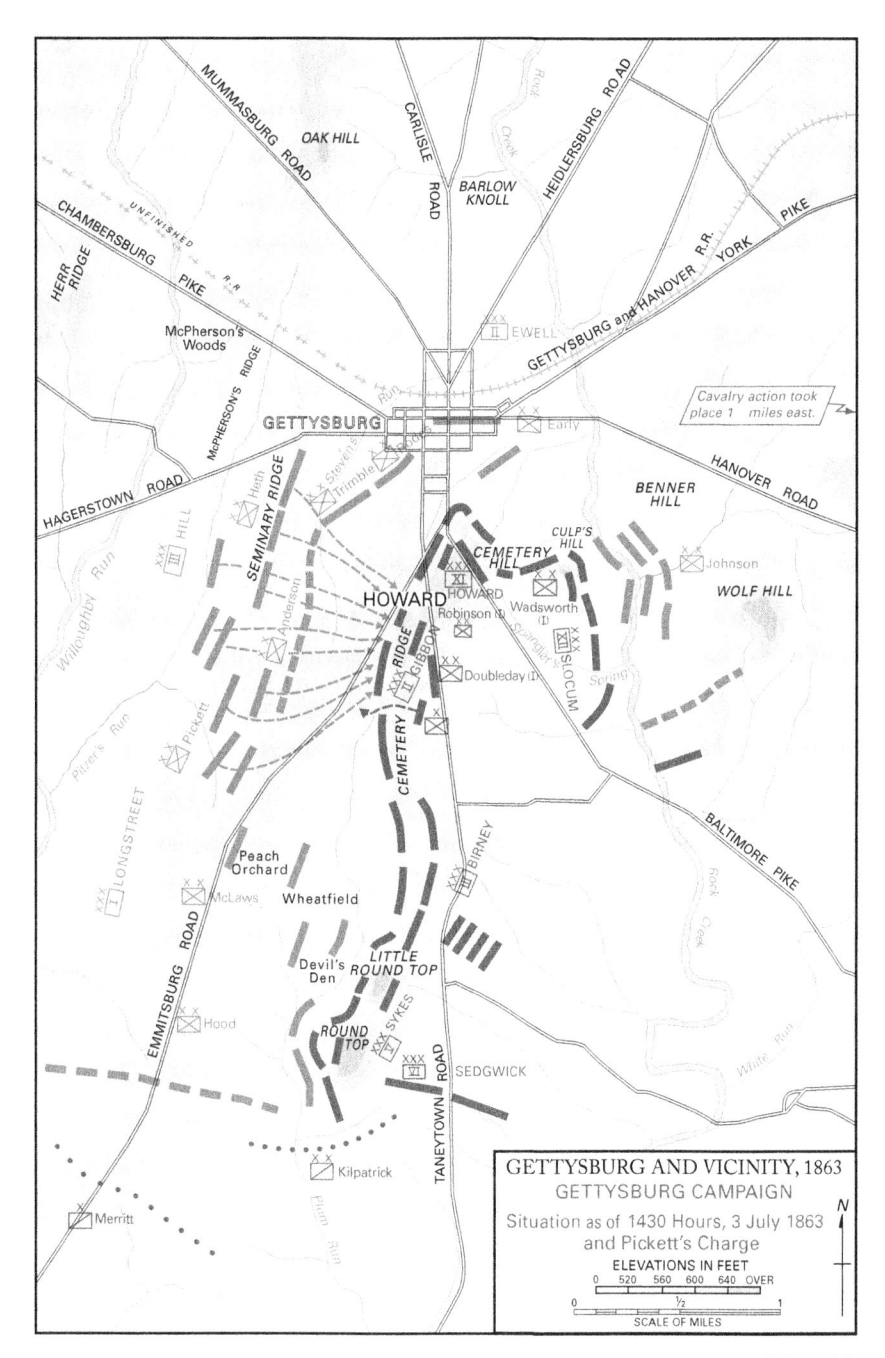

MAP 13

commanders. He gave each of them an opportunity to express his opinion on the next course of action. Only John Newton, the acting I Corps commander, indicated that the current positions were poor. The rest seemed determined to stay and fight. The three-hour meeting tended to ramble; finally, Meade's chief of staff, Butterfield, posed three alternatives to the group and asked the commanders to vote on each one. Essentially, the alternatives were to attack, defend, or withdraw. Meade was surprised by his chief's interjection but allowed the vote to proceed. The result was overwhelmingly in favor of defending the current positions and waiting for at least a day to see what Lee would do. Meade closed the meeting by commenting, "Such, then, is the decision." As the commanders filed out of his headquarters, Meade stopped the acting II Corps commander, Maj. Gen. John Gibbon. He told Gibbon that since Lee had attacked both the right and left flanks, his next move probably would be against the center, the location of Gibbon's corps. Everyone returned to their headquarters to await the next day's events.[75]

Lee rode with Longstreet along his attack positions twice during the morning of 3 July. He wanted to make sure that the artillery and infantry were properly positioned and ready for the decisive blow. Approximately 172 Confederate guns were on line to deliver a massive cannonade. After the guns had demoralized the Federal infantry and suppressed the enemy's artillery, the 13,500 soldiers from Longstreet's and Hill's corps who finally had been massed for the attack would charge across a mile-wide open field. A little after 1300 the Confederate artillery opened fire.[76]

Pickett's Charge is probably the most famous attack of the entire war. Its fame was achieved by the heroism displayed by the Confederates, who had to withstand the furious Federal artillery and musket fire, and by the belief that the few men who finally stumbled over the stone wall along the Union front line had reached the "high water mark" of the Confederacy. While all of this is true, it is equally important to remember that Meade's defense, both tactically and operationally, was extremely effective because of strong Union leadership, creative command and control, and the fighting spirit of the soldiers. The Army of Northern Virginia did everything that Robert E. Lee asked of it. The Army of the Potomac was its equal, and the Battle of Gettysburg finally demonstrated this beyond a reasonable doubt. While very famous, Pickett's Charge was futile.

Stuart's cavalry attack against the Union rear was equally futile. On a field about two miles east of Gettysburg, Federal cavalry easily turned back Stuart's troopers in a mounted clash. The Confederate defeat on 3 July was of immense proportions.[77]

Back on Seminary Ridge, Generals Lee and Longstreet rallied the remnants of Pickett's assault force as they streamed back across the field under artillery fire. Both officers exerted a calming influence on the men, and within an hour the Army of Northern Virginia had gotten itself back together again. Longstreet tightened his lines, pulling McLaws' and Hood's divisions westward across the Emmitsburg Road to a shorter line. He also shifted the artillery so it was ready to receive any counterattacks that Meade might attempt. Throughout the remainder of that day and night and for most of 4 July, the Confederates awaited a Federal counterattack that never materialized.

Late in the afternoon of 3 July Meade had directed the V Corps commander to make a reconnaissance of the Confederate right. Sykes sent a reinforced brigade forward, but an enemy brigade posted in front of the Confederate line quickly stopped the Federals. Meade, still unsure of Lee's next move but certain that a rebel retreat was imminent, ordered seven of his eight brigades of cavalry against the enemy's rear and lines of communications on 4 July. In the meantime, he unscrambled the units that had been jumbled together during the rapid shifting of forces over the past three days. For him, 4 July was also a day of reorganization and of waiting to see what the enemy would do.[78]

Lee's situation on 4 July was precarious. Although Lee was certain he could repulse any Federal attack, his lines of communications were vulnerable. If he remained in position too long, the larger Army of the Potomac might eventually work its way around one of his flanks and cut off his line of retreat. When it became clear that the Yankees were not going to attack, he ordered a retreat to the crossing sites over the Potomac at Williamsport. Ambulances carrying the wounded and wagons carrying the plunder from the Pennsylvania farmlands departed first. The seventeen-mile-long train moved out, and after dark on the fourth, Hill's corps withdrew, followed soon after by Longstreet's and Ewell's corps.[79]

On that same evening Meade, wanting to gain the initiative, held a council of war. He proposed moving against the Confederates on the next day. All the corps commanders still advised against an attack if Lee continued to hold a position along Seminary Ridge. Nevertheless, Meade directed the VI Corps to conduct a reconnaissance in force on the morning of the fifth. When it moved forward at a little before noon, it did not run into any resistance until the corps reached Fairfield. Sedgwick reported to Meade that he suspected that the Confederates were going to wait for a Union attack there.[80]

This upset the plans Meade already had set in motion. In addition to sending his cavalry out to harass the enemy's rear areas and directing the VI Corps to make its reconnaissance, he had directed a Federal force at Frederick, Maryland, to advance to the vicinity of Harpers Ferry. This could block Lee's retreat. Deciding also that it would be too costly to try to force the passes into the Cumberland Valley and advance directly against Lee's rear, Meade ordered his army to march southward on the east side of the mountains and assemble at Middletown. In anticipation of this move, he directed his supply base to be shifted from Westminster to a railhead at Frederick. But Sedgwick's report of the results of his reconnaissance as far as Fairfield seemed to indicate that Lee was still looking for a fight in Pennsylvania. Meade halted his army for a day and a half until he determined that the Army of Northern Virginia was in fact withdrawing. By the time his army was on the move again, the Confederates were safely approaching their crossing point at Williamsport.

Lee's army had about half the distance that Meade's had to travel to reach Williamsport. Unfortunately for the Confederates, when they reached there, they found that their pontoon bridge had been destroyed in a Federal raid and that recent heavy rains swelled the Potomac River. Lee ordered crossings to be prepared and his army to entrench. He was still hopeful that Meade would attack.[81]

Meade finally had his army assembled in front of the Confederate positions at Williamsport on 12 July. During the evening he met with his corps commanders and found them still reluctant to attack prepared enemy positions. Not having seen the ground over which an attack would have to be made, Meade withheld his decision to attack and on the next day conducted a personal reconnaissance with his chief of staff. Determining that an assault was feasible, he directed the army to attack on 14 July. By then, Lee was safely back on Virginia soil.

Lincoln and Stanton were furious. In Washington, it appeared that Meade had missed the opportunity for which everyone in the North had been waiting—the complete destruction of the Army of Northern Virginia. Lincoln was quoted as saying that Meade looked like an old lady trying to shoo her geese across a creek. The Joint Congressional Committee on the Conduct of the War later held hearings hostile to Meade, accusing him of cowardice. Meade was taken aback by this attitude in the capital. Instead of being a great hero, he was being characterized as just the opposite. The final proof of Meade's excellent abilities, however, was the ultimate honor bestowed on him. The Northern leadership stopped looking for a new commander for the Army of the Potomac. When Lee surrendered the Army of Northern Virginia at Appomattox Court House almost two years later, Meade still commanded the army that ultimately trapped and defeated him. The Army of the Potomac was to be Meade's for the duration of the war.[82]

Operational Artists

Many commentators on the Gettysburg campaign have focused on the tactics of Meade and Lee. For these analysts, the campaign only provides the backdrop against which to view the events of 1–3 July. They have examined the commanders' battlefield decisions often in excruciating detail to discover the reasons for the successes and failures of both sides. They have identified key tactical events and decisions that shaped Lee's ultimate failure and Meade's success. Often in these analyses, Lee's subordinates appear as important reasons for the Army of Northern Virginia's defeat. Richard Ewell and James Longstreet most often appear on their list of villains. The commentators contend that Ewell was indecisive throughout much of the battle; his failure to follow up the initial success on 1 July made it very difficult for Lee to regain the upper hand that his army initially had gained at great cost. They have turned to Longstreet's infatuation with his concept of an offensive-defensive and believe that this hampered the I Corps commander's performance. Some have characterized his actions as bordering on outright insubordination. By focusing on the battle, however, they have misunderstood the importance of expert performance at the operational level. The conduct of the campaign provides more than a backdrop. It provides many of the reasons for the success of George G. Meade and the failure of Robert E. Lee.

At the center of the entire campaign lies the issue of objectives. Lee developed his objectives in consultation with the Confederate president and the cabinet. It was an excellent forum for mixing the military's views (as expressed by Lee) and the political views (as expressed by the members of the cabinet and the president). There should not have been any question in Lee's mind as to what he was trying to achieve during the invasion. Indeed, it appears that he was quite clear on those things that his army had to accomplish during the campaign. The objectives reflect an interesting mix of political and military goals. On the military side, his army was to gather supplies from Northern farmers, draw the Army of the Potomac away from defensive lines along Virginia's river lines, and win an important battle on Northern soil.

This last military objective supported the political goals as well. A great victory in the North might still convince some European nations to recognize the Confederacy as an independent nation. If Lee effectively threatened Philadelphia, Baltimore, or Washington, the potential for European recognition might be increased. Other political goals supported the concept of an invasion. The invasion could increase Northern war weariness and thus foster some initiatives from a peace movement. Additionally, either a successful battle or threats to Philadelphia, Baltimore, and Washington might reinforce Northern feelings of war weariness. This blend of military and political objectives was a reasonable and feasible goal for the use of military power.

Meade's objectives were much more narrowly focused. His objectives were given to him without his being consulted, but General Halleck's participation in Washington insured that the military as well as the political view was well represented. Meade was told to operate against the invading force of rebels and to screen Baltimore and Washington. Although the accomplishment of each objective would have clear political results, both objectives translated into precise military objectives. The results of the application of military power against them could be easily measured.

Applying these objectives to the theater setting provides an interesting contrast between Lee's and Meade's orientations. Lee's objectives did not automatically focus either him or his army on the enemy. In fact, in order to gather supplies, the Army of Northern Virginia had to operate out of the range of the Army of the Potomac. Therefore, it was important not to operate in the enemy's presence. Naturally, Lee knew that the Federals would pursue him once they had determined the extent of his operations. During the Maryland campaign in September 1862, even the overly cautious George B. McClellan finally pursued Lee's invading army. Lee knew that once the Yankees had substantial combat power in Pennsylvania, widespread foraging was out of the question among the hostile population and in unfamiliar territory.

To accomplish both the objective of gathering supplies and the objective of fighting a battle, Lee needed at least to know the Yankees' movements if not their intentions. Lee's poor use of his cavalry during the latter half of June was devastating. His substandard use of his cavalry meant that he did not know the enemy's dispositions and had no way of inferring their intentions. Even after Hill's corps had engaged the vanguard of the Army of the Potomac on 1 July, Lee still did not know the extent of the damage that he could inflict or that could be inflicted upon him.

There is no evidence to suggest that Lee prioritized any of the conflicting objectives he was trying to accomplish during the campaign. There also is no evidence to suggest that either he or his staff analyzed the consistencies and inconsistencies between the objectives. Because of the complex relationships between his political and military objectives, an analysis to prioritize and to determine inconsistencies was absolutely essential. At the time, this probably was not seen as being particularly important because everyone believed that the Army of Northern Virginia could do virtually anything it wanted when confronted by the Army of the Potomac. Unfortunately for the Confederacy, past experiences were irrelevant. The Army of the Potomac had a new commander on 28 June.

Meade's objectives focused him only on the enemy. Within the theater setting, the objective to cover Washington and Baltimore for political reasons still meant that he must remain oriented on the locations and movements of the Army of Northern Virginia. His aggressive intent, excellent combat command experience at all levels of command, and absolute attention on the enemy meant that the Army of the Potomac was not going to be distracted by anything like Stuart's cavalry raid. In addition, Meade's political guidance translated quite readily into military terms: find, fix, and fight Lee's army.

Initially, Lee's concept of operations masked the weaknesses in his plan. It was excellent up to the point where an aggressive opponent put it to the test. He had integrated alacrity and deception; and as long as Joe Hooker was opposite him, his operational vision was as brilliant as ever. But this concept depended on poor performance and timidity by the enemy army's leadership. When that leadership changed, the whole concept was faulty.

During the march north through Maryland into Pennsylvania, it appeared that Lee masterfully synchronized his forces. He outmaneuvered Joe Hooker and kept the enemy commander constantly in a state of uncertainty. The full meaning of Stuart's absence just prior to the battle was not obvious at the time because some Confederate cavalry still screened the army's movements and Hooker was in a quandary about what to do. But other trusted subordinates were not clear about Lee's intent. With the general knowledge that a battle with the Yankees was inevitable, it is no wonder that first Heth, then Hill, and finally Ewell piled on the Federals when they saw an opportunity on 1 July. Integration of forces at all levels of command was not achieved. Moreover, operational intelligence did not play a role in Heth's, Hill's, or Ewell's decisions. They were simply trying to achieve tactical success. When Lee finally arrived on the battlefield, he sensed the operational problem and tried to slow down the tactical development of the battle. By then it was too late. His subordinates already had committed him to battle, and they were urging further aggressiveness. The extent of the tactical commitment was too much to allow him to slow down the operational development of the campaign.

Meade's concept of operations was borne out by events. But he had an easier task than Lee. By the time Meade assumed command, he knew what the enemy was doing. He did not know all of the important details, but he had the capability to find the answers he needed. His army was operating on friendly territory; intelligence collection was much easier than it had been in the past in Virginia. Meade, however, personally brought something to the campaign that had been lacking so far. He had an acute knowledge of the capabilities of the Army of the Potomac, which he learned during his earlier years in command at various levels. He knew it was a good army. Thus, the scanty intelligence did not hinder his aggressiveness. His conduct of the movement to contact was brilliantly conceived and flawlessly executed. After assuming command on 28 June, Meade quickly formulated a plan of campaign and focused on operational attainment of the objectives, using mutually supporting corps to offensively find and fight Lee. He brought forces to bear at critical times at the right place.

In the opening stages of the battle, operational maneuver played an interesting role. Lee was caught generally unaware of the enemy, and Meade was looking for a fight. But Lee had numerical superiority throughout 1 July. His army won the battle. Aggressive leadership by Hill and Ewell drove the Federals off the field. Even though unprepared, Lee won because his forces were deployed for successful maneuver at the operational level. If Lee had decided to withdraw on 2 July instead of 4 July, we might be analyzing the Battle of Gettysburg as another Confederate victory. Lee would have outmaneuvered Meade, driven the Federals off the battlefield at Gettysburg, and then, having gathered substantial supplies and won a battle, could have withdrawn southward. The extent of the victory certainly would have been equal to the victory at Chancellorsville. But once Lee decided on the evening of 1 July that the tactical victory was not great enough, Meade outmaneuvered him operationally. Rapidly, Meade brought superior combat and logistical power to bear at the operationally decisive place and time.

Meade's ability to generate operational reserves permitted him to achieve superiority at the critical points. During the movement toward Gettysburg from 28 June to 1 July, he deployed his corps on a wide front but kept them close enough together to avoid defeat in detail. Covering his supply base at Westminster, Maryland, Meade could respond in any direction and reasonably expect success. More important, his dispositions meant that even if he made unexpected contact with Lee's army, the campaign would still unfold in accordance with his long-range operational vision. He effectively operated against the invading force of rebels. Furthermore, he also was in a position to shift eastward to cover Baltimore and Washington, his other primary objectives. The positioning of his corps in relation to each other and in support of his two objectives allowed Meade to use uncommitted forces to respond flexibly and creatively, regardless of the Confederate reaction to contact with the Army of the Potomac.

The Army of Northern Virginia's immediate reaction to the unexpected contact with the Army of the Potomac on 1 July also demonstrated Lee's understanding of the effective use of operational reserves. Even though he was only vaguely aware of the location of the enemy, Lee had sensibly deployed his army so combat power could be built up wherever it was needed when battle occurred. Perhaps an argument could be made that his forces were deployed too well: When battle was joined, it was too difficult for Lee to slow down its development. Aggressive subordinates made use of the operational reserves that Lee should have kept firmly under his control. Nevertheless, Lee's understanding of the importance of operational reserves and their effective use was a hallmark of his repeated successes throughout the war. Gettysburg demonstrated once again his understanding of their importance.

Of particular interest is the comparison between the operational reserves available to Lee and Meade on the evening of 3 July. Lee had run out of them. Meade still had operational reserves available. Faced with this reality, Lee only had one alternative: Withdraw to Virginia. Meade, on the other hand, possessed numerous alternatives. He could attack Lee directly. He could maneuver against Lee's line of communications. He could remain on the defensive and cover Washington and Baltimore. As it turned out, Meade chose to remain on the defensive, undoubtedly influenced by the tactical realities of the Civil War. Having experienced combat command at all major levels, Meade knew that attacks against prepared positions were extremely costly. This attitude caused him problems with the leadership in Washington. They wanted Lee's army destroyed in place. They believed that Meade had the forces available. While they were correct — Meade had the operational reserves — they did not understand the tactical realities that Meade knew so well.

The second day further illustrates the interplay between the use of operational reserves and tactical realities. Here Meade excelled. He brought forces from one flank to be plugged into another to stem Longstreet's attack. He force-marched Sedgwick's corps, covering a greater distance than Longstreet's missing division (Pickett) to arrive in the nick of time on the battlefield. By contrast, Pickett remained at Chambersburg too long to be an effective operational reserve.

Tactical realities also demanded logistical feasibility. At the operational level, both Lee and Meade understood the profound influence of logistics. For this reason, in most histories of the campaign, one finds little comment on operational logistical constraints. Each commander's long-range logistical vision permitted him to operate creatively. But it is operational logistics that lends an air of incredibility to Longstreet's repeated proposal for an offensive defense. From a purely tactical standpoint, Longstreet's concept made good sense. But it suffered from a blind spot on logistics. Operating on foreign soil, Lee could not afford to separate his army from its logistical tail for an extended period. If he did and Meade chose not to attack, Lee would be in an impossible operational situation. Longstreet's arguments notwithstanding, there was no suitable location between the Army of the Potomac and Washington for Lee to position his Army. Longstreet's vague references to such a location avoided the crucial questions. Which location would be so important that Meade would be forced to attack? What would Lee do logistically if Meade chose not to attack? Operating in hostile territory, Lee had to assess operational logistical considerations to which his subordinates were not accustomed.

Lee's relationships to his subordinates during the battle trouble many people. It is in those relationships that many observers find the most fault. They argue that Lee should have been more decisive with Ewell and firmer with Longstreet. And Lee should not have reorganized his command structure just prior to a type of campaign with which no one had any previous successful experience. These arguments, however, concern Lee the tactician; off the field of battle, both the command structure and Lee's relationships with his subordinates were highly effective. Obviously, the campaign was lost at the tactical level. Lee felt that he could only accomplish his campaign objectives by winning a battle more spectacular than his defensive stroke at Chancellorsville. He believed that this required him to attack if he was going to win a more clear-cut victory. But it is by no means obvious that a firmer, more decisive Robert E. Lee would have made any tactical difference. The experience of the commanders in the Civil War repeatedly demonstrated that an attacker was at a severe disadvantage. Technology favored the defender. Furthermore, in the area where there can be a search for alternative outcomes, one can overlook the importance of the enemy in determining the original outcome. A competent commander led the Army of the Potomac; Lee was facing a fundamentally different situation than he had in previous confrontations with Union commanders.

George G. Meade's relationships with his subordinates were highly effective. Throughout the campaign, he selected trusted subordinates to command several corps in order to reduce his span of control. Reynolds commanded a "wing" of the Army of the Potomac while it was moving in the direction of Gettysburg. After Reynolds was killed and Meade had received word that a battle was in progress at Gettysburg, he directed Hancock to ride to the scene and take charge, even though Hancock was junior to other corps commanders already on the field. He used councils of war to cement relationships. Rather than being signs of weakness and lack of command presence, they tended to ensure that his senior commanders understood that Meade knew and valued their views on key decisions. By contrast, Joe Hooker and other preceding commanders had kept their subordinates in the dark on their operational concept. Meade demonstrated effective operational command.

In the final analysis, making an overall comparison of the two opponents is very difficult. Each commander faced different problems, not the least of which is that they faced each other. Measuring performance against objectives, however, narrows the evaluation considerably. Meade accomplished the objectives given to him by his military commander, Henry W. Halleck. He operated effectively against the invading force of rebels and effectively covered Washington and Baltimore. But he did not achieve total success. He did not achieve the objective of his political leaders: the destruction of the Army of Northern Virginia. It is possible to argue that this was an implied task subordinate to his specified task to operate against the invaders, and therefore he should have pursued this objective without specific instructions. It is interesting to note, however, that the experienced combat leaders, Halleck and Meade, did not identify this implied task. Perhaps their previous Civil War experiences taught them that a single crushing blow in a Napoleonic battle was an impossible task.

Even though he lost the battle and thus lost the campaign, Lee accomplished almost everything he intended. He had gathered supplies from Northern farmers. He drew the Army of the Potomac away from the natural defensive barriers in northern Virginia. By the evening of 1 July, he had won a battle on Northern soil. At the cost of 8,000 casualties, his army had captured 4,500 Yankees, had killed or wounded another 4,500 enemy, and seized all the terrain that the enemy held at the outset of the battle. But Lee decided to continue the fight offensively. That decision changed the statistics significantly. Outnumbering the Federals on 1 July by 28,000 to 18,000, Confederate relative combat superiority was reversed by 3 July. By then, the Union had mustered 85,500 to the Confederate 75,000. Casualty figures were even more dramatic. Confederate losses were over 28,000, more than 37 percent of the forces engaged. Federal casualties were more than 23,000, or 26 percent of Meade's force. Lee's decision to pursue the implied task of destroying the Army of the Potomac cost him dearly, in terms of both casualties and the overall outcome of the campaign.[83]

Implied tasks for both commanders produced an interesting turn of events. Lee's implied task hurt him militarily. Meade's implied task hurt him politically. As is always the case, if a commander does not precisely know all of his objectives, any road will lead him to them, including the road to ruin. Clearly defined and attainable objectives are crucial for the operational commander.

Notes

1. Histories of the Gettysburg campaign abound. Because this chapter is only a synopsis of the more important events that shaped the campaign at the operational level, I have omitted many details. I have used citations that will direct the reader to sources helpful for those who desire a more complete understanding of the events. For a description of the Confederate cabinet discussions with Lee, see, for example, John H. Reagan, *Memoirs, With Special Reference to Secession and the Civil War* (New York: The Neale Publishing Co., 1906), p. 121. The best overall source for the Gettysburg campaign is Edwin B. Coddington, *The Gettysburg Campaign: A Study in Command* (New York: Scribner's, 1968). This was published in a paperback edition in 1984 and is widely available.
2. Stephen Sears, *George B. McClellan: The Young Napoleon* (New York: Ticknor & Fields, 1988), pp. 339–40; T. Harry Williams, *Lincoln and His Generals* (New York: Knopf, 1952), p. 212.
3. It is interesting to note that these discussions reflect precisely what Clausewitz advocated in one section of *On War*. Lee, the commander, was participating in strategic discussions with the cabinet. Did the results of these discussions support or refute Clausewitz's admonition? Instead of adding clarity, the discussions may have contributed to cloudy strategic thinking. See Carl von Clausewitz, *On War*, ed. and trans. Michael Howard and Peter Paret (Princeton: Princeton University Press, 1984), p. 608.
4. Archer Jones, *Confederate Strategy From Shiloh to Vicksburg* (Baton Rouge: Louisiana State University Press, 1961), pp. 199–200.
5. Douglas S. Freeman, *R. E. Lee: A Biography*, 4 vols. (New York: C. Scribner's Sons, 1934), 2: 19; U.S. War Department, *The War of the Rebellion: A Compilation of the Official Records of the Union and Confederate Armies*, 69 vols. (Washington, D.C.: Government Printing Office, 1880–1901), ser. 1, vol. 25, pt. 2, p. 782 (hereafter cited as *OR*); Jones, *Confederate Strategy*, pp. 205–06.
6. *OR*, vol. 25, pt. 2, pp. 791–92; Armistead L. Long, *Memoirs of Robert E. Lee* (New York: J. M. Stoddart & Co., 1886), p. 267.
7. J. William Jones, ed., *Southern Historical Society Papers*, 52 vols. (Richmond: Virginia Historical Society, 1877), 4: 153.
8. Clifford Dowdey and Louis H. Manarin, eds., *Wartime Papers of R. E. Lee* (Boston: Little, Brown, 1961), p. 508.
9. Reagan, *Memoirs*, pp. 121–22; Jones, *Historical Society Papers*, 4: 153; Long, *Memoirs of Robert E. Lee*, pp. 268–69.
10. Dowdey and Manarin, *Wartime Papers*, p. 490; Jones, *Historical Society Papers*, 4: 160.
11. *OR*, vol. 25, pt. 2, p. 810.
12. Douglas S. Freeman, *Lee's Lieutenants: A Study in Command*, 3 vols. (New York: C. Scribner's Sons, 1942), 2: 712; *OR*, vol. 25, pt. 2, p. 840.
13. Herman Hattaway and Archer Jones, *How the North Won: A Military History of the Civil War* (Urbana: University of Illinois Press, 1983), pp. 382–83.
14. *OR*, vol. 25, pt. 2, p. 438.
15. Williams, *Lincoln and His Generals*, pp. 243–46.

16. Dowdey and Manarin, *Wartime Papers*, pp. 501–03. On 7 June Lee asked President Davis to return to his army Pickett's division of Longstreet's corps. Even at this late date, the unit had been proposed to be sent to help the situation at Vicksburg and still had not returned to Lee's control. It is impossible to tell how important the proposal to reinforce the west was in Lee's recommendation to invade the North. Detaching forces from Lee's army had been a strong possibility, supported initially by the Secretary of War. Lee had to do something spectacular to convince the government that he needed more forces than he previously had available to him at Chancellorsville. A proposal simply to continue to defend along the Rappahannock River probably would not prove that he could not afford to send part of his army to someone else. The invasion of the North provided him with that proof.
17. Dowdey and Manarin, *Wartime Papers*, p. 496. In Washington, General in Chief Halleck hoped Dix would accomplish much more than he did. Dix believed that his force was too small to accomplish much. He burned some bridges near Ashland, Virginia, and captured some supplies at Hanover Court House, but that was the extent of the threat. See *OR*, vol. 27, pt. 1, pp. 18–19.
18. Ibid., pt. 3, pp. 12–13.
19. Ibid., pt. 1, p. 30.
20. Ibid., pt. 1, pp. 31–32.
21. Ibid., pt. 3, pp. 27–28, and pt. 1, p. 904; Henry B. McClellan, *The Life and Campaigns of Major General J. E. B. Stuart* (New York: Houghton, Mifflin and Co., 1885), pp. 264–69, 294; Freeman, *R. E. Lee*, 3: 8–13, 19.
22. *OR*, vol. 27, pt. 1, pp. 34–35.
23. Ibid., pt. 2, pp. 297–98; Kenneth P. Williams, *Lincoln Finds a General: A Military Study of the Civil War*, 5 vols. (New York: Macmillan, 1959), 2: 630; John W. Thomason, *Jeb Stuart* (New York: C. Scribner's Sons, 1930), pp. 413–21; Coddington, *Gettysburg Campaign*, pp. 69–70.
24. *OR*, vol. 27, pt. 3, pp. 924–25, and pt. 1, p. 77.
25. Ibid., pt. 3, p. 88. George G. Meade, ed., *The Life and Letters of George Gordon Meade*, 2 vols. (New York: Charles Scribner's Sons, 1913), 1: 385.
26. *OR*, vol. 27, pt. 1, p. 40.
27. Coddington, *Gettysburg Campaign*, p. 119.
28. Williams, *Lincoln Finds a General*, 2: 668–69; Edward J. Stackpole, *They Met at Gettysburg* (Harrisburg, Pa.: Eagle Books, 1956), pp. 22–23; Coddington, *Gettysburg Campaign*, pp. 139–40.
29. E. B. Long and Barbara Long, *Civil War Day by Day: An Almanac, 1861–1865* (New York: Doubleday, 1971), p. 371.
30. Williams, *Lincoln and His Generals*, p. 258.
31. Ibid.; Williams, *Lincoln Finds a General*, 2: 641–42.
32. *OR*, vol. 27, pt. 1, p. 58.
33. Ibid.
34. Ibid.
35. Ibid.
36. Meade, *Life and Letters*, 2: 11.
37. Williams, *Lincoln and His Generals*, p. 247.
38. *OR*, vol. 27, pt. 3, p. 374, and pt. 1, p. 61.
39. Ibid.
40. George R. Agassiz, ed., *Inside Meade's Headquarters, 1863–1865: Letters of Colonel Theodore Lyman* (Boston: The Atlantic Monthly Press, 1922), p. 25; W. A. Swanberg, *Sickles the Incredible* (New York: Scribner, 1956), p. 195.

41. Emerson G. Taylor, *Gouverneur Kemble Warren* (New York: Houghton Mifflin Co., 1959), pp. 119–20.
42. Frederick H. Dyer, *A Compendium of the War of the Rebellion*, 3 vols. (New York: T. Yoseloff, 1959), 1: 287, 301, 323, 318; Meade, *Life and Letters*, 1: 389; *OR*, vol. 25, pt. 2, pp. 471–72.
43. Freeman Cleaves, *Meade of Gettysburg* (Norman: University of Oklahoma Press, 1960), pp. 129–30; *OR*, vol. 27, pt. 1, p. 65.
44. James Longstreet, *From Manassas to Appomattox: Memoirs of the Civil War in America* (Philadelphia: J. B. Lippincott Co., 1896), pp. 346–47.
45. Thomason, *Jeb Stuart*, pp. 421–24.
46. *OR*, vol. 27, pt. 3, p. 923.
47. Much historical controversy surrounds the misuse of the Confederate cavalry during this stage of the campaign. The safest to say is that Lee and Stuart share the blame. Lee had sufficient cavalry with the army to keep him informed. Their orders, however, did not tell them specifically to maintain contact with the Union army and report its movements. Stuart's share of the blame is that he actually did not pass around the Union army without hindrance. Soon after setting out, he ran into part of Hancock's II Federal Corps and had to make a detour. Arguably, he also took the best brigade commanders with him. Moreover, he captured 125 supply wagons, which he decided to take with him. This seriously decreased his rate of march. Clearly, the Confederate cavalry was not used properly during this stage of the campaign; the eyes and ears of the Army of Northern Virginia were not focused on the campaign objectives.
48. *OR*, vol. 27, pt. 2, p. 316.
49. Coddington, *Gettysburg Campaign*, pp. 186–93.
50. Ibid., pp. 194–95.
51. *OR*, vol. 27, pt. 1, pp. 62–63.
52. Ibid.
53. Edward J. Nichols, *Toward Gettysburg: A Biography of General John F. Reynolds* (University Park: Pennsylvania State University Press, 1956), p. 196; *OR*, vol. 27, pt. 1, p. 69.
54. James L. Morrison, Jr., ed., *The Memoirs of Henry Heth* (Westport, Conn.: Greenwood Press, 1974), p. 173.
55. During a courtesy call at Chambersburg by one of Longstreet's division commanders, John B. Hood, Lee exclaimed "Ah! General, the enemy is a long time finding us; if he does not succeed soon, we must go in search of him." See John B. Hood, *Advance and Retreat* (New Orleans, La.: G. T. Beauregard, 1886), p. 55; Coddington, *Gettysburg Campaign*, p. 195.
56. Coddington, *Gettysburg Campaign*, pp. 309–10.
57. Nichols, *Toward Gettysburg*, pp. 200–02; Cleaves, *Meade of Gettysburg*, pp. 134–35.
58. Coddington, *Gettysburg Campaign*, pp. 294–97; Oliver O. Howard, *Autobiography of Oliver Otis Howard* (New York: The Baker & Taylor Co., 1908), pp. 417–18.
59. *OR*, vol. 27, pt. 2, p. 318.
60. Shelby Foote, *The Civil War: A Narrative*, 3 vols. (New York: Random House, 1963), 2: 479–80; Jones, *Confederate Strategy*, pp. 207–08.
61. After the battle, many Southerners searched for opportunities they had missed during the battle—opportunities that would have turned the defeat into a victory. (Ewell's decision not to attack was generally viewed as a missed opportunity.) See, for example, Henry Kyd Douglas, *I Rode with Stonewall* (Chapel Hill: University of North Carolina

Press, 1940), p. 247. It is impossible to say with any degree of certainty that Ewell's attack would have been successful. The report of the approach of the Federal V Corps later turned out to be false. But the positions on Cemetery Hill were formidable. Ewell and his division commanders were experienced combat leaders who at that time considered an attack not practicable. See also Jubal A. Early, *Autobiographical Sketch and Narrative of the War Between the States* (Philadelphia: J. B. Lippincott Co., 1912), p. 270.

62. Foote, *The Civil War*, 2: 487.
63. Freeman, *R. E. Lee*, 3: 103.
64. Coddington, *Gettysburg Campaign*, p. 321.
65. Foote, *The Civil War*, 2: 486, 494.
66. Hood, *Advance and Retreat*, p. 56; Foote, *The Civil War*, 2: 491–93.
67. Harry W. Pfanz, *Gettysburg: The Second Day* (Chapel Hill: University of North Carolina Press, 1987), pp. 104–11; Freeman, *R. E. Lee*, 3: 113.
68. Pfanz, *The Second Day*, p. 111.
69. Hood, *Advance and Retreat*, pp. 57–59.
70. Swanberg, *Sickles*, pp. 208–11.
71. Coddington, *Gettysburg Campaign*, pp. 347–49; Taylor, *Kemble Warren*, pp. 122–23.
72. *OR*, vol. 27, pt. 2, p. 320; Douglas, *I Rode with Stonewall*, p. 249; Coddington, *Gettysburg Campaign*, pp. 446–48.
73. Freeman, *R. E. Lee*, 3: 144–45; Coddington, *Gettysburg Campaign*, pp. 454–64.
74. Early, *Autobiographical Sketch*, p. 275.
75. John Gibbon, *Personal Recollections of the Civil War* (New York: G. P. Putnam's Sons, 1928), pp. 140–45.
76. E. Porter Alexander, *Military Memoirs of a Confederate* (Bloomington: Indiana University Press, 1962), pp. 418–21.
77. Coddington, *Gettysburg Campaign*, pp. 520–23.
78. *OR*, vol. 27, pt. 1, p. 916.
79. Lee's situation on the fourth was similar to that which might have faced him if he had adopted Longstreet's earlier proposal to move around the Federal flank, set up in a defensive position, and let the Federals attack the Confederates. In theory, it was an interesting plan. But if the Federals chose not to attack and instead looked for the enemy's lines of communications, the Army of Northern Virginia had few alternatives except to retreat. Even after decisively defeating the rebels on 1–3 July, Meade was reluctant to attack frontally. There is no reason to believe that he would have decided differently if he had faced the situation Longstreet had advocated earlier in the campaign.
80. Coddington, *Gettysburg Campaign*, pp. 545–52, 559–60.
81. Ibid., pp. 570–72.
82. Williams, *Lincoln and His Generals*, p. 288.
83. Coddington, *Gettysburg Campaign*, pp. 249–50; Thomas L. Livermore, *Numbers and Losses in the Civil War in America, 1861–1865* (New York: Houghton, Mifflin and Co., 1901), p. 103.

Normandy to Falaise

A Critique of Allied Operational Planning in 1944[1]

Russell F. Weigley

American and British military thought before World War II neglected the operational art to focus instead on strategy and tactics. It is almost certainly not coincidental that the Anglo-American campaign in France in 1944 conspicuously fell short of achieving all it might have because of a series of controversial command decisions on the operational level.

The Americans and British won spectacular victories, from their landing in France on 6 June 1944 to their arrival at the western frontier of Germany in the late summer and early autumn. But the victories were less spectacular than the Allies had hoped they might be, because they failed to accomplish the complete defeat of Germany before the end of 1944. The hope that Germany might surrender unconditionally before 1945 was by no means unrealistic. It was a hope that might have been fulfilled, with the consequent saving of thousands of lives on both sides and the shortening of the Holocaust—had Allied operational decision-making been more effective.

Overlord

The planning for Operation Overlord encompassed the Anglo-American invasion of northwest France, from the amphibious and airborne assault of the Normandy beaches through the occupation of a lodgment area comprising the rough rectangle west and north of the Rivers Seine and Loire. (See *Map 14.*) The amphibious assault phase of Overlord, code-named Neptune, became the most spectacular of all the Allied successes of the 1944 campaign in France. It was so impressive a success largely because a great deal of fear of failure had shadowed the planning for it.

The Gallipoli fiasco of 25 April–20 December 1915, during World War I, had engendered a belief among most of the armed forces of the world—the United States Marine Corps for reasons of service self-preservation excepted—that in modern war against modern defenses, amphibious assaults cannot succeed. This belief persisted throughout the interwar period. It emphasized that amphibious assaults must be essen-

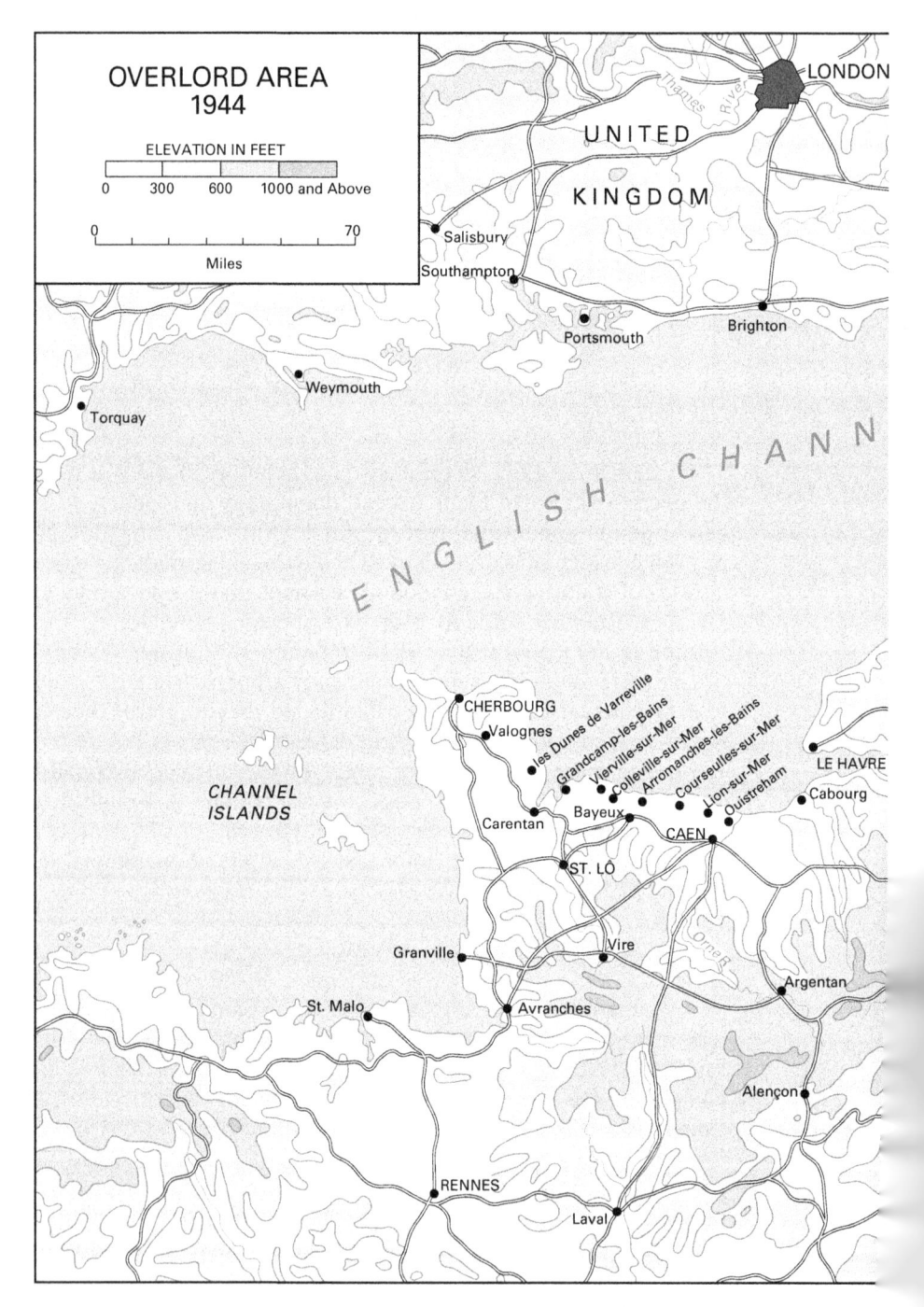

MAP 14

NETHERLANDS
ANTWERP
Ostende
Brugge
Ghent
Dover
DUNKERQUE
CALAIS
BRUSSELS
BELGIUM
LILLE
E L
Mons
Arras
Abbeville
le Tréport
DIEPPE
Somme
AMIENS
River
ST. QUENTIN
FRANCE
ROUEN
REIMS
Seine
Marne River
EVREUX
River
PARIS
Chartres
Seine River
TROYES
Châteaudun

tially like the innumerable failed frontal assaults on the Western Front of 1914–1918, because inherently an amphibious assault must be a head-on attack and not a flanking maneuver. An amphibious assault would be yet more hopeless than attacks on the old Western Front because of the necessity to attack out of the water, with soldiers' movement impeded and even minor wounds likely to lead to death by drowning. Moreover, there was the necessity to reinforce and resupply by transshipment out of the water. When the planning for the cross-Channel invasion of 1944 began in earnest during the winter of 1943–1944, the Gallipoli syndrome had not yet been exorcised to the extent that we may now imagine. The only amphibious assaults of that time in World War II that had contended against serious resistance on the beaches were Salerno in Italy on 9 September and Tarawa in the Gilbert Islands in the Pacific on 20 November 1943; both had brushed uncomfortably close to failure. Neither Salerno nor Tarawa had presented defenses nearly so formidable as those with which the Germans would guard the northwest coast of France by the spring of 1944.

Finally, fear clouded the NEPTUNE planning. An Anglo-American defeat on the Normandy beaches so late in the war might produce incalculably grave effects upon the whole remaining course of World War II, particularly upon the resolve of war-weary Great Britain and the fate of Prime Minister Winston Churchill's government. For the very reason that the fears were so deep-rooted and severe, to overcome them NEPTUNE became the most meticulously planned endeavor in all military history.

Fortunately for the Allies, NEPTUNE—translated into action on D-Day, 6 June 1944—rewarded the care of its planners by proceeding so smoothly and effectively that the D-Day invasion was almost an anticlimax. The losses in the invading force that day, somewhat over 10,000 in total with about 2,000 dead,[2] were obviously not inconsiderable, but they were certainly fewer than most of the Allied planners and commanders had anticipated. On four of the five assault beaches, there was never any question following the first waves of the landing force that the invasion would stay and would not be pushed back into the water. Even on the Americans' OMAHA Beach, the only place where during the morning there seemed to be danger of a reversal, doubts were resolved by noon.

But the NEPTUNE planning had been tactical and technological rather than operational. D-Day had been almost anticlimactic in its success because there had been intricately detailed calculation of such tactically important minutiae as considerations of the proper timing of the first landings in relation to tidal conditions—preferably at midpoint on a rising tide so that landing vessels disembarking troops and cargo could readily be re-floated. This also meant that troops would not have to advance the excessive distance across open beaches under enemy fire that would result from landings at low tide. At the same time, the enemy's beach obstacles were being built from high tide outward and would not yet have advanced far enough to interfere seriously with disembarkation. There were considerations of the appropriate hour of the day for the first landings—about an hour after dawn, so that aerial bombardment and naval gunfire support could have a last go at the enemy during daylight. Thus, the first wave had to go ashore on a day when midpoint of a rising tide occurred about an hour after dawn. There also was reliance on a full or near-full moon during the night before the amphibious landings, so there would be enough light for predawn airborne assaults on both flanks of the landing sites. Therefore, the invasion could occur only when the phase of the moon and the timing of the tides all fitted together like the pieces of a complex jigsaw puzzle.[3] The technological aspects of the NEPTUNE planning included development of duplex drive (DD) amphibious tanks and other specially fitted tanks for the assault out of the water.[4]

While NEPTUNE received such exceptionally careful tactical planning, certainly OVERLORD had been the object of the most searching strategic scrutiny. The cross-Channel invasion, a direct strategic thrust against the strongest bulwarks of Germany's European conquests in the west as the most effective strategy toward the rapid and complete defeat of Germany, had gained British as well as American acceptance as the centerpiece of Allied strategy only after debates in the highest Allied military councils. This had gone on continually from the ARCADIA Conference of American and British leaders in Washington 24 December 1941 to 14 January 1942.[5] But there was no consideration of the operational implications of OVERLORD and NEPTUNE comparable in care and scale to the tactical and strategic planning.

Operations in Normandy after D-Day: The Deadlock

Consideration of the operational implications should have begun with the issue of operational exploitation of a hoped-for tactical success in the landings on the Normandy beaches. Pre-invasion planning discussions had included a certain amount of more or less casual speculation about the possibility of a rapid drive inland, particularly by General Sir Bernard Law Montgomery, whose command of 21st Army Group made him de facto commander of Allied ground forces throughout the early phases of OVERLORD. Montgomery spoke of pressing from the British beaches on through Caen and toward Falaise in the first few days.[6] In spite of the success of the landings, nothing of the sort occurred, and Caen was not cleared until 18–21 July.[7]

Operations inland from the beaches would entail overcoming the defensive advantages accorded the Germans by the geography of the bocage region of Normandy. There had been good reason to choose Normandy as the invasion target. The province offered the major port of Cherbourg to logisticians who believed that the early capture of a large seaport would be vital to winning the battle of the logistical buildup against the enemy. Normandy also was within the combat radius from English bases of all the aircraft required for aerial support, including the relatively short-ranging Supermarine Spitfire. Indeed, Allied planners choosing the invasion site had long since concluded that there was no practical alternative to Normandy.[8]

But going to Normandy meant, especially in the American zone to the west of the British, at the base of the Cotentin or Cherbourg Peninsula and just east of there, the necessity to press from the beaches into the hedgerows of the bocage. The hedgerows divided the Norman countryside into innumerable separate earthen-walled enclosures, some about as large as an American football field, most considerably smaller. The hedgerows were often as much as two meters thick at the base and two to three meters high. Hawthorn bushes and other vegetation springing out from them might reach as much as four meters above the ground. All but the most important roads through the hedgerow country tended to be sunken lanes, worn down by centuries of wagon traffic to make the adjacent hedgerows more commanding still, with foliage overarching the lanes. In this terrain the Allies' strong suit of mobility could not be appropriately exploited. Truck and even tank movement could be too readily blocked. Tanks could not break through the hedgerows. The enemy could shelter himself against artillery fire. Combat would tend to resolve itself into a series of field-by-field infantry battles, the foot soldiers having to fight for each hedgerow in turn, then having to move across the exposed intervening ground to reach the next hedgerow.[9]

On the right of the American sector, around the base of the Cotentin or Cherbourg Peninsula, the hedgerows gave way to different but equally difficult obstacles of terrain. Here, low-lying land could be and in the event was readily inundated by the German defenders, so that only occasional causeways afforded dry passage across flooded prairies. An entire division might have to advance on a front not much more than one tank wide.[10]

The OVERLORD planners gave almost no thought to the terrain obstacles of the bocage, and only slightly more to the inundated prairies. Certainly the obstacles were visible in aerial photographs. There were occasional references to them in preinvasion discussions, especially by British planners who had traveled in Normandy before the war. But there was no effective operational planning to cope with Norman geography. Allied ground commanders were left to improvise responses to the bocage after the invasion began to press inland from the beaches. Indeed, not only operational but also tactical and technological responses were left to be tinkered out under the pressures of costly and nearly stalemated combat. Only after the hedgerows had frustrated attempts to break through with ordinary tanks did the troops in the field improvise devices to mount on their prows to undercut and uproot the earthen walls. Then, such devices could not be fashioned and distributed rapidly enough to prevent their absence from contributing to a costly deadlock of seven weeks' duration disturbingly reminiscent of the Western Front of World War I.[11] Under such conditions, the 90th Infantry Division in its first six weeks in combat suffered nearly 90 percent casualties among its combat riflemen and nearly 150 percent casualties among its company grade officers.[12] The casualty rates in other divisions could not have been much lower.[13]

On the operational level, one possible way in which the Allied planners might conceivably have confronted the problems of the hedgerows and of the flooded base of the Cotentin Peninsula would have involved allocation of Allied armor and potential for mobility. The American buildup in Normandy soon included greater armored strength than the British.[14] Sufficient armored divisions were available in the U.S. Army to have accelerated the American buildup still more. The American forces had mobility superior to the British in trucks of greater ruggedness and durability, as well as more plentiful stream-crossing and bridging equipment. Yet the American forces, the more mobile of the Allies, had to cope with the worst of the hedgerows and the inundations, while the British faced somewhat less difficult terrain but with an inferior capacity to exploit such an advantage. The Allies helped undercut their own trump card of American mobility.

The Americans were on the Allied right, coping with the harsher terrain obstacles, and the British were on the left, in another situation to which the planners had never given adequate forethought. It had simply been taken for granted that because American resources came to Europe from the west, the Americans should occupy the Allies' western flank; while as the advance across France should proceed eastward, the British would be on the left, hugging the Channel coast and their lifeline to England, as they had done in both 1914–1918 and 1939–1940. This alignment gave the British the more favorable terrain not only in Normandy but also throughout the coming campaigns across France, the Low Countries, and Germany. It may well be that logistics made the alignment inevitable. But the operational implications of penalizing the more mobile of the Allied armies surely deserved consideration when OVERLORD received so much strategic and tactical preparation.[15]

COBRA

For seven weeks from 6 June until late July, the battle for Normandy was a brutal slugging match fought for painfully gradual, daily gains forward along the causeways, from one hedgerow to the next, from one block of rubble to the next in the towns. Little opportunity for the exercise of operational imagination offered itself until the Americans had not only struggled through the worst of the bocage but carried their front, between the towns of St. Lô and Périers, to a stretch of Route Nationale 800 that ran for some 23 kilometers from east-southeast to west-northwest as straight as an arrow. This highway feature presented the American command with an uncommonly apt invitation to exploit another Allied trump card, superior airpower, in support of the ground battle. The straight road could serve as a landmark readily enough visible from the air. While American troops gathered, poised for assault, just north of the highway, aircraft including heavy bombers could saturation-bomb an area just south of the road so thoroughly that the defenders might be pulverized or stunned into helplessness and the possibility thus be opened to rupture the German lines.

Upon this tactical conception the American command built an ambitious operational design, the work largely of Lt. Gen. Omar N. Bradley, commanding the First U.S. Army (as well as the 12th Army Group, not yet fully operational), and Maj. Gen. J. Lawton "Lightning Joe" Collins, commanding the VII Corps. These formations were to have three infantry divisions—from right to left, the 9th, 4th, and 30th—deployed and ready to assail the German defenders in the area of the saturation bombing, a rectangle 7,000 yards wide and 2,500 yards deep (approximately the same dimensions in meters) immediately after the bombardment. Behind the three assaulting infantry divisions waited three mechanized divisions: the 1st Infantry Division, motorized for the occasion, with Combat Command B of the 2d Armored Division attached; the remainder of the 2d Armored Division; and the 3d Armored Division with the 22d Infantry attached. Once the three forward divisions had punched a hole in the German lines, the mechanized divisions were to exploit the breakthrough into a breakout that would end the near deadlock persisting since D-Day. This was to be Operation COBRA.[16]

It was, incidentally, one of the few occasions during the European campaign when the Americans, inclined by their consciousness of bountiful overall strength to attack on broad fronts, acted in recognition of the value of concentration.

Tragedy, however, twice stained the launching of COBRA. The operation was scheduled to begin on 24 July but had to be postponed because of bad weather. Before word of the postponement could reach the headquarters of all the relevant air commands of the Allied Expeditionary Air Forces, the heavy bombers had commenced their bombing runs, and enough bombs fell short of their targets to kill 25 men and wound 131 infantrymen attached to the 30th Division. The short bombing was the result partly of the bombers making their approach perpendicular to the target area and thus over the heads of the American infantry, although Bradley thought that the air chieftains had assured him that the bombers would fly parallel to the Périers–St. Lô road. Now an irate Bradley learned that for various technical reasons the airmen were unwilling to make their approach in any way except perpendicular to the road. The ground commanders reluctantly and angrily acquiesced in their proposition, whereupon when COBRA got off to a new start on 25 July, the bombers killed another 111 American troops and wounded another 490 while hitting all three assault divisions.[17]

Moreover, those divisions made slow progress in spite of advancing into a desolated landscape and against obviously shocked and shaken enemy troops. By nightfall of 25 July the breaking of the deadlock seemed decidedly uncertain. At this juncture General Collins intervened with a decision that helped stamp him as the most capable American corps commander in the European theater of operations. With the intuition essential to a great commander, he had sensed that the appearance of the events and reports of 25 July were misleading, and that the German resistance in his front was ready to collapse. During the afternoon, therefore, he had decided to commit the 1st Infantry and the 2d and 3d Armored Divisions on the morning of 26 July. His intuition was sound. The mechanized divisions not only broke quickly through the remaining enemy defensive crust, but they promptly transformed the breakthrough into a breakout, beginning to race deep behind the German lines.[18]

But now the failure to plan adequately in operational terms — to fully explore the operational implications of an excellent tactical plan — proved to undermine in part that very excellence.

The Brittany Diversion

The mechanized columns breaking out into open country south of the Périers–St. Lô road, and the growing numbers that followed them, spread out west and east.

Strong columns moved south and then turned the westward corner from Normandy into Brittany. They did so because the OVERLORD planners, always deeply concerned about gaining sufficient port capacity to win the battle of the logistical buildup, consistently kept their eyes on the wealth of ports in Brittany, particularly Brest near the western tip of the peninsula and largely undeveloped Quiberon Bay on the south coast, but indeed dotted all along the shore. Therefore, Bradley followed up the COBRA breakout by informally activating Lt. Gen. George S. Patton, Jr.'s U.S. Third Army. When the activation became formal at noon on 1 August, Bradley's 12th Army Group headquarters also became fully activated, and Lt. Gen. Courtney H. Hodges assumed command of the First Army; Patton was to thrust into Brittany with an oversized corps, Maj. Gen. Troy H. Middleton's VIII. It was oversized in that it contained two armored divisions, the 4th and the 6th, rather than one such division as usually assigned to an American corps.[19]

General Montgomery was to remain Allied ground commander through his 21st Army Group headquarters until General Eisenhower set up headquarters on the Continent and assumed direct ground command. This transition occurred at noon on 1 September, whereupon Bradley's army group passed altogether from Montgomery's control (the British government compensated Montgomery by promoting him to field marshal as of that date).[20] Meanwhile, however, Montgomery believed that for reasons of diplomacy he must hold the reins much more loosely when he dealt with American rather than British subordinates. Wisely, Montgomery perceived that the breakout went far toward negating the need for the Breton ports. With Allied forces now able to drive rapidly eastward, other ports could be secured much closer to the main front; by the time the Breton ports were captured and cleared of the predictable German demolitions, better logistical facilities would be available. Thus Montgomery deemed the commitment of an exceptionally large corps to Brittany a misuse of scarce resources.[21]

Contrary to the American impression of Montgomery as an inveterately cautious commander, he was willing to take risks where Brittany was concerned for the sake of a more powerful drive east toward Berlin and, it could be hoped, a prompt end to the war. Bradley and the principal American commanders were unwilling to take those risks. The OVERLORD plan, developed when a breakout could not be counted on, called for the westward turn from Normandy into Brittany, and the Americans remained locked into the plan. They failed to develop the operational possibilities of their own tactical success with COBRA.

As Montgomery feared, the Breton ports ended up having little relevance to the campaign eastward, particularly because a tenacious German defense held Brest until 20 September. The consequences were serious. One of the two armored divisions in Brittany, the 4th, turned back eastward after pressing only about halfway into the Peninsula, but in the meantime it contributed to the Brittany offensive's heavy consumption for dubious purposes of supplies that would soon become desperately scarce elsewhere. This description applies particularly to fuel. The Allied drive across France unleashed by the COBRA breakout was destined to halt at about the borders of Germany and the Low Countries, because there it ran out of fuel. The Allies had to pause, and the pause lasted just long enough to permit the Germans to regroup in their Westwall defenses and to impose a new deadlock upon the Allies in the autumn. Even relatively small additional amounts of gasoline, certainly those amounts that powered the VIII Corps drive across Brittany, might conceivably have provided enough additional impetus to the Allies to deny the enemy the respite he needed after his flight from France.[22]

Meanwhile, another flaw in the operational followup to COBRA contributed yet more substantially to preventing the complete defeat of Germany before the end of 1944.

The Argentan-Falaise Pocket

It was implicit in the desire that COBRA should produce not only a breakthrough, rupturing the German lines, but a breakout from Normandy deep into France. Then the breakout forces could fan out widely, east toward Germany, as well as, more dubiously, west into Brittany. But while the American high command meticulously planned the tactical problem of breaking through and out, once more they did not explore as they might have the operational implications of the tactical plan: how best to exploit the prospect of pushing fast and far into the interior of France.

As the breakout developed, and American spearheads indeed ranged swiftly eastward, improvisation in response to opportunity led to a design to trap the bulk of the German forces, the Seventh Army and Fifth Panzer Army, in northwest France. (*See Map 15.*) The design might well have been better conceived and better executed. By neglecting operational thinking and planning beforehand, the opportunities that COBRA ought to have opened were not grasped, and a genuine chance to end the war in a matter of weeks was lost.

If American forces breaking out from Normandy were in part to race toward the east, the planners might well have pondered the evident prospects they might seize if those rapidly moving forces should at some point turn north to become a hammer smashing the enemy in their path against the anvil of Montgomery's British Second and Canadian First Armies in the eastern sector of Normandy. Such a northward turn posed also the prospect of enveloping a large portion of the German forces still fighting farther west, as many were bound to be doing because of the relative immobility of the German Army as compared with the American, and because of the impediments to movement imposed upon the Germans by Allied air power as well as by defeat.

The COBRA planners could not have foreseen that the German Führer, Adolf Hitler, would enhance the latter opportunity, but they should have contemplated more clearly than they did that the opportunity would be presented to them in some form. As events actually developed, Hitler's effort to repair the disaster of the American breakout took the form of a strong counterattack aimed at the inevitably narrow passageway through which for a time the Americans had to advance south along the southwest coast of Normandy, through Avranches, before turning west into Brittany or east toward Germany. Hitler hoped to drive across that narrow corridor from Mortain through Avranches to the sea and thus to cut off those Americans south of his thrust. The true effect of his scheme, how-

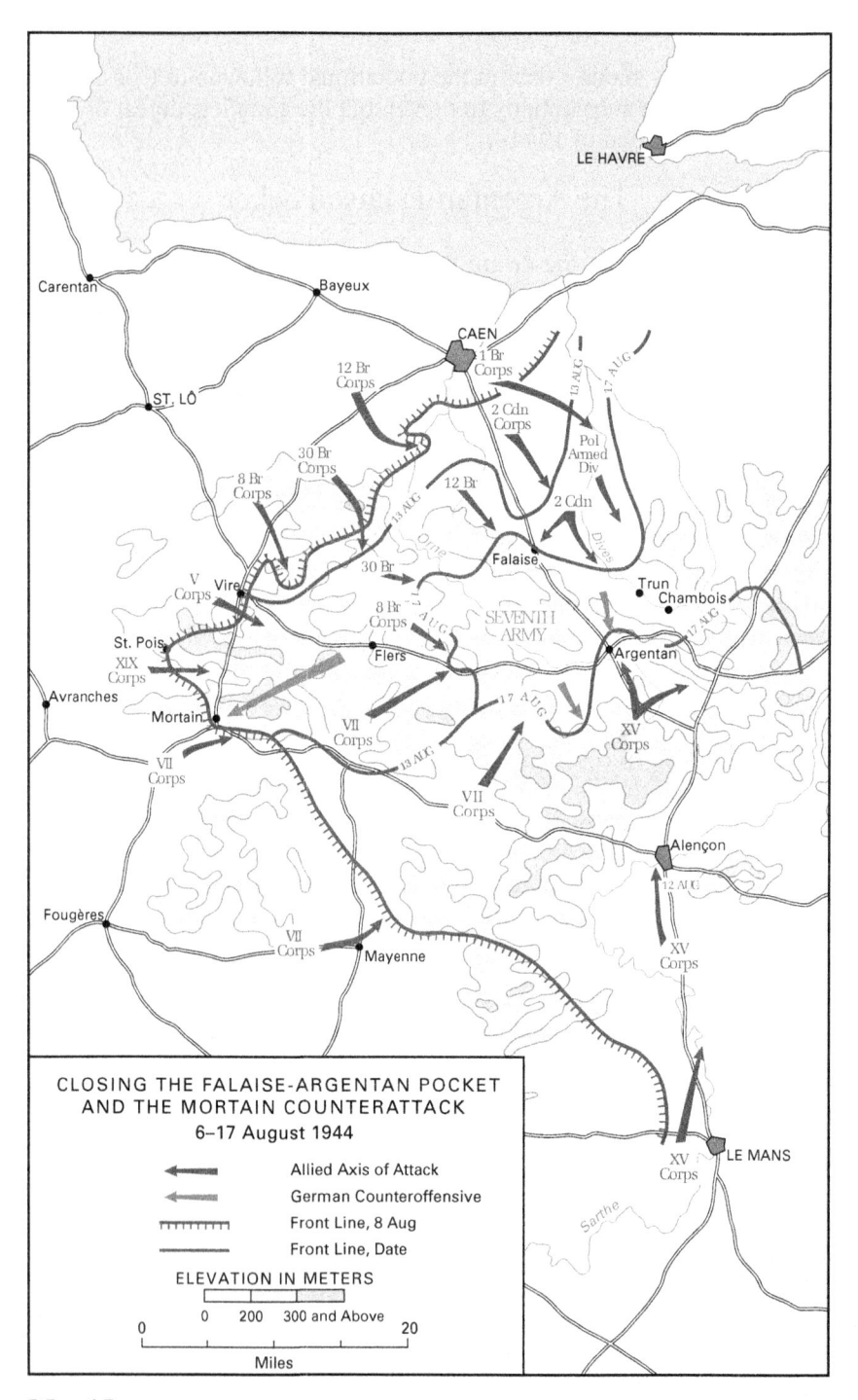

MAP 15

ever, was to push more German troops more deeply into a noose that an American northward turn to meet the British in eastern Normandy might then close.

It was observation of the Germans' enhancing Allied opportunity that especially stimulated the American command to improvise an envelopment design. The fact that the Americans never clearly settled on a choice between a short or a long envelopment demonstrates the improvisational nature of this operational plan, however. Military planning should never grow so rigid, of course, that it arbitrarily closes off promising options. We are dealing here with a situation in which the Americans were so far from having explored their options through foresighted operational thinking, and so far from making up their minds, that they did not pursue either the short or the long envelopment idea purposefully enough to succeed as much as they might have.

The short envelopment involved turning the Americans' easterly spearheads north toward Argentan, there to meet an offensive by Montgomery advancing south through Falaise. The long envelopment envisaged instead an American left turn down the River Seine to meet the British along its lower reaches. The willingness of the enemy to thrust himself deep into a westward noose encouraged an initial preference for the short envelopment.[23]

Either envelopment plan involved risks, particularly the risk that the Germans might succeed in pushing through Avranches. But Allied signals intelligence, the ULTRA interception, and decrypting of German wireless communications informed the American command just enough about enemy intentions and strength that, while not quite looking over Hitler's shoulder at the cards in his hand, Bradley and his subordinates could feel reasonably comfortable about holding at Mortain with minimum strength while continuing to move most of his forces into Brittany and toward Argentan. Stout defensive fighting by the 30th Infantry Division at Mortain on 6–8 August vindicated accepting the risk.[24]

Meanwhile Maj. Gen. Wade H. Haislip's XV Corps of Patton's Third Army led the race toward Argentan. On 13 August, however, the corps encountered unexpectedly strong resistance just south of that place, and Bradley decided to halt its advance for the time being. This decision proved to be a critical turning point in the evolution of the short envelopment into the battle of the Argentan-Falaise Pocket.

Two considerations overtly shaped Bradley's halt order. First, the Germans by now were responding to the danger of envelopment through the closing of Allied pincers between Argentan and Falaise. Having failed at Mortain, they were hastening their eastward withdrawal. Because the XV Corps was well in advance of the American center of gravity, Bradley feared that the German columns on the march eastward might break through the exposed American left flank stretching south and west from near Argentan. He preferred to pause to consolidate along that shoulder. Second, when the short envelopment began, the Canadians to the north had been much closer to Argentan than the Americans, so the boundary between the 12th and 21st Army Groups lay just over ten kilometers south of that town. To advance farther, Haislip would have to press into the zone of the British army group, and Bradley feared a costly collision between Allied troops.

Behind the latter two overt reasons for Bradley's halting the XV Corps lay factors of personality of the sort that can readily inject elements of irrationality into otherwise rational planning—factors not reflected on neat maps displaying combat formations as orderly rectangles. Montgomery was a vain and egotistical man, continually attempting to appropriate to himself as much credit as possible for everything that went well in his vicinity, whether or not the credit rightly belonged to him. He was not widely liked, even among his fellow British officers (although he had created a bond of rapport with his British soldiers—he got along much better with those separated from him by a wide gap in rank and age than with his peers or his immediate subordinates). Among the Americans, the distance occasioned by his headline-hunting and by his vanity and acerbity more generally was aggravated by the condescension he affected toward those with less combat experience than himself and his countrymen (which was largely experience in losing, the cynical might respond).

Patton had come to loathe Montgomery when they commanded the U.S. Seventh and British Eighth Armies, respectively, in Sicily and raced each other for the port of Messina. Notwithstanding Montgomery's forbearance in handling the Americans since D-Day in Normandy, numerous points of friction had exacerbated bad feelings, with Bradley as well as with Patton. The latter two, estranged over Patton's soldier-slapping escapades in Sicily and other indications of his instability of character, had renewed their friendship in no small degree on the basis of their shared aversion to Montgomery. By August 1944 Patton was playing upon and encouraging Bradley's preference for keeping his distance from Montgomery.

Under the command structure prevailing in August, Bradley would have needed Montgomery's permission to alter the interarmy group boundary to facilitate an American advance through Argentan and beyond. But Bradley would not pick up the telephone to ask Montgomery for the change, so wide a chasm had opened between the senior American and British field commanders. Nor would General Dwight D. Eisenhower intervene: His conception of his and his subordinates' command responsibilities required that matters of direct concern to the army groups be left to the heads of the army groups—probably excessive self-denial on the part of the Supreme Commander, Allied Expeditionary Forces. This interplay of personalities among the generals may well do more to explain the events of the Argentan-Falaise Pocket than Bradley's overt reasons for halting.

In any event, the American halt south of Argentan proved to be the first and crucial step toward a failure to close the Argentan-Falaise gap promptly enough to entrap the main German forces with a completeness that could have broken the back of the enemy's power in the west. The halt was also the first and crucial symptom of the lack of adequate operational planning to exploit COBRA. Forethought could have averted Bradley's making a hasty decision based at least in part on his personal feelings toward Montgomery. Bradley was later to blame Montgomery for the incomplete grasping of opportunity, pointing out that the advance of the First Canadian Army through Falaise and on toward Argentan was much slower than the Third Army's progress nearly as far as Argentan. Such criticism of Montgomery overlooked, however, the much tougher resistance of the Germans who faced the Canadians as compared with those confronting the Americans. The difference in strength of resistance was predictable, because it was inherent in the fact that the enemy front opposite the 21st Army Group had never been broken, unlike the front before the Americans. Appropriate forethought would have included this predictable circumstance in developing the operational design.[25]

Without such forethought, the halt south of Argentan led in turn to Bradley's reaching a second crucial and highly consequential hasty decision. On the next day, 14 August, he shifted his sights from the short toward the long envelopment. He decided to keep only two divisions of the XV Corps near Argentan while moving the other two east toward the Seine and the longer turning maneuver. Significantly, he made this important decision and ordered it into effect without consulting Montgomery.[26] Again, furthermore, Bradley's decision coincided with the inclinations of his newly restored friend, General Patton, not only because of their attitudes toward Montgomery, but also because Patton, a cavalryman by training and temperament with the cavalryman's thirst for continual movement, was always impatient of delays like that around Argentan and eager to sidestep them for the sake of moving again.

Informed of Bradley's new decision by telephone, Patton sent Haislip and his corps headquarters east with the two divisions on his right, the 5th Armored and the 79th Infantry. Bradley's and Patton's use of these divisions was at odds with Bradley's professed fear of a German onslaught against the left shoulder of the Argentan front, but it accorded with the real situation, which in turn was at least by now at odds with Bradley's first overt explanation for the halt. Collins' VII Corps of the First Army had sufficiently bolstered the shoulder, and the Germans were sufficiently and obviously intent on merely escaping the pocket, that fear for the shoulder could be discarded.[27]

On 16 August Montgomery belatedly took the initiative to restore the short envelopment. His belatedness underlines once more the absence of sustained operational forethought and planning, on the part of both the principal Allies, the British as well as the Americans. Montgomery telephoned Bradley—note the direction of the call—to suggest a renewed push to close the encirclement of the Germans remaining in the Falaise-Argentan Pocket by closing the pincers between Falaise and Argentan. To this end the British command took the initiative also in suggesting a revised interarmy group boundary, so that the Americans would meet the Canadians about eleven kilometers northeast of Argentan, near Trun and Chambois.[28] (*See Map 15.*)

Unfortunately for the Allies, because the Germans were rushing to escape from the pocket they were now in considerably greater strength between the Allied pincers than they would have been if the Americans had persisted in the attack on the thirteenth or fourteenth. Bradley accepted Montgomery's suggestion, but German resistance was a good deal stiffer than it would have been likely to be a few days earlier. The departure of General Haislip compelled the Americans to shuffle their command structure around Argentan, which caused further delay. On 16 August Patton created a provisional corps under his chief of staff, Maj. Gen. Hugh J. Gaffey, to take over the French *2ème Division Blindée* and the American 90th Infantry Division from the XV Corps, along with the 80th Infantry Division. Gaffey ordered his troops to be ready to attack by 1000 hours on 17 August, but before the effort could get under way, Maj. Gen. Leonard T. Gerow arrived by Bradley's orders with his V Corps headquarters of the First Army to take over from Gaffey and Patton the three divisions scheduled to make the Argentan drive. Gerow took command by daybreak on the seventeenth, but his desire for an improved line of departure postponed the main attack until the early hours of 18 August.[29]

The Falaise-Argentan pincers closed at last the next day, 19 August, near Chambois. The closing sealed, after all, an impressive Allied victory. Some 50,000 Germans were caught in the envelopment and became prisoners. About 10,000 German dead lay within the encirclement area. As the pocket had narrowed, Allied tactical air power had battered the enemy's equipment within it mercilessly, and the tanks, self-propelled guns, and other heavy materiel not wrecked from the air largely had to be abandoned as the last Germans fled through the closing jaws. The German defeat was complete enough that the long envelopment on the Seine, on which Patton's Third Army embarked after the shift from Argentan, produced far less spectacular results, because the spectacular prizes were no longer available.[30]

Nevertheless, the enemy was able to extricate nearly all his army, corps, and division headquarters staffs, which meant that he retained the cadres around which to rebuild his shattered formations. As the Allies did not yet quite realize, the Germans possessed a remarkable capacity for such rebuilding. Given the skeleton of a formation, they could restore the formation itself within a few weeks. It was particularly for this reason that the consequences of the Allies' faulty operational planning for the Falaise-Argentan Pocket were to prove tragic. By September, along the German frontier, the cadres that had escaped the pocket had become the nuclei of a restored German resistance. Given respite when the Americans and British had to halt near the frontier after their fuel tanks ran dry—a problem worsened by the faulty operational planning that perpetrated the large commitment to Brittany—the resistance in the Westwall of the German formations that had fled past Argentan, rebuilt and augmented by new formations, imposed on the Allies the costly autumn stalemate of 1944: the legacy of the faulty operational planning behind the short and long envelopments.[31]

When the Allies landed in Normandy on 6 June, they hoped for an end to the war against Germany before winter closed in. The hope was not unrealistic. Foresighted operational planning—as well as the tactical and technological triumph of D-Day—could well have shortened the seven weeks' stalemate in Normandy, so that the Allies might have reached the German frontier before the close of summer and good campaigning weather. Foresighted operational planning to exploit the tactical triumph of COBRA could well have denied the Germans much of their ability to extract from France the cadres upon which to build the defense of their western frontier. Although the possibilities were more limited, foresighted operational planning might also have found ways to minimize the fuel crisis that obliged the Allied pursuit across France to halt as it approached the Westwall.

The tragedy in all these circumstances lay especially in the strong likelihood that the prolongation of the war through the winter of 1944–1945 and into the spring of 1945 was unnecessary. Consequently, many thousands died who might have lived, not only among the soldiers of both sides but among the civilian victims of the war's last harsh winter, as well as among the targets of the last frenzied workings of the death camps that perpetrated the Holocaust.

The Allied, mainly American, strategy that had focused on the cross-Channel invasion as the most expeditious means of confronting and then overthrowing Germany's main strength in the West to swiftly end World War II was an eminently sound strategy. While Allied tactics were not always so sound as the cross-Channel invasion strategy, the executions of D-Day and of COBRA both demonstrated an admirable tactical prowess. The principal shortcomings of the American and British forces in the 1944 campaign in northwest Europe lay not surprisingly in the intermediate area between strategy and tactics that prewar military thought in the West had neglected, in the area of the operational art. Here, repeated failures to exploit tactical advantages as fully as possible to implement the strategic design for the destruction of German power in the West, failures to link tactics to strategy by way of a refined, thoughtful, coherent operational art, probably prolonged World War II. The Allied campaign in northwest Europe in 1944 was a triumphant military endeavor on a grand scale, and its commanders and soldiers merit the heroic stature that history has usually accorded them. But the triumph could have been more complete.

Notes

1. This essay, with minor revisions, originally was published under the title "From the Normandy Beaches to the Falaise-Argentan Pocket," *Military Review* 70, no. 9 (September 1990): 45–64. It is reprinted with the permission of the author and the editors of *Military Review*.
2. Cornelius Ryan, *The Longest Day: June 6, 1944* (New York: Simon and Schuster, 1959). "A Note on Casualties," p. 279, gives carefully considered estimates of casualties; the number of killed given here is my own estimate projected from Ryan's figures. The planning for the cross-Channel invasion is examined in minute detail in Gordon A. Harrison, *Cross-Channel Attack*, U.S. Army in World War II (Washington, D.C.: U.S. Army Center of Military History, 1951), pp. 54–82, 164–97.
3. Harrison, *Cross-Channel Attack*, pp. 188–90.
4. Ibid., p. 192; Chester Wilmot, *The Struggle for Europe* (New York: Harper and Brothers Publishers, 1952), pp. 182, 195, 291–92; Robin Higham, "Technology and D-day" in Eisenhower Foundation, *D-day: The Normandy Invasion in Retrospect* (Lawrence: The University of Kansas Press, 1971), pp. 221–46.
5. Harrison, *Cross-Channel Attack*, p. 48.
6. Carlo D'Este, *Decision in Normandy* (New York: E. P. Dutton, 1987), p. 78, is strong in demonstrating Montgomery's intent to take Caen on the first day; see also Omar N. Bradley, *A Soldier's Story* (New York: Henry Holt and Co., 1951), p. 251.
7. Martin Blumenson, *Breakout and Pursuit*, U.S. Army in World War II (Washington, D.C.: U.S. Army Center of Military History, 1961), p. 193; D'Este, *Decision in Normandy*, pp. 356, 363, 390–99.
8. Harrison, *Cross-Channel Attack*, pp. 71–73; D'Este, *Decision in Normandy*, pp. 32–33.
9. Harrison, *Cross-Channel Attack*, p. 284; Blumenson, *Breakout and Pursuit*, pp. 13, 41–44.
10. Harrison, *Cross-Channel Attack*, pp. 286–87; Blumenson, *Breakout and Pursuit*, pp. 78–88.
11. D'Este, *Decision in Normandy*, pp. 85, 87, 153–54, and Max Hastings, *OVERLORD: D-day and the Battle for Normandy* (New York: Simon and Schuster, 1984), pp. 36, 146, for such anticipation as occurred; but, see again Harrison, *Cross-Channel Attack*, p. 284.
12. Blumenson, *Breakout and Pursuit*, p. 201; see also pp. 175–76, 200.
13. See Roland G. Ruppenthal, *Logistical Support of the Armies, May 1941–September 1944*, 2 vols., U.S. Army in World War II (Washington, D.C.: U.S. Army Center of Military History, 1953), 1: 460–61, for the large and largely unanticipated replacement problem.
14. In the Normandy fighting, the British deployed the 7th and 11th Armored Divisions (in addition to the specialized 79th used in the landings); D'Este, *Decision in Normandy*, index, p. 535. The United States deployed or had ready to participate by the time of the COBRA breakout the 2d, 3d, 4th, 5th, and 6th Armored Divisions (index, p. 554).
15. So much was the alignment of the British on the left and the Americans on the right taken for granted that the literature contains almost no discussion of the issue. It is touched

upon, mainly as it determined the subsequent occupation zones in Germany, in Cornelius Ryan, *The Last Battle* (New York: Simon and Schuster, 1966), pp. 144–45.

16. Blumenson, *Breakout and Pursuit*, pp. 185–223; Bradley, *A Soldier's Story*, pp. 329–34, 338–42; J. Lawton Collins, *Lightning Joe: An Autobiography* (Baton Rouge: Louisiana State University Press, 1979), pp. 233–38; D'Este, *Decision in Normandy*, pp. 337–51.

17. Blumenson, *Breakout and Pursuit*, pp. 228–33 (p. 229, for casualties); Bradley, *A Soldier's Story*, pp. 346–47; Collins, *Lightning Joe*, pp. 238–39.

18. Blumenson, *Breakout and Pursuit*, pp. 231–66 (particularly p. 241, for Collins' decision); Collins, *Lightning Joe*, pp. 241–46 (particularly p. 242, for the same decision); D'Este, *Decision in Normandy*, pp. 403–07.

19. See Blumenson, *Breakout and Pursuit*, pp. 343–44, for the new command arrangements; see pp. 347–49 for the plans for the Third Army and VIII Corps to advance into Brittany.

20. Forrest C. Pogue, *The Supreme Command*, U.S. Army in World War II (Washington, D.C.: U.S. Army Center of Military History, 1954), pp. 204, 261–63; Blumenson, *Breakout and Pursuit*, pp. 343–44, 684, and 684, for Montgomery's promotion.

21. On Montgomery's wishes to throw the overwhelming bulk of the Allied armies eastward with no emphasis on Brittany, see *The Memoirs of Field-Marshal the Viscount Montgomery of Alamein, K.G.* (Cleveland: The World Publishing Co., 1958), pp. 238–40; Nigel Hamilton, *Master of the Battlefield: Monty's War Years, 1942–1944* (New York: McGraw Hill, 1983), pp. 778–79.

22. For the American belief in the importance of the Breton ports, see Blumenson, *Breakout and Pursuit*, pp. 209–10, 343–44; for the operations in Brittany, see pp. 337–415, 631–56; for the end of resistance at Brest on 20 September, see p. 652; for the inutility of the Breton ports as events unfolded, see pp. 655–56. For subsequent Allied logistical problems, see pp. 657–75, 676–702, and Ruppenthal, *Logistical Support of the Armies*, 2: 3–21.

23. For Allied envelopment plans, see Pogue, *The Supreme Command*, pp. 208–09; Blumenson, *Breakout and Pursuit*, pp. 479–81, 492–99. For the German counterattack, see Blumenson, *Breakout and Pursuit*, pp. 457–75.

24. D'Este, *Decision in Normandy*, pp. 415–17, 420–21; Ralph Bennett, U*ltra* *in the West: The Normandy Campaign of 1944–45* (New York: Charles Scribner's Sons, 1980), pp. 115–19.

25. For the halt on 13 August, see Blumenson, *Breakout and Pursuit*, p. 505. For Bradley's and the Allies' decision-making and the problems of inter-Allied command relations, see Bradley, *A Soldier's Story*, pp. 373–79; Dwight D. Eisenhower, *Crusade in Europe* (Garden City, N.Y.: Doubleday and Co., 1948), pp. 276–79; Blumenson, *Breakout and Pursuit*, pp. 506–09, 523–24, 527; D'Este, *Decision in Normandy*, pp. 439–60. For Bradley's blaming Montgomery, see Bradley, *A Soldier's Story*, p. 377; Blumenson, *Breakout and Pursuit*, p. 508.

26. Blumenson, *Breakout and Pursuit*, p. 523.

27. Ibid., p. 524.

28. Ibid., p. 527.

29. Ibid., pp. 527, 529–30.

30. Ibid., pp. 537–42, for 19 August; p. 557, for the number of Germans captured; p. 558, for the German dead and losses of equipment.

31. Ibid., pp. 530–35, 538, 540, 542–58, and Wilmot, *Struggle for Europe*, pp. 423–44 on the escape of German cadres. For the implications, see Wilmot, *Struggle for Europe*,

pp. 477–82, 545–61; Charles B. MacDonald, *The Siegfried Line Campaign*, U.S. Army in World War II (Washington, D.C.: U.S. Army Center of Military History, 1963), pp. 18–19; Hugh M. Cole, *The Lorraine Campaign*, U.S. Army in World War II (Washington, D.C.: U.S. Army Center of Military History, 1950), pp. 31–35. On the Allies' supply, particularly fuel problems, see the references in note 21, supra, and especially Blumenson, *Breakout and Pursuit*, pp. 691–92, 696–97.

After Inch'on

MacArthur's 1950 Campaign in North Korea

Stanlis David Milkowski

Operational Command and Control in the Korean War

The Korean War offers an excellent case for investigation of operational art not only as a historical exercise, but also as a paradigm with particular relevance to current strategic thinking. General Douglas MacArthur, Commander in Chief (CINC) of joint and combined forces in the theater, was, until the ascension of General H. Norman Schwarzkopf, Jr., in the Desert Shield/Storm campaign during the Gulf War, the last American operational-level commander.[1] Paradoxically, the experience of operational planning in a global backwater at the midpoint of the twentieth century has possibly greater applicability to the dangerous world of the future than do the barely cold after-action reviews and lessons learned of the brief Gulf War. Since the breakup of the Soviet Union, the basic premise that underlies much strategic planning at the national level and that makes a virtue of budgetary necessity to reduce military force structure is that we must be prepared to deploy limited forces to strange corners of the world for ambiguous missions within ad hoc coalitions. The likelihood, therefore, is very great that operational planners may in the future find themselves dealing with a campaign on unfamiliar terrain, in a logistics- and intelligence-bare theater, without a command and control system tailored to the mission at hand. The task, in short, would be very much like that which confronted the operational commander ordered to undertake the pursuit into North Korea after Inch'on.

This essay examines the command and control system General Douglas MacArthur used to conduct operations in Korea and will determine how far it was to blame for the disaster which befell United Nations Command (UNC) deep in North Korea in November 1950. In doctrinal terms, UNC was defeated when it passed beyond the operational culminating point without achieving its objectives.[2] Interpretative historical accounts variously tend to blame this near-catastrophic setback on MacArthur's hubris, or on "schizophrenia at GHQ" (General Headquarters), or on intelligence failure, or on the misplaced trust in air power to isolate the battlefield.[3] Arguably, there were elements of all these in MacArthur's defeat, but they offer little help to either serious students of military history or the serving professionals who seek to understand how UNC came to find itself in such disarray on the eve of the Chinese counterstroke and why miscalculation so quickly turned into calamity. Certainly, they cannot be assigned appropriate weight unless one first asks what demands were made on the command and control system adapted for operations in North Korea and its adequacy for the purpose. Analysis of the reverses suffered by UNC in fact shows that it was the failure of the operational command and control system more than MacArthur's often-cited single-mindedness that made inevitable a defeat of the magnitude the Chinese inflicted. That the latter contributed to the former is indisputable, given the dominance of MacArthur's personality; yet UNC would not have come so close to catastrophe with less flawed command and control.

This essay concentrates on the period from the recapture of Seoul at the end of September 1950 to the withdrawal of UN and Republic of Korea (ROK) forces from North Korea completed in late December. The transition to the offensive from the stubborn, not infrequently desperate, defense of the Pusan Perimeter began with the Inch'on landings on 15 September and subsequent breakout from the Perimeter by Eighth Army; it was completed with the linkup of forces south of the Han River and consolidation at Seoul on 27 September. The same day, MacArthur received from the Joint Chiefs of Staff (JCS) the mission to destroy the North Korean armed forces and the authority to conduct military operations north of the 38th Parallel to this end. (*Map 16*) Further, the JCS directive specified the political and military constraints on UNC operations and described actions to be taken in the event of contingent Soviet or Chinese intervention.

Crossing the 38th Parallel in early October, UN and ROK forces drove into North Korea in an aggressive pursuit across a broad front that encountered no serious checks until the surprise Chinese counterattacks at the end of the month against extended forces. After a period of consolidation and adjustment of unit boundaries dictated by tactical withdrawals of forward elements, the final UN offensive designed to achieve the military objectives of the campaign opened on 24 November. Within seventy-two hours, the Chinese had struck hard at several points on UNC's extended front and threatened to cut off major forces deep in North Korea. Though UNC was able to keep open its lines of communications (LOC) and extricate most forces in danger of encirclement, it was at the cost of heavy casualties, abandonment or destruction of large quantities of materiel, and the ultimate loss of all the hard-won gains of the offensive. By Christmas Day, UNC found itself almost where it had started three months earlier. It was, as MacArthur himself had reported to the JCS on 28 November, "an entirely new war."[4]

KOREA

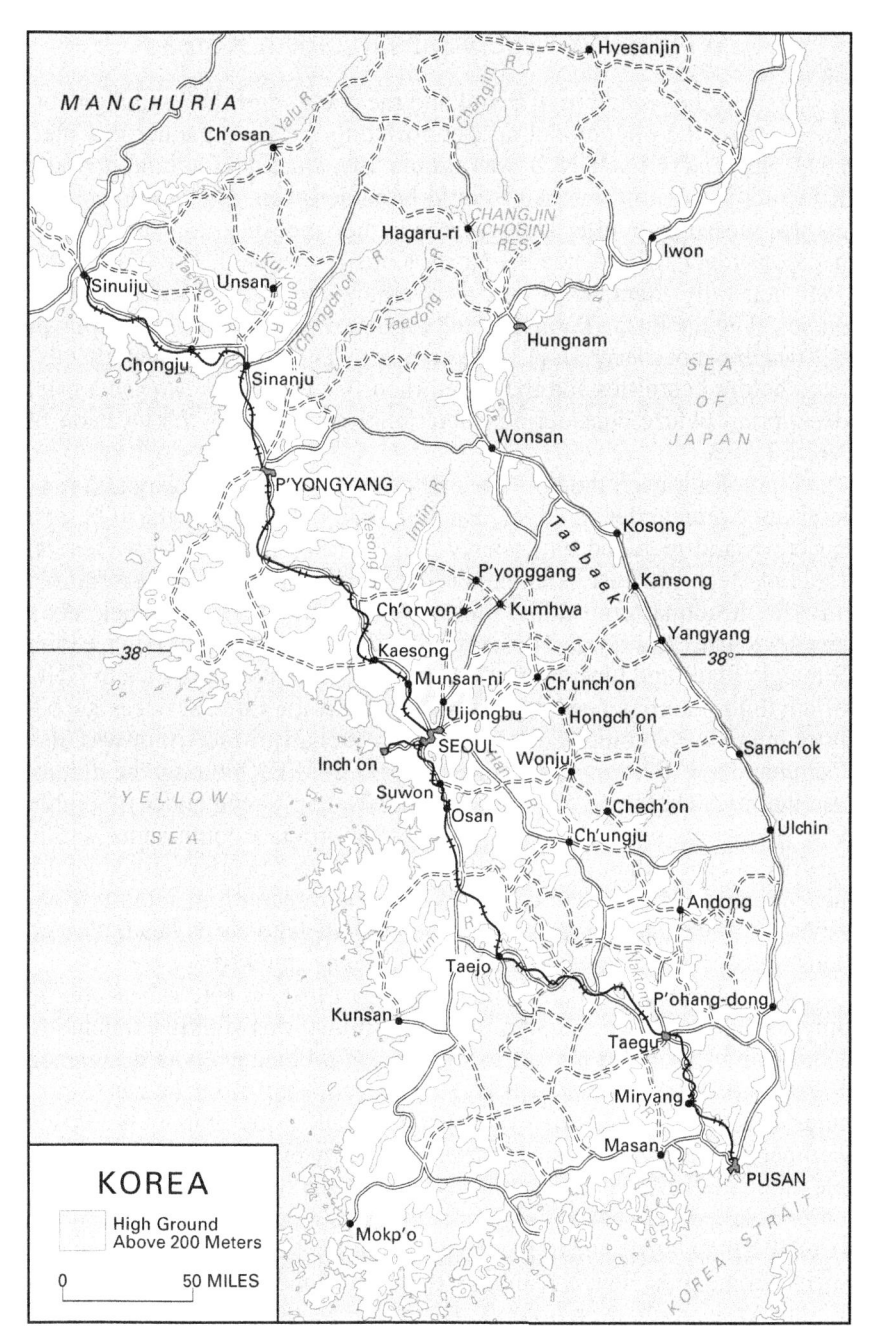

High Ground Above 200 Meters

0   50 MILES

MAP 16

Genesis of Operations in North Korea

Prior to the recapture of Seoul and the opening of the campaign outlined above, the operational task confronting the Commander in Chief, UN Command (CINCUNC), was simple: to maintain a foothold in South Korea until a counteroffensive could be undertaken. The command and control measures in effect represented ad hoc modifications of the organizations that existed when the North Koreans attacked. These measures were generally adequate as long as operations were confined to the area enclosed by the Pusan Perimeter and logistical support was uncomplicated (which is not to say easy).[5] The command and control system that existed before hostilities and the initial modifications for war merit a brief description before considering operational planning for the invasion of North Korea.

First of all, even though MacArthur received his authority and missions as Commander in Chief, Far East (CINCFE), from the JCS, and his command included major navy and air force headquarters, General Headquarters, Far East Command (GHQ FEC), in Tokyo was essentially an army headquarters, staffed almost entirely by army personnel.[6] As a gesture toward "jointness," the staff coordinated planning through a Joint Strategic Plans and Operations Group (JSPOG), but the absence in GHQ of anything like balanced representation from the three services kept it from being a true joint headquarters.[7] Functionally, MacArthur was also Commander, U.S. Army Forces Far East (USAFFE), although he did not use the title. Therefore, Lt. Gen. Walton Walker, Commander of Eighth U.S. Army, was merely the senior major subordinate commander within USAFFE, rather than the ground component commander within a joint headquarters.[8] Walker had under his direct command four infantry divisions, all garrisoned in Japan, with no intermediate corps headquarters. This was the situation when the North Koreans attacked.

When Walker was named commander of ground forces in Korea in July 1950, Eighth Army's area of responsibility was simply extended to Korea, and this geographical extension (or subtheater) was designated Eighth U.S. Army Korea (EUSAK) to differentiate it from the base structure.[9] While Walker effectively controlled ROK army units in the Pusan Perimeter, he had no formal command authority over them (a good example of the improvised nature of initial operations). As quickly as skeleton corps headquarters could be organized in the Continental United States (CONUS), it was rushed to the theater, with Walker's immediate requirements taking precedence. Although there was doubt in some quarters that Eighth Army could even hold the Perimeter, MacArthur early conceived the Inch'on landing as an operational maneuver to regain the initiative. This turning movement would isolate the bulk of the North Korean Army in the south, recover Seoul, and facilitate immediate offensive operations against North Korea. To carry out the turning movement he envisioned, MacArthur needed to create a corps headquarters separate from EUSAK. Despite his staff's fears of a "half-baked affair," he determined to form a corps staff from GHQ FEC personnel and selected his chief of staff, Maj. Gen. Edward M. Almond, to command it.[10] This organization was designated X Corps, assigned one Marine and one Army division, and placed in GHQ Reserve until the Inch'on operation commenced. Given the circumstances of its creation and the fact that nearly all key staff personnel were on loan from GHQ, JSPOG planners assumed that X Corps tactical elements would come under Walker's command after the linkup with EUSAK. But the staff's assumption proved to be wholly erroneous, as the CINC had quite different plans for X Corps.[11]

Prior to welcome confirmation in Washington that Inch'on was not going to become a miniature Gallipoli or worse, the political object shaping military operations in Korea had been simply to prevent the destruction of the Republic of Korea and the ejection of UN forces from the peninsula. Now for the first time it was necessary to consider in concrete terms the basis for terminating hostilities and in particular whether or not to invade North Korea. The guidance conveyed in the 27 September JCS directive contained a clear mission that reflected the political consensus finally thrashed out within National Command Authority (NCA) councils and approved by the president. That mission was the destruction of the North Korean armed forces.[12] UNC operations north of the 38th Parallel were explicitly authorized, but there was one major constraint and two significant caveats contained in the directive. Above all, no forces under MacArthur's command were permitted to enter Manchuria or the USSR, and no air or naval actions were to be undertaken against those areas. Furthermore, in the conduct of his campaign, the CINCUNC was free to undertake military operations anywhere in North Korea only so long as there was no sign of entry by "major" Chinese or Soviet forces. Finally, "as a matter of policy," he was prohibited from using non-Korean ground forces in the northernmost provinces bordering Manchuria and the USSR. As long as these conditions obtained, CINCUNC was enjoined "to feel unhampered tactically and strategically to proceed north of the 38th Parallel." MacArthur confirmed his understanding of the mission, responding: "Unless and until the enemy capitulates, I regard all of Korea open for our military operations."[13]

MacArthur, of course, had anticipated the 27 September mission and the operational latitude he could expect in selecting military objectives to accomplish it. Likewise, the FEC staff in Tokyo had earlier completed a preliminary estimate of the post-Inch'on situation. Already they were in the process of drafting proposed courses of action based on the assumption that the National Command Authority (NCA) would not settle for restoration of the 38th Parallel as the basis for calling off the UN intervention.[14]

The CINC, however, obviously had not communicated his concept of operations to his staff; nor had the staff validated the planning assumptions upon which they were proceeding. For, one day prior to receipt of the JCS directive, MacArthur surprised the staff with instructions to plan an offensive into North Korea that would feature a deep amphibious envelopment (à la Inch'on), in conjunction with a cross-country advance across the 38th. Although MacArthur did not specify the formation to be used for the amphibious landing, there was obviously only one candidate: X Corps.

A New Concept of Operations

MacArthur's principal staff had assumed that he intended to give Walker command of X Corps; the FEC deputy chief of staff, the G–3 (assistant chief of staff for operations), and G–4 (assistant chief of staff for logistics) all strongly favored such a course.[15] The Eighth Army staff also shared this mistaken assumption and had planned accordingly: After Seoul was retaken, X Corps was to continue the attack north toward the enemy capital, P'yongyang, maintaining the momentum of the offensive, while Eighth Army moved up behind it. Depending upon the development of the situation, X Corps might continue the attack in the west toward the Yalu, or move laterally along the P'yongyang-Wonsan corridor to assist ROK units advancing northward along the east coast. In either event, operations of both forces would be coordinated under Walker's command.[16]

Because Inch'on had originally been conceived as only one pincer of a vast double envelopment, with a second amphibious operation on the east coast, JSPOG already had current data on likely landing sites, and within hours of receiving CINCUNC's guidance was able to present MacArthur with an outline plan.[17] The most likely candidate was Wonsan, an excellent deepwater port on the opposite side of the peninsula's waist from P'yongyang and connected to it by the only east-west LOC of any consequence north of the 38th Parallel. MacArthur readily accepted the hybrid plan prepared by JSPOG, calling for X Corps to make an amphibious landing at Wonsan and prepare either to effect a juncture with Eighth Army (advancing in the west to capture P'yongyang) or to advance north to the key coast industrial complex, Hamhung-Hungnam.[18] The X Corps would constitute an operational maneuver force under command of the CINCUNC. MacArthur apparently based his concept of operations on four assumptions, which seem not to have been explicitly stated at the time but tacitly accepted as the general conditions for operations in North Korea. First, the extremely difficult, nearly trackless mountain terrain running generally north-south divides maneuver into eastern and western compartments. Second, given the primitive condition of the transport system and the efficient work of Far East Air Forces (FEAF) on LOC interdiction, logistical support of operations throughout North Korea could not be sustained from Inch'on and Pusan alone. Third, a turning movement on the east coast still might cut off large numbers of North Koreans who had escaped across the 38th Parallel. Fourth, there would be no Soviet or Chinese interference with UNC operations.[19] MacArthur clearly had identified the remnants of the North Korean Army as the enemy center of gravity—which was true, as long as his fourth assumption remained valid.

Walker was soon disabused of the expectation that he would get X Corps under his command. Informed of GHQ's new plan, Eighth Army staff objected vigorously. They believed that X Corps could reach Wonsan faster moving overland by road from Seoul; this was substantiated by the report on 1 October that ROK troops under Walker's command had already crossed the 38th Parallel on the east coast highway against negligible enemy resistance. Furthermore, Eighth Army would be forced to delay its offensive for lack of supplies because the requirements to embark X Corps elements through the ports of Inch'on and Pusan would slow incoming cargo to a trickle (thus canceling the presumed logistical advantages accruing to amphibious seizure of Wonsan).[20] Adding their voices, the Commander, Naval Forces, Far East (ComNavFE), and his staff objected to the amphibious operation as unnecessary, holding, with the army, that X Corps could march there faster than they could be lifted.[21] Perhaps navy planners, realizing that they no longer enjoyed the element of surprise as at Inch'on, foresaw the slow and dangerous process of clearing Wonsan harbor of mines. But, MacArthur held to his plan for a Wonsan amphibious landing, not persuaded by the objections to that operation—if he was aware of them.

There is strong evidence that the organization of the FEC staff was unequal to the demands of supporting an operational commander. First, it had been raided for officers to serve the nascent X Corps headquarters, and these losses had not been made good. Second, there was a fundamental lack of joint service expertise on the staff. Professional air and naval planners served their respective component commanders; thus, the GHQ tended to perceive them as outsiders.[22] The absence of a joint campaign plan was most conspicuous in the realm of air-ground coordination. During the summer, throughout the Pusan Perimeter fighting, command and control of air assets was confused, often wasteful, and sometimes ineffective. To some extent this was understandable, given the improvisation that characterized the initial period of U.S. intervention. But as late as the start of the Wonsan operation there was still no formal, clearly delineated command arrangement at theater level to centralize air operations over Korea. Finally, CINCUNC formally designated Lt. Gen. George E. Stratemeyer, Commander, Far East Air Forces (FEAF), as "operational controller" of all land-based air operations and "coordination controller" of all carrier-based naval and marine air operations over Korea. This arrangement was the fruition of air force efforts to centralize theater air allocation and targeting that had been going on since July—resisted by the navy and GHQ FEC itself. At no time, however, through the end of the UNC's withdrawal from North Korea was the air campaign fully integrated into planning at operational level.[23]

Finally, there seems not to have been a mechanism to disseminate to the staff principals planning guidance by which they in turn could have provided timely, thorough estimates and mission analyses to the CINC (as witness the staff's confusion about the direction of future operations after Seoul's recapture and MacArthur's apparent ignorance of serious doubts concerning the feasibility of a second amphibious thrust). Perhaps this was due to the failure to name a permanent replacement for General Almond, who had been FEC chief of staff when he was selected to command X Corps: He was expected to resume his former post upon conclusion of the campaign. Given MacArthur's Olympian style of command, in which access to his telephoneless office in the Tokyo Dai Ichi Building was limited to a few trusted advisers, there was no conduit for the routine exchange of critical information between the CINC and his staff.[24]

Signs of Strain

On 2 October the CINCUNC issued orders assigning to Eighth Army the main attack in the west, with the initial objective of capturing P'yongyang. The X Corps was to land amphibiously at Wonsan to encircle enemy forces escaping north across the 38th Parallel. Once in possession of their respective objectives, each organization was to attack toward the other along the east-west LOC across the waist of the peninsula, cutting off all escape routes. The X Corps would remain under the direct command of General MacArthur.[25] Adding insult to injury, as the Eighth Army staff saw it, Walker was also ordered on 2 October to provide logistical support to X Corps—without having any control over the corps' operations. This added significantly to the burden on Eighth Army, which was already feeling the strain caused by the requirement to give priority at Inch'on and Pusan to outloading X Corps units. From 1–17 October the total tonnage unloaded was negligible, and most of that was necessarily diverted to X Corps.[26] Throughout October, Eighth Army's advance would be limited by the adverse logistical situation; its troops had nearly reached P'yongyang before it could get any supplies through Inch'on.[27] Yet Eighth Army was not relieved of logistical support responsibility for X Corps until well after the corps had landed at Wonsan and commenced operations in North Korea.

It is impossible, without reading the detailed after-action reports and without some firsthand knowledge of the terrain, to appreciate the serious difficulties Eighth Army faced in making equitable distribution to X

Corps. So onerous was the burden, in Ridgway's estimation, that to have given Walker tactical control of X Corps "would have added little to the load already awarded him."[28] Distance, terrain, lack of regular communications between the two fronts, guerrilla activity, and a fragile transportation net frustrated the best efforts of Eighth Army to carry out its responsibility. Inevitably, a significant degree of mutual resentment came to exist among staff officers of the two commands. This was occasioned by incidents like the one in which X Corps got CINCUNC to overrule an Eighth Army decision that it be held to the same level of a shortage of supplies as I and IX Corps.[29]

On the X Corps side, the staff wrestled with problems beyond its organizational abilities: It was performing army-type functions with a corps-size staff.[30] As the Corps G–4 later wrote, in order to perform its logistical mission over wide frontages, with limited routes of communication, in support of joint and combined forces, "the book just had to be thrown out the window." He found it inexplicable that GHQ FEC had tasked Eighth Army with logistical support in preference to X Corps' direct contact with the theater logistics agency, Japan Logistics Command, which had been the arrangement from the formation of the corps through its commitment at Inch'on. "Detailed supply plans had been completed [with Japan Logistics Command] to meet unexpected difficulties. The introduction of Eighth Army into channels interrupted these arrangements at a critical time." He concludes that, at a time when all staffs were overworked and involved in a very complicated operation requiring the closest liaison, many difficulties could have been avoided if X Corps had continued to receive logistic support directly from Japan, at least until the initial landings at Wonsan had been established.[31] MacArthur's decision to coordinate the operations of both the eastern and western maneuver forces from Tokyo was presumably based on an appreciation of the near-impassable terrain that separated them. Yet the assignment of theater logistical responsibility to Eighth Army indicates a lack of any such understanding. One must conclude that GHQ FEC was out of touch with the situation as the campaign shifted to the offensive.

Dash for the Yalu

In the final event, those who had expressed doubts concerning the efficacy of the Wonsan operation were proven right: ROK troops advancing up the east coast took Wonsan on 11 October—several days before the last X Corps units had even boarded transports. Apparently undeterred by this development, the CINCUNC merely announced his intention to detach ROK elements in northeastern Korea (ROK I Corps) from Eighth Army and place them under the operational control of X Corps, once it had landed at Wonsan.[32] If the merits of the Wonsan landing already appeared dubious, the operation was soon to take on the aspect of a débâcle. The Navy found Wonsan Harbor to have been skillfully and heavily mined; after arriving off the objective area on 19 October, X Corps troops steamed back and forth until they were finally able to begin landing on the twenty-fifth.[33] But probably the most pernicious effect of the ill-starred operation was on Eighth Army's pursuit in the west: not until 9 October did the spearhead division strike across the 38th Parallel for P'yongyang, a delay caused primarily by supply shortages.[34]

The objective of the Wonsan landing was to permit X Corps to rapidly strike west toward P'yongyang, as Eighth Army drove north, thereby cutting off the withdrawal of the main North Korean forces that had been committed against the Pusan Perimeter. When it became clear that the North Korean capital could fall to UN forces long before X Corps debarked, CINCUNC issued a new operations order on 17 October that drew a proposed boundary between Eighth Army and X Corps, to become effective on his further order. The boundary ran north-south, generally along the watershed of the Taebaek Mountain range, to an objective line deep in North Korea that corresponded to the JCS-directed limit of advance for non-Korean elements of the UNC. Eighth Army was to advance to the western extension of the line, X Corps to the eastern.[35] On the eve of X Corps' landing, MacArthur modified his instructions, ordering both commanders to drive forward to the Yalu River as rapidly as possible with all forces under their command—the old objective line was to be regarded as merely "an initial objective."[36] (*Map 17*)

The failure of the Wonsan operation to achieve the objective for which it was designed demonstrated the soundness of the view that Walker should have been given X Corps and designated the ground component commander for the post-Inch'on exploitation phase. But, with Wonsan and P'yongyang in friendly hands, the CINCUNC's concept of two operational forces, maneuvering independently on either side of the Taebaek range, was eminently sound. It minimized the extremely formidable difficulties imposed by terrain and promised the rapid destruction of the North Korean Army as an organized force, assuming the continued forbearance of the Soviets and Chinese. Events almost immediately called into question the validity of that assumption. On 25 October Eighth Army units encountered Chinese Communist Forces (CCF) troops for the first time, north of the Ch'ongch'on River (just as the U.S. I Corps published its order for the advance to the Yalu).[37] The following night Chinese units struck hard at the ROK II Corps on Eighth Army's right and over the next three days caused the ROKs to pivot northeast to face in the direction of the Chinese main attack. This opened a gap in Eighth Army's front, leaving the U.S. I Corps' right flank open. Some 1st Cavalry Division elements were moved in to shore up the ROKs, and one regiment was badly mauled in the pro-

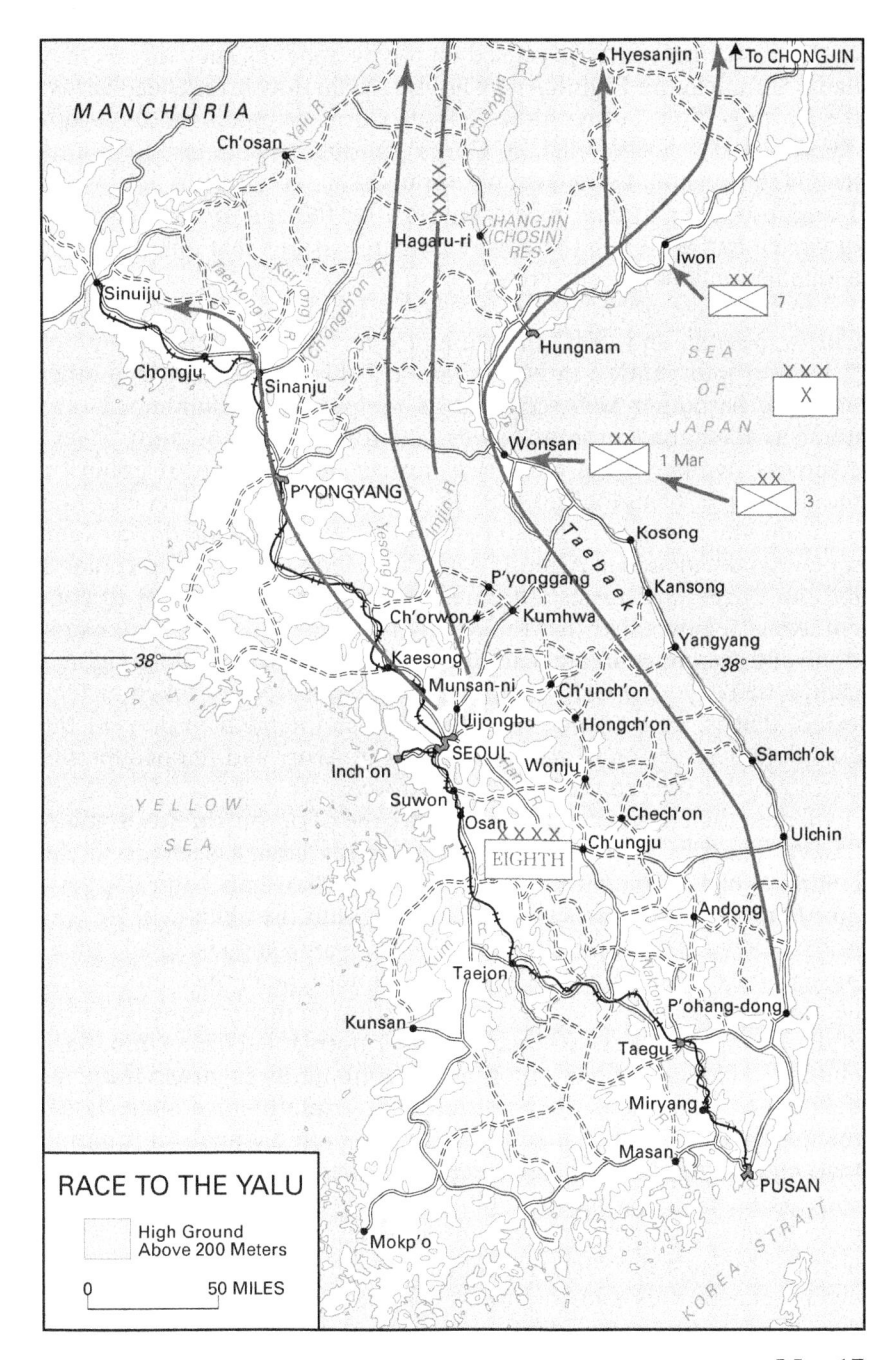

MAP 17

cess. The Chinese attacks ceased on 6 November as suddenly as they had begun, leaving Eighth Army holding a shallow bridgehead across the Ch'ongch'on, but with the ROK II Corps crippled and its troops demoralized.[38] To the east, X Corps' marines encountered Chinese troops in divisional strength, but repulsed them with limited losses. There, too, the Chinese broke contact after the end of the first week in November, although there were numerous signs that unknown size elements remained in the area.

In the wake of the Chinese "tap," Eighth Army was shaken, X Corps sobered, and GHQ unsure as to the "present actual scope of [Chinese] intervention in North Korea."[39] On 14 November another ominous harbinger was recorded as temperatures plummeted—as much as 40 degrees in some places—to lows well below zero.[40] Nevertheless, Walker made clear that he had no intention of going on the defensive, bringing the U.S. IX Corps up in the center in order to renew the advance in greater strength.[41] Similarly, there was soon renewed confidence in Almond's headquarters: Diminishing contacts led the Corps G–2 (assistant chief of staff for intelligence) to conclude on 18 November that the enemy had ended his delaying operations and was once again withdrawing to the north.[42] Most significantly, in Tokyo the CCF intervention was clearly not taken at face value, that is, as evidence that the Chinese intended to prevent the complete destruction of the North Korean Army and the occupation of all North Korea to the Yalu by UN forces.

Under the circumstances, such a degree of optimism was extraordinary. The FEC G–2 (despite MacArthur's later assertions to the contrary) had sufficient intelligence by mid-November to raise serious doubts about the wisdom of plunging into the unknown. He was privy to key national intelligence reports, which suggested a hardening resolve by the Chinese leadership to intervene in the conflict, and he possessed generally accurate information on the movement of several additional Chinese armies from their normal garrisons into Manchuria.[43] That the national intelligence community regarded these indicators as ambiguous does not let theater intelligence analysts off the hook, for they were also receiving concrete tactical information that, taken with national reporting, suggested grounds for the greatest caution in renewing the offensive.[44] Yet the FEC G–2 seems to have been unable to move off dead center: neither an unqualified positive forecast nor clear warnings of danger. Indecisiveness about enemy capabilities and intentions was reflected in the vacillating, even self-contradictory, daily intelligence estimates provided CINCUNC at this time. In the absence of solid intelligence estimates from his G–2, MacArthur's reliance on his intuitive conviction that the Chinese were bluffing is perhaps more understandable.[45]

"Withdrawals Unnecessarily Precipitous"

MacArthur's concept of dividing UNC into two maneuver forces operating on multiple lines, dictated by the compartmented terrain, was perfectly suited to the pursuit and destruction of a weakened enemy whose remnant forces were fugitive deep in North Korea. The commitment of Chinese troops, however, altered the equation. Regardless of how one interpreted Chinese intentions, the check to Eighth Army's advance had been serious enough to suggest that UNC had reached the culminating point of the offensive. But when they vanished as suddenly as they had appeared, CINCUNC, after getting a scare, determined that the CCF intervention was token—a face saving gesture. Despite the rebounding optimism, there was at least recognition within GHQ FEC of the prudence in a closer examination of UNC's dispositions and some adjustment of the original plan. Given that UNC's main effort had to be made in the west, the only alteration of Eighth Army's offensive scheme was to delay its resumption long enough to accumulate sufficient supplies to sustain it to the Yalu. The real question was what modification should be made in X Corps' mission. This the GHQ FEC planners now took under consideration.

The CINCUNC directive to drive to the border with all possible speed following the Wonsan landing necessitated a wide deployment of X Corps troops. General Almond planned to conduct the dash to the Yalu by sending the ROK I Corps up the main east coast road to the Soviet border; the U.S. 1st Marine Division up the road from Hamhung to the Chosin Reservoir, from whence it could drive north; and the U.S. 7th Infantry Division, which had landed farthest up the coast at Iwon, straight north to the border.[46] By mid-November X Corps covered a 400-mile front. Since most combat units were committed to reaching distant objectives, few troops were available for rear area security and anti-guerrilla missions, and the corps reserve was very small. It was also necessary for the X Corps commander to devote a great deal of time and some part of his limited resources to problems of civil government and rehabilitation of heavily damaged cities and ports.[47] Thus, two basic alternative courses of action presented themselves after the Chinese broke contact. First, X Corps would continue its mission without regard to Eighth Army's progress in the west or for flank security of its own columns, relying on momentum to reach its objectives before either winter or the Chinese could force a halt. Second, X Corps would consolidate its forces on its supply base of Hungnam, pulling back the most extended elements (some of which were rapidly closing on the Yalu) to positions from which they would provide mutual support in the event of trouble, and wait until Eighth Army could develop the situation in its sector. Almond, whose poor opinion of the Chinese infantryman's fighting qualities inclined him toward CINCUNC's interpretation of China's intervention, was clearly set on resuming his offensive.

The JSPOG, however, tended to look at X Corps' deployment from the standpoint of "how can X Corps best assist Eighth Army?"—even though the terrain separating them made such support a dubious proposition at best. From that point of view, there was little to recommend Almond's plan.[48] But its disadvantages were significant: X Corps' advance, as currently oriented (almost due north), risked becoming seriously overextended; should progress by Eighth Army's right flank be delayed, X Corps' left flank would be completely exposed. On the other hand, X Corps could assist Eighth Army if Almond attacked to the northwest, thereby threatening enemy forces north of the Ch'ongch'on River with envelopment. It was estimated that Almond could make available two divisions for this purpose by calling off his advance north.[49] This was the essence of the JSPOG recommendation to MacArthur, which was implemented on 16 November by a message directing X Corps to develop as an alternative a plan for reorienting the main attack west on reaching the Chosin Reservoir area.[50]

There were serious problems with the course of action recommended by the JSPOG staff. Perhaps most obvious is that it assigned a mission fundamentally incompatible with the scheme of operational maneuver: The main reason for control of X Corps as a separate force by the operational commander was the extreme impracticability of coordinating its operations with those of Eighth Army. Far worse from the maneuver commander's point of view, the ground over which JSPOG intended that X Corps should attack in support of Eighth Army is the worst on the peninsula. Avenues of approach from the line of contact were extremely restricted due to the rugged, compartmented terrain, the paucity of even fair roads, and the virtual impossibility of cross-country motorized movement.[51] Some indication of the difficulty involved in mounting mutually supporting operations across the Taebaek Mountains could have been received from the fact that, despite several efforts following the October Chinese attacks, it had not been possible to establish patrol contact between Eighth Army and X Corps. There was, in fact, an almost complete lack of liaison between the two fronts in November.[52] The GHQ FEC was apparently ignorant of such nuances, probably because of their isolation in Tokyo: After Seoul was retaken JSPOG personnel seem rarely to have visited the theater and consequently had few firsthand impressions to guide their efforts.[53]

Whether it was cause or symptom of intelligence shortcomings is hard to judge, but operations planning seems to have been done in a vacuum within the staff as well. For example, on 12 November, when JSPOG began to develop their proposed branch to X Corps' plan, planning assumptions credited the Chinese with less than a third of the strength G–2 had estimated to Washington that same day (whether they were unwitting or disbelieving of G–2's figures is a matter of conjecture).[54] And if the limitations imposed by terrain upon friendly forces were poorly understood, there was virtually no comprehension of the manner in which Chinese forces made use of it. Whereas the JSPOG plan envisioned striking the Chinese force's "flank," threatening its "rear," and cutting the enemy's "main supply route," these were meaningless abstractions when applied to the Chinese campaign plan. The lightly armed, well-disciplined Chinese troops carried four or five days' rations and ammunition; when these were exhausted a fresh unit relieved them. All reinforcing units deployed directly from bases or assembly areas located north of the Yalu in Manchuria. They moved on foot in widely dispersed columns, usually at night. They attacked from the march and maneuvered rapidly over even the most difficult terrain.[55]

The JSPOG's fundamental misunderstanding of enemy strengths and weaknesses reflected the isolation of GHQ FEC from the theater, its lack of firsthand familiarity with the ground on which United Nations forces were maneuvering, and a near complete breakdown of the operations-intelligence interface. There seems to have been little comprehension in Tokyo that once in motion X Corps forward elements might find themselves out on the end of some very long and precarious limb if anything went wrong. As Almond later put it, "the principal problem facing me as X Corps commander, with a fighting force extended over a 400 mile front, was how to concentrate these forces to meet a rapidly deteriorating tactical situation."[56]

Upon assurance from Walker that his supply levels were adequate, the CINCUNC approved Eighth Army's plan to resume the advance on 24 November. On that date Almond's representatives briefed MacArthur in Tokyo on X Corps' plan to support Eighth Army's attack: basically a reorientation to the west of the corps main attack by 1st Marine Division from their positions south of the Chosin Reservoir. This he approved with only one modification, a corresponding shift of the proposed boundary between the two commands, and then he directed its implementation. The X Corps scheduled its supporting attack to commence at 0800 on 27 November.[57] But even as the 1st Marine Division launched its attack west on the morning of the twenty-seventh, Eighth Army's offensive was halted by strong Chinese counterattacks on its right and center.[58] Within twenty-four hours, the ROK II Corps had collapsed on Eighth Army's right and numerous penetrations elsewhere had forced a general withdrawal by the U.S. I and IX Corps to defensive positions. In X Corps, the 1st Marine Division's attack had been halted by heavy Chinese counterattacks and its route of withdrawal cut in several places, while major elements of 7th Infantry Division were isolated and under heavy pressure.

"Having done everything humanly possible within the capabilities of [the] Command," MacArthur announced that his plan for the immediate future was to pass from the offensive to the defensive, with such adjustments as were dictated by a "constantly fluid situation." He concluded that the ultimate objective of the Chinese Communists was "undoubtedly" the complete destruction of all UN forces in Korea and that it was "quite evident" that his present strength was insufficient to meet this "undeclared war by the Chinese with the inherent advantages which accrue thereby to them."[59] But an infantry lieutenant's recollection of the ordeal east of the Chosin Reservoir cuts straight to the heart of the UN Command's defeat: "Once the battle was joined with the overwhelming but unorganized Chinese forces, our withdrawals were unnecessarily precipitous and uncontrolled."[60]

Thoughts for the Operational Artist

Near the end of his discourse on military genius, Clausewitz characterizes the qualities demanded of the commander in chief in terms that precisely sum up the challenge of the theater commander in 1950. He must also be a statesman, but he must not cease to be a general. "On the one hand, he is aware of the entire political situation; on the other, he knows exactly how much he can achieve with the means at his disposal."[61] That MacArthur's leadership and judgment after Inch'on do not pass this test is fundamentally attributable to the fault Clausewitz identifies as "obstinacy." "Stubbornness and intolerance of criticism result from a special form of egotism, which elevates above everything else the pleasure of its autonomous intellect, to which others must bow." Unlike vanity, which is content with appearances, "obstinacy demands the material reality." Strength of character becomes obstinacy when the commander resists another's point of view "not from superior insight or attachment to some higher principle, but because he objects instinctively."[62]

This is the hard kernel of MacArthur's flaw as operational commander. His overriding belief in his mission and willingness to call what he surely regarded as a Chinese bluff in order to carry out that mission became the dominant factors influencing campaign planning for operations in North Korea.[63] But, even so, the flaw need not have been fatal, if MacArthur's command and control system had left him some margin for rashness, accidents—or chance.[64] The main point of this study is that command and control of UNC operations was itself fatally flawed; the command system was simply unequal to the demands on it. In essence, it lacked both the structure and the flexibility to be successful in the unique circumstances obtaining in the fall of 1950. These shortcomings may be summarized as follows.

The GHQ FEC had not been a joint headquarters when the war began, nor did it become one until long afterward.[65] The staff, not surprisingly, tended to see the war almost exclusively in terms of the ground component, usually leaving air and naval coordination as afterthoughts. Certainly, the operations of the four services were never synchronized into a single operational campaign plan (although the brilliantly executed Inch'on operation was clear evidence of the tactical merits of such synchronization). This points out probably the hardest task in a contingency of the sort Korea represents: to tailor a joint operational staff functionally organized to deal with the specific problem at hand.

The lack of a joint campaign plan is also evident in the failure to plan ahead to exploit the success of the Inch'on turning movement. This resulted in loss of momentum at the critical point when, it is clear in hindsight, the balance might have been tipped irreversibly in UNC's favor. Because a "seam" was introduced in operations, the effects of friction were greatly increased. And unquestionably the greatest cause of friction was the decision to continue X Corps' independent existence. MacArthur's failure to ensure unity of effort by the ground component at this juncture is hard to understand. Perhaps it can be partially explained by the fact that he had not seen the ground on which the campaign was to be fought. Prior to Inch'on he had visited Korea only three times, and there is no indication that he conducted a personal reconnaissance of the area north of Seoul.

If allocation of resources is the key logistical problem at operational level, control of the logistical spigot also gives the operational commander the means to weight the main effort or to change the direction of that effort by reinforcing success. By making the commander of Eighth Army responsible for resupply of X Corps, a force not under his control, CINCUNC reduced his own flexibility to exploit a tactical advantage developed on either front, quite apart from seriously encumbering Eighth Army at the critical point in the campaign. The Eighth Army–X Corps situation demonstrates a major difficulty with multiple lines of operation in a single campaign: It tends to produce competition for resources which might better be concentrated in support of one commander or the other.[66] Had Walker been designated ground component commander after the recapture of Seoul, it would have made sense to vest him with logistical responsibility for all forces in the peninsula. Otherwise, it was inexplicable.

The single operational failure that had the direst consequences for the offensive into North Korea was, of course, intelligence. The function performed by the operational intelligence officer is unique. He represents the point of convergence of national and tactical intelligence collection. His is the key responsibility to collate intelligence from above and below, to correlate it with weather and terrain, and to disseminate to subordinate commanders what they need to know. Above all, he is responsible for estimates of enemy intentions as well as capabilities. By this standard, it is hard not to conclude that the CINCUNC was badly served by his G–2. In general, the greater the degree to which a theater lacks prior "strategic intelligence preparation of the battlefield," the more likely it is that the operational G–2 will have a better feel for enemy intentions than national intelligence agencies.

What gave the Korean War its unique character was that it was fought at the margin of U.S. strategy, beyond the line that demarcated America's vital interests. It was also fought on the margin in the sense that resources were limited—borrowed from strategic missions elsewhere. In a dangerous world, future crises may overtake us in the same way, at places where map sheets end and where there is no contingency planning worthy of the name. Against that day, operational planners might do worse than to consider the lessons of 1950.

Notes

1. Certainly in the classic sense of the term. Although the definition of the operational level of command is somewhat elastic, nevertheless, certain criteria can be adduced. The operational commander is responsible for selecting military objectives that will accomplish the strategic goals assigned by the NCA. His forces will be joint and very likely combined as well. Distances involved in movement, fire, and maneuver are likely to be very great. The operational commander allocates logistics within the theater and is the focal point for integration of national and tactical intelligence. Using these criteria, no one between MacArthur and Schwarzkopf fully qualifies as an operational commander. Westmoreland and Abrams in Vietnam come close, but it is hard to argue that either had the latitude as Commander, U.S. Military Assistance Command, Vietnam (COMUSMACV), to select his military objectives.
2. The culminating point is that at which the attacker's strength no longer significantly exceeds the defender's, and beyond which, therefore, offensive operations risk overextension, counterattack, and defeat. Department of the Army (DA), Field Manual (FM) 100–5, *Operations* (Washington, D.C.: Department of the Army, 1986), p. 181.
3. For instance, General Matthew B. Ridgway, *The Korean War* (Garden City, N.Y.: Doubleday, 1967), p. 63, on hubris; Dean Acheson, *The Korean War* (New York: W. W. Norton, 1971), pp. 64–67, on schizophrenia in GHQ; Roy E. Appleman, *South to the Naktong, North to the Yalu*, U.S. Army in the Korean War (Washington, D.C.: Government Printing Office, 2000), pp. 765, on air power. Nearly every account of the Korean War faults intelligence to a greater or lesser degree.
4. James F. Schnabel, *Policy and Direction: The First Year*, U.S. Army in the Korean War (Washington, D.C.: Government Printing Office, 1990), p. 275.
5. The conflict began on 25 June with the surprise North Korean attack across the 38th Parallel. The first U.S. reinforcements arrived from Japan on 1 July and were in combat as rapidly as they could be moved to the front. The defensive line known as the Pusan Perimeter came into being when the delaying U.S. forces withdrew east across the Naktong River on 1 August. It remained in existence until Eighth Army's breakout after Inch'on. A rectangular area measuring 100 miles north to south and about 50 miles east to west, the Perimeter contained a good interior LOC radiating from Taegu and included an excellent deepwater port, Pusan.
6. Naval Forces, Far East, was commanded by Vice Adm. C. Turner Joy, and Far East Air Forces came under Lt. Gen. George Stratemeyer. Schnabel, *Policy and Direction*, p. 49.
7. Robert F. Futrell, *The United States Air Force in Korea, 1950–1953* (Washington, D.C.: Government Printing Office, 1983), pp. 44, 52; Schnabel, *Policy and Direction*, pp. 46–49.
8. Schnabel, *Policy and Direction*, pp. 47–49.
9. Appleman, *South to the Naktong*, p. 114. Prior to the North Korean invasion, FEC had no operational responsibility for the defense of the ROK. Per recommendation of the JCS, the president appointed MacArthur Commander in Chief, United Nations Command, on 10 July. Schnabel, *Policy and Direction*, p. 102.
10. Schnabel, *Policy and Direction*, p. 157.

11. Ibid., pp. 187–89.

12. Not, as MacArthur subsequently claimed, to reunify Korea. In fact, the 27 September directive carefully left open the question of the future political sovereignty of North Korea, reflecting caution in regard to possible Soviet or Chinese counters.

13. Schnabel, *Policy and Direction*, pp. 182–84.

14. Although the fight to retake Seoul was more bitter than expected and the breakout of Eighth Army from the Perimeter slower than planned, the success of the Inch'on operation had not been in doubt since the seventeenth. However, in operational terms, planning for future operations was tardy and, because of the failure to rapidly exploit success at Inch'on, necessitated pursuit into North Korea of enemy forces that should not have been allowed to escape. See Ridgway, *The Korean War*, pp. 41–43.

15. Schnabel, *Policy and Direction*, p. 189. Several years later, however, MacArthur stated these officers never expressed any such views at the time. Appleman, *South to the Naktong*, p. 612.

16. Appleman, *South to the Naktong*, p. 612.

17. Ibid., p. 610. Sufficient forces for two simultaneous amphibious operations were not available.

18. Schnabel, *Policy and Direction*, p. 188.

19. Appleman, *South to the Naktong*, pp. 609–11; Schnabel, *Policy and Direction*, pp. 187–91.

20. Despite his staff's urging, Walker did not formally raise objections to the CINCUNC's plan; nor is there any evidence that he ever discussed alternative courses of action with MacArthur. Appleman, *South to the Naktong*, p. 611; Schnabel, *Policy and Direction*, p. 190.

21. Appleman, *South to the Naktong*, p. 612.

22. The success of the complex Inch'on operation seems due to the extraordinary skill and competence of the component planners entrusted with the details and not a little luck.

23. Futrell, *Air Force in Korea*, pp. 49–55, 213.

24. Almond was reputed to have kept the staff on a very short leash and to have been a man feared by many. His deputy, Maj. Gen. Doyle Hickey, who was designated acting FEC chief of staff, though capable, did not possess Almond's formidable talents or obviously the same degree of authority. See Appleman, *South to the Naktong*, p. 490. For a most revealing account of MacArthur's command style and his relations with his confidants and staff, see D. Clayton James, *The Years of MacArthur: Volume III: Triumph and Disaster, 1945–1964* (Boston: Houghton Mifflin, 1985).

25. Schnabel, *Policy and Direction*, pp. 196–98.

26. HQ Eighth U.S. Army, Korea, *Monograph: Special Problems in the Korean Conflict* (APO 301: Eighth Army Historical Service Detachment [Provisional], 1952), pp. 37–38.

27. Although the overall situation improved subsequently, as late as mid-November one corps was operating with only a one-day supply of ammunition in reserve. See Appleman, *South to the Naktong*, p. 640; Schnabel, *Policy and Direction*, p. 258.

28. Ridgway, *The Korean War*, p. 48.

29. So strong was the animosity that when, after the withdrawal from North Korea, Eighth Army redistributed some X Corps supplies that were no longer required, some X Corps officers referred to it as "confiscation." Eighth Army, *Special Problems*, pp. 42–48.

30. The X Corps got control of the ROK I Corps once the Wonsan landings had been completed. Schnabel, *Policy and Direction*, p. 206.

31. Eighth Army, *Special Problems*, p. 52.
32. HQ X Corps, *War Diary (WD)*, Monthly Summary: 1–31 Oct 50, "Wonsan-Iwon Landings," p. 48.
33. The mine laying had been planned and supervised by Soviet technicians. Clearing operations cost not only time, but the loss of several U.S. and ROK vessels and many casualties. Marines waiting to debark called it Operation Yo-yo. See Appleman, *South to the Naktong*, pp. 633–737; Schnabel, *Policy and Direction*, pp. 209–10.
34. Schnabel, *Policy and Direction*, p. 202.
35. Appleman, *South to the Naktong*, p. 612; Schnabel, *Policy and Direction*, p. 216.
36. HQ X Corps, *WD*, 1–31 Oct 50, pp. 50–51. This order constituted a clear violation of the prohibition on employment of "non-Korean" troops in proximity to the border. The JCS response, however, was almost apologetic: while realizing that CINCUNC "undoubtedly had sound reasons for issuing these instructions [JCS] would like to be informed of them, as your action is a matter of some concern here." MacArthur responded that the guidance to "feel unhampered tactically and strategically" constituted a modification of his instructions. Schnabel, *Policy and Direction*, p. 218; Acheson, *The Korean War*, pp. 62–63. For some understanding of how MacArthur could defy the orders of his nominal superiors, see Ridgway's comments on perceptions of his "infallibility," Acheson, *The Korean War*, p. 63, and Omar Bradley and Clay Blair, *A General's Life* (New York: Simon & Schuster, 1983), pp. 585–90.
37. Appleman, *South to the Naktong*, p. 676.
38. Certain ROK regiments had been literally atomized by the Chinese attack, and one division lost nearly all its artillery, vehicles, and heavy equipment. JCS, Joint Daily SITREP no. 123, 30 Oct 50; Appleman, *South to the Naktong*, pp. 672–715.
39. JCS, Joint Daily SITREP no. 132, Nov 50.
40. HQ X Corps, *Periodic Intelligence Report (PIR)* no. 49, 14 Nov 50.
41. Schnabel, *Policy and Direction*, p. 256.
42. X Corps, *PIR* no. 53, 18 Nov 50.
43. In the Senate hearings following MacArthur's relief, he stated that "the intelligence that a nation is going to launch war, is not an intelligence that is available to a commander, limited to a small area of combat. That intelligence should have been given to me." U.S. Congress, Senate, *Committee on Armed Services and Committee on Foreign Relations, Military Situation in the Far East, Hearings* (New York: Arno Press, 1979), p. 18.
44. There were, for example, several interrogation reports that contained ominous signs of full-fledged intervention. In one such report, two Korean civilian refugees from a town situated at a major Yalu River crossing point told of seeing "a continuous flow of CCF troops" passing into Korea since 12 October and of being informed by a Chinese officer that 200,000 CCF troops were coming to the aid of the North Koreans. In another, a Chinese prisoner claimed that his unit had been greeted upon its arrival in North Korea in early October by a man "his platoon leader said was Kim Il Sung." This man told them, "I am in a difficult position and have lost the war," after which he welcomed them to Korea and wished them victory. X Corps, *PIR* no. 49, 14 Nov, and no. 53, 18 Nov 50.
45. The most common explanation for the gross failure of theater intelligence to accurately assess either Chinese intentions or capabilities is that MacArthur simply refused to credit intelligence indicators suggesting that he might have to delay or even cancel his offensive. See Schnabel, *Policy and Direction*, p. 277; Ridgway, *The Korean War*, pp. 76–77. While there is no question of the dominance of MacArthur's personality, a close reading of the intelligence estimates he was receiving shows good reason for confusion as to the actual enemy situation. See Schnabel, *Policy and Direction*, p. 276. Finally, where-

as CINCUNC was aware of a substantial number of Chinese soldiers in North Korea, estimates fell far short of the reality: FEC G–2 was estimating about 76,800 total Chinese troops in Korea, when in fact there were approximately 180,000 concentrated in front of Eighth Army and 120,000 in front of X Corps. JCS, Joint Daily SITREP no. 133, 13 Nov 50; Appleman, *South to the Naktong*, p. 769.

46. HQ X Corps, *WD*, 1–30 Nov 50, "Drive to the Yalu: CCF Counter Attack," p. 2. U.S. troops at the time called the reservoir Chosin, which is the Japanese rendering of the Korean name, because that is what was on their maps. It is today usually called by its proper Korean name, Changjin. For purposes of consistency it will be referred to here as Chosin, as it was invariably rendered in contemporary documents.

47. Ibid., p. 3. For these rear-area missions, the X Corps commander had available after 17 November the entire U.S. 3d Infantry Division, the last reinforcing combat unit to arrive from CONUS.

48. Schnabel, *Policy and Direction*, pp. 260–62. The "advantages" to Almond's plan, which the staff developed during the course-of-action analysis, were, as the author dryly puts it, "so innocuous as to seem fabricated."

49. Ibid., pp. 260–61.

50. HQ X Corps, WD, 1–30 Nov 50, p. 5.

51. Ibid., p. 19.

52. At the daily EUSAK briefings held at 1330 in Seoul, X Corps liaison reports were read. These reports ended as of 0600 on the previous morning. Nor was radio contact between the two commands apparently any better than "occasional." Eighth Army believed that this situation materially contributed to the intelligence failure. Eighth Army, *Special Problems*, pp. 41–42, 50. MacArthur seems to have been unaware of this communications gap: When questioned on the subject during the congressional investigation that followed his relief from command, he testified that "there was as complete coordination as I have ever known between enveloping movements." U.S. Congress, Senate, *Military Situation in the Far East*, pp. 192, 248.

53. X Corps *War Diaries*, which contain detailed lists of important conferences and visitors to the command, show no record of GHQ FEC staff visits after early October.

54. Schnabel, *Policy and Direction*, p. 260.

55. X Corps, *PIR* no. 49, 14 Nov 50. See also Nicholas A. Canzona and Lynn Montross, *U.S. Marine Operations in Korea, 1950–1953: Volume III: The Chosin Reservoir Campaign* (Washington, D.C.: Government Printing Office, 1957); Allen S. Whiting, *China Crosses the Yalu: The Decision to Enter the Korean War* (New York: Macmillan, 1960).

56. "Recollections of Hungnam and Chosin," *Korean War Historical Commentary*, Edward M. Almond Papers, U.S. Army Military History Institute, Carlisle Barracks, Pa.

57. HQ X Corps, Special Rpt on the Chosin Reservoir, 27 Nov–10 Dec 50, p. 10.

58. JCS, Joint Daily SITREP no. 142, 27 Nov 50.

59. JCS, Joint Daily SITREP no. 143, 28 Nov 50.

60. Roy E. Appleman, *East of Chosin: Entrapment and Breakout in Korea* (College Station: Texas A&M University Press, 1987), p. 318.

61. Carl von Clausewitz, *On War*, ed. and trans. Michael Howard and Peter Paret (Princeton: Princeton University Press, 1984), p. 112.

62. Ibid., pp. 108–09.

63. Schnabel, *Policy and Direction*, pp. 227–78.

64. As evidence that this is true, consider the accomplishments of the 1st Marine Division. Isolated in extremely restricted terrain on X Corps' left flank when the Chinese struck, the division withdrew in good order despite its reliance on a precarious main

supply route. Further, it inflicted very heavy casualties, causing the CCF to break contact in order to reconstitute. This successful fighting withdrawal was due primarily to the commander's healthy appreciation of the risks involved in his earlier advance and the prudent measures he took to ensure the security of his force. See Canzona and Montross, *Marine Operations in Korea*.

65. And it was most certainly not a combined headquarters. Not only were UN and ROK officers excluded from the staff, but as late as the beginning of October the commander of Eighth Army was in doubt as to the degree of control he held over ROK units in his area. Schnabel, *Policy and Direction*, pp. 192, 205.

66. DA, FM 100–5, p. 180.

The Maturation of Operational Art

Operations Desert Shield and Desert Storm

John S. Brown

Earlier authors in this collection have made the point that American commanders conducted campaigns at the operational level long before they conceptualized an operational level as such.[1] The belated American doctrinal recognition of the operational level of war in 1982 and operational art in 1986 was part of an overall post-Vietnam renaissance in the United States' military thinking that focused heavily on a Soviet adversary and took Soviet doctrine into account.[2] In emerging from its Vietnam experience, the United States Army in particular had to shake off the trauma of ten wearying years of a war generally won at the tactical level but overwhelmingly lost at the strategic level.[3] It also had to recover from a generation wherein little doctrinal thinking beyond the tactical had occurred at all. The Korean War had featured an operational component, but Eisenhower's "New Look" soon had ground forces flailing to establish strategic relevance.[4] The "Flexible Response" of the Kennedy and Johnson years promised to consider the full spectrum of military options, but in practice it was about low intensity conflict—counterguerrilla, pacification, nation building, Green Berets, and the like.[5]

Post-Vietnam developments made a rethinking of doctrinal principles likely. Whatever World War II hubris had been left in the Army had hemorrhaged out during the fighting in Southeast Asia, and the Army found itself struggling to articulate the value it would bring to future quarrels.[6] The 1973 Arab-Israeli War crystallized the recognition that mid-to-high-intensity conventional combat was not only possible, but likely.[7] The return to a European focus again juxtaposed the United States with the Soviet Union, which not only wielded superior conventional capabilities, but also had refined and elaborated doctrine at the tactical, operational, and strategic levels.[8] Finally, embarrassing shortcomings with respect to joint and operational performance during the muddled-through invasion of Grenada led to Congress' bullying the Department of Defense into the Goldwater-Nichols reforms—reforms that the services could not seem to come up with themselves.[9] The story of this post-Vietnam military renaissance and its translation into a collective canon labeled AirLand Battle has already been told.[10] In this article, we hope to describe how this newly refined doctrine translated into practical capabilities and how Operations DESERT SHIELD and DESERT STORM played out as examples of the operational art. Although its focus is the U.S. Army's experience, it takes into account the jointness of the campaign and parallel developments in other services.

Operational Ingredients

Combat veterans will tell you there is a difference between having a plan and carrying it through to successful conclusion, between "knowing what right looks like" and "making it happen." Given the comparatively recent American articulation of the operational art and the distances in time separating most of DESERT STORM's senior commanders from their last exposures to service school systems, their success at implementing contemporary classroom doctrine would have been surprising had there not been additional mechanisms at work to translate newly developed theory into practical operational capabilities. Five such mechanisms stand out: the proliferation of officers trained in the new doctrine onto the staffs wherein operational decisions are effectively made; the general adaptation of a vocabulary that reflected the new doctrine; the Battle Command Training Program (BCTP) and similar simulations-driven exercises; the development of technical capabilities commensurate with the doctrine; and the evolution of the Capable Corps.

Most senior American leaders of DESERT STORM had little exposure to the operational art in the Army educational system. Key, albeit relatively junior, members of their staffs had. The United States has long had a love-hate relationship with staff specialization such as that represented by the German General Staff. On the one hand, theorists and commentators since at least as far back as Emory Upton have praised the efficiency of the German General Staff and advocated it as a model — a model many European militaries in fact adopted.[11] On the other hand, frontier and maritime traditions of greater vintage characterized service with troops or sailors as "where the action was," and service on a senior staff as somehow less manly. Indeed, General George S. Patton, Jr.'s comments on the subject capture a stereotype quite nicely:

> The typical staff officer is a man past middle life, spare, wrinkled, intelligent, cold, noncommittal, with eyes like a codfish, polite in contact, but at the same time unresponsive, cool, calm, and as damnably composed as a concrete post or plaster of Paris cast; a human petrification with a heart of feldspar and without charm or the friendly germ; minus bowels, passions or a sense of humor. Happily they never reproduce and all of them finally go to hell.[12]

Twentieth-century Americans adopted an egalitarian attitude toward military staff work; rather than evolving a small, highly specialized elite cadre, they rotated officers between staff and line assignments fairly routinely. In the views of the officers themselves, they "did their time" on staff in order to return to the troop, flight, or sea duty they truly preferred.[13] In keeping with this egalitarian attitude toward staff work, the American Army trained virtually all its middle-grade officers in such skills. The Command and General Staff College (CGSC) and its predecessors at Fort Leavenworth, Kansas, have turned out tens of thousands of officers since 1881, and tens of thousands more have received the same training in a nonresident status.[14] The Navy and Air Force developed similar institutions at Newport, Rhode Island, and Maxwell Air Force Base, Alabama, respectively. As the staff complexities of the operational art became more apparent to those attempting to promulgate it, the year given over to such programs as resident CGSC instruction seemed too brief to develop a proper mastery. The School of Advanced Military Studies (SAMS) graduated its first students from an extended two-year version of the CGSC in 1985, featuring intense emphasis upon the operational art, higher-level command and staff coordination, and historical precedents. By 1990 SAMS was graduating about fifty students a year. In addition, students in the one-year CGSC course were offered the opportunity to compete, with extra work and effort, for a Master of Military Arts and Science (MMAS) degree within the time frame of their CGSC attendance.[15]

How did the Army attract talented middle-grade officers to intense staff training in an organization inclined to denigrate staff work? In many cases the attraction was to return to troop duty earlier than otherwise would have been possible. During the 1980s Army force structure featured heavy requirements for the field-grade officer in branch-immaterial nominative assignments or assignments drawing on a secondary Military Occupational Specialty (MOS). A major who had just been with troops had little prospect of returning to troop duty soon. An additional year at Leavenworth in SAMS, however, virtually guaranteed an immediate return to an operational unit, albeit generally on a corps or division staff. Once there, the major could reasonably hope to make a favorable impression and be returned to a battalion within a year or so, when the next SAMS class graduated to replace the officer. The mathematics worked out to a return to troops as a field-grade officer within two to three as opposed to four to five years. A fraction of SAMS's popularity was its exploitation of a time-honored American technique: Seduce talented officers into staff work by promising to make them line officers in due course.[16]

Whatever their motives, SAMS graduates proliferated throughout the Army and enhanced staff proficiency—particularly with respect to the operational art heavily emphasized at the time. They were reinforced by an emphasis upon the operational art in the basic course, and thus the tendency of all recent officer graduates of the service school systems to use concepts and vocabulary that facilitated its use. The 1986 edition of Field Manual (FM) 100–5, *Operations*, deployed an array of historical operational vignettes to make its points; such terms as Center of Gravity, Lines of Operation, and Culminating Point were recommended as key concepts for operational design. Although they did not develop a precise equivalent to SAMS, Navy and Air Force educators also gave due attention to the operational art and campaign planning during this period and developed appropriate literature for their student officers as well.[17]

Although initially a tactical construct, the categorization of the Battlefield Operating Systems (BOS)—maneuver, fire support, intelligence, command and control, air defense, mobility-countermobility, and combat service support—gave planners a convenient checklist and matrix that had operational implications as well. Soviet theorists, with their heavy emphasis on the operational art and their advocacy of such instruments as the operational maneuver group, were carefully studied, as were the alleged operational superiorities of the German World War II *Wehrmacht*. Woe be unto the Leavenworth student who did not have something intelligent to say about *Auftragstaktik* or *Schwerpunkt*. In a relatively brief period of time the Army school system had permeated grades captain through colonel with an appreciation of the operational art and a vocabulary appropriate to that appreciation.[18]

The intellectual residue of a service school system fades quickly unless it is put to use. Prior to the 1980s the operational level of war was not much amenable to rehearsal. Field and fleet exercises at that level, even if actual troop and sailor participation were scaled back, were extraordinarily expensive.[19] War games using blocks of wood or paper chits to represent units or ships had been in use since the nineteenth century, but these tended to be torpidly paced, heavily dependent upon umpires for scenario depiction and combat resolution, and deficient in placing appropriate pressure on combat support and combat service support assets.[20] The introduction and rapid maturation of computer simulations changed this situation. The BCTP, for example, began as a tactical-level simulation capable of forcing battalion staffs to cope with the full range of circumstances they might encounter. Computer-generated battlefield circumstances were reported through keyboard operators to subordinate commanders, who in turn passed them higher. These subordinate commanders, not umpires, had the mission of bringing the computer developments to life, reporting them through doctrinal communications systems in such a manner that they seemed real to commanders and staffs above them.[21] Computer simulation developed considerable sophistication, in particular with respect to resolving the probabilities of combat results quickly and thus driving combat support and combat service support commanders and staffs to perform in real time as well. Within a decade simulations were the preferred—and economical—way to drill staffs in their battlefield responsibilities. One seldom saw entire units maneuvering in the field at greater than the battalion level.[22]

Originally a tactical training asset, simulations soon drove staff training at all levels. Division and corps staffs found themselves commanding and controlling fast-paced battles with an intensity they never before had experienced during training. Rather than being training supervisors or spectators, senior officers now found themselves to be training subjects—their successes and shortcomings analyzed with excruciating precision.[23] Simulations-driven exercises expanded to accommodate joint assets, joint headquarters, and major commands at the highest level. For the first time it was truly feasible to "rehearse" short of war at the operational level. Indeed, before the Iraqi invasion of Kuwait, General H. Norman Schwarzkopf, Jr., had conducted a major joint simulations-driven exercise, INTERNAL LOOK 90, that eerily anticipated circumstances he would face several months later. He attributed some fraction of his subsequent success to the insights gained and staff skills honed in this particular exercise.[24]

Computers were not driving training alone, of course. They also were part of a larger modernization effort that radically enhanced technical capabilities to pursue warfare at the operational level.[25] Communications, benefiting from revolutionary advances in microchips and computer integration, were more sophisticated, capable, pervasive, and redundant than ever before. Intelligence gathered through satellite imagery, from airborne platforms with multiple sensors and from signal intercepts—as well as from more traditional means—allowed unprecedented precision in one's appreciation of the enemy. Aviation with the AH–1 Apache attack helicopter and artillery with the Multiple Launch Rocket System (MLRS) acquired ranges and capabilities that made "deep battle" deep enough to be significant at the operational level. A sophisticated new generation of tactical vehicles, to include the redoubtable M1A1 Abrams tank and formidable M2/M3 Bradley fighting vehicle, concentrated far more fighting power into far less frontage than ever before. This is not to mention the considerable role of hastily procured, largely commercial, global positioning systems in assuring that fighting power did not get lost in the desert when maneuvering through operational distances. Even combat service support had, in the highly mobile M977 and M978 Heavy Expanded Mobility Tactical Trucks (HEMTTs) and ubiquitous High Mobility Multipurpose Wheeled Vehicle (HMMWV), achieved technical advances with operational implications. Now food, fuel, ammunition, and logistical services stood a reasonable chance of keeping pace with combat vehicles advancing quickly through challenging terrain.

Technical advance altered the level of command at which the operational level of war was fought. Historically, the corps was the ground operational building block and the army or army group the level at which the operational art was pursued.[26] By 1990 American heavy divisions had acquired a depth, breadth, and potency of geographical reach that elevated them into operational building blocks. Indeed, the 1990 division readily occupied the terrain and assumed the mission of the 1945 corps and the 1990 corps that of the 1945 army.[27] This trend had been recognized, and by the late 1980s had matured into the concept and then into the reality of the Capable Corps. Such a corps featured a sizable inventory of combat support and combat service support units that rendered it capable of sustaining combat operations for a prolonged period. Unlike the thinly manned command and control headquarters of World War II, the late twentieth-century corps had logistical attributes of the World War II army group.[28] The net result was that DESERT STORM was fought on the ground with divisions as operational building blocks and corps as practitioners of the operational art.

Americans were late in coming to grips with the theory of the operational art. Although better with actual practice than with theory, they nevertheless suffered from the lack of a conceptual framework when campaigning on a grand scale. By 1990 this imbalance no longer obtained. Not only had they sharpened an appreciation of the operational level of war in their doctrine, they also had trained a cadre of mid-level officers in its use, spread relevant concepts and vocabulary broadly through the officer corps, drilled staffs at every level using simulations that captured much of the challenge of actual operations, exploited technology that considerably enhanced operational capabilities, and driven the level of operational practitioner down to the Capable Corps. They would soon face the requirement to bring this growth and change to bear in combat.

DESERT SHIELD

It has become fashionable to characterize the American deployment during DESERT SHIELD as lethargic, successful only because of the incredible inertia of Saddam Hussein through six long months.[29] This is more sound bite to facilitate contemporary budget battles than it is historical analysis to assess relative performance. In fact, the DESERT SHIELD deployment progressed at least twice as fast as previous efforts to project such heavy forces overseas, albeit in the Army's case half as fast as the standard Chief of Staff General Eric K. Shinseki set in 1998 for the Army of 2015.[30] DESERT SHIELD represented considerable progress along a continuum running from World War II through this future Army. The deployment also represented considerable operational finesse, allowing thoughtful progression from forces capable of deterrence alone through those capable of delay, of defense, and, finally, of attack.

The 2 August 1990 Iraqi seizure of Kuwait had been swift and sure, but it had not been without challenges. In part to achieve surprise and in part to operate within Iraq's logistical means, the Iraqis had assaulted with three *Republican Guard* heavy divisions, several special forces units, and about 1,000 tanks.[31] This was enough to quickly dispatch the 20,000-man Kuwaiti Army, but hardly sufficient to garrison a nation of 2 million people and secure a dozen major oil fields scattered across eight thousand square miles of desert. Within days four *Republican Guard* motorized divisions had joined their armored brethren to assist in securing Kuwait, and by mid-September Iraqi forces had built up to 360,000 men, 2,800 tanks, and 800 combat aircraft in or near Kuwait.[32] The Iraqis moved to the Saudi border and attempted to reinforce their fait accompli by intimidating that neighbor, but a similarly swift conquest of Saudi Arabia was no sure thing. Saudi Arabia's population of 14 million was more proximate to Iraq's 19 million, its Army of 10 brigades and 550 tanks at least three times as strong as that of Kuwait had been, and securing its most important oil fields would require a further 250-kilometer advance on the part of the Iraqis.[33] Perhaps more important, the American buildup progressed just quickly enough to render a painless Iraqi win doubtful—while guaranteeing that the shedding of American blood would eventually bring the full weight of an American response to bear.

The Americans were surprised by but not altogether unprepared to respond to the Iraqi invasion. As mentioned earlier, Central Command's (CENTCOM's) General Schwarzkopf had directed that the simulations-driven exercise INTERNAL LOOK 90 depart from a Soviet threat and instead examine an attack of six Iraqi heavy divisions through Kuwait into Saudi Arabia. In this war game the hastily deployed XVIII Airborne Corps lost many key oilfields and the port of Al Jubayl but succeeded in keeping a toehold at Ad Damman. The simulated Iraqis ground to a halt after being mauled by helicopters and tactical aircraft but inflicted an appalling 50 percent attrition upon the American ground combat forces in theater. Sobered by these results, CENTCOM planners resolved to frontload heavy ground combat units into scarce shipping, build up heliborne and other antiarmor capabilities quickly, and achieve effective cooperation with potential Arab allies early in the case of an actual contingency.[34]

The CENTCOM planners, reinforced as the crisis unfolded by further drafts of SAMS graduates—Schwarzkopf's famous "Jedi Knights"—soon had the opportunity to put their simulations-derived insights to practical use. Exercise INTERNAL LOOK 90 concluded on 28 July 1990. Iraq invaded Kuwait 2 August, and on 3 August President George H. W. Bush concluded that forcible response would be necessary. King Fahd bin Abdul Azziz al-Saud invited U.S. troops into his country on 7 August, and on 8 August President Bush announced that troops were on their way. At 1000 on 8 August the initial contingent of the 82d Airborne Division's 2d Brigade lifted off from Pope Air Force Base, North Carolina. Perhaps more important, by that time a heavy brigade of the 24th Infantry Division (Mechanized) was en route to the port of Savannah, Georgia, preparing to embark.[35] By the time it arrived air superiority would already have been achieved in theater, in part because of the 180 combat aircraft of the Saudis, in part because of about 600 American Air Force combat aircraft that swiftly reinforced them, in part because of the dispatch of 6 American aircraft carriers to nearby waters, and in part because of the worldwide reach of such American bombers as the B–1, B–52, and F–111. This is not to mention the maturing allied naval blockade that was evermore effective in choking off Iraq's external sources of supply.[36]

The American buildup progressed quickly and, despite its unprecedented nature and scope, reasonably smoothly. American operational planners had long experience with the notions of rapidly deploying forces to Europe or Korea to offset a Warsaw Pact or North Korean buildup. They had matured elaborate automated data systems to prioritize and track units deploying by sea and air and to associate manpower, equipment, tonnage, and volume with them.[37] Legislation was available to make civilian commercial lift available to military transporters when military means would not suffice. Indeed, DESERT STORM saw the first-ever crisis activation of the Civilian Reserve Air Fleet (CRAF), and unit load-masters soon found themselves wrestling with Boeing 747 load-plans as well as with those of the more familiar C–5s and C–141s.[38] The deployment challenged the leadership and supervision of military transporters and load-masters. At the unit end of the hierarchy these were bright young officers and NCOs tracking company equipment and load plans as an extra duty. The hierarchy progressed through grizzled Air Force NCOs and Navy or Merchant Marine petty officers—who had absolute authority concerning what went where on their plane or vessel—up a ladder of technical responsibility that culminated in the four-star commander of the Transportation Command (TRANSCOM), activated in 1987.

The deployment was not without its quirks and shortcomings, with too little airlift and sealift for all that the operational planners would have liked to accomplish, but it was an impressive and unprecedented accomplishment nevertheless. In less than six months the Army alone loaded and unloaded 500 ships and 9,000 aircraft that delivered 1,800 army aircraft; 12,400 tracked vehicles; 114,000 wheeled vehicles; 38,000 containers; 1,800,000 tons of cargo; and 350,000 personnel. The small but capable fleet of eight newly designed Fast Sealift Ships (FSS) greatly facilitated this effort.[39] The deployment exercised techniques and systems that had matured during dozens of training exercises hypothesizing the speedy dispatch of Cold War reinforcements. Indeed, the working mechanics were so familiar that staff pundits characterized the movement from Europe to Saudi Arabia as DEFORGER 90, a play on words with respect to numerous REFORGER exercises wherein Europe itself was in receipt of reinforcements.[40] One difference, however, was that most heavy units deploying to REFORGER fell in on equipment pre-positioned in Europe. When going to Saudi Arabia, they took everything with them.

At its middle levels the TRANSCOM hierarchy managing the DESERT SHIELD deployment was populated by alumnae of the Command and General Staff College and its sister service schools, graduated recently enough to have been exposed to the emphasis placed upon the operational art during the 1980s. Even those officers who were not SAMS graduates themselves had the operational vision and vocabulary appropriate to support CENTCOM schemes that phased from deterrence through delay, defense, and ultimately attack. Broad features of the deployment that had operational implications included the front loading of antiarmor systems, the incremental construction of a logistical support base, and the ultimate development of a defense in depth.

The soldiers of the 82d Airborne Division were a mere trip-wire in the sand for about a week. During that brief period their deterrence value was the sure knowledge that an Iraqi attack wherein Americans were killed would guarantee war with the United States and preclude a speedy diplomatic solution to the Kuwaiti crisis favorable to Iraq. This thin psychological deterrence soon shaded into the capability to conduct a classic delay, as wings of combat aircraft and battalions of attack helicopters converged on Saudi airfields and the Saudis hastily redeployed their widely scattered ground units to thicken the screen opposing the Iraqis. Table 1 compares the Iraqi and allied buildups throughout the DESERT SHIELD period.[41] By the end of August an Iraqi attack would have rolled forward into a robust screen of mobile allied antitank systems and into the teeth of allied air and aviation superiority as well. Sufficient ground forces did not exist to actually stop the Iraqi armor, but it would have been severely attrited while crossing 300 kilometers of open desert to reach valuable oil fields and significant built-up areas. There, they would have become entangled with enclaves of dug-in American paratroopers and marines armed with a proliferation of medium- and short-range antitank weapons while still being punished from the air. Although the overall odds favored the Iraqis, the only guarantee was that the combat would be brutal, sustained, and bloody.

By mid-September the operational picture had again changed. The debarkation of the 24th Infantry Division (Mechanized) put a force on the ground that could stand fast, rather than retire, in the face of all but the most massive of Iraqi attacks. Positioned far enough to the rear to assure the Iraqis would have sustained significant attrition from the air before closing, the tankers and mechanized infantrymen of the 24th had reasonable prospects that Iraqi attacks would be too weakened to force them off their positions. If they did, subsequent positions arranged in depth afforded the likelihood of progressively attriting and then stopping the attack short of vital logistical installations. Firing from defilade positions with superb fields of fire and state-of-the-art weapons that accurately outranged Iraqi counterparts by hundreds of meters, they could anticipate loss ratios of better than a dozen to one in their favor, thus considerably offsetting Iraqi numerical superiorities.[42] Within a few weeks Egyptian and Syrian heavy divisions equipped equivalently to the Iraqis arrived, as did the 1st Cavalry Division out of Fort Hood, Texas. Within two months of their attack on Kuwait, Iraqi prospects for a successful follow-on thrust deep into Saudi Arabia had plummeted from high to zero.

As Saudi security stabilized behind an ever more formidable DESERT SHIELD, the National Command Authority concluded that a diplomatic resolution of the crisis was unlikely and that the combination of blockade and economic sanctions also would not yield timely results. Iraqi forces had continued to build up in Kuwait. Although Iraqi prospects for a successful offensive had faded, their prospects for a successful defense had not. Line infantry replaced mechanized units in the border areas, and Iraqi engineers constructed arrays of minefields, obstacles, and fighting positions in depth. Saddam himself opined that the American people would not stand for 10,000 casualties and seemed determined to exact at least that number if forced to defend the country he had seized.[43] American squeamishness over casualties might ultimately provide him the diplomatic leverage he sought. Determined to avoid this, on 8 November President Bush committed to an additional buildup of forces to provide an offensive option. Implied within this further buildup was the need to accumulate forces so potent they could crush the Iraqis with minimal losses to themselves. Within days the 2d Armored Cavalry Regiment, 1st Infantry Division (Mechanized), 1st Armored Division, 3d Armored Division, the brigade-size 2d Armored Division (Forward), and the remainder of the U.K. 1st Armoured Division were on their way to Saudi Arabia. This doubling of American forces in theater progressed at about the same pace as the deployment that had preceded it. By mid-February 1991 a second Capable Corps, the VII, had joined the XVIII Airborne Corps in theater.[44] (*See Map 18.*)

As important as the speedy buildup of combat forces was the buildup of a logistical apparatus to support them. Accustomed to dealing with transoceanic distances, American logisticians had ample experience planning for and supporting operations in austere theaters. They had developed a notion of "above the line" and "below the line" forces. Above the line were the maneuver units operational commanders mentally perceived as the "chips" on their board. Below the line were the logistical units necessary to sustain them. In an austere theater, the ratio with respect to troops between the two was 1.6 to 1 in favor of those below the line. In DESERT SHIELD and DESERT STORM the required ratio was 1.3 to 1 because of the Saudi capability to provide important support services.[45] Through the long years of planning for Cold War reinforcement, tables and formulae had developed for interweaving combat, combat support, and combat service support in such a manner that the combat forces never went short. Combat units deployed with a prescribed number of "days of supply" on board, and logistical units arrived, set up for operations, and replenished the combat units' days of supply before they were exhausted. They also provided the requisite array of logistical services: maintenance, medical support, communications, transportation, etc. The organizing principles for assuring that logistical assets kept pace with the buildup of tactical units were robust organic logistical capabilities at the battalion and division level and a Corps Support Command (COSCOM) capable of supervising the diverse logistical units tailored for the specific circumstances.

The COSCOM provided the overhead necessary to coordinate division logistical activities, supplied support beyond the technical capabilities of the divisions, replenished division stocks, and compensated for the quantitative differences between the means the division brought with it and the means the theater required. Numerous exercises and simulations during the 1980s developed leaders and staffs capable of guaranteeing a complementary buildup of combat and logistical assets. The XVIII Airborne Corps headquarters elements deployed with the first waves of the 82d Airborne Division and synchronized a remarkably smooth growth through the point that a four-plus division corps was on the ground. Behind this shield, VII Corps, Third Army, and CENTCOM eventually deployed and built up their own logistical structures as well.[46]

Another deployment technique that acquired operational significance was an emergent capability to train en route. During World War II divisions shipped men and equipment together and generally took six months to get from their training to stations overseas.[47] During that time little meaningful training occurred—in particular with respect to maneuver training or firing crew-served weapons. Fortunate units had the opportunity to take a month or so and retrain overseas, as happened in England prior to Normandy or North Africa prior to shipment to Italy; unfortunate units deployed into combat cold, as happened at Kasserine Pass or Buna.[48] During DESERT SHIELD heavy units shipped their equipment, and then trained intensively on others units' hardware while the ships were en route. At the appointed time the soldiers deployed by air to intercept their heavy equipment as it arrived at the port of debarkation and moved from there to the field recently trained. This technique proved particularly useful for integrating replacements that inevitably arrived to fill out units preparing to deploy. American units from Europe, for example, rotated through gunnery training at Grafenwöhr and tactical training at Hohenfels hosted by the 3d Infantry Division (Mechanized), which was not deploying.[49] This had the operational significance of rapidly accelerating the pace at which distant adversaries faced American units fully prepared for combat.

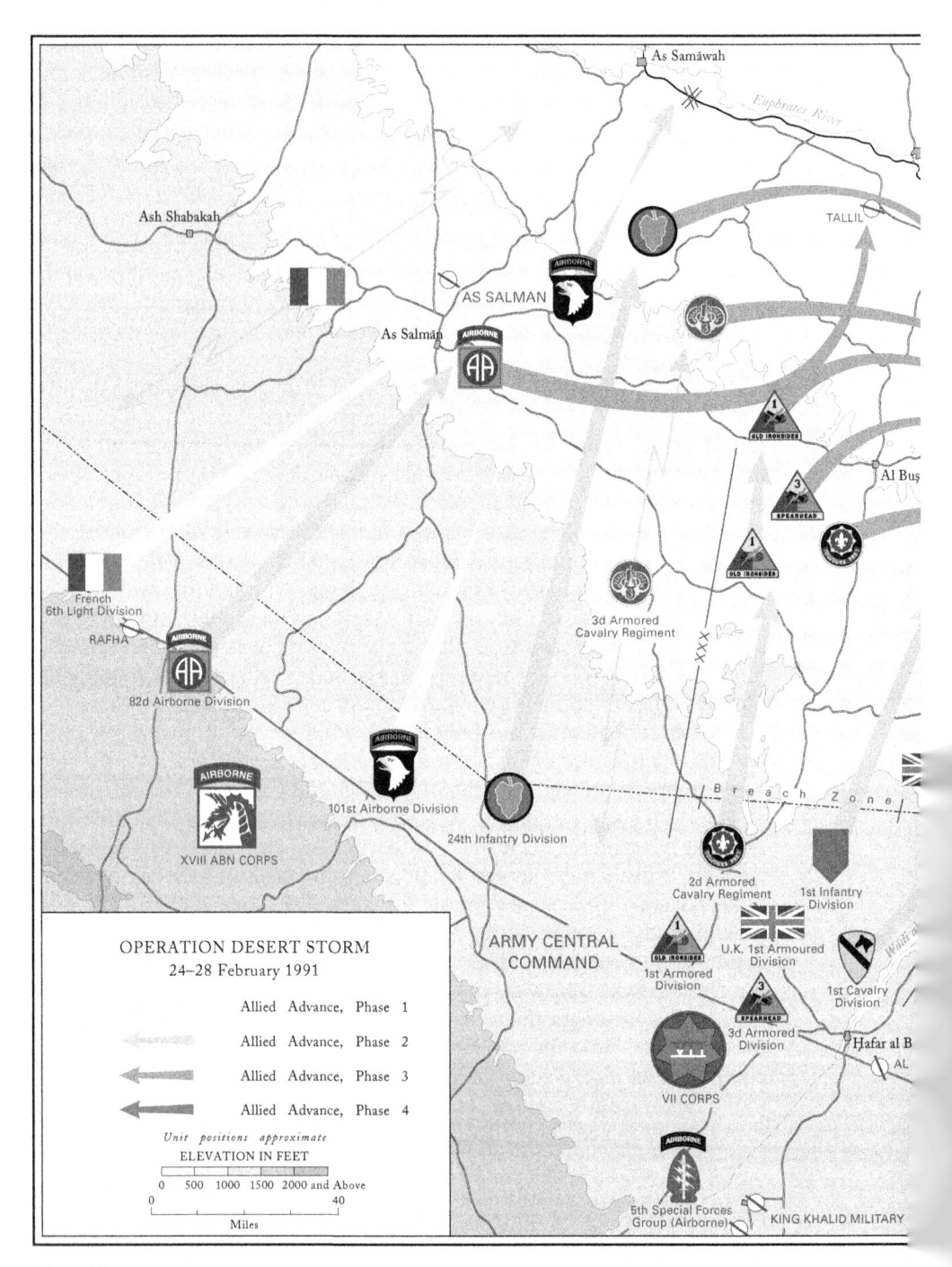

MAP 18

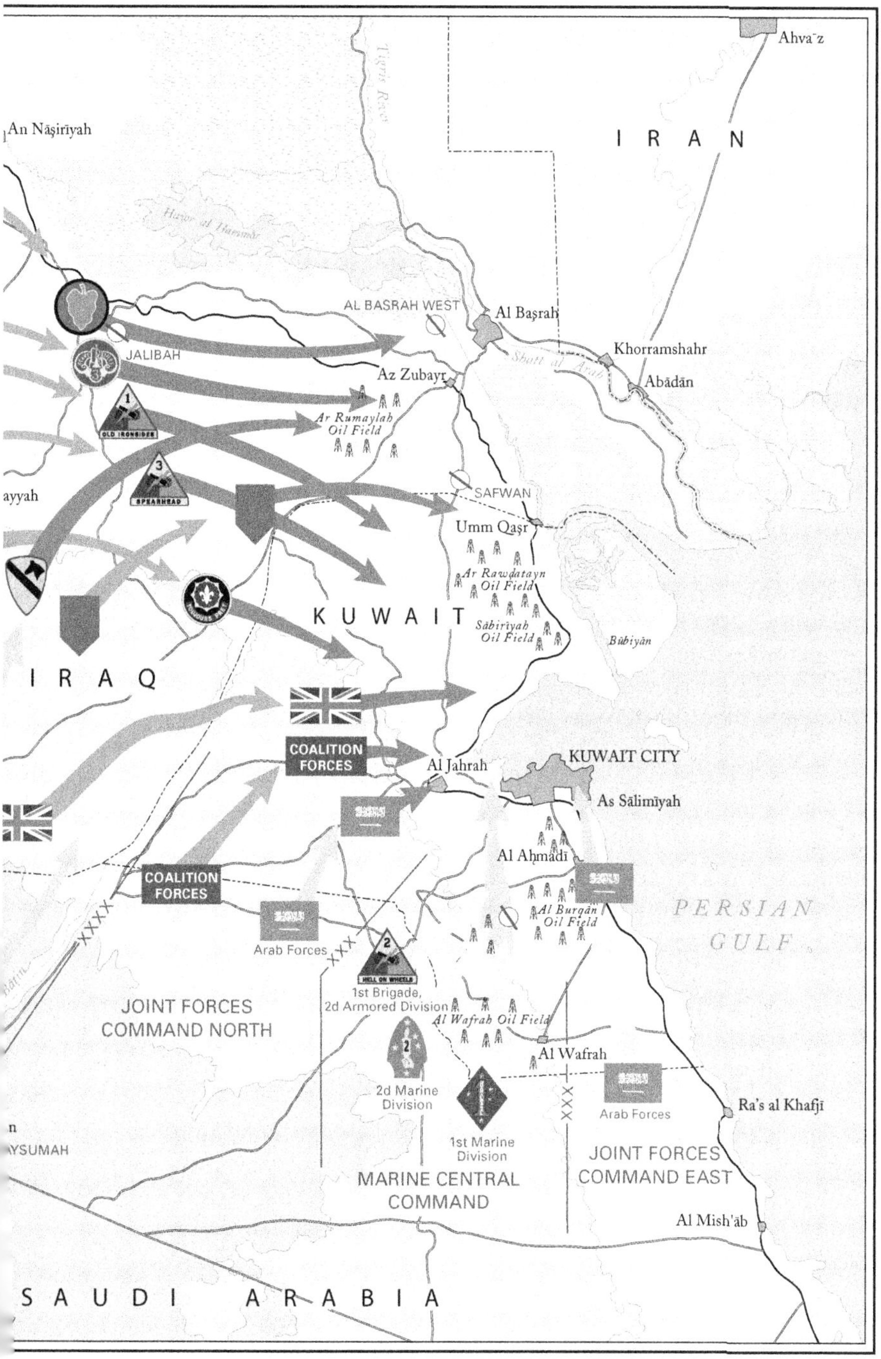

Ahvāz
IRAN
An Nāşirīyah
AL BASRAH WEST
Al Başrah
JALIBAH
Khorramshahr
Abādān
Az Zubayr
Ar Rumaylah Oil Field
SAFWAN
Umm Qaşr
Ar Rawdatayn Oil Field
KUWAIT
Sābirīyah Oil Field
Būbiyān
IRAQ
COALITION FORCES
Al Jahrah
KUWAIT CITY
As Sālimīyah
Al Aḩmadī
COALITION FORCES
Arab Forces
PERSIAN GULF
Al Burqān Oil Field
1st Brigade, 2d Armored Division
JOINT FORCES COMMAND NORTH
Al Wafrah Oil Field
Al Wafrah
2d Marine Division
1st Marine Division
Arab Forces
Ra's al Khafjī
JOINT FORCES COMMAND EAST
MARINE CENTRAL COMMAND
Al Mish'āb
SAUDI ARABIA

Desert Shield demonstrated the American appreciation of and contributions to the operational art. From a cold start operational planners deployed a force that was able to successively deter, delay, defend, and attack its Iraqi opponent. Given that the Iraqis had their deployment challenges as well, the window of likely allied defeat was narrow indeed. This operational planning was effected by a cadre of mid-level officers who had had significant education with respect to the operational art and implemented by a much greater number who understood its basic concepts and vocabulary. War plans changed almost weekly, with the area to be secured growing from small desert enclaves through the entirety of Saudi Arabia itself. Computer simulations assisted in operational analysis through each step in the planning and associated war-gaming process, most notably in the Internal Look 90 exercise that defined key issues even before Saddam Hussein had seized Kuwait. The American achievement was greatly assisted by technological advances that provided a striking qualitative edge over the Iraqis and allowed a division to secure a sector formerly appropriate to a corps and a corps to secure a sector formerly appropriate to an army. Coincident with this advance with respect to weaponry was the maturation of the corps as a headquarters fully capable of integrating combat support, combat service support, and joint assets—again characteristics formerly associated with an army. With the mission of securing Saudi Arabia complete, American operational planners could now turn to their follow-on mission of liberating Kuwait.

Desert Storm Prepared

Desert Storm was a debilitating aerial and artillery preparation followed by a ground turning movement. On the map, the turning movement looks easy; broad arrows sweep in wide arcs to squeeze the hapless Iraqis into an evermore compressed pocket. Postwar commentators, particularly impressed with the several orders of magnitude difference in casualties, might lead one to believe it actually was easy. In fact it was far more difficult than one might think, and its eventual lopsided success was the result of a great deal of hard work by capable professionals well before the first armored vehicle crossed the line of departure. At the operational level plans were developed and refined, allies were incorporated into roles that were acceptable and suitable, units were trained and rehearsed for their missions, and the preconditions for a successful ground assault were achieved. While all this was going on, due precaution had to be taken against possible Iraqi actions to interfere with allied preparations. Let us examine these major prebattle efforts in turn.

The Jedi Knights conducting General Schwarzkopf's operational planning had a few basic options, all of which the commercial media appreciated and debated.[50] By November 1990 the Iraqis had matured a layered defense, with line infantry entrenched behind protective barriers along the border backed up by local mobile reserves of regular army tank and mechanized divisions. These local reserves were themselves backed up by the operational reserves of the heavily mechanized *Republican Guard*. Of these Iraqi forces, the line infantry was considered brittle, the regular army heavy divisions reliable, and the *Republican Guard* formidable. The most direct approach for the allies would have been an attack into the teeth of Iraqi defenses along the Saudi-Kuwait border. The avenues available for such an attack included north along the coastal road, from the "elbow" of the border northeast along the shortest route directly into Kuwait City, or along the Wadi al Batin in the far west of Kuwait. A more indirect approach would be an envelopment through Iraq, either close in by punching through thinly held defenses immediately west of the Wadi al Batin or deeper by altogether turning the Iraqi line in its far west. Both the direct approach and the envelopment could be complemented by amphibious landings on the Kuwaiti coast and airborne or air assault landings into the enemy's rear. Yet another alternative was not to attack seriously on the ground at all, but instead to rely upon air and naval bombardment, economic sanctions, and limited probes and attacks to wear down the Iraqi will to resist.

A factor complicating operational deliberations was the role allies were willing play. The United States, Great Britain, and France favored attacking Iraq directly. Their Arab allies believed the legitimate mission was to liberate Kuwait and were reluctant to commit their ground forces to a wider war.[51] The two U.S. Marine divisions already ashore were more comfortable operating proximate to the sea—and thus to their logistical support—but were short on the heavy equipment and firepower necessary to punch through the thicker Iraqi defenses they would face. Arabs and western allies alike supported an air campaign, although the Arabs inclined to emphasize defending Saudi air space while the western allies were eager to carry the war deep into Iraq. Over time a campaign plan emerged that accommodated allied preferences and borrowed heavily from each of the basic operational options available.[52] Fighting would begin with a multiphased air campaign to establish preconditions for ground assault. Allied air forces would successively smash Iraqi air defenses, secure air supremacy, suppress Iraqi command and control, isolate the Kuwaiti Theater of Operations, and attrit enemy ground forces in the path of the proposed offensive. The ground assault would begin with a division-size feint up the Wadi al Batin and a supporting attack by the marines reinforced with an Army armored brigade through the elbow of Kuwait. Arab thrusts equivalent in size to that of the marines would go in to their left and right. A marine amphibious feint would tie Iraqi units into coastal defenses, while an air assault deep into Iraq would isolate the Kuwaiti Theater of Operations from the Iraqi core around Baghdad. The main attack would be that of the VII Corps, consisting of five heavy divisions, four separate field artillery brigades, an armored cavalry regiment, and a separate aviation brigade. This mailed fist — a description the corps commander, Lt. Gen. Frederick M. Franks, Jr., had chosen — would envelope the Iraqi line at its far west end, turning east to annihilate the *Republican Guard* before sweeping across the northern half of Kuwait. The four-division XVIII Airborne Corps, already commanding the air assault intrusion into Iraq, would ride the VII Corps' left flank and continue to isolate the Kuwaiti Theater from the west, while assisting in closing the trap to the east.

The scheme of attack that emerged from Schwarzkopf's operational planners during the fall of 1990 and early winter of 1990–1991 seems as close to a "Leavenworth Solution" as one could hope to see. Every unit in theater had been given a role appropriate to its technical capabilities, doctrine, and, in some cases, national sensibilities. Elaborate matrices synchronized the actions of each of the battlefield operating systems: maneuver, fire support, mobility and countermobility, air defense, command and control, intelligence, and combat service support. A clever balance had been achieved amongst feints, supporting attacks, economy-of-force measures, and a main attack sufficiently weighted to achieve decisive results. Officers who had war-gamed dozens of campaigns in simulation war-gamed this one in simulation as well — time and again to refine details.[53] Shortcomings that ultimately emerged during the conduct of DESERT STORM would not result from officers and staffs insufficiently trained to develop doctrinally correct campaign plans.

One significant attribute of the DESERT STORM campaign plan was the extent to which it changed over time.[54] Word processors, improved duplication techniques, and modern communications made it feasible to edit and amend plans as disseminated documents. Space-age intelligence assets and ingrained habits of leadership rehearsal provided reasons to do so. Since DESERT STORM it has been fashionable to point out deficiencies in the shared intelligence picture. These complaints would ring hollow with such German generals as Alexander von Kluck approaching the Marne in 1914 or Hermann Hoth attacking the Kursk Salient in 1943 — commanders who had real intelligence dilemmas.[55] No army in history has had as precise and accurate a picture of how its adversary laid out on the ground as did the American Third Army on 24 February 1991. Prior to the 1st Infantry Division breach, for example, battalion commanders received aerial photos detailing Iraqi platoon positions in their sectors. Narrative descriptions concerning where units were and when one could expect to encounter them proved remarkably accurate.[56] Satellite imagery, aerial photography, unmanned aerial vehicle (UAV) feedback, and information drawn from a fistful of other sensors fed huge amounts of material into the voracious appetites of military intelligence analysts. At first the return from Signals Intelligence (SIGINT) was limited by the Iraqi practice of coordinating via secure landline, but eventually the air campaign so disrupted this network that the Iraqis were forced back into more readily intercepted radio communications if they were to communicate at all.[57] The Americans did not have much access to human intelligence (HUMINT), and a relatively small amount of information fed into the system through such traditional means as ground scouts, patrols, and reconnaissance units. This historically disproportionate reliance upon technical means of intelligence would have implications after the ground war started, as we shall see.

Ingrained habits of rehearsal were as important as updated intelligence in refining the campaign plan. Since 1981 American heavy units had been rotating through intense simulated combat at Fort Irwin's National Training Center (NTC). This superb facility was soon paralleled by a somewhat smaller Combined Arms Maneuver Training Center (CMTC) in Hohenfels, Germany.[58] There, realistic laser-gunnery exercises had revived an appreciation of the value of rehearsals as well as after-action reviews. Rehearsals ran the gamut from map exercises through "rock drills," wherein participants "maneuvered" through scaled-down versions of the terrain as if they were their entire units, to full-up rehearsals in like-type terrain with all men and equipment. As the ground war approached, successive levels of command were read into the plan, rehearsed their roles in it, and provided feedback. Updated intelligence interwove with rehearsal results to drive further refinements. A case in point at the operational level was the weighting of VII Corps with its fifth heavy division versus one heavy division left to the XVIII Airborne Corps.[59] Another example was the decision to continue with the breach and short left hook in the 1st Mechanized Infantry Division's sector even after it became apparent that Iraqi resistance farther west was so thin that divisions could sweep around that flank virtually unopposed.

Rehearsing VII Corps logisticians convincingly demonstrated that while the end run would provide important tactical advantages, a breach through the minefield would be necessary to sustain the attack logistically as it neared Kuwait. Yet another route farther east, perhaps up the Wadi al Batin, would have to be opened to sustain operations inside Kuwait. In the end it was decided that the 1st and 3d Armored Divisions and the XVIII Airborne Corps' 24th Mechanized Infantry Division would sweep around the minefield, the 1st Mechanized Infantry Division would breach it, and the U.K. 1st Armoured Division would pass through the breach, take a hard right, and roll up Iraqi defenses in such a manner that lanes through the minefields farther east could be safely cut later.[60]

Rehearsals became larger, more comprehensive, and more complex as plans matured. Units deploying from Germany had not actually maneuvered above the battalion level, and those from the United States had not actually maneuvered above the brigade level.[61] Once clear of their port of debarkation and bivouacked in the desert, all now had ample opportunity to conduct maneuver training at every level. Commanders carefully balanced the advantages of additional maneuver training against wear and tear on unit equipment. Most found the opportunity to maneuver their units on an unprecedented scale through extraordinary distances while pacing themselves in such a manner that they sustained high operational readiness rates as well.[62] When the air war had disrupted Iraqi intelligence collection and the time came to shift the VII Corps and XVIII Airborne Corps from DESERT SHIELD positions proximate to the east coast of Saudi Arabia to the staging areas for DESERT STORM farther inland, the respective corps commanders took the opportunity to maneuver on the grandest possible scale. The VII Corps, for example, rehearsed large-scale offensive movements through dozens of kilometers while moving west to its staging areas.[63]

This surrogate maneuver training was invaluable in itself and also provided the opportunity to resolve a number of technical issues with operational implications. Few soldiers, for example, had been familiar with the new GPS technology before DESERT SHIELD, but in short order virtually every platoon leader had one. This presented both training worries and doctrinal issues as several different makes of GPS were worked into the modus operandi of maneuver units. The results were dramatic. Suddenly units as small as platoons could maintain perfect alignment with each other while maneuvering in formations as large as a corps through hundreds of kilometers of trackless desert in the dark. The Iraqis would later be totally surprised by this unprecedented operational capability.[64] Similarly, the experience of the rehearsal allowed operational commanders to determine the pace at which such uninterrupted maneuver should progress: twelve miles an hour. It turned out that this speed was one of several smoothly riding interfaces between gear ratios on the M1A1 tank—and the fastest such interface at which linear formations of unlike vehicles in a battalion or brigade formation could be kept together. Because the M1A1 rode smoothly at that speed, its gyrostabilization was optimized and the tank could fire accurately while moving.[65] This yielded yet another operational capability unheard-of in earlier wars: the uninterrupted advance of a great mass of armor firing accurately on the move into a defender who could not hope to achieve the same range or accuracy even from fixed and surveyed positions. Twelve miles an hour may sound slow, but what historical army has ever sustained such an opposed rate of advance for days at a time?

Other training progressed collaterally with these first-in-a-generation corps-level maneuvers. A case in point was the 1st Infantry Division's elaborate rehearsal of the breach it was to conduct during the first day of the ground war—to include the carefully choreographed passage of the entire U.K. 1st Armoured Division through the Big Red One's positions.[66] Another case in point was live-fire gunnery, conducted across expanses commanders had theretofore only been able to dream about. M1A1 tank crews, for example, had their first opportunity to fire the high-performance M829A1 service sabot, as opposed to the far-less-potent training round.[67]

Much of this extraordinarily valuable ground force maneuver and tactical training occurred while the air war was already under way. The air war was intended to set the preconditions for ground assault: air supremacy, paralyzed Iraqi command and control, degraded Iraqi logistics, and severely mauled Iraqi armor and artillery formations. Air supremacy was readily achieved, and Iraqi command and control does in fact seem to have been nearly paralyzed by the time the ground war began. Logistical degradation wore unevenly, with Iraqi units nearest to the border being the most disadvantaged. In part this was because of the greater distances, every kilometer of which was exposed to allied attack, through which supply lines to these units passed. This was also because of the lower priority of line infantry units on the border and the absence of stockpiles in them comparable to those built up to support mechanized units and the *Republican Guard*. Indeed, the *Republican Guard* seems to have been well supplied and well fed until the VII Corps overran it. Attrition inflicted upon Iraqi armor and artillery was significant, but less than planners had hoped. Weather often interfered, as did the Iraqi energy in digging in or camouflaging this equipment, Iraqi use of decoys, and the high altitude at which allied aircraft flew to avoid losses. Precision-guided munitions were helpful in what came to be known as "tank-plinking," but these were too expensive and in too short supply to be useful against unremunerative targets.

A few vignettes make the point. The newly captured artillery commander of the Iraqi *49th Infantry Division* commented that he had lost less than 10 percent of his artillery prior to the ground war but had lost all the rest in a single day of American preparatory artillery fires prior to the breach. In another vignette, the G–3 of the 2d Armored Division (Forward) rewalked the battlefield of his brigade's Objective NORFOLK and found that virtually all the Iraqi tanks on it had been destroyed by American tank fire. Overall, the allied air campaign was a great success, but it did far less well against dug-in equipment than it did against command and control nodes and logistical assets. This situation changed radically, as we shall see, when ground fighting forced theretofore hidden Iraqi equipment into movement. Then the synergy to be achieved by employing ground and air assets in concert demonstrated itself with devastating effect.[68]

One limit on the operational success of the air campaign was the distraction presented by the urgent divergence of air assets to campaign against Iraqi missiles. Although the Iraqis launched only eighty-six

Scuds, these primitive missiles had an impact well beyond their numbers. Their range enabled them to reach, albeit inaccurately, soft and unprepared targets. Indeed, for Americans the bloodiest single incident of the war occurred when a Scud missile slammed into a barracks in Al Khobar, killing twenty-eight and wounding ninety-eight—almost half from a single unit, the 14th Quartermaster Detachment from Greensburg, Pennsylvania.[69] Perhaps as troubling, Scuds launched at Israel threatened to bring that embattled nation into the war, thus wrecking carefully constructed American alliances with Arab nations hostile to or suspicious of Israel.[70] Patriot air defense missiles hastily deployed to Saudi Arabia and Israel did destroy a number of incoming Scuds, but by 24 January 40 percent of all allied air sorties were nevertheless directed against the Scuds—as were significant intelligence, electronic warfare, and special operations resources.[71] A vast cat-and-mouse game developed throughout western Iraq as American intelligence and reconnaissance assets attempted to find Scuds for fighter bombers to engage, while Iraqis attempted to fire their mobile missiles quickly and then scoot out of harm's way. Planes hunting Scuds were not, of course, pursuing other previously agreed-upon targets whose destruction had been preconditions for the ground assault.

One frequent comment with respect to DESERT SHIELD and DESERT STORM was surprise that Saddam Hussein did not do more to interfere with the allied buildup.[72] We have already commented on the relative buildup of forces in the Kuwaiti Theater of Operations and on the narrow window of opportunity wherein a preemptive ground assault by Iraqis could have worked—if at all. The abortive Iraqi thrust at Khafji on 29–31 January 1991 reinforces this point. Terrorists and commandos could perhaps have been a viable threat to the logistical buildup, but the allies had given considerable time and attention to protecting themselves against them.[73] Maneuver units made a point of scattering themselves into the open desert as quickly as possible, thus presenting a poor target themselves while being able to readily target any person or vehicle approaching them.

Preemptive strikes and terrorist attacks simply do not seem to have been in the plan whereby Saddam Hussein intended to achieve his diplomatic objectives. He had presented the world with a fait accompli, and hoped he could consolidate his gains, in all or in part, without an actual fight. If he convinced the allies that the forcible liberation of Kuwait would be prohibitively costly, he could strike a favorable deal. Before the air campaign began, it served him no purpose to further provoke the allies. Indeed, he took a number of measures, to include releasing the last of some thirteen hundred western hostages, to appear conciliatory.[74] After the air attacks commenced, terrorist attacks and commando raids might have made more sense, but they would have had to overcome the extraordinary efforts the Saudis—possessed of a security apparatus with long experience in dealing with Middle Eastern terrorism—had undertaken to protect themselves and their guests, the great lengths to which the allies had gone to make themselves unattractive as targets, and the damage Iraqi command and control had already sustained. Ports, airfields, and sprawling desert encampments consciously isolated from the civilian population and swarming with armed men simply did not present an easy target. Convoys could have been more lucrative, but they too had undertaken appropriate security measures. Preemptive attacks on a larger scale, such as at Khafji, had even less chance of success and more potential for disaster. Saddam Hussein was not unreasonable in falling back on his initial diplomatic premise, that he could make the liberation of Kuwait too costly for the allies to sustain.[75]

DESERT STORM operational planners sought to liberate Kuwait and disable the Iraqi war machine without testing Saddam Hussein's chilling theory, "Yours is a society that cannot accept 10,000 deaths in one battle."[76] Plans were developed and refined to avoid so costly a battle, employing the latest and best in doctrine and simulations. Allies were given missions appropriate to their capabilities and inclinations. Training and rehearsal refined unit performance. Particular emphasis went into choreographing the breaches in the Iraqi defenses that were to occur, minimizing exposure to artillery when pushing down narrow lanes in the minefields and maximizing forces available to cope with expected counterattacks. The air campaign methodically paralyzed Iraqi command, control, and logistics while attriting front-line combat assets. This presented allied ground forces with a significantly weakened adversary. On 24 February 1991, the ground war began.

DESERT STORM Executed

It is a rare event for an operational plan to play out as designed. As the famous nineteenth-century German General Helmuth von Moltke said, "no plan ... extends with any degree of certainty beyond the first encounter with the main force."[77] History's victors were often embarrassed by differences between the campaign they intended to wage and the one that actually occurred. Its vanquished, of course, seldom intended the results they achieved. As an operational plan DESERT STORM was a bit of a historical anomaly: It worked as intended. Employing the parlance of the time, the ground operational scheme consisted of a *demonstration*, a *feint*, three *supporting attacks*, an *economy-of-force* measure to isolate—guard, if you will—the battlefield, and a main attack that featured a penetration early on and in itself was an envelopment.[78] Let us review the nature and success of each of these operational components in turn and then discuss how they fit into the larger whole—and why it was successful.

A *demonstration* is an operation wherein contact is not actually made, but sufficient force is visibly deployed to cause an adversary to allocate significant resources to meet it.[79] The U.S. Navy demonstrated with the 5th Marine Expeditionary Brigade (MEB) to create the impression that an amphibious assault was imminent. Like many, the Iraqis had been exposed to Marine Corps publicity concerning its ability to wreak havoc across the shore and had believed what they heard. Conscious exposure of the 5th MEB and its preparatory activities on the Cable News Network (CNN) and through other media heightened the Iraqi sense of anxiety, as did the visible presence of naval vessels in the Persian Gulf. The Iraqis dug in four divisions along their seaward flank specifically for the purpose of defending against amphibious assault, and as many more divisions were postured in such a manner that they might quickly intercede when the marines came across the beaches. Instead, once the ground war was well under way, the 5th MEB landed behind friendly lines and became an operational reserve for the supporting attacks discussed below.[80]

A *feint* is an operation wherein rounds are actually exchanged and fighting actually occurs, but the attacking force does not commit itself decisively in such a manner that it cannot readily extract itself.[81] Again, the intent is to deceive the enemy with respect to where an actual attack will occur. The 1st Cavalry Division began its ground war by attacking up the Wadi al Batin, ultimately drawing the attention of five Iraqi divisions. (*See Map 18.*) After exchanging shots and doing some damage, the 1st Cavalry backed out of the wadi and swung west to catch up with the VII Corps and serve as its operational reserve.[82]

Demonstrations and feints work best if the deception they are intended to promulgate is plausible and one the enemy is inclined to believe anyway. The Iraqis had reason to be anxious concerning their two-hundred-plus kilometer coastline, particularly since important supply routes ran along it. They also fully expected an attack up the Wadi al Batin, recognizing that that prominent terrain feature would facilitate land navigation deep into the heart of their theater. Indeed, when VII Corps did conduct its attack from the west, it came across mile after mile of vehicle defensive positions aligned precisely along the azimuth described by 240 degrees magnetic—facing in the direction of an attack up the Wadi al Batin.[83] Without much effort the theater deception plan had taken 20 percent of the Iraqi in-theater force structure out of the fight. By the time the Iraqis realized their mistake and attempted to redeploy, it was too late. The 5th MEB and 1st Cavalry Division, on the other hand, were readily available for operations elsewhere.

A *supporting attack* is a significant offensive effort intended to destroy units or to seize terrain and facilities that are important to the overall campaign scheme.[84] Supporting attacks are often timed in such a manner as to deceive an enemy into reacting to them as if they were the main attack. They may draw forces away from the main attack and, perhaps even more important, they may lead the enemy to malposition his reserves. Since a supporting attack involves significant resources and some risk, a single supporting attack is generally preferred. DESERT STORM featured three, largely because the two divisions of the I Marine Expeditionary Force, reinforced by the Tiger Brigade of the Army's 2d Armored Division, had lined up on the most direct approach from the elbow of Kuwait into Kuwait City. Suitable but independent missions were needed for the Arab allies to their left and right. These, the largely Saudi and Gulf Coalition Joint Forces Command–East (JFC-E) and the largely Egyptian, Syrian, and Saudi Joint Forces Command–North (JFC-N), were each assigned the mission of conducting a supporting attack as well.

The marines attacked at 0400 on 24 February with a tightly choreographed breaching effort into the Iraqi infantry defending to their front. These Iraqi units, brittle to start with, had been pummeled by air strikes and were at the farthest end of Iraq's tenuous logistical chain. They proved no match for the methodical Marine attack. M60A1 tanks with dozer blades breached the berms, while engineer line charges and M60A1 tanks with mine plows cleared lanes through the minefields. Marine artillery readily suppressed its Iraqi counterparts, and tanks and Tube-launched, Optically tracked Wire-guided (TOW) missiles quickly picked off the relatively few T–55s and T–62s that chose to fight. By the end of the first day the I Marine Expeditionary Force had advanced thirty-two kilometers, destroying dozens of armored vehicles, capturing 10,000 Iraqis, and seizing Al Jaber Airfield south of Kuwait City. The following morning an Iraqi heavy division attempted a counterattack but was quickly beaten off. By the third day of the ground war the I Marine Expeditionary Force had isolated Kuwait City, secured Kuwait International Airport, and seized Mutla Ridge, the dominant terrain feature overlooking Kuwait City, and roads north from it. Nothing that they encountered could cope with the marines' carefully synchronized and tightly focused supporting attack.[85]

The Arab allies of Joint Forces Command–East and Joint Forces Command–North paced themselves against the Marine Corps advance. They were less well equipped and supported, however, and found themselves trailing the marines on the first day. They did preoccupy substantial Iraqi units to their front, however, and as the extent of the marine penetration became clear these defending units collapsed as well. On 27 February JFC-E and JFC-N were abreast of the marines and expediently passed Saudi-led units through the marines to accomplish the liberation of Kuwait City. It seemed prudent to have those responsible for securing such a heavily populated built-up area speak the language and understand the culture of the inhabitants. With the Iraqis having fled or surrendered, this advance into Kuwait City took on a festive air.[86]

An *economy-of-force* mission, as the name implies, is an effort to accomplish a supporting purpose with a minimal investment of resources.[87] In the case of DESERT STORM the supporting purpose to be served was the isolation of the Kuwaiti Theater of Operations (KTO) from the rest of Iraq. Iraqi units and logistical assets from outside the KTO were not to be admitted, nor were Iraqi forces to be allowed to escape the theater. The XVIII Airborne Corps was ideally suited for such a role. The French 6th Light Armored Division, reinforced with paratroopers from the 82d Airborne Division and incorporating organic missile-firing Gazelle helicopters, had the general attributes of an American cavalry regiment. On day one of the ground war it rushed forward to seize As Salman in a spirited fight and then faced west to guard against Iraqi intrusion from that direction. At the same time the heliborne 101st Airborne Division (Air Assault) flew in to seize a forward operating base 176 kilometers deep into Iraq and then leaped a brigade forward to the Euphrates River Valley the following day. From these positions, swarms of Apache and Cobra attack helicopters fanned out to intercept and terrorize Iraqi ground movement along the northerly routes into the KTO. The dangerous east flank of the XVIII Airborne Corps was carried by the formidably heavy 24th Infantry Division (Mechanized) and the 3d Armored Cavalry Regiment. These units backstopped the French 6th Light Armored and 101st Airborne (Air Assault) Divisions until they were set, cleared the corps' right flank to the Euphrates, and then turned east to cooperate with the VII Corps in its main attack against the Iraqi *Republican Guard*. Given that its heavy division in effect became part of the main attack, the XVIII Airborne Corps had in fact isolated the KTO with minimal but well-chosen force.[88]

The main attack was that of the awesome Anglo-American VII Corps. This massive steel fist—five heavy divisions, an armored cavalry regiment, an aviation brigade, and four artillery brigades—boasted over 146,000 soldiers and almost 50,000 vehicles. Its divisions advanced with footprints twenty-four kilometers wide by forty-eight kilometers deep. Never before had so much firepower been concentrated into such an organization, and never before had such an organization featured such extraordinary tactical mobility. The purpose of a main attack generally is to crush an enemy's center of gravity, that asset or attribute that is most essential to their prospects for success. The Iraqi center of gravity was adjudged to be the *Republican Guard*, three heavy and five motorized divisions equipped and trained to the highest Iraqi standards. As formidable as the *Republican Guard* was, the even more superbly equipped and far more highly trained VII Corps seemed the right force to defeat them.[89]

The 1st Infantry Division (Mechanized) breach was as methodical and even more mechanized than that of the marines farther east. Tightly synchronized teams of M1A1 dozer tanks, M1A1 mine-plow tanks, combat engineer vehicles, and accompanying engineers in armored personal carriers bored through berms, minefields, and other obstacles while overwatched by sniper tanks and supported by the preparatory fires of fourteen battalions of field artillery. The carefully derived intelligence picture hopelessly compromised the Iraqi defenders, who found their crew-served weapons pounded into oblivion even before the first American target offered itself. The entire operation was a marvel of technology and technique. In a few hours the Big Red One had cut twenty-four lanes across a sixteen-kilometer front without the loss of a single soldier. In short order the division pulled its own units through the breach and passed the U.K. 1st Armoured Division through as well.[90]

Meanwhile, the 2d Armored Cavalry Regiment, 1st Armored Division, and 3d Armored Division had swept around the western margin of the obstacle belt and had swung east to envelop the Iraqi defenses. Finding little opposition short of Al Busayyah, the 1st Armored Division hammered that town with preparatory artillery and then swept through it, overrunning an Iraqi division and a corps headquarters en route. Farther east, the 3d Armored Division had made contact with the *Republican Guard's Tawakalna Mechanized Division*, as had the 2d Armored Cavalry Regiment screening to the east of the two armored divisions. Outnumbered but engaging accurately at extended ranges, the cavalrymen soon identified the basic contours of the *Republican Guard* defenses—to include several regular army heavy divisions that augmented their force structure. Within hours the 1st and 3d Armored Divisions rolling in from the west and the 1st Infantry Division (Mechanized) and U.K. 1st Armoured Division emerging from the breach were on line facing the east to deliver the decisive blow.[91]

The VII Corps attack on the *Republican Guard* was all that an armored assault is intended to be. From horizon to horizon, as far as the eye could see, redoubtable M1A1 Abrams tanks on line beetled purposely forward across the desert, alternating the crack of their main guns when they identified worthy targets with the chatter of machine guns for those of lesser import. As the tanks progressed, their crews turned the landscape in front of them ablaze with the flaming hulks of destroyed Iraqi vehicles and equipment, mirroring the devastated landscape through which they had recently passed. In the wake of the M1A1s, M2 Bradley infantry fighting vehicles scurried along to keep up, occasionally joining the chatter of the battle with their machine guns or disgorging infantrymen to clear a position or police up prisoners. Farther to the rear, M113 armored personnel carriers sped along with communicators, engineers, mortarmen, mechanics, and other supporting troops, accompanied by the occasional hulking M88A1 recovery vehicle capable of snatching immobile tanks from their predicaments. Even farther to the rear, generally out of sight, M109 howitzer artillerymen struggled to keep the lip of the advancing tanks under the umbrella of their supporting fires. Potential targets were destroyed by the tankers or surrendered to the infantrymen so quickly that the artillerymen seldom had an opportunity to fire, but when they did the effects were devastating. The *Republican Guard*—outflanked, surprised, outranged, and in any given exchange generally outgunned—had no more chance of reversing this inexorable advance than vegetation in the path of a magma flow. Their choices were to die, surrender, or flee. Those who fled found themselves horribly exposed to the attack helicopters and close-air-support aircraft that ranged forward to intercept Iraqis the ground troops had flushed out. The decisive attack achieved decisive results; in little more than a day the VII Corps smashed the *Republican Guard* and accompanying regular army units in its path and swept on across northern Kuwait.[92] (*See Map 18.*)

Americans reasonably expected to win the war with Saddam Hussein but nevertheless were surprised by the expediency of the victory and its low cost in American lives. A major fraction of that happy result can be explained by American mastery of the operational art. The operational plan we adopted was solid. A corporate product, it may not quite have demonstrated the personal genius of Alexander's timing at Arbela, Marlboro's poise at Blenheim, or Lee's eye for the ground at Fredericksburg.[93] The interplay between commander and staff in contemporary planning makes personal genius difficult to isolate. The DESERT STORM plan was a good piece of staff workmanship, however, and made thoughtful use of each of the operational components involved. The demonstration and the feint reinforced misperceptions the Iraqis were already inclined to believe: that an amphibious attack would occur and that the main attack would be up the Wadi al Batin. A fifth of the Iraqi force structure was neutralized by deception, whereas the demonstrating and feinting forces were restored into play elsewhere. The supporting attacks seized important objectives—Kuwait City, for example—while taking on adversaries within their means. The fact that there were three supporting attacks rather than one neatly accommodated national sensibilities without unduly straining military resources. Perhaps more important, the location of these attacks further reinforced the Iraqi conviction that the main attack was coming across the Kuwaiti border from the south and led the Iraqis to persist in malpositioning the *Republican Guard*—their operational reserves. The XVIII Airborne Corps neatly isolated the battlefield with forces ideally suited for guarding a lengthy frontage, and the VII Corps conducted the main attack with forces ideally suited to delivering a devastating blow. The parts of the plan came together nicely, and each unit involved was well suited to play its part.

The allied capacity for operational maneuver juxtaposed to an Iraqi incapacity to do the same. The relatively few advantages the Iraqis had—generally longer-range tube artillery, chemical stockpiles, prepared defenses and, in some cases, combat experience—had been quickly compromised. There is little evidence that the Iraqis attempted an operational-level counterstroke. The few Iraqi counterattacks that did occur seem to have been local and reflexive—certainly they were unsuccessful. The air campaign had seriously degraded Iraqi command and control at all levels, further aggravating inherent leadership shortcomings. The Iraqi command style was already ponderous and set piece. The line infantry divisions were virtually incapable of operational maneuver, and only the *Republican Guard* had ever demonstrated a capacity for it. Unsuccessful generals tended to be shot, so daring, creativity, and risk taking were unlikely Iraqi command attributes. Iraqi expectations were not for victory in the traditional sense, but rather to defend stubbornly enough that bloodied Americans opted for a diplomatic resolution.[94]

The American operational plan allowed the allies to fully capitalize on important technical advantages while negating the few the Iraqis might have had. The overall scheme fell into the classic three-phase battle advocated as early as by World War I's Sir Douglas Haig: preparatory attrition, decisive attack, and exploitation. Fortunately for the Americans, technology rendered this somewhat shopworn paradigm extraordinarily effective. Air supremacy, precision-guided munitions, deep-attack helicopters, long-range rocket artillery, and space-age intelligence assets delivered preparatory attrition unprecedented in its effectiveness. Newly introduced global positioning systems smoothly guided huge formations in a great arc through the trackless desert. The openness of the terrain in the chosen path of advance allowed M1A1 tank gunners to take full advantage of their superior range, superlative training, and phenomenal accuracy. These factors are multiplicative; when crews have twice the effective range, are twice as fast, and are three times as accurate, it is as if the odds favor them twelve to one before tactical circumstances are taken into account. This is not to mention thermal sights that rendered American crews as dangerous at night as they were in the day—unlike their night-blind Iraqi counterparts. The Americans had important technological advantages; they used them well.

The DESERT STORM operational plan was greatly facilitated by sustainment architecture that the Americans had matured through the years and brought with them into the theater. The logistical assets of the Capable Corps and the robust divisions were taxed without being overwhelmed by the rigors and distances of the desert fighting. Supplies and services proved sufficient to sustain a campaign that wreaked unprecedented destruction at an unprecedented pace.

DESERT STORM provides the intellectual inheritance of the operational art a rare thing, a plan that worked as designed. Part of the reason was the merits of the plan itself, part the capabilities and competence of those chosen to carry it out. DESERT STORM was not, however, a flawless performance. Let us next comment on some of its principal shortcomings, and then assess lessons the campaign seems to impart.

Shortcomings and Remediations

As successful an example of the operational art as DESERT STORM was, it was not flawless. Even in the midst of brilliant success, certain shortcomings became obvious: divergent pictures of the battlefield, fratricide, overwrought logistics, and differences in purpose and capability amongst coalition partners. Let us discuss each of these shortcomings in turn and then comment on the implications for the future of the operational art of postwar efforts to remediate them.

Once the ground war began in earnest and units were moving quickly and colliding with the enemy, appreciations of what was actually happening on the ground diverged. The theater headquarters in Riyadh had a different picture than that of the field-grade commanders in the direct-fire battle, with intermediate headquarters having their own snapshots as well.[95] This was no new thing; since time immemorial battlefield confusion has been so commonplace that terms such as "the fog of war" have been invented to describe it. DESERT STORM varied on this theme given that modern technology produced an illusion of clarity that was not actually there. Space-age intelligence assets—satellite imagery, aerial photography, long-range radio intercepts, and preliminary reports speeding through advanced communications systems—convinced Riyadh that the Iraqi Army was in full flight and that a hell-for-leather pursuit was an imperative. Field-grade commanders, on the other hand, encountering their own fierce little battles, characterized the Iraqis as offering various levels of resistance depending upon whom they had fought and assumed that because of modern communications their reports were being taken into account. Whatever their intent, Iraqi communications were so severely degraded they could not have coordinated a withdrawal if they chose. The Iraqis who did fight seem to have fought back instinctively, without much evidence they were responding to any recent guidance. The field-grade commanders who met such resistance were understandably loath to rush carelessly into it.[96]

The most obvious operational implication of this discoordinate appreciation of the battlefield was the alleged snit between the theater commander, General Schwarzkopf, and the VII Corps commander, General Franks, over the pace of the VII Corps advance.[97] Confident in his intelligence, Schwarzkopf set aside the customary usage of deferring to the commander closest to the action and with ever-increasing fervor admonished Lt. Gen. Joseph Yeosock, the Third Army commander, to have Franks pick up his pace. Franks recoiled from the idea of willy-nilly pursuit, particularly when his own subordinates suggested serious resistance was still prospective. Unfortunately, Franks' internal information flowed in patterns not much changed since World War II—land lines, radios, operations sergeants posting maps with stickers or grease pencils, and hurried huddles amongst commanders draping maps across the hoods of vehicles—whereas the operational tempo was considerably advanced over that of World War II. Franks had a reasonable feel for what was happening, but with all his tactical headquarters in some state of degradation due to continuous movement, he could never articulate this appreciation with the elegant precision that would have convinced Riyadh. Fortunately for the lives of many soldiers, Franks followed his instincts and met the *Republican Guard* with the irresistible onslaught of four divisions on line previously described. Postwar analysis determined that virtually all the *Republican Guard* tanks had been destroyed by ground fire; they had been ready for a fight until they were hit with overwhelming force.[98]

A near comedic example of the divergence of battlefield pictures involved an incident at Safwan Airfield. Schwarzkopf wanted Safwan controlled. Franks assumed control meant precluding retreat through it and put attack helicopters on the mission. Schwarzkopf subsequently deliberated with the Chairman of the Joint Chiefs of Staff General Colin Powell concerning the best location to accept the surrender of and stipulate terms to the Iraqis. The two four-star generals decided upon Safwan: inside the Iraqi border but allegedly controlled by Americans. It came as a post–cease-fire shock to VII Corps that Schwarzkopf wanted a media-worthy elaboration of tents, traffic controls, press support, and other facilities thrown up overnight on an airfield the Iraqis still occupied. With a bit of a wink at the terms of the cease-fire, Franks dispatched a heavy brigade to bloodlessly bully the Iraqis off of the airfield, and the show went on.[99]

Most battlefield confusion was not so amusing. Like wars before it, the Gulf War featured the horrors and agonies of fratricide. There is no reason to believe "blue-on-blue" engagements were more frequent during DESERT STORM than in earlier wars, and considerable evidence to suggest that they were less costly.[100] The low number of casualties overall made them far more noticeable, however, as did the forensic evidence left when American-made depleted uranium was in the lethal rounds.[101] Of ninety-six American combat dead, twenty-one were attributed to fratricide.[102] Indeed, virtually every brigade-size unit that found itself involved in serious intermingled combat with the Iraqis experienced blue-on-blue engagements, although not all of them were fatal.[103]

The traditional ingredients of fratricide—battlefield confusion, limited visibility, high-tempo, fluid operations, intermingled friend and foe, and mistaken target identity—were all present during DESERT STORM. In addition, weapons were accurate at much greater ranges than they had ever been before, and the capability to reliably engage distant targets had outpaced the ability to reliably identify them. This proved particularly true at night, when an M1A1 crew, for example, could accurately engage a thermal hot spot at two thousand meters but would be hard put to distinguish the actual features of a target at a quarter of that distance. The power of suggestion being as potent as it is, crews perpetrating fratricide seem to have "seen" enemy vehicles in shapes that would have been indistinct blobs under normal circumstances.[104]

In previous wars fratricide had generally been a tactical rather than an operational issue, often adjudged as an unfortunate cost of doing business.[105] DESERT STORM commanders, less tolerant of such casualties, went to elaborate lengths to preclude them. By the fourth day of the ground campaign, with units stung by fratricides that had nevertheless occurred, restrictions accumulated to render fire and movement—even at the operational level—far more cautious, methodical, and tentative than it had been in the first few days. One battalion commander spoke of clearing all fires personally, for example, and an officer in a different unit reported taking an hour to get clearance to fire at a unit that was firing at him.[106] Fortunately, this gingerly behavior occurred in the face of an enemy that was already defeated.

Another source of impedence in the closing hours of the ground war was a deteriorating logistical situation. At the battalion level, fuel, ammunition, and other supplies moved on the capable and relatively nimble HEMTT, a modern vehicle with outsized wheels, ample clearance, and good off-road performance. In the open desert, it readily kept up with the tanks. The vehicles designated to replenish the HEMTTs, however, were far less mobile. The 5,000-gallon tankers of the forward support battalion were road bound and awkward, as were most of the vehicles in the echelons of combat service support above it. M1A1 tanks were extremely fuel consumptive. Theoretically, they could achieve a 300-mile range on 500 gallons of fuel, but in practice they traveled perhaps half as far.[107] Their powerful turbine engines consumed about as much fuel idling as on the move, and engines needed to be kept idling to support the power requirements of their highly sophisticated sights, fire controls, hydraulics, and communications. Other armored vehicles consumed less fuel than the M1A1 but nevertheless put enormous demands upon the supply system. Indeed, a heavy division could easily require 500,000 gallons of fuel to conduct a day of offensive operations.[108]

Logistical planners identify constraints that operational planners are wise to acknowledge. No tanker, for example, wants to be low on fuel in the presence of the enemy. As a rule of thumb, sustaining vehicles half-full or more on fuel during a movement-to-contact precludes that possibility. In a DESERT STORM American heavy division this imperative dictated a rotation of fuel truckers forward and back as HEMTTs that refueled combat vehicles cycled to the rear to refill from the 5,000-gallon tankers of the support battalion and then returned, often passing newly emptied HEMTTs on their way back. The 5,000-gallon tankers in turn had to rotate even farther to the rear to replenish themselves from established stocks. Given the fuel consumption of the M1A1 and the working mechanics of truck capacities and rotations, the mathematics of fuel replenishment worked out to be a fuel stop every seventy kilometers—or about every four hours if progressing steadily in a linear formation at twelve miles an hour. A well-drilled task force can defend itself and nevertheless refuel in about fifteen minutes with two full fuel HEMTTs per company on hand.[109]

During the first several days of the ground war the carefully rehearsed refueling procedures smoothly supported the ground advance. Time and again American formations swept away Iraqi defenders so completely that the HEMTTs could follow closely upon the tanks without undue risk. During the climactic struggle with the *Republican Guard*, American units, in some cases after an advance of 150 kilometers, were at a logistical peak. Newly refueled M1A1s moved adroitly and speedily overran their adversaries—without fuel concerns affecting the pace of their maneuver. When Iraqi resistance collapsed and advance shaded into exploitation, however, fuel supplies became problematic. The road-bound 5,000-gallon tankers of the support battalions simply could not keep in supporting distance of the nimble HEMTTs traveling with the battalion task forces, and the logistical tether defined by the refueling return journeys stretched to the breaking point. In some cases a 150-kilometer gap separated the task forces from the convoys intended to refuel them. This distance not only greatly increased turnaround time for the cycling HEMTTs, but it also greatly increased the risk of hostile encounter or navigational error as miniature columns of HEMTTs, normally following a HMMWV with a radio and a GPS but without such equipment themselves, threaded their way back across the messy battlefield left in the wake of the tanks. It was not uncommon to encounter armed Iraqis who had not yet surrendered–some of whom still had fight left in them–and even less uncommon to risk flawed navigation as newly refueled HEMTTs rushed back through dust and darkness to intercept their steadily advancing task forces. One support platoon, for example, overshot its moving target and found itself between the advancing vanguard of M1A1s and the retreating Iraqis. Fortunately, the Iraqis were too committed to flight to take advantage of this situation, and alert M1A1 gunners recognized the HEMTTs rolling along in front of them for what they were. There nevertheless were tense moments as frantic task-force communicators jumped from one radio net to another trying to reestablish communications with this errant platoon.[110]

The operational result of this overly stretched fuel tether was that the allied advance had reached something of a culminating point by the hundredth hour of the ground war. Postwar critics made much of an allegation that the war ended too soon.[111] Perhaps, but a day or two more would not have made a significant difference. It would have taken that long to get M1A1s that were "running on fumes" by the time of the cease-fire back into a robust and sustainable fuel posture. This is not to mention the physical fatigue of soldiers who had been rolling for four days and the encumbrance upon speedy engagement caused by hastily minted precautions against fratricide. Ironically, other traditional ingredients of a Clausewitzian culminating point—casualties, ammunition shortages, maintenance attrition, and dwindling water supplies and rations—did not apply at this point in the Gulf War. Indeed, these factors reflected hardly any degradation at all.[112]

The integration of allies into the overall operational scheme was another feature of the campaign reflecting uneven performance. The U.K. 1st Armoured Division meshed fairly seamlessly into the VII Corps. The elaboration of doctrine, planning, rehearsal, and execution necessary for interoperability had ample precedent in the nearly continuous combined NATO training the two nations had participated in since 1949. The Americans found the British accents, diet, and support vehicles curious without being problematic. Indeed, British battalions stationed in Germany had long-standing partnerships with American counterparts, making it almost inevitable that Tommy's traditional irreverence for authority would slop over onto American soldiers. A case in point was a cheeky lance corporal returned from a forward reconnaissance who counseled an American battalion commander to make haste with debarkation because he was uncertain whether the Saudi Desert had room enough for the overbuilt American truck fleet and morale facilities.[113]

Integrating the French into the XVIII Airborne Corps was more difficult, with language being less of a problem than the lack of mutual training experience. France was a member of the NATO political structure without being a member of the NATO military structure. French soldiers had good reputations in combat and actual operations but were far less likely to have participated in the combined training NATO officers valued as a prelude. Doctrine, equipment, organization, and ways of doing business were different from that of other NATO allies. That having been said, American and French officers and soldiers nevertheless established a useful rapport at the working level, and the French emerged as valuable members of the XVIII Airborne Corps team.[114]

The Americans' integration with their Arab allies was not possible to the degree achieved with the British and French. Of the Arabs, only the Egyptians had conducted serious ground tactical training with the Americans, and that in the tightly choreographed and highly photogenic BRIGHT STAR Exercises over a number of years in Egypt.[115] Military-to-military relationships with other Arab nations had ranged from modest to hostile insofar as troop training was concerned, although there had been a considerable participation of Arab officers in American schools and of American officers in military assistance programs. The Syrians, Egyptians, and several others deployed Soviet-designed equipment that would have been virtually impossible to distinguish in combat from that of the

Iraqis, and the specter of Israeli participation was a constant source of anxiety to those most mindful of Arab-American goodwill and cohesiveness. The best that could be done with respect to ground integration was to negotiate workable lines of authority among the Arab allies, grouping them into the two joint task forces with their own sectors carefully defined and providing them with considerable autonomy in conducting missions complementary to but separate from the efforts of the western allies. Arab forces moved through the Americans, such as in the case of the liberation of Kuwait City, only after the most careful coordination. These constraints were not as rigorously felt in the air or at sea, wherein there were fewer moving parts, the equipment in use was western, the pilots and skippers spoke in or responded to English, and protocols for integration had been previously rehearsed.[116]

Following the Gulf War, America and its allies sought to remedy the shortcomings demonstrated during DESERT STORM. Significant investments in sensor information technology and a related process labeled digitization promised to improve upon the shared battlefield picture. Such advanced communications could guarantee that information available to platoons was simultaneously available at theater level and vice versa. Continuing experience with this hardware and software has clearly established that revolutionary means now exist to penetrate the fog of war. This progress is somewhat dampened by the following concerns:

- Accuracy of information so quickly shared;
- Potential to spoof or compromise sensors and computers;
- Affordability of equipping allies or later-deploying American units with the same new technologies;
- Possibility that the proliferation of available information will alter the speed and fidelity with which decisions targeting a capable component can be made;
- Likelihood of overwhelming decision makers with too much information.

Opinions vary, depending on whether one sees war as more science or art.[117]

One particularly promising aspect of advanced communications and information technology is its potential to radically reduce fratricide. If friendly positions are known by the virtue of a matrix of sensors and transponders generating visual displays accessible to all, the likelihood of blue-on-blue engagements theoretically could be driven to zero. This has worked out favorably in test environments, but not yet in training environments. Equipment malfunctions have been part of the problem, as has the fact that units drawn from different commands, components, or nations are seldom equivalently equipped. Digitization holds the greatest promise with respect to reducing fratricide in circumstances wherein those directing a strike can reasonably oversee a tactical display of unit or vehicle locations while doing so. Misplaced artillery and air strikes, traditionally the most appalling sources of fratricide, could become a thing of the past. However, visual tactical displays are of little use to the tank gunner or apache pilot sorting out intermingled friend and foe in direct-fire engagements. Only through-sight cues can prevent terrible mistakes on a messy battlefield wherein the separation of forces is measured in mils on an aiming reticle rather than in meters on a map. The fielded through-sight capability to separate friend from foe has not advanced since the Gulf War.[118]

The logistical tether—most specifically, the fuel tether—of American heavy forces has also received considerable attention since the Gulf War. The most promising advances have been with respect to the appetite of the fuel-guzzling M1A1 tank. Improvements include an auxiliary power unit that allows radios and turret to operate without the main engine running and externally mounted bladders that provide a supplemental fuel-carrying capability.[119] Significant advances have also been made with respect to fuel standardization, tactical fuel-handling equipment, and transmodal movement of fuel supplies.[120] Research initiatives that have not yet had practical effect stress the development of more fuel-efficient engines and the development of lighter, yet equally effective armor.[121] The dramatic differences in off-road mobility between fuel HEMTTs accompanying battalion task forces and the higher-echelon vehicles intended to refuel them remain, virtually guaranteeing that the logistical tether may be improved but will not be abolished as long as tanks are the decisive instrument of ground combat.

With respect to training with allies and potential allies, progress has been made—albeit not as much as one might hope in the Middle East. The Kuwaitis train seriously and consistently with American units. A brigade set of equipment is permanently on hand in their desert nation, and American task forces rotate through to train on it—and with their Kuwaiti colleagues—on a near continuous basis.[122] Similar brigade sets are now positioned in Qatar and Bahrain as well, albeit with less routine training. The BRIGHT STAR training with the Egyptians has evolved to yield considerably more promise of practical wartime combined operations, and arms sales to Saudi Arabia and other Arab nations guarantee a steady flow of American technical experts to them and of their students into American schools. Unfortunately, the Saudis and Jordanians are unreceptive to the idea of an American troop presence on their soil consistent enough to sustain effective combined training, and the Syrians have gravitated back into a posture of hostility toward such an idea.[123] It seems feasible to suggest integrating Kuwaitis and Egyptians on a modest scale into an American-led operational force, but an operation on the scale of DESERT SHIELD or DESERT STORM would probably require a return to the bifurcated command arrangements of the Gulf War. The prospects for effective combined operations with the traditional NATO allies remain promising. It is true that budget cuts and force downsizing have reduced the numbers, scale of, and opportunities for combined training, but this degradation seems more than offset by the practical experience of working together in the actual conduct of operations in the Balkans.[124] This is not to mention the broader maturation of the NATO Alliance as Poland, Hungary, and the Czech Republic have joined and many other nations participate through Partnership for Peace.[125]

In summary, the major operational shortcomings of DESERT STORM have been recognized and progress made with respect to them—without, however, the shortcomings' having been fully resolved. Battlefield digitization seems likely to guarantee a shared picture of the battlefield in "real time" and to radically reduce the fog of war. This shared picture remains vulnerable to inaccurate initial information, spoofing, the uneven distributions of relevant information technology, and human limits in the pace of decision making. Digitization's shared picture should allow units to reduce fratricide—radically in the case of artillery and air strikes, less so in the case of tanks and other direct-fire weapons. The logistical tether imposed by fuel resupply has lengthened by the virtue of initiatives to expend less; but difficulties remain in moving resupply vehicles forward through tactical terrain. Combined operations with allies are increasingly a part of our practical repertoire without, however, yet being broadly enough applied in the Middle East to represent much change since the Gulf War. What is a change is that Americans can have a heavy brigade on the ground in Kuwait in days rather than weeks, and in concert with the Kuwaiti Army can preclude an easy Iraqi fait accompli such as that of August 1990.

Conclusions

Taken together, DESERT STORM and DESERT SHIELD represented considerable advance in the American appreciation of the operational art. Wedded to an overall post-Vietnam renaissance in American military capabilities was a specific articulation of the operational art in doctrinal literature, the proliferation of middle-grade officers educated in its use, simulations-driven training exercises forcing evermore realistic training circumstances on operational leaders, enhanced weapons and communications technology, and the evolution of corps and division structures capable of successfully participating at the operational level of war. During DESERT SHIELD operational planners deployed a force that kept pace with the Iraqi buildup, offering Saddam Hussein little prospect of a successful seizure of the Saudi oilfields and no prospect of a painless one. During DESERT STORM the arms and services operated together with an unprecedented virtuosity that smashed a theretofore formidable opponent in a brief time—with astonishingly few casualties. One would be hard put to imagine a more effective demonstration of joint and combined operations than that turned in to liberate Kuwait.

The above having been said, such proficiencies are perishable. Were we now presented with another opponent as formidable as Iraq was then, could we cope as handily? Post–Cold War downsizing has slashed American ground forces by a third. It would obviously be more problematic to field the seven active Army divisions of DESERT STORM out of the year 2002 inventory of ten than it was to field them out of the 1990 inventory of sixteen. Perhaps more important, focus has drifted away from warfare at the operational level, driven by the twin engines of operations other than war and year-2002-vintage defense transformation. Somalia, Haiti, Bosnia, Kosovo, Macedonia, and Afghanistan have all been important operations; they have also been operations wherein the smallness of scale on the ground and the fluidity between the tactical and the strategic have been so extreme that an operational level of activity has never emerged. Transformation as it seems to be playing out within the Department of Defense emphasizes technology and the tactical applications of technology with relatively less thought to maneuvering units in the mass. Force structure is understandably easier to justify with the operational tempo of present requirements than with the anticipated demands of future ones.

Historically, American officers have lagged in their appreciation of the operational art for at least three reasons. First, they were too busy with frontier, constabulary, and imperial police functions to give much thought to subjects they considered esoteric. Second, they never had a peacetime force structure large enough to experience practical training beyond the tactical level. Third, they thought they would have ample time to mobilize in the face of a truly formidable adversary—and would acquire the intellectual skills necessary to fight one while doing so. The 1970s and 1980s, following upon the operational myopia of the New Look and the paramilitary and tactical preoccupations of Vietnam, represented a unique departure from this pattern. Given our post–DESERT STORM spate of constabulary responsibilities, radical armed forces downsizing, and cost cutting, as well as the reluctance to contemplate a near-peer adversary, are we reverting to our original habits? Where is the major headquarters that drives its officers to contemplate and rehearse an operational plan from the highest-ranking general through the lowest-ranking lieutenant—as did EUCOM and USAREUR at their Cold War pinnacles?

In fairness to our ancestors, it must be pointed out that after paying an initial price in blood, they became reasonably adept at the operational art—even if they never conceptualized it as such. The Vicksburg Campaign, the Meuse-Argonne Offensive, and the Normandy Breakout all offer useful lessons in campaign execution—as do many other battles Americans have fought on similar scale. American leaders proved creative enough to quickly overcome their shortcomings, in part because they were educated men who read widely enough to profit from experiences other than their own and in part because they had been exposed to the working mechanics of planning and execution in the Army school system. Contributing to such possible creativity is, after all, the purpose of this collection of readings—in keeping with the historian's responsibility to be the memory of institutions that might otherwise forget. It seems unlikely that in the near term we will be able to overcome the forces driving us away from 1991 levels of proficiency in the operational art. We hope the combination of professional reading habits, school instruction, creative use of simulations, and the innate adaptability of our officers and soldiers will enable us to again master the operational art quickly enough when our next occasion to use it comes. If so, the results at that time will resemble the relative bloodlessness of DESERT STORM rather than the bloodshed of Kasserine Pass.

Notes

1. Notably Brig. Gen. Harold W. Nelson, "The Origins of Operational Art," in this volume.
2. Clayton R. Newell, "On Operational Art," in *On Operational Art*, ed. Clayton R. Newell and Michael D. Krause (Washington, D.C.: U.S. Army Center of Military History, 1994), pp. 9–14.
3. Harry G. Summers, Jr., *On Strategy: A Cultural Analysis of the Vietnam War* (Novato, Calif.: Presidio Press, 1982), pp. 90–97.
4. Robert A. Doughty, *The Evolution of U.S. Army Tactical Doctrine, 1946–1976* (Washington, D.C.: U.S. Army Center of Military History, 2001), pp. 12–18.
5. Ibid., pp. 25–40.
6. Fred Franks, Jr., and Tom Clancy, *Into the Storm: A Study on Command* (New York: G. P. Putnam's Sons, 1997), pp. 84–127; Robert H. Scales, Jr., *Certain Victory: The United States Army in the Gulf War* (Washington, D.C.: Office of the Chief of Staff, U.S. Army, 1993), pp. 5–36.
7. Franks and Clancy, *Into the Storm*, pp. 93–94; Scales, *Certain Victory*, pp. 9–10; Ronnie L. Brownlee and William J. Mullen III, *Changing an Army: An Oral History of General William E. DePuy, U.S.A. Retired* (Washington, D.C.: U.S. Army Center of Military History, 1987).
8. David C. Glantz, "Soviet Operational Art Since 1936: The Triumph of Maneuver War," in Part Three of this anthology.
9. Gordon Nathaniel Lederman, *Reorganizing the Joint Chiefs of Staff: The Goldwater Nichols Act of 1986* (Westpoint, Conn.: Greenwood Press, 1999), pp. 65–84.
10. John Romjue, *From Active Defense to AirLand Battle: The Development of Army Doctrine, 1973–1982* (Fort Monroe, Va.: U.S. Army Training and Doctrine Command, 1984).
11. Emory Upton, *The Military Policy of the United States* (Washington, D.C.: Government Printing Office, 1912), pp. iii–xv.
12. John A. Shaud, "The 'Staff Experience' and Leadership Development," *Airpower Journal* (Spring 1993); see also William B. Skelton, *An American Profession of Arms: The American Officer Corps, 1784–1861* (Lawrence: University Press of Kansas, 1992), pp. 221–37; Robert M. Utley, *Frontier Regulars: The United States Army and the Indian, 1886–1891* (New York: Macmillan, 1973), pp. 10–36.
13. Boyd L. Dastrup, *The U.S. Army Command and General Staff College: A Centennial History* (Leavenworth, Kans.: Sunflower University Press, 1982), pp. 78–105.
14. Ibid., p. 128.
15. Electronic Interv, author with Capt. John Townsend, Combat Studies Institute Faculty, Fort Leavenworth, Kans., 14 Nov 01.
16. Intervs, author with Marcus Erlandson, Friedburg, Germany, 17 Apr 86, and Joe Martz, Fort Stewart, Ga., 15 Oct 92. Both are SAMS graduates and familiar with their own thinking and that of their colleagues.
17. Department of the Army (DA), Field Manual (FM) 100–5, *Operations* (Washington, D.C.: Headquarters, Department of the Army, 1986), pp. 179–82. For the Air Force view, see John A. Warden III, *The Air Campaign: Planning for Combat* (Washington, D.C.:

National Defense University Press, 1988); for the Navy, see Wayne P. Hughes, Jr., *Fleet Tactics: Theory and Practice* (Annapolis, Md.: Naval Institute Press, 1986).

18. Ibid.; see also note 15, above.

19. Jean R. Moenk, *A History of Large Scale Maneuvers in the United States, 1935–1964* (Fort Monroe, Va.: U.S. Army Continental Army Command, 1969).

20. James F. Dunnigan, *Complete Wargames Handbook: How to Play, Design and Find Them* (New York, William Morrow, 1992), pp. 145–47, 234–40.

21. Franks and Clancy, *Into the Storm*, pp. 98–104.

22. Ibid.

23. Ibid.

24. H. Norman Schwarzkopf and Peter Petre, *It Doesn't Take a Hero* (New York: Bantam Books, 1992), pp. 285–95.

25. Department of Defense (DOD), *Conduct of the Persian Gulf War: Final Report to Congress* (Washington, D.C.: Government Printing Office, 1992), pp. 359–65.

26. DA, FM 100–5, p. 185; John B. Wilson, *Maneuver and Firepower: The Evolution of Divisions and Separate Brigades* (Washington, D.C.: U.S. Army Center of Military History, 1998), pp. 371–72.

27. Compare, for example, the desert fighting frontages depicted in Vincent J. Esposito, ed., *The West Point Atlas of American Wars*, 2 vols. (New York: Praeger, 1959), 2: 73–88, with those of Frank N. Schubert and Theresa L. Kraus, eds., *The Whirlwind War* (Washington, D.C.: U.S. Army Center of Military History, 1995). See also the division footprint as depicted in Scales, *Certain Victory*, p. 239. For a depiction of corps assets, see John McGrath and Robert Wright, "Gulf War Build-up Briefing," Washington, D.C.: U.S. Army Center of Military History, 2001.

28. Ibid.

29. John S. Brown, "Desert Storm as History—and Prologue," *Army* (February 2001): 48–51.

30. Ibid. Scales, *Certain Victory*, pp. 57–65; DOD, *Conduct of the Persian Gulf War*, pp. 34–42; Dennis Steele, "The Army Magazine Hooah Guide to Army Transformation," *Army* (February 2001): 24–26.

31. McGrath and Wright, "Gulf War Build-up"; Scales, *Certain Victory*, pp. 44–45.

32. Ibid.

33. International Institute for Strategic Studies, *The Military Balance, 1990–1991* (London: Brassey's, 1990), pp. 108–09, 115–16.

34. Schwarzkopf and Petre, *It Doesn't Take a Hero*, pp. 285–95.

35. *Desert Victory: The U.S. Army in the Gulf* (Arlington, Va.: Association of the United States Army, 2001), p. 5; Jason K. Kamiya, *A History of the 24th Mechanized Infantry Division During Operation Desert Storm* (Fort Stewart, Ga.: Victory Division, 1992), pp. 2–3.

36. DOD, *Conduct of the Persian Gulf War*, pp. 48–62, 371–91; McGrath and Wright, "Gulf War Build-up."

37. See, for example, Russell F. Weigley, *History of the United States Army* (New York: Macmillan, 1967), pp. 538–42; see also William G. Pagonis and Harold E. Rough, "Good Logistics is Combat Power: The Logistical Sustainment of Operation Desert Storm," *Military Review* (September 1991): 28–39, and Peter C. Langenus, "Moving an Army: Movement Control for Desert Storm," *Military Review* (September 1991): 40–51.

38. *Desert Victory*, pp. 5–7.

39. Ibid., p. 3.

40. Author's personal experience as a tank battalion commander deploying from Europe to Saudi Arabia. See also *Desert Victory*, p. 9.

41. See note 34, above.
42. Bantz Craddock, ed., *24th Mechanized Infantry Division Combat Team Historical Reference Book: A Collection of Historical Letters, Briefings, Orders, and Other Miscellaneous Documents Pertaining to the Defense of Saudi Arabia and the Attacks To Free Kuwait* (Fort Stewart, Ga.: Victory Division, 1992), docs. 1, 7, 8, 9.
43. Bo Eldridge, "DESERT STORM, Mother of All Battles," *Command: Military History, Strategy and Analysis* (November–December 1991): 18.
44. DOD, *Conduct of the Persian Gulf War*, pp. 65–87.
45. David A. Fastabend, "An Appraisal of 'The Brigade Based New Army,'" *Parameters* (Autumn 1997): 73–81.
46. McGrath and Wright, "Gulf War Build-up."
47. John S. Brown, *Draftee Division: The 88th Infantry Division in World War II* (Lexington: The University Press of Kentucky, 1986), pp. 70–83.
48. John S. Brown, *Winning Teams: Correlates of Success in World War II Infantry Divisions* (Fort Leavenworth, Kans.: Master of Military Arts and Sciences Program, 1985).
49. Author's personal experience. See also Crosbie E. Saint, "War Adds New Dimensions to Europe's Role," *Army* (October 1991): 88–97.
50. Perhaps most notably in Trevor N. Dupuy et al., *How To Defeat Saddam Hussein: Scenarios and Strategies for the Gulf War* (New York: Warner Books, Inc., 1991).
51. Schwarzkopf and Petre, *It Doesn't Take a Hero*, pp. 388–89, 401–05. See also U.S. News and World Report, *Triumph Without Victory: The Unreported History of the Persian Gulf War* (New York: Random House, 1992), pp. 173–83.
52. Schwarzkopf and Petre, *It Doesn't Take a Hero*, pp. 353–406. See also Rick Atkinson, *Crusade: The Untold Story of the Gulf War* (New York: Houghton Mifflin, 1993), pp. 105–15.
53. Ibid.
54. Schwarzkopf and Petre, *It Doesn't Take a Hero*, pp. 406–50; Franks and Clancy, *Into the Storm*, pp. 171–245.
55. Esposito, *West Point Atlas*, sec. 1, pp. 9–12, sec. 2, p. 38.
56. Author's personal experience as a tank battalion commander participating in the First Infantry Division breach. See also Jim Tice, "Coming Through: The Big Red One Raid," *Army Times*, 26 Aug 91, pp. 12, 18–20.
57. Edward C. Mann III, *Thunder and Lightning: DESERT STORM and the Airpower Debates* (Maxwell Air Force Base, Ala.: Air University Press, 1995), pp. 145–59; Jerome V. Martin, *Victory from Above: Air Power Theory and the Conduct of Operations DESERT SHIELD and DESERT STORM* (Maxwell Air Force Base, Ala.: Air University Press, 1994), pp. 66–67, 75, 80.
58. Anne W. Chapman, *The Army's Training Revolution, 1973–1990: An Overview* (Fort Monroe, Va.: U.S. Army Training and Doctrine Command, 1991), pp. 9–10, 19–20.
59. Franks and Clancy, *Into the Storm*, pp. 225–35; Schwarzkopf and Petre, *It Doesn't Take a Hero*, p. 383.
60. DOD, *Conduct of the Persian Gulf War*, pp. 243–45.
61. Author's personal experience as a tank battalion commander deploying from Germany; Interv, author with Lt. Col. Gregory Fontenot, then a tank battalion commander deploying from Fort Riley, Kansas, 12 Aug 93.
62. Ibid. See also Franks and Clancy, *Into the Storm*, pp. 212–13.
63. Franks and Clancy, *Into the Storm*, pp. 236–38; DOD, *Conduct of the Persian Gulf War*, pp. 245–47.
64. Author's personal experience; Scales, *Certain Victory*, pp. 254–56, 362; DOD, *Conduct of the Persian Gulf War*, pp. 565–70.

65. Author's personal experience; U.S. Naval Institute, "Weapons/Systems/Platforms — Ground Combat Vehicles — Tanks — U.S. — M1A1," U.S. Navy Military Database, Mar 91.
66. Author's personal experience as a participant in the breach and as a battalion commander providing guides to the U.K. 1st Armoured Division for its passage; Tice, "Coming Through"; Patrick Cordingley, *In the Eye of the Storm: Commanding the Desert Rats in the Gulf War* (London: Hadder and Stoughton, 1996), pp. 217–25.
67. See note 62, above.
68. VII Corps Artillery Debrief to support USAREUR Desert Storm Training Conference, Grafenwöhr, Germany, 16 Jul 91; G–3, 2d Armd Div (Fwd), Battlefield Equipment Survey, Uqlat-al-Udhaybah (Norfolk) Battlefield, 14 Apr 91; Scales, *Certain Victory*, pp. 207–10; Eliot A. Cohen, *Gulf War Air Power Survey*, 5 vols. (Washington, D.C.: Government Printing Office, 1993), vol. 3, pt. 2, pp. 202–20.
69. Atkinson, *Crusade*, pp. 416–21.
70. U.S. News and World Report, *Triumph Without Victory*, pp. 244–50.
71. DOD, *Conduct of the Persian Gulf War*, pp. 166–68; Atkinson, *Crusade*, pp. 140–48; *Desert Victory*, p. 18.
72. Franks and Clancy, *Into the Storm*, pp. 240–45; James Blackwell, *Thunder in the Desert: The Strategy and Tactics of the Persian Gulf War* (New York: Bantam Books, 1991), pp. 102–07, 153–66.
73. DOD, *Conduct of the Persian Gulf War*, pp. 535–36; Atkinson, *Crusade*, p. 141.
74. Schwarzkopf and Petre, *It Doesn't Take a Hero*, pp. 313–93.
75. Blackwell, *Thunder in the Desert*, pp. 102–07, 153–60, 222.
76. See note 43, above.
77. DA, FM 3–0, *Operations* (Washington, D.C.: Headquarters, Department of the Army, 2001), pp. 6–7.
78. DOD, *Conduct of the Persian Gulf War*, pp. 243–45.
79. John I. Alger, *Definitions and Doctrine of the Military Art, Past and Present* (West Point, N.Y.: U.S. Military Academy Department of History, 1979), p. 42.
80. Blackwell, *Thunder in the Desert*, pp. 153–60; *Desert Victory*, p. 28.
81. Alger, *Military Art*, p. 42.
82. *Desert Victory*, p. 25; Franks and Clancy, *Into the Storm*, pp. 243–45.
83. Author's personal experience as a participant in that attack. See also G–3, 2d Armd Div (Fwd), Battlefield Equipment Survey.
84. Alger, *Military Art*, p. 40.
85. Schwarzkopf and Petre, *It Doesn't Take a Hero*, pp. 450–68; Atkinson, *Crusade*, pp. 376–81, 411–15, 457–61.
86. Schwarzkopf and Petre, *It Doesn't Take a Hero*, pp. 466–67; Atkinson, *Crusade*, p. 461.
87. Alger, *Military Art*, pp. 48, 126.
88. Scales, *Certain Victory*, pp. 216–21, 308; DOD, *Conduct of the Persian Gulf War*, pp. 260–62.
89. Franks and Clancy, *Into the Storm*, pp. 175–77; DOD, *Conduct of the Persian Gulf War*, pp. 10, 243–45.
90. Tice, "Coming Through"; author's personal experience as a tank battalion commander assigned to the 1st Infantry Division (Mechanized) and providing guides to the U.K. 1st Armoured Division.

91. Franks and Clancy, *Into the Storm*, pp. 286–362; Scales, *Certain Victory*, pp. 261–86; Steve Vogel, "Metal Rain: Old Ironsides and the Iraqis Who Wouldn't Back Down," *Army Times*, 16 Sep 91, pp. 8–22, 61; Steve Vogel, "A Swift Kick: The 2nd ACR's Taming of the Guard," *Army Times*, 5 Aug 91, pp. 10–18, 28–30, 61; Steve Vogel, "The Tip of the Spear," *Army Times*, 13 Jan 92, pp. 8–16, 54; Steve Vogel, "Hell Night: For the 2d Armored Division (Fwd) It Was No Clean War," *Army Times*, 7 Oct 91.

92. Ibid.; also Tice, "Coming Through," and author's personal experience as a tank battalion commander participating in that attack.

93. J. F. C. Fuller, *The Generalship of Alexander the Great* (New Brunswick, N.J.: Rutgers University Press, 1960), pp. 163–80. J. F. C. Fuller, *A Military History of the Western World*, 3 vols. (New York: Minerva Press, 1967), II: 127–55. Douglas Southall Freeman, *R. E. Lee: A Biography*, 4 vols. (New York: Charles Scribner's Sons, 1934), II: 443–74.

94. Blackwell, *Thunder in the Desert*, pp. 29–73, 213–23; Bo Eldridge, "DESERT STORM: Mother of All Battles," *Command: Military History, Strategy and Analysis* (November–December 1991): 18, 33, 35; Richard Jupa and James Dingeman, "The Iraqi Republican Guards: Just How Elite Were They," *Command: Military History, Strategy and Analysis* (November–December 1991): 44–50.

95. Schwarzkopf and Petre, *It Doesn't Take a Hero*, pp. 453–65; Franks and Clancy, *Into the Storm*, pp. 345–47.

96. Ibid.; also author's personal experience as a field-grade commander in the face of such resistance.

97. Ibid.

98. See note 68, above. See also Franks and Clancy, *Into the Storm*, pp. 474–75.

99. Schwarzkopf and Petre, *It Doesn't Take a Hero*, pp. 474–78; Franks and Clancy, *Into the Storm*, pp. 454–57.

100. Geoffrey Regan, *Blue on Blue: A History of Friendly Fire* (New York: Avon Books, 1995); Charles R. Shrader, *Amicide: The Problem of Friendly Fire in Modern War* (Fort Leavenworth, Kans.: U.S. Army Command and General Staff College Press, 1982).

101. DOD, *Conduct of the Persian Gulf War*, p. 591; David Bird, *Combat Identification Program* (Fort Meade, Md.: Combat Identification Division, 1991).

102. Memorandum, U.S. Army Center of Military History, Historical Resources Branch, 25 Feb 00, sub: U.S. Army Deaths and Prisoners of War (POW) in the Persian Gulf War, 1993–1991. DOD, *Conduct of the Persian Gulf War*, p. 591.

103. Ibid. See also notes 90 and 91, above, and Sean D. Naylor, "Friendly Fire: The Reckoning," *Army Times*, 21 Aug 91.

104. Bird, *Combat Identification Program*.

105. See note 100, above.

106. Vogel, "Metal Rain"; Vogel, "Hell Night"; Presentations, "Large Unit Maneuvers" and "Small Unit Maneuver," USAREUR DESERT STORM Training Conference, Grafenwöhr, Germany, 16 Jul 91.

107. U.S. Navy Military Database, "M1A1"; Andrew Leyden, *Gulf War Debriefing Book: An After Action Report* (Grants Pass, Oreg.: Hellgate Press, 1997), p. 46; author's personal experience.

108. DA, FM 101–10–1, *Staff Officers' Field Manual: Organizational, Technical, and Logistical Planning Factors*, 2 vols. (Washington, D.C.: Headquarters, Department of the Army, 1986), 2: Table 2–15.

109. Interv, author with Lt. Col. Steve Marshman, Commander of the 498th Support Battalion, Garlstadt, Germany (and DESERT STORM) from May 1989 to May 1991, 11 October 1991; U.S. Naval Institute (USNI), "Weapons/System/Platform (Menu)—Ground Com-

bat Vehicles—Support Vehicles—U.S.—HEMMT—HMMWV," USNI Military Database, Mar 91; author's personal experience.

110. Ibid.; John S. Brown, "The Hundred Hour End Point: An Operational Assessment" (Naval War College; Newport, Rhode Island; 19 June 1992).

111. Douglas Waller and John Barry, "The Day We Stopped the War," *Newsweek*, 20 Jan 92, pp. 16–25; Tom Donelly, "The Generals' War," *Army Times*, 2 Mar 92; U.S. News and World Report, *Triumph Without Victory*, pp. 399–415.

112. See note 110, above.

113. Interv, author with Lt. Col. John Sharples, Partnership Battalion Commander and Commander of the Royal Scots Dragoon Greys, Fallingbostel, Federal Republic of Germany, 12 Sep 90; author's personal experience as the battalion commander in question.

114. Scales, *Certain Victory*, pp. 134–44, 216–17.

115. U.S. Central Command, "Bright Star 01/02," *http://www.centcom.mil/Operations/Previous%20Exercises/brightstar2001/index.htm.*

116. DOD, *Conduct of the Persian Gulf War*, pp. 48–63, 161–79, 182–223, 487–521.

117. Steele, "Hooah Guide."

118. Bird, *Combat Identification Program*. Also compare, for example, the current version of DA, FM 17–12–1, *Tank Gunnery*, 2 vols. (Washington, D.C.: Department of the Army, 2001), with its 1990 counterpart.

119. "Bladders Carry Extra Fuel for the M1," *Armor* (January–February 1998); author's personal experience as an armor brigade commander, 1993–1995.

120. Charles C. Cannon, Jr., "Logistical Challenges on the Battlefield," *Army* (October 2000): 131–36.

121. Charles S. Mahan, Jr., "Revolution in Military Logistics," *Army* (May 2000): 25–28; Mark J. O'Konski, "Enhancing Army Deployability," *Army* (May 2000): 29–31.

122. Tommy R. Franks, "Full Spectrum—Fully Engaged," *Army* (October 2000): 181–86; Peter R. Mansoor, "Guarding America's Interests in the Gulf," *Army* (March 2000): 33–37.

123. Ibid.; author's personal experience as an armored brigade commander deployed to INTRINSIC ACTION and to CENTCOM Forward Headquarters in Kuwait, 1995.

124. Heidi B. Vierow, "From Peacekeeping to the QDR," *Army* (April 2001): 25–29. Nicholas Firoenza, "New NATO: Alliance Settles into Post-Kosovo Routine," *Armed Forces Journal International* (September 2000): 76–82.

125. Ibid.; Ed Smith and Tom Linn, "Continuing the Revolution: Defense Reform Measures in Eastern Europe Make Uneven but Steady Progress," *Armed Forces Journal International* (September 2000): 84–88.

Afterword

Historical analysis can be a rather slippery endeavor, with a broad spectrum of views from historians and military analysts alike looking at the same episodes and reaching entirely different conclusions. Adding a relatively new term, such as operational art, to the mix makes the process even more delicate. It seems clear that some military theorists and practitioners recognized an operational level of war (although no such term was used at the time) even as modern warfare began. But a century would pass before the term and its actual practice would be consciously applied, and then it would be on the battlefields of Western Europe. The operational level of war was a long time in being recognized and eventually studied. While France and Germany had an early start in the process, the marshals of the Soviet Union fully mastered the concept in World War II. The United States was a slow learner and did not officially recognize the operational level of war and incorporate it into its doctrine until 1982.[1]

The selective examples and narratives contained in this study have attempted to provide some historical perspective to a concept that always existed but only recently has been fully recognized and defined. The embryonic formulation of operational art developed under the keen eye of Napoleon Bonaparte, and further revisions followed with the French Army's grand tactics and the critical precision of the German Field Marshal Helmuth von Moltke. But the French and German military, perhaps still influenced by their past training and experiences, tended to overcentralize their resources and focus on recreating another Cannae—a climactic battle of annihilation that would resolve an entire campaign, or maybe even the war. Curiously, in spite of the tactical brilliance of the original battle, it did not resolve Hannibal's campaign in Italy—and the Carthaginians still lost the war. During the American Civil War, the leadership of both sides always seemed entranced with the prospect of fighting one defining engagement that would resolve the entire conflict. The lure of what some would view as the Jominian way of warfare has indeed been commonplace, if elusive. But in pursuing the scheme that would achieve both tactical and strategic success, the generals of the nineteenth century almost stumbled upon the method that later leadership would identify as the operational level of war.

[1.] Clayton R. Newell, "On Operational Art," in *On Operational Art*, ed. Clayton R. Newell and Michael D. Krause (Washington, D.C.: Government Printing Office, 1994), pp 9–10.

The Russians learned from these predecessors (and from their own mistakes as well) and eventually adapted a highly sophisticated operational art of war. The latter half of World War II demonstrated their masterful grasp of welding a series of tactical decisions together to form operational objectives that met the strategic goals of the Soviet Union — the defeat of Nazi Germany. In the years following World War II, the operational art of the Soviet military was refined to meet changing technology and national goals. Today, with the dissolution of the Soviet Empire, the Russian Army appears to be adjusting its military doctrine, and particularly its scope of the operational art, to a less grandiose scale.

In the United States, these doctrinal developments progressed more slowly. As one contributor already suggested in his discussion of the Gettysburg campaign, the concept was evident as early as the Civil War. Sadly, however, even by the time of the war in Korea nearly one hundred years later, American military leadership was still grasping to understand and implement the military connection that tied national strategy and battlefield tactics together. Poor intelligence and an awkward command and organizational structure — critical components of the operational art of war—clearly contributed to the American and United Nations reversals on the Korean Peninsula in November 1950. Those associated with the war in Vietnam are even more well known. One of the most obvious and successful demonstrations of the operational art was seen in the first Persian Gulf War (1991–1992).

The scope of this study was to introduce the origins of the operational art of war, and more importantly, highlight both the practice and the impact that it has had in modern military history. Now, over a decade after Operations DESERT SHIELD and DESERT STORM, the U.S. Army must be careful not to become enamored with sophisticated technology and limited (albeit successful) small-scale incursions that are designed to achieve short-term political solutions. Operational art is a proven and critical component of military doctrine, and it should not be sacrificed or forgotten in the wake of changing technology and political environments.

Words move people, but examples draw them on. In this anthology, the reader has encountered a variety of examples that may provide some additional perspective of how wars have been fought and won — or lost. Why did Napoleon and Moltke succeed, while defeat met the French at Sedan in May 1940 and the Americans were forced to retreat in Korea in November 1950? Operationally, what could have been done differently during the Gettysburg campaign, and what should have been done better during the contest in Normandy? With these historical examples and at least an introduction to the evolution of this concept, perhaps the reader may develop a clearer understanding of the operational level of war, particularly as it may be applied in current doctrine and practiced in future conflicts.

Contributors

John S. Brown is the current commander of the Center of Military History and chief of Military History. A graduate of the U.S. Military Academy, General Brown holds master's and doctorate degrees in history from Indiana University. He also has earned master's degrees from the U.S. Army Command and General Staff College and the U.S. Naval War College. He is the author of *Draftee Division*.

David G. Chandler received his doctorate from Oxford University and served for many years as the Head of the Department of War Studies at the Royal Military Academy in Sandhurst. He is president emeritus of the British Commission for Military History and a world-renowned expert on the Napoleonic Wars. Dr. Chandler is the author of numerous articles and books, including *The Campaigns of Napoleon, Dictionary of the Napoleonic Wars, World War II on Land*, and *The D-Day Encyclopedia* (coeditor).

Robert A. Doughty is head and professor of the Department of History at the U.S. Military Academy at West Point. A colonel in the U.S. Army, he graduated from the Military Academy in 1965 and earned a Ph.D. in European History from the University of Kansas. Colonel Doughty is the author of the two-volume series, *Warfare in the Western World*, and *The Breaking Point: Sedan and the Fall of France, 1940*.

Karl-Heinz Frieser is the head of Operational Art History at the German Military History Institute. Dr. Frieser authored *Blitzkrieg Legende*, as well as several articles on the operational level of war and military history. He is a lieutenant colonel in the German Army.

David M. Glantz, a retired colonel, U.S. Army, is the editor of the *Journal of Slavic Military Studies* and a prolific writer about military affairs in Eastern Europe and Russia. He is the author of *Zhukov's Greatest Defeat, Stumbling Colossus*, and *When Titans Clashed* (coauthor). Colonel Glantz is the former director of the U.S. Army Foreign Military Studies Office at Fort Leavenworth, Kansas.

Arthur V. Grant, formerly the minority staff director for the U.S. Senate Select Committee on Intelligence, is currently with the Raytheon Company. A retired colonel, U.S. Army, he was an instructor at the U.S. Military Academy and the National War College. Colonel Grant contributed to the revised edition of the West Point *Campaign Atlas to the American Civil War*.

Jacob W. Kipp received his Ph.D. in history in 1970 from Pennsylvania State University. He is the director of the U.S. Army Foreign Military Studies Office/Joint Reserve Intelligence Center at Fort Leavenworth, Kansas. He contributes frequently to various scholarly and military journals concerning Russian military history and military affairs in Eastern Europe.

Michael D. Krause is a former deputy commander of the U.S. Army Center of Military History and instructor at the National War College. He retired as a colonel from the Ordnance Corps. Colonel Krause received his Ph.D. in modern European history from Georgetown University in 1968. He coauthored *Theater Logistics and the Gulf War* and coedited *On Operational Art*.

Bruce W. Menning has written extensively on the formative period of the Soviet Red Army and is the author of *Bayonets Before Bullets: The Imperial Russian Army, 1861–1914*. Dr. Menning received his Ph.D. in history from Duke University. He is a former associate professor of History from the University of Miami, Ohio, and he currently serves as an instructor of strategy in the Department of Joint and Multinational Operations of the U.S. Army Command and General Staff College.

Stanlis David Milkowski recently retired from the U.S. Army as a colonel, after serving several tours of duty in a variety of intelligence assignments. A graduate of the National War College, he is the author of several articles dealing with military intelligence.

Harold W. Nelson, a retired brigadier general, U.S. Army, is a former chief of Military History and commander of the Center of Military History. Dr. Nelson also taught military history and operational art at the Army War College. He coauthored the *U.S. Army War College Guide to the Battle of Gettysburg* and similar studies on the Battles of Chancellorsville, Fredericksburg, and Antietam.

Gunter R. Roth is a brigadier general in the German Army and head of the German Military History Institute. Dr. Roth has written extensively on German military history and the operational art of war.

Graham H. Turbiville, Jr., is a former director of the U.S. Army Foreign Military Studies Office at Fort Leavenworth. Before that, he was the chief of the Soviet/Warsaw Pact Strategic Operations Branch in the Defense Intelligence Agency and editor of the *Low Intensity Conflict and Law Enforcement Journal*. Dr. Turbiville was the general editor of *The Voroshilov Lectures* and the coauthor of *CINC's Strategies: The Combatant Command Process*.

Russell F. Weigley was a professor of History at Temple University and a frequent lecturer at the U.S. Army War College. He authored several major studies in military history, including: *The Age of Battles*, *The American Way of War*, *History of the United States Army*, and *Eisenhower's Lieutenants*. Professor Weigley, a distinguished military historian, passed away in early 2004.

Index

Agapeyev, A. P.: 195–96
Air forces: 99, 172–73, 178
Air offensive operations: 172–73, 174
Aircraft: 80, 93
AirLand Battle doctrine: 15, 16, 333, 439
Al-Saud, King Fahd bin Abdul Azziz: 445
Albe, Bacler d': 29, 30
Almond, Maj. Gen. Edward M.: 419, 422, 426, 427, 428, 429, 434*n*, 436*n*
Alsace-Lorraine: 76–77, 78–79, 155, 156–57
Amphibious operations
   Korean War: 420, 421, 422, 434*n*
   World War II: 393, 396–97
Antinuclear maneuver, Soviet: 271–74, 276
Applied strategy: 199–200
Ardennes: 94, 96, 159, 160, 161, 171–72, 174
Argentan-Falaise pocket: 403, 405–10. *See also* Germany; World War II.
Army of Northern Virginia. *See* Civil War, U.S.
Army of the Potomac. *See* Civil War, U.S.
Artillery
   centralized control in the French Army: 90–92, 96
   French failure to coordinate with infantry: 77, 78
   French use of: 80, 83–86, 106*n*
   massed batteries of: 56
   Moltke's use of: 124, 125, 126
   Napoleon's use of: 29, 52, 56
   offensive use of: 98
   operational planning for the use of: 83–86, 90–92, 96, 102
   Pétain's use of: 86–87
   Prussian Army use of: 36, 38
   as strategic reserve: 90–91, 96
   World War I use of: 80, 82, 83–86, 88, 106*n*
   World War II use of: 96, 97–98
Auerstädt, Germany: 48, 57–60, 64
Auftragstaktik: 164, 175–76, 178–79, 442
Augereau, Marshal: 37, 40, 42, 46–47, 48, 51, 53, 60–61, 64

Austria: 40, 41, 43, 120–21, 123–24, 127

Babakov, A.: 291*n*
Babel, Isaac: 226
Bagramian, Marshal I. Kh.: 309–10, 323*n*
Battle Command Training Program (BCTP): 440, 442
Battlefield Operating System: 442
Bavaria, Germany: 120
Beauharnais, Eugène: 33, 43
Beauregard, General P. G. T.: 356–57
Belgium: 127, 150
   in World War I: 76–77, 78, 151, 155
   in World War II: 94, 96, 158–59, 160–61, 169–70, 171, 175, 176
Belorussia: 257–58, 260–63, 264, 287*n*
Berlin, Germany: 265–66, 289*n*
Bernadotte, Marshal: 37, 42, 44, 45, 46–47, 48, 49, 51–52, 57–61, 62–63, 64, 65
Berthier, Marshal: 28–29, 30–31, 37, 39–40, 42, 43, 49, 50–51, 58, 59, 61, 64
Beskrovnyi, Liubomir G.: 211*n*
Billotte, General Gaston: 96
Bismarck, Otto von: 120, 123, 131, 141–43, 144, 150
Blitzkrieg: 10–11, 14, 27, 158, 161, 170, 172, 175, 178–79, 247, 283*n*
Bloch, Jan S.: 195–96, 203
Blücher, General: 37, 38, 61, 62
Bogdanov, A. A.: 241*n*
Bolsheviks: 218–21, 222, 224
Bonnal, Henri: 74–75
Bourcet, General Pierre de: 70
Bradley, Lt. Gen. Omar N.: 400–401, 402, 405–07, 408
Breakthrough, as operational objective: 207, 232, 233, 244*n*
British Bomber Command: 99
British Expeditionary Forces: 78, 79, 80–81, 88, 94, 151, 152, 155, 166
Brittany, France: 401–02, 405, 409
Broglie, Marshal Victor de: 69
Brown, Brig. Gen. John S.: 331
Brunswick, Duke of: 36, 37, 38, 39, 45, 46, 48, 53, 58, 60

Budennyî, General S. M.: 225–28, 243*n*
Buford, Brig. Gen. John: 361, 365, 366
Bush, George H. W.: 445, 448
Butterfield, Maj. Gen. Daniel: 358, 361, 378

Cable News Network (CNN): 460
Caemmerer, Rudolf von: 337
Campaign planning
    for coalition warfare: 453–54
    as a field of military specialization in Germany: 136
    by Lee: 350–53, 369–70, 371–72, 374, 376, 378–79, 380, 382–83
    by Manstein: 158–60
    by Meade: 378, 379–80, 383, 384
    by Moltke: 118–19, 120–21, 123–24, 127, 130, 136–37, 138, 139, 140, 144–45
    by Napoleon: 31, 34, 39–44, 49–52
    for the Persian Gulf War: 453–55, 459, 464
    by Schlieffen: 150–51, 165
    Soviet: 219–20
    U.S. Army: 15–16
Cannae, Battle of: 150, 151, 155–56, 157, 158, 165, 166, 179, 483
Capable Corps: 440, 444, 448, 452, 465
Case Red: 159
Case Yellow: 158, 159, 164
Casualties
    Gettysburg: 370–71, 387
    Napoleonic wars: 53, 58, 61
    Operation OVERLORD: 396
    Russian in World War II: 251, 253, 254, 263, 288*n*
    World War I: 77, 78, 80, 82, 86, 87, 89
Cavalry units
    in the French Army: 95, 100, 101
    Lee's use of: 363, 365, 382, 390*n*
    Moltke's use of: 124, 125, 126
    Napoleon's use of: 32, 53
    in the Prussian Army: 36, 124
    used for intelligence gathering: 32, 44, 46, 47, 124, 125
    used for security of forces: 124, 125
Cemetery Hill: 367, 369–71, 372, 373, 374, 390*n*. *See also* Civil War, U.S.; Gettysburg, battle of.
Cemetery Ridge: 373, 374, 376. *See also* Civil War, U.S.; Gettysburg, battle of.

Center of Higher Military Studies: 92
Chancellorsville, Virginia: 350, 352, 353, 359, 360, 386
Chandler, David: 25
Charles, Archduke: 134
Chemin des Dames, France: 84, 85, 87
Cherbourg, France: 397–98
China, People's Republic of: 416, 419, 421, 424, 426, 427, 430, 434*n*, 435*n*
Churchill, Winston: 169, 177, 178, 396
Civil War, Soviet: 185–86, 218, 221, 222, 223–28, 232, 233, 244*n*
Civil War, Spanish: 11
Civil War, U.S. *See also* Campaign planning, by Lee; Casualties, Gettysburg; Cavalry units, Lee's use of; Deception, Lee's use of: Gettysburg, battle of; Gettysburg campaign.
    Army of Northern Virginia: 349, 350–51, 352, 379–80
        invasion of the North by: 354–65
        objectives in the Gettysburg campaign: 381
        organization of: 352–53, 361
        role of mutual support in the battle of Gettysburg: 366–67, 370, 372–73
        supplies for: 351, 365, 379, 381, 382, 386–87
        use of cavalry: 363–64, 365–66
    Army of the Potomac: 349, 350, 351, 352, 353, 357, 363–65, 379–80, 382, 386–87
    Pennsylvania, Confederate invasion of: 349, 350–53, 354–65, 379–80, 382
Civilian Reserve Air Fleet, U.S.: 446
Clausewitz, Carl von: 10, 13, 15–16, 36, 74, 115, 119–20, 126, 134, 139, 144, 145, 149, 150, 154, 158, 159, 161, 163, 165–66, 192–93, 198–99, 205, 333, 334, 388*n*, 430
COBRA. *See* Operations, military.
Cold War: 12–13, 16–17
Collins, Maj. Gen. J. Lawton: 400, 401, 407
Colmater (filling), failure of the concept of: 93, 96–101
Combined arms
    German concept of: 10–11

Combined arms—Continued
  Imperial Russian Army operations: 216
  Moltke's promotion of coordination of: 124–25, 126–27
  and Napoleon's *corps d'armée*: 33, 47, 70
  Soviet Army emphasis on: 233–34, 235, 237–39, 244*n*, 247, 251, 257, 260–61, 267–68, 269, 272–73, 275, 277, 290*n*, 300–301, 305, 307, 310, 312, 314
Combined Arms Maneuver Training Center: 455
Command and control
  decentralization of: 120, 125–26, 140–41
  effects of technology on: 443–44
  flexibility of in the German Army: 164, 174, 175–76, 179
  French centralization of: 90, 91, 92, 97
  Hitler's effect on in World War II: 162–63, 164–65, 166, 178–79
  in the Korean War: 415–16, 418–20, 421–22, 423–24, 430–32, 433*n*
  of logistical support in the Soviet Army: 295, 297–98, 301, 303, 305, 307, 309, 311, 313–14, 324*n*, 325*n*
  need to organize in peacetime: 125–26
  operational direction methodology: 140–43, 144–46
  Soviet Army: 274, 275, 282*n*, 284*n*
Commission for the Study and Use of the Experience of the War, 1914–1918 (Soviet Union): 220
Communications, battlefield
  collapse of German system in World War I: 79
  French system in World War I: 79
  Moltke's development of: 113
  in Napoleon's army: 29, 30, 64
Communist Forces, Chinese: 424, 426, 427, 428–29, 435*n*, 436*n*
Communist ideology and military strategy: 185–86
Communist Party of the Soviet Union, relationship with the Red Army: 222, 229, 230–31, 235
Computer simulations used in military training: 442–43, 444, 445, 452, 473

Computer simulations used in military training—Continued
  used in preparation for DESERT STORM: 454
Comte, Auguste: 201
Concentration of forces. *See* War, principles of.
Corps d'armée: 33, 47, 57, 58, 65, 70, 71. *See also* French Army; Napoleon Bonaparte.
Corps Support Command (U.S.): 449
Couch, Maj. Gen. Darius N.: 357–58, 364–65
Course of Instruction in the Elements of the Art and Science of War, A, by Junius B. Wheeler: 335
Creveld, Martin van: 65
Culmination point: 154, 155, 159, 161–62, 163
Culp's Hill: 370–71, 372, 374, 376. *See also* Civil War, U.S.; Gettysburg, battle of.

Daille, Maj. Marius: 88–89
Daru, Count: 28–29, 31
Davis, Jefferson: 350, 351, 356, 389*n*
Davout, Marshal Louis-Nicolas: 37, 42, 44, 46–47, 48, 49, 51–52, 57–59, 60–61, 62, 64, 65
Debeney, General Eugène: 87–89, 92, 102
Deception
  Lee's use of: 354–57, 360, 383
  Napoleon's use of: 32, 34, 41, 42–43
  U.S. use of in the Persian Gulf War: 460–61, 464
Decline and Fall of the Roman Empire, The, by Edward Gibbons: 116
Deep operations, Soviet
  air support for: 273
  concept of: 9–10, 213, 215, 231–32, 233, 247–48, 283*n*
  logistical support for: 308, 314
  use of in World War II: 256, 258–59, 260, 262, 289*n*, 304
Deep operations, successive
  theory of: 206, 215, 231–32, 233–34, 236–37, 238, 268, 242–43
  use of: 259, 260, 263–66, 302
Deep pursuit, Soviet concept of: 231
Defense
  French doctrine regarding: 93–94
  French planning for in World War II: 94–96

491

Delbrueck, Hans: 230, 236
Denmark: 118–19
DESERT SHIELD. *See* Operations, military.
DESERT STORM. *See* Operations, military.
Deterrence as a defense strategy: 114
Dix, Maj. Gen. John A.: 354, 356, 358, 389*n*
Doctrine
    French: 25, 74–76, 90–94, 96, 102, 103
    Soviet: 222–23, 228, 242*n*, 270–71, 276
    and technological change: 114
    U.S.: 13, 15–18, 336–42, 343–44, 345
Doctrine for Joint Operations: 16
Doctrine for Planning Joint Operations: 16
Doughty, Robert: 25
Dragomirov, M. I.: 185, 191, 193, 197, 199, 210*n*
Dragoons, Napoleon's use of: 32, 46
Drum, Hugh: 339

East Prussia: 262–64, 265
École Supérieure de Guerre: 74
Economic infrastructure and the ability to conduct war: 195, 196, 205
Economy of force. *See* War, principles of.
Egypt: 470, 472
Eisenhower, General Dwight D.: 12, 402, 406–07
Elbe River: 40, 41, 45, 60–61
Engineer units, battle use of: 124, 125
English Channel: 94, 98, 101
Envelopment
    counterattacks against: 162–64, 173–74, 178
    of German forces in World War II: 405–10
    German use of: 150–51, 155–56, 157–58, 160, 161–62, 163, 170, 174
    in the Korean War: 420–21, 422, 424, 428, 429–30, 436*n*
    Manstein's use of: 160
    Napoleon's use of: 34, 47, 51–52, 71
    as operational objective: 207
    in the Persian Gulf War: 453–54, 463
    Schlieffen's emphasis on: 150–51, 155–56, 157–58, 165, 166
    Soviet use of in World War II: 11, 259–61, 262, 263, 264, 265–66, 267, 285*n*, 288*n*
Espèrey, General Louis Franchet d': 80, 81

Essai général de tactique, by General Jacques Guibert: 70
"Essay on Strategy," by Moltke: 131, 134, 136
Ewell, Lt. Gen. Richard: 354, 356, 363, 364, 365–66, 367, 369–70, 373–74, 376, 381, 383, 385–86, 390*n*

Far East Command (U.S.): 418, 419–20, 421–22, 423, 426, 427, 428, 429, 430–31, 433*n*, 434*n*, 435*n*, 436*n*, 437*n*
Field Manual 100-5: 12, 14, 15, 442. *See also* Doctrine, U.S.
Field manuals, French: 73–74. *See also* Doctrine, French.
Field Service Regulations: 336–39. *See also* Doctrine, U.S.
Finland: 294
First Italian Campaign (1796): 32–33
Flavigny, General J. A. L. R.: 97, 99–100, 173–74
Flexibility of response: 136–38, 141, 143
Foch, Marshal Ferdinand: 80, 91, 154–55
Fort Leavenworth, Kansas, schools: 339–40
France. *See also* French Army; World War I.
    military doctrine, development of: 25, 75–76
    and the Persian Gulf War: 453, 462, 470
    and World War I: 76–89, 151–58
    and World War II: 94–101, 158, 169–79, 393
Franco-Prussian War (1870–1871): 25, 127–31, 136–37, 142–43, 144–45, 189–90, 191, 192, 197. *See also* Germany.
Franco-Russian Alliance: 76–77
Franks, Lt. Gen. Frederick M., Jr.: 454, 466–67
Fratricide: 467–68, 470, 471–72, 473
Frederick, Crown Prince of Prussia: 121, 123, 127
Frederick Charles, Prince: 121, 123, 127
Frederick Karl, Prince: 119, 147*n*
Frederick-Wilhelm, King of Prussia: 118, 123, 124
Frederick-William III: 36, 37, 38, 40, 42, 44, 48, 58, 61, 63
Fredericksburg, Virginia: 354–55, 356, 360

French, Sir John: 81
French Army
    ability to perform at the operational level in World War I: 82
    Chief of the General Staff: 88
    command and control system: 79, 80
    communications system in World War I: 79
    failure to coordinate land and air resources: 93
    failure to launch timely counterattacks at Sedan: 98–100
    flexibility of response: 79, 81–82, 91–92, 102–03
    mutiny: 86
    operational planning in World War I: 82–85, 86–87, 88–89
    in peacetime: 71–73
    use of successive operations: 88, 89, 92–93, 102
    and World War II: 178
French Army War College: 88–89
French High Command: 96–97
French Imperial Headquarters: 28–31, 34–35, 40, 50–51
Freycinet, Charles de: 72–73
Frieser, Karl-Heinz: 112
Frunze, M. V.: 221, 222, 223, 229, 230, 233, 242*n*, 243*n*
Frunze Military Academy: 215
Fulda Gap: 39, 41. *See also* World War II.
Fuller, General J. F. C.: 36, 174, 236–37

Gallieni, General Joseph: 80, 81
Gamelin, General Maurice: 91, 94, 107*n*, 177
Gaulle, Col. Charles de: 177–78
"General Disposition for the Assembly of the Grand Army," by Napoleon Bonaparte: 42
Georges, General Alphonse: 96, 97, 99, 100
German Army
    absence of a strategic reserve force: 161–62
    and attack on Sedan: 95–101
    collapse of communication system in World War I: 79
    ground air defense: 99
    operational planning in World War I: 84
    panzer units: 95–96, 98, 99–100, 101, 160–61, 162, 163–64, 169–79, 256, 259–63, 264, 289*n*

German General Staff: 150, 153, 154, 156, 158–60, 165–66, 170, 175, 176, 440
German Reich in the pre–World War I period: 149–51
Germany. *See also* German Army; World War I; World War II.
    and the Argentan-Falaise pocket: 405–10
    and development of military theories: 10–11
    and the Franco-Prussian War: 71–72, 74–75
    and invasion of the Soviet Union in World War II: 238–39, 248, 249–53, 283*n*, 296
    and World War I: 76–89, 150–58
    and World War II: 158–66, 238–39, 248–53, 296
Gerua, Col. Aleksandr: 199–200, 204, 210*n*
Gettysburg, battle of: 365–80. *See also* Civil War, U.S.
Gettysburg campaign: 329–30; 365–87. *See also* Civil War, U.S.
Gibbons, Edward: 116
Glantz, David M.: 186
Global positioning systems: 443, 456, 465
Goldwater-Nichols Department of Defense Reorganization Act of 1986: 16–17, 439
Goltz, Colmar von der: 144, 203, 205
Golushko, Col.-Gen. I. M.: 295, 300, 303, 315, 320*n*, 322*n*, 323*n*, 324*n*, 326*n*
Gorbachev, Mikhail S.: 314, 325*n*
Goretskiî, K. E.: 318*n*
Grand Armée: 38, 40, 42, 44, 48, 61–62, 65, 70, 104*n*. *See also* French Army; Napoleon Bonaparte.
Grandmaison, Col. Louis de: 75
Grant, Arthur: 329
Grant, Maj. Gen. Ulysses S.: 349–50. *See also* Civil War, U.S.
Great Britain
    and the Napoleonic wars: 40, 41, 43
    and the Persian Gulf War: 453, 462–63, 470
    and planning for Operation OVERLORD: 393, 396
    and World War I: 79, 80–81, 88, 151, 152, 155
    and World War II: 94, 158, 160, 393, 396

493

Guderian, General Heinz: 98, 100, 171, 172, 173, 175, 178, 179
Guibert, General Jacques: 70
Gulevich, Lt. Col. A. A.: 196, 203

Haig, Douglas: 465
Haislip, Maj. Gen. Wade H.: 405, 406, 407, 408
Halder, General Franz: 174, 176–77
Halleck, General Henry W.: 353, 355, 358–59, 360, 364–65, 371, 381, 386, 389*n*
Hancock, Maj. Gen. Winfield S.: 367, 386, 390*n*
Hardie, Col. James A.: 359, 360
Harpers Ferry, West Virginia: 358–59
Henry, Prince of Prussia: 118
Herr, General Frédéric G.: 90
Heth, Maj. Gen. Henry: 365, 366, 376, 383
Hill, Lt. Gen. A. P.: 354, 356, 364, 365–66, 367, 369, 370, 374, 376, 378, 383
Hindenburg Line: 84, 85. *See also* World War I.
Hitler, Adolf: 10, 11, 158, 162–63, 164–65, 166, 168*n*, 176–77, 178–79, 403. *See also* German Army; World War I; World War II.
Hoetzendorf, Conrad von: 230
Hohenlohe, Prince: 36, 37, 38, 39, 45, 46, 47–48, 52, 53, 56, 60, 61, 62, 64
Holland: 42–43, 161
Hood, Maj. Gen. John B.: 371, 373, 376, 379, 390*n*
Hooker, Maj. Gen. Joseph: 350, 353, 354, 355–59, 360, 361, 383, 386
Howard, Maj. Gen. Oliver O.: 366, 371
Hungary: 263, 303
Huntziger, General Charles: 94, 96, 97, 98, 100, 171–72
Hussein, Saddam: 444, 448, 452, 458, 459, 464, 473. *See also* Persian Gulf War.

Imperial Russian Army
 and concept of a unified supreme headquarters: 216
 failure to critically assess military history: 191–92
 and intermediary command to control operations of a group of armies: 216
 officers of in the Red Army: 218–19, 220–23, 225–26, 232–33

Imperial Russian Army—Continued
 and planning for future wars: 204–05
 and the Russo-Turkish War: 189–90
Inch'on, Korea: 418, 419, 420, 421, 422, 423, 430–31, 434*n*
Industrial revolution, effects on warfare: 4–5, 8–9, 111
Instruction on the Offensive Action of Large Units in Battle: 338. *See also* Doctrine, French; French Army.
Instructions of the Tactical Employment of Large Units: 92. *See also* Doctrine, French; French Army.
INTERNAL LOOK 90: 443, 445, 452
Iraq: 444–45, 447–53, 454. *See also* Operations, military, DESERT STORM; Persian Gulf War.
Iraqi forces: 444–45, 452–53, 454, 455, 456, 457, 458, 459, 460, 461, 462–65, 467, 469. *See also* Persian Gulf War; *Republican Guard* units.
Israel: 458, 470–71
Isserson, Georgiy S.: 8–9, 12, 17, 234–35, 245*n*
Italy: 32–33, 43, 120, 123
Ivanov, I.: 244*n*
Izmest'ev, P. I.: 219–20

Japan
 war with Russia in 1904–1905: 197–201
 and World War II: 266–67
Japan Logistics Command (U.S.): 423
Jena-Auerstädt campaign (1806): 25, 34, 45, 48–57, 64–65, 149. *See also* Napoleon Bonaparte; Napoleonic wars.
Joffre, General Joseph: 76–80, 81–82, 102–03, 151–52, 156, 160
Joint Chiefs of Staff (U.S.): 416, 418, 419–20, 424, 433*n*, 435*n*
Joint operations, U.S.: 16–18
Joint Strategic Plans and Operations Group: 418, 419, 420, 428–29
Jomini, Henri: 4, 15–16, 192–93, 198–99, 333, 334, 335
Joy, Vice Adm. C. Turner: 433*n*

Kamenev, S. S.: 221, 227–28
Kersnovskiy, Anton A.: 210*n*
Khar'kov, battle for: 250–51, 254–55, 256, 286*n*. *See also* World War II.
Khrulev, A. V.: 294, 295, 296, 297, 298, 299, 301, 317*n*, 318*n*, 319*n*, 323*n*

Khrushchev, Nikita S.: 13, 269, 270
Kipp, Jacob W.: 185–86
Kleist, General Ewald von: 169, 170, 171, 175
Kluck, General Alexander von: 80–81, 454
Kobbe, William: 335
Kokoshin, A. A.: 234
Konev, Marshal I. S.: 264, 265, 266
Königgrätz, Czechoslovakia: 123–24
Korea, People's Republic of (North Korea): 415–16, 419–22, 426
Korea, Republic of (South Korea): 416, 433*n*. *See also* South Korean Army.
Korean War: 13, 330–31, 415–32, 484. *See also* Amphibious operations; China, People's Republic of; Command and control; Envelopment; Joint Chiefs of Staff (U.S.); Logistical support; Military intelligence; Operational maneuver; Operational planning; Operational reserves; Terrain; United Nations Command; War, principles of.
Korotkov, I. A.: 219
Krause, Michael D.: 111
Kriegsakademie: 115, 135–36, 139. *See also* German Army.
Kulik Commission: 282*n*
Kuropatkin, General A. N.: 197, 206, 219
Kursk, Soviet Union: 164–65
Kursk, Battle of: 254, 256–58, 300, 301, 320*n*. *See also* World War II.
Kuwait: 331, 443, 444–45, 447, 448, 452–53, 454, 455, 458–59, 461–62, 464, 472, 473–74. *See also* Operations, military; Persian Gulf War.

La Malmaison, battle of: 87, 92, 102. *See also* World War I.
Lafontaine, General: 98–99
Landgrafen-Berg: 50, 51, 52
Lannes, Marshal: 37, 44, 45–46, 47, 48, 49–50, 51, 53, 56, 59, 60–61, 62, 64
Lee, General Robert E.: 329–30, 349, 389*n*, 391*n*. *See also* Civil War, U.S.
  committed to battle at Gettysburg by actions of subordinates: 365–67, 383
  concept of operations at Gettysburg: 369–70, 371–72, 374, 376, 378–79, 380, 382–83

Lee, General Robert E.—Continued
  and decision to invade the North: 350–53
  and the invasion of the North: 354, 356, 361, 363–65, 380–82, 389*n*
  lack of correct intelligence at Gettysburg: 363, 365–67, 372, 382, 390*n*
  objectives in the Gettysburg campaign: 381, 382, 386–87, 388*n*
  relationships with subordinates: 363, 365, 369–70, 373–74, 376, 383, 384, 385–86
  and reorganization of the Army of Northern Virginia: 352–53, 361, 385–86
  and supplies: 351, 365, 379, 381, 382, 386–87
  use of cavalry preliminary to the Gettysburg campaign: 363, 365, 382, 390*n*
  use of deception: 354–57, 360, 383
  use of operational reserves: 384
  use of the principle of concentration of forces: 370, 383–84. *See also* War, principles of.
Lefebvre, Marshal: 42, 44, 49–50, 58
Lenin, V. I.: 219, 220, 228, 229, 241*n*
Leyer, Genrikh Antonovich: 185, 189, 193–95, 197, 198, 199, 200, 201, 202, 204, 241*n*
Liddell Hart, Basil H.: 77, 155, 160–61, 169, 236–37
Liège, Belgium: 76
Lincoln, Abraham: 349, 353, 355–56, 357, 358, 359, 360, 380
Little Round Top: 370, 371, 372, 373, 374, 376. *See also* Civil War, U.S.; Gettysburg, battle of.
Lloyd, William: 193
Logistical support
  command and control of in the Soviet Army: 295, 297–98, 301, 303, 305, 307, 309, 311, 313–14, 324*n*, 325*n*
  "delivery forward" principle in the Soviet system: 301
  and early warfare: 5
  German failures during World War I: 154
  Korean War: 416, 418, 420–21, 422–23, 424, 427, 429, 431, 434*n*, 436*n*
  and Operation OVERLORD: 397–98, 402

495

Logistical support—Continued
  and Panzer Group Kleist: 170, 176
  and the Persian Gulf War: 446–47, 448–49, 453, 455, 465, 468–69, 472, 473
  planning for in the Soviet Army: 295, 297–98, 300, 302, 303, 305–06, 307–08, 310–14, 318n, 324n, 325n
  rear service establishment in the Soviet Army: 294–95, 296–97, 299, 300–303, 304, 305, 306, 307–08, 309, 311, 313–14, 315, 317n, 318n, 321n, 324n, 325n
  role in modern military operations: 8–9
  and the Russian Army in World War I: 216, 217
  and the Russo-Japanese War: 197–98
  self-sufficiency of corps in Napoleon's army: 35
  in the Soviet Army: 186–87, 227, 230, 231, 233, 253, 254, 256–57, 260, 263, 273, 282n, 285n, 293–316
  and Soviet planning for nuclear warfare: 310–11
  Soviet in World War II: 294–308, 317n, 318n, 322n, 324n
  and World War II: 11
Longstreet, Lt. Gen. James: 350, 354, 356, 361, 364, 365–66, 367, 369, 370, 371, 372, 373–74, 376, 378–79, 381, 385, 390n, 391n
Louis Bonaparte: 42–43
Louis Ferdinand, Prince: 39, 45, 46
Louise, Queen of Prussia: 36, 63
Ludendorff, General: 87
Luxembourg: 77, 78, 81, 127, 160, 169, 171
Lykke, Col. Arthur F., Jr.: 7

MacArthur, General Douglas: 12, 13, 330–31, 415–16, 418–32, 433n, 434n, 435n, 436n. *See also* Korean War; World War II.
  concept of operations: 420–22, 424, 427, 428, 429–30
  and logistics responsibilities in the Korean War: 422–23
McClellan, Maj. Gen. George B.: 349, 354, 382
McLaws, Maj. Gen. Lafayette: 371, 372, 376, 379
Magdeburg, East Germany: 45, 49, 61, 62, 63
Maginot Line: 94, 95, 96, 97, 98, 160, 175. *See also* World War I; World War II.
Malinovsky, R. Y.: 268
Mamontov, General K. K.: 225
Manchuria: 266–67, 304–07, 324n, 419, 426, 429
Manstein, Field Marshal Erich von: 112, 152, 155, 156, 158–65, 166, 168n, 170, 171, 174, 179, 254. *See also* SICKLE CUT Plan.
Manual for Commanders of Large Units (Provisional): 340
Marbot, Baron M. de: 52, 59
Marne Campaign (1914): 151–54. *See also* World War I.
Marne River: 79, 80–82, 151–54
Maunoury, General Michel J.: 80, 81
Meade, General George G.: 329, 330, 359, 360–61, 391n
  concept of operations at Gettysburg: 378, 379–80, 383, 384
  and development of the battle of Gettysburg: 364, 367
  failure of subordinates to coordinate with at Gettysburg: 373
  objectives in the Gettysburg campaign: 381–82, 386
  relationship with national command: 364–65
  relationship with subordinates: 374, 376, 378, 386
  use of operational reserves: 384–85
  use of the principle of concentration of forces: 367, 371, 383, 384. *See also* War, principles of.
  use of terrain: 372. *See also* Terrain.
Media, U.S. military use of: 460
Mekhlis, I.: 318n
Menning, Bruce W.: 185, 215
Methodical battle: 92–94, 102
Meuse River: 94, 95–96, 98, 99, 100–101, 159, 160, 169–70, 171–74, 175
Middle East War (1973) 13–14
Middleton, Maj. Gen. Troy H.: 401–02
Mikhnevich, General Nikolay Petrovich: 89, 194, 196–97, 201–04, 216
Military Academy of Rear and Supply (Soviet): 309, 322n, 323n
Military Dictionary, by Henry L. Scott: 334
Military Encyclopedia, by Joachim Stocqueler: 333

Military intelligence
   and the Korean War: 426, 428–29, 431, 433*n*, 435*n*, 436*n*
   in Napoleon's army: 29–31, 32, 39–40, 44, 46, 47, 48, 50, 64
   and the Persian Gulf War: 454–55, 458, 463, 465, 466–67, 471–72
   and the U.S. Civil War: 363, 365–67, 372, 382, 390*n*
Military scientific societies, Russian: 229–30, 233
Military strategy. *See also* War, principles of.
   and civilian support: 195
   and Communist ideology: 185–86
   defensive operations used by Manstein: 162–64
   definitions of: 4, 7, 334
   of exhaustion: 195, 203
   extended line: 5, 6
   French in World War I: 76–79
   German in World War I: 77–79
   Hitler's preference for offensive operations: 164–65
   Moltke's understanding of: 118–19, 120, 131, 134, 136, 138, 144
   Napoleonic: 5, 28
   and nuclear war: 269–70
   for Operation OVERLORD: 397
   Russian thinking: 191–95, 202–04
   and strategic deployment of forces: 205
Milkowski, Stanlis D.: 330–31
Milroy, Maj. Gen. Robert H.: 356, 357
"Miracle of the Marne": 79–82, 102, 107*n*, 151
Mission-oriented tactics: 175–76, 178–79. *See also Auftragstaktik.*
Mobility
   effects of artillery on: 82, 90–91
   effects of railroads on. *See* Railroads.
   effects on operational level of war in World War I: 82
   and French doctrine: 90–91, 92–93
   German in World War II: 163, 249–50
Mobilization
   effects of the industrial revolution on: 4–5
   of Napoleon's army: 39–40, 42
   of Prussian forces in 1866: 120, 121
   of Soviet society during peacetime: 10
Moltke, Field Marshal Helmuth von: 77–78, 79, 81, 111–12, 113–46, 185, 190, 191, 198–99, 459. *See*

Moltke, Field Marshal Helmuth von—Continued
   also German Army; Operational level of war.
   campaign planning: 118–19, 120–21, 123–24, 127, 130
   command relationships: 125–26, 140–41
   and the Franco-Prussian War: 127–31
   and organization of the General Staff: 140–41
   and theory of operational conduct: 131, 134–40
   writings: 131, 134, 136, 147*n*
Moltke, Helmuth von (the younger): 151, 153, 154–55, 156–58
Montdidier, battle of: 87–89, 92–93, 102. *See also* World War I.
Montgomery, General Bernard Law: 397, 402, 405, 406, 407, 408
Moreau, General Jean: 70
Mortier, Marshal: 37, 43
Moscow, battle for: 161–62. *See also* World War II.
Murat, Marshal: 45, 47, 48–50, 51, 53, 56, 57, 60–61, 62
Mutual support, principle of
   Moltke's emphasis on: 125, 139
   Napoleon's use of: 34–35, 43–48, 51–52, 53

Napoleon Bonaparte: 27–66. *See also Corps d'armée; Grand Armée;* Napoleonic wars.
   battle headquarters: 29–30, 50–51
   campaign planning by: 31, 34, 39–44, 49–52
   effect on French operational art in the twentieth century: 74–75
   errors in judgment: 64–66
   and the First Italian Campaign (1796): 32–33
   flexibility of plans: 44, 49, 64–66
   and the Jena-Auerstädt campaign: 34–36, 48–66
   logistical support: 32, 40, 61
   as master of operational art: 39–44, 50–51, 60–66, 70–71, 74–75
   military objectives of: 4, 25
   and need "to make war a real science": 27–28
   and organization of forces: 104*n*
   philosophy of war: 27

Napoleon Bonaparte—Continued
   relationship with subordinates: 28, 49–51, 56, 58–60, 71, 74–75
   Russian emphasis on the ideas of: 192, 193, 195, 198
   staff: 28–31, 33, 50–51
   use of deception and surprise: 32–33, 34, 41, 42. *See also* War, principles of, surprise.
   use of mass: 33–34, 50–51. *See also* War, principles of, concentration.
   use of mutually supporting formations: 34–35, 43–48, 51–52, 53
   use of reserve forces above the tactical level: 60–63
Napoleonic wars. *See also* Military strategy; Napoleon Bonaparte; Operational formations of military units; Prussian Army.
   casualties: 53, 58, 61
   disposition of Prussian Army: 44–46
   and Great Britain: 40, 41, 43
   prisoners of war: 46, 53, 56, 58, 61, 62–63
   and Russia: 40–41, 62, 63
   and Saxony: 41, 42, 44, 63
Nation in Arms, The, by Colmar von der Goltz: 144
National Command Authority: 419–20, 433*n*, 448
National Training Center: 455
Nelson, Harold W.: 329
NEPTUNE: 393, 396–97
Ney, Marshal: 40, 42, 44, 46–47, 48, 49–50, 51, 53, 56, 60–61, 62, 63, 65
Neznamov, Lt. Col. Aleksandr Aleksandrovich: 185, 189, 200–201, 204–08, 211*n*, 216, 219, 221, 222, 228
Nicholas Academy of the General Staff: 191–92, 193, 196–97, 200, 214, 216–17, 218, 219
Nimitz, Admiral Chester W.: 12
Nivelle, General Robert G.: 83–86, 102
Normandy, France, invasion of: 330, 393–98, 403. *See also* World War II.
North Atlantic Treaty Organization (NATO): 14–15, 470, 472–73
Novikov, Lt. Gen. M.: 310–11
Nuclear weapons
   effect on theories regarding possible military operations: 12–13, 14–15, 17, 269–74

Nuclear weapons—Continued
   Soviet military reliance on: 13, 269–74
Nuclear warfare, Soviet planning for logistical support of: 310–11, 312

Offensive à outrance: 75, 77
Ogarkov, Marshal N. V.: 311–12
Operational art
   definitions of: 6, 7–8
      French: 70
      German: 8
      Soviet: 8, 342–44
      Svechin: 214, 230
      U.S. Army: 15–16, 333
      Varfolomeev: 214–15
   development of French thinking on: 69–71, 73–76, 87–89, 90–92, 101–03
   early Russian thoughts on: 200–201
   effect of theories of nuclear war on: 269–70
   effects of technology on: 443–44
   Gerua's early ideas on: 199–200
   Soviet development of theories regarding: 7–10, 185–86, 213, 214, 228–34, 238–39, 247, 342–44, 484
   U.S. Army development of vocabulary relating to: 441–42, 444, 447, 452, 473
   as U.S. military doctrinal concept: 13, 15–18, 484
   U.S. military training in: 440–42, 444, 447, 452, 473, 474–75
   U.S. study of Soviet theorists: 442
Operational commanders, Moltke's definition of the role of: 125–26, 127, 140–42
Operational formations of military units
   French development of: 69–71, 74–76, 90, 91, 95
   Napoleonic: 33–35, 44, 45–48, 57, 58, 65, 70–71
   Soviet: 255
   square battalion: 33–35, 44, 45–48, 65
Operational level of war: 483–84
   American development of the concept of: 333–45
   definition of: 333–35
   French Army publications regarding: 73–74
   French misunderstandings of: 69, 75, 91–92, 101–03

Operational level of war—Continued
  Moltke's development of the concept of: 113–14, 118–19, 131, 134–40, 144–46
Operational logistics
  and the Gettysburg campaign: 385
  and the Soviet Army: 293–94, 297–98, 299, 300–301, 303–04, 306–08, 316
Operational maneuver
  allied capacity for in the Persian Gulf War: 464–65, 466–67, 469–70, 473–74
  incompatibility with mission in the Korean War: 428
  Iraqi incapacity for in the Persian Gulf War: 461, 464–65, 466
  irrelevance of in a nuclear-war scenario: 270
  logistical support for: 186–87, 216, 217, 293–94, 297–98, 299, 300–301, 302, 303–04, 306, 307–08, 316, 385
  Soviet practice in a continuous sequence: 186
  definition of: 269, 288*n*, 342–44
  doctrine after World War II: 269
  reorganization of forces to improve: 255
  response to high-precision weaponry: 274
  theories of antinuclear maneuver: 271–73
  in World War II: 249–51, 253, 256, 257–59, 260–63, 264–66
Operational objective, Moltke's definition of: 118, 119, 120, 125
Operational planning deficiencies in Operation OVERLORD: 330, 393, 396, 397–99, 401, 402, 403, 405, 406–10
  by the French in World War I: 82–85, 86–87, 88–89
  by the Germans in World War II: 163, 169–70
  in the Korean War: 415–16, 418, 420, 421–22, 427, 428–29, 430–31, 434*n*
  by Manstein: 163
  by Nivelle: 83–84
  for the Persian Gulf War: 444–49, 452–55, 459, 464–65, 473–74
  by Pétain: 86–87
  Soviet: 219–20

Operational reserves. *See also* Reserve forces.
  at Gettysburg: 384–85
  in the Korean War: 427
  Napoleon's use of: 60–63
  U.S. use of in the Persian Gulf War: 460, 464
Operations, military
  BAGRATION: 260–61
  CITADEL: 164–65
  COBRA: 399–401, 402, 403, 407, 409, 411*n*
  DESERT SHIELD: 17, 331, 444–52, 473–74
  DESERT STORM: 17, 331, 440, 444, 446, 448, 452–75. *See also* Computer simulations; Persian Gulf War.
  OVERLORD: 393–97. *See also* World War II.
  SICKLE CUT: 164–65, 169, 174, 176–77. *See also* SICKLE CUT Plan.
Order of battle, Moltke's call for standardization of: 124–25

Panzer Group Kleist: 169–79
Panzer units. *See* German Army.
Paris, France: 76, 80, 81, 130–31, 142–43, 144
Patton, Lt. Gen. George S., Jr.: 12, 401–02, 405, 406, 407, 408, 440
Peacetime armies
  in France: 71–73
  Moltke's understanding of the role of: 125
Pershing, Maj. Gen. John J.: 87
Persian Gulf War: 17, 331, 440, 444–75. *See also* Campaign planning; Deception; Envelopment; France; Great Britain; Kuwait; Iraq; Logistical support; Military intelligence; Operational maneuver; Operational planning; Operational reserves; Operations, military, DESERT STORM; *Republican Guard* units; Saudi Arabia; Training; Transportation; War, principles of.
  Arab countries allied with the United States: 453, 461–62, 470–71, 472
  American air superiority: 446, 447, 453, 455, 457, 465
  campaign planning for: 453–55, 459, 464

499

Persian Gulf War—Continued
  coalition warfare: 453–54, 461–62, 463, 464–65, 470–71
  implementation of the campaign plan for: 459–65
Pétain, General: 84, 86–87, 90–91, 92, 102
Petrovsky, D.: 222–23
Pettigrew, Brig. Gen. James: 365
Pickett, Maj. Gen. George E.: 371, 373, 376, 378, 385, 389*n*
Pickett's Charge: 376, 378. *See also* Civil War, U.S.; Gettysburg, battle of.
Pilsudski, Marshal: 227, 228
Pleasonton, Brig. Gen. Alfred: 355, 357–58, 361
Poland: 158
  and the Soviet Civil War: 226–28, 231, 232
  and World War II: 260, 261, 262, 264, 265, 303
Ponte Corvo, Duke of: 37, 42, 44, 45, 46–47, 48, 49, 51–52, 57–61, 62–63, 64, 65
Potomac River: 361, 363, 364, 380
Powell, General Colin: 467
Principes de la guerre de montagnes, by General Pierre de Bourcet: 70
Provisional Instructions for the Tactical Employment of Large Units (1921): 88
Provisional Use of Armored Divisions, The: 93. *See also* Doctrine, French; French Army.
Prussia: 35–36, 118–19, 121, 123
Prussian Army
  and the battle at Jena: 34
  and cult of the past: 36–37
  disposition in the Napoleonic wars: 44–46
  and incorporation of the Saxon Army: 37, 38, 42, 45, 47
  lack of planning for war with France: 37–39, 40
  leadership problems: 36–39
  lines of communication: 46, 47–48, 51
  Moltke as chief of the general staff: 118–19, 120–21
Puzyrevskii, A. K.: 195, 196
P'yongyang, Korea: 420, 422, 424

Radzievskii, Alekseî Ivanovich: 324*n*
Railroads
  French Army use of: 79, 85, 151

Railroads—Continued
  and mobility of armies: 111, 113, 121, 145, 190
  Moltke's use of: 113, 116–17, 121, 127, 140, 145, 147*n*, 190
  in Russia: 196
  and the Russo-Japanese War: 198
  Soviet use of in World War II: 294–95, 299, 301, 302, 303, 305, 306
Rappahannock River: 350–51, 352, 353, 355, 356, 357, 360
Rawlinson, General Henry: 88
Rear Services, Soviet Armed Forces: 295, 297
Red Army of Workers and Peasants: 218. *See also* Soviet Army.
Regulation on Maneuver of Artillery: 90, 91. *See also* Doctrine, French; French Army.
Regulation on the Conduct of Large Units: 73–74, 92. *See also* Doctrine, French; French Army.
Regulations on the Service of Armies in the Field: 73. *See also* Doctrine, French; French Army.
Republican Guard units: 444–45, 452–53, 454, 457, 462–65, 467, 469. *See also* Iraqi forces; Operation DESERT STORM; Persian Gulf War.
Reserve forces. *See also* Operational reserves.
  artillery as: 90–91, 96, 102
  efforts to prevent effective use of in World War I: 82–83
  French lack of in World War I: 79
  French lack of in World War II: 177–78
  French use of: 93, 96, 97, 98, 102
  German lack of in battle for Moscow: 161–62
  German use of in World War I: 82–83, 85–86, 87, 88
  Moltke's reasons for not having: 137
  Napoleon's use of: 34–35, 43, 44, 46–47, 51, 53, 56, 60–63
  in the Prussian Army: 39, 47, 48
  Soviet Army use of in World War II: 165
Reynolds, Maj. Gen. John: 361, 365, 366, 367, 386
Reznichenko, V. G.: 273–74, 275, 291*n*
Rhine, Confederation of the: 35–36
Rice, Condoleeza: 213
Ritter, Gerhard: 150, 157

500

Rochade: 152–53, 161–64
Rokossovsky, General K. K.: 254
Romania: 260, 262–63, 288*n*, 303
Rommel, General Erwin: 175–76, 178, 179
Roon, Albrecht von: 141–43
Rosecrans, Maj. Gen. William S.: 350
Roth, Günter R.: 112
Rothenberg, Gunther: 191
Rotmistrov, Marshal P. A.: 267
Royal Air Force: 99
Rüchel, General: 38, 39, 45, 48, 53, 56, 60
Rupprecht, Crown Prince of Bavaria: 77–78
Russia. *See also* Civil War, Soviet; Russian Army; Union of Soviet Socialist Republics; World War I; World War II.
    alliance with France before World War I: 76–77
    effect of economic backwardness on the ability to wage war: 195, 196, 205
    and the Napoleonic wars: 40–41, 62, 63
    nationalist school of military thought: 201, 202, 204, 207
    Provisional Government (September–October 1917): 213–14
    railroads: 196
    War Ministry's Historical Commission: 191–92
    and World War I: 151, 154, 216–18, 223
Russian Army (after 1991): 277–81. *See also* Soviet Army.
Russian Federation: 277–81
Russo-Japanese War (1904–1905): 197–201, 203, 215–16
Russo-Turkish War (1877–1878): 189–90, 191–92

Saale River: 45–46, 47, 49–50, 51, 52, 57, 58–59
St. Lô, France: 330, 400–401, 403
Saudi Arabia: 445–46, 447–49, 452, 453, 455–56, 458–59, 472. *See also* Operations, military, DESERT SHIELD, DESERT STORM; Persian Gulf War.
Saxony: 120
    allied with Austria: 120–21
    and the Napoleonic wars: 41, 42, 44, 63
Scharnhorst, Colonel: 37, 38, 39, 62, 149
Schlichting, Sigismund W. von: 8, 201, 205
Schlieffen, General Alfred von: 76, 77, 80, 112, 145, 149–54, 156–57, 158, 159, 160, 161, 165–66, 179
Schlieffen Plan: 150–52, 154–55, 157–58, 160, 161, 165–66
School of Advanced Military Studies: 441–42, 445, 447
Schwarzkopf, General H. Norman, Jr.: 443, 445, 452–53, 454, 466, 467. *See also* Operations, military, DESERT SHIELD, DESERT STORM; Persian Gulf War.
Scientific positivism: 192–93, 201, 202
Scott, Col. Henry L.: 334
Security. *See* War, principles of.
Sedan, France: 94–101, 130–31, 150, 160, 161, 164, 165, 169, 171–74, 177, 191
Seddon, James: 350
Sedgwick, Maj. Gen. John: 354, 355, 371, 374, 379–80, 385
Seeckt, General Hans von: 158
Seminary Ridge: 369, 378–79. *See also* Civil War, U.S.; Gettysburg, battle of.
Shaposhnikov, Boris Mikhailovich: 200–201, 230–31
Sheinovo, Bulgaria: 190, 191
Sheridan, General Philip H.: 140–41
Shinseki, General Eric K.: 444
SICHELSCHNITT. *See* Operations, military, SICKLE CUT.
SICKLE CUT Plan: 155, 156, 160–61, 162, 166, 178. *See also* Manstein, Field Marshal Erich von; Operations, military, SICKLE CUT.
Sickles, Maj. Gen. Daniel E.: 371, 373, 374
Siegfried Line: 84, 85. *See also* World War II.
Simpkin, Brig. Richard E.: 213
Slocum, Maj. Gen. Henry W.: 371
Sokolovsky, Marshal V. D.: 269
Soult, Marshal Nicolas Jean-de-Dieu: 37, 40, 42, 44, 45–46, 47, 49–50, 51, 53, 60–61, 62, 65
South Korean Army: 418, 419, 420, 423–24, 426, 427, 429, 434*n*, 435*n*, 437*n*
Soviet Army
    Academy of the General Staff: 214, 215, 218, 220–21, 222–23
    airborne forces: 257, 270, 271, 273
    armored formations: 247
    cavalry units: 224–28, 231, 243*n*, 249, 250–51, 253, 255, 257–58, 259, 260, 261–63

Soviet Army—Continued
  combined-arms emphasis: 233–34, 35, 237–39, 244*n*, 247, 251, 257, 260–61, 267–68, 269, 272–73, 275, 277, 290*n*, 300–301, 305, 307, 310, 312, 314
  command and control issues: 274, 275, 282*n*, 284*n*
  Communist Party relationship: 222, 229, 230–31, 235
  doctrine: 186–87, 222–23, 228, 242*n*, 270–71, 276–77
  effect of nuclear war theories on: 269–70
  field regulations: 233–34, 238, 288*n*
  force structure: 224–28, 248–53, 255, 266, 267–68, 269–70, 272–73, 274, 275, 276–77, 283*n*, 286*n*, 290*n*
  logistics: 186–87, 227, 230, 231, 233, 253, 254, 256–57, 260, 263, 273, 282*n*, 285*n*, 293–316, 324*n*
  mechanization of: 213–14, 234–39, 269, 273
  mechanized units: 247, 249, 251, 253, 254, 255, 256, 257, 258, 259, 260–63, 267–68, 282*n*, 285*n*, 287*n*, 289*n*
  military operations theory: 7–10, 11, 14–15
  mobile units in World War II: 253–55, 256–57, 258–59, 260–63, 264–66, 267, 289*n*, 290*n*, 303–04, 325*n*
  modernization after World War II: 13
  and national preparation for war: 230–31
  operational maneuver forces: 8, 249–51
  organization of: 186, 224–28, 248–49
  purges of officers: 11, 238, 239, 247–48, 282*n*
  reorganized for the atomic age: 13, 268–69
  role of the tsarist general staff in: 218–19, 220–23, 225–26, 232–33, 318*n*
  ski units: 249, 250, 254, 284*n*
  and the Soviet Civil War: 223–28, 233–34
  and study of military history: 3, 7, 229–30, 233
  tank units: 249, 250–53, 254, 255, 56–63, 264–66, 267, 268, 269, 270, 272–73, 277, 282*n*, 284*n*, 285*n*, 286*n*, 287*n*, 288*n*, 289*n*, 290*n*. *See also* Tank units.

Soviet Army—Continued
  and the technological revolution in weaponry: 273–76
  training of officers: 221–22, 231–32
  in World War II: 161–62, 238–39, 247–48, 283*n*, 319*n*
Soviet General Staff
  and logistical support: 295, 296–97, 318*n*
  and logistical support for nuclear warfare: 310
Soviet High Command
  and conceptualization of future battle: 274, 276–77
  failure to achieve strategic ends in World War II: 253–55, 257–58
  and logistical support: 303, 305
  and the Manchurian offensive: 266–67
  and offensives against the Germans: 253–66
  and organization of forces at the beginning of World War II: 249–53, 254, 255
  planning for the 1944–1945 winter offensive: 263–64
  and restructuring of forces after World War II: 267–68
  use of deception and surprise: 259, 260–63, 264, 274–75, 276, 287*n*. *See also* War, principles of.
Soviet Navy: 299, 319*n*
Soviet Staff Academy, Conduct of Operations Department: 8, 186
Soviet Union. *See* Union of Soviet Socialist Republics.
Staff rides: 135, 139, 140, 145, 157
Staff system
  Moltke's use of: 140–41
  in Napoleon's army: 29–31, 33
  in the Prussian Army: 36–37
Stalin, Joseph: 10, 226, 228, 236, 237, 243*n*
  and logistical support for the Soviet Army: 297, 298, 318*n*, 319*n*, 320*n*
  and military forces after World War II: 13
  and plan for mechanization of the Soviet Army: 235
  and purges of military officers: 11, 238, 239, 247–48, 282*n*
  and Soviet Army leadership: 238

Stalingrad, battle of: 251, 253, 285*n*, 300–301. *See also* World War II.
Steinmetz, General: 127, 141
Stocqueler, Joachim: 333
Strategiya, by A. A. Svechin: 230
Strategy, by G. A. Leyer: 193
Strategy, by N. P. Mikhnevich: 202
Stratemeyer, Lt. Gen. George E.: 421–22, 433*n*
Stuart, Maj. Gen. Jeb: 355–56, 357, 360, 361, 363, 364, 374, 376, 378, 382, 383, 390*n*
Sukhomlinov, General: 217, 241*n*
Surprise. *See* War, principles of.
Svechin, Col. Aleksandr A.: 8, 189, 192, 195, 200, 207–08, 210*n*, 214, 219, 220, 222, 229, 230–31, 232, 234–35, 236, 238, 240*n*
Sverdlov, Col. F. D.: 271
Sweden: 59–60, 62–63
Swift, Eben: 117, 337–38
Tactical and Strategic Studies, by Hugh Drum: 339
Tactics, grand: 69–71
Tank units
    British: 107*n*
    French use of in World War II: 96–99, 100–101
    German use of in World War II: 169–79, 249–50
    Soviet: 268
    use at the operational level: 169–79
Tauenzien, General Bolesas Friedrich: 45, 46, 53
Technology
    and need for new military doctrine: 14, 114, 116–17
    and need for new tactical and organizational structures: 9, 203–04
    and pursuit of war at the operational level: 443–44, 452, 456, 465, 466, 471–72, 473, 474
Telegraph: 113, 145, 190, 198, 204
Temporary Field Regulations of the Workers' and Peasants' Red Army, 1936, The: 215
Terrain
    effect on operations of armies: 70
    Meade's use of: 372
    Moltke's appreciation of the role of in military operations: 115
    role in the Korean War: 420–21, 422–23, 424, 428–29, 431

Thüringer Wald, Germany: 34, 38, 41, 42, 44–45
Timoshenko, S. K.: 247–48, 283*n*
Touchon, General Robert: 100–101
Training
    for French soldiers: 71, 72–73, 74–75
    for German officers: 135–36, 139, 140, 145
    lack of for officers in Napoleon's army: 31
    NATO exercises: 470
    of Soviet Army officers: 221–22, 231–32
    of U.S. forces with allied forces: 470, 472
    for U.S. soldiers after arrival in Saudi Arabia: 455–57, 459
    for U.S. soldiers en route to the Persian Gulf: 449
Transportation
    in the Persian Gulf War: 446–47, 449
    Soviet improvements to for military use: 313
    Soviet organization of in World War II: 299, 301, 302, 303, 305, 306, 307
    Soviet use of air transport in World War II: 301, 302, 304, 306, 307, 319*n*
    Soviet use of animals for in World War II: 302, 308
Trench warfare: 75–76, 77, 78
Triandafillov, V. K.: 19*n*, 186, 228, 229, 232–34, 236, 238, 244*n*, 246*n*
Trotsky, Leon D.: 219, 222, 224–25, 228, 229, 242*n*, 243*n*
Tsiffer, R.: 224
Tukhachevsky, Marshal Mikhail N.: 8, 186, 215, 221, 223–24, 227, 228, 229, 231, 232, 233, 234–38, 242*n*, 244*n*, 245*n*, 257
Turbiville, Graham H.: 186–87
Turkey: 115–16, 119, 189–90
Turkish Army: 115–16

Ukraine: 259–60, 261
Union of Soviet Socialist Republics. *See also* Korean War; Soviet Army; World War II.
    Civil War: 185–86. *See also* Civil War, Soviet.
    defense industrial facilities: 301–02

Union of Soviet Socialist Republics—Continued
  economic effects on military doctrine: 276, 277
  infrastructure: 10
  and the Korean War: 419, 421, 424, 426, 434n, 435n
  and militarization of the national economy: 10, 230–31, 234–35, 236–37, 313, 317n, 321n
  military purges: 282n. *See also* Soviet Army, purges of officers.
  and relationship between civilian and military leadership: 230–31
  revolution in military affairs (1960–1970): 17, 269–70, 291n, 309
  and war of annihilation: 230, 231, 234–39
  and World War II: 161–64, 248–67
United Nations Command: 415–16, 418, 419–20, 422, 424, 427, 429, 430, 431, 437n. *See also* Korean War.
United Nations Command, Commander in Chief: 418–20, 421–22, 423–24, 426, 427, 429–30, 431, 433n, 434n, 435n
Unity of command. *See* War, principles of.
U.S. Air Force: 15, 16
U.S. Army. *See also* Korean War; Operations, military; Persian Gulf War; World War I; World War II.
  campaign planning: 15–17, 453–55, 459, 464
  doctrinal evolution in the post–World War II period: 13–14
  doctrine for large units: 338–42, 343–44, 345
  and planning for Operation OVERLORD: 393, 396
U.S. Army Command and General Staff College: 441, 447
U.S. Army Command and General Staff School: 12, 16
U.S. Army Training and Doctrine Command: 13–14
U.S. Army War College: 16, 339, 341–42
U.S. Central Command: 445, 447, 449
U.S. Eighth Army: 418–19, 420, 421, 422–23, 424, 426, 427–28, 429, 431, 433n, 434n, 435n, 436n, 437n

U.S. Military Academy: 335
U.S. Navy: 12, 16, 460
U.S. X Corps: 419, 420, 421, 422–24, 426, 427–30, 431, 434n, 435n, 436n
Varfolomeev, N. E.: 214–15, 229, 231, 232, 238, 244n
Vasilevskiĭ, Marshal A. M.: 305, 323n
Verdun, France: 83, 87
Verkhovsky, Aleksandr I.: 213–14, 228, 236
Vietnam War: 13, 439
Vinogradov, General V. I.: 186–87, 305, 309, 323n
Vistula Campaign: 227–28, 231, 232, 243n. *See also* World War II.
Voroshilov, Marshal K. E.: 226, 228, 235, 236, 243n, 295

Wagner, Arthur: 337–38
Walker, Lt. Gen. Walton: 418, 419, 420, 421, 422–23, 424, 426, 429, 431, 434n
Wallach, Jehuda: 157–58
War, industrialization of: 203–04, 205–06, 215
War, principles of
  concentration
    German use of in World War II: 164
    German violations of in World War I: 154–55
    Lee's use of at Gettysburg: 370, 383–84
    Meade's use of at Gettysburg: 367, 383
    Moltke's understanding of the role of: 120, 121, 123, 125, 139–40
    Napoleon's use of: 33–35, 42–44, 50–51, 119, 120
    Red Army failure to practice in World War II: 163
    U.S. failure to use in the Korean War: 427–28, 429
    U.S. use of in the breakout from St. Lô: 400–401
    U.S. use of in the Persian Gulf War: 462–65
  economy of force
    Moltke's use of: 131

War, principles of—Continued
    Napoleon's understanding of: 27
    Persian Gulf War use of: 462
    Red Army use of in World War II: 264
  security: 32, 34, 42–43
  surprise
    German use of in World War I: 151
    German use of in World War II: 160, 163–64, 170, 172–73, 175–76, 178–79, 248, 249
    Lee's use of: 354–57, 360, 383
    Napoleon's use of: 32
    Soviet use of in World War II: 259, 260–63, 264, 267
  unity of command
    absence in planning for Operation OVERLORD: 393, 396, 405–10
    absence in Soviet command structure: 253
    failure to practice during the Korean War: 330–31, 420–21, 422–23, 424, 427, 429, 431–32

War Communism: 223
War planning. *See also* Operational planning.
  importance of the staff process in: 219–20
  Neznamov's concept of: 205–08
  Russian: 205–08, 216–17
  Soviet: 219–20
Warren, Brig. Gen. Gouverneur K.: 361, 367, 374
Warsaw, Miracle of: 227–28, 231. *See also* World War II.
Warsaw Pact: 13–14, 15. *See also* Hungary; Poland; Romania; Union of Soviet Socialist Republics.
Wehrmacht: 10, 161, 163, 165, 170
Weigley, Russell F.: 330
Wheeler, Junius B.: 335
Wilhelm, King of Prussia: 130, 131, 140, 141–43, 144, 190
Wilhelm, Thomas: 334
Wilkinson, Spencer: 140
Wonsan, Korea: 420, 421, 422, 423–24, 427, 434*n*, 435*n*
World War I: 5, 6, 8, 76–89, 150–58. *See also* Belgium; Casualties;

World War I—Continued
  Communications, battlefield; French Army; German Army; Germany; Great Britain; Logistical support; Military strategy; Mobility; Operational planning; Reserve forces; War, principles of.
  and France: 76–89
  German strategy: 76–79, 150–54
  and Russia: 216–18, 223
  U.S. Army lessons from: 338–39
World War II. *See also* Amphibious operations; Belgium; Casualties; Command and control; Deep operations, Soviet; Defense; Envelopment; France; French Army; Germany; Great Britain; Japan; Logistical support; Mission-oriented tactics; Mobility; Operational maneuver; Operational planning; Poland; Railroads; Reserve forces; Soviet High Command; Stalin, Joseph; Tank units; Transportation; Union of Soviet Socialist Republics; War, principles of.
  Allied operational decision-making during Operation OVERLORD: 393
  effects of poor Allied operational planning on the length of: 405–10
  German campaign against the Soviet Union: 11, 238–39, 248, 249–53, 283*n*
  Normandy invasion: 330, 393–97, 411*n*
  Soviet Army in: 11, 161–62, 238–39, 247–59, 283*n*, 319*n*
  Soviet deficiencies in organization and command and control in the early years: 249–59, 296. *See also* Soviet Army.
  U.S. operations in: 12, 393–410

Yalu River: 424, 426, 427
Yelchaninov, A. G.: 205–06
Yeosock, Lt. Gen. Joseph: 466
Young Turks (Russia): 201, 204

Zaionchkovskiy, General: 216–17
Zhukov, Marshal G. I.: 253, 259–60, 264, 265–66, 268–69, 282*n*, 295, 296–97, 318*n*, 320*n*

CPSIA information can be obtained
at www.ICGtesting.com
Printed in the USA
BVOW04s0228221217
503439BV00010B/87/P

9 781507 635049